COMPUTER SYSTEMS

An Integrated Approach to Architecture and Operating Systems

Umakishore RAMACHANDRAN
Georgia Institute of Technology

William D. LEAHY, Jr.
Georgia Institute of Technology

Addison-Wesley

Boston   Columbus   Indianapolis   New York   San Francisco   Upper Saddle River
Amsterdam   Cape Town   Dubai   London   Madrid   Milan   Munich   Paris   Montreal   Toronto
Delhi   Mexico City   Sao Paulo   Sydney   Hong Kong   Seoul   Singapore   Taipei   Tokyo

Editor in Chief: Michael Hirsch
Acquisitions Editor: Matt Goldstein
Editorial Assistant: Chelsea Bell
Managing Editor: Jeffrey Holcomb
Senior Production Project Manager:
  Marilyn Lloyd
Director of Marketing: Margaret Waples
Marketing Coordinator: Kathryn Ferranti
Senior Operations Supervisor: Alan Fischer

Text Designer: Sandra Rigney
Cover Designer: Kristine Carney
Cover Image: Heart—Elise Gravel/Shutterstock
  Images; Brain—Elise Gravel/Shutterstock
  Images; Shoulder—Mark Strozier/iStockphoto
Project Management: Dennis Free/
  Aptara®, Inc.
Full Service Vendor: Aptara®, Inc.
Printer/Binder: Courier Stoughton

Credits and acknowledgments borrowed from other sources and reproduced, with permission, in this textbook appear on appropriate page within text.

The interior of this book was set in QuarkXPress 6.5, Berkeley Book and ITC Franklin Gothic.

Library of Congress Cataloging-in-Publication Data
Ramachandran, Umakishore.
   Computer systems : an integrated approach to architecture and operating systems/
Umakishore Ramachandran, William Leahy.
      p. cm.
   ISBN 978-0-321-48613-4
   1. Computer systems.   2. Computer architecture.   3. Systems software.   4. System design.
5. Operating systems (Computers)   I. Leahy, William.   II. Title.
   QA75.5.R37 2010
   005.4'3—dc22
                                                                          2010020509

10 9 8 7 6 5 4 3 2 1—CRS—14 13 12 11 10

Addison-Wesley
is an imprint of

www.pearsonhighered.com

ISBN 10:   0-321-48613-7
ISBN 13: 978-0-321-48613-4

To,

Amma,
Our Parents and Families

Preface

Why a New Book on Computer Systems?

There is excitement when you talk to high school students about computers. There is a sense of mystery as to what is "inside the box" that makes the computer do such things as play video games with cool graphics, play music—be it rap or symphony—send instant messages to friends, and so on. The purpose behind this textbook is to take the journey together to discover the mystery of what is inside the box. As a glimpse of what is to come, let us say at the outset that what makes the box interesting is not just the hardware, but also how the hardware and the system software work in tandem to make it all happen. Therefore, the path we take in this book is to look at hardware and software together to see how one helps the other and how together they make the box interesting and useful. We call this approach "unraveling the box"—that is, resolving the mystery of what is inside the box: We look inside the box and understand how to design the key hardware elements (processor, memory, and peripheral controllers) and the OS abstractions needed to manage all the hardware resources inside a computer, including processor, memory, I/O and disk, multiple processors, and network. Hence, this is a textbook for a first course in **computer systems** embodying a novel **integrated approach** to these topics.

The book is intended to give the breadth of knowledge in these topics at an early stage in a student's undergraduate career (in computer science or computer engineering). This text serves the need for teaching a course in an integrated fashion so that students can see the connection between the architecture and the system software. The material may be taught as a four-credit semester course, as a five-credit quarter course, or as a two-quarter three-credit course sequence. A course based on this textbook would serve well to prepare a student for more in-depth senior-level or graduate-level courses that go deeper into computer architecture, operating systems, and networking, to cater to specialization in those areas. Further, such a course kindles interest in systems early that can be capitalized on to involve students in undergraduate research.

Key features of the book (in addition to processor and memory systems) include the following:

1. a detailed treatment of storage systems;
2. an elaborate chapter devoted to networking issues; and
3. an elaborate chapter devoted to multiprocessing and multithreaded programming.

Pedagogical Style

The pedagogical style taken in the book is one of "discovery" as opposed to "instruction" or "indoctrination." Further, the presentation of a topic is "top down" in the sense that the reader is first exposed to the problem we are trying to solve and then initiated into the solution approach. Take, for example, memory management (Chapter 8). We first start with the question, "What is memory management?" Once the need for memory management is understood, we start identifying software techniques for memory management and the corresponding hardware support needed. Thus, the textbook almost takes a storytelling approach to presenting concepts, which students seem to love. Where appropriate, we have included worked-out examples of problems in the different chapters in order to elucidate a point.

Our focus in writing the textbook has always been on the students. One can see this commitment to students in the number of worked-out examples in the textbook that help solidify the concepts that were just discussed. In our experience as educators, we have seen that students really appreciate getting a historical context (names of famous computer scientists and organizations that have been instrumental in the evolution of computing) to where we are today and how we got here. We sprinkle such historical nuggets throughout the textbook. Additionally, we include a section on historical perspective in several chapters where it makes sense. Another thing that we learned and incorporated from listening to students is giving references to external work to amplify a point in context, rather than as an afterthought. One can see this in the number of footnotes throughout the textbook. Additionally, we also give bibliographic notes and pointers to further reading at the end of each chapter in a section devoted to external references (textbooks and seminal work) that may or may not be directly cited in the text, but should be useful to increasing the students' knowledge base. Today, with the abundance of information via the Internet, it is often tempting to point to URLs for additional information. However, we have desisted from this temptation (except for the inclusion of reliable links published by authoritative sources). Having said that, we know that students of this generation will go to the web first, before they go to the library, and of course, they should. In this context, we would like to share a note of caution to the students: Be judicious in your use of the Internet as a resource for information. Often, a Google search may be the quickest way to get information that you are seeking. However, you have to sift the information to ensure its veracity. As a rule of thumb, use the information from the web to answer curiosity questions or gossip. (How did DEC go out of business? Why did Linux succeed while Unix BSD did not? What is the history of the Burroughs corporation? Who are the real pioneers in computer systems?) For technical references (What is the pipeline structure of the Pentium 4? What is the instruction-set architecture of the VAX 11/780?), seek out published books and refereed conference and journal papers (many of which are available online, of course).

Incidentally, this textbook grew out of teaching such an integrated course, every semester from the fall of 1999, in the College of Computing at Georgia Institute of Technology. In the beginning, the authors developed a comprehensive set of notes and slides for the course and used two standard textbooks (one for architecture and one for operating systems) as background reference material for the students to supplement the course material. In the spring of 2005, we turned our courseware into a manuscript for a textbook, because the students continually communicated to us a need for a textbook that matched the style and contents of our course. An online version of this textbook has been in use at Georgia Tech since the spring of 2005 for this course that presents an integrated introduction to systems. The course is offered three times every year (including summers), with over 80 students taking the course every semester. Thus, the manuscript has received continuous feedback and improvement from students taking the course, for over 15 consecutive semesters, before going to print.

In designing the course from which this book was born, as well as in writing the book, we have learned a lot from the way a first course in systems is taught at other institutions, and from a number of excellent textbooks. For example, the first course in systems taught at MIT[1] has a long history and tradition, and is truly one of a kind. The book [Saltzer, 2009] that grew out of that course is a great resource for students aspiring to specialize in computer systems. In writing our book, we will freely admit that we have been inspired by the pedagogical styles of [Ward, 1989] and [Kurose, 2006].

The Structure of the Book and Possible Pathways Through the Book

The intellectual content of the book is broken up into five modules. The roadmap that follows suggests a possible pathway through the material. The pathway assumes a roughly equal coverage of the architecture and operating systems topics.

1. **Processor:** The first module deals with the processor, and software issues associated with the processor. We start by discovering how to design the brain inside the box[2], the processor. What are the software issues? Since computers are programmed, for the most part, in high-level language, we consider the influence of high-level language (HLL) constructs on the instruction set of the processor (Chapter 2). Once we understand the design of the instruction set, we focus on the hardware issue of implementing the processor. We start with a simple implementation of the processor (Chapter 3), and then go on to consider a performance-conscious implementation with the use of pipelining techniques (Chapter 5). The processor is a precious resource that has to be multiplexed among several competing programs that may need to run on it, as illustrated by the video-game example in Chapter 1 (see Section 1.3). It is the OS's responsibility to use this resource well. The module concludes with OS algorithms for processor scheduling (Chapter 6).

    We expect each of Chapters 2, 3, 5, and 6 to require three hours of classroom instruction, with an hour of recitation help for each chapter.

2. **Memory System:** The second module deals with memory systems and memory hierarchies. A computer program comprises code and data, and therefore needs space in which to reside. The memory system of a computer is perhaps the most crucial factor in determining its performance. The processor speed (measured in gigahertz these days) may mean nothing if the memory system does not match that speed by providing, in a timely manner, the code and data necessary for executing a program. Whereas the size of memory systems is growing by leaps and bounds, thanks to advances in technology, applications' appetite for using memory is growing equally fast, if not faster. Thus, memory also is a precious resource, and it is the responsibility of the OS to manage this resource well. The first part of this module concerns the OS

---

1. http://mit.edu/6.033/www/.

2. The anatomical allusion in the cover design is meant to illustrate the analogy of computing to the networked distributed processing that happens so naturally in the human body.

algorithms for efficient management of memory and the architectural assists for supporting it (Chapters 7 and 8); the second part deals with the memory hierarchies that help to reduce the latency seen by the processor when accessing code and data (Chapter 9).

We expect each of Chapters 7, 8, and 9 to require three hours of classroom instruction, with an hour of recitation help for each chapter.

3. **Storage System:** The third module deals with the I/O (particularly, stable storage) and the file system. What makes the computer useful and interesting is being able to interact with it. First, we deal with hardware mechanisms for grabbing the attention of the processor away from the currently executing program (Chapter 4). These mechanisms deal with both external events and internal exceptions encountered by the processor during program execution. Associated with the hardware mechanisms are software issues that address "discontinuities" in the normal program execution, which include remembering our location in the original program and the current state of the program execution. Next, we delve into the mechanisms for interfacing the processor to I/O devices and the corresponding low-level software issues such as device drivers (Chapter 10), with a special emphasis on the disk subsystem. This is followed by a comprehensive treatment of the file system (Chapters 11) built on stable storage such as the disk.

We expect each of Chapters 4 and 10 to require three hours of classroom instruction and an hour each of recitation help; Chapter 11 should require six hours of classroom instruction and two hours of recitation help.

4. **Parallel System:** Computer architecture is a fast-changing field. Chip density, processor speed, memory capacity, etc., have all been showing exponential growth over the last two decades and are expected to continue that trend for the foreseeable future. Parallel processing is no longer an esoteric concept reserved for supercomputers. With the advent of multicore technology that houses multiple CPUs inside a single chip, parallelism is becoming a commodity. Therefore, understanding the hardware and software issues surrounding parallelism is necessary to answer the question "What is inside a box?" This module deals with operating systems issues and the corresponding architectural features in multiprocessors for supporting parallel programming (Chapter 12).

We expect Chapter 12 to require six hours of classroom instruction, with two hours of recitation help.

5. **Networking:** In the world we live in, a box is almost useless unless it is connected to the outside world. The multiplayer video game (introduced in Chapter 1), with your friends as fellow players on the network, is a nice motivating example, but even in our everyday mundane activities, we need the network for e-mail, web browsing, etc. What distinguishes the network from other input/output devices is the fact that your box is now exposed to the world! You need a language to talk to the outside world from your box and deal with the vagaries of the network, such as temporary or permanent disconnections. This module deals with the evolution of networking hardware, and the features of the network protocol stack (which is part of the operating system) for dealing with the vagaries of the network (Chapter 13).

We expect Chapter 13 to require six hours of classroom instruction, with two hours of recitation help.

In a nutshell, Chapters 2 through 10 will require one week of instruction each; Chapters 11, 12 and 13 will require two weeks of instruction each, rounding up a 15-week semester. The hardware and software issues for each of the five modules are treated together in this textbook. The suggested pathway above through the material follows this treatment.

It is possible to tilt the coverage unevenly between architecture and operating systems topics if one so chooses, without loss of continuity. Let us consider the processor module. Chapters 3 and 5 deal with the hardware implementation issues of the processor. For a course that is more OS-oriented, Chapter 5, which deals with pipelined processor implementation (starting from Section 5.7), may be lightly covered or skipped altogether (depending on time constraints), without loss of continuity. Similarly, in a course that is more architecture oriented, Chapter 6, dealing with processor scheduling issues, may be skipped altogether, without loss of continuity.

In the memory module, Chapter 8 deals with details of page-based memory management, from an OS perspective. An architecture-oriented course could skip this chapter if it so chooses, without loss of continuity. Similarly, an OS-oriented course may choose to tone down the detailed treatment of cache memories in Chapter 9.

In the storage module, an architecture-oriented course may choose to tone down the treatment of file systems coverage in Chapter 11, without concern over loss of continuity.

In the parallel module (Chapter 12), an architecture-oriented course may skip topics such as OS support for multithreading and advanced topics such as multiprocessor scheduling, deadlocks, and classic problems and solutions in concurrency; similarly, an OS-oriented course may choose to skip advanced topics in architecture, such as multiprocessor cache coherence, taxonomy of parallel machines, and interconnection networks. Given the importance of parallelism, it would be prudent to cover the chapter as completely as possible, subject to time constraints, in any course offering.

In the networking module (Chapter 13), an architecture-oriented course offering may skip the detailed treatment of the transport and network layers (Sections 13.6 and 13.7, respectively). An OS-oriented course may choose to cover less of the link layer of the protocol stack (Section 13.8) and the networking hardware (Section 13.9).

Where Does This Textbook Fit into the Continuum of CS Curriculum?

Figure P.1 shows the levels of abstraction in a computer system. We can try to relate the levels of abstraction in Figure P.1 to courses in a typical CS curriculum. Courses such as basic programming, object-oriented design and programming, graphics, and HCI

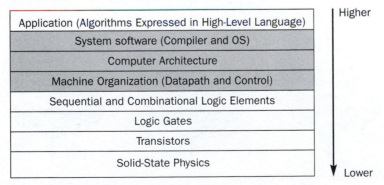

Figure P.1 Levels of abstraction in a computer system.

generally deal with higher layers of abstraction. Typically, computer science and computer engineering curricula offer courses dealing with the fundamentals of digital electronics and logic design, followed by a course on computer organization that deals purely with the hardware design of a computer. Beyond the computer organization course (moving up the levels of abstraction shown in Figure P.1), most curricula take a stovepipe approach: distinct courses dealing with advanced concepts in computer architecture, operating systems, and computer networks, respectively.

Design of computer systems is such an integrated process today that one has to seriously question this stovepipe approach, especially in the early stages of the development of a student in an undergraduate curriculum in computer science.

A course structured around the topics covered in this book is a unique attempt to present concepts in the middle (covering topics in the shaded area of Figure P.1— systems software and their relationship to computer architecture) in a unified manner in an introductory systems course. Such a course would serve as a solid preparation for students aspiring to learn advanced topics in computer architecture, operating systems, and networking (Figure P.2).

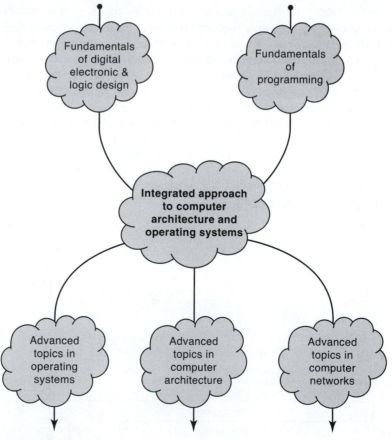

Figure P.2   Systems course sequence.

The prerequisites for a course structured around the topics covered in this textbook are quite straightforward: basic logic design and programming, using a high-level language (preferably, C). In other words, a fundamental understanding of the levels of abstractions above and below the topics covered in this book (see Figure P.1) is required.

There are excellent textbooks that cater to the fundamentals of digital electronics and logic design, as well as fundamentals of programming. Similarly, there are excellent textbooks that deal with advanced topics in computer architecture, operating systems, and computer networking. **What is missing is a simplified and integrated introduction to computer systems that serves as the bridge between the fundamentals and the advanced topics. The aim of this textbook is to serve as this bridge.**

The boundary of computer science as a discipline has expanded. Correspondingly, students coming into this discipline have varied interests. There is a need for CS curricula to offer choices for students to pursue in their undergraduate careers. At the same time, there is a responsibility to ensure that students acquire "core" knowledge in systems (broadly defined) regardless of these choices. We believe that a course structured around this textbook would fulfill such a core systems requirement. If taught right, it should give ample opportunity for students to pursue deeper knowledge in systems, through further coursework. For example, our recommendation would be to have a course based on this textbook in the sophomore year. In the junior year, the students may be ready to take courses that are more design oriented—specializing in architecture, operating systems, and/or networking—building on the basic concepts they learned in their sophomore year via this textbook. Finally, in their senior year the students may be able to take more conceptual courses on advanced topics in these areas.

The textbook balances the treatment of both architecture and operating systems topics. It is the belief of the authors that students majoring in computer science should get an equal treatment of the two topics early in their undergraduate preparation, regardless of their career objectives. Certainly, students aspiring to becoming system architects, must understand the interplay between hardware and software, as laid out in this textbook. Even for students aspiring to specialize in software development, such an understanding is essential to becoming better programmers. However, it is up to individual instructors how much emphasis to place on the two topics. The good news is that the textbook allows instructors to go into as much depth as they deem necessary, commensurate with the curricular structure existing in their institutions. For example, if an instructor chooses to scale back on the architecture side, it would be quite easy to tread lightly on the implementation chapters addressing the processor (Chapters 3 and 5), without losing continuity in the discourse. In discussing the structure of this textbook, we have already given similar suggestions for each of the five modules that this textbook comprises.

Supplementary Material for Teaching an Integrated Course in Systems

The authors fully understand the challenge an instructor faces in teaching an integrated course in computer systems that touches on architecture, operating systems, and networking.

To this end, we make available a set of online resources. Since we have been teaching this course—three offerings in each calendar year for the last 11 years—as a requirement for all computer science majors, we have amassed a significant collection of online resources:

1. We have PowerPoint slides for all the topics covered in the course, making preparation and transition (from the stovepipe model) easy.

2. A significant project component dovetails each of the five modules. We have detailed project descriptions of several iterations of these projects, along with software modules (such as simulators) for specific aspects of the projects.

3. In addition to the problems at the end of each chapter, we have additional problem sets for the different modules of the course, as well as homework problems and midterm and final exams used thus far in the course.

Example Project Ideas Included in the Supplementary Material

Processor Design

Students are supplied with a data path design that is 90% complete. Students complete the data path to help them become familiar with the design. Then they design the microcode-based control logic (using a logic design software such as LogicWorks) for implementing a simple instruction set using the data path. This allows the students to get a good understanding of how a data path functions and to appreciate some of the design tradeoffs. The students get actual circuit design experience and functionally test their design, using the built-in functional simulator of the logic design software.

Interrupts and Input/Output

Students take the design from the first project and add circuitry to implement an interrupt system. Then they write (in assembly language) an interrupt handler. The circuit design part of the project is once again implemented and functionally simulated using LogicWorks software system. In addition, the students are supplied with a processor simulator that they enhance with the interrupt support, and use it in concert with the interrupt handler, which they write in assembly language. This project not only makes operation of the interrupt system clear, but also illustrates fundamental concepts of low-level device input/output.

Virtual Memory Subsystem

Students implement a virtual memory subsystem that operates with a supplied processor simulator. The students get the feel for developing the memory-management part of an operating system through this project by implementing and experimenting with different page replacement policies. The project is implemented in the C programming language.

Multi-Threaded Operating System

Students implement the basic modules of a multithreaded operating system, including CPU and I/O scheduling queues, on top of a simulator that we supply. They experiment with different processor scheduling policies. The modules are implemented in C, using pthreads. The students get experience with parallel programming, as well as exposure to different CPU scheduling algorithms.

Reliable Transport Layer

Students implement a simple reliable transport layer on top of a simulated network layer provided to them. Issues that must be dealt with in the transport layer include corrupt packets, missing packets, and out-of-order delivery. This project is also implemented in C, using pthreads.

A Note of Caution

We offer one word of caution as we launch on our journey to explore the insides of a computer system: In a textbook that presents computer system design, it is customary to back up concepts with numerical examples to illustrate the concepts. The past is indicative of the future. If there is a constant in the technology landscape, it is *change*. When you buy a new car, the minute it rolls out of the showroom, it becomes a used car. In the same manner, any numbers we may use in the numerical examples as to the speed of the processor, or the capacity of memory, or the transfer rate of peripherals become outdated instantly. What endure are the *principles,* which is the focus of this textbook. A comfort factor is that whereas the absolute numbers may change with time—from megaHertz to gigaHertz, and megabytes to gigabytes—the *relative* numbers stay roughly the same as technology advances, thus making the numerical examples in the textbook endure with time.

Acknowledgments

We are deeply indebted to several colleagues, nationally and internationally, who have been either directly or indirectly responsible for the creation of this textbook. First and foremost, we would like to thank Yale Patt, who, back in the summer of 2004 when we described the course that we teach at Georgia Tech, told us in his inimitable forceful style that we should write a textbook because there is a crying need for a book that presents the systems concepts in an integrated manner. We can honestly say that, but for his encouragement, we may not have embarked on this path. Our colleagues at other institutions who deserve special mention for encouraging us to write this textbook include Jim Goodman (University of Wisconsin-Madison and University of Auckland, New Zealand), Liviu Iftode (Rutgers University), Phil McKinley (Michigan State University), and Anand Sivasubramaniam (Pennsylvania State University and TCS). We are particularly thankful to Jim Goodman for his careful reading of an early draft of the manuscript and providing detailed feedback that helped improve the discourse tremendously. Besides these folks, we received much positive reinforcement for our project from several colleagues in other institutions who helped to get us started.

The first step was creating a manuscript for internal consumption by students at Georgia Tech. We cannot thank the students of CS 2200 at Georgia Tech enough. The feedback from several generations of students, who have used the online version of this textbook since the spring of 2005, has been immensely useful in improving the presentation clarity, refining specific worked-out examples in the text, providing historical pointers that would interest the reader, and other contributions. In addition, three undergraduate students helped with some of the artwork in this textbook: Kristin Champion, John Madden, and Vu Ha.

Several colleagues in the College of Computing, including Nate Clark, Tom Conte, Constantine Dovrolis, Gabriel Loh, Ken Mackenzie, and Milos Prvulovic, have given suggestions and insightful comments that have helped clarify the discourse in this textbook. We owe a lot to Constantine Dovrolis for suggestions and feedback on early drafts of the networking chapter that have helped improve both the content and the ordering of its presentation in that chapter. Ken Mackenzie's suggestions helped us to come up with a simple control regime for processor design in Chapter 3. Tom Conte gave detailed comments on the pipelining chapter that helped in improving the clarity and the content. Eric Rotenberg of North Carolina State University provided very useful feedback on early drafts of the pipelining chapter. Junsuk Shin wrote the simple client–server socket code that appears in the appendix. Our special thanks go to all of them.

We wish to thank Georgia Tech, and the vision of the College of Computing that encourages such creative thinking on the teaching side. Indeed, it is the revision of the entire undergraduate curriculum back in 1996 which started us on the path of looking critically at how we teach our undergraduates and understanding what we are missing in the curriculum that ultimately led us to develop a first course in systems as an integrated offering spanning architecture, operating systems, and networking.

Being novices at book publishing, we turned to successful textbook authors to learn from their experiences. Yale Patt (University of Texas), Jim Kurose (University of Massachusetts), Jim Foley (Georgia Tech), Andy van Dam (Brown University), Sham Navathe (Georgia Tech), Rich LeBlanc (Georgia Tech), and Larry Snyder (University of Washington) deserve special mention. We cannot thank them enough for their generosity in sharing their experiences as authors and guiding us through the various aspects of book publishing, including choosing a publisher, working with an editor, framing questions for potential reviewers, and effectively using the reviews in revising the manuscript.

The manuscript went through several rounds of external review. Most of the anonymous reviewers were thoughtful and skillfully surgical in pointing out ways to improve the manuscript. We are extremely grateful for their time and help in shaping the final product.

Our special thanks to Addison-Wesley for publishing our textbook. As our manuscript editor in charge of overseeing the review process and giving us feedback on how to improve the manuscript, Matt Goldstein has been superb. His style of looking over our shoulders without being overbearing is unique. He has been patient with us when we let schedules slip and has been unwaveringly supportive of the vision behind this book project. Our thanks to Marilyn Lloyd, senior production manager at Pearson, who was in charge of our textbook production. Our thanks go also to Jeff Holcomb, Chelsea Bell, and Dan Parker of Pearson. As the project manager overseeing the day-to-day details of the production process, Dennis Free of Aptara and the Aptara staff, including Jawwad Ali Khan and Rajshri Walia, and Brian Baker of Write With, Inc., deserve special mention for bringing the production of this book to fruition in a timely manner.

Finally, we would like to thank our families for their love, understanding, and support, which sustained us throughout the writing of this book. As an aside, Umakishore's father was a famous novelist (with the pen-name "Umachandran") with several fictional books in Tamil to his credit; memories of him served as an inspiration for undertaking this book-writing project.

Umakishore Ramachandran
William D. Leahy, Jr.

Contents

Chapter 4 Interrupts, Traps, and Exceptions   129

Chapter 5 Processor Performance and Pipelined Processor Design   156

Chapter 6 Processor Scheduling   233

Chapter 10 Input/Output and Stable Storage   423

Chapter 11 File System   469

Chapter 12 Multithreaded Programming and Multiprocessors   521

Chapter 13 Fundamentals of Networking
and Network Protocols   620

Chapter 14 Epilogue: A Look Back at the Journey   720

Introduction

Computers are ubiquitous, from cell phones to automobiles to laptops to desktops to machines that power search engines such as Google, eBay, and Amazon. *Computer architecture* relates to the design of the hardware inside each of these instantiations of computing machines. In the early days of computing, there was a clean separation between the hardware design and the software systems. However, a confluence of factors now is making this separation impractical and inefficient. From the hardware side, the two most significant, interlinked developments are on-chip power dissipation and multicore processors. For over 40 years, there was an unabated increase in processing power, fulfilling Intel cofounder Gordon Moore's prediction back in 1965 that chip density (and, indirectly, the processing speed) would double roughly every two years. The side effect of this increase in chip density and processing speed is the corresponding increase in power dissipation. As a result, in recent times architects have turned their focus to achieving better utilization of the increased chip density by putting more processors on the same chip, a technique that, in computing jargon, is referred to as *multicore* (since each core is an independent processor). Simultaneously, software has been growing in complexity: Today we find computing seeping into different aspects of our everyday life. From the software side, application complexity, increased interactivity, real-time response, and the need to tackle parallelism from the get-go rather than as an afterthought are the contributing factors. What these developments from the hardware and software sides mean is that each side can no longer afford to treat the other side as a black box. There is a compelling need to train the next generation of *system architects*, who understand the interrelationship between system software and computer architecture.

The sooner we introduce this interrelationship to the students, the better equipped they will be as computer scientists, regardless of their ultimate career pursuits.

Figure 1.1   What's in the box?

1.1 What Is Inside a Box?

Making up a computer are a processor (called the central processing unit, or CPU), the memory subsystem, all the various peripherals (such as the keyboard, monitor, mouse, disk, and DVD[1] player), and the network interface that allows you to connect the box to the outside world. Then there are the system software (such as the operating system, compiler, and runtime systems for high-level programming languages) that allows you to do what you want to do at the application level. In this text, we will often refer to the computer system, as just defined, as a box.[2]

1.2 Levels of Abstraction in a Computer System

Consider an application you may be familiar with, such as Google Earth (Figure 1.2). You can pretty much navigate visually over the entire surface of the earth simply by moving your mouse on the earth's terrain with the help of the graphical user interface (GUI) provided by Google Earth. You move the mouse over any specific region of the earth you are interested in—say, Mount Everest—and click. Suddenly, you get a 3-D view of the tallest mountain range in the world filling your screen, satellite imagery of the terrain, pictures of the area, etc. What is happening inside the box that gives you this visual experience?

---

1. DVD stands for Digital Versatile Disk or Digital Video Disk, which uses optical technology to store large multimedia data such as movie files.

2. Figure 1.1 is a comical picture of the surprise that awaits us when we open the box and look inside.

Figure 1.2   Screen shots from the Google Earth application.[3]

Consider another, more complex example, a multiplayer video game (Figure 1.3), Baseball. This is a multi-player video game version of the great American pastime. The object of the game is pretty straightforward, namely, to score more runs than the other team to win the game. However, there are complicated rules and penalties that govern the actual play.

Let us consider the software architecture for developing such an application. Imagine a (logically) central software component, which we will call a *server*, that maintains the state of the game. Each player is represented by a software component, which we will call a *client*. Since this is a multiplayer game, the clients and server are not executing on the same machine, but they execute on different machines interconnected by a local area network. It is natural to program such an application in some High Level Language (HLL).

Figure 1.3   A video game (Baseball).

3. © 2010 Google Earth.

We may add some audio/visual content to the video game we are designing. As you can see in Figure 1.4, in addition to our own code (shown in gray boxes on the right side of the figure), a number of other things have to come together for the video game software to work. The CPU, of course, does not understand anything other than machine language; therefore, a compiler has to translate the HLL program to the instruction set understood by the processor so that the programs can be run on the processor hardware.

Now let us look at the processor, from the bottom up (left side of Figure 1.4). At the lowest level of the abstraction hierarchy, there are electrons and holes that make up the semiconductor substrate. The transistor abstraction brings order to the wild world of electrons and holes. Logic gates are made up of transistors. Combinational and sequential logic elements are realized out of basic logic gates and are then organized into a datapath. A finite state machine controls the datapath to implement the repertoire of instructions in the instruction-set architecture of the processor. Thus, the instruction set is the meeting point of the software and the hardware. It serves as the abstraction needed by the compiler to generate the code that runs on the processor; the software does not care how the instruction set is actually implemented by the hardware. Similarly, the hardware implementation does not care what program runs on the processor. It simply fulfills the contract of realizing the instruction-set architecture in the hardware.

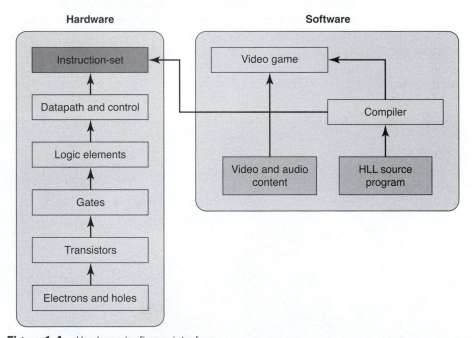

Figure 1.4   Hardware/software interface.

The left half shows the levels of abstractions in hardware, starting with electrons and holes at the bottom and working up to the instruction set at the top. The instruction set is the "contract" between hardware and software. The right half shows the software components that come together from concept to implementation of an application such as a video game.

As can be seen, the successive levels of abstraction (instruction set, datapath and control, logic elements, gates, and transistors) allow us to control the probabilistic behavior of electrons and holes in the semiconductor substrate from a high-level language program. Figure 1.5 shows how a networked video game goes through these several levels of abstractions to manipulate the electrons and holes on the semiconductor substrate. This is the power of abstraction, which is at the heart of dealing with the complexity in design, be it the hardware subsystem or the software subsystem. Both Figures 1.4 and 1.5 are meant to show the conceptual steps for converting a high-level language program through a series of abstraction layers to the point where it is ready to execute on a processor.

Now let us get back to the networked video game example and understand the role of the operating system in the life cycle of the game development to the point where actual users are playing the game.

1.3 The Role of the Operating System

Where does the operating system figure in the life cycle of the networked video game development and actual use? The operating system is the resource manager responsible for orchestrating the use of the hardware resources for the whole endeavor, from the design of the game to the actual game playing.

Using the networked video game example, let us understand the program development and deployment life cycle. We have written the client–server application in a high-level language. We may use a simple text editor or a sophisticated program development system such as Visual Studio to develop our video game. Once the game is developed, we compile the program to the instruction set of the processor. The text editor, the compiler, and other such programs involved in the program development life cycle need to run on the processor. For example, the compiler has to run on the processor, taking the HLL program as the input and producing machine code as the output. The operating system makes the processor available for each program to do its job. Now let us see what happens when you actually play the game.

In the video game, you click the mouse button that results in the batter striking out on your screen and the screens of every one of the players (see Figure 1.6). What is going on? First, the hardware device controller on your box records your mouse click. The controller then *interrupts* the processor. Remember that the processor is currently running your client program. An *interrupt* is a hardware mechanism for alerting the processor that something external to the program is happening that requires the processor's attention. It is like a doorbell in a house. Someone has to see who is at the door and what he or she wants. The operating system (which is also a collection of programs) schedules itself to run on the processor so that it can answer this doorbell. The operating system fields this interrupt, recognizes that it is from the mouse and is intended for the client program, and passes it on to the client program. The client program packages this interrupt as a message, to the server program, through the network. The server program processes the message; updates the state of the game, incorporating the new information; and sends messages to all the clients, with the updated state. The clients, through their respective operating systems, update their respective displays to show the new world state. As can be seen, several hardware resources (processor, memory for the programs and data, mouse, display, network connections) are

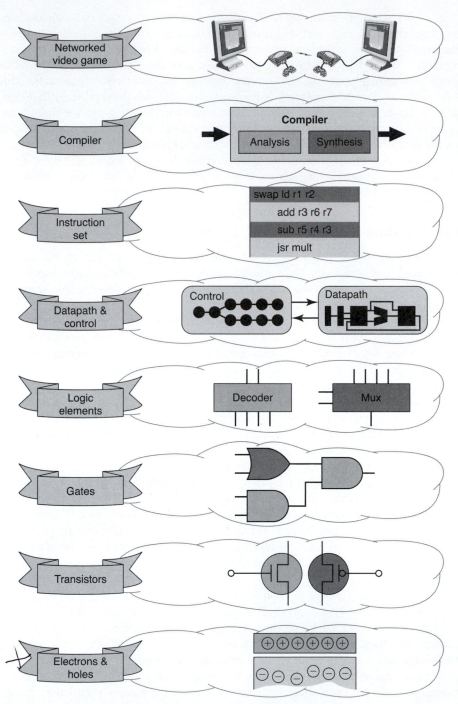

Figure 1.5 From electrons and holes to a multiplayer video game.

A video game application works through the levels of hardware abstractions to get the electrons and holes to do what it wants.

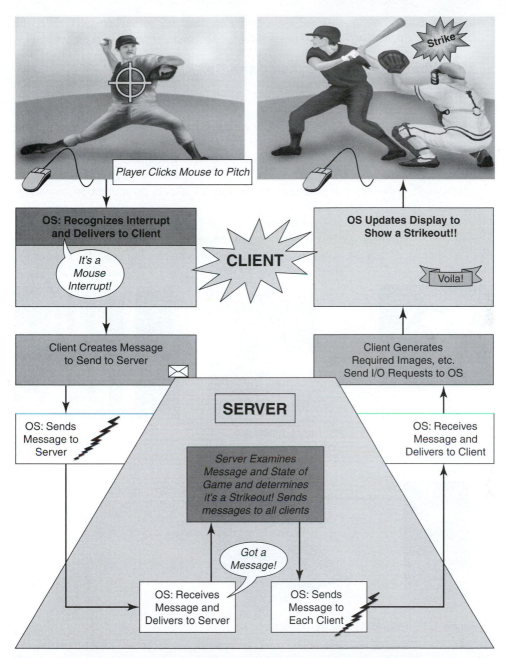

Figure 1.6 Application–hardware–OS interactions in a distributed video game.

The interactions happen among the client side of the application program, the
server side of the application program, the OS at each end, and the hardware
on which the client and the server are executing.

all being allocated and de-allocated in the course of the mouse button being clicked, to the point where the display changes. The operating system orchestrates all of these actions.

1.4 What Is Happening Inside the Box?

The video game example serves as a teaser for our further understanding of the interactions between applications, operating system, and hardware. For us to better understand what is going on inside the box, we have to get a good handle on what is happening with both the system software and the hardware architecture.

First, it is useful to understand that there are several instantiations of computer systems, ranging from handheld devices such as cell phones and PDAs,[4] to tablet PCs,[5] notebook PCs, desktop computers, parallel machines, cluster computers, to supercomputers, as shown in Figure 1.7.

Irrespective of these different manifestations and sizes, the organization of the hardware inside computer systems is pretty much the same. There are one or more central processing units (CPUs), memory, and input/output devices. Conduits for connecting

Figure 1.7   From PDAs to supercomputers.

Several instantiations of computer systems, ranging from handheld devices to supercomputers that occupy an entire floor of a building, such as the server farm powering the search engines at Yahoo! and Google or performing climate-change simulations at National Labs.

---

4. PDA stands for Personal Digital Assistant, a generic name that is used to denote cell phones, pagers, etc.
5. PC stands for Personal Computer.

these units together are called buses, and the device controllers act as the intermediary between the CPU and the respective devices. The specifics of the computational power, memory capacity, and the number and types of input/output (I/O) devices may change from one manifestation of the computer system to the next. For example, commensurate with its intended use, a PDA may have very limited I/O capabilities such as a touch-screen display, microphone, and speakers. A high-end supercomputer used for running large-scale scientific applications such as modeling climate changes may employ thousands of CPUs, incorporate several terabytes[6] of memory, and be connected to an array of disks with storage capacity on the order of several petabytes.[7] Figure 1.8 shows the organization of the hardware in a typical desktop computer system.

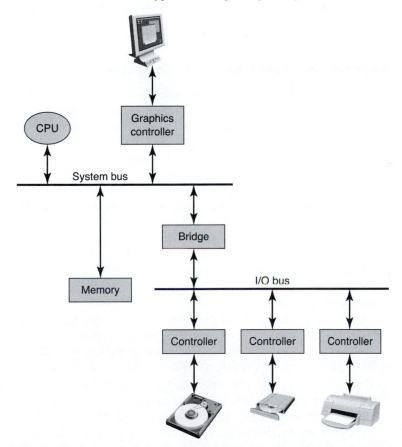

Figure 1.8 Organization of hardware in a desktop computer system.

Despite the vast landscape of various computing platforms, the basic organization of all computer systems is pretty similar. Notice that the organization opens up the possibility for supporting simultaneous activities among the hardware components.

---

6. 1 terabyte $= 2^{40}$ bytes. (Sometimes, a terabyte is also meant to signify 10^{12} bytes.)

7. 1 petabyte $= 2^{50}$ bytes. (Sometimes, a petabyte is also meant to signify 10^{15} bytes.)

The organization suggests that there is scope for simultaneous activity of the hardware elements (i.e., concurrency). For example, it should be possible for the printer to be printing your document while the hard drive is reading an MP3[8] file from the disk in order to play your desired music while you are reading a news story from CNN[9] through your Web browser. The CPU is the brain of the entire system. Everything that happens in the computer system is a result of some program that runs on the CPU. You may observe that, simultaneously with your watching CNN on your computer screen, the printer is busy printing your document from a document-editing program. A Web browser is an application program, and so is the document editor. The operating system allots time on the CPU for each of these programs to initiate its activities; hence, the hardware concurrency suggested by the organization shown in Figure 1.8 is actually realized in practice.

1.4.1 Launching an Application on the Computer

Let us understand how the various entities shown in Figure 1.8, working with the operating system, come together to give you a simple computing experience—say, of watching a video on the display device. This is an intentionally simplified description for the purpose of illustration. The box in the figure labeled "memory" holds any program that you wish to execute on the CPU. In the absence of any user program, the operating system, which is also a program, is always executing on the CPU, ready for work that the user may want the computer system to carry out. First, with your mouse you may click on an icon on the display device labeled "movie player." The movement of the mouse and the mouse click are fielded by the operating system. From the icon clicked, the operating system knows which program the user wishes to execute. All such programs are resident on some storage device, most likely the hard drive of the computer. The operating system "loads" the executable image of the movie player program into the memory and transfers control of the CPU to start executing this program.

The execution of the movie player program results in a graphics window opening on your display, which asks you to specify the movie file that you wish to watch. You then probably use a keyboard to type the name of the file, including the drive on which the file may be found (say, the DVD drive). The program opens the file on the DVD drive and plays it, and you now watch your favorite movie on the display device. The operating system is involved every step of the way, to deliver you the movie-watching experience, including (a) updating the graphics display, (b) capturing the user inputs on the keyboard and delivering them to the movie player program, and (c) moving the data from a storage device such as the DVD drive to memory. The actual mechanics of data movement to and from the I/O devices to and from the memory and/or the CPU may depend on the speed characteristics of the

---

8. MP3, which stands for MPEG-1 Audio Layer 3, is the de facto standard for digitally storing music.
9. CNN is the Atlanta-based Cable News Network.

devices. We will discuss these aspects in much more detail in Chapter 10 on the I/O subsystem.

The I/O bus and system bus shown in Figure 1.8 serve as the conduits by which data are moved among the various sources and destinations depicted by the hardware elements. Just as highways and surface streets may have different speed limits, the buses may have different speed characteristics for transporting data. The box labeled "bridge" in Figure 1.8 serves to smooth the speed differences between the different conduits in use inside a computer system organization.

1.5 Evolution of Computer Hardware

With the ubiquity of computing in our everyday living, it is difficult to imagine a time when computers were not commonplace. Yet, not so long ago, the computational power in your current-day laptop, which you may have purchased for less than $1000, cost over a million dollars and occupied a room the size of a large dance floor, with elaborate cooling and raised floors for the cabling.

In the early 1940s, ENIAC (the Electronic Numerical Integrator and Computer) was built at the University of Pennsylvania. The ENIAC is widely considered to be the very first programmable electronic digital computer (Figure 1.9).

Figure 1.9   ENIAC, the first electronic digital computer.[10]

Built in secrecy at the University of Pennsylvania under funding from the U.S. Army, the world's first computer carried out calculations to support the Allies in the World War II effort.

10. Used by permission of the School of Engineering and Applied Science of the University of Pennsylvania.

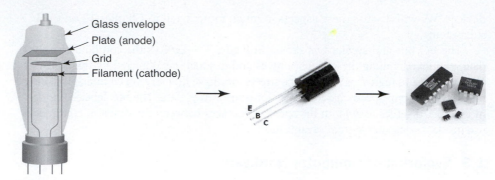

Glass envelope
Plate (anode)
Grid
Filament (cathode)

E
B
C

Figure 1.10   From vacuum tube to transistor to microchip.

The evolution of the fundamental switching component allowed the form factor of a single processor to shrink from occupying an entire room to the size of a penny.

Built with over 18,000 vacuum tubes[11] and 1000 bits of random access memory implemented by tiny magnetic ferrite cores (usually referred to as "core memory"), and consuming around 170 Kilowatts of electrical power, the ENIAC had a processing power roughly equal to what you may find in a modern-day musical greeting card! This is how far computing technology has progressed in a little over six decades since the time of ENIAC.

One can attribute the rapid progress of computer hardware to the ingenuity of scientists and engineers from complementary, yet diverse, fields, including physics, chemistry, electrical engineering, mathematics, and computer science. Of course, the most visible technological revolution that has spurred the rapid advancement of the computer industry is the semiconductor revolution. Digital computers had their modest beginnings, using vacuum tubes and magnetic core memory, in the 1940s. With the invention of a switching device called the transistor,[12] at Bell Laboratories in 1947, the semiconductor revolution began to take shape. The practice of building digital computers with discrete transistors gave way to the integration of several such transistors onto a single piece of silicon. The development of microchips—single-chip microprocessors based on CMOS[13] transistors employing *very large scale integration* (VLSI) introduced in the late 1980s and early 1990s—was perhaps the tipping point in the computer hardware revolution (see Figure 1.10). Today every computing device from cell phones to supercomputers uses the microchip as the basic building block, and semiconductor memory (typically, several hundreds of megabytes or even gigabytes) has completely replaced magnetic core memory (see Figure 1.11).

---

11. Vacuum tubes, consisting of electrodes inside a small sealed vacuum-tubular chamber often made of glass, served as the digital switching devices prior to the semiconductor revolution.

12. In 1956, John Bardeen, Walter H. Brattain, and William Shockley, the inventors of the transistor, received the Nobel Prize in Physics for their pioneering work at Bell Telephone Laboratories.

13. CMOS stands for Complementary Metal-Oxide Semiconductor, the most widely used technology for realizing transistors in integrated circuits (ICs).

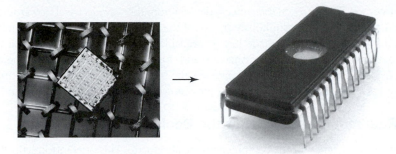

Figure 1.11   From magnetic core memory to semiconductor memory.

The evolution of memory technology enabled a megabit of storage to be packed in a chip roughly the size of a piece of bubblegum.

1.6 Evolution of Operating Systems

Operating system evolution dovetails the evolution of the processor and of the computer systems built around the processor. Operating systems had their modest beginnings in the 1950s, with offerings such as FMS (Fortran Monitoring System) and IBSYS (IBM 7094 operating system). Today, of course, operating systems span the domain of the computing devices shown in Figure 1.7. Microsoft Windows and Mac OS dominate the PC market. Linux has a strong foothold in the enterprise-computing arena. Embedded devices such as cell phones and PDAs have their own unique requirements, and there are specialized operating systems that cater to those needs. Examples of specialized embedded operating systems include Symbian OS and Blackberry OS. Many embedded operating systems are derivatives of desktop operating systems. Examples of such derived operating systems include Mac iPhone OS and Windows CE.

One can trace the evolution of operating systems with the class of computer systems that they were designed to support and with the increasing expectations of the user community. *Batch-oriented* operating systems supported the mainframe class of computers. *Multiprogrammed* operating systems emerged to better utilize the available hardware resources in mainframes and minicomputer systems. *Timeshared* operating systems evolved as a response to the user community's desire to get interactive response from the computer systems. With the advent of personal computers and the graphical user interface (GUI), operating systems for PCs integrated the GUI into the operating system, as exemplified by Microsoft Windows 95 and its successors.[14]

Ultimately, operating systems are concerned with providing computational resources, namely, processing, memory, storage, and other I/O devices for end users. A trend that has emerged in recent times is to make the computing resources available via the Internet. This trend had its beginnings with *grid* computing, which was purely a research endeavor to make high-performance computing resources available across administrative boundaries

---

14. The interested reader should see a documentary called "Triumph of the Nerds" (produced and aired in 1996 by the U.S. Public Broadcasting Station, PBS) to get a perspective on the personal computer revolution: www.pbs.org/nerds/. One can get the video by going to Google videos.

via the Internet. The term *grid computing*—derived from the way electrical power is distributed and made available ubiquitously by use of the power grid—is meant to signify that computing power should be made just as available and ubiquitous as electrical power. Today several vendors, such as Amazon and Microsoft, are offering computational resources (processing power and storage) via the Web. *Cloud computing* is the industry buzzword associated with this new way of providing computational resources to end users.

1.7 Roadmap of the Rest of the Book

These are exciting times for the computer system aficionado. This brief introduction unambiguously shows the intimate relationship between computer hardware and system software. Correspondingly, the rest of the book presents hardware and software issues pertaining to processor, memory, I/O, parallel systems, and networking in an integrated fashion.

Part I: Processor

Chapters 2–5 address processor design and hardware issues.

Chapter 6 discusses processor-scheduling issues that are addressed by an operating system.

Part II: Memory Subsystem

Chapters 7–8 deal with memory management issues addressed by an operating system with corresponding architectural assists.

Chapter 9 addresses memory hierarchy, specifically dealing with processor caches.

Part III: I/O Subsystem

Chapter 10 is about I/O issues in general as they pertain to interfacing to the processor, with specific emphasis on disk subsystem.

Chapter 11 discusses file system design and implementation, a key component of an operating system to manage persistent storage.

Part IV: Parallel System

Chapter 12 deals with programming, system software, and hardware issues as they pertain to parallel processors.

Part V: Networking

Chapter 13 is about operating system issues encountered in the design of the network protocol stack, as well as the supporting hardware issues.

Exercises

1. Consider the Google Earth application. You launch the application, move the mouse on the earth's surface, and click on Mount Everest to see an up-close view of the mountain range. Identify, in layman's terms, the interactions between the operating system and the hardware during this sequence of actions.

2. How does a high-level language influence the processor architecture?

3. Answer True or False, with justification: "The compiler writer is intimately aware of the details of the processor implementation."

4. Explain the levels of abstractions found inside the computer, from the silicon substrate to a complex multiplayer video game.

5. Answer True or False, with justification: "The internal hardware organization of a computer system varies dramatically, depending on the specifics of the system."

6. What is the role of a "bridge" between computer buses, as shown in Figure 1.8?

7. What is the role of a "controller" in Figure 1.8?

8. Using the Internet, research and explain five major milestones in the evolution of computer hardware.

9. Using the Internet, research and explain five major milestones in the evolution of the operating system.

10. Compare and contrast *grid computing* and the *power grid*. Explain how the analogy between the terms makes sense. Also, explain how the analogy breaks down.

11. Match the left-hand and right-hand sides.

UNIX operating system	Torvalds
Microchip	Bardeen, Brattain, and Shockley
FORTRAN programming language	Kilby and Noyce
C programming language	De Forest
Transistor	Lovelace
World's first programmer	Thompson and Ritchie
World's first computing machine	Mauchley and Eckert
Vacuum tube	Backus
ENIAC	Ritchie
Linux operating system	Babbage

Bibliographic Notes and Further Reading

The term *von Neumann architecture* has become synonymous with *stored program computer*, which consists of a CPU and a memory to store instructions and data. Computer historians dispute this association. The ideas in the model, proposed by John von Neumann in an article widely distributed in 1945, were in fact inspired by the ENIAC architecture developed at the University of Pennsylvania by J. Presper Eckert and John Mauchly. Even predating the ENIAC, a mathematician named Alan Turing wrote an article in 1936 in which he hypothesized a "universal computing machine." This hypothetical machine had infinite memory for storing instructions and data. Today this hypothetical machine bears his name as the "Turing machine," and is the foundation for theoretical computer science. Alan Turing is considered the "father of theoretical computer science," and every year the Association for Computing Machinery (ACM) confers the prestigious Turing Award to an individual who has made a lasting contribution to the field of computer science. The award is considered equivalent in prestige to the Nobel Prize.

It is always fun to hunt down some really classic references to see the thought processes that existed at a previous time. John Backus and his team proposed the FORTRAN programming language to his superior at IBM back in 1953, and the earliest article on FORTRAN is dated 1954 [Backus, 1954]. Backus received the Turing Award in 1977 for this work. The ENIAC architecture was conceived by Eckert and Mauchly in 1943, and an article describing it can be found in the IEEE *Annals of the History of Computing* [Burke, 1981].

Charles Babbage, considered the "father of the computer," lived between 1791 and 1871, and is credited with inventing the first mechanical computer (called the difference engine) that uses wheels and gears to perform simple calculations fed to it via punched cards. Ada Lovelace, often referred to as the world's first computer programmer, lived between 1815 and 1852, and is credited with having written the first algorithm for use with Babbage's analytical engine (which was never completed in his lifetime). Those were the modest beginnings of the computer revolution.

The invention of the integrated circuit, or the microchip, by Jack Kilby in 1958 (independently invented by Robert Noyce six months later), which launched the "real" computer revolution, is chronicled in T. R. Reid's book [Reid, 2001]. Shown here is Gordon Moore's chart[15] from his *Electronic* magazine article dated 1965 [Moore, 1965], illustrating his prediction regarding chip density as a function of time:

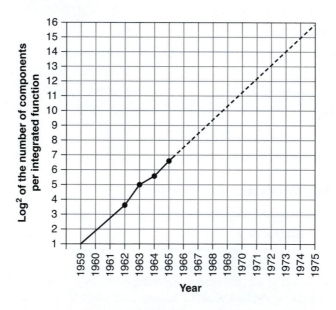

15. See Gordon Moore's plenary address entitled "No exponential is forever," at ISSCC 2003, the 50th Anniversary of Moore's law, Intel Corporation. http://sscs.org/History/MooresLaw.htm.

Dennis Ritchie and Ken Thompson at Bell Labs developed the UNIX operating system [Ritchie, 1974]. Brian Kernighan and Dennis Ritchie at Bell Labs developed the C programming language [Kernighan, 1978]. Andrew Tanenbaum, professor of computer science at Vrije University, Netherlands, developed an open source version of the UNIX operating system, called it MINIX (short for MIni-uNIX), and released it in 1987 as an appendix to his well-respected operating systems textbook [Tanenbaum, 1987]. This opened up a whole user community around the operating system. A Finnish student, Linus Torvalds, inspired by MINIX, developed his own version of an open source UNIX operating system and released it as Linux in 1991, with a simple, unassuming message to comp.os.minix newsgroup [Torvalds, 1991].

We wrap this chapter up with some pointers to recent operating systems. Windows Version 7 is the latest offering from Microsoft for PC platforms [Windows Version 7, 2010]. Microsoft's Windows CE (CE stands for Compact Edition) is meant for embedded applications such as medical devices, automobiles, and cell phones [Windows CE, 2010]. Apple has its own operating system offerings for its PC platform [Mac OS X, 2010] and for the iPhone [iPhone OS X, 2010]. Symbian OS [Symbian OS, 2010] is an open source operating system that is popular for smartphones. Blackberry OS is a proprietary software platform designed by the company Research in Motion (RIM) for its Blackberry line of mobile phones [Blackberry OS, 2010].

Processor Architecture

Two architectural issues surround processor design: the instruction set and the organization of the machine. There was a time, in the early days of computing (circa 1960s and 1970s), when processor design was viewed entirely as an exercise in hardware left to electrical engineers. Computers were programmed largely in assembly language, so, the fancier the instruction set was, the simpler the application programs tended to be. That was the prevailing conventional wisdom. With the advent of modern programming languages, such as Algol in the 1960s, and rapid advances in compiler technology, it became very clear that processor design is not simply a hardware exercise. In particular, the instruction set design is intimately related to how effectively the compiler can generate code for the processor. In this sense, programming languages have exerted a considerable influence on instruction set design.

Let us understand how the programming language influences instruction set design. The constructs in high-level language such as assignment statements and expressions map to arithmetic and logic instructions and load/store instructions. High-level languages support data abstractions that may require different precision levels of operands and addressing modes in the instruction set. Conditional statements and looping constructs would require conditional and unconditional branching instructions. Further, supporting modularization constructs such as procedures in high-level language may require additional supporting abstractions from the processor architecture.

Applications have a significant influence on the instruction set design as well. For example, the early days of computing were dominated by scientific and engineering applications. Correspondingly, high-end systems of the 1970s and 1980s supported floating-point arithmetic in the instruction set. For some time now, the dominant use of computing has been in cell phones and other embedded systems, and this trend will no doubt continue as computing weaves its way into the very fabric of society. Streaming applications such as audio and video are becoming commonplace in handheld gadgets. Naturally, the requirements of such applications (e.g., a single instruction operating on a set of data items) are starting to influence the instruction set design.

It may not always be feasible or cost effective to support the need of a particular system software or application directly in hardware. For example, in the early days of computing, low-end computers supported floating-point arithmetic via software libraries implemented by the use of integer arithmetic available in the instruction set. Even to this day, complex operations such as finding the cosine of an angle might not be supported directly by the instruction set in a general-purpose processor. Instead, special system software called *math libraries* implements such complex operations by mapping them to simpler instructions that are part of the instruction set.

The operating system has influence on instruction set design as well. A processor may appear to be running several programs at the same time. Think about your PC or PDA. There are several programs running, but there may not be several processors. Therefore, there needs to be a way of remembering what a particular program is doing before we go on to another program. You may have seen an efficient cook working on four woks simultaneously, making four different dishes. She remembers what state each dish is in and at appropriate times adds the right ingredients to the dishes. The operating system is the software entity (i.e., a program in itself) that, like the cook managing different dishes, orchestrates different program executions on the processor. The operating system has its own influence on processor design, as will become apparent in later chapters that deal with program discontinuities and memory management.

2.1 What Is Involved in Processor Design?

From a course on logic design, we know about such hardware resources as registers, the arithmetic/logic unit, and the datapath that connects all the resources together. Of course, there are other resources such as main memory for holding programs and data, multiplexers for selecting from a set of input sources, buses for interconnecting the processor resources to the memory, and drivers for putting information from the resources in the datapath onto the buses. We will visit datapath design shortly.

As an analogy, we can think of these hardware resources as the alphabet of a language like English. Words use the alphabet to make up the lexicon of the English language. In a similar manner, the instruction set of the processor uses hardware resources to give shape and character to a processor. Just as the repertoire of words in a natural language allows us to express different thoughts and emotions, the instruction set allows us to orchestrate the hardware resources to do different things in a processor. Thus, the instruction set is the key element that distinguishes an Intel x86 processor from a Power PC, and so on.

As computer users, we know that we can program a computer at different levels: in languages such as C, Python, and Java; in assembly language; or directly in machine language.

The instruction set is the prescription given by the computer architect, specifying the capabilities needed in the machine, which should be made visible to the machine language programmer. Therefore, the instruction set serves as a contract between the software (i.e., the programs that run on the computer at any level) and the actual hardware implementation. There is a range of choices in terms of implementing the instruction set, and we will discuss these choices in later chapters. First, we will explore the issues inherent in designing an instruction set.

2.2 How Do We Design an Instruction Set?

Computers evolved from calculating machines, and during the early stages of computer design the choice of instructions to have in a machine was largely dictated by whether it was feasible to implement the instruction in hardware. This was because the hardware was very expensive and the programming was done directly in assembly language. Therefore, the design of the instruction set was largely within the purview of the electrical engineers, who had a good idea of the implementation feasibilities. However, hardware costs came down, and, as programming matured, high-level languages were developed such that the question shifted from implementation feasibility to whether the instructions were actually useful—that is, useful from the point of view of producing highly efficient and/or compact code for programs written in high-level languages.

It turns out that, whereas the instruction set orchestrates what the processor does internally, users of computers seldom have to deal directly with the instruction set. Certainly, while you are playing a video game you are not worried about what instructions the processor is executing when you hit at a target. It is common knowledge that programming is more error prone in assembly language than in a high-level language.

The shift from people writing assembly language programs to compilers translating high-level language programs into machine code has been a primary influence on the evolution of the instruction-set architecture. This shift implies that we look to a simple set of instructions that will result in efficient code for high-level language constructs.

A note of caution is important here. Elegance of an instruction set is important, and the architecture community has invested a substantial intellectual effort in that direction. However, an equally important and perhaps overarching concern is the efficacy of the implementation of the instruction set. In particular, the regularity of the instruction-set architecture is an important consideration in striving to achieve simpler and faster implementation. We will revisit this matter when we discuss implementation details in Chapters 3 and 5.

Each high-level language has its own unique syntactic and semantic flavor. Nevertheless, we can identify a baseline set of features that are common across most high-level languages. We will identify such a feature set first. We will use compiling this feature set as a motivating principle in our discussion and development of an instruction set for a processor. As we already mentioned in the beginning of this chapter, instruction set design is influenced by a number of other factors beyond compilation of high-level language constructs. We will discuss these other factors in Section 2.11.

2.3 A Common High-Level Language Feature Set

Let us consider the following feature set:

1. **Expressions and assignment statements:** Compiling such constructs reveals many of the nuances in an instruction-set architecture (ISA, for short), from the kinds of arithmetic and logic operations to the size and location of the operands needed in an instruction.

2. **High-level data abstractions:** Compiling an aggregation of simple variables (usually called *structures* or *records* in a high-level language) reveals additional nuances that may be needed in an ISA.

3. **Conditional statements and loops:** Compiling such constructs results in changing the sequential flow of execution of the program and requires additional machinery in the ISA.

4. **Procedure calls:** Procedures allow the development of modular and maintainable code. Compiling a procedure call/return brings additional challenges in the design of an ISA, including remembering the state of the program before and after execution of the procedure and passing parameters to the procedure and receiving results from the called procedure.

In Sections 2.4–2.8, we will consider each of these features and develop the machinery needed in an ISA, from the point of view of efficiently compiling them. In Section 2.10 we will wrap up these discussions by presenting the LC-2200 ISA, a simple instruction set that will serve as a basis for exploring processor implementation details in later chapters.

2.4 Expressions and Assignment Statements

We know that any high-level language (such as Java, C, or Perl) has arithmetic and logical expressions, and assignment statements:

```
a = b + c; /* add b and c and place in a */          (1)
d = e - f; /* subtract f from e and place in d */    (2)
x = y & z; /* AND y and z and place in x */          (3)
```

Each of the preceding statements takes *two operands* as inputs, performs an operation on them, and then stores the result in a *third operand*.

Consider the following three instructions in a processor instruction set:

```
add a, b, c; a ← b + c                               (4)
sub d, e, f; d ← e - f                               (5)
and x, y, z; x ← y & z                               (6)
```

The high-level constructs in (1), (2), and (3) directly map to the instructions (4), (5), and (6), respectively.

Such instructions are called *binary* instructions, because they work on two operands to produce a result. They are also called *three-operand* instructions, because there are three operands (two source operands and one destination operand). Do we always need three operands in such binary instructions? The short answer is no, but in the sections that follow we elaborate on the answer to this question.

2.4.1 Where To Keep the Operands?

Let us discuss the location of the program variables in the previous set of equations: $a, b, c, d, e, f, x, y,$ and z. A simple model of a processor is shown in Figure 2.1.

Inside the processor is an arithmetic/logic unit, or ALU, that performs the operations such as ADD, SUB, AND, OR, and so on. We will now discuss where to keep the operands for these instructions. Let us start the discussion with a simple analogy.

Suppose that you have a toolbox containing a variety of tools. Most toolboxes come with a tool tray. If you are working on a specific project (say, fixing a leak in your kitchen faucet), you transfer a set of screwdrivers and pipe wrenches from the toolbox to the tool tray. You take the tool tray to the kitchen sink. You work on the leak and then return the tools in the tool tray back to the toolbox when you are all done. Of course, you do not want to run back to the toolbox for each tool you need, but instead hope that it is already there in the tool tray. In other words, you optimize the number of times you have to run to the toolbox by bringing the minimal set you need in the tool tray.

We want to do exactly that in the design of the instructions. We have heard the term *registers* used to describe the resources available within a processor. These are like memory, but they are inside the processor, so they are physically (and, therefore, electrically) close to the ALU and are made of faster parts than memory (see Figure 2.2). Therefore, if the operands of an instruction are in registers, they are much quicker to access than if they are in memory. But that is not the whole story.

There is another compelling reason for using registers, especially in modern processors with very large memories. We refer to this problem as the *addressability* of operands. Let us return to the toolbox/tool-tray analogy. Suppose that you are running

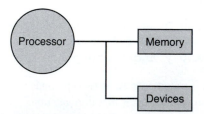

Figure 2.1   A basic computer organization.

The processor contains the Arithmetic/Logic Unit (ALU) that fetches the instructions and operands from memory.

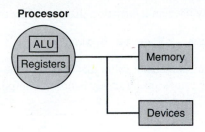

Figure 2.2   Adding registers inside the processor.

Proximity of the registers reduces the access time to the operands from the ALU.

an automobile repair shop. Now your toolbox is really big. Your project requires pretty much all the tools in your toolbox, but at different times as you work on the project. So, as you work on different phases of your project, you will return the current set of tools in your tool tray to the toolbox and bring the appropriate ones for the new phase. Of course, every tool has its unique place in the toolbox. On the other hand, you don't have a unique location in the tool tray for each tool. Instead, you are reusing the space in the tool tray for different tools from your toolbox.

An architect faces this same dilemma with respect to uniquely addressing operands. A modern processor has a very large memory system. As the size of memory grows, the size of a memory address (the number of bits needed to name uniquely a memory location) also increases. Thus, if an instruction has to name three memory operands, that increases the size of each individual instruction. This addressability of operands is a big problem. Each instruction must occupy several memory locations in order to uniquely name all the memory operands it needs.

On the other hand, by having a small set of registers that cater to the immediate program need (*á la* the tool tray), we can solve this memory addressability problem, because the number of bits required to uniquely name a register in this set is small. As a corollary to the memory addressability problem, the size of the register set must be small in order to limit the number of addressing bits necessary for naming the operands in an instruction (even if the level of integration would permit more registers to be included in the architecture).

Therefore, we may have instructions that look like this:

```
add r1, r2, r3; r1 ← r2 + r3
sub r4, r5, r6; r4 ← r5 − r6
and r7, r8, r9; r7 ← r8 & r9
```

In addition, there is often a need to specify constant values for use in the program. For example, initializing a register to some starting value is a routine requirement. The easiest way to meet this need is to have such constant values be part of the instruction itself. Such values are referred to as *immediate* values.

For example, we may have an instruction that looks like this:

```
addi r1, r2, imm;  r1 ← r2 + imm
```

In this instruction, an immediate value that is part of the instruction becomes the third operand. Immediate values are extremely handy in compiling high-level languages.

Example 2.1

Given the instructions

ADD	Rx, Ry, Rz	;	Rx ← Ry + Rz
ADDI	Rx, Ry, Imm	;	Rx ← Ry + Immediate value
NAND	Rx, Ry, Rz	;	Rx ← NOT (Ry AND Rz)

show how you can use them to achieve the effect of the following instruction:

SUB	Rx, Ry, Rz	;	Rx ← Ry − Rz

Answer:

NAND	Rz, Rz, Rz	;	1's complement of Rz in Rz
ADDI	Rz, Rz, 1	;	2's complement of Rz in Rz
		;	Rz now contains −Rz
ADD	Rx, Ry, Rz	;	Rx ← Ry + (−Rz)
		;	The next two instructions restore
		;	the original value of Rz:
NAND	Rz, Rz, Rz	;	1's complement of Rz in Rz
ADDI	Rz, Rz, 1	;	2's complement of Rz in Rz

All the operands are in registers for these arithmetic and logic operations. We will introduce the concept of *addressing mode*, which refers to how the operands are specified in an instruction. The addressing mode used in this case is called *register addressing* because the operands are in registers.

Now, with respect to the high-level constructs (1), (2), and (3), we will explore the relationship between the program variables a, b, c, d, e, f and x, y, z and these processor registers. As a first order, let us assume that all these program variables reside in memory, placed at well-known locations by the compiler. Because the variables are in memory and the arithmetic/logic instructions work only with registers, the variables have to be brought into the registers somehow. Therefore, we need additional instructions to move data back and forth between the memory and the processor registers. These are called *load* (into registers from memory) and *store* (from registers into memory) instructions.

For example,

```
ld   r2, b; r2 ← b
st   r1, a; a  ← r1
```

With these load/store instructions and the arithmetic/logic instructions, we can now "compile" a construct such as

```
a = b + c
```

into

```
ld   r2, b                                          (7)
ld   r3, c                                          (8)
add r1, r2, r3                                      (9)
st   r1, a                                          (10)
```

One may wonder, why not simply use memory operands and avoid the use of registers? After all, the single instruction

```
add  a, b, c
```

seems so elegant and efficient compared with the four-instruction sequence shown in (7)–(10).

The reason can be best understood with our toolbox/tool tray analogy. You knew that you would need to use the screwdriver several times in the course of the project. So, rather than going to the toolbox every time, you paid the cost of bringing the screwdriver once in the tool tray, and you *reused* it several times before returning it back to the toolbox.

The memory is like the toolbox, and the register file is like the tool tray. You expect that the variables in your program may be used in several expressions. Consider the following high-level language statement:

```
d = a * b + a * c + a + b + c;
```

You can see that, once **a, b,** and **c** are brought from the memory into the registers, they will be *reused* several times in just this one expression evaluation. Try compiling the preceding expression evaluation into a set of instructions (assuming a multiply instruction similar in structure to the add instruction). What does such a reuse of program variables available in the registers buy us? The answer is, speed. As we already noted earlier in this subsection, since the registers are inside the processor itself, access time to the program variables is much shorter than it would be if the instructions required going to memory every time to access a program variable.

In a load instruction, one of the operands is a memory location and the other is a register that is the destination of the load instruction (see Figure 2.3). Similarly, in a store instruction, the destination is a memory location.

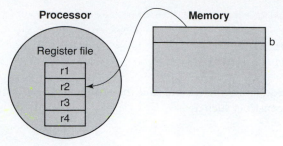

Figure 2.3   Loading a register from memory.

The processor specifies in a load instruction the memory address to load from and the destination register.

Example 2.2

An architecture has one register called an Accumulator (ACC) and instructions that manipulate memory locations and the ACC as follows:

LD	ACC,	a	;	ACC ← contents of memory location a
ST	a,	ACC	;	memory location a ← ACC
ADD	ACC,	a	;	ACC ← ACC + contents of memory location

Using the preceding instructions, show how to realize the semantics of the following instruction:

ADD a, b, c; memory location a ← contents of memory location b + contents of memory location c

Answer:

LD	ACC, b
ADD	ACC, c
ST	a, ACC

2.4.2 How Do We Specify a Memory Address in an Instruction?

Let us consider how to specify the memory address as part of the instruction. Of course, we can embed the address in the instruction itself. However, there is a problem with this approach. As we mentioned in Section 2.4.1, the number of bits needed to represent a memory address in an instruction is already large and will only get worse as the memory size keeps growing. For example, if we have a petabyte (roughly 2^{50} bytes) of memory, we will need 50 bits for representing each memory operand in an instruction. Further, as we will see in Section 2.5, when compiling a program written in a high-level language (especially an object-oriented language), the compiler may know only the offset (relative to the base address of the structure) of each member of a complex data structure, such as an array or an object. Therefore, we introduce an addressing mode that alleviates the need to have the entire memory address of an operand in each instruction.

Such an addressing mode is ***base+offset*** mode. In this addressing mode, a memory address is computed in the instruction as the sum of the contents of a register in the processor (called a base register) and an offset (contained in the instruction as an immediate value) from that register. This is usually represented mnemonically as

```
ld   r2, offset(rb);    r2 ← MEMORY[rb + offset]
```

If rb contains the memory address of variable b, and the offset is 0, then the preceding instruction is equivalent to loading the program variable b into the processor register r2.

Note that rb can simply be one of the registers in the processor.

The power of the base+offset addressing mode is that it can be used to load/store simple variables, as shown before, and also elements of compound variables (such as arrays and structs), as we will see shortly.

Example 2.3

Given the following instructions

LW	Rx, Ry, OFFSET	;	Rx ← MEM[Ry + OFFSET]
ADD	Rx, Ry, Rz	;	Rx ← Ry + Rz
ADDI	Rx, Ry, Imm	;	Rx ← Ry + Immediate value

show how you can realize a new addressing mode, called autoincrement, for use with the load instruction that has the following semantics:

LW	Rx, (Ry)+	;	Rx ← MEM[Ry];
		;	Ry ← Ry + 1;

Your answer should show how the LW instruction using autoincrement will be realized with the given instructions.

Answer:

LW	Rx, Ry, 0	;	Rx ← MEM[Ry + 0]
ADDI	Ry, Ry, 1	;	Ry ← Ry + 1

2.4.3 How Wide Should Each Operand Be?

The width is often referred to as the *granularity* or the *precision* of the operands. To answer this question, we should once again go back to the high-level language and the data types supported in the language. Let's use C as a typical high-level language. The base data types in C are **short, int, long, char**. Whereas the width of these data types are implementation dependent, it is common for **short** to be 16 bits; **int** to be 32 bits; and **char** to be 8 bits. We know that the **char** data type is used to represent alphanumeric characters in **C** programs. There is a historic reason that the **char** data type is 8 bits. ASCII was introduced as the digital encoding standard for alphanumeric characters (found in typewriters) for information exchange between computers and communication devices. ASCII code uses 7 bits to represent each character. So, one would have expected **char** data type to be 7 bits. However, the popular instruction-set architectures at the time **C** language was born used 8-bit operands in instructions. Therefore, it was convenient for **C** to use 8 bits for the **char** data type. Similarly, the reason an **int** data type in most implementations of the **C** compilers is 32 bits is simply the fact that 32-bit processor architecture is quite common.

The next issue is the choice of granularity for each operand. This depends on the desired precision for the data type. Let us informally define *data precision*. Suppose that, in your program, you have a variable **x** which can take on unsigned integer values from 0 to 255. You need just 8 bits to represent such a variable. Thus, the required precision for **x** is 8 bits. Similarly, if you have in your program a signed integer variable **y** that can take on values from -2^{31} to $+(2^{31} - 1)$, then you need 32-bit precision to represent the variable **y** (assuming a 2's complement notation for the representation). The data types in high-level languages (e.g., int, short, and char in C) give programmers the flexibility to tailor their data precision needs for the different program variables. You might wonder about the necessity for this tailoring; why not simply use the maximum precision available in the architecture? The answer is that this is an opportunity to optimize space and time. The less precision there is, the less space is occupied by a program variable in memory. Further, there is often a time advantage, both in ferrying the operands back and forth between the processor and memory, and for arithmetic and logic operations that need less precision. This is particularly true for floating-point arithmetic operations. Therefore, to optimize space and time, it is best if the operand size in the instruction matches the precision needed by the data type. This is why processors support multiple precisions in the instruction set: word, half-word, and byte. **Word** precision usually refers to the *maximum precision* the architecture can support in hardware for arithmetic/logic operations. The other precision categories allow for optimization of space and time.

For the purposes of our discussion, we will assume that a word is 32 bits, a half-word is 16 bits, and a byte is 8 bits. These precision categories respectively map to *int, short,* and *char* in most C implementations. This choice is based on the fact that, circa 2009, the most common hardware word size was 32 bits. We already introduced the concept of addressability of operands, in Section 2.4.1. When an architecture supports multiple precision operands, there is a question of *addressability* of memory operands. *Addressability* refers to the smallest precision operand that can be individually addressed in memory. For example, if a machine is byte addressable, the smallest precision that can be addressed individually is a byte; if it is word addressed, then the smallest precision that can be addressed individually is a word. We will assume byte addressability for our discussion.

So, a word in memory will look as follows:

MSB			LSB

There are 4 bytes in each word. (MSB refers to *most significant byte*; LSB refers to *least significant byte*). So, if we have an integer variable in the program with the value

0x11223344,

then its representation in memory will look as follows:

11	22	33	44

Each byte can be individually addressed. Presumably, there are instructions for manipulating at this level of precision in the architecture.

So, the instruction set may include instructions at multiple precision levels of operands, such as the following:

```
ld    r1, offset(rb);     load a word at address rb+offset into r1
ldb   r1, offset(rb);     load a byte at address rb+offset into r1
add   r1, r2, r3;         add word operands in registers r2 and r3 and place
                          the result in r1
addb  r1, r2, r3;         add byte operands in registers r2 and r3 and place
                          the result in r1
```

There must be a correlation between the architectural decision of supporting multiple precision for the operands and the hardware realization of the processor. The hardware realization includes specifying the width of the datapath and the width of the resources in the datapath, such as registers. We will discuss processor implementation in much more detail in Chapters 3 and 5. Because, for our discussion we said that a word (32 bits) is the maximum precision supported in hardware, it is convenient to assume that the datapath is 32 bits wide. That is, all arithmetic and logic operations take 32-bit operands and manipulate them. Correspondingly, it is convenient to assume that the registers are 32-bits wide to match the datapath width. It should be noted that it is not necessary, but just convenient and more efficient, for the datapath and the register widths to match the chosen word width of the architecture. Additionally, the architecture and implementation have to follow some convention for supporting instructions that manipulate precisions smaller than the chosen word width. For example, an instruction such as *addb* that works on 8-bit precision may take the lower 8 bits of the source registers, perform the addition, and place the result in the lower 8 bits of the destination register.

It should be noted that modern architectures have advanced to 64-bit precision for integer arithmetic. Even the C programming language has introduced data types with 64-bit precision, although the name of the data type may not be consistent across different implementations of the compiler. However, the conceptual discussion of the instruction set design in this chapter is orthogonal to actual hardware precision supported in the architecture.

2.4.4 Endianness

An interesting question in a byte-addressable machine is the ordering of the bytes within the word. With 4 bytes in each word, if the machine is byte addressable, then four consecutive bytes in memory, starting at address 100, will have addresses 100, 101, 102, and 103.

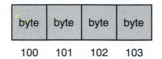

The composite of these 4 bytes make up a word whose address is 100.

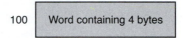

Let us assume that the word at location 100 contains the values 0x11223344. The individual bytes within the word may be organized two possible ways:

Organization 1:

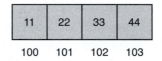

In this organization, the MSB of the word (containing the value 11_{hex}) is at the address of the word operand, namely, 100. This organization is called *big endian*.

Organization 2:

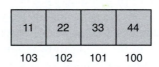

In this organization, the LSB of the word (containing the value 44_{hex}) is at the address of the word operand, namely, 100. This organization is called *little endian*.

So, the endianness of a machine is determined by which byte of the word is at the word address. If it is MSB, then it is big endian; if it is LSB, then it is little endian.

In principle, from the point of view of programming in high-level languages, this should not matter so long as the program uses the data types in expressions in exactly the same way as they are declared.

However, in a language like C it is possible to use a data type differently from the way it was originally declared.

Consider the following code fragment:

```
int i = 0x11223344;
char *c;

c = (char *) &i;
printf("endian: i = %x; c = %x\n", i, *c);
```

Let us investigate what will be printed as the value of c. This depends on the endianness of the machine. In a big-endian machine, the value printed will be 11_{hex}; in a little-endian machine, the value printed will be 44_{hex}. The moral of the story is that, if you declare a datatype of a particular precision and access it as another precision, then it could be a recipe for disaster, depending on the endianness of the machine. Architectures such as IBM PowerPC and Sun SPARC are examples of big endian; Intel x86, MIPS, and DEC Alpha are examples of little endian. In general, the endianness of the machine should not have any bearing on program performance, although one could come up with pathological examples in which a particular endianness may yield a better performance for a particular program—often during string manipulation.

For example, consider the memory layout of the strings "RAMACHANDRAN" and "WAMACHANDRAN" in a big-endian architecture (see Figure 2.4). Assume that the first string starts at memory location 100.

```
char a[13] = "RAMACHANDRAN";
char b[13] = "WAMACHANDRAN";
```

Now consider the memory layout of the same strings, but in a little-endian architecture as shown in Figure 2.5. Inspecting Figures 2.4 and 2.5, one can see that the memory layout of the strings is from left to right in big-endian, whereas it is from right to left in little-endian. To compare the strings, one could use the layout of the strings in memory to achieve some coding efficiency in the two architecture styles.

	+0	+1	+2	+3
100	R	A	M	A
104	C	H	A	N
108	D	R	A	N
112	W	A	M	A
116	C	H	A	N
120	D	R	A	N

Figure 2.4 Big endian layout.

The MSB of the word is at the word address (e.g., R at memory address 100).

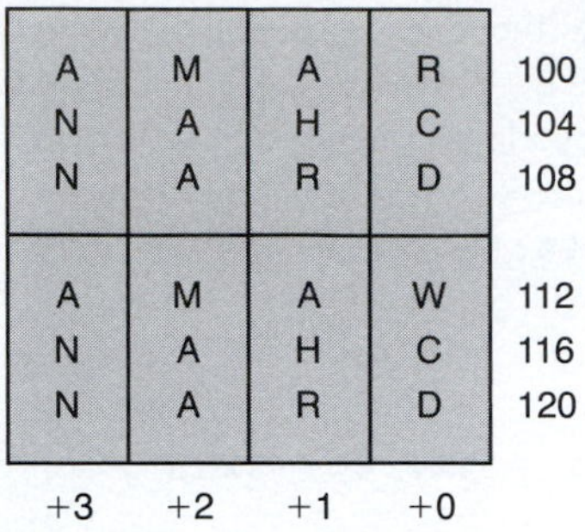

A	M	A	R	100
N	A	H	C	104
N	A	R	D	108
A	M	A	W	112
N	A	H	C	116
N	A	R	D	120

+3   +2   +1   +0

Figure 2.5   Little endian layout.

The LSB of the word is at the word address (e.g., R is at memory address 100).

As we mentioned earlier, so long as you manipulate a data type commensurate with its declaration, the endianness of the architecture should not matter to your program. However, there are situations in which, even if the program does not violate the previously mentioned rule, endiannesss can come to bite the program behavior. This is particularly true for network codes that necessarily cross machine boundaries. If the sending machine is little-endian and the receiving machine is big-endian, there even could be correctness issues in the resulting network code. It is for this reason that network codes use format conversion routines between host to network format, and vice versa, to avoid such pitfalls.[1]

The reader may be wondering why all the box makers couldn't just pick one endianness and go with it? The problem is that such choices become quasi-religious argument so far as a box maker is concerned, and because there is no standardization, the programmers have to just live with the fact that there could be endianness differences in the processors they are dealing with.

To keep the discussion simple, henceforth we will assume a little-endian architecture for the rest of the chapter.

2.4.5 Packing of Operands and Alignment of Word Operands

Modern computer systems have large amounts of memory. Therefore, it would appear that there is plenty of memory to go around, so there should be no reason to be stingy about the use of memory. However, this is not quite true. As memory size is increasing, so is the appetite of applications for memory. The amount of space occupied by a program in memory is often referred to as its *memory footprint*. A compiler, if so directed during compilation, may try to *pack* operands of a program in memory

---

1. If you have access to Unix source code, look up routines called hton and ntoh, which stand for format conversion between *host to network* and *network to host,* respectively.

in order to conserve space. This is particularly meaningful if the data structure consists of variables of different granularities (e.g., `int`, `char`, etc.), and if an architecture supports multiple levels of precision of operands. As the name suggests, *packing* refers to laying out the operands in memory, ensuring that no space is wasted. However, we will also explain in this section why packing may not always be the right approach.

First, let us discuss how the compiler may lay out operands in memory in order to conserve space. Consider the data structure:

```
struct {
    char    a;
    char    b[3];
}
```

One possible layout of this structure in memory, starting at location 100, is shown as follows:

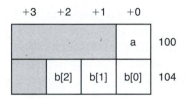

Let us determine the amount of memory actually needed to lay out this data structure. Because each char is 1 byte, the size of the actual data structure is only 4 bytes, but the layout shown wastes 50% of the space required to hold the data structure. The shaded region is the wasted space. This is the unpacked layout.

An efficient compiler may eliminate this wasted space and pack the previous data structure in memory, starting at location 100, as follows:

b[2]	b[1]	b[0]	a
103	102	101	100

The packing done by the compiler is commensurate with the required precision for the data types and the addressability supported in the architecture. In addition to being frugal with respect to space, this layout would result in fewer memory accesses needed to move the whole structure (consisting of the two variables **a** and **b**) back and forth between the processor registers and memory. Thus, packing operands could result in time efficiency, in addition to space efficiency.

As we said before, packing may not always be the right strategy for a compiler to adopt.

Consider the following data structure:

```
struct {
    char    a;
    int     b;
}
```

We will once again determine how much memory is needed to lay out this data structure in memory. A char is 1 byte, and an int is 1 word (4 bytes); so, in total, 5 bytes are needed to store the structure in memory. Let's look at one possible layout of the structure in memory, starting at location 100.

+3	+2	+1	+0	
b...	b...	b_{lsb}	a	100
			b_{msb}	104

The problem with this layout is that **b** is an int, and it starts at address 101 and ends at address 104. To load **b**, two words have to be brought from memory (from addresses 100 and 104). This is inefficient, whether it is done in hardware or in software. Architectures will usually require that word operands start at word addresses. This is referred to as *alignment restriction* of word operands to word addresses.

An instruction

```
ld   r2, address
```

will be an illegal instruction if the address is not on a word boundary (100, 104, etc.). Although the compiler can generate code to load two words (at addresses 100 and 104) and do the necessary manipulation to get the int data type reconstructed inside the processor, this is inefficient timewise. So, typically, the compiler will lay out the data structures such that data types which need word precision are at word address boundaries.

Therefore, a compiler will most likely lay out the previous structure in memory, starting at address 100, as follows:

+3	+2	+1	+0	
			a	100
b_{msb}	b...	b...	b_{lsb}	104

Note that this layout wastes space (37.5% wasted space), but is more efficient from the point of view of time needed to access the operands.

You will see that this classic space–time tradeoff will surface in computer science at all levels of the abstraction hierarchy presented in Chapter 1, from applications down to the architecture.

2.5 High-Level Data Abstractions

Thus far, we have discussed simple variables in a high-level language such as *char, int,* and *float*. We refer to such variables as *scalars*. The space needed to store such a variable is known *a priori*. A compiler has the option of placing a scalar variable in a register or in a memory location. However, when it comes to data abstractions such as arrays and structures that are usually supported in high-level languages, the compiler may have no option except to allocate them in memory. Recall that, due to the addressability problem, the register set in a processor is typically only a few tens of registers. Therefore, the sheer size of such data structures precludes allocating them in registers.

2.5.1 Structures

Structured data types in a high-level language can be supported with **base+offset** addressing mode.

Consider the following C construct:

```
struct {
    int   a;
    char  c;
    int   d;
    long  e;
}
```

If the base address of the structure is in some register **rb**, then accessing any field within the structure can be accomplished by providing the appropriate offset relative to the base register. The compiler knows how much storage is used for each data type and knows the alignment of the variables in the memory.

2.5.2 Arrays

Consider the following declaration:

```
int a[1000]; an array of integers a[0] through a[999]
```

The name **a** refers not to a single variable, but to an array of variables a[0], a[1], etc. For this reason arrays are often referred to as *vectors*. The storage space required for such variables may or may not be known at compile time, depending on the semantics of the high-level programming language. Many programming languages allow arrays to be dynamically sized at run time as opposed to compile time. What this means is that at compile time, the compiler may not know the storage requirement of the array. Contrast this with scalars whose storage size requirement is always known to the compiler at compile time. Thus, a compiler will typically use memory to allocate space for such vector variables.

The compiler will lay this variable **a** out in memory as follows:

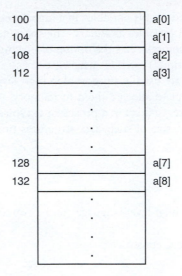

Consider the following statement that manipulates the array:

```
a[7] = a[7] + 1;
```

To compile the preceding statement, assuming that the instruction set allows only ALU operations using registers, first we have to load **a[7]** from memory. It is easy to see that this is doable, given the **base+offset** addressing mode that we already introduced:

```
ld   r1, 28(rb)
```

With **rb** initialized to **100**, the foregoing instruction accomplishes loading **a[7]** into **r1**.

Typically, arrays are used in loops. In this case, there may be a loop counter (say, *j*) that may be used to index the array. Consider the following statement:

```
a[j] = a[j] + 1;
```

In the preceding statement, the offset to the base register is not fixed. It is derived from the current value of the loop index. Although it is possible to still generate code for loading **a[j]**,[2] this requires additional instructions before the load can be performed to compute the effective address of **a[7]**. Therefore, some computer architectures provide an additional addressing mode to let the effective address be computed as the sum of the contents of two registers. This is called the **base+index** addressing mode.

---

2. Basically, the loop index has to be multiplied by 4 and added to rb to get the effective address. Generating the code for loading a[j] by using only base+offset addressing mode is left as an exercise to the reader.

Every new instruction and every new addressing mode adds to the complexity of the implementation; thus, the pros and cons have to be weighed very carefully. This is usually done by cost/performance analysis. For example, to add **base+index** addressing mode, we have to ask the following questions:

1. How often will this addressing mode be used during the execution of a program?
2. What is the advantage (in terms of number of instructions saved) of using **base+index** versus **base+offset**?
3. What, if any, is the penalty paid (in terms of additional time for execution) for a load instruction that uses **base+index** addressing compared with **base+offset** addressing?
4. What additional hardware is needed to support **base+index** addressing?

Answers to these four questions will give us a quantitative handle on whether or not including the **base+index** addressing mode is a good idea.

We will come back to the issue of how to evaluate adding new instructions and addressing modes to the processor in later chapters, when we discuss processor implementation and performance implications.

2.6 **Conditional Statements and Loops**

Before we talk about conditional statements, it is important that we understand the concept of flow of control during program execution. Program execution proceeds sequentially in the normal flow of control:

100	I_1
104	I_2
108	I_3
112	I_4
116	I_5
120	I_6
124	I_7
128	I_8
132	.

Execution of instruction I_1 is normally followed by I_2, then I_3, I_4, and so on. We utilize a special register called *Program Counter (PC)*. Conceptually, we can think of the PC pointing to the currently executing instruction.[3] We know that program execution does not follow this sequential path of flow of control all the time.

---

3. We will see in Chapter 3 that, for efficacy of the implementation we present, the PC contains the memory address of the instruction immediately following the currently executing instruction. However, it should be noted that this is simply a design choice used in this textbook and not a necessity in the instruction set design.

2.6.1 If-Then-Else Statement

Consider the following statements:

```
        if (j == k) go to L1;
        a = b + c;
L1:     a = a + 1;
```

Let us investigate what is needed for compiling the preceding set of statements. The "if" statement has two parts:

1. Evaluation of the predicate "$j == k$": This can be accomplished through the instructions that we identified already for expression evaluation.

2. If the predicate evaluates to TRUE, then it changes the flow of control from going to the next sequential instruction to the target L1. The instructions identified so far do not accomplish this change of flow of control.

Thus, there is a need for a new instruction that changes the flow of control in addition to evaluating an arithmetic or logic expression. We will introduce a new instruction:

beq r1, r2, L1;

The semantics of this instruction are as follows:

1. Compare r1 and r2.
2. If they are equal, then the next instruction to be executed is at address L1.
3. If they are unequal, then the next instruction to be executed is the next one textually following the *beq* instruction.

BEQ is an example of a conditional branch instruction to change the flow of control. We need to specify the address of the target of the branch in the instruction. While describing arithmetic and logic instructions, we discussed addressability (see Section 2.4.1) and suggested that it is a good idea to keep the operands in registers rather than memory in order to reduce the number of bits needed in the instruction for operand specifiers. This naturally raises the question of whether the target of the branch instruction should also be in a register instead of being part of the instruction. That is, should the address L1 be kept in a register? A branch instruction takes the flow of control away from the current instruction (i.e., the branch) to another instruction that is usually not too far from it. We know that the PC points to the currently executing instruction. So, the target of a branch can be expressed, relative to the current location of the branch instruction, by the provision of an *address offset* as part of the instruction. Since the distance to the target of the branch from the current instruction is not too large, the address offset needs only a few bits in the branch instruction. In other words, it is fine to use a memory address (actually, an address offset) as part of the instruction for branch instructions to specify the target of the branch.

Thus, the branch instruction has the following format:

```
beq r1, r2, offset
```

The effect of this instruction is as follows:

1. Compare r1 and r2.
2. If they are equal, then the next instruction to be executed is at address $PC+offset_{adjusted}$[4].
3. If they are unequal, then the next instruction to be executed is the next one textually following the *beq* instruction.

<mark>We have essentially added a new addressing mode to compute an effective address.</mark> This is called ***PC-relative*** addressing.

The instruction-set architecture may have different flavors of conditional branch instructions such as BNE (branch on not equal), BZ (branch on zero), and BN (branch on negative).

Quite often, there may be an "else" clause in a conditional statement.

```
      if (j == k) {
            a = b + c;
      }
      else {
            a = b - c;
      }
L1:  .....
      .....
```

It turns out that we do not need anything new in the instruction-set architecture to compile the preceding conditional statement. The conditional branch instruction is sufficient to handle the predicate calculation and branch associated with the "if" statement. However, after the set of statements in the body of the "if" clause is executed, the flow of control has to be unconditionally transferred to **L1** (the start of statements following the body of the "else" clause).

To enable this, we will introduce an "unconditional jump" instruction,

```
j    rtarget
```

where r_{target} contains the target address of the unconditional jump.

The requirement for such an unconditional jump instruction needs some elaboration, since we have a branch instruction already. After all, we could realize the effect

---

4. PC is the address of the beq instruction; $offset_{adjusted}$ is the offset specified in the instruction adjusted for any implementation specifics, which we will see in the next chapter.

of an unconditional branch by using the conditional branch instruction **beq**. When the two operands of the **beq** instruction are used to name the same register (e.g., **beq r1, r1, offset**), the effect is an unconditional jump. However, there is a catch. The range of the conditional branch instruction is limited to the size of the offset. For example, with an offset size of 8 bits (and assuming that the offset is a 2's complement number, in which case both positive and negative offsets are possible), the range of the branch is limited to PC-128 and PC+127. This is the reason for introducing a new unconditional jump instruction, wherein a register specifies the target address of the jump.

The reader should feel convinced that, by using the conditional and unconditional branches, it is possible to compile any level of nested if-then-else statements.

2.6.2 Switch Statement

Many high-level languages provide a special case of conditional statement exemplified by the "switch" statement of C.

```
switch (k) {
    case 0:
    case 1:
    case 2:
    case 3:
    default:
}
```

If the number of cases is limited and/or sparse, then it may be best to compile this statement similar to a nested if-then-else construct. On the other hand, if there are a number of contiguous, nonsparse cases, then compiling the construct as a nested

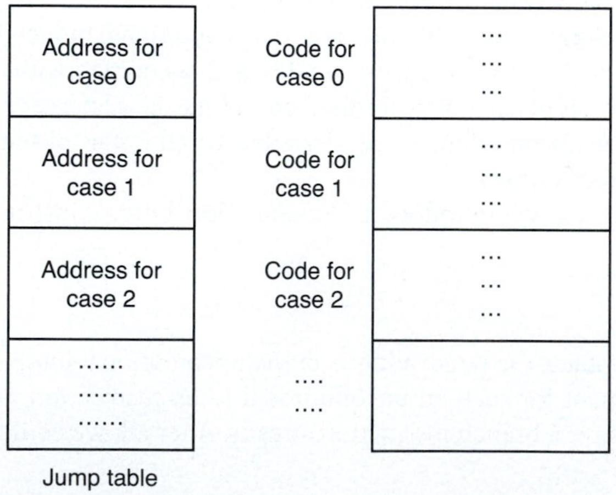

Jump table

Figure 2.6   Implementing switch statement with a jump table.

Each entry in the table points to the first instruction corresponding to that case value.

if-then-else will result in inefficient code. As an alternative, using a jump table that holds the starting addresses for the code segments of each of the cases will make it possible to get an efficient implementation. (See Figure 2.6.)

In principle, nothing new is needed architecturally to accomplish this implementation. Whereas nothing new may be needed in the instruction-set architecture to support the switch statement, it may be advantageous to have unconditional jump instruction that works with one level of indirection.

That is,

```
J    @(rtarget)
```

where **rtarget** contains the address of the target address to jump to (unconditionally).

Additionally, some architectures provide special instructions for bounds checking. For example, MIPS architecture provides a set-on-less-than instruction

```
SLT s1, s2, s3
```

which works as follows:

```
if s2 < s3 then set s1 to 1
else set s1 to 0
```

This instruction is useful to do the bounds checking in implementing a switch statement.

2.6.3 Loop Statement

High-level languages provide different flavors of looping constructs. Consider the code fragment

```
        j = 0;
loop:   b = b + a[j];
        j = j + 1;
        if (j != 100) go to loop;
```

Assuming that a register **r1** is used for the variable **j**, and the value 100 is contained in another register **r2**, we can compile the preceding looping construct as follows:

```
loop:    ...
         ...
         ...
         bne r1, r2, loop
```

Thus, no new instruction or addressing mode is needed to support the aforesaid looping construct. The reader should feel convinced that any other looping construct (such as "for," "while," and "repeat") can similarly be compiled by using conditional and unconditional branch instructions that we have introduced so far.

2.7 Checkpoint

So far, we have seen the following high-level language constructs:

1. Expressions and assignment statements
2. High-level data abstractions
3. Conditional statements, including loops

We have developed the following capabilities in the instruction-set architecture to support the efficient compilation of the constructs discussed:

1. Arithmetic and logic instructions using registers
2. Data movement instructions (load/store) between memory and registers
3. Conditional and unconditional branch instructions
4. Addressing modes: register addressing, base+offset, base+index, PC-relative

2.8 Compiling Function Calls

Compiling procedures or function calls in a high-level language require some special attention.

First, let us review the programmer's mental model of a procedure call. The program is in *main* and makes a call to function *foo*. The flow of control of the program is transferred to the entry point of the function; upon exiting *foo*, the flow of control returns to the statement following the call to *foo* in *main*. Here is what the model looks like:

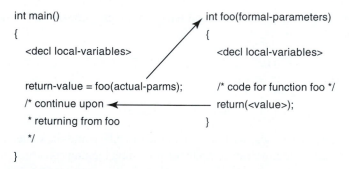

```
int main()                              int foo(formal-parameters)
{                                       {
    <decl local-variables>                  <decl local-variables>

    return-value = foo(actual-parms);       /* code for function foo */
    /* continue upon                        return(<value>);
     * returning from foo                }
     */

}
```

First, let us define some terms: *caller* is the entity that makes the procedure call (*main* in our example); *callee* is the procedure that is being called (*foo* in our example).

Let us enumerate the steps in compiling a procedure call:

1. Ensure that the state of the caller (i.e., processor registers used by the caller) is preserved for resumption upon return from the procedure call.

2. Pass the actual parameters to the callee.

3. Remember the return address.

4. Transfer control to callee.

5. Allocate space for callee's local variables.

6. Receive the return values from the callee and give them to the caller.

7. Return to the point of call.

Can the preceding set of requirements be handled with the capabilities we have already identified in the instruction-set architecture of the processor? To answer this question, let us look at each of the listed items one by one. We will first understand the ramifications of preserving the state of the caller in Section 2.8.1 and then consider the remaining chores in Section 2.8.2.

2.8.1 State of the Caller

Let us first define what we mean by the *state of the caller*. To execute the code of the callee, the resources needed are memory (for the code and data of the callee) and processor registers (since all arithmetic/logic instructions use them). The compiler will ensure that the memory used by the caller and callee are distinct (with the exception of any sharing that is mandated by the semantics of the high-level language). Therefore, the contents of the processor registers are the "state" we are worried about, because partial results of the caller could be sitting in them at the time of calling the callee. Since we do not know what the callee may do to these registers, it is prudent to *save* them prior to the call and *restore* them upon return.

Now we need a place to save the registers. Let us try a hardware solution to the problem. We will introduce a *shadow register set* into which we will save the processor registers prior to the call; we will restore the processor registers from this shadow register set upon return from the procedure call. (See Figure 2.7.)

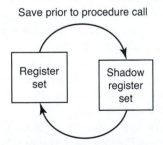

Save prior to procedure call

Register set

Shadow register set

Restore upon procedure return

Figure 2.7   State save/restore for procedure call/return.

Upon a procedure call, save the registers in the shadow register set; restore upon return.

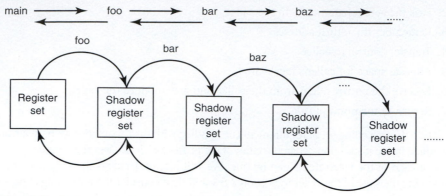

Figure 2.8   State save/restore for a nested procedure call.

Extend the idea of shadow register set to a sequence of nested procedure calls.

We know that procedure calls are frequent in modular codes, so rapid save/restore of state is important. Since the shadow register set is located inside the processor, and the save/restore is happening in hardware, the shadow register set seems like a good idea.

The main problem with this idea is that it assumes that the called procedure is not going to make any more procedure calls itself. We know from our experience with high-level languages that this is a bad assumption. In reality, we need as many shadow register sets at the level of nesting that is possible in procedure call sequences. (See Figure 2.8.)

Let us discuss the implications of implementing these shadow register sets in hardware. The level of nesting of procedure calls (i.e., the chain of calls shown in Figure 2.8) is a dynamic property of the program. A hardware solution necessarily has to be finite in terms of the number of such shadow register sets. Besides, this number cannot be arbitrarily large, due to the cost and complexity of a hardware solution. Nevertheless, some architectures, such as Sun SPARC, implement a hardware mechanism called *register windowing* precisely for this purpose. Sun SPARC provides 128 hardware registers, out of which only 32 registers are visible at any point in time. The invisible registers form the shadow register sets to support the procedure calling mechanism shown in Figure 2.8.

Figure 2.8 also suggests a solution that can be implemented in software: the *stack* abstraction that you may have learned about in a course on data structures. We save the state in a stack at the point of call and restore it upon return. Because the stack has the *last-in-first-out (LIFO)* property, it fits nicely with the requirement of nested procedure calls.

The stack can be implemented as a software abstraction in memory; thus, there is no limitation on the dynamic level of nesting.

The compiler has to maintain a pointer to the stack for saving and restoring state. This does not need anything new from the architecture. The compiler may dedicate one of the processor registers as the *stack pointer*. Note that this is not an architectural restriction, but just a convenience for the compiler. Besides, each compiler is free to choose a different register to use as a stack pointer. What this means is that the compiler will not use this register for hosting program variables, since the stack pointer serves a dedicated internal function for the compiler.

What we have just done with dedicating a register as the stack pointer is to introduce a software *convention* for register usage.

Well, one of the good points of the hardware solution was the fact that it was done in hardware and, hence, fast. If the stack is now implemented in software, then it is going to incur the penalty of having to move the data back and forth between processor registers and memory on every procedure call/return. Let us see whether we can have the flexibility of the software solution while keeping the performance advantage of the hardware solution. The software solution cannot match the speed advantage of the hardware solution, but we can certainly try to reduce the amount of wasted effort.

Let us understand whether we really do need to save all the registers at the point of call and restore them upon return. This approach implies that the caller (i.e., the compiler on behalf of the caller) is responsible for save/restore. If the callee does not use *any* of the registers, then the whole chore of saving and restoring the registers would have been wasted. Therefore, we could assign the chore to the callee and let the callee save/restore the registers that *it is going to use* in its procedure. Once again, if the caller does not need any of the values in those registers upon return, then the effort of the callee is wasted.

To overcome this dilemma, let us carry the idea of software convention a little further. Here again, an analogy may help. This is the story of two lazy roommates. They would like to get away with as little house chores as possible. However, they have to eat every day, so they come to an agreement. They have a frying pan for common use, and each has a set of her own dishes. The convention they decide to adopt is the following:

- The dishes that are their own, they never have to clean.
- If they use the other person's dishes, then they have to leave them clean after every use.
- There is no guarantee that the frying pan will be clean; it is up to each person to clean and use it if they need it.

With this convention, each can get away with very little work—if they do not use the frying pan or the other person's dishes, then practically no work at all!

The software convention for procedure calling takes an approach similar to the lazy roommates analogy. Of course, a procedure call is not symmetric, as is the lazy roommates analogy (since there is an ordering—caller to callee). The caller gets a subset of the registers (the **s** registers) that are its own. The caller can use them any way it wants without worrying about the callee trashing them. The callee, if it needs to use the **s** registers, has to save and restore them. As in the case of the frying pan, there is a subset of registers (the **t** registers) that are common to both the caller and the callee. Either of them can use the **t** registers without worrying about saving or restoring them. Now, as in the analogy to the lazy roommates, if the caller never needs any values in the **t** registers upon return from a procedure, then it has to do no work on procedure calls. Similarly, if the callee never uses any of the **s** registers, then it has to do no work for saving/restoring registers.

The saving/restoring of registers will be done on the stack. We will return to the complete software convention for procedure call/return after we address the other items in the list of things to be done for procedure call/return.

2.8.2 Remaining Chores with Procedure Calling

1. **Parameter passing:** An expedient way of passing parameters is via processor registers. Once again, the compiler may establish a software convention and reserve some number of processor registers for parameter passing.

   Of course, a procedure may have more parameters than are allowed by the convention. In this case, the compiler will pass the additional parameters on the stack. The software convention will establish where exactly on the stack the callee can find the additional parameters with respect to the stack pointer.

2. **Remember the return address:** We introduced the processor resource, Program Counter (PC), early on in the context of branch instructions. None of the high-level constructs we have encountered thus far have required remembering where we are in the program. So now, there is a need to introduce a new instruction for saving the PC in a well-known place so that it can be used for returning from the callee.

   We introduce a new instruction:

   ```
   JAL rtarget, rlink
   ```

   The semantics of this instruction is as follows:

   - Remember the return address in r_{link} (which can be any processor register).
   - Set PC to the value in r_{target} (the start address of the callee).

   We return to the issue of software convention. The compiler may designate one of the processor registers to be r_{target} to hold the address of the target of the subroutine call and designate another of the processor registers to be r_{link} to hold the return address. That is, these registers are not available to house normal program variables.

   So, at the point of call, the procedure call is compiled as

   ```
   JAL rtarget, rlink; /* rtarget containing the address
                               of the callee */
   ```

   Returning from the procedure is straightforward. Since we already have an unconditional jump instruction,

   ```
   J rlink
   ```

   accomplishes the return from the procedure call.[5]

3. **Transfer control to callee:** Step 3 transfers the control to the callee via the JAL instruction.

---

5. Actually, given that we now have a JAL instruction, we can simply use this instruction to do an unconditional jump. JAL r_{link}, $r_{dont-care}$, where $r_{dont-care}$ is simply ignored, accomplishes an unconditional jump to the location pointed to by r_{link}.

4. **Space for callee's local variables:** The stack is a convenient area to allocate the space needed for any local variables in the callee. The software convention will establish where exactly on the stack the callee can find the local variables with respect to the stack pointer.[6]

5. **Return values:** An expedient way for this to be done is for the compiler to reserve some processor registers for the return values. As in the case of parameters, if the number of returned values exceeds the registers reserved by the convention, then the additional return values will be placed on the stack. The software convention will establish where exactly on the stack the caller can find the additional return values with respect to the stack pointer.

6. **Return to the point of call:** As we mentioned earlier, a simple jump through r_{link} will get the control back to the instruction that follows the point of call.

2.8.3 Software Convention

Just to make this discussion concrete, we introduce a set of processor registers and the software convention used:

- Registers **s0–s2** are the caller's s registers.
- Registers **t0–t2** are the temporary registers.
- Registers **a0–a2** are the parameter passing registers.
- Register **v0** is used for return value.
- Register **ra** is used for return address.
- Register **at** is used for target address.
- Register **sp** is used as a stack pointer.

Before illustrating how we will use the preceding conventions to compile a procedure call, we need to recall some details about stacks. A convention that is used by most compilers is that the stack grows down from high addresses to low addresses. The basic stack operations are as follows:

- *Push* decrements the stack pointer and places the value at the memory location pointed to by the stack pointer.
- *Pop* takes the value at the memory location pointed to by the stack pointer and increments the stack pointer.

Figures 2.9–2.20 show the way the compiler will produce code to build the stack frame at run time. In all the figures, **LOW** address is at the top of the stack and **HIGH** address is at the bottom of the stack, consistent with the stack growing from high address to low address.

---

6. See Exercise 18 for a variation of this description.

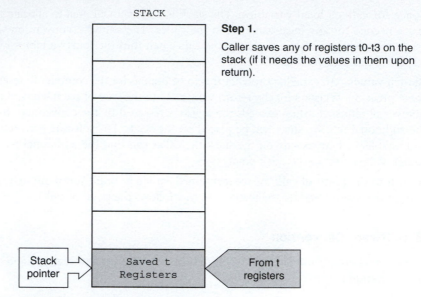

Step 1.

Caller saves any of registers t0-t3 on the stack (if it needs the values in them upon return).

Figure 2.9 Procedure call/return—Step 1.

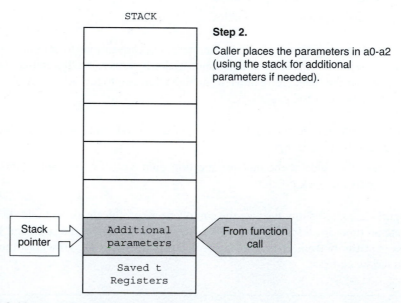

Step 2.

Caller places the parameters in a0-a2 (using the stack for additional parameters if needed).

Figure 2.10 Procedure call/return—Step 2.

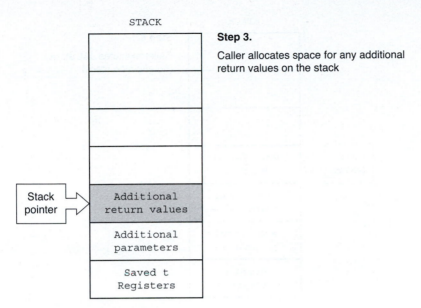

Figure 2.11   Procedure call/return—Step 3.

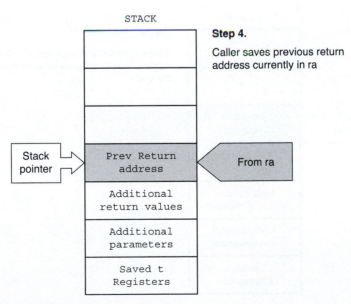

Figure 2.12   Procedure call/return—Step 4.

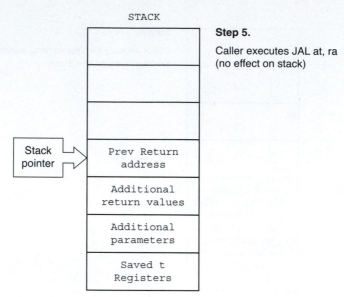

Figure 2.13   Procedure call/return—Step 5.

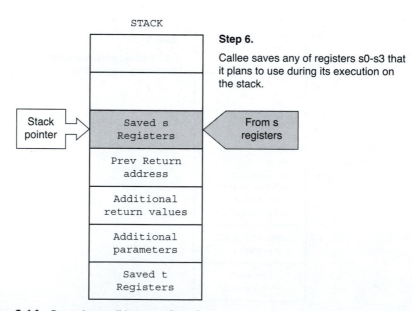

Figure 2.14   Procedure call/return—Step 6.

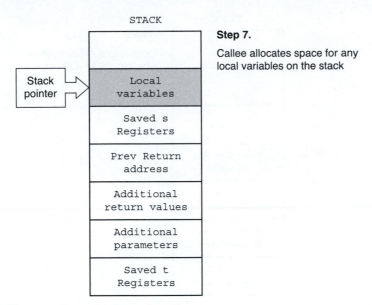

Figure 2.15 Procedure call/return—Step 7.

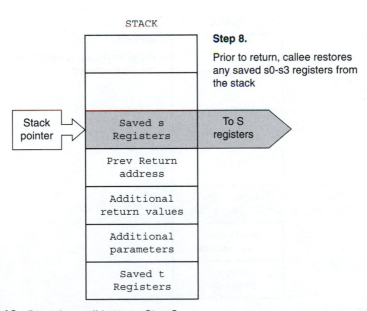

Figure 2.16 Procedure call/return—Step 8.

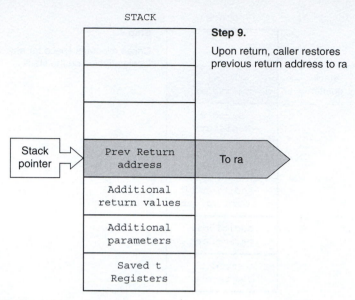

Figure 2.17   Procedure call/return—Step 9.

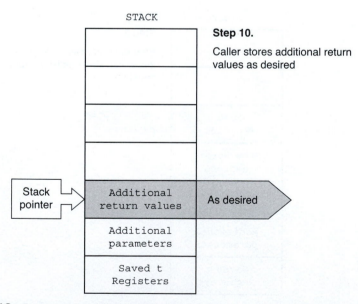

Figure 2.18   Procedure call/return—Step 10.

STACK

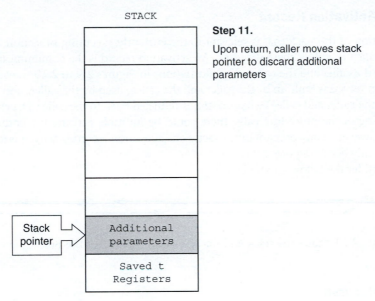

Step 11.

Upon return, caller moves stack pointer to discard additional parameters

Figure 2.19   Procedure call/return—Step 11.

STACK

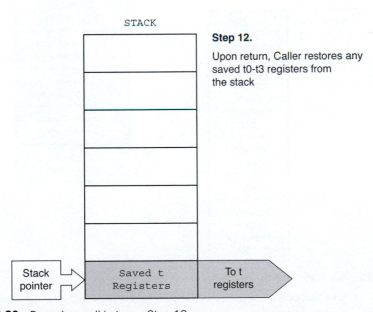

Step 12.

Upon return, Caller restores any saved t0-t3 registers from the stack

Figure 2.20   Procedure call/return—Step 12.

2.8.4 Activation Record

The portion of the stack that is relevant to the currently executing procedure is called the *activation record* for that procedure. An activation record is the communication area between the caller and the callee. The illustrations in Figures 2.9 to 2.19 show how the activation record is built up by the caller and the callee, used by the callee, and dismantled (by the caller and callee) when control is returned back to the caller. Depending on the nesting of the procedure calls, there could be multiple activation records on the stack. However, at any point of time exactly one activation record is active pertaining to the currently executing procedure.

Consider the following sequence:

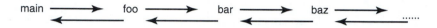

Figure 2.21 shows the stack and the activation records for the preceding sequence of calls.

2.8.5 Recursion

One of the most powerful tools for a programmer is recursion. We do not need anything special in the instruction-set architecture to support recursion. The stack mechanism

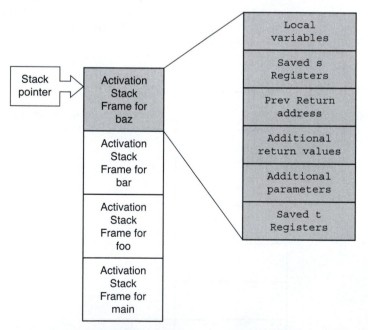

Figure 2.21   Activation records for a sequence of calls.

Note that only the topmost activation record is meaningful for the currently executing procedure.

ensures that every instantiation of a procedure, whether it is the same procedure or a different one, gets a new activation record. Of course, a procedure that could be called recursively has to be coded in a manner that supports recursion. This is in the purview of the programmer. The instruction set need not be modified in any way to specially support recursion.

2.8.6 Frame Pointer

During execution of a program, it is, obviously, essential to be able to locate all of the items that are stored on the stack by the program. Their absolute location cannot be known until the program is executing. It might seem obvious that they can be referenced as being at some offset from the stack pointer, but there is a problem with this approach. Certain compilers may generate code that will move the stack pointer during the execution of the function (after the stack frame is constructed). For example, a number of languages permit dynamic allocation on the stack. Whereas it would be possible to keep track of this stack movement, the extra bookkeeping and execution time penalties would make this a poor choice. The common solution is to designate one of the general-purpose registers as a *frame pointer* that contains the address of a known point in the activation record for the function. This address will never change during execution of the function. An example will help to clarify the problem and the solution. Consider the following procedure:

```
int foo(formal-parameters)
{
    int a, b;

    /* some code */
    if (a > b) {                    (1)
        int c = 1;                  (2)
        a = a + b + c;              (3)
    }

    printf("%d\n, a);               (4)

    /* more code for foo */

    /*
     * return from foo
     */
    return(0);
}
```

Let us assume that the stack pointer (denoted as $sp) contains 100 after step 6 (Figure 2.14) in a call sequence to foo. In step 7, the callee allocates space for the local variables (a and b). Assuming the usual convention of the stack, growing from high addresses to low addresses, a is allocated at address 96 and b is allocated at address 92. Now $sp contains 92. This situation is shown in Figure 2.22.

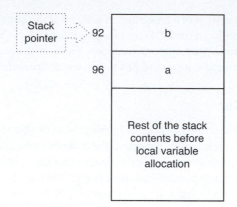

Figure 2.22   State of the stack after the local variables are allocated in the procedure. Note that the stack pointer value is 92 at this time.

Procedure foo starts executing. The compiled code for the "if" statement needs to load a and b into processor registers. This is quite straightforward for the compiler. The following two instructions

```
ld      r1, 4($sp);      /* load r1 with a; address of a = $sp+offset = 92+4 = 96 */
ld      r2, 0($sp);      /* load r2 with b; address of b = $sp+offset = 92+0 = 92 */
```

load a and b into processor registers r1 and r2, respectively.

Note what happens next in the procedure if the predicate calculation turns out to be true. The program allocates a new variable c. As one might guess, this variable will also be allocated on the stack. Note, however, that this is not part of the local variable allocation (step 7, Figure 2.15) prior to beginning the execution of foo. This is a conditional allocation subject to the predicate of the if statement evaluating to true. The address of c is 88. Now $sp contains 88. This situation is shown in Figure 2.23.

Inside the code block for the "if" statement, we may need to load/store the variables *a* and *b*. (See statement 3 in the code block.) Generating the correct addresses for *a* and *b* is the tricky part. The variable *a* was originally at an offset of 4 with respect to $sp. However, it is at an offset of 8 with respect to the current value in $sp. Thus, in order to load variables *a* and *b* in statement (3), the compiler will have to generate the following code:

```
ld      r1, 8($sp);      /* load r1 with a; address of a = $sp+offset = 88+8 = 96 */
ld      r2, 4($sp);      /* load r2 with b; address of b = $sp+offset = 88+4 = 92 */
```

Once the "if" code block execution completes, *c* is de-allocated from the stack and the $sp changes to 92. Now *a* is at an offset of 4 with respect to the current value in $sp. This situation is the same as that shown in Figure 2.22.

The reader can see that, from the point of writing the compiler, the fact that the stack can grow and shrink makes the job harder. The offset for local variables on the stack changes, depending on the current value of the stack pointer.

This is the reason for dedicating a register as a frame pointer. The frame pointer contains the first address on the stack that pertains to the activation record of the called

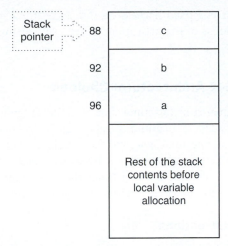

Figure 2.23 State of the stack after the variable c is allocated, corresponding to statement (2) in the procedure.

Note that the stack pointer value is 88 at this time.

procedure and never changes while this procedure is in execution. Of course, if a procedure makes another call, then its frame pointer has to be saved and restored by the callee. Thus, the very first thing that the callee does is to save the frame pointer on the stack and copy the current value of the stack pointer into the frame pointer. This is shown in Figure 2.24.

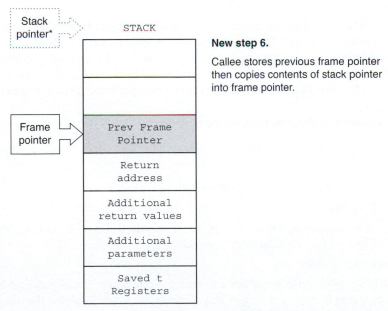

* Stack pointer may change during procedure execution

Figure 2.24 Frame Pointer.

The frame pointer is a fixed harness on the stack (for a given procedure) and points to the first address of the activation record (AR) of the currently executing procedure.

2.9 Instruction-Set Architectural Choices

In this section, we summarize architectural choices in the design of instruction sets. The choices range from a specific set of arithmetic and logic instructions in the repertoire to the addressing modes, architectural style, and the actual memory layout (i.e., format) of the instruction. Sometimes, these choices are driven by current technology trends and implementation feasibility, while at other times they are determined by the goal of elegant and/or efficient support for high-level language constructs.

2.9.1 Additional Instructions

Some architectures provide additional instructions to improve the space and time efficiency of compiled code.

- For example, in the MIPS architecture, load/store instructions are always for an entire word of 32 bits. Nevertheless, once the instruction is brought into a processor register, special instructions are available for *extracting* a specific byte of the word into another register; similarly, a specific byte of the word can be *inserted* into the word.
- The DEC Alpha architecture includes instructions for loading and storing at different operand sizes: byte, half-word, word, and quad-word.
- Some architectures may have some predefined immediate values (e.g., 0, 1, and other small integers) available for direct use in instructions.
- DEC VAX architecture has a single instruction to load and store all the registers in the register file to and from memory. As one might guess, such an instruction would be useful for storing and restoring registers at the point of procedure call and return. The reader should think about the utility of such an instruction in light of the discussion of procedure calling conventions presented earlier in the chapter.

2.9.2 Additional Addressing Modes

In addition to the addressing modes we already have discussed, there are fancier addressing modes provided by some architectures:

- Many architectures provide an indirect addressing mode.
  - `ld @(ra)`

    In this instruction, the contents of the register ra will be used as the address of the address of the actual memory operand.
- Pseudo-direct addressing
  - MIPS provides this particular addressing mode where the effective address is computed by taking the top 6 bits of the PC and concatenating them with the bottom 26 bits of the instruction word, to get a 32-bit absolute address:

Early architectures such as IBM 360, PDP-11, and VAX 11 supported many more addressing modes than we covered in this chapter. Most modern architectures have taken a minimalist approach toward addressing modes for accessing memory. This is mainly because over the years it has been seen that very few of the more complex addressing modes are actually used by the compiler. Even base+index is not found in MIPS architecture, though IBM PowerPC and Intel Pentium do support this addressing mode.

2.9.3 Architecture Styles

Historically, there have been several different kinds of architecture styles:

- **Stack oriented:** Burroughs Computers introduced the stack-oriented architecture, in which all the operands are on a stack. All instructions work on operands that are on the stack.

- **Memory oriented:** IBM 360 series of machines focused on memory-oriented architectures wherein most (if not all) instructions work on memory operands.

- **Register oriented:** As discussed in this chapter, most instructions in this architecture style deal with operands that are in registers. With the maturation of compiler technology, and the efficient use of registers within the processor, this style of architecture has come to stay as the instruction-set architecture of choice. DEC Alpha, and MIPS are modern-day examples of this style of architecture.

- **Hybrid:** As is always the case, one can make a case for each of the styles of architecture, with specific applications or set of applications in mind. So, naturally, a combination of these styles is quite popular. Both the IBM PowerPC and the Intel x86 families of architectures are a hybrid of the memory-oriented and register-oriented styles.

2.9.4 Instruction Format

Depending on the instruction repertoire, instructions may be grouped into the following classes:

1. **Zero-operand instructions**
   Examples include
   - HALT (halts the processor) and
   - NOP (does nothing).

   Also, if the architecture is stack-oriented, then it has only implicit operands for most instructions (except for pushing and popping values explicitly on the stack). Instructions in such an architecture would look like the following:
   - ADD (pops the top two elements of the stack, adds them, and pushes the result back onto the stack)

- PUSH <operand> (pushes the operand onto the stack)
- POP <operand> (pops the top element of the stack into the operand)

2. **One-operand instructions**
   Examples include instructions that map to unary operations in high-level languages:

   - INC/DEC <operand> (increments or decrements the specified operand by a constant value)
   - NEG <operand> (2's complement of the operand)
   - NOT <operand> (1's complement of the operand)

   Also, unconditional jump instructions usually have only one operand:

   - J <target> (PC ← target)

     Also, some older machines (such as DEC's PDP-8) used one implicit operand (called the *accumulator*) and one explicit operand. Instructions in such architecture would look like the following:

   - ADD <operand> (ACC ← ACC + operand)
   - STORE <operand> (operand ← ACC)
   - LOAD <operand> (ACC ← operand)

3. **Two-operand instructions**
   Examples include instructions that map to binary operations in a high-level language. The basic idea is that one of the operands is used as both source and destination in a binary operation:

   - ADD R1, R2 (R1 ← R1 + R2)

   Data movement instructions also fall into this class:

   - MOV R1, R2 (R1 ← R2)

4. **Three-operand instructions**
   This is the most general kind; we have seen examples of it throughout the chapter. Examples include the following:

   - ADD R_{dst}, R_{src1}, R_{src2} (R_{dst} ← R_{src1} + R_{src2})
   - LOAD R, Rb, offset (R ← MEM[Rb + offset])

Instruction format deals with how the instruction is laid out in memory. An architecture may include a mixture of the styles that we discussed earlier and may comprise various types of instructions that need a different number of operands in every instruction.

A typical instruction has the following generic format:

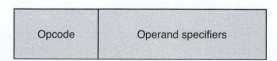

| Opcode | Operand specifiers |

At the point of designing the instruction format, we are getting to the actual implementation. This is because the choice of the instruction format has a bearing on the space and time efficiency of the design. A related choice is the actual *encoding* of the fields within an instruction, which pertains to the semantic meaning associated with each bit pattern for a given field—for example, the bit pattern corresponding to ADD, etc.

In a broad sense, instruction formats may be grouped under two categories:

- **All instructions are of the same length.** In this format, all instructions have the same length (e.g., one memory word). What this means is that the same bit position in an instruction may have a different meaning, depending on the instruction.

  - *Pros:*

    - This simplifies the implementation due to the fixed size of the instruction.

    - Interpretation of the fields of the instruction can start as soon as the instruction is available, as all instructions have the same, fixed length.

  - *Cons:*

    - Because all instructions do not need all the fields (for example, single operand versus multiple operand instructions), there is the potential for wasted space in each instruction.

    - We may need additional glue logic (such as decoders and multiplexers) to apply the fields of the instruction to the datapath elements.

    - The instruction-set designer is limited by the fact that all instructions have to fit within a fixed length (usually, one word). The limitation becomes apparent in the size of the immediate operands and address offsets specifiable in the instruction.

MIPS is an example of an architecture that uses instructions of the same length.

Here are examples of instructions from MIPS:

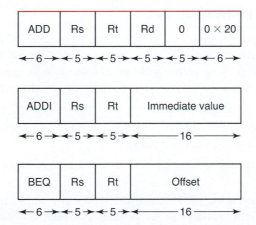

In the preceding ADD instruction, the 5-bit field following Rd serves no purpose in the instruction, but is there due to the fixed-word length requirement of each instruction.

- **Instructions may be of variable length.** In this format instructions are of variable length; that is, an instruction may occupy multiple words.
  - *Pros:*
    - There is no wasted space, because an instruction occupies exactly the space required for it.
    - The instruction-set designer is not constrained by limited sizes (for example, the size of immediate fields).
    - There is an opportunity to choose different sizes and encoding for the opcodes, addressing modes, and operands, depending on their observed usage by the compiler.
  - *Cons:*
    - This format complicates the implementation, because the length of the instruction can be discerned only after decoding the opcode. This could lead to a sequential interpretation of the instruction and its operands.

  The DEC VAX 11 family and the Intel x86 family are examples of architectures with variable-length instructions. In VAX 11, the instructions can vary in size from 1 byte to 53 bytes.

It should be emphasized that our intent here is not to suggest that all architectural styles and instruction formats covered in this section are feasible today. Rather, our intent is to give the reader an exposure to the variety of choices that have been explored in instruction set design. For example, there have been commercial offerings in the past of stack-oriented architectures (with zero operand instruction format) and accumulator-based machines (with one-operand instruction format). However, such architectures are no longer in the mainstream of general-purpose processors.

2.10 LC-2200 Instruction Set

As a concrete example of a simple architecture, we define the LC-2200. This is a 32-bit register-oriented little-endian architecture with a fixed-length instruction format. There are 16 general-purpose registers as well as a separate program counter (PC) register. All addresses are word addresses. The purpose of introducing this instruction set is three-fold:

- The LC-2200 serves as a concrete example of a simple instruction set that can cater to the needs of any high-level language.
- It serves as a concrete architecture for our discussion of implementation issues in Chapters 3 and 5.
- Perhaps most important, the LC-2200 also serves as a simple, unencumbered vehicle for adding other features to the processor architecture for our discussion, in later chapters, of interrupts, virtual memory, and synchronization issues. This add-on capability is particularly attractive as a learning tool because it exposes the reader to the process by which a particular feature may be added to the processor architecture to serve a specific functionality.

2.10.1 **Instruction Format**

The LC-2200 supports four instruction formats. The R-type instruction includes **add** and **nand**. The I-type instruction includes **addi, lw, sw,** and **beq**. The J-type instruction is **jalr**, and the O-type instruction is **halt**. Thus, in total, LC-2200 has only eight instructions. Table 2.1 summarizes the semantics of these instructions.

R-type instructions (add, nand):

bits 31-28:   opcode

bits 27-24:   reg X

bits 23-20:   reg Y

bits 19-4:   unused (should be all 0s)

bits 3-0:   reg Z

31 28	27 24	23 20	19 4 3	0
Opcode	Reg X	Reg Y	Unused	Reg Z

I-type instructions (addi, lw, sw, beq):

bits 31-28:   opcode

bits 27-24:   reg X

bits 23-20:   reg Y

bits 19-0:   immediate value or address offset (a 20-bit, 2s complement number with a range of −524288 to +524287)

31 28	27 24	23 20	19 0
Opcode	Reg X	Reg Y	(Signed) immediate value or address offset

J-type instructions (jalr):[7]

bits 31-28:   opcode

bits 27-24:   reg X (target of the jump)

bits 23-20:   reg Y (link register)

bits 19-0:   unused (should be all 0s)

31 28	27 24	23 20	19 0
Opcode	Reg X	Reg Y	Unused

---

7. The LC-2200 does not have a separate, unconditional jump instruction. However, it should be easy to see that we can realize such an instruction by using JALR R_{link}, $R_{dont\text{-}care}$; where R_{link} contains the address to jump to and $R_{dont\text{-}care}$ is a register whose current value you don't mind trashing.

Table 2.1 LC-2200 Instruction Set

Mnemonic Example	Format	Opcode	Action Register Transfer Language
add add $v0, $a0, $a1	R	0 0000_2	Add contents of reg Y with contents of reg Z, store results in reg X. RTL: $v0 ← $a0 + $a1
nand nand $v0, $a0, $a1	R	1 0001_2	Nand contents of reg Y with contents of reg Z, store results in reg X. RTL: $v0 ← ~($a0 && $a1)
addi addi $v0, $a0, 25	I	2 0010_2	Add immediate value to the contents of reg Y and store the result in reg X. RTL: $v0 ← $a0 + 25
lw lw $v0, 0×42($fp)	I	3 0011_2	Load reg X from memory. The memory address is formed by adding OFFSET to the contents of reg Y. RTL: $v0 ← MEM[$fp + 0×42]
sw sw $a0, 0×42($fp)	I	4 0100_2	Store reg X into memory. The memory address is formed by adding OFFSET to the contents of reg Y. RTL: MEM[$fp + 0×42] ← $a0
beq beq $a0, $a1, done	I	5 0101_2	Compare the contents of reg X and reg Y. If they are the same, then branch to the address PC+1+OFFSET, where PC is the address of the beq instruction. RTL: if($a0 == $a1) PC ← PC+1+OFFSET

Note: For programmer convenience (and implementer confusion), the assembler computes the OFFSET value from the number or symbol given in the instruction and the assembler's idea of the PC. In the example, the assembler stores done-(PC+1) in OFFSET so that the machine will branch to label "done" at run time.

Mnemonic Example	Format	Opcode	Action Register Transfer Language
jalr jalr $at, $ra	J	6 0110_2	First store PC+1 into reg Y, where PC is the address of the jalr instruction. Then branch to the address now contained in reg X. Note that if reg X is the same as reg Y, the processor will first store PC+1 into that register and then end up branching to PC+1. RTL: $ra ← PC+1; PC ← $at Note that an **unconditional jump** can be realized by using **jalr $ra, $t0** and discarding the value stored in $t0 by the instruction. This is why there is no separate jump instruction in LC-2200.
nop	n.a.	n.a.	Actually a pseudo instruction (i.e., the assembler will emit the following: add $zero, $zero, $zero)
halt halt	O	7 0111_2	

O-type instructions (halt):

bits 31-28:   opcode

bits 27-0:   unused (should be all 0s)

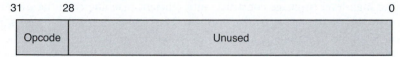

2.10.2 LC-2200 Register Set

As we mentioned already, LC-2200 has 16 programmer-visible registers. It turns out that zero is a very useful small integer in compiling high-level language programs. For example, it is needed for initializing program variables. For this reason, we dedicate register R0 to always contain the value 0. Writes to R0 are ignored by the architecture.

    We give mnemonic names to the 16 registers, consistent with the software convention that we introduced in Section 2.8.3. Further, since the assembler needs it, we introduce a "$" sign in front of the mnemonic name for a register. The registers, their mnemonic names, their intended use, and the software convention are summarized in Table 2.2.

Table 2.2 Register Convention

Reg #	Name	Use	Callee-Save?
0	$zero	always zero (by hardware)	n.a.
1	$at	reserved for assembler	n.a.
2	$v0	return value	No
3	$a0	argument	No
4	$a1	argument	No
5	$a2	argument	No
6	$t0	Temporary	No
7	$t1	Temporary	No
8	$t2	Temporary	No
9	$s0	Saved register	Yes
10	$s1	Saved register	Yes
11	$s2	Saved register	Yes
12	$k0	reserved for OS/traps	n.a.
13	$sp	Stack pointer	No
14	$fp	Frame pointer	Yes
15	$ra	return address	No

2.11 Issues Influencing Processor Design

2.11.1 Instruction Set

Throughout this chapter, we have focused on instruction set design. We also have made compiling high-level language constructs into efficient machine code the overarching concern in the design of an instruction set. This concern is valid up to a point. However, compiler technology and instruction set design have evolved to the point where such a concern is not what is keeping the computer architects awake at nights in companies such as Intel or AMD. In fact, the 1980s and 1990s saw the emergence of many ISAs, some more elegant than the others, but all driven by the kinds of concerns we articulated in the earlier sections of this chapter. Perhaps one of the favorites, from the point of view of elegance and performance, is Digital Equipment Corporation's Alpha architecture. The architects of DEC Alpha gave a lot of thought to code generation that is intuitive and efficient from the viewpoint of the compiler writer, as well as to an ISA design that will lend itself to an efficient implementation. With the demise of DEC, a pioneer in minicomputers throughout the 1980s and 1990s, the Alpha architecture also met its end.

The decade of the 1980s saw the debate between *Complex Instruction Set Computers (CISC)* and *Reduced Instruction Set Computers (RISC)*. With CISC-style ISA, the task of a compiler writer is complicated by the plethora of choices that exist for compiling high-level constructs into machine code. Further, the complexity of the ISA makes efficient hardware implementation a significant challenge. Choices for the compiler writer are generally good, of course, but if the programmer does not know the implication in terms of performance *a priori*, then such choices become questionable. With the maturation of compiler technology, it was argued that a RISC-style ISA both would be easier to use for the compiler writer and would lead to better implementation efficiency, than a CISC-style ISA.

As we all know, an ISA that has stood the test of time is Intel's x86. It represents a CISC-style ISA. Yet, x86 is still the dominant ISA, while many elegant ones, such as DEC Alpha, have disappeared. The reason is that there are too many other factors (market pressure[8] being a primary one) which determine the success or failure of an ISA. Performance is an important consideration, of course, but the performance advantage of a really good ISA, such as Alpha, over that of x86 is not large enough to be a key determinant. Besides, despite the implementation challenge posed by the x86 ISA, smart architects at Intel and AMD have managed to come up with efficient implementation, which, when coupled with the prevailing high clock speeds of processors, make the performance advantage of a "good" ISA not that significant—at least, not significant *enough* to displace a well-entrenched ISA such as x86.

Ultimately, the success or failure of an ISA largely depends on market adoption. Today, computer software powers everything from commerce to entertainment. Therefore, adoption of an ISA by major software vendors (such as Microsoft, Google,

---

8. Part of the reason for this market pressure is the necessity to support legacy code—i.e., software developed on older versions of the same processor. This *backward compatibility* of a processor contributes to the bloated nature of the Intel x86 ISA.

IBM, and Apple) is a key factor that determines the success of an ISA. An equally important factor is the adoption of processors embodying the ISA by "box makers" (such as Dell, HP, Apple, and IBM). In addition to the traditional markets (laptops, desktops, and servers), embedded systems (such as game consoles, cell phones, PDAs, and automobiles) have emerged as dominant players in the computing landscape. It is not easy to pinpoint why an ISA may or may not be adopted by each of these segments (software giants, box makers, and builders of embedded systems). Although it is tempting to think that such decisions are based solely on the elegance of an ISA, we know from the history of computing that this is not exactly true. Such decisions are often based on pragmatics: availability of good compilers (especially for C) for a given ISA, need to support legacy software, etc.

2.11.2 Influence of Applications on Instruction Set Design

Applications have in the past influenced, and continue to date to influence, the design of instruction set. In the 1970s, and perhaps into the 1980s, computers were used primarily for number crunching in scientific and engineering applications. Such applications rely heavily on floating-point arithmetic. Whereas high-end computers (such as IBM 370 series and Cray) included such instructions in their ISA, the so-called *minicomputers* of that era (such as DEC PDP 11 series) did not. There were successful companies (e.g., *Floating Point Systems, Inc.*) that made attached processors for accelerating floating-point arithmetic for the minicomputers. Nowadays, floating-point instructions are a part of any general-purpose processor. Processors (e.g., StrongARM, ARM) that are used in embedded applications such as cell phones and PDAs may not have such instructions. Instead, they realize the effect of floating-point arithmetic by integer instructions for supporting math libraries.

Another example of applications' influence on the ISA is the MMX instructions from Intel. Applications that process audio, video, and graphics deal with *streaming data*—that is, continuous data such as a movie or music. Such data would be represented as arrays in the memory. The MMX instructions, first introduced by Intel in 1997 in their Pentium line of processors, aimed at dealing with streaming data efficiently by the CPU. The intuition behind these instructions is pretty straightforward. As the name *stream data* suggests, audio, video, and graphics applications require the same operation (such as addition) to be applied to corresponding elements of two or more streams. Therefore, it makes sense to have instructions that mimic this behavior. The MMX instructions originally introduced in the Pentium line and its successors do precisely that. There are 57 instructions, grouped into categories such as arithmetic, logical, comparison, conversion, shift, and data transfer, and each one takes two operands (each of which is not a scalar, but a vector of elements). For example, an add instruction will add the corresponding elements of the two vectors.[9]

---

9. As a historical note, the MMX instructions evolved from a style of parallel architectures called Single Instruction Multiple Data (SIMD, for short), which was prevalent until the mid 1990s for catering to the needs of image-processing applications. (See Chapter 12 for an introduction to the different parallel architecture styles.)

A more recent example comes from the gaming industry. Interactive video games have become very sophisticated. The graphics and animation processing required for real-time gaming consoles has progressed beyond the capability of the general-purpose processors. Of course, you wouldn't want to lug around a supercomputer on your next vacation trip, to play video games! Enter *Graphics Processing Units* (*GPUs*, for short). These are special-purpose attached processors that perform the needed arithmetic for gaming consoles. Basically, the GPU comprises a number of functional units (implementing primitive operations required in graphics rendering applications) that operate in parallel on a stream of data. A recent partnership between Sony, IBM, and Toshiba unveiled the Cell processor that takes the concept of GPUs a step further. The Cell processor comprises several processing elements on a single chip, each of which can be programmed to do some specialized task. The Cell processor architecture has made its way into PlayStation (PS3).

2.11.3 Other Issues Driving Processor Design

ISA is only one design issue, and perhaps not the most riveting one, in the design of modern processors. Some of the more demanding issues are listed here, and some of these will be elaborated on in later chapters:

1. **Operating system:** We have already mentioned that the operating system plays a crucial role in the processor design. One manifestation of that role is the illusion, given to the programmer, of memory space that is larger than the actual amount of memory present in the system. Another manifestation is the responsiveness of the processor to external events such as interrupts. As we will see in later chapters, to efficiently support such requirements stemming from the operating system, the processor may include new instructions as well as new architectural mechanisms that are not necessarily visible via the ISA.

2. **Support for modern languages:** Most modern languages such as Java, C++, and C# provide the programmer with the ability to dynamically grow and shrink the data size of the program. Dubbed *dynamic memory allocation,* this is a powerful feature from the point of view of both the application programmer and resource management by the operating system. Reclaiming memory when the data size shrinks, referred to as *garbage collection*, is crucial from the point of view of resource management. Mechanisms in the processor architecture for automatic garbage collection are another modern-day concern in processor design.

3. **Memory system:** As you know, processor speeds have been appreciating exponentially over the past decade. For example, a Sun 3/50 had a processor speed of 0.5 MHz circa 1986. Circa 2007, laptops and desktops had processor speeds in excess of 2 GHz. Memory density has been increasing at an exponential rate, but memory speed has not increased at the same rate as processor speed. This disparity between processor and memory speeds often is referred to as the *memory wall*. Clever techniques in the processor design to overcome the memory wall are one of the most important issues in processor design. For example, designing cache memories and integrating them into the processor

design is one such technique. We will cover these issues in a later chapter on memory hierarchies.

4. **Parallelism:** With increasing density of chips, usually measured in millions of transistors on a single piece of silicon, it is becoming possible to pack more and more functionality into a single processor. In fact, the chip density has reached a level where it is possible to pack multiple processors on the same piece of silicon. These architectures, called *multi-cores* and *many-cores*, bring to the fore a whole new set of processor design issues.[10] Some of these issues, such as parallel programming and memory consistency, are carried over from traditional multi-processors (a box comprising several processors), which we will discuss in a later chapter.

5. **Debugging:** Programs have become complex. An application such as a web server, in addition to being parallel and having a large memory footprint, may also have program components that reach into the network and databases. Naturally, developing such applications is not trivial. A significant concern in the design of modern processors is support for efficient debugging, especially for parallel programs.

6. **Virtualization:** As applications have increased in complexity, their needs have become more complex as well. For example, an application may need some services that are available in only one particular operating system. If you want to run multiple applications simultaneously, each having its own unique requirements, then there may be a need for simultaneous support by multiple application-execution environments. You may have a dual-boot laptop and your own unique reason for having this capability. It would be nice if you could have multiple operating systems coexisting simultaneously, without your having to switch back and forth. *Virtualization* is the system concept for supporting multiple, distinct execution environments in the same computer system. Architects are now paying attention to efficiently supporting this concept in modern processor design.

7. **Fault tolerance:** As the hardware architecture becomes more complex, with multi- and many-cores and large memory hierarchies, the probability of component failures increases. Architects are paying more attention to processor design techniques that will hide such failures from the programmer.

8. **Security:** Computer security is a big issue in this day and age. We normally think of network attacks when we are worried about protecting the security of our computer. It turns out that the security can be violated even within a box (between the memory system and the CPU). Architects are working to alleviate such concerns by incorporating encryption techniques for processor-memory communication.

---

10. Architecturally, there is not a major difference between multi- and many-cores. However, the programming paradigm needs a radical rethinking if there are more than a few (up to 8 or 16) cores. Hence, the distinction: multi-core may have up to 8 or 16 cores; anything beyond that is a many-core architecture.

Summary

The instruction set serves as a contract between the hardware and the software. In this chapter, we started from the basics to understand the issues in the design of an instruction set. The important points to take away from the chapter are summarized as follows:

- The influence of high-level language constructs in shaping the ISA
- Minimal support needed in the ISA for compiling arithmetic and logic expressions, conditional statements, loops, and procedure calls
- Pragmatic issues (such as addressing and access times) that necessitate the use of registers in the ISA
- Addressing modes for accessing memory operands in the ISA commensurate with the needs of efficient compilation of high-level language constructs
- Software conventions that guide the use of the limited register set available within the processor
- The concept of a software stack and its use in compiling procedure calls
- Possible extensions to a minimal ISA
- Other important issues guiding processor design in this day and age

Exercises

1. Having a large register file is detrimental to the performance of a processor because it results in a large overhead for procedure call/return in high-level languages. Do you agree or disagree? Give supporting arguments.

2. Distinguish between the frame pointer and the stack pointer.

3. In the LC-2200 architecture, where are operands normally found for an add instruction?

4. This question pertains to endianness. Let's say you want to write a program for comparing two strings. You have a choice of using a 32-bit byte-addressable big-endian or little-endian architecture to do this. In either case, you can pack four characters into each word of 32 bits. Which one would you choose and how will you write such a program? [Hint: Normally, you would do string comparison, one character at a time. If you can do it a word at a time instead of a character at a time, that implementation will be faster.]

5. An ISA may support different flavors of conditional branch instructions, such as BZ (branch on Zero), BN (branch on negative), and BEQ (branch on equal). Figure out the predicate expressions in an *if* statement that may be best served by these different flavors of conditional branch instructions. Give examples of such predicates in an *if* statement and how you would compile them, using these different flavors of branch instructions.

6. We have said that endianness will not affect your program performance or correctness, so long as the use of a (high-level) data structure is commensurate with its

declaration. Are there situations where, even if your program does not violate this rule, you could be "bitten" (pun intended) by the endianness of the architecture? [Hint: Think of programs that cross network boundaries.]

7. Work out the details of implementing the *switch* statement of C, using jump tables in assembly and using any flavor of conditional branch instruction. [Hint: After ensuring that the value of the switch variable is within the bounds of valid case values, jump to the start of the appropriate code segment corresponding to the current switch value, execute the code, and, finally, jump to exit.]

8. Procedure A has important data in both S and T registers and is about to call procedure B. Which registers should A store on the stack? Which registers should B store on the stack?

9. Consider the usage of the stack abstraction in executing procedure calls. Do all actions on the stack happen only via pushes and pops to the top of the stack? Explain circumstances that warrant reaching into other parts of the stack during program execution. How is this accomplished?

10. Answer True/False, with justification: Procedure call/return cannot be implemented without a frame pointer.

11. DEC VAX has a single instruction for loading and storing all the program visible registers from/to memory. Can you see a reason for such an instruction pair? Consider both the pros and the cons.

12. Show how you can simulate a subtract instruction by using the existing LC-2200 ISA.

13. The BEQ instruction restricts the distance you can branch to from the current position of the PC. If your program warrants jumping to a distance farther than that allowed by the offset field of the BEQ instruction, show how you can accomplish such "long" branches by using the existing LC-2200 ISA.

14. What is an ISA and why is it important?

15. What are the influences on instruction set design?

16. What are conditional statements and how are they handled in the ISA?

17. Define the term *addressing mode*.

18. In Section 2.8, we mentioned that local variables in a procedure are allocated on the stack. Although this description is convenient for keeping the exposition simple, modern compilers work quite differently. Search the Internet and find out exactly how modern compilers allocate space for local variables in a procedure call. [Hint: Recall that registers are faster than memory. So, the objective should be to keep as many of the variables in registers as possible.]

19. We use the term *abstraction* to refer to the stack. What is meant by this term? Does the term *abstraction* imply how it is implemented? For example, is a stack used in a procedure call/return a hardware device or a software device?

20. Given the following instructions

    BEQ   Rx, Ry, offset ;   if (Rx == Ry) PC = PC+offset

    SUB   Rx, Ry, Rz   ;   Rx ← Ry – Rz

    ADDI   Rx, Ry, Imm ;   Rx ← Ry + Immediate value

    AND   Rx, Ry, Rz   ;   Rx ← Ry AND Rz

    show how you can realize the effect of the following instruction:

    BGT   Rx, Ry, offset ;   if (Rx > Ry) PC = PC+offset

    Assume that the registers and the immediate fields are 8 bits wide. You can ignore overflow that may be caused by the SUB instruction.

21. Given the following load instruction

    LW   Rx, Ry, OFFSET ;   Rx ← MEM[Ry + OFFSET]

    show how to realize a new addressing mode, called *indirect*, for use with the load instruction that is represented in assembly language as follows:

    LW   Rx, @(Ry) ;

    The semantics of this instruction is that the contents of register Ry is the address of a pointer to the memory operand that must be loaded into Rx.

22. Convert the statement

    ```
    g = h + A[i];
    ```

    into an LC-2200 assembler, with the assumption that the address of A is located in $t0, g is in $s1, h is in $s2, and, i is in $t1.

23. Suppose that you design a computer called the Big Looper 2000 that will never be used to call procedures and that will automatically jump back to the beginning of memory when it reaches the end. Do you need a program counter? Justify your answer.

24. Consider the program that follows, and assume that the following statements are true for this processor:
    * All arguments are passed on the stack.
    * Register V0 is for return values.
    * The S registers are expected to be saved; that is, a calling routine can leave values in the S registers and expect it to be there after a call.
    * The T registers are expected to be temporary; that is, a calling routine must not expect values in the T registers to be preserved after a call.

    ```
    int bar(int a, int b)
    {
      /* Code that uses registers T5, T6, S11-S13; */
      return(1);
    }
    ```

```
int foo(int a, int b, int c, int d, int e)
{
  int x, y;
  /* Code that uses registers T5-T10, S11-S13; */
  bar(x, y); /* call bar */
  /* Code that reuses register T6 and arguments a, b, and c;
  return(0);
}

main(int argc, char **argv)
{
  int p, q, r, s, t, u;
  /* Code that uses registers T5-T10, S11-S15; */
  foo(p, q, r, s, t); /* Call foo */
  /* Code that reuses registers T9, T10; */
}
```

Shown next is the stack when bar is executing. Indicate clearly in the spaces provided which procedure (main, foo, bar) saved specific entries on the stack.

main	foo	bar	
____	____	____	p
____	____	____	q
____	____	____	r
____	____	____	s
____	____	____	t
____	____	____	u
____	____	____	T9
____	____	____	T10
____	____	____	p
____	____	____	q
____	____	____	r
____	____	____	s
____	____	____	t
____	____	____	x
____	____	____	y
____	____	____	S11

		S12
_____	_____	_____ S12
_____	_____	_____ S13
_____	_____	_____ S14
_____	_____	_____ S15
_____	_____	_____ T6
_____	_____	_____ x
_____	_____	_____ y
_____	_____	_____ S11
_____	_____	_____ S12
_____	_____	_____ S13 ◄——— Top of Stack

Bibliographic Notes and Further Reading

The introduction to instruction-set design in this chapter is intentionally kept simple and reachable for students in a first course on systems. There have been a number of influential ISAs. The IBM 360 series [IBM System/360, 1964] was one of the milestones in the development of mainframe computers. Shortly thereafter, IBM followed this with the IBM 370 series [IBM System/370, 1978]. The 360 and 370 series exemplified the CISC-style of ISA design. Another influential company in the evolution of computers was Digital Equipment Corporation (DEC) [Bell Web page, 2010]. DEC's PDP-8 was a 12-bit computer introduced in the 1960s that had an instruction set built around a single register in the CPU called the accumulator [PDP-8, 1973]. DEC's PDP-11 was a 16-bit successor to PDP-8 and dominated the minicomputer market between 1970 and 1990. The PDP-11's ISA is built around a set of eight registers [Bell, 1970]. DEC introduced the VAX 11 architecture in the mid-to-late 1970s as a 32-bit offering for midrange computer applications [Strecker, 1978]. It is a classic example of a CISC-style architecture.

The 1980s saw the introduction of RISC-style architectures. William Joy, cofounder of Sun Microsystems, wrote an interesting article[11] chronicling the RISC revolution. In 1980, Professor David Patterson started the Berkeley RISC project [Patterson, 1981], which later became the foundation for Sun Microsystem's SPARC architecture [SPARC Architecture, 2010]. MIPS started out as a university project at Stanford in the early 1980s [Hennessy, 1981]. Professor John Hennessy, who led the project, founded the company MIPS Computer Systems in 1984, which was later acquired by Silicon Graphics (SGI).

IBM 801 [Cocke, 2000; Radin, 1982] started out in the late 1970s as an experimental project led by John Cocke, a computer pioneer at IBM and winner of the

---

11. See http://www.cs.washington.edu/homes/lazowska/cra/risc.html.

Turing Award. In the 1980s, many of the ideas from this project appeared in a commercial offering from IBM as the POWER architecture. An alliance among Apple, IBM, and Motorola resulted in an extension of the POWER architecture to PCs. This line of processors, called the PowerPC, was used in the Apple's Macs until 2006. HP came up with its own RISC architecture in the mid-1980s, the Precision Architecture, or PA-RISC [Mahon, 1986], which powered its line of workstations until 2008. The Alpha processor is a 64-bit RISC architecture from DEC [Sites, 1992]. Despite the interesting architecture and novel implementation, this processor has been taken off the market due to nontechnical reasons (company acquisitions and mergers).

Intel's 80x86 architecture, introduced in the 1980s, is still the dominant processor in the marketplace. It is a CISC-style architecture. The best way of getting details on the x86 instruction set is by going to the source [Intel Instruction set, 2008].

The textbook by [Patterson, 2008] is an excellent source for understanding basic computer organization and design, especially regarding the topic of this chapter, namely, instruction-set design and the role played by the compiler in guiding the design.

Processor Implementation

The previous chapter dealt with issues involved in designing the instruction-set architecture of the processor. This chapter deals with the implementation of the processor once we have developed an instruction set. The instruction set is not a description of the implementation of the processor; rather, it serves as a contract between hardware and software. For example, once the instruction-set is designed, a compiler writer can generate code for different high-level languages to execute on a processor that implements the contract. Naturally, we can we have different implementations of the same instruction set. As we will see in this chapter, a number of factors go into the implementation choice that one may make.

3.1 Architecture versus Implementation

First let us understand why this distinction between architecture and implementation is important.

1. Depending on cost/performance, several implementations of the same architecture may be possible and even necessary to meet market demand. For example, it may be necessary to have a high-performance version of the processor for a server market (such as a web server); at the same time, there may be a need for a lower performance version of the same processor for an embedded application (such as a printer). This is why we see a *family* of processors adhering to a particular architecture description, some of which may even be unveiled by a vendor simultaneously (e.g., Intel Xeon series, IBM 360 series, DEC PDP 11 series, etc.).

2. Another important reason for decoupling architecture from implementation is that it allows for parallel development of system software and hardware. For example,

through decoupling, it becomes feasible to validate system software (such as compilers, debuggers, and operating systems) for a new architecture, even prior to the time when an implementation of the architecture is available. This drastically cuts down the time needed to market a computer system.

3. Customers of high-performance servers make a huge investment in software. For example, the Oracle database is a huge and complex database system. Such software systems evolve slowly, compared with generations of processors. Intel cofounder Gordon Moore predicted, in 1965, that the number of transistors on a chip would double every two years. In reality, the pace of technology evolution has been even greater, with processor speed doubling every 18 months. This means that a faster processor could hit the market every 18 months. You will have observed this phenomenon if you have been paying attention to the speed rating of the processors when new ones are introduced into the market year after year. Software changes more slowly than hardware technology; therefore, it is important that *legacy* software run on new releases of processors. This suggests that we want to maintain the contract (i.e., the instruction-set) so that much of the software base (such as compilers and related tool sets, as well as fine-tuned applications) remains largely unchanged from one generation of processor to the next. Decoupling architecture from implementation allows this flexibility to maintain binary compatibility for legacy software.

3.2 What Is Involved in Processor Implementation?

There are several factors to consider in implementing a processor: price, performance, power consumption, cooling considerations, operating environment, etc. For example, a processor for military applications may require a more rugged implementation capable of withstanding harsh environmental conditions. The same processor inside a laptop may not require as rugged an implementation.

There are primarily two aspects to processor implementations:

1. The first concerns the organization of the electrical components (ALUs, buses, registers, etc.), commensurate with the expected price–performance characteristic of the processor.

2. The second concerns thermal and mechanical issues, including cooling and physical geometry for placement of the processor in a printed circuit board (often referred to as a *motherboard*).

These two issues specifically relate to a single-chip processor. Of course, the hardware "inside a box" is much more than a processor. There is a host of other issues to consider for the box as a whole, including printed circuit boards, backplanes, connectors, chassis design, etc. In general, computer system design is a tradeoff along several axes. If we consider just the high-end markets (supercomputers, servers, and desktops) then the tradeoff is mostly one of *price–performance*. However, in embedded devices such as cell phones, a combination of three dimensions, namely, *power* consumption, *performance,* and *area* (i.e., size)—commonly referred to as *PPA*—has been the primary guiding principle for design decisions.

Super Computers	Servers	Desktops & Personal Computers	Embedded
High perform- ance primary objective	Intermediate performance and cost	Low cost primary objective	Small size, performance, and low power consumption primary objectives

Computer design is principally an empirical process, riddled with tradeoffs along the various dimensions.

In this chapter, we focus on processor implementation—in particular, the design of the datapath and control for a processor. The design presented in this chapter is a basic one. In Chapter 5, we explore pipelined processor implementation.

Now we will review some key hardware concepts that are usually covered in a first course on logic design.

3.3 Key Hardware Concepts

3.3.1 Circuits

Combinational logic. The output of a circuit with this logic is a Boolean combination of the inputs to the circuit. That is, there is no concept of a *state* (i.e., memory). Basic logic gates (AND, OR, NOT, NOR, NAND) are the building blocks for realizing such circuits. Another way of thinking about such circuits is that there is no *feedback* from output of the circuit to the input.

Consider a patch panel that mixes different microphone inputs and produces a composite output to send to the speaker. The output of the speaker depends on the microphones selected by the patch panel to produce the composite sound. The patch panel is an example of a combinational logic circuit. Other examples of combinational logic circuits, found in the datapath of a processor, include multiplexers, demultiplex-ers, encoders, decoders, and ALU's.

Sequential logic. The output of a sequential logic circuit is a Boolean combination of the current inputs to the circuit and the current *state* of the circuit. A memory element, called a *flip-flop,* is a key building block of such a circuit, in addition to the basic logic gates that make up a combinational logic circuit.

Consider a garage door opener's control circuit. The "input" to the circuit is the clicker, with a single push-button, and some switches that indicate whether the door is all the way up or all the way down. The "output" is a signal that tells the motor to raise or lower the door. The direction of motion depends on the "current state" of the door. Thus, the garage door opener's control circuit is a sequential-logic circuit. Examples of sequential-logic circuits usually found in the datapath of a processor include registers and memory.

3.3.2 Hardware Resources of the Datapath

The datapath of a processor consists of combinational- and sequential-logic elements. With respect to the instruction set of the LC-2200 that we summarized in Chapter 2, let us identify the datapath resources that we will need.

We need **memory** to store the instructions and operands. We need an **arithmetic logic unit (ALU)** to do the arithmetic and logic instructions. We need a **register file**, because it is the focal point of action in most instruction-set architectures. Most instructions use register files. We need a **program counter** (henceforth referred to simply as a **PC**) in the datapath to point to the current instruction and for use in implementing the branch and jump instructions we discussed in Chapter 2. When an instruction is brought from memory, it has to be kept somewhere in the datapath; so we will introduce an **instruction register (IR)** to hold the instruction.

As the name suggests, a register file is a collection of architectural registers that are visible to the programmer. We need control and data lines to manipulate the register file. These include address lines to name a specific register from that collection, and data lines for reading from or writing into that register. A register file that allows a single register to be read at a time is called a *single-ported register file (SPRF)*. A register file that allows two registers to be read simultaneously is referred to as a *dual-ported register file (DPRF)*. Example 3.1 sheds light on all the control and data lines needed for a register file.

Example 3.1

Shown next is a dual-ported register file (DPRF) containing 64 registers. Each register has 32 bits. $A_{address}$ and $B_{address}$ are the register addresses given for reading the 32-bit register contents onto Ports A and B, respectively. $C_{address}$ is the register address given for writing Data_in into a chosen register in the register file. RegWrEn is the write-enable control for writing into the register file. How many wires are represented by each of the arrows in this Figure?

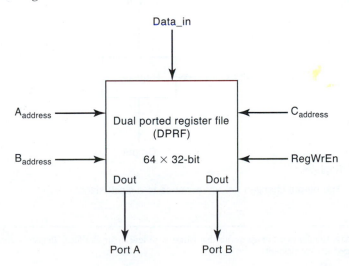

Answer:

a. Data_in has _____32_____ wires

b. Port A has _____32_____ wires

c. Port B has _____32_____ wires

d. $A_{address}$ has _____6_____ wires

e. $B_{address}$ has _____6_____ wires

f. $C_{address}$ has _____6_____ wires

g. RegWrEn has _____1_____ wires

3.3.3 Edge-Triggered Logic

The contents of a register changes from its current *state* to its new *state* in response to a clock signal. (See Figure 3.1.)

The precise moment when the output changes state in response to a change in the input depends on whether a storage element works on *level logic*[1] or *edge-triggered logic*. With level logic, the change happens as long as the clock signal is *high*. With edge-triggered logic (see Figure 3.2), the change happens only on the *rising* or the *falling* edge of the clock. If the state change happens on the rising edge, we refer to it as *positive-edge-triggered logic;* if the change happens on the falling edge, we refer to it as *negative-edge-triggered logic*.

From now on in our discussion, we will assume positive-edge-triggered logic for all the registers used in the datapath. We will discuss the details of choosing the width of the clock cycle in Section 3.4.2.

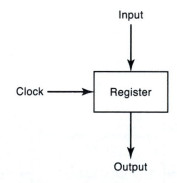

Figure 3.1   Register.

   The output changes only in response to a clock signal.

---

1. It is customary to refer to a storage device that works with level logic as a *latch*. Registers usually denote edge-triggered storage elements.

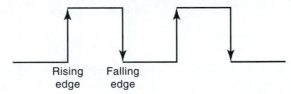

Figure 3.2 Clock.

The cycle time of the clock is the time between two consecutive rising (or falling) edges.

Example 3.2

The following circuit, with three registers A, B, and C, is connected as shown:

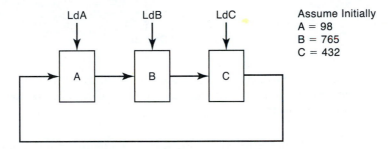

LdA, LdB, and LdC are the clock signals for registers A, B, and C, respectively. In the circuit shown, if LdA, LdB, and LdC are enabled in a given clock cycle, what are the contents of A, B, and C in the next clock cycle?

Answer:

Whatever contents are at the input of the registers will appear at the registers' respective outputs.

Therefore,

```
A = 432; B = 98; C = 765
```

The **memory** element is special. (See Figure 3.3.) As we saw in Chapter 1, in the discussion of the organization of the computer system, the memory subsystem is, in fact, completely separate from the processor. However, for the sake of simplicity in developing the basic concepts in processor implementation, we will include memory in the datapath design. For the purposes of this discussion, we will say that memory is not edge triggered.

For example, to read a particular memory location, you supply the "Address" and the "Read" signal to the memory; after a finite amount of time (called the read access time of the memory), the contents of the particular address become available on the "Data out" lines. Similarly, to write to a particular memory location, you supply the "Address,"

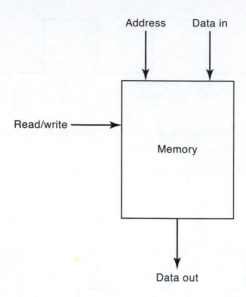

Figure 3.3   Memory.

The specific contents of the memory appear on the "Data out" lines, after a finite amount of time, once the "Address" has been supplied and the operation specified is "Read."

the "Data in," and the "Write" signal to the memory; after a finite amount of time (the write access time), the particular memory location will have the value supplied via "Data in." We will deal with memory systems in much more detail in Chapter 9.

3.3.4 Connecting the Datapath Elements

Let us consider what needs to happen to execute an ADD instruction of the LC-2200 and, from that, derive how the datapath elements ought to be interconnected.

1. **Step 1:** We need to use the PC to specify to the memory what location contains the instruction (Figure 3.4).

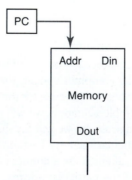

Figure 3.4   Step 1.

PC supplies instruction address to memory.

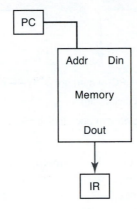

Figure 3.5 Step 2.

Instruction is read out of memory and clocked into IR.

2. **Step 2:** Once the instruction is read from the memory, then it has to be stored in the IR (Figure 3.5).

3. **Step 3:** Once the instruction is available in IR, we can use the register numbers specified in the instruction (contained in IR) to read the appropriate registers from the *register file* (dual ported, similar to the one in Example 3.1), perform the addition by using the ALU, and write the appropriate register into the register file (Figure 3.6).

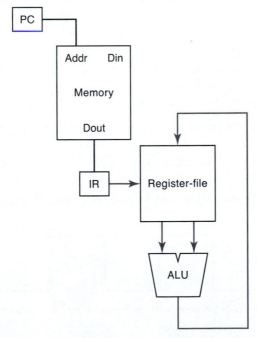

Figure 3.6 Step 3.

Perform ADD two register values and store in third register.

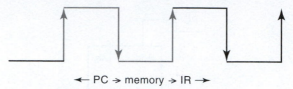

Figure 3.7   Steps 1 and 2 (first clock cycle).

Both steps are completed in one clock cycle.

The previous three steps show the roadmap of the ADD instruction execution. Let us see if the three steps can be completed in one clock cycle. As mentioned earlier, all the storage elements (except memory) are positive-edge triggered. What this means is that, in one clock cycle, we can transfer information from one storage element to another (going through combinational logic elements and/or memory), so long as the clock signal is long enough to account for all the intervening latencies of the logic elements. So, for instance, Steps 1 and 2 can be completed in one clock cycle; but step 3 cannot be completed in the same clock cycle. For step 3, we have to supply the register-number bits from IR to the register file. However, due to the edge-triggered nature of IR, the instruction is available in IR only at the beginning of the **next** clock cycle (see Figure 3.7).

It turns out that step 3 can be done in one clock cycle. At the beginning of the next clock cycle, the output of IR can be used to index the specific source registers needed for reading out of the register file. The registers are read (similar to how memory is read when an address is given in the same cycle), they are passed to the ALU, the ADD operation is performed, and the results are written into the destination register (pointed to by IR again). Figure 3.8 illustrates the completion of step 3 in the second clock cycle.

Determining the clock cycle time. Let us reexamine steps 1 and 2, which we said could be completed in one clock cycle. How wide should the clock cycle be to accomplish these steps? With reference to Figure 3.7, from the first rising edge of the clock, we can enumerate all the combinational delays encountered when accomplishing steps 1 and 2:

- amount of time that has to elapse for the output of PC to be stable for reading ($D_{r\text{-output-stable}}$);
- wire delay, to allow for the address to propagate from the output of PC to the Addr input of the memory ($D_{wire\text{-PC-Addr}}$);
- access time of the memory to read the addressed location ($D_{mem\text{-read}}$);

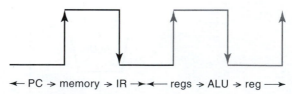

Figure 3.8   Step 3 (second clock cycle).

The ALU result appears in the register at the end of second clock cycle.

- wire delay, to allow time for the value read from the memory to propagate to the input of IR ($D_{wire-Dout-IR}$);
- amount of time that has to elapse for the input of IR to be stable before the second rising edge shown in Figure 3.7, usually called the setup time ($D_{r-setup}$); and
- amount of time that the input of IR needs to remain unchanged after the second rising edge, usually called the hold time (D_{r-hold}).

The width of the clock necessary for accomplishing steps 1 and 2 should be greater than the sum of all the delays:

$$Clock\ width > D_{r-output-stable} + D_{wire-PC-Addr} + D_{mem-read} + D_{wire-Dout-IR} + D_{r-setup} + D_{r-hold}$$

We do such an analysis for each of the potential paths of signal propagation in every clock cycle. Thereafter, we choose the clock width to be greater than the *worst case delay for signal propagation* in the entire datapath. In Section 3.4.2, we will formally define the terms involved in computing the clock cycle time.

Example 3.3

Given the following parameters (all in picoseconds), determine the minimum clock width of the system (consider only steps 1–3 of the datapath actions):

$D_{r-output-stable}$	(PC output stable)	–	20 ps
$D_{wire-PC-Addr}$	(wire delay from PC to Addr of Memory)	–	250 ps
$D_{mem-read}$	(Memory read)	–	1500 ps
$D_{wire-Dout-IR}$	(wire delay from Dout of Memory to IR)	–	250 ps
$D_{r-setup}$	(setup time for IR)	–	20 ps
D_{r-hold}	(hold time for IR)	–	20 ps
$D_{wire-IR-regfile}$	(wire delay from IR to Register file)	–	250 ps
$D_{regfile-read}$	(Register file read)	–	500 ps
$D_{wire-regfile-ALU}$	(wire delay from Register file to input of ALU)	–	250 ps
D_{ALU-OP}	(time to perform ALU operation)	–	100 ps
$D_{wire-ALU-regfile}$	(wire delay from ALU output to Register file)	–	250 ps
$D_{regfile-write}$	(time for writing into a Register file)	–	500 ps

Answer:

Steps 1 and 2 are carried out in one clock cycle.

Clock width needed for steps 1 and 2 is

$$C_{1-2} > D_{r-output-stable} + D_{wire-PC-Addr} + D_{mem-read} + D_{wire-Dout-IR} + D_{r-setup} + D_{r-hold}$$
$$> 2060\ ps$$

Step 3 is carried out in one clock cycle.

Clock width needed for step 3 is

$$C_3 > D_{\text{wire-IR-regfile}} + D_{\text{regfile-read}} + D_{\text{wire-regfile-ALU}} + D_{\text{ALU-OP}} + D_{\text{wire-ALU-regfile}}$$
$$+ D_{\text{regfile-read}}$$
$$> 1850 \text{ ps}$$

Minimum clock width $>$ worst case signal propagation delay,

$$> \text{MAX} (C_{1\text{-}2}, C_3)$$
$$> 2060 \text{ ps}$$

The preceding parameters were fairly accurate as of circa 2007. What should be striking about these numbers is the fact that wire delays dominate.

3.3.5 Toward Bus-Based Design

We made up ad hoc connections among the datapath elements to get one instruction executed. To implement another instruction (e.g., LD), we may have to create a path from the memory to the register file. If we extrapolate this line of thought, we can envision every datapath element connected to every other one. As it turns out, this is neither necessary nor the right approach. Let us examine what is involved in connecting the ALU to the register file. We have to run as many wires as the number of bits in the width of the datapath between the two elements. For a 32-bit machine, this means 32 wires. You can see that wires quickly multiply as we increase the connectivity among the datapath elements. Wires are expensive in terms of taking up space on silicon, and we want to reduce the number of wires so that we can use the silicon real estate for active datapath elements. Further, just having more wires does not necessarily improve the performance. For example, the fact that there are wires from the memory to the register file does not help the implementation of ADD instruction in any way.

Therefore, it is clear that we have to think more carefully through the issue of connecting datapath elements. In particular, the previous discussion suggests that, perhaps, instead of dedicating a set of wires between every pair of datapath elements, we should think of designing the datapath to share the wires among the datapath elements. Let us investigate how many sets of wires we need and how we can share them among the datapath elements.

Single bus design. One extreme is to have a single set of wires and have all the datapath elements share it. This is analogous to what happens in a group meeting: One person talks, and the others listen. Everyone takes a turn talking during the meeting if he or she has something to contribute to the discussion. If everyone were to talk at the same time, there would be chaos, of course. This is exactly how a *single bus system*—a single set of wires shared by all the datapath elements—works. Figure 3.9 shows such a system.

Bus denotes that the set of wires is shared. The first thing to notice is that the gray line is a single bus, electrically—that is, any value put on the bus becomes available on

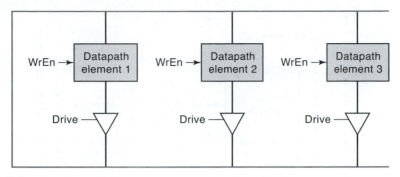

Figure 3.9   Single bus design.

Exactly one datapath element can place its output on the bus, by asserting the associated "Drive" signal.

all segments of the wire. The second thing to notice is that there are triangular elements that sit between the output of a datapath element and the bus. These are called *drivers* (also referred to as *tristate*[2] buffers). There is one such driver gate for each wire coming out from a datapath element that needs to be connected to a bus, and they isolate electrically the datapath element from the bus. Therefore, to electrically "connect" datapath element 1 to the bus, the associated driver must be "on." This is accomplished by selecting the "Drive" signal associated with this driver. When this is done, we say that datapath element 1 is "driving" the bus. It would be a mistake to have more than one datapath element driving the bus at a time. So the designer of the control logic has to ensure that only one of the drivers connected to the bus is "on" in a given clock cycle. If multiple drivers are "on" at the same time, then, apart from the fact that the value on the bus becomes unpredictable, there is potential for seriously damaging the circuitry. On the other hand, multiple data elements may choose to grab what is on the bus in any clock cycle. To accomplish this, the WrEn (write enable) signal associated with the respective data elements (shown in Figure 3.9) has to be turned "on."

Two-bus design. Figure 3.10 illustrates a two-bus design. In this design, the register file is a dual-ported one similar to that shown in Example 3.1. That is, two registers can be read and supplied to the ALU in the same clock cycle. Both the gray (top) and black dotted (bottom) buses may carry address or data values, depending on the need in a particular cycle. However, nominally, the gray bus carries address values and the black dotted bus carries data values between the datapath elements.

Although not shown in the figure, there is a driver at the output of each of the datapath elements that are connected to either or both of the buses. How many cycles will be needed to carry out steps 1–3 described at the beginning of Section 3.3.4? What needs to happen in each cycle?

Let us explore these two questions.

---

2. A binary signal is in one of two states: 0 or 1. The output of a driver when not enabled is in a third state, which is neither a 0 nor a 1. This is a high-impedance state where the driver electrically isolates the bus from the datapath element that it is connected to. Hence the term *tristate buffer*.

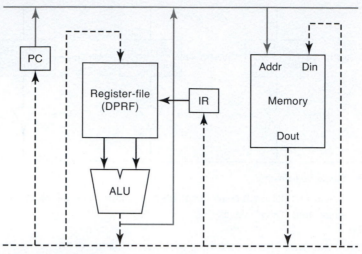

Figure 3.10 Two-bus design.

Opportunity for two simultaneous, independent conversations to go on among the datapath elements.

First clock cycle:

- PC to Gray bus (Note: No one else can drive the Gray bus in this clock cycle.)
- Dark gray bus to Addr of Memory
- Memory reads the location specified by Addr
- Data from Dout to Black dotted bus (Note: No one else can drive the Black dotted bus in this clock cycle.)
- Black dotted bus to IR
- Clock IR

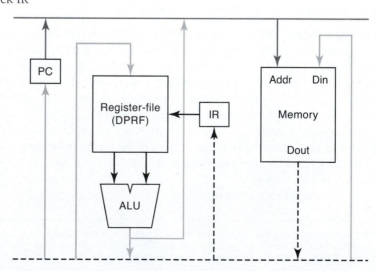

We have accomplished all that is needed in steps 1 and 2 in one clock cycle.

Second clock cycle:

- IR supplies register numbers to Register file (see the dedicated wires represented by the arrow from IR to Register file); two source registers; one destination register
- Read the Register file and pull out the data from the two source registers
- Register file supplies the data values from the two source registers to the ALU (see the dedicated wires represented by the arrows from the Register file to the ALU)

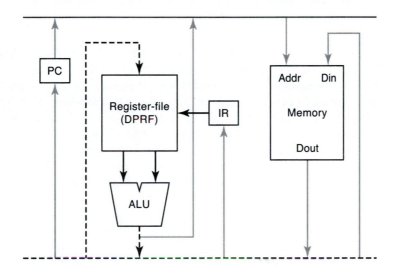

- Perform the ALU ADD operation
- ALU result to Black dotted bus (Note: No one else can drive the Black dotted bus in this clock cycle.)
- Black dotted bus to Register file
- Write to the register file at the destination register number specified by IR

We have accomplished all that is needed for step 3 in one clock cycle.

The key thing to take away from the preceding discussion is that we have accomplished steps 1–3 without having to run dedicated wires connecting every pair of datapath elements (except for the register-file-to-ALU connections, and the register selection wires from IR) by using the two shared buses.

3.3.6 Finite State Machine (FSM)

Thus far, we have summarized the circuit elements and how they could be assembled into a datapath for a processor. That is just one part of the processor design. The other, equally important, aspect of processor design is the control unit. It is best to understand the control unit as a finite state machine, because it takes the datapath through successive stages in order to accomplish instruction execution.

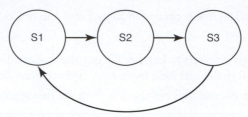

Figure 3.11 A finite state machine (FSM).

The circles represent the states, and the arrows show the transitions among them.

A finite state machine, as the name suggests, has a *finite* number of states. In Figure 3.11, the circles labeled S1, S2, and S3 are the *states* of the FSM. The arrows are the *transitions* between the states. FSM is an *abstraction* for any sequential logic circuit. It captures the desired behavior of the logic circuit. The state of the FSM corresponds to some physical state of the sequential logic circuit. Two things characterize a transition: (1) the external *input* that triggers that state change in the actual circuit, and (2) the *output* control signals generated in the actual circuit during the state transition. Thus, the FSM is a convenient way of capturing all the hardware details in the actual circuit.

For example, the simple FSM shown in Figure 3.12 represents the sequential logic circuit for the garage door opener that we introduced earlier. Table 3.1 shows the state transition table for this FSM, with inputs that cause the transitions and the corresponding outputs they produce.

The "up" state corresponds to the door being up, while the "down" state corresponds to the door being down. The input is the clicker push button. The outputs are the control signals to the up and down motors, respectively. The transitions labeled "0" and "1" correspond to an absence of clicker action. The transitions labeled "2" and "3" correspond to the clicker being pushed. The former state transition "2" is accompanied by an "output" control signal to the up motor, and the latter transition "3" is accompanied by an "output" control signal to the down motor. Anyone who has taken a logic design course knows that it is a straightforward exercise to

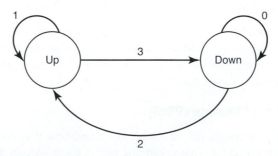

Figure 3.12 An FSM for the garage door opener.

The transitions correspond to the entries shown in the State Transition Table (Table 3.1).

Table 3.1   State Transition Table for the FSM in Figure 3.12

		State		
Transition Number	**Input**	**Current**	**Next**	**Output**
0	None	Down	Down	None
1	None	Up	Up	None
2	Clicker	Down	Up	Up motor
3	Clicker	Up	Down	Down motor

design the sequential logic circuit, given the FSM and the state transition diagram. (See the two exercise problems at the end of this chapter that relate to the garage door opener.)

We know that sequential logic circuits can be either *synchronous* or *asynchronous*. In the former, a state transition occurs, synchronized with a clock edge, whereas in the latter, a transition occurs as soon as the input is applied.

The control unit of a processor also is a sequential logic circuit. We can represent the control unit by the FSM shown in Figure 3.13.

FETCH: This state corresponds to fetching the instruction from the memory.

DECODE: This state corresponds to decoding the instruction brought from the memory in order to determine the operands needed and the operation to be performed.

EXECUTE: This state corresponds to carrying out the instruction execution.

We will revisit the control unit design in Section 3.5.

3.4 Datapath Design

The central processing unit (CPU) consists of the datapath and the control unit. The datapath has all the logic elements, and the control unit supplies the control signals to orchestrate the datapath, commensurate with the instruction set of the processor.

The datapath is the combination of the hardware resources and their connections. Let us review how to identify the hardware resources needed in the datapath. As we

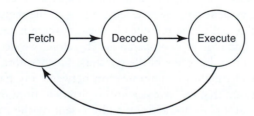

Figure 3.13   An FSM for controlling the CPU datapath.

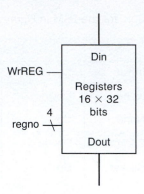

Figure 3.14 Register file with a single output port.

The 4-bit "regno" uniquely addresses one of the 16 registers; the "WrREG" signal specifies whether the operation is read or write for the addressed register.

already mentioned, the instruction-set architecture itself explicitly selects some of the hardware resources. In general, we would need more hardware resources than those which are apparent from the instruction set, as we will see shortly.

To make this discussion concrete, let us start by specifying the hardware resources needed by the instruction set of the LC-2200:

1. **ALU** capable of ADD, NAND, SUB;

2. **register file** with 16 registers (32-bit), as shown in Figure 3.14;

3. **PC** (32-bit); and

4. **Memory** with $2^{32} \times 32$ bit words.

Memory is a hardware resource that we need in LC-2200 for storing instructions and data. The size of the memory is an implementation choice. The architecture specifies only the maximum size of memory that can be accommodated, on the basis of addressability. Given 32-bit addressing in the LC-2200, the maximum amount of memory that can be addressed is 2^{32} words of 32 bits each.

Let us figure out what additional hardware resources may be needed. We already mentioned that, when an instruction is brought from the memory, it has to be kept someplace in the datapath. IR serves this purpose. Let us assume that we want a single bus to connect all these datapath elements. Regardless of the number of buses, one thing should be evident right away when we look at the register file. We can get only one register value out of the register file because there is only one output port (Dout). ALU operations require two operands. Therefore, we need some temporary register in the datapath to hold one of the registers. Furthermore, with a single bus, there is exactly one channel of communication between any pair of datapath elements. This is the reason that we have **A** and **B** registers in front of the ALU. By similar reasoning, we need a place to hold the address sent by the ALU to the memory. The **memory address register (MAR)** serves this purpose. The purpose of the **Z**

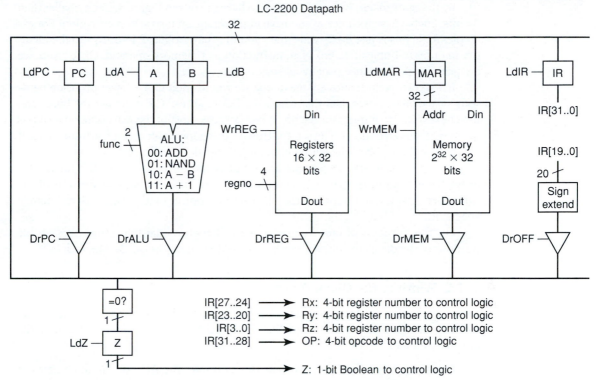

Figure 3.15   The LC-2200 Datapath.

Some of the resources get specified by the ISA; others are needed to remedy
the limitation due to a single bus.

register (a 1-bit register) will become evident later on when we discuss the implementation of the instruction set. The zero-detect combination logic in front of the Z register (Figure 3.15) checks to see whether the value on the bus is equal to zero.
Depending on the resources needed by the instruction set, the limitations of the datapath, and the implementation requirements of the instruction set, we end up with a
single bus design, as shown in Figure 3.15.

3.4.1 ISA and Datapath Width

We have defined the LC-2200 to be a 32-bit instruction-set architecture. Accordingly,
all instructions, addresses, and data operands are 32 bits in width. We will now explore
the implication of this architectural choice on the datapath design. Let us understand
the implication on the size of the buses and other components such as the ALU.

Purely from the point of view of logic design, it is conceivable to implement higher-
precision arithmetic and logic operations with lower-precision hardware. For example,
if you so chose, you could implement a 32-bit addition by using a 1-bit adder. It would
be slow, but you could do it.

By the same token, you could choose to have the bus in Figure 3.15 be smaller than 32 bits. Such a design choice would have implications on instruction execution. For example, if the bus is just 8 bits wide, then you may have to make four trips to the memory in order to bring all 32 bits of an instruction or a memory operand. Once again, we are paying a performance penalty for making this choice.

It is a cost–performance argument that we would want to use lower precision hardware or narrower buses than that which the ISA requires. The narrower the buses are, the cheaper it is to implement the processor, because most of the real estate on a chip is taken up by interconnects. The same is true for using lower-precision hardware, since it will reduce the width of the wiring inside the datapath as well.

Thus, the datapath design represents a price–performance tradeoff. This is why, as we mentioned in Section 3.1, a chip maker may bring out several versions of the same processor, each representing a different point in the price–performance spectrum.

For the purposes of our discussion, we will assume that the architecture-visible portions of the datapath (PC, register file, IR, and memory) are all 32 bits wide.

3.4.2 Width of the Clock Pulse

Earlier, in Section 3.3 (see Example 3.3), we informally discussed how to calculate the clock cycle width. Let us formally define some of the terms involved in computing the clock cycle time:

- Every combinational logic element (for example, the ALU or the drive gates in Figure 3.15) has latency for propagating a value from its input to the output, namely, *propagation delay*.

- Similarly, there is latency (called *access time*) from the time a register is enabled for reading (for example, by application of a particular *regno* value to the register file in Figure 3.15) until the contents of that register appear on the output port (Dout).

- For a value to be written into a register, the input to the register has to be *stable* (meaning the value does not change) for some amount of time (called *set up time*) before the rising edge of the clock.

- Similarly, the input to the register has to continue to be stable for some amount of time (called *hold time*) after the rising edge of the clock.

- Finally, there is a *transmission delay* (also referred to as *wire delay*) for a value placed at the output of a logic element to traverse on the wire and appear at the input of another logic element (for example, from the output of a drive gate to the input of the PC in Figure 3.15).

Thus, if, in a single clock cycle, we wish to perform a datapath action that reads a value from the register file and puts it into the A register, we have to add up all the constituent delays. We compute the worst-case delay for any of the datapath actions that needs to happen in a single clock cycle. This gives us a *lower bound* for the clock cycle time.

3.4.3 Checkpoint

So far, we have reviewed the following hardware concepts:

- basics of logic design, including combinational and sequential logic circuits;
- hardware resources for a datapath such as register file, ALU, and memory;
- edge-triggered logic and arriving at the width of a clock cycle;
- datapath interconnection and buses; and
- finite state machines.

We have used these concepts to arrive at a datapath for the LC-2200 instruction-set architecture.

3.5 Control Unit Design

Take a look at the picture in Figure 3.16. The role of the orchestra conductor is to pick out the members of the orchestra who should be playing or singing at any point in time. Each member knows what he or she has to play, so the conductor's job, essentially, is keeping the timing and order, and not managing the content itself. If the datapath is the

Figure 3.16 An orchestral arrangement.

The conductor's role is akin to that of a processor's control unit. She gives "timing cues" to each member of the orchestra.

orchestra, then the control unit is the conductor. The control unit gives cues for the various datapath elements to carry out their respective functions. For example, if the DrALU line is asserted (i.e., if a 1 is placed on this line), then the corresponding set of driver gates will place whatever is at the output of the ALU on the corresponding bus lines.

Inspecting the datapath, we can list the control signals needed from the control unit:

- **Drive signals:** DrPC, DrALU, DrREG, DrMEM, DrOFF
- **Load signals:** LdPC, LdA, LdB, LdMAR, LdIR, LdZ
- **Write memory signal:** WrMEM
- **Write registers signal:** WrREG
- **ALU function selector:** func
- **Register selector:** regno

There are several possible alternative designs to generate the control signals, all of which are the hardware realization of the FSM abstraction for the control unit of the processor.

3.5.1 ROM Plus State Register

Let us look at a very simple design. First, we need a way of knowing what **state** the processor is in. Earlier, we introduced an FSM for the control unit, consisting of the states FETCH, DECODE, and EXECUTE. These are the **macro** states of the processor in the FSM abstraction. In a real implementation, several **microstates** may be necessary to carry out the details of each of the macro states, depending on the capabilities of the datapath. For example, let us assume that it takes three microstates to implement the FETCH macro state. We can then encode these microstates as

```
ifetch1   0000,
ifetch2   0001, and
ifetch3   0010.
```

We now introduce a **state register**, the contents of which hold the encoding of these microstates. So, at any instant, the contents of this register show the state of the processor.

The introduction of the state register brings us a step closer to hardware implementation from the FSM abstraction. Next, to control the datapath elements in each microstate, we have to generate the control signals, which we just listed. Let us discuss how to accomplish the generation of control signals.

One simple way is to use the state register as an index into a table. Each entry of the table contains the control signals needed in that state. Returning to the analogy of an orchestra, the conductor has the music score in front of her. She maintains the "state" of the orchestra with respect to the piece that the musicians are playing. Each line of the music score tells the conductor who should be playing at any point in time, just as an entry in the table of the control unit signifies the datapath elements that should participate in the datapath actions in that state. Each individual player knows what he or she has to play. In the same manner, each datapath element knows what it has to do. In

	Drive signals					Load signals						Write signals			
Current State	PC	ALU	Reg	MEM	OFF	PC	A	B	MAR	IR	Z	MEM	REG	func	regno

Figure 3.17   An entry of the table of control signals.

both cases, they need someone to tell them when to act. So, the conductor and the control unit have exactly similar jobs, in that they both give the timing necessary (the "when" question) for the players and the datapath elements to do their respective parts at the right time. This appears quite straightforward, so let us represent each control signal by **one bit** in this table entry. If the value of the bit is 1, then the control signal is generated; if it is 0, then it is not generated. Of course, the number of bits in **func** and **regno** fields corresponds to their width in the datapath (2 and 4, respectively; see Figure 3.15). Figure 3.17 shows a layout of the table entry for the control signals.

The control unit has to transition from one state to another. For example, if the FETCH macro state needs three micro states, then we have the following situation:

Current state	Next state
ifetch1	ifetch2
ifetch2	ifetch3

It is relatively straightforward to accomplish this next state transition by making the next state part of the table entry. So now our table looks as shown in Figure 3.18.

Let us investigate how to implement this table in hardware.

The table is nothing but a memory element. The property of this memory element is that, once we have determined the control signals for a particular state, we can *freeze* the contents of that table entry. We refer to this kind of memory as *read-only memory*, or *ROM*.

Therefore, our hardware for the control unit looks as shown in Figure 3.19. On every clock tick, the state register advances to the next state as specified by the output of the ROM entry accessed in the current clock cycle. This is the same clock that drives all the edge-triggered storage elements in the datapath (see Figure 3.15). All the load signals coming out of the ROM (LdPC, LdMAR, etc.) serve as *masks* for the clock signal in that they determine whether the associated storage element which they control should be clocked in a given clock cycle.

The next thing to do is to combine the datapath and the control. This is accomplished by simply *connecting* the *correspondingly named entities* in the datapath (see Figure 3.15) to the ones coming out of the ROM.

	Drive signals					Load signals						Write signals				
Current State	PC	ALU	Reg	MEM	OFF	PC	A	B	MAR	IR	Z	MEM	REG	func	regno	Next state
...																

Figure 3.18   Next state field added to the control signals table.

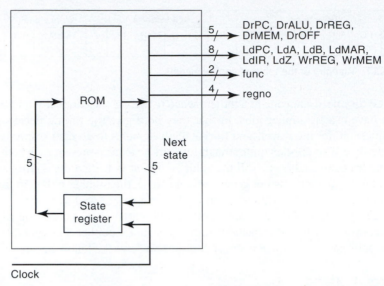

Figure 3.19   Control unit, composed of a state register plus ROM.

Each row of the ROM contains the control signals that have to be generated in a given clock cycle (i.e., "state") and sent to the datapath.

The way this control unit works is as follows:

1. The state register names the state that the processor is in for this clock cycle.
2. The ROM is accessed to retrieve the contents at the address pointed to by the state register.
3. The output of the ROM is the current set of control signals to be passed on to the datapath.
4. The datapath carries out the functions as dictated by these control signals in this clock cycle.
5. The *next state* field of the ROM feeds the state register so that it can transition to the next state at the beginning of the next clock cycle.

These five steps are repeated in every clock cycle.

Figure 3.13 introduced the control unit of the processor as an FSM. Figure 3.20 is a reproduction of the same figure for convenience. Now let us examine what needs to happen

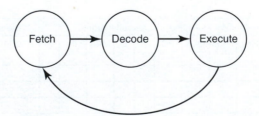

Figure 3.20   FSM for the CPU datapath reproduced.

in every macro state, represented by the FSM in Figure 3.20, and how our control unit can implement this. For each microstate, we will show the datapath actions alongside.

3.5.2 FETCH Macro State

The FETCH macro state fetches an instruction from memory at the address pointed to by the program counter (PC) into the instruction register (IR); it subsequently increments the PC, in readiness for fetching the next instruction.

Now let us list what needs to be done to implement the FETCH macro state:

- Send PC to the memory.
- Read the memory contents.
- Bring the memory contents read into the IR.
- Increment the PC.

With respect to the datapath, it is clear that, with a single-bus datapath, all of these steps cannot be accomplished in one clock cycle. We can break this up into the following microstates, each executed in one clock cycle:

- **ifetch1**
     $PC \rightarrow MAR$
- **ifetch2**
     $MEM[MAR] \rightarrow IR$
- **ifetch3**
     $PC \rightarrow A$
- **ifetch4**
     $A + 1 \rightarrow PC$

With a little bit of reflection, we will be able to accomplish the actions of the FETCH macro state in fewer than four cycles. Observe what is being done in **ifetch1** and **ifetch3**. The content of the PC is transferred to the MAR and A registers in both cases. These two states can be collapsed into a single state because the contents of the PC, once put on the bus, can be clocked into both the registers in the same cycle. Therefore, we can simplify the previous sequence to the following one:

- **ifetch1**
     $PC \rightarrow MAR$
     $PC \rightarrow A$
- **ifetch2**
     $MEM[MAR] \rightarrow IR$
- **ifetch3**
     $A + 1 \rightarrow PC$

Now that we have identified what must be done in the datapath for the microstates that implement the FETCH macro state, we can write down the control signals needed to effect the desired actions in each of these microstates. For each microstate, we highlight the datapath elements and control lines that are activated.

- **ifetch1**
    PC → MAR
    PC → A
    Control signals needed:
        DrPC
        LdMAR
        LdA

Following figure shows the datapath actions for **ifetch1** microstate.

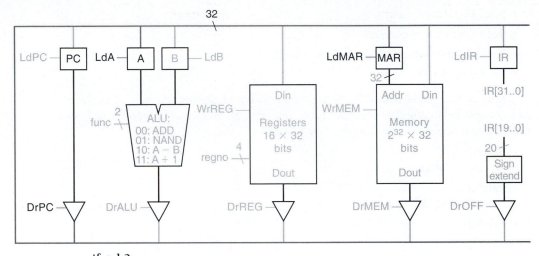

- **ifetch2**
    MEM[MAR] → IR
    Control signals needed:
        DrMEM
        LdIR

Following figure shows the datapath actions for **ifetch2** microstate.

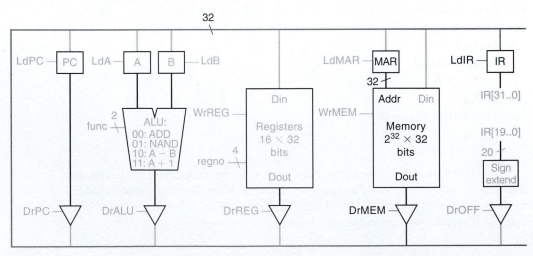

Note: With reference to the datapath, the default action of the memory is to read (i.e., when WrMEM is 0). Also, the memory implicitly reads the contents of the memory at the address contained in MAR and has the result available at *Dout* in **ifetch2**.

- **ifetch3**
    A + 1 → PC
    Control signals needed:
        func = 11
        DrALU
        LdPC

Following figure shows the datapath actions for **ifetch3** microstate.

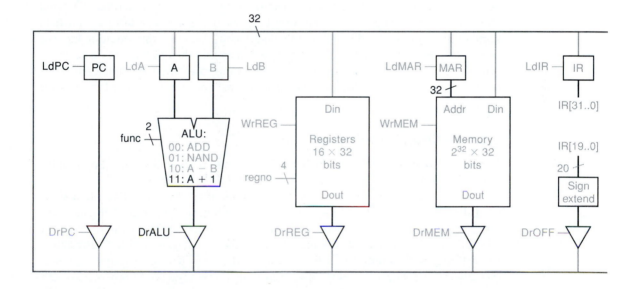

Note: If the func selected is 11, then the ALU implicitly performs A + 1 (see Figure 3.15).

Now we can fill out the contents of the ROM (see Figure 3.21) for the addresses associated with the microstates **ifetch1**, **ifetch2**, and **ifetch3**. (X denotes "don't care.") The next-state field of **ifetch3** is intentionally marked TBD (to be determined), and we will come back to that shortly.

This is starting to look like a *program,* albeit at a much lower level than those we may have learned about in our first computer-programming course. Every ROM location contains a set of commands that actuate different parts of the datapath. We will call each table entry a *microinstruction,* and we will call the entire contents of the ROM a *micro program.* Each microinstruction also contains the (address of the) next microinstruction to be executed. Control unit design has now become a programming exercise. It is the ultimate concurrent program, because we are exploiting all the hardware concurrency that is available in the datapath in every microinstruction.

Current State	State num	Drive signals					Load signals						Write signals		func	regno	Next state
		PC	ALU	Reg	MEM	OFF	PC	A	B	MAR	IR	Z	MEM	REG			
Ifetch1	00000	1	0	0	0	0	0	1	0	1	0	0	0	0	xx	xxxx	00001
Ifetch2	00001	0	0	0	1	0	0	0	0	0	1	0	0	0	xx	xxxx	00010
Ifetch3	00010	0	1	0	0	0	1	0	0	0	0	0	0	0	11	xxxx	TBD

Figure 3.21   ROM with some entries filled in with control signals.

Notice that there is a structure to each microinstruction. For example, all the drive signals can be grouped together; similarly, all the load signals can be grouped together. There are opportunities to reduce the space requirement of this table. For example, it may be possible to combine some of the control signals into one encoded field. Because we know that only one entity can drive the bus at any one time, we could group all the drive signals into one 3-bit field; each unique code of this 3-bit field signifies the entity selected to put its value on the bus. Whereas this would reduce the size of the table, it adds a decoding step, which increases the delay in the datapath for generating the drive control signals. We cannot group all the load signals into one encoded field, because multiple storage elements may need to be clocked in the same clock cycle.

3.5.3 DECODE Macro State

Once we are done with fetching the instruction, we are ready to decode it. So, from the **ifetch3** microstate, we want to transition to the DECODE macro state.

In this macro state, we examine the contents of IR (bits 31–28) to figure out what the instruction is. Once we know the instruction, we can go to that part of the micro program which implements that particular instruction. So we can think of the DECODE process as a multiway branch based on the OPCODE of the instruction. We will redraw the control unit FSM to depict the DECODE as a multiway branch. (See Figure 3.22.) Each leg of the multiway branch takes the FSM to the macro state corresponding to the execution sequence for a particular instruction. To keep the diagram simple, we show the multiway branch taking the FSM to a particular class of instruction.

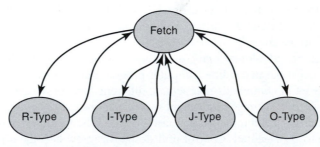

Figure 3.22   Extending the FSM with the DECODE macro state fleshed out.

We soon will come back to the question of implementing the multiway branch in the control unit. Let us first address the simpler issue of implementing each of the instructions.

3.5.4 EXECUTE Macro State: ADD Instruction (Part of R-Type)

R-type has the following format:

Recall that the ADD instruction does the following:

$$R_X \leftarrow R_Y + R_Z$$

To implement this instruction, we have to read two registers from the register file and write to a third register. The registers to be read are specified as part of the instruction and are available in the datapath as the contents of IR. However, as can be seen from the datapath, there is no path from the IR to the register file. There is a good reason for this omission. Depending on whether we want to read one of the source registers or write to a destination register, we need to send different parts of the IR to the **regno** input of the register file. As we have seen, **multiplexer** is the logic element that will let us make such selections.

Therefore, we add the element shown in Figure 3.23 to the datapath.

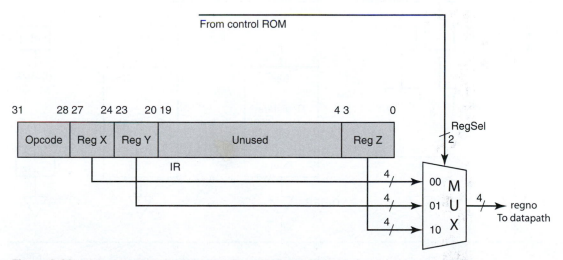

Figure 3.23   Using the IR bit fields to specify register selection.

The multiplexer allows selecting the specific field of the IR that is needed to be sent as the "regno" address to the register file.

	Drive signals					Load signals						Write signals				
Current State	PC	ALU	Reg	MEM	OFF	PC	A	B	MAR	IR	Z	MEM	REG	func	RegSel	Next state
...																

Figure 3.24   RegSel field added to the ROM control signals.

The **RegSel** control input (2 bits) comes from the microinstruction. The inputs to the multiplexer are the three different register-specifier fields of the IR. (See Chapter 2 for the format of the LC-2200 instructions.) It turns out that the register file is never addressed directly from the microinstruction. Therefore, we replace the 4-bit **regno** field of the microinstruction with a 2-bit **RegSel** field. (See Figure 3.24.)

Now we can write the datapath actions and the corresponding control signals needed in the microstates to implement the ADD execution macro state:

- **add1**
  Ry → A
  Control signals needed:
  RegSel = 01
  DrREG
  LdA

Following figure shows the datapath actions for **add1** microstate.

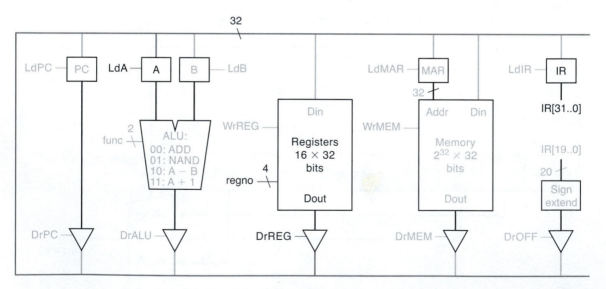

Note: The default action of the register file is to read the contents of the register file at the address specified by **regno** and make the data available at *Dout*.

- **add2**
  Rz → B

Control signals needed:
   RegSel = 10
   DrREG
   LdB

Following figure shows the datapath actions for **add2** microstate.

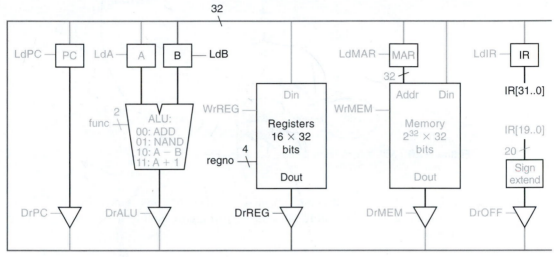

- **add3**

   $A + B \rightarrow Rx$

   Control signals needed:
      func = 00
      DrALU
      RegSel = 00
      WrREG

Following figure shows the datapath actions for **add3** microstate.

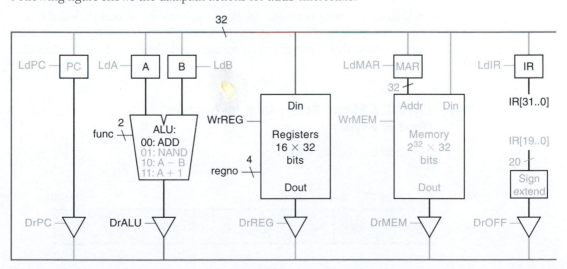

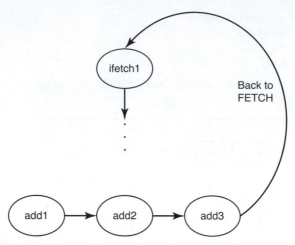

Figure 3.25   ADD macro state fleshed out in the FSM.

The ADD macro state is implemented by the control unit sequencing through the microstates **add1, add2, add3,** and then returning to the FETCH macro state. (See Figure 3.25.)

3.5.5 EXECUTE Macro State: NAND Instruction (Part of R-Type)

Recall that the NAND instruction does the following:

$$R_X \leftarrow R_Y \text{ NAND } R_Z$$

The NAND macro state is similar to ADD and consists of **nand1, nand2,** and **nand3** microstates. We leave it as an exercise to the reader to figure out what changes are needed in those microstates, compared with the corresponding states for ADD.

3.5.6 EXECUTE Macro State: JALR Instruction (Part of J-Type)

J-type instruction has the following format:

31 28	27 24	23 20	19 0
Opcode	Reg X	Reg Y	Unused

Recall that JALR instruction was introduced in the LC-2200 for supporting the sub-routine calling mechanism in high-level languages. JALR stashes the return address in a register and transfers control to the subroutine by doing the following:

$R_Y \leftarrow PC + 1$
$PC \leftarrow R_X$

Here are the microstates, datapath actions, and control signals for the JALR instruction:

- **jalr1**
    $PC \rightarrow Ry$
    Control signals needed:
        DrPC
        RegSel = 01
        WrREG

Following figure shows the datapath actions for **jalr1** microstate.

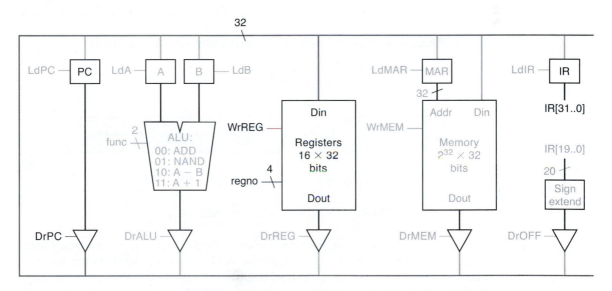

Note: PC + 1 needs to be stored in Ry. Recall that we already incremented PC in the FETCH macro state.

- **jalr2**
    $Rx \rightarrow PC$
    Control signals needed:
        RegSel = 00
        DrREG
        LdPC

Following figure shows the datapath actions for **jalr2** microstate.

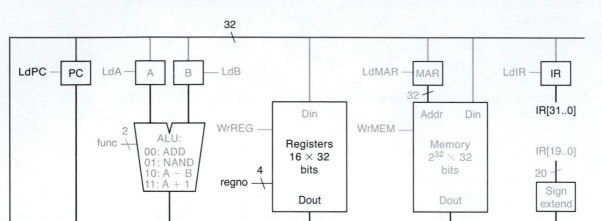

3.5.7 EXECUTE Macro State: LW Instruction (Part of I-Type)

I-type instruction has the following format:

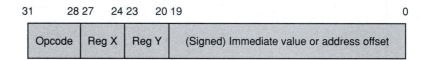

Recall that LW instruction has the following semantics:

```
Rx ← MEMORY[Ry + signed address-offset]
```

In the I-type instruction, the signed address offset is given by an immediate field that is part of the instruction. The immediate field occupies IR 19-0. As can be seen from the datapath, there is a **sign-extend** hardware that converts this 20-bit 2's complement value to a 32-bit 2's complement value. The **DrOFF** control line enables this sign-extended offset from the IR to be placed on the bus.

Here are the microstates, datapath actions, and control signals for the LW instruction:

- **lw1**

   Ry → A
   Control signals needed:
      RegSel = 01
      DrREG
      LdA

Following figure shows the datapath actions for **lw1** microstate.

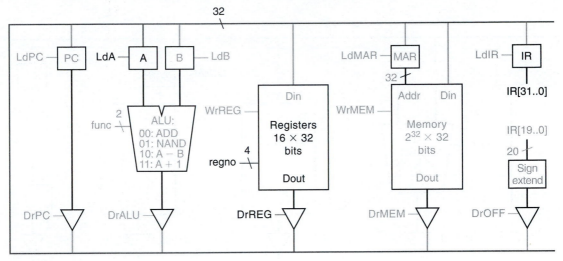

- **lw2**

    Sign-extended offset → B
    Control signals needed:
        DrOFF
        LdB

Following figure shows the datapath actions for **lw2** microstate.

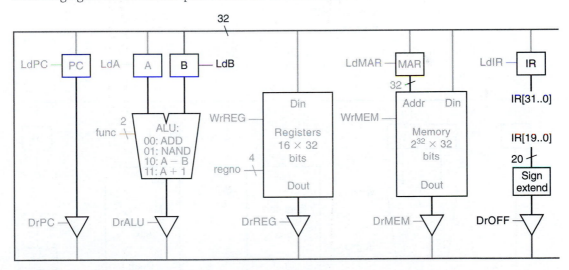

- **lw3**

    A + B → MAR
    Control signals needed:
        func = 00
        DrALU
        LdMAR

Following figure shows the datapath actions for **lw3** microstate.

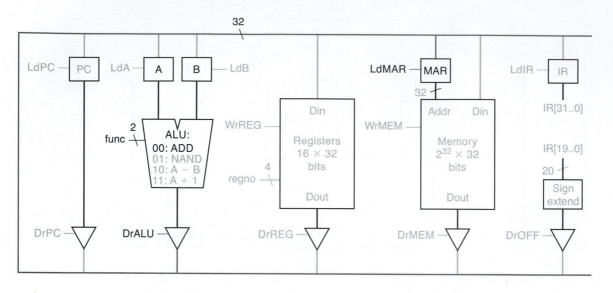

- **lw4**

    MEM[MAR] → Rx
    Control signals needed:
    DrMEM
    RegSel = 00
    WrREG

Following figure shows the datapath actions for **lw4** microstate.

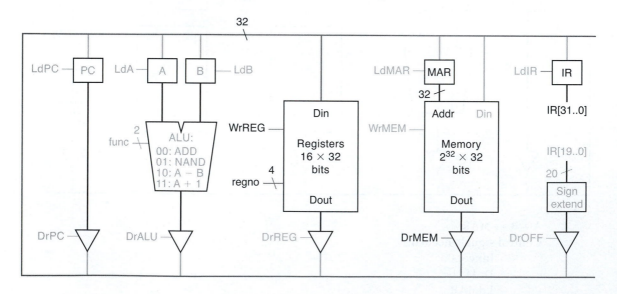

Example 3.4

We have decided to add another addressing mode, **autoincrement**, to the LC-2200. This mode comes in handy for LW/SW instructions. The semantics of this addressing mode with LW instruction is as follows:

```
LW  Rx, (Ry)+    ;       Rx ← MEM[Ry];
                 ;       Ry ← Ry + 1;
```

The instruction format is as follows:

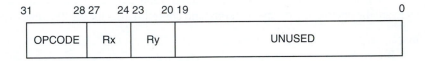

Write the sequence for implementing the LW instruction with this addressing mode. (You will need to write the sequence for the EXECUTE macro state of the instruction.) For each microstate, show the datapath action (in register transfer format such as A ← Ry), along with the control signals you will need to enable the datapath action (such as DrPC).

Answer:

```
LW1:    Ry → A, MAR
        Control Signals:
              RegSel=01; DrReg; LdA; LdMAR

LW2:    MEM[Ry] → Rx
        Control Signals:
              DrMEM; RegSel=00; WrREG

LW3:    A + 1 → Ry
        Control Signals:
              Func=11; DrALU; RegSel=01; WrREG
```

3.5.8 EXECUTE Macro State: SW and ADDI Instructions (Part of I-Type)

Implementation of the SW macro state is similar to the LW macro state. Implementation of the ADDI macro state is similar to the ADD macro state, with the only difference that the second operand comes from the immediate field of the IR as opposed to another register. The development of the microstates for these two instructions is left as an exercise to the reader.

3.5.9 EXECUTE Macro State: BEQ Instruction (Part of I-Type)

BEQ instruction has the following semantics:

```
If (Rx == Ry) then PC ← PC + 1 + signed address-offset
else nothing
```

This instruction needs some special handling. The semantics of this instruction calls for comparing the contents of two registers (Rx and Ry) and branching to a target address generated by adding the sign-extended offset to PC + 1 (where PC is the address of the BEQ instruction) if the two values are equal.

In the datapath, there is hardware to detect whether the value on the bus is a zero. The microstates for BEQ use this logic to set the Z register upon comparing the two registers.

Here are the microstates, datapath actions, and control signals for the BEQ macro state:

- **beq1**
    Rx → A
    Control signals needed:
        RegSel = 00
        DrREG
        LdA

Following figure shows the datapath actions for **beq1** microstate.

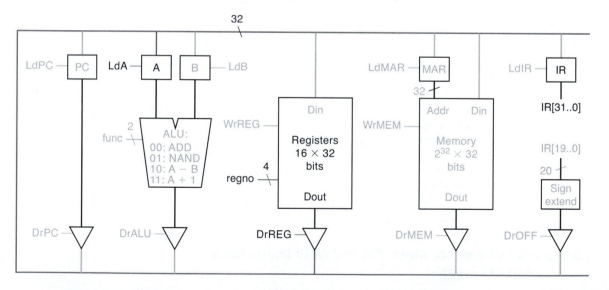

- **beq2**
    Ry → B
    Control signals needed:
        RegSel = 01
        DrREG
        LdB

Following figure shows the datapath actions for **beq2** microstate.

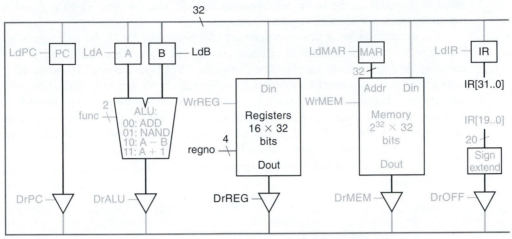

- beq3

    A − B

    Load Z register with result
    of zero detect logic

    Control signals needed:
    func = 10
    DrALU
    LdZ

Following figure shows the datapath actions for **beq3** microstate.

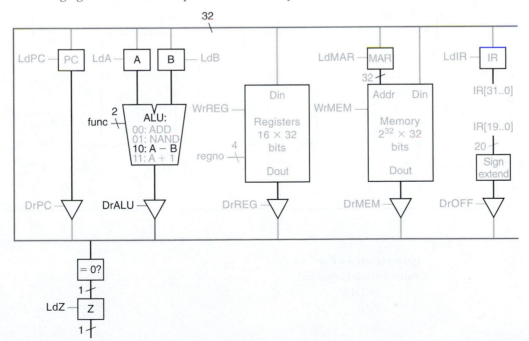

Note: The zero-detect combinational logic element in the datapath is always checking whether the value on the bus is zero. By asserting LdZ, the Z register (1-bit register) is capturing the result of this detection for later use.

The actions following this microstate get tricky compared with the microstates for the other instructions. In the other instructions, we simply sequence through all the microstates for that instruction and then return to the FETCH macro state. However, BEQ instruction causes a control flow change that depends on the outcome of the comparison. If the Z register is not set (i.e., Rx != Ry), then we simply return to **ifetch1** to continue execution with the next sequential instruction. (PC is already pointing to that instruction.) On the other hand, if Z is set, then we continue with the microstates of BEQ to compute the target address of the branch.

First let us go ahead and complete the microstates for BEQ, assuming that a branch has to be taken.

- **beq4**
    PC → A
    Control signals needed:
        DrPC
        LdA

Following figure shows the datapath actions for **beq4** microstate.

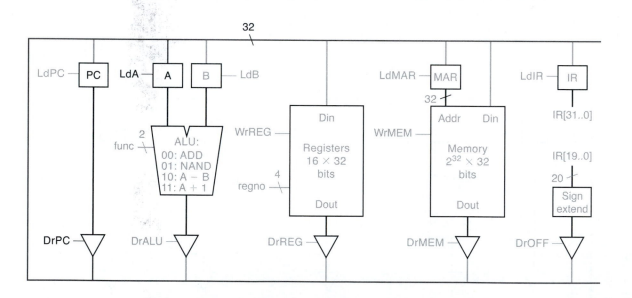

- **beq5**
    Sign-extended offset → B
    Control signals needed:
        DrOFF
        LdB

Following figure shows the datapath actions for **beq5** microstate.

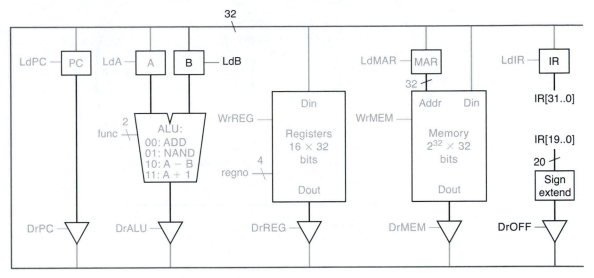

- **beq6**

    A + B → PC

    Control signals needed:

    func = 00

    DrALU

    LdPC

Following figure shows the datapath actions for **beq6** microstate

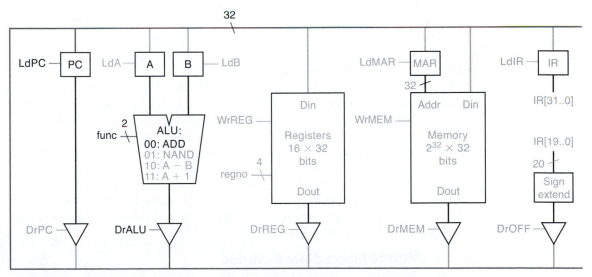

Note: In the FETCH macro state itself, PC has been incremented. Therefore, we simply add the sign-extended offset to PC to compute the target address.

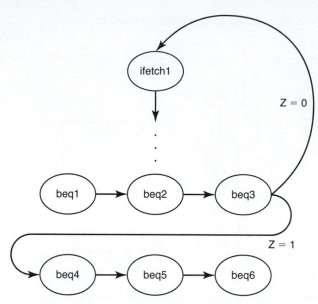

Figure 3.26   Desired state transitions in the BEQ macro state.

We have to go to either ifetch1 or beq4, depending on the result of the arithmetic done in beq3, which is captured in the Z register at the end of beq3.

3.5.10 Engineering a Conditional Branch in the Microprogram

Figure 3.26 shows the desired state transitions in the BEQ macro state. The **next-state** field of the **beq3** microinstruction will contain **beq4**. With only one **next-state** field in the microinstruction, we need to engineer the transition from **beq3** to **ifetch1** or **beq4**, depending on the state of the Z register. A time-efficient way of accomplishing this task is to use an additional location in the ROM to duplicate the microinstruction corresponding to **ifetch1**. We will explain how this is done.

Let us assume that the state register has 5 bits, **beq4** has the binary encoding $\underline{0}1000$, and the next state field of the **beq3** microinstruction is set to **beq4**. We will prefix this encoding with the contents of the Z register to create a 6-bit address to the ROM. If the Z bit is 0, then the address presented to the ROM will be 001000; and if the Z bit is 1, then the address will be $\underline{1}01000$. The latter address (101000) is the one in which we will store the microinstruction corresponding to the **beq4** microstate. In the location 001000 (let us call this **ifetch1-clone**), we will store the exact same microinstruction as in the original **ifetch1** location. Figure 3.27 shows this pictorially.

We can extend this idea (cloning a microinstruction) whenever we need to take a conditional branch in the micro program.

3.5.11 DECODE Macro State Revisited

Let us return to the DECODE macro state. Recall that this is a multiway branch from **ifetch3** to the macro state corresponding to the specific instruction contained in IR. We

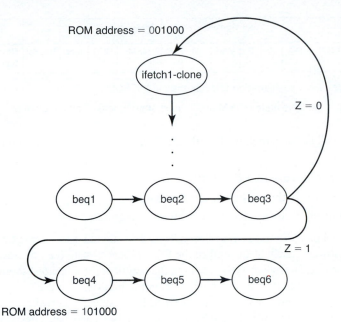

Figure 3.27   Engineering the conditional micro branch.

Pick a 5-bit base address (01000) and prefix it with the output of the Z register.

adopt a trick similar to the one with the Z register for implementing the 2-way branch for the BEQ instruction.

Let us assume that 10000 is the encoding for the *generic* EXECUTE macro state.

The **next-state** field of **ifetch3** will have this generic value. We prefix this generic value with the contents of the OPCODE (IR bits 31-28) to generate a 9-bit address to the ROM. Thus, the ADD macro state will start at ROM address **000**10000, the NAND macro state will start at ROM address **001**10000, the ADDI at ROM address **001**10000, and so on. This is shown pictorially in Figure 3.28.

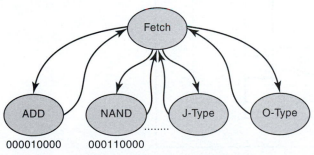

Figure 3.28   Effecting the multiway branch of DECODE macro state.

Use a 5-bit base address (10000) and prefix it with the (4-bit) opcode field from the IR.

	Drive signals					Load signals						Write signals				NextState and modifiers		
Current State	PC	ALU	Reg	MEM	OFF	PC	A	B	MAR	IR	Z	MEM	REG	func	RegSel	Next State	M	T

Figure 3.29   Final configuration of each entry in the ROM.

We have added the M and T "next state modifier" bits to each entry in the ROM.

Putting all this together, we find that the control logic of the processor has a 10-bit address:

- **The top 4 bits are rom IR 31-28.**
- **The next bit is the output of the Z register.**
- **The bottom 5 bits are from the 5-bit state register.**

The top 4 bits (shown as coming from IR 31-28) should be zero, except when we want to do a multiway branch at the end of the FETCH macro state (i.e., microstate **ifetch3**). Similarly, the next bit (shown as coming from the output of the Z register) should be zero except when we want to do the two-way branch in the **beq3** microstate. To ensure the selective modification of the top 5 bits of the ROM address, we will add two more 1-bit fields to each entry in the ROM, called M and T. (See Figure 3.29.) These fields, respectively, control whether the 4 bits from IR and the 1 bit from Z are to be used as ROM address modifiers in

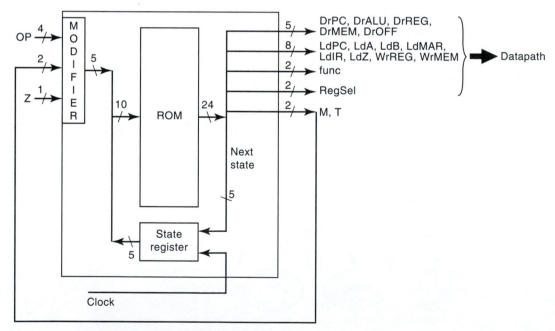

Figure 3.30   The LC-2200 control unit.

This shows the complete addressing scheme for the ROM as well as all the control signals that need to be generated and sent to the datapath.

a given clock cycle. Working out the modifier circuitry shown in Figure 3.30 to complete the control unit design by using these bits is left as an exercise for the reader. (See Exercise 17.)

The lines coming in and out of the control unit depicted in Figure 3.30 connect directly to the corresponding signal lines of the datapath shown in Figure 3.15.

3.6 Alternative Style of Control Unit Design

Let us consider different styles of implementing the control unit of a processor.

3.6.1 Microprogrammed Control

In Section 3.5, we presented the microprogrammed style of designing a control unit. This style has a certain elegance, simplicity, and ease of maintenance. The advantage we get with the microprogrammed design is that the control logic appears as a program contained in a ROM and thus lends itself to better maintainability. There are two potential sources of inefficiency with microprogrammed design. The first relates to **time**. To generate the control signals in a particular clock cycle, an address has to be presented to the ROM, and only after a delay referred to as the **access time** of the ROM are the control signals available for operating on the datapath. This time penalty is in the critical path of the clock cycle time and hence is a source of performance loss. However, the time penalty can be masked by the employment of prefetching of the next microinstruction while the current one is being executed. The second source of inefficiency relates to **space**. The design presented in the previous section represents one specific style of microprogramming called *horizontal microcode*, wherein there is a bit position in each microinstruction for every control signal needed in the entire datapath. From the sequences we have developed so far, it is clear that in most microinstructions most of the bits are 0 and only a few bits are 1, corresponding to the control signals that are needed for that clock cycle. For example, in **ifetch1**, only **DrPC**, **LdMAR**, and **LdA** are 1; all the other bits in the microinstruction are 0. The space inefficiency of horizontal microcode could be overcome by a technique called *vertical microcode* that is akin to writing assembly-language programming. Basically, the bit position in each microinstruction may represent a different control signal, depending on an opcode field in each vertical microinstruction. Vertical microcode is trickier, because the control signals corresponding to a particular bit position in the microinstruction have to be mutually exclusive.

3.6.2 Hardwired Control

It is instructive to look at what exactly the ROM represents in the horizontal microcode developed in Section 3.5. It really is a **truth table** for all the control signals needed in the datapath. The rows of the ROM represent the states, and the columns represent the functions (one for each control signal). From previous exposure to logic design, the reader may know how to synthesize the minimal Boolean logic function for each column. Such logic functions are more efficient than a truth table.

We can implement the Boolean logic functions corresponding to the control signals by using combinational logic circuits. The terms of this function are the conditions under which a specific control signal needs to be asserted.

For example, the Boolean function for **DrPC** will look as follows:

```
DrPC = ifetch1 + jalr1 + beq4 + ...
```

Using AND/OR gates, or universal gates such as NAND/NOR, we can generate all the control signals. We refer to this style of design as **hardwired control** because the control signals are implemented by combinational logic circuits (and hence are hardwired; i.e, they are not easy to change). Such a design leads to efficiency in both time (no access-time penalty for ROM lookup) and space (no wasted space for signals that are *not* generated in a clock cycle). There has been some criticism in the past that such a design leads to a maintenance nightmare because the Boolean functions are implemented by random logic.

However, the advent of **programmable logic arrays (PLAs)** and **field programmable gate arrays (FPGAs)** has largely nullified this criticism. For example, PLAs give a structure to the random logic by organizing the required logic as a structured two-dimensional array. We show this organization in Figure 3.31.

The outputs are the control signals needed to actuate the datapath (**DrPC, DrALU,** etc.). The inputs are the state the processor is in (**ifetch1, ifetch2**, etc.) and the conditions generated in the datapath (contents of the IR, Z, etc.). Every gate in the AND plane has *all* the inputs (true and complement versions). Similarly, every gate in the OR plane has as inputs *all* the product terms generated by the AND plane. This is called a PLA because the logic can be "programmed" by the selection or nonselection of the inputs to the AND and OR planes. Every PLA *output* is a **SUM-of-PRODUCT** term. The PRODUCT terms are implemented in the AND plane. The SUM terms are implemented in the OR plane. This design concentrates all the control logic in one place and thus has the structural advantage of the microprogrammed design. At the same time, since the control signals are generated by the use of combinational-logic circuits, there is no penalty to this hardwired design. There is

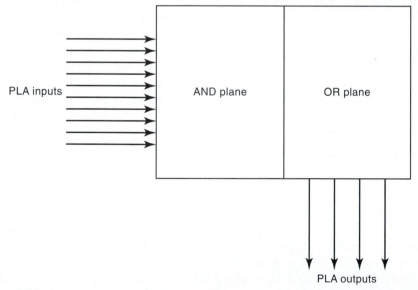

Figure 3.31   PLA.

The inputs on the left come from the state register and the datapath elements that affect the state of the processor such as IR and Z; each output is expressed as the sum of products of the inputs; the outputs are the control signals that need to be sent to the datapath.

a slight space disadvantage, compared with a true random-logic design, because every AND gate has a fan-in equal to *all* the PLA inputs and every OR gate has a fan-in equal to the number of AND gates in the AND plane. However, the structural advantage and the regularity of the PLA lend itself to compact VLSI design and far outweigh any slight disadvantage.

More recently, FPGAs have become very popular as a way of quickly prototyping complex hardware designs. An FPGA is really a successor to the PLA and contains logic elements and storage elements. The connections among these elements can be programmed "in the field"; hence, the name. This flexibility allows any design bugs to be corrected more easily, even after deployment, thus improving the maintainability of hardwired design.

3.6.3 Choosing Between the Two Control Design Styles

The choice for control design between the two styles depends on a variety of factors. We have given the pros and cons of both control styles. It would appear that, with the advent of FPGAs, much of the maintainability argument against hardwired control has disappeared. Nevertheless, for basic implementation of processors (i.e., nonpipelined), as well as for the implementation of complex instructions (such as those found in the Intel x86 architecture), microprogrammed control is preferred due to its flexibility and amenability to quick changes. On the other hand, as we will see in the chapter on pipelined processor design, hardwired control is very much the preferred option for high-end pipelined processor implementation. Table 3.2 summarizes the pros and cons of the two design approaches.

Table 3.2 Comparison of Control Regimes

Control Regime	Pros	Cons	Comment	When to Use	Examples
Microprogrammed	Simplicity, maintainability, flexibility Rapid prototyping	Potential for space and time inefficiency	Space inefficiency may be mitigated with vertical microcode Time inefficiency may be mitigated with prefetching	For complex instructions, and for quick nonpipelined prototyping of architectures	PDP 11 series, IBM 360 and 370 series, Motorola 68000, complex instructions in Intel x86 architecture
Hardwired	Amenable for pipelined implementation Potential for higher performance	Potentially harder to change the design Longer design time	Maintainability can be increased with the use of structured hardware such as PLAs and FPGAs	For high-performance pipelined implementation of architectures	Most modern processors, including Intel Xeon series, IBM PowerPC, MIPS

Summary

In this chapter, we got a feel for implementing a processor, given an instruction set. The first step in the implementation is the choice of the datapath and the components that comprise the datapath. We reviewed the basic digital logic elements in Section 3.3 and the datapath design in Section 3.4. Once the datapath is fixed, we turn our attention to the design of the control unit that drives the datapath to realize the instruction set. Assuming a microprogrammed control unit, Section 3.5 walked us through the microstates for implementing the instructions found in the LC-2200 ISA. In Section 3.6, we reviewed the difference between hardwired control and microprogrammed control.

Historical Perspective

It is instructive to look back in time to see how the performance tradeoffs relate to economic and technological factors.

In the 1940s and 1950s, the logic elements for constructing the hardware and memory were extremely expensive. Vacuum tubes and, later, discrete transistors served as the implementation technology. The instruction-set architecture was very simple and typically featured a single register called an *accumulator*. Examples of machines from this period include the EDSAC and the IBM 701.

In the 1960s, we started seeing the first glimmer of "integration." The IBM 1130, introduced in 1965, featured *solid logic technology (SLT),* a precursor to integrated circuits. This decade saw a drop in hardware prices, but memory was still implemented by magnetic cores (called *core memory*) and was a dominant cost of a computer system.

The trend continued in the 1970s with the initial introduction of SSI (small scale integrated), and then MSI (medium scale integrated), circuits as implementation technologies for the processor. Semiconductor memories started making their way in the 1970s as a replacement for core memory. It is interesting to note that, circa 1974, the prices per bit for core memory and for semiconductor memory were about equal ($0.01 per bit). Semiconductor memory prices started dropping rapidly from then on, and the rest is history!

The 1970s was an era for experimenting with a number of different architecture approaches, such as stack-oriented, memory-oriented, and register-oriented architectures. Examples of machines from this era include the IBM 360 and the DEC PDP-11 for hybrid memory- and register-oriented architectures; and the Burroughs B-5000 for a stack-oriented approach. All of these are variants of a *stored program computer,* which is often referred to as *von Neumann* architecture, named after computer pioneer John von Neumann.

In parallel with the development of the stored program computer, computer scientists were experimenting with radically new architectural ideas. These include *dataflow* and *systolic* architectures. These architectures were aimed at giving the programmer control over performing several instructions in parallel, breaking the mold of sequential execution of instructions that is inherent in the stored-program model. Both dataflow and systolic architectures focus on data rather than instructions. The dataflow approach allows all instructions whose input data are ready and available to execute and pass the results of their respective executions to other instructions that are waiting for these results. The systolic approach allows parallel streams of data to flow through an array of functional units prearranged to carry out a specific computation on the data streams (e.g., matrix multiplication). Whereas the dataflow architecture is a realization of a general model of computation, the systolic is an algorithm-specific model of synthesizing architectures. Although these alternative styles of architecture did not replace the stored-program computer, they had tremendous impact on computing as a whole, from algorithm design to processor implementation.

In the 1980s, there were several interesting developments. In the first place, high-speed LSI (large scale integrated) circuits using bipolar transistors were becoming commonplace. This was the implementation technology of choice for high-end processors such as the IBM 370 and the DEC VAX 780. In parallel with this trend, VLSI (very large scale integrated) circuits using CMOS transistors (also called field effect transistors or FETs) were making their way as vehicles for single-chip microprocessors. By the end of the decade, and into the early 1990s, these *killer micros* started posing a real threat to high-end machines in terms of price–performance. The 1980s also saw rapid advances in compiler technologies and the development of a true partnership between system software (as exemplified by compilers) and instruction-set design. This partnership paved the way for RISC (reduced instruction-set computer) architectures. The IBM 801, the Berkeley RISC, and the Stanford MIPS processors led the way in the RISC revolution. It is interesting that there was still a strong following for the CISC (complex instruction-set computer) architecture, as exemplified by the Motorola 68000 and the Intel x86 series of processors. The principle of pipelined processor design (see Chapter 5), which until the 1980s was reserved for high-end processors, made its way into microprocessors, as the new level of integration allowed placing more and more transistors into one piece of silicon. The debate over RISC versus CISC petered out, and the issue became one of striving to achieve an instruction throughput of one per clock cycle in a pipelined processor.

The decade of the 1990s firmly established the microchip (single-chip microprocessors based on CMOS technology) as the implementation technology of choice in the computer industry. By the end of the decade, the Intel x86 and the Power PC instruction sets (curiously, both of these processor families are CISC-style architectures that incorporated a number of the implementation techniques from the RISC-style architectures) became the industry standard for making "boxes," be they desktops, servers, or supercomputers. It is important to note that one of the most promising architectures of this decade was the DEC Alpha. Unfortunately, due to the demise of DEC in the late 1990s, the Alpha architecture also rests in peace!

With the advent of personal communication devices (cell phones, pagers, and PDAs) and gaming devices, embedded computing platforms have been growing in importance since the 1980s. A significant number of embedded platforms use descendants of a RISC architecture called ARM (short for Acorn RISC Machine, originally designed by Acorn Computers). Intel makes XScale processors that are derived from the original ARM architecture. A point to note is that ARM processors were originally designed with PCs and workstations in mind.

Superscalar and *VLIW* (very large instruction word architectures) processors represent technologies that grew out of the RISC revolution. Both are attempts to increase the throughput of the processor. They usually are referred to as *multiple issue* processors. The superscalar processor relies on the hardware to execute a fixed number of mutually independent, adjacent instructions in parallel. In the VLIW approach, as the name suggests, an instruction actually contains a number of operations that are strung together in a single instruction. VLIW relies heavily on compiler technology to reduce the hardware design complexity and exploit parallelism. First introduced in the late 1980s, the VLIW technology has gone through significant refinement over the years. The most recent foray of VLIW architecture is the IA-64 offering from Intel, targeting the supercomputing marketplace. VLIW architectures are also popular in the high-end embedded computing space, as exemplified by DSP (digital signal processing) applications.

We have reached the end of the first decade of the new millennium. There is little debate over instruction sets these days. Most of the action is at the level of micro-architecture, namely, how to improve the performance of the processor by various hardware techniques. Simultaneously, the level of integration has increased to allow placing multiple processors on a single piece of silicon. Dubbed *multicore*, such chips have started appearing in most computer systems that we purchase today.

Exercises

1. What is the difference between level logic and edge-triggered logic? Which do we use in implementing an ISA? Why?

2. Given the FSM and state-transition diagram for a garage door opener (Figure 3.12 and Table 3.1), implement the sequential logic circuit for the garage door opener. [Hint: The sequential logic circuit has two states and produces three outputs, namely, next state, up motor control, and down motor control.]

3. Reimplement the logic circuit of Exercise 2, using the ROM-plus-state-register approach detailed in this chapter.

4. Compare and contrast the various approaches to control-logic design.

5. One of the optimizations to reduce the space requirement of the control-ROM-based design is to club together independent control signals and represent them by an encoded field in the control ROM. What are the pros and cons of this approach? Which control signals can be clubbed together and which ones cannot be? Justify your answer.

6. What are the advantages and disadvantages of a bus-based datapath design?

7. Consider a three-bus design. How would you use it for organizing the datapath elements of the two-bus design shown in Figure 3.10? How does this help, compared with the two-bus design?

8. Explain why internal registers, such as the instruction register (IR) and memory address register (MAR), may not be usable for temporary storage of values in implementing the ISA by the control unit.

9. An engineer would like to reduce to two the number of microstates required for implementing the FETCH macro state. How would she able to accomplish that goal?

10. What is the advantage of fixed-length instructions?

11. Assume that, for the portion of the datapath shown next, all the lines are 16 bits wide. Fill in the table that follows the diagram.

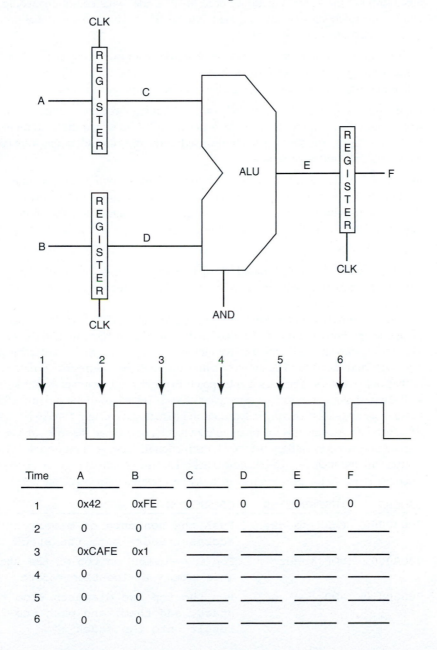

Time	A	B	C	D	E	F
1	0x42	0xFE	0	0	0	0
2	0	0	___	___	___	___
3	0xCAFE	0x1	___	___	___	___
4	0	0	___	___	___	___
5	0	0	___	___	___	___
6	0	0	___	___	___	___

12. In the LC-2200 processor, why is there not a register after the ALU?

13. Extend the LC-2200 ISA to include a subtract instruction. Show the actions that must be taken in microstates of the subtract instruction, assuming the datapath shown in Figure 3.15.

14. In the datapath diagram shown in Figure 3.15, why do we need the A and B registers in front of the ALU? Why do we need MAR? Under what conditions would you be able to do without any of these registers? [Hint: Think of additional ports in the register file and/or buses.]

15. Core memory used to cost $0.01 per bit. Consider your own computer. What would be a rough estimate of its cost if memory cost is $0.01/bit? If memory were still at that price, what would be the effect on the computer industry?

16. If computer designers focused entirely on speed and ignored cost implications, what would the computer industry look like today? Who would the customers be? Now consider the same question reversed: If the only consideration were cost, what would the industry be like?

17. In Section 3.5.11, we introduced two additional fields, M and T, as next-state modifier bits. These bits allow the top half of the ROM address to be modified selectively in a given cycle. Complete the logic for the control unit shown in Figure 3.30 by using these next-state modifier bits.

18. (Design Question)

    Consider a CPU with a stack-based instruction set. Operands and results for arithmetic instructions are stored on the stack; the architecture contains no general-purpose registers.

    The data path shown next uses two separate memories: a 65,536 (2^{16}) byte memory to hold instructions and (nonstack) data, and a 256-byte memory to hold the stack. The stack is implemented with a conventional memory and a stack pointer register. The stack starts at address 0, and grows upward (to higher addresses) as data are pushed onto the stack. The stack pointer points to the element on top of the stack (or is −1 if the stack is empty). You may ignore issues such as stack overflow and underflow.

    Memory addresses referring to locations in program/data memory are 16 bits. All data are 8 bits. Assume that the program/data memory is byte addressable; that is, each address refers to an 8-bit byte. Each instruction includes an 8-bit opcode. Many instructions also include a 16-bit address field. The instruction set is given. Here, "memory" refers to the program/data memory (as opposed to the stack memory).

OPCODE	INSTRUCTION	OPERATION
00000000	PUSH \<addr>	Push the contents of memory at address \<addr> onto the stack
00000001	POP \<addr>	Pop the element on top of the stack into memory at location \<addr>
00000010	ADD	Pop the top two elements from the stack, add them, and push the result onto the stack

```
00000100  BEQ <addr>       Pop top two elements from the
                           stack; if they're equal, branch
                           to memory location <addr>
```

Note that the ADD instruction is only 8 bits, but the others are 24 bits. Instructions are packed into successive byte locations of memory (i.e., do *not* assume that all instructions use 24 bits).

Assume that memory is 8 bits wide; that is, each read or write operation to main memory accesses 8 bits of instruction or data. This means that the instruction fetch for multibyte instructions requires multiple memory accesses.

(a) Datapath

Complete the partial design shown.

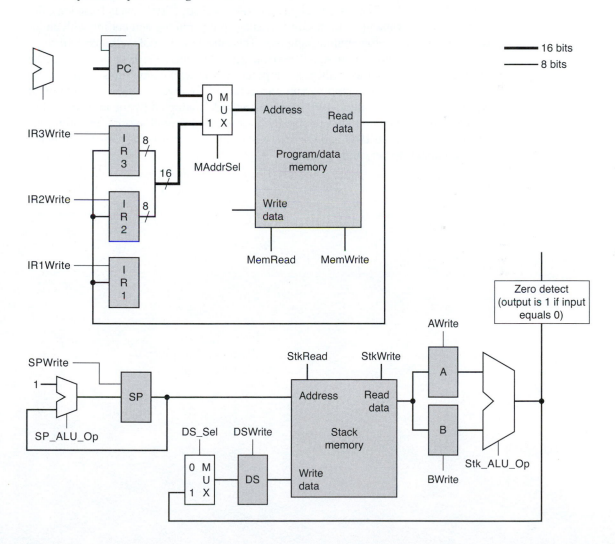

Assume that reading or writing the program/data memory or the stack memory requires a single clock cycle to complete (actually, slightly less, in order to allow time to read/write registers). Similarly, assume that each ALU requires slightly less than one clock cycle to complete an arithmetic operation, and the zero detection circuit requires negligible time.

(b) Control Unit

Show a state diagram for the control unit, indicating the control signals that must be asserted in each state of the state diagram.

Bibliographic Notes and Further Reading

There are a number of good textbooks covering the fundamentals of logic design [Katz, 2004; Mano, 2007]. The textbook by Patt and Patel [Patt, 2004] covers basic logic design topics, following up with machine language programming and ending with an introduction to the C programming language. There are a number of textbooks that cover computer organization and design [Patterson, 2008; Stallings, 2010; Tanenbaum, 2005; Hamacher, 2001]. Maurice Wilkes, a computer pioneer with many "firsts" to his credit, was the inventor of the microprogramming technique for organizing the control unit of a processor in 1951 [Wilkes, 1951], which was widely adopted by the industry to implement complex computer structures. Wilkes received several awards, including the ACM Turing Award in 1967 and the Eckert-Mauchly Award in 1980, the latter from the IEEE Computer Society and ACM.

Interrupts, Traps, and Exceptions

In the previous chapter, we discussed the implementation of the processor. In this chapter, we will discuss how the processor can handle discontinuities in program execution. In a sense, branch instructions and subroutine calls are discontinuities as well. However, the programmer consciously introduces such discontinuities as part of the program. The discontinuities we will look into in this chapter are those which are unplanned for and often may not even be part of the program that experiences the discontinuities.

Let us look at a simple analogy, a *classroom*. The professor is giving a lecture on computer architecture. To encourage class participation, he wants students to ask questions. He could do one of two things: (1) Periodically, he could stop lecturing and poll the students to see whether they have any questions; or (2) he could tell the students that, whenever they have a question, they should put up their hand to signal that they have a question. Clearly, the first approach inhibits the spontaneity of the students. By the time the professor gets around to polling the students, they may have forgotten that they had a question. Worse yet, they had so many questions, one after another, that they are now completely lost! The second approach will ensure that the students remain engaged and that they do not lose their train of thought. However, there is a slight problem. When should the professor take a student's question? He could take it immediately, as soon as someone puts up a hand, but he may be in mid-sentence. Therefore, he should finish his train of thought and then take the question. He has to be careful to remember where he was in his lecture so that, after answering the student's question, he can return to the point at which he left off in the lecture. What if another student asks a question while the professor is in the middle of answering the first student's question? That will soon spiral out of control; therefore, as a first-order principle, the professor should not take another question until he is finished answering the first one. So, there are two things to take away from the classroom analogy: Remember where to return in the lecture, and disable further questions.

The processor that we designed executes instructions, but unless it can talk to the outside world for I/O, it is rather useless. Building on the previous analogy, we can have the processor periodically poll an input device (such as a keyboard). On the one hand, polling is error prone, since the device could be generating data at a rate faster than the polling rate. On the other hand, it is extremely wasteful for the processor to be doing the polling if the device has no data to deliver. Therefore, we can apply the classroom analogy and let the device *interrupt* the processor to let it know that it has something to say to the processor. As in the classroom analogy, the processor should remember where it is in its current program execution and disable further interruptions until it services the current one.

4.1 Discontinuities in Program Execution

In Chapter 3, we defined the terms *synchronous* and *asynchronous* in the context of logic circuit behavior. Consider a real-life example. Let's say that you walk to the fridge and pick up a soda. That's a *synchronous* event. It is part of your intended activities. On the other hand, while you are working on your homework in your room, your roommate comes in and gives you a soda. That's an *asynchronous* event, because it was not part of your intended activities. Making a phone call is a synchronous event; receiving one is an asynchronous event.

We can generalize the definitions of *synchronous* and *asynchronous* events observed in a system, be they in hardware or software. A *synchronous* event is an event that occurs (if it occurs at all) at well-defined points of time, aligned with the intended activities of the system. The state changes from one microstate to the next in the sequences that we discussed in Chapter 3 and are all examples of synchronous events in a hardware system. In a similar way, opening a file in your program is a synchronous software event.

An *asynchronous* event is an event that occurs (if it occurs at all) unexpectedly with respect to other ongoing activities in the system. As we will see shortly, interrupts are asynchronous hardware events. An e-mail arrival notification while you are in the middle of your assignment is an asynchronous software event.

A system may compose synchronous and asynchronous events. For example, the hardware may use polling (which is synchronous) to detect an event and then generate an asynchronous software event.

Now we are ready to discuss discontinuities in program execution that come in three forms: *interrupts, exceptions,* and *traps.*

1. **Interrupts**

    An *interrupt* is the mechanism by which devices catch the attention of the processor. This is an unplanned discontinuity for the currently executing program and is asynchronous with the processor execution. Furthermore, the device I/O may be intended for a program altogether different from the current one. For the purposes of clarity of discourse, we will consider as interrupts only discontinuities caused by external devices.

2. **Exceptions**

    Programs may unintentionally perform certain illegal operations (for example, *divide by zero*) or follow an execution path unintended in the program specification. In such cases, once again it becomes necessary to discontinue the original sequence of instruction execution of the program and deal with the unplanned discontinuity—in this case, an *exception.* Exceptions are internally generated conditions and are synchronous with the processor execution. They are usually unintended by the current program and are the result of some erroneous condition encountered during execution. However, programming languages such as Java define an exception mechanism to allow error propagation through layers of software. In this case, the program *intentionally* generates an exception to signal some unexpected program behavior. In either case, we define *exception* to be some condition (intentional or unintentional) that deviates from normal program execution.

3. **Traps**

    Programs often make *system calls* to read/write files or to request other services from the system. System calls are like procedure calls, but they need some special handling because the user program will be accessing parts of the system whose integrity affects a whole community of users, and not just this program. Further, the user program may not know where in memory the procedure corresponding to this service exists and may have to discern that information at the point of call. Trap, as the name suggests, allows the program to *fall into* the operating system, which will then decide what the user program wants. Another term often used in computer literature for program-generated traps is *software interrupts.* For the purposes of our discussion, we will consider software interrupts to be the same as traps. Similar to exceptions, traps are internally generated conditions and are synchronous with the processor execution. Some traps could be intentional—for example, as a manifestation of a program making a system call. Some traps could be unintentional, as far as the program is concerned. We will see examples of such unintentional traps in later chapters when we discuss memory systems.

Table 4.1 Program Discontinuities

Type	Sync/Async	Source	Intentional?	Examples
Exception	Sync	Internal	Yes and No	Overflow, Divide by zero, Illegal memory address, Java exception mechanism
Trap	Sync	Internal	Yes and No	System call, Software interrupts, Page fault, Emulated instructions
Interrupt	Async	External	Yes	I/O device completion

Whereas the understanding of the term *interrupt* is fairly standardized, the same cannot be said about the other two terms in the literature. In this book, we have chosen to adopt a particular definition of these three terms, which we use consistently, but acknowledge that the definition and use of these terms may differ in other books. Specifically, in our definition, a *trap* is an internal condition that the currently running program has no way of dealing with on its own, and, if anything, the system has to handle it. On the other hand, it is the currently running program's responsibility to handle an *exception*.

Table 4.1 summarizes the characteristics of these three types of program discontinuities. The second column characterizes whether it is synchronous or asynchronous; the third column identifies the source of the discontinuity as internal or external to the currently running program; the fourth column specifies whether the discontinuity was intentional, irrespective of the source; and the last column gives examples of each type of discontinuity.

4.2 Dealing with Program Discontinuities

As it turns out, program discontinuity is a powerful tool. First, it allows the computer system to provide input/output capabilities; second, it allows the computer system to perform resource management among competing activities; third, it allows the computer system to aid the programmer in developing correct programs. Interrupts, traps, and exceptions serve the three functions, respectively.

Dealing with program discontinuities is a partnership between the processor architecture and the operating system. Let us understand the division of labor. Detecting program discontinuity is the processor's responsibility. Redirecting the processor to execute code to deal with the discontinuity is the operating system's responsibility. As we will see throughout this book, such a partnership exists between the hardware and the system software for handling each subsystem.

Let us now figure out what needs to happen to deal with program discontinuities—specifically, the actions that need to happen implicitly in hardware, and those which need to happen explicitly in the operating system.

It turns out that most of what the processor has to do to deal with program discontinuity is the same regardless of the type of discontinuity. Recall that a processor is

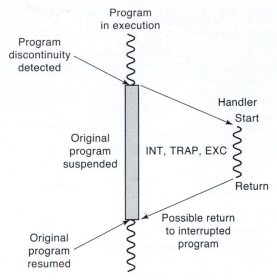

Figure 4.1   Program discontinuity.

There are similarities and differences between program discontinuities and the normal procedure call.

simply capable of executing instructions. To deal with any program discontinuity, the processor has to start executing a different set of instructions than the ones it is currently executing. A *handler* is the procedure executed when a discontinuity occurs. The code for the handler is very much like any other procedure that you may write. In this sense, a discontinuity is very much like a procedure call. (See Figure 4.1.) However, it is an unplanned procedure call. Moreover, the control may or may not return to the interrupted program (depending on the nature of the discontinuity). Yet, it is necessary to observe all the formalities (the procedure-calling convention) for this unplanned procedure call and subsequent resumption of normal program execution. Most of what needs to happen is straightforward, similar to normal procedure call/return.

Four things are tricky about discontinuities:

1. They can happen anywhere during the instruction execution. That is, the discontinuity can happen in the middle of an instruction execution.

2. The discontinuity is unplanned for and, quite possibly, completely unrelated to the current program in execution. Therefore, the hardware has to save the program counter value implicitly before the control goes to the handler.

3. At the point of detecting the program discontinuity, the hardware has to determine the address of the handler to transfer control from the currently executing program to the handler.

4. Because the hardware saved the PC implicitly, the handler has to discover how to resume normal program execution.

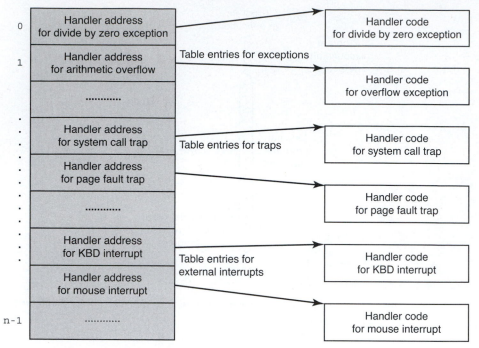

Figure 4.2 Interrupt vector table (IVT)—OS sets up this table at boot time.

This ensures that when a program discontinuity occurs, the hardware can determine "where" to go by consulting this table.

What makes it possible to address these four issues is the partnership between the operating system and the processor architecture. The basis for this partnership is a data structure, maintained by the operating system somewhere in memory, that is known to the processor. This data structure is a *fixed-size table* of handler addresses, one for each type of anticipated program discontinuity. (See Figure 4.2.) The size of the table is architecture dependent. Historically, the name given to this data structure has been *interrupt vector table (IVT)*.[1] Each discontinuity is given a *unique* number, often referred to as a *vector*. This number serves as a unique index into the IVT. The operating system sets up this table at boot time. This is the explicit part of getting ready for dealing with program discontinuities. Once set up, the processor uses this table during normal program execution in order to look up a specific handler address when it detects a discontinuity.

In the case of traps and exceptions, the hardware generates this vector internally. We introduce an *exception/trap register (ETR)*, internal to the processor, for storing this vector (Figure 4.3). When an exception or a trap is encountered, the unique number associated with that exception or trap will be placed in ETR. For example, upon detecting a "divide by zero" exception, the FSM for divide instruction will

---

1. Different vendors give this data structure a different name. Intel calls this data structure Interrupt Descriptor Table (IDT), with 256 entries.

Figure 4.3   Exception/trap register—number set by the processor upon detecting an exception/trap; used by the processor to index into the IVT to get the handler address.

place the vector corresponding to this exception in ETR. Similarly, a system call may manifest as a "trap instruction" supported by the processor architecture. In this case, the FSM for the trap instruction will place the vector corresponding to the specific system call in ETR.

To summarize, the essence of the partnership between the operating system and the hardware for dealing with program discontinuities is as follows:

1. The architecture may itself define a set of exceptions and specify the numbers (vector values) associated with them. These are usually due to run-time errors encountered during program execution (such as arithmetic overflow and divide by zero).

2. The operating system may define its own set of exceptions (software interrupts) and traps (system calls) and specify the numbers (vector values) associated with them.

3. The operating system sets up the IVT at boot time with the addresses of the handlers for dealing with different kinds of exceptions, traps, and interrupts.

4. During the normal course of execution, the hardware detects exceptions/traps and stashes the corresponding vector values in ETR.

5. During the normal course of execution, the hardware detects external interrupts and receives the vector value corresponding to the interrupting device.

6. The hardware uses the vector value as an index into the IVT to retrieve the handler address in order to transfer control from the currently executing program.

In the case of an external interrupt, the processor has to do additional work to determine the vector corresponding to the device that is interrupting, in order to dispatch the appropriate device-handling program. Section 4.3 discusses the enhancements to the processor architecture and instruction set designed to deal with program discontinuities. Section 4.4 deals with hardware design considerations for dealing with program discontinuities.

4.3 Architectural Enhancements to Handle Program Discontinuities

Let us first understand the architectural enhancements needed to take care of these program discontinuities. Because the processor mechanism is the same regardless of the type of discontinuity, we will henceforth refer to these discontinuities simply as *interrupts*.

1. When should the processor entertain an interrupt? This is analogous to the classroom example. We need to leave the processor in a clean state before going to the handler. Even if the interrupt happens in the middle of an instruction execution,

the processor should wait until the instruction execution is complete before check-ing for an interrupt.

2. How does the processor know there is an interrupt? We can add a *hardware line* on the datapath bus of the processor. At the end of each instruction execution, the processor samples this line to see whether there is an interrupt pending.

3. How do we save the return address? How do we manufacture the handler address? Every instruction execution FSM enters a special macro state, **INT**, at the end of in-struction execution if there is an interrupt pending.

4. How do we handle multiple cascaded interrupts? We will discuss the answer to this question in Section 4.3.3.

5. How do we return from the interrupt? We will present ideas for this question in Section 4.3.4.

4.3.1 Modifications to FSM

In Chapter 3, the basic FSM that we discussed for implementing a processor consisted of three macro states—Fetch, Decode, and Execute—as shown in Figure 4.4(a).

Figure 4.4(b) shows the modified FSM that includes a new macro state for handling interrupts. As we mentioned in Section 4.2, an interrupt may have been generated at any time during the execution of the current instruction. The FSM now checks at the point of completion of an instruction if there is a pending interrupt. If there is (INT = y), then the FSM transitions to the INT macro state; if there is no interrupt pending (INT = n),

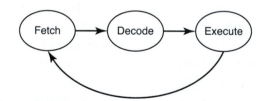

Figure 4.4(a)   Basic FSM of a processor.

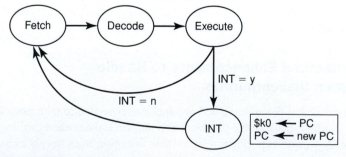

Figure 4.4(b)   Modified FSM for handling interrupts.

The processor enters the INT state at the completion of the current instruction if an INT is pending.

then the next instruction execution resumes by returning to the Fetch macro state. A possibility is to check for interrupts after each macro state. This is analogous to the professor completing his or her thought before recognizing a student with a question in the classroom example. However, checking for interrupts after each macro state is problematic. In Chapter 3, we saw that the datapath of a processor includes several internal registers that are not visible at the level of the instruction-set architecture of the processor. We know that, once an instruction execution is complete, the values in such internal registers are no longer relevant. Thus, deferring the check for interrupt until the completion of the current instruction leaves the processor in a clean state. In order for the interrupted program execution to be resumed after the interrupt is serviced, two things are needed: the state-of-the-program visible registers, and the point-of-program resumption.

Example 4.1

Consider the following program:

100	ADD
101	NAND
102	LW
103	NAND
104	BEQ

An interrupt occurs when the processor is executing the ADD instruction. What is the PC value that needs to be preserved to resume this program after the interrupt?

Answer:

Even though the interrupt occurs during the execution of the ADD instruction, the interrupt will be taken only **after** the instruction execution is complete. Therefore, the PC value to be preserved to resume this program after the interrupt is **101**.

Let us now discuss what needs to happen in the INT macro state. To make the discussion concrete, we will make enhancements to the LC-2200 processor for handling interrupts.

1. We have to save the current PC value somewhere. We reserve one of the processor registers, $k0 (general-purpose register number 12 in the register file), for this purpose. The INT macro state will save PC into $k0.
2. We receive the PC value of the handler address from the device, load it into the PC, and go to the Fetch macro state. We soon will elaborate on the details of accomplishing this step.

4.3.2 A Simple Interrupt Handler

Figure 4.5 shows a simple interrupt handler. The save/restore of processor registers is exactly similar to the procedure-calling convention discussed in Chapter 2.

```
Handler:
    save processor registers;
    execute device code;
    restore processor registers;
    return to original program;
```

Figure 4.5   A simple interrupt handler.

Example 4.2

Consider the following program:

100	ADD
101	NAND
102	LW
103	NAND
104	BEQ

An interrupt occurs when the processor is executing the ADD instruction. At this time, the only registers in use by the program are R2, R3, and R4. What registers are saved and restored by the interrupt handler?

Answer:

Unfortunately, because an interrupt can happen at any time, the interrupt handler has no way of knowing which registers are currently in use by the program. Therefore, it saves and restores *all* the program-visible registers, even though this program needs only R2, R3, and R4 to be saved and restored.

4.3.3 Handling Cascaded Interrupts

There is a problem with the simple handler code given in Figure 4.5. If there is another interrupt while the current one is being serviced, then we will lose the PC value of the original program (currently in $k0). This essentially would make it impossible to return to the original program that incurred the first interrupt. Figure 4.6 depicts this situation.

By the time we get to the second interrupt handler, we have lost the return address to the original program. This situation is analogous to the classroom example when the professor has to handle a second question before completing the answer to the first one. In that analogy, we simply took the approach of disallowing a second questioner before the answer to the first questioner was complete. Maybe the second question needs to be answered right away in order to help everyone understand the answer to the original

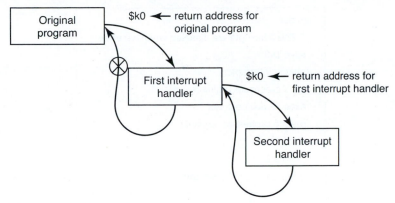

Figure 4.6 Cascaded interrupts.

With the return address stored in $k0, nested interrupts will lose the return address to the original program that incurred the first interrupt.

question. Being unable to entertain multiple interrupts is just not a viable condition for a computer system. Devices are heterogeneous in their speed. For example, the data rate of a disk is much higher than that of a keyboard or a mouse. Therefore, we cannot always afford to turn off interrupts while servicing the current one. At the same time, there has to be a window *devoid of interrupts* available to any handler, wherein it can take the necessary actions to avoid the situation shown in Figure 4.6.

Therefore, two things become clear in terms of handling cascaded interrupts:

1. A new instruction to turn off interrupts, namely, `disable interrupts`.
2. A new instruction to turn on interrupts, namely, `enable interrupts`.

Further, the hardware should implicitly turn off interrupts while in the INT state and hand over control to the handler. Figure 4.7 shows the modified FSM with the disable interrupt added to the INT macro state.

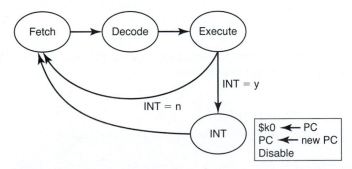

Figure 4.7 Modified FSM with disable interrupts added.

The hardware turns off interrupts before handing over control to the interrupt handler program.

```
Handler:
    /* The interrupts are disabled when we enter */
    save $k0;
    enable interrupts;
    save processor registers;
    execute device code;
    restore processor registers;
    disable interrupts;
    restore $k0;
    return to original program;
```

Figure 4.8   Modified interrupt handler.

Handler enables interrupts explicitly, using the new instruction, as soon as the return address is saved.

Let us now investigate what the handler should do to avoid the situation shown in Figure 4.6. The handler should save the return address to the original program contained in $k0 while the interrupts are still disabled. Once it does that, it can then enable interrupts in order to ensure that the processor does not miss interrupts which are more important. Before leaving the handler, the handler should restore $k0, with interrupts disabled. Figure 4.8 shows this modified interrupt handler. As in the procedure-calling convention discussed in Chapter 2, saving or restoring registers uses the stack.

Example 4.3

Consider the following program:

100	ADD
101	NAND
102	LW
103	NAND
104	BEQ

An interrupt occurs when the processor is executing the ADD instruction. The handler code for handling the interrupt is as follows:

1000	Save $k0
1001	Enable interrupts
1002	/* next several instructions save processor registers */
......	
1020	/* next several instructions execute device code */
......	
1102	/* next several instructions restore processor registers */

......
1120   restore $k0
1121   return to original program

Assume that a second interrupt occurs at the instruction "restore $k0" (PC = 1120). When will the original program be resumed?

Answer:

The original program *will never be resumed*. Note that the second interrupt will be taken immediately on completion of "restore $k0." Upon completion of this instruction, the handler $k0 = 101, which is the point of resumption of the original program. Now the second interrupt is taken. Unfortunately, the second interrupt (see Figure 4.7) will store the point of resumption of the first handler (memory address = 1121) into $k0. Thus, the point of resumption of the original program (memory address = 101) is lost forever. The reason is that the interrupt handler in this example does not have the crucial "disable interrupts" instruction of Figure 4.8.

It should be noted, however, that it might not always be prudent to entertain a second interrupt while servicing the current one. For example, in Section 4.4.1 we will introduce the notion of multiple interrupt levels. According to their relative speeds, devices will be placed on different interrupt priority levels. For example, a high-speed device such as a disk will be placed on a higher priority level compared with a low-speed device such as a keyboard. When the processor is serving an interrupt from the disk, it may temporarily ignore an interrupt coming from a keyboard.

The role of the hardware is to provide the necessary mechanisms for the processor to handle cascaded interrupts correctly. The partnership between the handler code (which is part of the operating system) and the processor hardware determines how best to handle multiple simultaneous interrupts, depending on what the processor is doing at a given point in time.

Basically, the choice is twofold:

- Ignore the interrupt for a while (if the operating system is currently handling a higher priority interrupt), or
- attend to the interrupt immediately, as described in this subsection.

Ignoring an interrupt temporarily may be implicit, as warranted by the hardware priority levels, or explicit, via the "disable interrupt" instruction that is available to the handler program.

4.3.4 Returning from the Handler

Once the handler completes execution, it can return to the original program by using the PC value stored in $k0. At first glance, it appears that we should be able to apply the mechanism used for returning from a procedure call, to return from the interrupt as well. For example, in Chapter 2, to return from a procedure call, we introduced the following instruction[2]:

```
J    rlink
```

Naturally, we are tempted to use the same instruction to return from the interrupt:

```
J    $k0
```

However, there is a problem. Recall that the interrupts should be in the enabled state when we return to the original program. Therefore, we may consider the following sequence of instructions to return from the interrupt:

```
Enable interrupts;
J    $k0;
```

There also is a problem with using this sequence of instructions to return from an interrupt. Recall that we check for interrupts at the end of each instruction execution. Therefore, between "**Enable Interrupts**" and "**J $k0**," we may get a new interrupt that will trash **$k0**.

Thus, we introduce the following new instruction:

```
Return from interrupt (RETI)
```

The semantics of this instruction are as follows:

```
Load PC from $k0;
Enable interrupts;
```

The important point to note is that this instruction is _atomic_; that is, the instruction executes fully before any new interrupts can occur. With this new instruction, Figure 4.9 shows the correct interrupt handler that can handle nested interrupts.

```
Handler:
    /* The interrupts are disabled when we enter */
    save $k0;
    enable interrupts;
    save processor registers;
    execute device code;
    restore processor registers;
    disable interrupts;
    restore $k0;
    return from interrupt;
    /* interrupts will be enabled by return from interrupt */
```

Figure 4.9   Complete interrupt handler.

---

2. Recall that the LC-2200 does not have a separate unconditional jump instruction. We can simulate it with the JALR instruction available in the LC-2200.

4.3.5 Checkpoint

To summarize, we have made the following architectural enhancements to the LC-2200 to enable it to handle interrupts:

1. The three new instructions to the LC-2200 are as follows:

   ```
   Enable interrupts
   Disable interrupts
   Return from interrupt
   ```

2. Upon an interrupt, store the current PC implicitly into a special register $k0.

We now turn to the discussion of the hardware needed to accommodate these architectural enhancements. We already detailed the changes to the FSM at the macro level. We will leave, as an exercise to the reader, working out the details of the INT macro state in the context of the LC-2200 datapath. To complete this exercise, the reader must identify the microstates needed to carry out all the actions required in the INT macro state, and then generate the control signals needed in each microstate.

4.4 Hardware Details for Handling Program Discontinuities

As we mentioned in Section 4.2, the architectural enhancements discussed thus far are neutral as to the type of discontinuity, namely, exception, trap, or interrupt. In this section, we discuss the hardware details needed to deal with program discontinuities in general, and to handle external interrupts in particular. We already introduced the interrupt vector table (IVT) and exception/trap register (ETR). We investigate the datapath modifications for interrupts, as well as the ability to receive the interrupt vector from an external device. We intentionally keep this discussion simple. The interrupt architecture in modern processors is very sophisticated, and we review this briefly in the chapter summary.

4.4.1 Datapath Details for Interrupts

We will now discuss the implementation details for handling interrupts. In Chapter 3, we introduced and discussed the concept of a bus for connecting the datapath elements. Let us expand on that concept, because it is necessary to understand the datapath extensions for handling interrupts. Specifically, let us propose a bus that connects the processor to the memory and the I/O devices. For the processor to talk to the memory, we need address and data lines. Figure 4.10 shows the datapath with additional lines on the bus for supporting interrupts. There is a wire labeled INT on the bus. Any device that wishes to interrupt the CPU *asserts* this line. In Chapter 3, we emphasized the importance of ensuring that only one entity accesses a shared bus at any point in time. The INT line, on the other hand, is different. Any number of devices can simultaneously assert this line to indicate their intent to talk to the

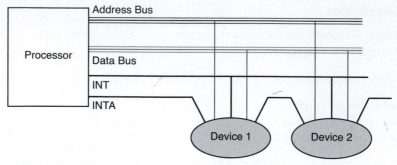

Figure 4.10 Datapath enhancements for handling interrupts.

All the devices are connected to an INT line in "wired-OR" fashion; the INTA line from the processor is daisy-chained through all the devices. An interrupting device that is electrically closest to the processor gets priority if multiple devices interrupt the processor simultaneously. The "vector" is placed on the data bus by the selected device.

processor (analogous to multiple students putting up their hand in the classroom example). An electrical circuit concept called *wired-OR* logic makes it possible for several devices to assert the INT line simultaneously. (The details of this electrical trick are outside the scope of this course, and the interested reader should refer to a textbook on logic design (e.g., [Katz, 2004; Mano, 2007; Patt, 2004] for more details.)

Upon an interrupt, the processor asserts the INTA line (in the INT macro state). Exactly one device should get this acknowledgement, though multiple devices may have signaled their intent to interrupt the processor. Notice the wiring of the INTA. It is not a shared line (like INT), but a chain from one device to another, often referred to as a *daisy chain*. The electrically closest device (Device 1 in Figure 4.10) gets the INTA signal first. If it has requested an interrupt, then it knows that the processor is ready to talk to it. If it has not requested an interrupt, then it knows that some other device is waiting to talk to the processor and passes the INTA signal down the chain. Daisy chain has the virtue of simplicity, but it suffers from latency for the propagation of the acknowledgement signal to the interrupting device, especially in this day and age of very fast processors. For this reason, this method is not used in modern processors.

A generalization of this design principle allows multiple INT and INTA lines to exist on the bus. Each distinct pair of INT and INTA lines corresponds to a *priority level*. Figure 4.11 shows an eight-level priority-interrupt scheme. Notice that there is still exactly one device that can talk to the processor at a time (the INTA line from the processor is routed to the INTA line corresponding to the highest priority, pending interrupt). Device priority is linked to the speed of the device. The higher the speed of the device, the greater will be the chance of data loss, and hence the greater will be the need to give prompt attention to that device. Thus, the devices will be arranged on the interrupt lines according to their relative priorities. For example, a disk would

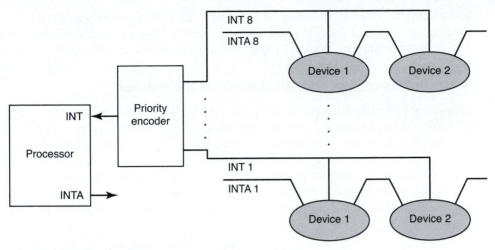

Figure 4.11 Priority interrupt.

> To cater to the needs of devices with different speeds, modern computer sys-
> tems have multiple priority levels. The devices are arranged on the different
> levels according to their speeds. In addition to the multiple levels, within each
> level there may be multiple devices.

be at a higher priority than a keyboard. However, despite there being multiple interrupt levels, they are insufficient to accommodate all the devices, due to the sheer
number of devices on dedicated interrupt lines. Besides, by definition, a device on a
higher priority level is more important than one on a lower priority level. However,
there may be devices with similar speed characteristics that belong to the same equivalence class as far as priority goes. Consider a keyboard and a mouse, for instance.
Thus, it may still be necessary to place multiple devices on the same priority level, as
shown in Figure 4.11.

As we mentioned earlier, daisy-chaining the acknowledgement line through the devices may not be desirable due to the latency associated with the signal propagation.
Besides, a processor is a precious resource, and every attempt is made nowadays to shift
any unnecessary burden away from the processor and onto supporting glue logic outside
the processor. Therefore, in modern processors, the burden of determining which device
needs attention is shifted to an external hardware unit called the *interrupt controller*. The
interrupt controller fields the interrupts, determines the highest priority one to report to
the processor, and handles the basic handshake for responding to the devices. Instead of
daisy-chaining the devices in hardware, the operating system chains the interrupt-service
routines for a given priority level in a linked list. Servicing an interrupt now involves
walking through the linked list to determine the first device that has an interrupt pending and choosing that one for servicing.

You are probably wondering how all of this relates to the way you plug a device
(say, a memory stick or a pair of headphones) into your laptop. Actually, there is no
magic. The position of the device (and, hence, its priority level) is already predetermined

in the I/O architecture of the system (as in Figure 4.11), and all you are seeing is the external manifestation of the device slot where you have to plug in your device. We will further discuss computer buses in Chapter 10, which deals with input/output.

4.4.2 Details of Receiving the Address of the Handler

Let us now look at how the processor receives the vector from an external device. As we mentioned in Section 4.2, the interrupt vector table (IVT), set up by the operating system at boot time, contains the handler addresses for all the external interrupts. Although a device does not know where in memory its handler code is located, it knows the table entry that will contain it. For example, the keyboard may know that its vector is 80, and the mouse may know that its vector is 82.[3] Upon receiving the INTA signal from the processor (see Figure 4.12), the device puts its

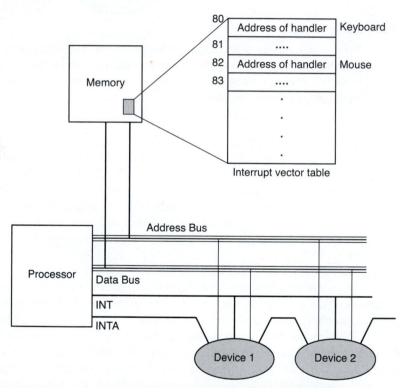

Figure 4.12   Processor–device interaction to receive the interrupt vector.

The processor receives the vector from the selected device and uses the vector as the address to retrieve the starting address of the handler associated with this device from the IVT in memory.

---

3. The OS typically decides the table entry for each device, which is then "programmed" into the device interface. We will revisit this topic in Chapter 10, which deals with input/output.

vector on the data bus. Recall that the processor is still in the INT macro state. The processor uses this vector as the index to look up in the vector table and retrieve the handler address, which is then loaded into the PC. The operating system reserves a portion of the memory (usually, low memory addresses) for housing this vector table. The size of the vector table is a design choice of the operating system. Thus, with this one level of indirection through the interrupt vector table, the processor determines where in memory the handler address is that points to the code for executing the procedure associated with this specific interrupt. Figure 4.12 pictorially shows this interaction between the device and the processor for receiving the handler address.

The handshake between the processor and the device is summarized as follows:

1. The device asserts the INT line whenever it is ready to interrupt the processor.

2. The processor, upon completion of the current instruction—Execute macro-state in Figure 4.4(b)—checks the INT line (Figure 4.4(b) shows this check as INT = y/n in the FSM) for pending interrupts.

3. If there is a pending interrupt—INT = y in the FSM, as shown in Figure 4.4(b)— then the processor enters the INT macro state and asserts the INTA line on the bus.

4. The device, upon receiving the INTA from the processor, places its vector on the data bus. (For example, keyboard will put out 80 as its vector.).

5. The processor receives the vector and looks up the entry, in the interrupt vector table, corresponding to this vector. Let's say that the address of the handler found in this entry is 0x5000. This is the PC value for the procedure that needs to be executed for handling this interrupt.

6. The processor (which is still in the INT macro state) completes the action in the INT macro state, as shown in Figure 4.4(b), saving the current PC in $k0 and loading the PC with the value retrieved from the interrupt vector table.

4.4.3 Stack for Saving/Restoring

Figure 4.9 shows the handler code, which includes saving and restoring of registers (similar to the procedure-calling convention). The stack seems like an obvious place to store the processor registers. However, there is a problem. How does the handler know which part of the memory is to be used as a stack? The interrupt may not even be intended for the currently running program, after all.

For this reason, it is usual for the architecture to have two stacks: *user stack* and *system stack*. Quite often, the architecture may designate a particular register as the stack pointer. Upon entering the INT macro state, the FSM performs *stack switching*.

Let us see what hardware enhancements are needed to facilitate this stack switching:

1. **Duplicate stack pointer:** Really, all that needs to be done is to duplicate the register designated by the architecture as the stack pointer. In Chapter 2, we designated an architectural register $sp as the stack pointer. We will duplicate that register: one

for use by the user program, and the other for use by the system. The state saving in the interrupt handler will use the system version of $sp, while the user programs will use the user version of $sp. This way, the state saving will not disturb the user stack, because all the saving/restoring happens on the system stack. At system startup (i.e., boot time), the system initializes the system version of $sp with the address of the system stack, allocating sufficient space to deal with interrupts (including nested interrupts).

2. **Privileged mode:** Remember that the interrupt handler is simply a program. We need to let the processor know which version of $sp to use at any point in time. For this reason, we introduce a *mode* bit in the processor. The processor is in *user* or *kernel* mode, depending on the value of this bit. If the processor is in user mode, the hardware implicitly uses the user version of $sp. If it is in kernel mode, it uses the kernel version of $sp. The FSM sets this bit in the INT macro state. Thus, the handler will run in kernel mode and, hence, use the system stack. Before returning to the user program, RETI instruction sets the mode bit back to "user" to enable the user program to employ the user stack when it resumes execution.

The mode bit also serves another important purpose. We introduced three new instructions to support interrupt. It would not be prudent to allow any program to execute these instructions. For example, the register $k0 has a special connotation, and any arbitrary program should not be allowed to write to it. Similarly, any arbitrary program should not be allowed to enable and disable interrupts. Only the operating system executes these instructions, referred to as *privileged instructions*. We need a way to prevent normal user programs from trying to execute these privileged instructions, either accidentally or maliciously. An interrupt handler is part of the operating system and runs in the "kernel" mode. (The FSM sets the mode bit in the INT macro state to "kernel.") If a user program tries to execute these instructions, an illegal instruction trap will result.

We need to address two more subtle points of detail to complete the discussion of interrupt handling. First, recall that interrupts could be nested. Since all interrupt

```
INT macro state:
  $k0 ← PC;
  ACK INT by asserting INTA;
  Receive interrupt vector from device on the data bus;
  Retrieve address of the handler from the interrupt vector table;
  PC ← handler address retrieved from the vector table;
  Save current mode on the system stack;
  mode = kernel; /* noop if the mode is already kernel */
  Disable interrupts;
```

Figure 4.13   Actions in the INT macro state.

```
RETI:
    Load PC from $k0;
    /* since the handler executes RETI, we are in the kernel mode */
    Restore mode from the system stack; /* return to previous mode */
    Enable interrupts;
```

Figure 4.14   Semantics of RETI instruction.

handlers run in the kernel mode, we need to do the mode switching (and the implicit stack switching due to the mode bit) in the INT macro state only when the processor is going from a user program to servicing interrupts. Further, we need to remember the current mode of the processor in order to take the appropriate action (whether to return to user or kernel mode) when the handler executes the RETI instruction. The system stack is a convenient vehicle for remembering the current mode of the processor.

The INT macro state and the RETI instruction respectively push and pop the current mode of the processor onto the system stack. The INT macro state and the RETI instruction take actions commensurate with the current mode of the processor. Figure 4.13 summarizes all the actions taken in the INT macro state; Figure 4.14 summarizes the semantics of the RETI instruction.

4.5 Putting It All Together

4.5.1 Summary of Architectural/Hardware Enhancements

To deal with program discontinuities, we added the following architectural/hardware enhancements to the LC-2200:

- an interrupt vector table (IVT), to be initialized by the operating system with handler addresses;
- an exception/trap register (ETR) that contains the vector for internally generated exceptions and traps;
- a hardware mechanism for receiving the vector for an externally generated interrupt;
- user/kernel mode and associated mode bit in the processor;
- user/system stack corresponding to the mode bit;
- a hardware mechanism for storing the current PC implicitly into a special register $k0, upon an interrupt, and for retrieving the handler address from the IVT, using the vector (either internally generated or received from the external device); and
- three new instructions to LC-2200:

```
Enable interrupts
Disable interrupts
Return from interrupt
```

4.5.2 Interrupt Mechanism at Work

We present a couple of examples to bring all these concepts together and give the reader an understanding of how the interrupt mechanism works. For clarity of presentation, we will refer to the system version of $sp as SSP and the user version of $sp as USP. However, architecturally (i.e., from the point of view of the instruction set), they refer to the same register. The hardware knows (via the mode bit) whether to use USP or SSP as $sp.

Example 4.4

The example sketched in Figure 4.15(a)–(d) illustrates the sequence of steps involved in interrupt handling. Some program called **foo** is executing. (See Figure 4.15(a).)

A keyboard device interrupts the processor. The processor is currently executing an instruction at location 19999. It waits until the instruction execution completes. It then goes to the INT macro state (see Figure 4.15(b)) and saves the current PC (whose value is 20000) in $k0. Upon receipt of INTA from the processor, the device puts out its vector on the data bus. The processor receives the vector from the device on the data bus, as shown in Figure 4.15(b).

Let us say that the value received is 40. The processor looks up memory location 40 to get the handler address (let this be 1000). Let the contents of the SSP be 300. In the INT macro state, the FSM loads 1000 into PC, 300 into $sp, saves the current mode on the system stack, and goes back to the Fetch macro state. The handler code at location 1000 (similar to Figure 4.9) starts executing using $sp = 299 as its stack. (See Figure 4.15(c).)

The original program will resume execution at PC = 20000 when the handler executes return from interrupt (Figure 4.15(d).)

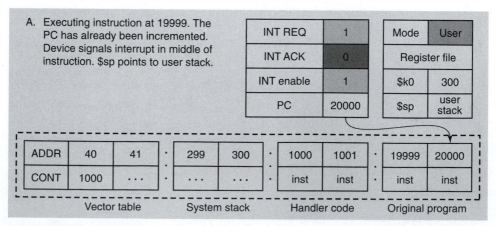

Figure 4.15(a)   Interrupt handling (INT received).

B. Interrupt has been sensed. $k0 gets PC. Interrupts are disabled. Interrupt is acknowledged. Device puts vector on bus.

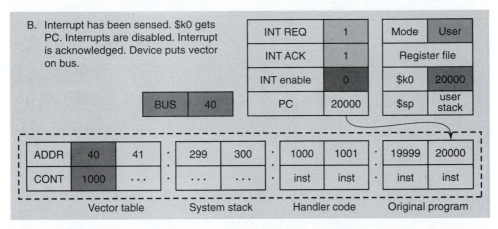

Figure 4.15(b) Interrupt handling (INT macro state—receive vector).

C. Handler address is put into PC; Current mode is saved in system stack; New mode is set to kernel; $sp now points to system stack; interrupt code at 1000 is set to handle the interrupt.

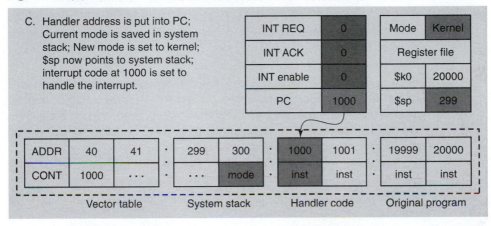

Figure 4.15(c) Interrupt handling (transfer control to handler code).

D. RETI instruction restores mode from system stack; since returning to user program in this example, $sp now points to user stack; also, copies $k0 into PC, re-enables interrupts and sets Mode to User.

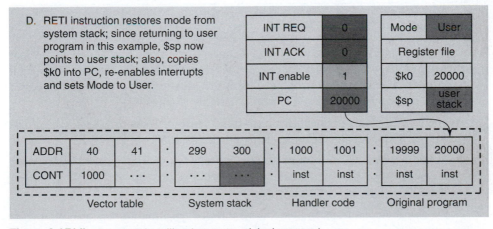

Figure 4.15(d) Interrupt handling (return to original program).

Example 4.5

Consider the following:

  Assume that the memory addresses are consecutive integers.

  User program executing instruction at memory location 7500

  User Stack pointer ($sp) value 18000

  SSP value 500

  Vector for keyboard = 80

  Vector for disk = 50

  Handler address for keyboard interrupt = 3000

  Handler address for disk interrupt = 5000

  a. Pictorially represent the preceding information in a manner similar to that shown in Figure 4.15.

  b. An interrupt occurs from the keyboard. Show the relevant state of the processor (similar to Figure 4.15(c)) when the interrupt handler for the keyboard is about to start executing.

  c. A higher priority interrupt from the disk occurs while the keyboard handler is running after it has reenabled interrupts. Assume that it is executing an instruction at memory location 3023 and that the stack pointer ($sp) value is 515. Show the relevant state of the processor (similar to Figure 4.15(c)) when the interrupt handler for the disk is about to start executing.

  d. Show the relevant state of the processor when the disk handler executes RETI instruction (similar to Figure 4.15(d)).

  e. Show the relevant state of the processor when the keyboard handler executes RETI instruction (similar to Figure 4.15(d)).

  This example is left as an exercise for the reader.

Summary

In this chapter, we introduced an important concept, interrupts, that allows a processor to communicate with the outside world. An *interrupt* is a specific instance of program discontinuity. We discussed the minimal hardware enhancements, inside the processor as well as at the bus level, needed to handle nested interrupts.

- The processor enhancements included (three) new instructions, a user stack, a system stack, a mode bit, and a new macro state called INT.

- At the bus level, we introduced special control lines, called INT and INTA, for the device to indicate to the processor that it wants to interrupt and for the processor to acknowledge the interrupt, respectively.

  We also reviewed traps and exceptions that are synchronous versions of program discontinuities. The interesting thing is that the software mechanism needed to handle all such discontinuities is similar. We discussed how to write a generic interrupt handler that can handle nested interrupts.

We have intentionally simplified the presentation of interrupts in this chapter to make it accessible to students in a first systems course. Interrupt mechanisms in modern processors are considerably more complex. For example, modern processors categorize interrupts into two groups: *maskable* and *nonmaskable*.

- The former refers to interrupts that can be temporarily turned off by the disable interrupt mechanism (e.g., a device interrupt).

- The latter corresponds to interrupts that cannot be turned off, even with the disable interrupt mechanism (e.g., an internal hardware error detected by the system).

We presented a mechanism by which a processor learns the starting address of the interrupt handler (via the vector table) and the use of a dedicated register for stashing the return address for the interrupted program. We also presented a simple hardware scheme by which a processor may discover the identity of the interrupting device and acknowledge the interrupt. The main intent of this discussion is to give confidence to the reader that designing such hardware is simple and straightforward.

We presented *mode* as a characterization of the internal state of a processor. This is also an intentionally simplistic view. The processor state may have a number of other attributes available as discrete bits of information (similar to the mode bit). Usually, a processor aggregates all of these bits into one register, called *processor status word (PSW)*. Upon an interrupt and its return, the hardware implicitly pushes and pops, respectively, both the PC and the PSW on the system stack.[4]

We also presented a fairly simple treatment of the interrupt handler code to convey what needs to be done in the processor architecture to deal with interrupts. The handler would typically do a lot more than save processor registers. In later chapters, we will revisit interrupts in the context of operating-system functionalities such as processor scheduling (Chapter 6) and device drivers (Chapter 10).

Interrupt architecture of modern processors is much more sophisticated than what is presented here. First of all, since the processor is a precious resource, most of the chores associated with interrupt processing, except for executing the actual handler code, are kept outside the processor. For example, a device called *programmable interrupt controller (PIC)* aids the processor in dealing with many of the nitty-gritty details involved in handling external interrupts, including

- dealing with multiple interrupt levels,
- fielding the actual interrupts from the devices,
- selecting the highest-priority device among the interrupting devices,
- getting the identity (vector table index) of the device selected to interrupt the processor, and
- acknowledging the selected device.

---

4. In the LC-2200, we designate a register $k0 for saving PC in the INT macro state. An alternative approach adopted in many modern processors is to save the PC directly on the system stack.

The PIC provides processor-readable registers, one of which contains the identity of the device selected to interrupt the processor. The use of PIC simplifies what the processor has to do on an interrupt. Upon an interrupt, the return address either is placed on a system stack or is made available in a special processor register, and control is simply transferred to a well-defined address set by the operating system, which corresponds to a generic first-level interrupt handler of the operating system. This handler simply saves the return address for the interrupted program, reads the identity of the interrupting device from the PIC, and jumps to the appropriate handler code. Usually, this first-level operating system handler is noninterruptible and may run in a special mode called *interrupt mode,* so the operating system does not have to worry about nested interrupts. In general, it is important that a device driver—software that actually manipulates a device—do as little work in an interrupt handling code as possible. This is to make sure that the processor is not tied up forever in interrupt processing. Device drivers are written such that only the time-sensitive code is in the interrupt handler. For example, the Linux operating system defines *top-half* and *bottom-half* handlers. By definition, the bottom-half handlers do not have the same sense of urgency as the top-half handlers. A device which has a significant amount of work to do that is not time critical will do it in the bottom-half handler.

Exercises

1. Upon an interrupt, what has to happen implicitly in hardware before control is transferred to the interrupt handler?

2. Why not use JALR to return from the interrupt handler?

3. Put the following steps in the correct order:

   actual work of the handler

   disable interrupt

   enable interrupt

   restore ko from stack

   restore state

   return from interrupt

   save ko on stack

   save state

4. How does the processor know which device has requested an interrupt?

5. What instructions are needed to implement interruptible interrupts? Explain the function and purpose of each, and explain what would happen if you didn't have them.

6. In the following interrupt handler code, select the items that do **not** belong.

   _____   disable interrupts;

   _____   save PC;

   _____   save $k0;

_____	enable interrupts;
_____	save processor registers;
_____	execute device code;
_____	restore processor registers;
_____	disable interrupts;
_____	restore $k0;
_____	disable interrupts;
_____	restore PC;
_____	enable interrupts;
_____	return from interrupt;

7. In the following actions in the INT macrostate, select the items that do *not* belong.

_____	save PC;
_____	save SP;
_____	$k0 ← PC;
_____	enable interrupts;
_____	save processor registers;
_____	ACK INT by asserting INTA;
_____	Receive interrupt vector from device on the data bus;
_____	Retrieve PC address from the interrupt vector table;
_____	Retrieve SP value from the interrupt vector table;
_____	disable interrupts;
_____	PC ← PC retrieved from the vector table;
_____	SP ← SP value retrieved from the vector table;
_____	disable interrupts;

Bibliographic Notes and Further Reading

We have only scratched the surface of issues relating to interrupt architecture of processors and the operating system mechanisms that efficiently deal with them. The interested reader is referred to more advanced textbooks on computer organization (e.g., [Patterson, 2008]) for details on how the interrupt architecture is implemented in modern processors, as well as to books on operating system concepts and implementation [Rubini, 2001; Tanenbaum, 2006; Silberschatz, 2008], to get a deeper knowledge on interrupt handling. A good discussion of the interrupt architecture of the Intel processor can be found in the Intel documentation [Intel System Programming Guide 3A, 2008].

Processor Performance and Pipelined Processor Design

In Chapter 3, we presented a basic design of a processor intended to implement the LC-2200 ISA. We hinted at how to achieve good performance when we talked about selecting the width of the clock cycle time and reducing the number of microstates in implementing each macro state (fetch, decode, and instruction-specific execute states).

Processor design and implementation is a quantitative exercise. An architect is constantly evaluating the decision to include an architectural feature in terms of its impact on performance. Therefore, we will first explore the performance metrics that are relevant in processor design. We will then look at ways to improve processor performance, first in the context of the simple design we presented in Chapter 3, and then in the context of a new concept called *pipelining*.

First, let's introduce some metrics to help us understand processor performance.

5.1 Space and Time Metrics

Let's say that you are building an airplane. You want to ferry a certain number of passengers on every trip, so you have to provide adequate space inside the aircraft to accommodate the passengers, their baggage, and food for them en route. In addition, you want to engineer the aircraft to take the passengers from point A to point B in a certain amount of time. The number of passengers to be accommodated in the plane has a bearing on the time it takes to ferry them. The more passengers there are, the more time it would take to ferry them to the destination for a given engine horsepower of the airplane, due to the drag caused by the collective weight of the passengers and their baggage.

Let's see how this analogy applies to processor performance. Due to the popular hype about processor speed, we always think of *Mhz*, *Ghz*, and *THz* whenever we think of processor performance. These terms, of course, refer to the clock rate of the processor. We know from Chapter 3 that the clock cycle time (inverse of clock rate) is determined by estimating the worst-case delay in carrying out the datapath actions in a single clock cycle.

It is important to understand why processor speed is not the only determinant of performance. Let's say that you wrote a program "foo" and are running it on a processor. The two performance metrics that you would be interested in are how much memory foo occupies (**space metric**) and how long foo takes to run (**time metric**). *Memory footprint*[1] quantifies the space metric, whereas *execution time* quantifies the time metric. We define the former as the space occupied by a given program and the latter as the running time of the program. Let us relate these metrics to what we have seen about processor design so far.

The instruction-set architecture of the processor has a bearing on the memory footprint of the program. First, let us understand the relationship between the two metrics. There is a belief that the smaller the footprint, the better the execution time will be. The conventional wisdom in the 1970s was that this premise is true, and it led to the design of *complex instruction set computer* (CISC) architectures. In defense of CISC architecture, compiler technology was in its infancy in the 1970s. There was a perceived semantic gap between the high-level languages and the instruction-set architecture. In hindsight, we can see that efficient compilation does not need exotic instructions; however, this fact was not self-evident at that time. Compounding this line of thinking, memory was very expensive; therefore, frugality in memory usage was sought in the design of instructions.

The criterion in CISC architecture was to make the datapath and control unit do more work for each instruction fetched from memory. This imperative gave rise to a set of instructions in which different instructions took different numbers of microstates to complete execution, depending on their complexity. For example, an *ADD* instruction will take a smaller number of microstates to execute, whereas a *MULTIPLY* instruction will take more. Similarly, an *ADD* instruction that uses register operands will take fewer microstates to execute, but the same instruction using memory to operands will take more. With more complex instructions, it is conceivable that the intended program logic could be contained in fewer instructions, leading to a smaller memory footprint.

Commonsense reasoning and advances in computer technology weakened the premise regarding the connection between the memory footprint and the execution time:

- This is where the airplane analogy breaks down. The passengers in the analogy are akin to instructions in memory. All the passengers in the airplane need to be ferried to the destination, and each of them contributes to the airplane's weight, which in turn determines the flying time to the destination. However, not all instructions

---

1. As used in Chapter 5 and Chapter 6, memory footprint pertains to the *static* space created in memory by the operating system, for a program, at the time of program creation.

that make up a program are necessarily executed. For example, it is well known that in many production programs a significant percentage of the program deals with error conditions which may arise during program execution. You know from your own programming experience that a good software engineering practice is to check for return codes on systems calls. The error-handling portion of such checks may rarely be executed. Just to drive home that point, as a pathological example, consider a program that consists of a million instructions. Suppose that there is a tight loop in the program, with just 10 instructions in which 99% of the execution time is spent; in such a case, the size of the program does not matter from the point of view of the execution time.

• Second, advances in processor implementation techniques (principally, the idea of pipelining instruction execution, which we will discuss in this chapter) blurred the advantage which a complex instruction holds over a sequence of simple instructions that accomplish the same end result.

• Third, with the shift in programming in assembly language to programming in high-level languages, the utility of an instruction set was measured by how useful it is to the compiler writer. In many ways, the advance in compiler technology was a primary factor that made the semantic gap, which we alluded to earlier, seem less onerous, and shifted the design of instruction sets away from CISC. It is worth noting that John Hennessy and John Cocke, two of the pioneers of the reduced-instruction-set revolution (to be described shortly), were compiler researchers in addition to being architecture researchers.

• Fourth, with advances in semiconductor technology and VLSI, memory costs started going down, thus making program size less of a concern. This took away the space argument for CISC. Coupled with this development, cache memories (which we will cover in detail in Chapter 9), introduced in the late 1960s, became more viable to deploy, due to the advances in semiconductor technology. With the advent of cache memories, the number of trips to the main memory from the processor was reduced, thus weakening another fundamental premise of CISC: that execution time is minimized by the fetching of a complex instruction, as opposed to a set of simple instructions.

These arguments gave rise to the *reduced instruction set computer (RISC)* architecture in the late 1970s and early 1980s. Although there was a lot of debate over CISC versus RISC in the 1980s, such arguments have become largely irrelevant today. The reality is that each side has shifted to include good features from the other camp. As we will see shortly when we discuss pipelining, the ISA is not as important as ensuring that the processor maintains a throughput of one instruction every clock cycle. For example, the dominant ISA today is the Intel x86, a CISC architecture, but implemented with the RISC philosophy. The CISC instructions are translated internally, by the hardware, into RISC instructions in the Intel x86 line of processors, starting with the PentiumPro/PentiumII. Another influential ISA today is ARM (Acorn RISC Machine). Whereas ARM started out as a RISC architecture, the prevalent version of this architecture today has a number of complex instructions.

We will have a more detailed discussion on memory footprint in Chapter 9, which discusses memory hierarchy. At this point, let us simply observe that there is not a strong correlation between the memory footprint of a program and its execution time.

What determines the execution time of the program? The number of instructions executed by the processor for a program is one component of the execution time. The second component is the number of microstates needed for executing each instruction. Because each microstate executes in one CPU clock cycle, the execution time for each instruction is measured by the clock cycles taken for each instruction (usually referred to as *CPI—clocks per instruction*). The third component is the *clock cycle time* of the processor.

So, if n is the total number of instructions executed by the program, then,

$$\text{Execution time} = \left(\sum \text{CPI}_j \right) * \text{clock cycle time, where } 1 \leq j \leq n \qquad (1)$$

Sometimes, it is convenient to think of an average CPI for the instructions that are executed by the program. So, if CPI_{Avg} is the average CPI for the set of instructions executed by the program, we can express the execution time as follows:

$$\text{Execution time} = n * \text{CPI}_{Avg} * \text{clock cycle time} \qquad (2)$$

Of course, it is difficult to quantify what an average CPI is, since this really depends on the frequency of execution of the instructions. We will discuss this aspect in more detail in the next section. Execution time of a program is the key determinant of processor performance. Perhaps more accurately, because the clock cycle time changes frequently, *cycle count* (i.e., the total number of clock cycles for executing a program) is a more appropriate measure of processor performance. In any event, it should be clear that the processor performance is much more than simply the processor speed. Processor speed is no doubt important, but the cycle count, which is the product of the number of instructions executed and the CPI for each instruction, is an equally, if not more, important metric in determining the execution time of a program.

Example 5.1

A processor has three classes of instructions:

$$A, B, C; \text{CPI}_A = 1; \text{CPI}_B = 2; \text{CPI}_C = 5.$$

For example, A may be arithmetic and logical operations, B may be memory operations such as load and store, and C may be complex operations such as multiplication or division.

A compiler produces two different, but functionally equivalent, code sequences for a program:

Code sequence 1 executes:

A-class instructions = 5

B-class instructions = 3

C-class instructions = 1

Code sequence 2 executes:

A-class instructions = 3

B-class instructions = 2

C-class instructions = 2

Which is faster?

Answer:

Code sequence 1 results in executing 9 instructions and takes a total of 16 cycles.

Code sequence 2 results in executing 7 instructions, but takes a total of 17 cycles.

Therefore, code sequence 1 is faster.

5.2 Instruction Frequency

It is useful to know how often a particular instruction occurs in programs. *Instruction frequency* is the metric for capturing this information. *Static* instruction frequency refers to the number of times a particular instruction occurs in the compiled code. *Dynamic* instruction frequency refers to the number of times a particular instruction is executed when the program is actually run. Let us understand the importance of these metrics. Static instruction frequency has an impact on the memory footprint. So, if we find that a particular instruction appears frequently in a program, then we may try to optimize the amount of space it occupies in memory by clever instruction-encoding techniques in the instruction format. Dynamic instruction frequency has an impact on the execution time of the program. So, if we find that the dynamic frequency of an instruction is high, we may try to make enhancements to the datapath and control to ensure that the CPI taken for its execution is minimized.

Static instruction frequency has become less important in general-purpose processors, since reducing the memory footprint is not as important a consideration as increasing the processor performance. In fact, techniques to support static instruction frequency, such as special encoding, will have a detrimental effect on performance. Special encoding destroys the uniformity of the instructions, which is crucial for a pipelined processor (see Section 5.10). However, static instruction frequency may still be an important factor in embedded processors, wherein optimizing on the available limited memory space may be necessary.

Example 5.2

Consider the following program, which consists of 1000 instructions:

```
I₁:
I₂:
```

```
  ..
  ..
  ..
I₁₀:
I₁₁: ADD
I₁₂:              ⎫ loop
I₁₃:              ⎬
I₁₄: COND BR I₁₀  ⎭
  ..
  ..
I₁₀₀₀:
```

ADD instruction occurs exactly once in the program as shown. Instructions I_{10}–I_{14} constitute a loop that gets executed 800 times. All other instructions execute exactly once.

   a. What is the static frequency of ADD instruction?

Answer:

The memory footprint of the program is 1000 instructions. Out of these 1000 instructions, ADD occurs exactly once.

Hence, the static frequency of ADD instruction $= 1/1000 * 100 = \textbf{0.1\%}$.

   b. What is the dynamic frequency of ADD instruction?

Answer:

The total number of instructions executed $=$ loop execution $+$ other instruction execution

$$= (800 * 5) + (1000 - 5) * 1$$
$$= 4995.$$

ADD is executed once every time the loop is executed. So, the number of ADD instructions executed $= 800$.

The dynamic frequency of ADD instruction

$= $ (number of ADD instructions executed/total number of instructions executed) $* 100$

$= (800/(995 + 4000)) * 100 = \textbf{16\%}$.

5.3 Benchmarks

We will now discuss how to compare the performance of machines. One often sees marketing hype such as "Processor X is 1 GHz" or "Processor Y is 500 MHz." How do we know which processor is better, given that execution time is not entirely determined by processor speed? *Benchmarks* are a set of programs that are representative of the workload for a processor. For example, for a processor used in a gaming console, a video game may be the benchmark program. For a processor used in a scientific application, matrix operations may be benchmark programs. Quite often, *kernels* of real programs are used as benchmarks. For example, matrix multiply may occur in several scientific applications and may be the biggest component of the execution time of such applications. In that case, it makes sense to benchmark the processor on the matrix multiply routine. The performance of the processor on such kernels is a good indicator of the expected performance of the processor on an application as a whole.

It is often the case that a set of programs constitutes the benchmark. There are several possibilities for deciding how best to use these benchmark programs to evaluate processor performance.

1. Suppose that you have a set of programs, and all of them must be run one after the other to completion. In that case, a useful summary metric is **total execution time**, which is the cumulative total of the execution times of the individual programs.

2. Let's say that you have a set of programs, and you would want to run them at different times, but not all at the same time. In this case, *arithmetic mean (AM)* would be a useful metric, which is simply an average of all the individual program execution times. It should be noted, however that this metric may bias the summary value toward a time-consuming benchmark program (e.g., execution times of programs: P1 = 100 secs; P2 = 1 sec; AM = 50.5 secs).

3. Imagine that you have a situation similar to the previous one, but you have an idea of the frequency with which you may run the individual programs. In this case, a useful metric would be *weighted arithmetic mean (WAM)*, which is a weighted average of the execution times of all the individual programs. This metric takes into account the relative frequency of execution of the programs in the benchmark mix (e.g., for the same programs P1 = 100 secs; P2 = 1 sec; f_{P1} = 0.1; f_{P2} = 0.9; WAM = 0.1 * 100 + 0.9 * 1 = 10.9 secs).

4. Let's say that you have a situation similar to (2), but you have no idea of the relative frequency with which you may want to run one program versus another. In this case, using the arithmetic mean may give a biased view of the processor performance. Another summary metric that is useful in this situation is *geometric mean (GM)*, which is the pth root of the product of p values (e.g., for the same programs P1 = 100 secs; P2 = 1 sec; GM = sqrt (100 * 1) = 10 secs). This metric removes the bias (toward large values) present in the arithmetic mean.

5. *Harmonic mean (HM)* is another useful composite metric. Mathematically, it is computed by taking the arithmetic mean of the reciprocals of the values being considered, and then taking the reciprocal of the result. This also helps slant the bias toward high values present in the arithmetic mean. The HM for the example we are considering (execution times of programs: P1 = 100 secs; P2 = 1 sec), is

$$HM = 1/(\text{arithmetic mean of the reciprocals})$$
$$= 1/(((1/100) + (1/1))/2) = 1.9801.$$

Harmonic means are considered especially useful when the dataset consists of ratios.

If the dataset consists of all equal values, then all three composite metrics (AM, GM, and HM) will yield the same result. In general, AM tends to bias the result toward high values in the dataset, HM tends to bias the result toward low values in the dataset, and GM tends to be in between. A useful rule of thumb is to use HM when the absolute values in the dataset are large, and use AM when the absolute values in the dataset are small. The moral of the story is that one has to be very cautious about using a single composite metric to judge an architecture.

Over the years, several benchmark programs have been created and used in architectural evaluations. The most widely accepted ones for engineering/scientific workstations are the SPEC benchmarks developed by an independent, nonprofit entity called *Standard Performance Evaluation Corporation* (SPEC), whose goal is "to establish, maintain and endorse a standardized set of relevant benchmarks that can be applied to the newest generation of high-performance computers."[2] The SPEC benchmarks consist of a set of generic applications, including scientific applications, transaction processing, and web servers, that represents the workload for general-purpose processors.[3]

What makes benchmarking hard is the fact that processor performance is not determined just by the clock cycle rating of the processor. For example, the organization of the memory system and the processor-memory bus bandwidth are key determinants, beyond the clock cycle time. Further, the behavior of each benchmark application poses different demands on the overall system. Therefore, when we compare two processors with similar, or even the same, CPU clock cycle rating, we may find that one does better on some benchmark programs, whereas the second does better on some others. This is the reason a composite index is useful when we want to compare two processors without knowing the exact kind of workload we are going to run on them. We have to be very cautious on the overuse of metrics, as has been suggested in a famous saying, "Lies, damned lies, and statistics."[4]

Example 5.3

The SPECint2006 integer benchmark consists of 12 programs for quantifying the performance of processors on integer programs (as opposed to floating-point arithmetic). The following table[5] shows the performance of the Intel Core 2 Duo E6850 (3 GHz) processor on the SPECint2006 benchmark:

---

2. Source: www.spec.org/.

3. See www.spec.org/cpu2006/publications/CPU2006benchmarks.pdf for a description of the SPEC2006 benchmark programs for measuring the integer and floating-point performance of processors.

4. See www.york.ac.uk/depts/maths/histstat/lies.htm.

5. Source: www.spec.org/cpu2006/results/res2007q4/cpu2006-20071112-02562.pdf.

Program Name	Description	Time in Seconds
400.perlbench	Applications in Perl	510
401.bzip2	Data compression	602
403.gcc	C Compiler	382
429.mcf	Optimization	328
445.gobmk	Game based on AI	548
456.hmmer	Gene sequencing	593
458.sjeng	Chess based on AI	679
462.libquantum	Quantum computing	422
464.h264ref	Video compression	708
471.omnetpp	Discrete event simulation	362
473.astar	Path-finding algorithm	466
483.xalancbmk	XML processing	302

a. Compute the arithmetic mean and the geometric mean.

Answer:

Arithmetic mean = $(510 + 602 + \cdots + 302)/12 =$ **491.8 secs**.
Geometric mean = $(510 * 602 * \cdots * 302)^{1/12} =$ **474.2 secs**.

Note how arithmetic mean biases the result toward the larger execution times in the program mix.

b. One intended use of the system has the following frequencies for the 12 programs:
  • 10% video compression
  • 10% XML processing
  • 30% path-finding algorithm
  • 50% all the other programs

Compute the weighted arithmetic mean for this workload.

Answer:

The workload uses 9 programs equally 50% of the time. The average execution time of these nine programs

$$= (510 + 602 + 382 + 328 + 548 + 593 + 679 + 422 + 362)/9$$
$$= 491.8 \text{ secs}.$$

Weighted arithmetic mean $= (0.1 * 708 + 0.1 * 302 + 0.3 * 466 + 0.5 * 491.8)$
$$= \textbf{486.7 secs.}$$

One reason that metrics are so useful is that they give a basis for comparison of machines with different architectures, implementation, and hardware specifications. However, raw numbers, as shown in Example 5.3, make it difficult to compare different machines. For this reason, SPEC benchmark results are expressed as ratios with respect to some reference machine. For example, if the time for a benchmark on the target machine is **x** secs, and the time on the reference machine for the same benchmark is **y** secs, then the SPECratio for this benchmark on the target machine is defined as

SPECratio

> **= execution time on reference machine/execution time on target machine**
>
> **= y/x**

The SPEC organization chose Sun Microsystems Ultra5_10 workstation, with a 300-MHz SPARC processor and 256-MB of memory, as a reference machine for the SPEC CPU 2000 performance test results. The same reference machine is used for the SPEC CPU 2006.

The SPECratios for different benchmarks may be combined through one of the statistical measures (arithmetic, weighted arithmetic, geometric, or harmonic) to get a single composite metric. Because we are dealing with ratios when using SPEC benchmarks as the standard way of reporting performance, it is customary to use harmonic mean.

The nice thing about SPECratio is that it serves as a basis for a comparison of machines. For example, if the mean SPECratios of two machines A and B are R_A and R_B, respectively, then we can directly draw relative conclusions regarding the performance capabilities of the two machines.

5.4 Increasing the Processor Performance

To explore avenues for increasing the processor performance, a good starting point is the equation for execution time. Let us look at each term individually and understand the opportunity for improving the performance that each offers.

- **Decreasing the clock cycle time:** The clock cycle time is determined by the worst-case delay in the datapath. Decreasing the clock cycle time is the same as increasing the clock frequency. We could rearrange the datapath elements such that the worst-case delay is reduced (for example, bringing them closer together physically in the layout of the datapath). Further, we could reduce the number of datapath actions taken in a single clock cycle. However, such attempts at reducing the clock cycle time have an impact on the number of CPIs needed to execute the different instructions. To get any more reduction in clock cycle time beyond these ideas, one has to shrink the feature size of the individual datapath elements. This avenue of optimization requires coming up with new chip fabrication processes and device technologies that help in reducing the feature sizes.

- **Datapath organization leading to lower CPI:** In Chapter 3, the implementation uses a single bus. Such an organization limits the amount of hardware concurrency among the datapath elements. We alluded to designs using multiple buses to increase the hardware concurrency. Such designs help in reducing the CPI for each instruction. Once again, any such attempt may have a negative impact on the clock cycle time and therefore would require careful analysis. Designing the microarchitecture of a processor and optimizing the implementation to maximize the performance is a fertile area of research, both in academia and in industries.

The preceding two bullet points focus on reducing the *latency* of individual instructions so that, cumulatively, we end up with a lower execution time. Another opportunity for reducing the execution time is to reduce the number of instructions.

- **Reduction in the number of executed instructions:** One possibility for reducing the number of instructions executed in the program is to replace simple instructions by more complex instructions. This would reduce the number of instructions executed by the program overall. We already saw a counterexample to this idea. Once again, any attempt to introduce new complex instructions has to be carefully balanced against the CPI, the clock cycle time, and the dynamic instruction frequencies. Compiler optimization is another approach to reducing the number of executed instructions, and in modern computer systems this plays a crucial role in determining the execution times of long-running programs.

It should be clear from the discussion so far that all three components of the execution time are interrelated, and have to be optimized simultaneously and not in isolation.

Example 5.4

An architecture has three types of instructions that have the following CPI:

Type	CPI
A	2
B	5
C	1

An architect determines that he can reduce the CPI for B to 3 with no change to the CPIs of the other two instruction types, but with an increase in the clock cycle time of the processor. What is the maximum permissible increase in clock cycle time that will make this architectural change still worthwhile? Assume that all the workloads executing on this processor use 30% of A, 10% of B, and 60% of C types of instructions.

Answer:

Let Co and Cn be the clock cycle times of the old (Mo) and new (Mn) machines, respectively. Let N be the total number of instructions executed in a program.

Execution time of the old machine is

$$ET_{Mo} = N * (F_A * CPI_{Ao} + F_B * CPI_{Bo} + F_C * CPI_{Co}) * Co,$$

where F_A, CPI_{Ao}, F_B, CPI_{Bo}, F_C, and CPI_{Co} are the dynamic frequencies and CPIs of each type of instruction, respectively.

Execution time of the old machine is

$$ET_{Mo} = N * (0.3 * 2 + 0.1 * 5 + 0.6 * 1) * Co$$
$$= N * 1.7 \, Co.$$

Execution time of the new machine is

$$ET_{Mn} = N * (0.3 * 2 + 0.1 * 3 + 0.6 * 1) * Cn$$
$$= N * 1.5 \, Cn.$$

For design to be viable,

$$ET_{Mn} < ET_{Mo}$$
$$N * 1.5 \, Cn < N * 1.7 \, Co$$
$$Cn < 1.7/1.5 * Co$$
$$Cn < 1.13 \, Co.$$

Max permissible increase in clock cycle time = **13%**.

___

5.5 Speedup

Comparing the execution times of processors for the same program or for a benchmark suite is the most obvious method for understanding the performance of one processor relative to another. Similarly, we can compare the improvement in execution time before and after a proposed modification in order to quantify the performance improvement which can be attributed to that modification.

We define

$$Speedup_{AoverB} = \frac{\text{Execution Time on Processor B}}{\text{Execution Time on Processor A}} \qquad (3)$$

Speedup of processor A over processor B is the ratio of execution time on processor B to the execution time on processor A.

Similarly,

$$Speedup_{improved} = \frac{\text{Execution Time Before Improvement}}{\text{Execution Time After Improvement}} \qquad (4)$$

Speedup due to a modification is the ratio of the execution time before improvement to that after the improvement.

Example 5.5

Here are the CPIs of instructions in an architecture:

Instruction	CPI
ADD	2
SHIFT	3
Others	2 (average of all instructions, including ADD and SHIFT)

Profiling the performance of a program, an architect realizes that the sequence ADD followed by SHIFT appears in 20% of the dynamic frequency of the program. He designs a new instruction, an ADD/SHIFT combo that has a CPI of 4.

What is the speedup of the program with all {ADD, SHIFT} replaced by the new combo instruction?

Answer:

Let N be the number of instructions in the original program. Then the execution time of the original program is

$$= N * \text{frequency of ADD/SHIFT} * (2 + 3) + N * \text{frequency of others} * 2$$
$$= N * 0.2 * 5 + N * 0.8 * 2 = 2.6 \, N.$$

With the combo instruction replacing {ADD, SHIFT}, the number of instructions in the new program shrinks to 0.9 N. In the new program, the frequency of the combo instruction is 1/9 and the other instructions are 8/9.

The execution time of the new program is

$$= (0.9 \, N) * \text{frequency of combo} * 4 + (0.9 \, N) * \text{frequency of others} * 2$$
$$= (0.9 \, N) * (1/9) * 4 + (0.9 \, N) * (8/9) * 2$$
$$= 2 \, N.$$

Speedup of the program = old execution time/new execution time
$$= (2.6 \, N)/(2 \, N)$$
$$= 1.3.$$

Another useful metric is the performance improvement due to a modification:

$$\text{Improvement in execution time} = \frac{\text{old execution time} - \text{new execution time}}{\text{old execution time}} \tag{5}$$

Example 5.6

A given program takes 1000 instructions to execute, with an average CPI of 3 and a clock cycle time of 2 ns. An architect is considering two options. (1) She can reduce the average CPI of instructions by 25% while increasing the clock cycle time by 10%; or (2) she can reduce the clock cycle time by 20% while increasing the average CPI of instructions by 15%.

   a. You are the manager deciding which option to pursue. Give the reasoning behind your decision.

Answer:

Let E0, E1, and E2 denote the execution times with base machine, first option, and second option, respectively.

$$E0 = 1000 * 3 * 2 \text{ ns}$$
$$E1 = 1000 * (3 * 0.75) * 2 (1.1) \text{ ns} = 0.825 \text{ E0}$$
$$E2 = 1000 * (3 * 1.15) * 2 (0.8) \text{ ns} = 0.920 \text{ E0}$$

Option E1 is better, because it results in less execution time than E2.

   b. What is the improvement in execution time of the option you chose, compared with the original design?

Answer:

$$\text{Improvement of option 1 relative to base} = (E0 - E1)/E0$$
$$= (E0 - 0.825 \text{ E0})/E0$$
$$= 0.175;$$

therefore, **17.5%** improvement.

Another way of understanding the effect of an improvement is to take into account the extent of the impact that the change has on the execution time. For example, the change may have an impact on only a portion of the execution time. A law associated with Gene Amdahl, a pioneer in parallel computing, can be adapted for capturing this notion:

> Amdahl's law:
>
> $$\text{Time}_{after} = \text{Time}_{unaffected} + \text{Time}_{affected}/x$$

(6)

In the foregoing equation, Time_{after}, the total execution time as a result of a change, is the sum of the execution time that is unaffected by the change ($\text{Time}_{unaffected}$) and the ratio of the affected time ($\text{Time}_{affected}$) to the extent of the improvement (denoted by x). Basically, Amdahl's law suggests an engineering approach to improving processor performance, namely, to spend resources on critical instructions that will have the maximum impact on the execution time.[6]

Table 5.1 summarizes the processor-related performance metrics that we have discussed so far.

Table 5.1 Summary of Performance Metrics

Name	Notation	Units	Comment
Memory footprint		Bytes	Total space occupied by the program in memory
Execution time	$(\Sigma\ CPI_j)$ * clock cycle time, where $1 \le j \le n$	Seconds	Running time of the program that executes n instructions
Arithmetic mean	$(E_1 + E_2 + \cdots + E_p)/p$	Seconds	Average of execution times of constituent p benchmark programs
Weighted arithmetic mean	$(f_1 * E_1 + f_2 * E_2 + \cdots + f_p * E_p)$	Seconds	Weighted average of execution times of constituent p benchmark programs
Geometric mean	p^{th} root $(E_1 * E_2 * \cdots * E_p)$	Seconds	p^{th} root of the product of execution times of p programs that constitute the benchmark
Harmonic mean	$1/(((1/E_1) + (1/E_2) + \cdots + (1/E_p))/p)$	Seconds	Arithmetic mean of the reciprocals of the execution times of the constituent p benchmark programs
Static instruction frequency		%	Occurrence of instruction i in compiled code
Dynamic instruction frequency		%	Occurrence of instruction i in executed code
Speedup (M_A over M_B)	E_B/E_A	Number	Speedup of Machine A over B
Speedup (improvement)	E_{Before}/E_{After}	Number	Speedup after improvement
Improvement in Exec time	$(E_{old} - E_{new})/E_{old}$	Number	New vs. old
Amdahl's law	$Time_{after} = Time_{unaffected} + Time_{affected}/x$	Seconds	x is amount of improvement

---

6. Amdahl's law has serious implications for achieving speedup for a program on a parallel machine. See Exercise 16 in Chapter 12, which deals with parallel systems.

Example 5.7

A processor spends 20% of its time on ADD instructions. An engineer proposes to improve the ADD instruction by four times. What is the speedup achieved because of the modification?

Answer:

The improvement applies only for the ADD instruction, so 80% of the execution time is unaffected by the improvement.

Original normalized execution time = 1.

New execution time = (time spent in ADD instruction/4)
+ remaining execution time

$$= 0.2/4 + 0.8$$

$$= 0.85.$$

Speedup = Execution time before improvement/Execution time after improvement

$$= 1/0.85 = \mathbf{1.18}.$$

5.6 Increasing the Throughput of the Processor

Thus far, we have focused on techniques to reduce the latency of individual instructions in order to improve processor performance. A radically different approach to improving processor performance is to focus not on the *latency* for individual instructions (i.e., the CPI metric), but on *throughput*—that is, the number of instructions executed by the processor per unit time. Latency answers the question of how many clock cycles the processor takes to execute an individual instruction (i.e., CPI). On the other hand, throughput answers the question as to how many instructions the processor executes in each clock cycle (i.e., *IPC*, or *instructions per clock cycle*). The concept called *pipelining* is the focus of the rest of this chapter.

5.7 Introduction to Pipelining

Welcome to Bill's Sandwich Shop! Bill has a huge selection of breads, condiments, cheeses, meats, and veggies to choose from in his shop, all neatly organized into individual stations. When Bill was starting out in business, he was a one-man team. He took the orders, went through the various stations, and made the sandwiches according to the specs. Now his business has grown. He has five employees, one for each of the five stations involved with the sandwich assembly: order taking, bread and condiments selection, cheese selection, meat selection, and veggies selection. The following table shows the sandwich assembly process:

Station 1 (place order)	Station II (select bread)	Station III (cheese)	Station IV (meat)	Station V (veggies)
New (5th order)	4th order	3rd order	2nd order	1st order

Each station is working on a different order; while the last station (Station V) is working on the very first order, the first station is taking a new order for a sandwich. Each station, after "doing its thing" for the sandwich, passes the partially assembled sandwich to the next station, along with the order. Bill is a clever manager. He decided against dedicating an employee to any *one* customer. That would require each employee to have his or her own stash of *all* the ingredients needed to make a sandwich and would unnecessarily increase the inventory of raw materials, since each customer may want only a subset of the ingredients. Instead, Bill carefully designed the work to be done in each station to be roughly the same, so that no employee would be twiddling his thumbs. Of course, if a particular sandwich order does not need a specific ingredient (say, cheese), then the corresponding station simply passes on the partially assembled sandwich to the next station. Nevertheless, most of the time (especially during peak time), all of Bill's employees are kept busy rolling out sandwiches in rapid succession.

Bill has quintupled the rate at which he can serve his customers.

5.8 Toward an Instruction-Processing Assembly Line

You can see where we are going with Bill's sandwich shop analogy. In the simple implementation of the LC-2200, the FSM executes one instruction at a time, taking it all the way through the fetch, decode, and execute macro states before starting on the next instruction. The problem with this approach is that the datapath resources are under-utilized. This is because, for each macro state, not all the resources are needed. Let us not worry about the specific datapath we used in implementing the LC-2200 ISA in Chapter 3. Regardless of the details of the datapath, we know that any implementation of the LC-2200 ISA would need the following datapath resources: memory, PC, ALU, register file, IR, and sign extender. Figure 5.1 shows the hardware resources of the datapath that are in use for each of the macro states for a couple of instructions:

We can immediately make the following two observations:

1. The IR is in use in every macro state. This is not surprising because IR contains the instruction, and parts of the IR are used in different macro states of its execution. IR is equivalent to the "order" being passed from station to station in the sandwich assembly line.

2. At the macro level, we can see that a different amount of work is being done in each of the three macro states. Each state of the FSM is equivalent to a station in the sandwich assembly line.

Macro State	Datapath Resources in Use				
FETCH	IR	ALU	PC	MEM	
DECODE	IR				
EXECUTE (ADD)	IR	ALU	Reg-file		
EXECUTE (LW)	IR	ALU	Reg-file	MEM	Sign extender

Figure 5.1 Datapath resources in use for different macro states.

```
I₁:   LW R1, MEM [1000];    R1 ← Memory at location 1000

I₂:   LW R2, MEM [2000];    R2 ← Memory at location 2000

I₃:   ADD R3, R5, R4;       R3 ← R4 + R5

I₄:   NAND R6, R7, R8;      R6 ← R7 NAND R8

I₅:   SW R9, MEM [3000];    R9 → Memory at location 3000

I₆:   . . . . .

I₇:   . . . . .

I₈

I₉

I₁₀

I₁₁

I₁₂

I₁₃
```

Figure 5.2   A Program is a sequence of instructions.

We want to use all the hardware resources in the datapath all the time if possible. In our sandwich assembly line, we kept all the stations busy by assembling multiple sandwiches simultaneously. We will try to apply the sandwich-assembly-line idea to instruction execution in the processor. A program is a sequence of instructions, as shown in Figure 5.2.

With the simple implementation of the FSM, the time line for instruction execution in the processor will look as shown in Figure 5.3(a). A new instruction processing starts only after the previous one is fully completed. Using our sandwich assembly line idea, we can see that, in order to maximize the utilization of the datapath resources, we should have multiple instructions in execution in our instruction *pipeline,* as shown in Figure 5.3(b). The question arises immediately as to whether this is even possible. If you are an employee in a sandwich assembly line, assembling your sandwich is completely independent of what your predecessor or your successor in the line wants for his/her sandwich. Are the successive instructions in a program similarly independent of one another? *No* is the immediate answer that comes to mind, because the program is sequential. However, look at the sequence of instructions shown in Figure 5.2. Even though the program is sequential, one can see that instructions I_1 through I_5 happen to be independent of one another. That is, the execution of one instruction does not depend on the results of the execution of the previous instruction in the sequence. We quickly point out that this happy state of affairs is not the norm, and we will deal with such dependencies in a processor pipeline in Section 5.13. For the moment, however, it is convenient to think that the instructions in sequence are independent of one another, in order to illustrate the possibility of adopting the sandwich-assembly-line-idea for the purpose of designing the processor pipeline.

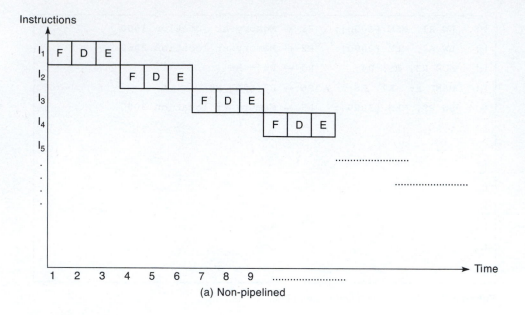

(a) Non-pipelined

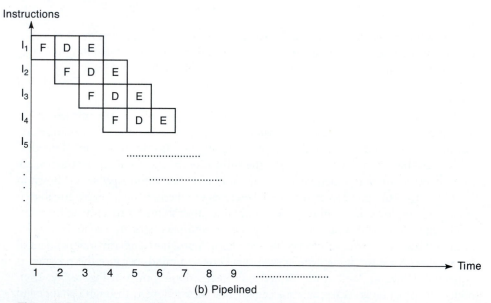

(b) Pipelined

Figure 5.3   Execution Timeline.

In (a), the processor deals with one instruction at a time. I_1 goes through F, D, E macro states completely, then I_2, and so on. In (b), multiple instructions are at various stages of processing. For example, at time = 3, I_1 is in E state, I_2 is in D state, and I_3 is in F state.

Notice that in the pipeline execution timeline shown in Figure 5.3(b), we start the processing of a new instruction as soon as the previous instruction moves to the next macro state. If this were possible, we could triple the throughput of the instructions processed. The key observations are that the datapath resources are akin to individual ingredients in the sandwich assembly line and the macro states are akin to the employees at specific stations of the sandwich assembly line.

5.9 Problems with a Simple-Minded Instruction Pipeline

The following are problems with the simple-minded application of the assembly line idea to the instruction pipeline.

1. The different stages often need the same datapath resources (e.g., ALU, IR).

2. The amount of work done in the different stages is not the same. For example, compare the work done in the DECODE and EXECUTE (LW) states in Figure 5.1. The former is simply a combinational function to determine the type of instruction and the resources needed for it. On the other hand, the latter involves address arithmetic, memory access, and writing to a register file. In general, the work done in the execute state will far outweigh the work done in the other stages.

Let us understand the implication of the first point, which is that we have resource contention among the stages. This is often referred to as a *structural hazard* and is a result of limitations in the datapath, such as having a single IR, a single ALU, and a single bus to connect the datapath elements. In the sandwich assembly line, the individual order (equivalent to the contents of IR) is on a piece of paper that is passed from station to station, and the partially assembled sandwich (equivalent to an instruction in partial execution) is passed directly from one station to the next (i.e., there is no central "bus" as in our simple datapath). We can use similar ideas to fix this problem with our instruction pipeline. For example, if we add an *extra* ALU, an *extra* IR, and an *extra* MEM to the datapath dedicated to the fetch stage, then that stage will become independent of the other stages. An extra ALU is understandable because both the fetch and execute stages need to use it, but we need to understand what it means to have an extra IR. Just as the order is passed from station to station in the sandwich assembly line, we are passing the contents of the IR from the fetch to the decode stages, and so on, to keep the stages independent of one another.

There is another serious structural hazard posed by the fetch and execute stages of the pipeline. The fetch stage needs access to the memory for instructions in every clock cycle. Additionally, if there is a load or a store instruction in the execute stage, then that stage also needs access to the memory. How can we solve this problem? One simple solution is to keep distinct the regions of memory accessed by the fetch and execute stages. Such a design is reasonable because (a) it is a good programming practice to keep the two separate, and (b) most modern processors (e.g., memory segmentation in the Intel x86 architecture, discussed in Chapter 7) separate the memory space into distinct regions to ensure inadvertent modifications to instruction memory by a program.

Therefore, we split the total memory into an I-MEM for instruction memory and a D-MEM for data memory in order to make the fetch stage independent of the execute stage. Instructions of the program now come from the I-MEM, and the data structures that the program manipulates come from the D-MEM. Thus, by design, we have eliminated this particular structural hazard.

The second point implies that the time needed for each stage of the instruction pipeline is different. Recall that Bill carefully engineered his sandwich assembly line to ensure that each employee did the same amount of work in each station. The reason is that the slowest member of the pipeline limits the throughput of the assembly line. Therefore, for our instruction assembly line to be as efficient, we should break up the instruction processing so that each stage does roughly the same amount of work.

5.10 Fixing the Problems with the Instruction Pipeline

Consider now the decode stage. This stage does the least amount of work in the current setup. To spread the work more evenly, we have to assign more work to this stage. We have a dilemma here. We cannot really do anything until we know what instruction is the focus of this stage. However, we can do something opportunistically, so long as the semantics of the actual instruction is not affected.

We expect most instructions to use register contents. Therefore, we can go ahead and read the register contents from the register file without actually knowing what the instruction is. In the worst case, we may end up not using the values read from the registers. However, to do this, we need to know which registers to read. This is where the instruction format chosen during instruction-set design becomes crucial. If you go back to Chapter 2 and look at the instructions which use registers in the LC-2200 (ADD, NAND, BEQ, LW, SW, and JAL), you will find that the source register specifiers for arithmetic/logic operations or for address calculations always occupy the *same* bit positions in the instruction format. We can exploit this fact and opportunistically read the registers as we decode what the actual instruction is. In a similar vein, we can break up the execute stage, which potentially does a lot of work, into smaller stages.

Using such reasoning, let us subdivide the processing of an instruction into the following five functional components, or stages:

- **IF:** This stage fetches the instruction pointed to by the PC from I-MEM and places it into IR; it also increments the current PC in readiness for fetching the next instruction.

- **ID/RR:** This stage decodes the instruction and reads the register file to pull out the registers that are needed by the instruction currently being decoded. The LC-2200 has 1 operand, 2 operand, and 3 operand instructions. However, the key thing to note is that *at most* two register values are needed by *any* of the instructions. For example, ADD, NAND, and BEQ need two source operands in order to be read out of the register file. Similarly, SW requires one register value for address calculation, and a second register value that needs to be stored in memory. To enable this functionality, the register file has to be *dual-ported,* meaning that two register addresses can be given simultaneously and two register contents can be read out in the same clock cycle. We will call such a register file a *dual-ported register file (DPRF)*. Now, which register addresses need to be given to the DPRF for reading varies with the specific instruction, because they come from different parts of IR, depending on the instruction type (R-type, I-type, and J-type; see Section 2.10.1). This is not an issue, as we can apply combination logic in this stage to choose the right register specifiers out of IR, using the opcode field of the instruction. Since this stage contains the logic for decoding the instruction, as well as for reading the register file, we have given it a hybrid name.

- **EX:** This is the stage that does all the arithmetic and/or logic operations that are needed for processing the instruction. We will see in Section 5.11 that, in the EX stage, one ALU may not suffice to cater to the needs of all the instructions.

- **MEM:** This stage either reads from or writes to the D-MEM for LW and SW instructions, respectively. Instructions that do not have a memory operand will not need the operations performed in this stage.

- **WB:** This stage writes the appropriate destination register (Rx) if the instruction requires it. Instructions in the LC-2200 that require writing to a destination register include arithmetic and logic operations, as well as load.

Pictorially, the passage of an instruction through the pipeline is shown in Figure 5.4. Similar to what we expect from the sandwich assembly line, we expect every instruction to pass through each of these stages in the course of the processing. At any point in time, five instructions are in execution in the pipeline: When instruction I_1 is in the WB stage, instruction I_5 is in the IF stage. This is a synchronous pipeline in the sense that, on each clock pulse, the partial results of the instruction execution are passed on to the next stage. The inherent assumption is that the clock pulse is wide enough to allow the slowest member of the pipeline to complete its function within the clock cycle time.

Every stage works on the partial results generated in the *previous clock cycle* by the preceding stage. Not every instruction needs every stage. For example, an ADD instruction does not need the MEM stage. However, this simply means that the MEM stage does nothing for one clock cycle when it gets the partial results of an ADD instruction. (Here, one can clearly see the analogy to the sandwich assembly line).

You might think that this is an inefficient design if you look at the passage of specific instructions. For example, this design adds one more cycle to the processing of an ADD instruction. However, the goal of the pipelined design is to increase the throughput of instruction processing and *not* to reduce the latency for each instruction. To return to our sandwich assembly line example, the analogous criterion in that example was to keep the customer line moving. The number of customers served per unit of time in

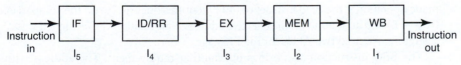

Figure 5.4   Passage of instructions through the pipeline.

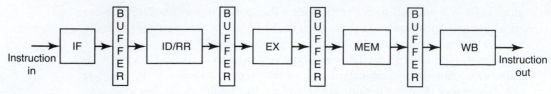

Figure 5.5 Instruction pipeline with buffers between stages.
The buffers give autonomy and independence to the stages.

that example is analogous to the number of instructions processed per unit of time in the pipelined processor.

Because each stage is working on a different instruction, once a stage has completed its function, it has to place the results of its function in a well-known location for the next stage to pick it up in the next clock cycle. This is called *buffering* the output of a stage. Such buffering is essential for the independence of each stage. Figure 5.5 shows the instruction pipeline with the buffers added between the stages. The *pipeline register* is the term commonly used to refer to the buffer between the stages. We will use *pipeline register* and *buffer* interchangeably in this chapter. In our sandwich assembly line example, the partially assembled sandwich serves as the buffer and gives independence and autonomy to each stage.

5.11 Datapath Elements for the Instruction Pipeline

The next step is to determine the datapath elements needed for each stage of the instruction pipeline and the contents of the buffers between the stages that provide the isolation between them.

- In the IF stage we need a PC, an ALU, and an I-MEM. The output of this stage is the instruction fetched from the memory; therefore, the pipeline register between the IF and ID/RR stages should contain the instruction.

- In the ID/RR stage, we need the DPRF. The output of this stage is the contents of the registers read from the register file (call them A and B) and the results of decoding the instruction (the opcode of the instruction, and the offset, if needed by the instruction). These constitute the contents of the pipeline register between ID/RR and EX stages.

- The EX stage performs any needed arithmetic for an instruction. Since this is the only stage that performs all the arithmetic for an instruction execution, we need to determine the worst-case resource need for this stage. This depends on the instruction-set repertoire.

  In our case (LC-2200), the only instruction that required more than one arithmetic operation is the BEQ instruction. BEQ requires one ALU to do the comparison (A == B) and another to do the effective address computation (PC + signed-offset). Therefore, we need two ALU's for the EX stage.

  The BEQ instruction also brings out another requirement. The address arithmetic requires the value of the PC that corresponds to the BEQ instruction.

(Incidentally, the value of PC is required for another instruction as well, namely, JALR.) Therefore, the value of PC should also be communicated from stage to stage (in addition to the other things being communicated) through the pipeline.

The output of the EX stage is the result of the arithmetic operations carried out and is therefore instruction specific. The contents of the pipeline register between the EX and MEM stages depends on such specifics. For example, if the instruction is an ADD instruction, then the pipeline register will contain the result of the ADD, the opcode, and the destination register specifier (Rx). We can see that the PC value is not required after the EX stage for any of the instructions. Working out the details of the pipeline register contents for the other instructions is left as an exercise to the reader.

- The MEM stage requires the D-MEM. If the instruction processed by this stage in a clock cycle is not LW or SW, then the contents of the input buffer are simply copied to the output buffer at the end of the clock cycle. For the LW instruction, the output buffer of the stage contains the D-MEM contents read, the opcode, and the destination register specifier (Rx), whereas, for the SW instruction, the output buffer contains the opcode. With a little reflection, we can easily see that no action is needed in the WB stage if the opcode is SW.

- The WB stage requires the register file (DPRF). This stage is relevant only for the instructions that write to a destination register (such as LW, ADD, and NAND). This poses an interesting dilemma. We know that every stage in every clock cycle is working on a different instruction. Therefore, with reference to Figure 5.4, at the same time that WB is working on I_1, ID/RR is working on I_4. Both of these stages need to access the DPRF simultaneously on behalf of different instructions. (For example, I_1 may be ADD R1, R3, R4; and I_4 may be NAND R5, R6, R7.) Fortunately, WB is writing to a register while ID/RR is reading registers. Therefore, there is no conflict in terms of the logic operation being performed by these two stages, and both can proceed simultaneously, as long as the same register is not being read and written to in a given cycle. It is a semantics conflict when the same register is being read and written to in the same cycle. (For example, consider I_1 to be ADD R1, R3, R4 and I_4 to be ADD R4, R1, R6.) We will address such semantic conflicts shortly in Section 5.13.2.

Pictorially, we show the new organization of the resources for the various stages in Figure 5.6. Note that DPRF in the ID/RR and WB stages refers to the same logic element in the datapath. In Figure 5.6, both stages include DPRF just to clarify the resources needed. Here are some things to note for our pipelined processor design. In the steady state, there are five instructions in different stages of processing in the pipeline. We know that, in the simple design of the LC-2200, the FSM transitioned through the microstates such as **ifetch1**, **ifetch2**, etc. In a given clock cycle, the processor was in *exactly* one state. In a pipelined implementation, the processor is simultaneously in all the states represented by the stages of the pipelined design. Every instruction takes five clock cycles to execute. Each instruction enters the pipeline at the IF stage and is *retired* (i.e., completed successfully) from the WB stage. In the ideal situation, the pipelined processor retires one new instruction in every clock cycle. Thus, the effective

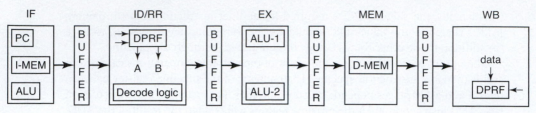

Figure 5.6   Organization of hardware resources for various stages.

CPI of the pipelined processor is 1. Inspecting Figure 5.6, one might guess that MEM stage could be the slowest. However, the answer to this question is more involved. We discuss considerations in modern processors with respect to reducing the clock cycle time in Section 5.15.

The performance of the pipelined processor is crucially dependent on the memory system. Memory access time is the most dominant latency in a pipelined processor. To hide this latency, processors employ caches. Recall the toolbox and tool tray analogy from Chapter 2. We mentioned that registers serve the role of the tool tray, in that we *explicitly* bring the memory values which the processor needs into the registers, using the load instruction. Similarly, caches serve as *implicit* tool trays. In other words, whenever the processor brings something from the memory (instruction or data), it implicitly places it into high-speed storage areas called caches, inside the processor. By creating an implicit copy of the memory location in the cache, the processor can subsequently reuse values in these memory locations without making trips to the memory. We will discuss caches in much more detail in Chapter 9, together with their effect on pipelined processor implementation. For the purpose of this discussion on pipelined processor implementation, we will simply say that caches allow for the hiding of the memory latency and make pipelined processor implementation viable. In spite of the caches and high-speed registers, the combinational logic delays (ALU, multiplexers, decoders, etc.) are significantly smaller than access to caches and general-purpose registers. In the interest of making sure that all stages of the pipeline have roughly the same latency, modern processor implementation comprises much more than five stages. For example, access to storage elements (cache memory, register file) may take multiple cycles in the processor pipeline. We will discuss such issues in Section 5.15. Because this is the first introduction to pipelined implementation of a processor, we will keep the discussion simple.

5.12 Pipeline-Conscious Architecture and Implementation

The key points to note in designing a pipeline-conscious architecture are as follows:

- **Need for an easily-decodable instruction format:** This property allows the implementation to make some decisions even before the instruction is fully decoded. A symmetric instruction format is an example that preserves such a property. This

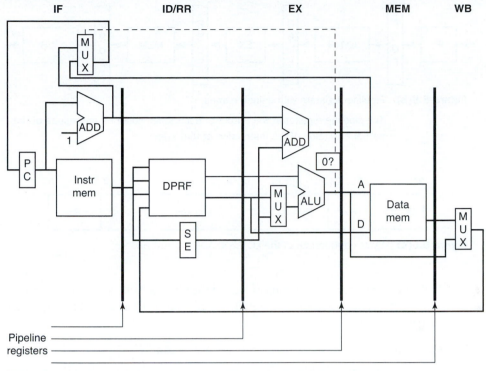

Figure 5.6(a)   Datapath for a pipelined LC 2200, showing all the connections between the stages in addition to the resources needed in each stage.

format ensures that the locations of certain fields in the instruction (e.g., register specifiers, size and position of offset, etc.) remain unchanged for groups of instructions (e.g., R-type or I-type in the LC-2200), independently of the specific instruction. As we saw, this was a key property that we exploited in the ID/RR stage for the LC-2200.

- **Need to ensure equal amounts of work in each stage:** This property ensures that the clock cycle time is optimal, since the slowest member of the pipeline determines it.

Figure 5.6(a) shows the full datapath for a pipelined LC-2200 implementation.

5.12.1 Anatomy of an Instruction Passage Through the Pipeline

In this subsection, we will trace the passage of an instruction through the five-stage pipeline. We will denote the buffers between the stages with unique names, as shown in Figure 5.6(b).

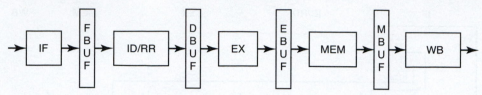

Figure 5.6(b)   Pipeline registers with unique names.

The pipeline register at the output of each stage contains the results of the partial execution of the instruction at that stage.

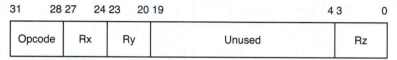

Figure 5.6(c)   Syntax and format of the LC 2200 ADD instruction.

Table 5.2 summarizes the function of each of the pipeline buffers between the stages. Let us consider the passage of the ADD instruction that has the following syntax and format:

ADD   Rx, Ry, Rz;   Rx ← Ry + Rz

Each stage performs the actions summarized next, to contribute toward the execution of the ADD instruction:

IF stage (cycle 1):

I-MEM[PC] → FBUF   // The instruction at memory address given by PC is fetched and placed in FBUF (which is essentially the IR); the contents of FBUF after this action will be as shown in Figure 5.6(c).

PC + 1 → PC   // Increment PC

ID/RR stage (cycle 2):

DPRF[FBUF[Ry]] → DBUF [A];   // read Ry into DBUF[A]
DPRF[FBUF[Rz]] → DBUF [B];   // read Rz into DBUF[B]
FBUF[OPCODE] → DBUF[OPCODE];   // copy opcode from FBUF to DBUF
FBUF[Rx] → DBUF[Rx];   // copy Rx register specifier from FBUF to DBUF

EX stage (cycle 3):

DBUF[A] + DBUF [B] → EBUF[Result]; // perform addition
DBUF[OPCODE] → EBUF[OPCODE];   // copy opcode from DBUF to EBUF
DBUF[Rx] → EBUF[Rx];   // copy Rx register specifier from DBUF to EBUF

Table 5.2 Pipeline Buffers and Their Contents

Name	Output of Stage	Contents
FBUF	IF	Primarily contains instruction read from memory
DBUF	ID/RR	Decoded IR and values read from register file
EBUF	EX	Primarily contains result of ALU operation plus other parts of the instruction, depending on the instruction specifics
MBUF	MEM	Same as EBUF if instruction is not LW or SW; if instruction is LW, then buffer contains the contents of memory location read

MEM stage (cycle 4):

DBUF → MBUF;   // The MEM stage has nothing to contribute toward the execution
                                of the ADD instruction; so simply copy the DBUF to MBUF.

WB stage (cycle 5):

MBUF[Result] → DPRF [MBUF[Rx]];   // write back the result of the addition
                                                        into the register specified by Rx

Example 5.8

Considering only the ADD instruction, quantify the sizes of the various buffers between the stages of the preceding pipeline.

Answer:

Size of FBUF (same as the size of an instruction in the LC-2200) = **32 bits**

Size of DBUF:

Size of contents of Ry register in DBUF[A] = 32 bits

Size of contents of Rz register in DBUF[B] = 32 bits

Size of opcode in DBUF[opcode]   = 4 bits

Size of Rx register specifier in DBUF[Rx] = 4 bits

Total size (sum of all the fields)   = **72 bits**

Size of EBUF:

Size of result of addition in EBUF[result] = 32 bits

Size of opcode in EBUF[opcode]   = 4 bits

Size of Rx register specifier in EBUF[Rx] = 4 bits

Total size (sum of all the fields)   = **40 bits**

Size of MBUF (same as EBUF)   = **40 bits**

5.12.2 Design of the Pipeline Registers

Although in the previous section we looked at the passage of a single instruction through the pipeline, it should be clear that each stage of the pipeline is working on a different instruction in each clock cycle. The reader should work out the actions taken by each stage of the pipeline for the different instructions in the LC-2200. (See the problems at the end of this chapter.) This exercise is similar to the design of the FSM control sequences that we undertook in Chapter 3 for the sequential implementation of the LC-2200. Once such a design is complete, then the size of the pipeline register for each stage can be determined as the maximum required for the passage of any instruction. The pipeline register at the output of the ID/RR stage will have the maximal content, since we do not yet know what the instruction is. The interpretation of the contents of a pipeline register will depend on the stage and the opcode of the instruction that is being acted upon by that stage.

A generic layout of the pipeline register is as shown in Figure 5.6(d). Opcode will always occupy the same position in each pipeline register. In each clock cycle, each stage interprets the remaining fields of the pipeline register at its input in accordance with the opcode and takes the appropriate datapath actions (similar to what we detailed for the ADD instruction in Section 5.12.1).

Example 5.9

Design the DBUF pipeline register for the LC-2200. Do not attempt to optimize the design by overloading the different fields of this register.

Answer:

DBUF has the following fields:

Opcode (needed for all instructions)	4 bits
A (needed for R-type)	32 bits
B (needed for R-type)	32 bits
Offset (needed for I-type and J-type)	20 bits
PC value (needed for BEQ)	32 bits
Rx specifier (needed for R-, I-, and J-type)	4 bits

Layout of the DBUF pipeline register:

Opcode	A	B	Offset	PC	Rx
4 bits	32 bits	32 bits	20 bits	32 bits	4 bits

Opcode	Other fields

Figure 5.6(d)   A generic layout of a pipeline register.

5.12.3 Implementation of the Stages

In a sense, the design and implementation of a pipeline processor may be simpler than a nonpipelined processor. This is because the pipelined implementation modularizes the design. This modularity leads to the same design advantages that accrue in writing a large software system as a composite of several smaller modules. Just as a large software team may work on the development of a complex software system (e.g., Microsoft Word), the modularity of a pipelined processor design allows multiple independent hardware teams to work on implementing the processor, each team working on a specific stage of the processor. The layout and interpretation of the pipeline registers are analogous to well-defined interfaces between components of a large software system. Once we complete the layout and interpretation of the pipeline registers, we can get down to the datapath actions needed for each stage in complete isolation from the other stages. Further, since the datapath actions of each stage happen in one clock cycle, the design of each stage is purely combinational. At the beginning of each clock cycle, each stage interprets the input pipeline register, carries out the datapath actions by using the combinational logic for this stage, and writes the result of the datapath action into its output pipeline register.

Example 5.10

Design and implement the datapath for the ID/RR stage of the pipeline to implement the LC-2200 instruction set. You can use any available logic design tool to do this problem.

Answer:

Figures 5.6, 5.6(a), and 5.6(b) are the starting points for solving this problem. The datapath elements have to be laid out. Using the format of the instruction, the register files have to be accessed and put into the appropriate fields of DBUF. The offset and the opcode fields of the instruction have to be copied from FBUF to DBUF. The PC value has to be put into the appropriate field of DBUF. Completing this example is left as an exercise for the reader.

5.13 Hazards

Although the sandwich assembly line serves as a good analogy for the pipelined processor, there are several twists in the instruction pipeline that complicate its design. These issues are summed up as *pipeline hazards*. Specifically, there are three types of hazards: **structural**, **data** and **control**.

As we will see shortly, the effect of all these hazards is the same, namely, to **reduce** the pipeline efficiency. In other words, the pipeline will execute less than one instruction every clock cycle. Recall, however, that the pipeline is synchronous. That is, in each clock cycle every stage is working on an instruction that has been placed on the pipeline register by the preceding stage. Just like air bubbles in a water pipe, if a stage is not ready to send a valid instruction to the next stage, it should place the equivalent of an "air bubble," a dummy instruction that does nothing, in the pipeline register. We refer to this as a *NOP (no-operation)* instruction.

We will include a NOP instruction in the repertoire of the processor. In subsequent discussions on hazards, we will address how the hardware automatically generates such NOPs when warranted by the hazard encountered. However, this need not always be the case. By exposing the structure of the pipeline to the software, we can make the system software—namely, the compiler—responsible for including such NOP instructions in the source code itself. We will return to this possibility in Section 5.13.4.

Another way of understanding the effect of bubbles in the pipeline is to realize that the average CPI of instructions is above 1. It is important to add a cautionary note to the use of the CPI metric. Recall that the execution time of a program in clock cycles is the product of CPI and the number of instructions executed. Thus, CPI by itself does not tell the whole story of how good an architecture or the implementation is. In reality, the compiler and the architecture, in close partnership, determine the program execution time. For example, unoptimized code that a compiler generates may have a lower CPI than the optimized code. However, the execution time may be much more than that of the optimized code. The reason is that the optimization phase of the compiler may have gotten rid of a number of useless instructions in the program, thus reducing the total number of instructions executed. But this may have come at the cost of increasing the three kinds of hazards and, hence, the average CPI of the instructions in the optimized code. Yet, the net effect of the optimized code may be a reduction in program execution time.

5.13.1 Structural Hazard

We already alluded to the structural hazard. This comes about primarily due to the limitations in the hardware resources available for concurrent operation of the different stages. For example, a single data bus in the nonpipelined version is a structural hazard for a pipelined implementation. Similarly, a single ALU is another structural hazard. There are two possible solutions to this problem: Live with it and fix it. If the hazard is likely to occur only occasionally (for some particular combinations of instructions passing through the pipeline simultaneously), then it may be prudent not to waste additional hardware resources to fix the problem. As an example, let us assume that our pointy-haired manager has told us that we can use only one ALU in the EX unit. So, every time we encounter the BEQ instruction, we spend two clock cycles in the EX unit, carrying out the two arithmetic operations that are needed, one for the comparison and the other for the address computation. Of course, the preceding and succeeding stages should be made aware that the EX stage will occasionally take two cycles to do its operation. Therefore, the EX unit should tell the stages preceding it (namely, IF and ID/RR) not to send a new instruction in the next clock cycle. Basically, there is a *feedback line* that each of the preceding stages looks at to determine whether it should just "pause" in a given cycle or do something useful. If a stage decides to "pause" in a clock cycle, it simply does not change anything in the output buffer.

The succeeding stages need to be handled differently than the preceding stages. Specifically, the EX stage will write a NOP opcode in its output buffer for the opcode field. A NOP instruction is a convenient way of making the processor execute a "dummy" instruction that has no impact on the actual program under execution. Via the NOP instruction, we have introduced a *bubble* in the pipeline between the BEQ and the instruction that preceded it.

The passage of a BEQ instruction is pictorially shown in a series of timing diagrams in Figure 5.7. We pick up the action from cycle 2, when the BEQ instruction is in the ID/RR stage. A value of STAY (equal to binary 1) on the feedback line tells the preceding stage to remain in the same instruction and not to send a new instruction at the end of this cycle. Such a bubble in the pipeline brings down the pipeline efficiency because the effective CPI goes above 1 due to the bubble.

If, on the other hand, it is determined that such an inefficiency is unacceptable, then we can fix the structural hazard by throwing hardware at the problem. This is what we did in our earlier discussion when we added an extra ALU in the EX stage to overcome this structural hazard.

Here are three quick notes on terminology:

- The pipeline is *stalled* when an instruction cannot proceed to the next stage.
- The result of such a stall is to introduce a *bubble* in the pipeline.
- A NOP instruction is the manifestation of the bubble in the pipeline. A stage executing a NOP instruction does nothing for one cycle. Its output buffer remains unchanged from the previous cycle.

You may notice that we use the terms *stalls, bubbles,* and *NOPs* interchangeably in this textbook. They all mean the same thing.

5.13.2 Data Hazard

Consider Figure 5.8(a). In the first equation, notice the two instructions occurring in the execution order of a program. I_1 reads the values in registers R2 and R3 and writes the result of the addition into register R1. The next instruction, I_2, reads the values in registers R1 (written into by the previous instruction I_1) and R5 and writes the result of the addition into register R4. The situation presents a *data hazard*, because there is a dependency between the two instructions. In particular, this kind of hazard is called a *read after write (RAW)* data hazard. Of course, the two instructions need not occur strictly next to each other. So long as there is a data dependency

Cycle 2

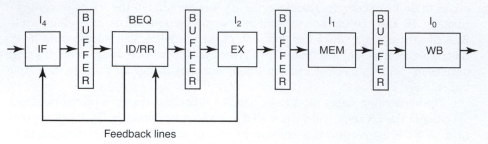

Cycle 3

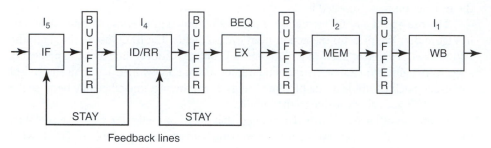

Cycle 4

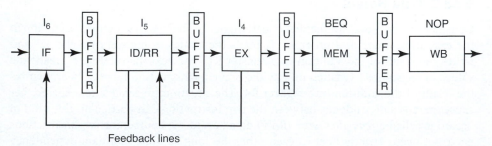

Cycle 5

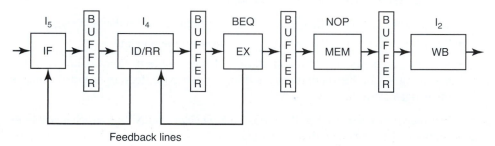

Figure 5.7   Illustration of a structural hazard.

$$I_1: R1 \leftarrow R2 + R3$$

(7)

$$I_2: R4 \leftarrow R1 + R5$$

Figure 5.8(a)   RAW hazard.

$$I_1: R4 \leftarrow R1 + R5$$

(8)

$$I_2: R1 \leftarrow R2 + R3$$

Figure 5.8(b)   WAR hazard.

$$I_1: R1 \leftarrow R4 + R5$$

(9)

$$I_2: R1 \leftarrow R2 + R3$$

Figure 5.8(c)   WAW hazard.

between any two instructions in the execution order of the program, it amounts to a data hazard.

There are two other kinds of data hazard. The situation presented in Figure 5.8(b) is called a *write after read (WAR)* data hazard. I_2 is writing a new value to a register, while I_1 is reading the old value in the same register. The situation presented in Figure 5.8(c) is called a *write after write (WAW)* data hazard. I_2 is writing a new value to a register that is also the target of a previous instruction.

This is an opportunity to amplify the relationship between hardware and software. RAW, WAR, and WAW hazards are properties of the processor pipeline. However, the occurrence of these hazards during the execution of a program depends on the intrinsic property of the program itself. The program properties that could lead to these hazards are, respectively, *flow dependence, anti dependence*, and *output dependence*.

We define these terminologies as follows:

1. A statement S2 is flow or true dependent on S1 if and only if the following two conditions are satisfied:

   - S1 precedes S2 in execution order, and
   - S1 modifies a resource read by S1.

2. A statement S2 is anti dependent on S1 if and only if the following two conditions are satisfied:

   - S1 precedes S2 in execution order, and
   - S2 modifies a resource that is read by S1.

3. A statement S2 is output dependent on S1 if and only if the following two conditions are satisfied:

- S1 precedes S2 in execution order, and

- both S1 and S2 modify the same resource.

A compiler performs data dependence analysis to identify these program properties and reorders instructions (if need be) to mitigate the ill effects of data dependencies on the pipelined processor.

These data dependencies pose no problem if the instructions execute one at a time in program order, as would happen in a nonpipelined processor. However, they could lead to problems in a pipelined processor, as explained in the next paragraph. It turns out that, for the simple pipeline which we are considering, WAR and WAW hazards do not pose much of a problem, and we will discuss solutions to deal with them later in this section. First, let us deal with the RAW hazard.

RAW hazard. Let us trace the flow of instructions represented by Equation (7) shown in Figure 5.8(a), through the pipeline:

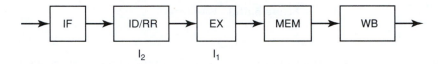

When I_1 is in the EX stage of the pipeline, I_2 is in ID/RR stage and is about to read the values in registers R1 and R5. This is problematic because I_1 has not computed the new value of R1 yet. In fact, I_1 will write the newly computed value into R1 only in the WB stage of the pipeline. If I_2 is allowed to read the value in R1, as shown in the preceding picture, it will read to an erroneous execution of the program. We refer to this situation as *semantic inconsistency*, when the intent of the programmer is different from the actual execution. Such a problem would never occur in a nonpipelined implementation, where the processor executes one instruction at a time.

The problem may not be as severe if the two instructions are not following one another.

For example, consider the following sequence:

$$I_1: R1 \longleftarrow R2 + R3$$
$$I_x: R8 \longleftarrow R6 + R7$$
$$I_2: R4 \longleftarrow R1 + R5$$

In this case, the pipeline looks as follows:

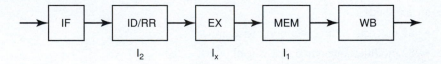

I_1 has completed execution. However, the new value for R1 will be written into the register only when I_1 reaches the WB stage. Thus, if there is a RAW hazard for any of the subsequent three instructions following I_1, it will result in a semantic inconsistency.

Example 5.11

Consider the following sequence of four instructions:

I_1: LW R1, MEM
<2 unrelated instructions>
I_4: R4 ← R1 + R5

I_4 and I_1 are separated by two unrelated instructions as shown in the preceding sequence. How many bubbles will result in the pipeline for that sequence of instructions?

Answer:

The state of the pipeline when I_4 gets to ID/RR stage is as follows:

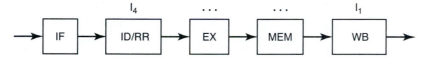

I_1 will write the value into R1 only at the end of the current cycle. Therefore, I_4 cannot read the register in this cycle and get the correct value.

Thus, there is a 1-cycle delay leading to one bubble (NOP instruction passed down from the ID/RR stage to the EX stage).

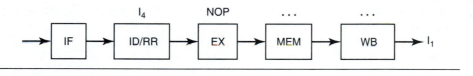

Example 5.12

I_1: R1 ← R2 + R3
I_2: R4 ← R4 + R3
I_3: R5 ← R5 + R3
I_4: R6 ← R1 + R6

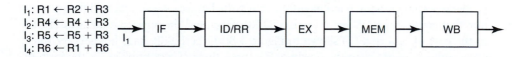

As shown, the sequence of instructions I_1 through I_4 is just about to enter the five-stage pipeline.

a. In the table that follows, show the passage of these instructions through the pipeline until all four instructions have been completed and retired from the pipeline. *Retired* from the pipeline means that the instruction is not in any of the five stages of the pipeline.

Answer:

Cycle Number	IF	ID/RR	EX	MEM	WB
1	I_1	–	–	–	–
2	I_2	I_1	–	–	–
3	I_3	I_2	I_1	–	–
4	I_4	I_3	I_2	I_1	–
5	–	I_4	I_3	I_2	I_1
6	–	I_4	NOP	I_3	I_2
7	–	–	I_4	NOP	I_3
8	–	–	–	I_4	NOP
9	–	–	–	–	I_4

b. Assuming that the program contains just these four instructions, what is the average CPI achieved for the previous execution?

Answer:

Four instructions are retired from the pipeline in nine cycles. Therefore, the average CPI experienced by these instructions is

```
Avg CPI = 9/4 = 2.25
```

Solving the RAW data hazard problem: Data forwarding. A simple solution to this problem is similar to the handling of the structural hazard. We simply stall the instruction that causes the RAW hazard in the ID/RR stage until the register value is available. In the case of Equation (7) shown in Figure 5.8(a), the ID/RR stage holds I_2 for three cycles until I_1 retires from the pipeline. For those three cycles, bubbles (in the form of NOP instructions manufactured by the ID/RR stage) are sent down the pipeline. For the same reason, the preceding stage (IF) is told to stay on the same instruction and not to fetch new instructions.

The series of pictures shown in Figure 5.9 illustrates the stalling of the pipeline due to the data hazard posed by Equation (7) in Figure 5.8(a).

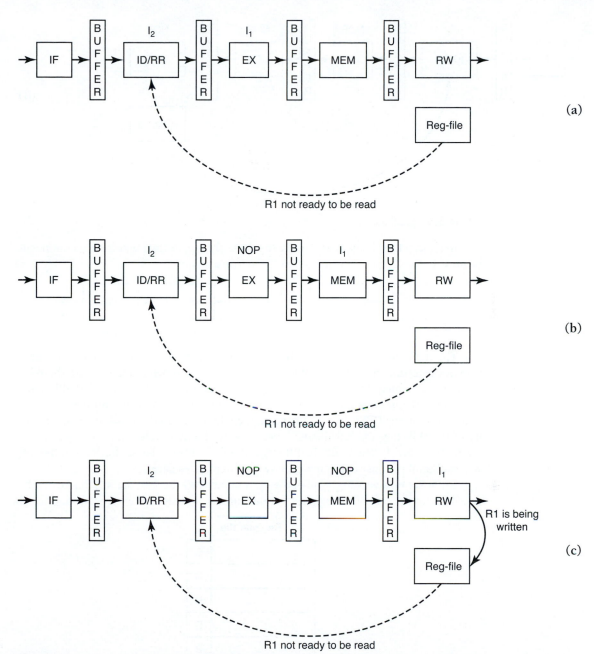

Figure 5.9 RAW hazard due to Equation (7) shown in Figure 5.8(a).

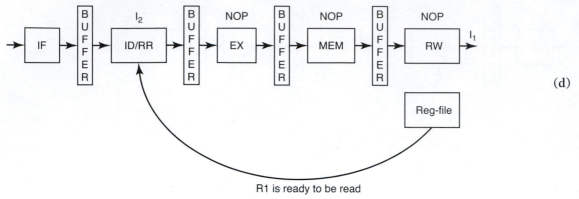

(d)

R1 is ready to be read

Figure 5.9 *(Continued)*

In the clock cycle following the next picture shown, normal pipeline execution will begin with the IF stage as it starts to fetch new instructions.

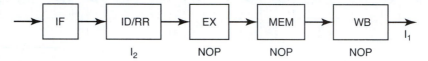

The ID/RR stage needs some hardware help to know that it has to stall. The hardware for detecting this is very simple. In the register file shown in Figure 5.10, the **B** bit is the register **busy** bit, and there is one bit per processor register. The ID/RR stage determines the destination register for an instruction and sets the appropriate B bit for that register in the DPRF. I_1 would have set the B bit for register R1. It is the responsibility of the WB stage to clear this bit when it writes the new value into the register file. Therefore, when I_2 gets to the ID/RR stage, it will find the B bit set for R1 and, hence, will stall until the busy condition goes away (three cycles later).

Let us see how we can get rid of the stalls induced by the RAW hazard. It may not be possible to get rid of stalls altogether, but the number of stalls can certainly be minimized

Register file

	B
	B
	B
	B
	B
	B
	B
	B

Figure 5.10 Register file with busy bits for each register.

Register file

	B	RP
	B	RP
	B	RP
	B	RP
	B	RP
	B	RP
	B	RP
	B	RP

Figure 5.11   Register file with busy and read-pending bits for each register.

with a little bit of hardware complexity. The original algorithm, which bears the name of its inventor, Tomasulo, made its appearance in the IBM 360/91 processor in the 1960s. The idea is quite simple. In general, a stage that generates a new value for a register looks around to see whether any other stage is awaiting this new value. If it finds one, it will *forward* the value to the stages that need it.[7]

With respect to our simple pipeline, the only stage that reads a register is the ID/RR stage. Let us examine what we need to do to enable this data forwarding. We add a bit called RP (read pending) to each of the registers in the register file (see Figure 5.11).

When an instruction hits the ID/RR stage, if the B bit is set for a register it wants to read, then it sets the RP bit for the same register. If any of the EX, MEM, or WB stages sees that the RP bit is set for a register for which it is generating a new value, it supplies the generated value to the ID/RR stage. The hardware complexity comes from the necessity of running wires from these stages back to the ID/RR stage. One might wonder, why not let these stages simply write to the register file if the RP bit is set? In principle, they could do so; however, as we said earlier, writing to the register file and clearing the B bit is the responsibility of the WB stage of the pipeline. Allowing any stage to write to the register file will increase the hardware complexity. Besides, this increased hardware complexity does not result in any performance advantage, because the instruction (in the ID/RR stage) that may need the data is getting the data via the forwarding mechanism.

Revisiting the RAW hazard shown in Figure 5.8(a), we see that data forwarding completely eliminates any bubbles, as shown in Figure 5.12.

Consider the following stream of instructions:

$$I_1$$
$$I_2$$
$$I_3$$
$$I_4$$

---

7. The solution we describe for the RAW hazard for our simple pipeline is inspired by the Tomasulo algorithm, but it is nowhere near the generality of that original algorithm.

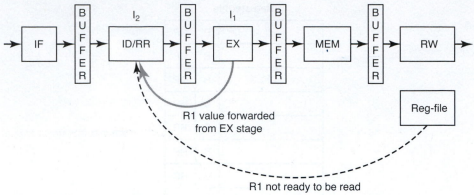

Figure 5.12   Data forwarding[8] to solve the RAW hazard shown in Figure 5.8(a).

Table 5.3 Bubbles Created in Pipeline due to RAW Hazard Shown in Figure 5.8(a)

Number of Unrelated Instructions Between I_1 and I_2	Number of Bubbles Without Forwarding	Number of Bubbles With Forwarding
0	3	0
1	2	0
2	1	0
3 or more	0	0

Here, if I_1 is an arithmetic/logic instruction that generates a new value for a register, and any of the subsequent three instructions (I_2, I_3, or I_4) need the same value, then this forwarding method will eliminate any stalls due to the RAW hazard. Table 5.3 summarizes the number of bubbles introduced in the pipeline with and without data forwarding, for the RAW hazard shown in Figure 5.8(a), as a function of the number of unrelated instructions separating I_1 and I_2 in the execution order of the program.

Example 5.13

This is the same sequence of instructions as given in Example 5.12. Assuming data forwarding, show the passage of instructions in the chart that follows. What is the average CPI experienced by these instructions?

I_1: R1 ← R2 + R3
I_2: R4 ← R4 + R3
I_3: R5 ← R5 + R3
I_4: R6 ← R1 + R6

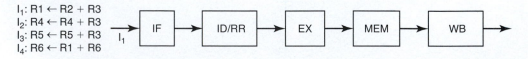

---

8. *Forwarding* seems counterintuitive, given that the arrow is going backwards! I_1 is ahead of I_2 in the execution order of the program, and it *forwards* the value it computed to I_2.

Answer:

As we see in Table 5.3, with data forwarding, there will be no more bubbles in the pipeline due to a RAW hazard posed by arithmetic and logic instructions, since there is data forwarding from every stage to the preceding stage. Thus, as can be seen in the chart, there are no more bubbles in the pipeline for the given sequence.

Cycle Number	IF	ID/RR	EX	MEM	WB
1	I_1	–	–	–	–
2	I_2	I_1	–	–	–
3	I_3	I_2	I_1	–	–
4	I_4	I_3	I_2	I_1	–
5	–	I_4	I_3	I_2	I_1
6	–	–	I_4	I_3	I_2
7	–	–	–	I_4	I_3
8	–	–	–	–	I_4

Average CPI = 8/4 = **2**.

Dealing with RAW data hazard introduced by load instructions. Load instructions introduce data hazard as well. Consider the following sequence:

$$I_1: \text{LW}\ \ \text{R1, 0(R2)}$$

$$I_2: \text{ADD}\ \ \text{R4, R1, R4} \tag{10}$$

In this case, the new value for R1 is not available until the MEM stage. Therefore, even with forwarding, a one-cycle stall is inevitable if the RAW hazard occurs in the immediately following instruction, as shown in Equation (10). Example 5.14 goes into the details of bubbles experienced due to a load instruction in the pipeline.

Example 5.14

Consider the following sequence of instructions:

I_1: LW R1, MEM
I_2: R4 ← R1 + R5

a. I_2 immediately follows I_1, as shown in the graphic. Assuming that there is register forwarding from each stage to the ID/RR stage, how many bubbles will result with the preceding execution?

b. How many bubbles will result with the preceding execution if there was no register forwarding?

Answer:

a. The state of the pipeline when I_2 gets to ID/RR stage is as follows:

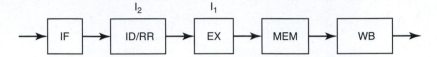

I_1 will have a value for R1 only at the end of the MEM cycle. Thus, there is a one-cycle delay leading to one bubble (NOP instruction passed down from the ID/RR stage to the EX stage), as shown:

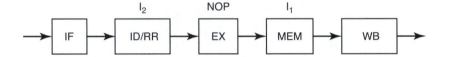

The MEM stage will simultaneously write to its output buffer (MBUF) and forward the value it read from the memory for R1 to the ID/RR stage, so that the ID/RR stage can use this value (for I_2) to write into the pipeline register (DBUF) at the output of the ID/RR stage. Thus, there is no further delay in the pipeline. This is despite the fact that I_1 writes the value into R1 only at the end of the WB stage. The following chart shows the progression of the two instructions through the pipeline:

Cycle Number	IF	ID/RR	EX	MEM	WB
1	I_1	–	–	–	–
2	I_2	I_1	–	–	–
3	–	I_2	I_1	–	–
4	–	I_2	NOP	I_1	–
5	–	–	I_2	NOP	I_1
6	–	–	–	I_2	NOP
7	–	–	–	–	I_2

So, the total number of bubbles for this execution with forwarding = **1**.

b. Without the forwarding, I_2 cannot read R1 until I_1 has written the value into R1. Writing into R1 happens at the end of the WB stage. Note that the value written into R1 is available for reading only in the following cycle. The next chart shows the progression of the two instructions through the pipeline.

Cycle Number	IF	ID/RR	EX	MEM	WB
1	I_1	–	–	–	–
2	I_2	I_1	–	–	–
3	I_3	I_2	I_1	–	–
4	I_4	I_2	NOP	I_1	–
5	–	I_2	NOP	NOP	I_1
6	–	I_2	NOP	NOP	NOP
7	–	–	I_2	NOP	NOP
8	–	–	–	I_2	NOP
9	–	–	–	–	I_2

So, the total number of bubbles for this execution without forwarding $= 3$.

Table 5.4 summarizes the number of bubbles introduced in the pipeline with and without data forwarding for a RAW hazard due to a load instruction, as a function of the number of unrelated instructions separating I_1 and I_2 in the execution order of the program.

Other types of data hazards. The other types of hazards, WAR and WAW, pose their own set of problems for the pipelined processor. However, these problems are much less severe than the RAW problem in terms of affecting pipeline processor performance. For example, WAR is not a problem at all, because the instruction that needs to read the data has already copied the register value into the pipeline buffer when it was in the ID/RR stage. For

Table 5.4 Bubbles Created in Pipeline due to Load-Instruction-Induced RAW Hazard

Number of Unrelated Instructions Between I_1 and I_2	Number of Bubbles Without Forwarding	Number of Bubbles With Forwarding
0	3	1
1	2	0
2	1	0
3 or more	0	0

the WAW problem, a simple solution would be to stall an instruction that needs to write to a register in the ID/RR stage if it finds the B bit set for the register. This instruction will be able to proceed once the preceding instruction that set the B bit clears it in the WB stage.

Let us understand the source of a WAW hazard. WAW means that a given register which was written into by one instruction is being overwritten by a subsequent instruction, with no intervening read of that register. One can safely conclude that the first write was a useless one to start with. After all, if there were a read of the register after the first write, then the ensuing RAW hazard would have overshadowed the WAW hazard. This begs the question as to why a compiler would generate code with a WAW hazard. There are several possible answers to this question. Earlier, we alluded to the program properties that lead to pipeline hazards in the first place. Flow dependencies are intrinsic to the program itself, while anti dependencies and output dependencies are induced largely by the compiler due to its aggressive use of registers to hold program variables. Recall that register accesses are faster than memory accesses; further, registers are limited in number. Thus, the compiler may reuse registers to hold program variables that could lead to anti and output dependence, which in turn lead to WAR and WAW hazards during execution in a pipelined processor. We will discuss this issue in more detail in Section 5.15.4 and present possible hardware solutions to the problem.

5.13.3 Control Hazard

This hazard refers to breaks in the sequential execution of a program due to branch instructions. Studies of the dynamic frequency of instructions in benchmark programs show that conditional branch instructions occur once in every four to six instructions. Branches cause disruption to the normal flow of control and are detrimental to pipelined processor performance. The problem is especially acute with conditional branches, because the outcome of the branch is typically not known until much later in the pipeline.

Let us assume that the stream of instructions coming into the pipeline, in program order, is as follows:

```
BEQ
ADD
NAND
LW
. . .
. . .
```

One conservative way of handling branches is to stop new instructions from entering the pipeline when the decode stage encounters a branch instruction. Once the branch is resolved, normal pipeline execution can resume, either along the sequential path of control or along the target of the branch. Figure 5.13 shows the flow of instructions for such a conservative arrangement. For a BEQ instruction, we know the outcome of the branch at the end of the EX cycle. If the *branch is not taken* (i.e., we continue along the sequential path), then the IF stage already has the right instruction, fetched from memory and ready to be passed on to the ID/RR stage. Therefore, we stall the pipeline for one cycle and continue

Cycle	IF*	ID/RR	EX	MEM	WB
1	BEQ				
2	ADD	BEQ			
3	ADD+	NOP	BEQ		
4	NAND	ADD	NOP	BEQ	
5	LW	NAND	ADD	NOP	BEQ

* We do not actually know what the instruction is in the fetch stage.

+ ADD instruction is stalled in the IF stage until the BEQ is resolved. The preceding schedule assumes that the branch was unsuccessful, allowing instructions in the sequential path to enter the IF stage once BEQ is resolved. There will be one more cycle delay to access the nonsequential path, if the branch was successful.

Figure 5.13   A conservative approach to handling branches.

with the ADD instruction, as shown in Figure 5.13. However, if the *branch is taken*, then we have to start fetching the instruction from the newly computed address of the PC, which is clocked into the PC only at the end of the EX cycle for the BEQ instruction. So, in cycle four, we will start fetching the correct next instruction from the target of the branch. Hence, there will be a two-cycle stall if the branch is taken according to the preceding scheme.

Example 5.15

Consider the following sequence of instructions:

$$
\begin{array}{ll}
& \text{BEQ} \quad \text{L1} \\
& \text{ADD} \\
& \text{LW} \\
& \text{....} \\
\text{L1} & \text{NAND} \\
& \text{SW}
\end{array}
$$

The hardware uses a conservative approach to handling branches.

a. Assuming that the branch is not taken, show the passage of instructions through the pipeline by filling in the chart that follows, until three instructions have successfully retired from the pipeline. What is the observed CPI for these three instructions?

b. Assuming that the branch is taken, show the passage of instructions through the pipeline by filling in the chart that follows, until three instructions have successfully retired from the pipeline. What is the observed CPI for these three instructions?

Answer:

a. The time chart for the given sequence when the *branch is not taken* is shown next. Note that the ADD instruction is stalled in IF stage for one cycle, until the BEQ instruction is resolved at the end of the EX stage.

Cycle Number	IF	ID/RR	EX	MEM	WB
1	BEQ	–	–	–	–
2	ADD	BEQ	–	–	–
3	ADD	NOP	BEQ	–	–
4	LW	ADD	NOP	BEQ	–
5	–	LW	ADD	NOP	BEQ
6	–	–	LW	ADD	NOP
7			–	LW	ADD
8				–	LW

The average CPI for these three instructions = 8/3 = **2.666**.

b. The time chart for the given sequence when the *branch is taken* is shown next. Note that the ADD instruction in the IF stage has to be converted into a NOP in cycle four, since the branch is taken. A new fetch has to be instantiated from the target of the branch in cycle four, thus resulting in a two-cycle stall of the pipeline.

Cycle Number	IF	ID/RR	EX	MEM	WB
1	BEQ	–	–	–	–
2	ADD	BEQ	–	–	–
3	ADD	NOP	BEQ	–	–
4	NAND	NOP	NOP	BEQ	–
5	SW	NAND	NOP	NOP	BEQ
6	–	SW	NAND	NOP	NOP
7	–	–	SW	NAND	NOP
8			–	SW	NAND
9				–	SW

The average CPI for the three instructions = 9/3 = **3**.

Of course, we can do even better if we are ready to throw some hardware at the problem. In fact, there are several different approaches to solving hiccups due to branches in pipelines. This has been a fertile area of research in the computer architecture community. Especially because modern processors may have deep pipelines (with more than 20 stages), it is extremely important to have a speedy resolution of branches in order to ensure high performance.

In this chapter, we will present a small window into the range of possibilities for solving this problem. You will have to wait to take a senior-level course in computer architecture to get a more detailed treatment of this subject.

Dealing with branches in the pipelined processor. Delayed branch and branch prediction are two approaches to dealing with this problem in a pipelined processor.

1. **Delayed branch:** The idea here is to assume that the instruction following the branch executes, irrespective of the outcome of the branch. This simplifies the hardware since there is no need to terminate the instruction that immediately follows the branch instruction. The responsibility of ensuring the semantic correctness underlying this assumption shifts to the compiler from the hardware. The default is to stash a NOP instruction in software (i.e., in the memory image of the program) following a branch. You may question the usefulness of this approach. The answer is that a smart compiler will do a program analysis and find a useful instruction that does not affect the program semantics to take the place of the NOP instruction. The instruction slot that immediately follows the branch is called a **delay slot**. Correspondingly, this technique is called **delayed branch**.

   The code fragments shown in Figures 5.14 and 5.15 illustrate how a compiler may find useful instructions to stick into delay slots. In this example, every time there is branch instruction, the instruction that immediately follows the branch is

```
;       Code before optimization to fill branch delay slots
;       Add 7 to each element of a ten-element array
;       whose address is in a0
addi   t1,  a0, 40              ; When a0=t1 we are done
loop:  beq  a0, t1, done
       nop                      ; branch delay slot        [1]
       lw   t0, 0(a0)                                       [2]
       addi t0, t0, 7
       sw   t0, 0(a0)
       addi a0, a0, 4                                       [3]
       beq  zero, zero, loop
       nop                      ; branch delay slot        [4]
done:  halt
```

Figure 5.14 Delayed branch: Delay slots with NOPs.

```
;       Code after optimization to fill branch delay slots
;       Add 7 to each element of a ten-element array
;       whose address is in a0
addi  t1,  a0, 40                        ; When a0=t1 we are done
loop: beq  a0, t1, done
      lw   t0, 0(a0)                     ; branch delay slot        [2]
      addi t0, t0, 7
      sw   t0, 0(a0)
      beq  zero, zero, loop
      addi a0, a0, 4                     ; branch delay slot        [3]
done: halt
```

Figure 5.15   Delayed branch: NOPs in delay slots replaced with useful instructions.

executed, regardless of the outcome of the branch. If the branch is unsuccessful, the pipeline continues without a hiccup. If the branch is successful, then (as in the case of branch misprediction) the instructions following the branch, except for the immediate next one, are terminated.

With reference to Figure 5.14, the compiler knows that the instructions labeled [1] and [4] are always executed. Therefore, the compiler initially sticks NOP instructions as placeholders in those slots. During the optimization phase, the compiler recognizes that instruction [2] is benign[9] from the point of view of the program semantics, since it simply loads a value into a temporary register. Therefore, the compiler replaces the NOP instruction [1] by the load instruction [2] in Figure 5.15. Similarly, the last branch instruction in the loop is an unconditional branch, which is independent of the preceding ADD instruction [3]. Therefore, the compiler replaces the NOP instruction [4] by the ADD instruction [3] in Figure 5.15.

Some machines may use even multiple delay slots to increase pipeline efficiency when branch penalties are high. The greater the number of delay slots, the lesser will be the number of instructions that need terminating upon a successful branch. However, this increases the burden on the compiler to find useful instructions to fill in the delay slot, which may not always be possible.

Delayed branch seems like a reasonable idea, especially for shallow pipelines (fewer than 10 stages), since it simplifies the hardware. However, there are several issues with this idea. The most glaring problem is that it exposes the details of the microarchitecture to the compiler writer, thus making a compiler not just ISA-specific, but processor-implementation specific. Either it necessitates rewriting parts of the compiler for each generation of the processor, or it limits evolution of the microarchitecture for

---

9. This is for illustration of the concept of the delayed branch. Strictly speaking, executing the load instruction after the loop has terminated may access a memory location that is nonexistent.

Cycle	IF*	ID/RR	EX	MEM	WB
1	BEQ				
2	ADD	BEQ			
3	NAND	ADD	BEQ		
4	LW	NAND	ADD	BEQ	
5	...	LW	NAND	ADD	BEQ

* We do not actually know what the instruction is in the fetch stage.

Figure 5.16 Branch prediction.

reasons of backward compatibility. Further, modern processors use deep pipelining. For example, the recent Intel Pentium line of processors has pipeline stages in excess of 20. Whereas the pipelines have gotten deeper, the sizes of basic blocks in the program that determine the frequency of branches have not changed. If anything, the branches have become more frequent with object-oriented programming. Therefore, delayed branch has fallen out of favor in modern processor implementation.

2. **Branch prediction:** The idea here is to assume the outcome of the branch to be one way and to start letting instructions into the pipeline, even upon detection of a branch. For example, for the same sequence shown in Figure 5.13, let us predict that the outcome is negative (i.e., the sequential path is the winner). Figure 5.16 shows the flow of instructions in the pipeline with this prediction. As soon as the outcome is known (when BEQ is in the EX stage), the result is fed back to the preceding stages. Figure 5.16 shows the happy state when the outcome is as predicted. The pipeline can continue without a hiccup.

   Of course, there are chances of misprediction, and we need to be able to recover from such mispredictions. Therefore, we need a hardware capability to terminate the instructions that are in partial execution in the preceding stages of the pipeline and to start fetching from the alternate path. This termination capability is often referred to as *flushing*. Another feedback line labeled "flush," shown pictorially in Figure 5.17, implements this hardware capability. Upon receiving this flush signal, both the IF and ID/RR stages abandon the partial execution of the instructions that

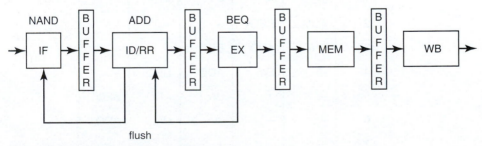

flush

Figure 5.17 Pipeline with flush control lines.

they are currently dealing with and start sending bubbles down the pipeline. There will be two bubbles (i.e., a two-cycle stall), corresponding to the ADD and NAND instructions in Figure 5.17, before normal execution can begin.

Example 5.16

Consider the following sequence of instructions:

```
            BEQ    L1
            ADD
            LW

            ....

L1          NAND
            SW
```

The hardware uses branch prediction (branch will not be taken).

a. Assuming that the prediction turns out to be true, show the passage of these instructions through the pipeline by filling in the chart that follows until three instructions have successfully retired from the pipeline. What is the observed CPI for these three instructions?

b. Assuming that the prediction turns out to be false, show the passage of these instructions through the pipeline by filling in the chart that follows until three instructions have successfully retired from the pipeline. What is the observed CPI for these three instructions?

Answer:

a. The time chart for the given sequence, when the prediction is true, is shown next. The branch prediction logic starts feeding the instructions from the sequential path into the pipeline, and they all complete successfully.

Cycle Number	IF	ID/RR	EX	MEM	WB
1	BEQ	–	–	–	–
2	ADD	BEQ	–	–	–
3	LW	ADD	BEQ	–	–
4	–	LW	ADD	BEQ	–
5	–	–	LW	ADD	BEQ
6	–	–	–	LW	ADD
7	–	–	–	–	LW

At the end of seven cycles, three instructions complete execution, yielding an average CPI of $7/3 = $ **2.333**.

b. The time chart for the given sequence, when the prediction turns out to be false, is shown next. Note that the ADD and LW instructions are flushed in their respective stages as soon as the BEQ determines that the outcome of the branch has been mispredicted. This is why, in cycle four, ADD and LW have been replaced by NOPs for the successive stages. The PC is set at the end of the EX cycle by the BEQ instruction (cycle three), in readiness to start fetching the correct instruction from the target of the branch in cycle four.

Cycle Number	IF	ID/RR	EX	MEM	WB
1	BEQ	–	–	–	–
2	ADD	BEQ	–	–	–
3	LW	ADD	BEQ	–	–
4	NAND	NOP	NOP	BEQ	–
5	SW	NAND	NOP	NOP	BEQ
6	–	SW	NAND	NOP	NOP
7	–	–	SW	NAND	NOP
8			–	SW	NAND
9				–	SW

The average CPI for the three instructions $= 9/3 = $ **3**.

Note that this value for average CPI is the same as the one we obtained earlier, with no branch prediction and the branch taken.

You may be wondering how we can predict the outcome of a branch, since on the surface the odds seem evenly split between taking and not taking. However, programs have a lot more structure that aids prediction. For example, consider a loop. This usually consists of a series of instructions; at the end of the loop, a conditional branch takes control back to the top of the loop or out of the loop. We can immediately see that the outcome of this conditional branch is heavily biased toward going back to the top of the loop. Thus, the branch prediction technique relies on such structural properties of programs.

There has been considerable research invested in understanding the properties of branches that occur in programs and designing prediction schemes to support them. As we already mentioned, loops and conditional statements are the high-level constructs that lead to conditional branch instructions. One strategy for

Address of branch instruction	Taken/not taken	Address of target of branch instruction

Figure 5.18 An entry in the branch target buffer.

branch prediction is to predict that the branch is likely to be taken if the target address is *lower* than the current PC value. The flip side of this statement is that if the target address is *higher* than the current PC value, then the prediction is that the branch will not be taken. The motivation behind this strategy is that loops usually involve a backward branch to the top of the loop (i.e., to a lower address), and there is a higher likelihood of this happening since loops are executed multiple times. On the other hand, forward branches are usually associated with conditional statements, and they are less likely to be taken.

Branch prediction is in the purview of the compiler and is performed on the basis of program analysis. The ISA has to support the compiler by providing a mechanism for conveying the prediction to the hardware. To this end, modern processors include two versions of many, if not all, branch instructions, the difference being a prediction on whether the branch will be taken or not. The compiler will choose the version of a given branch instruction that best meets its need.

3. **Branch prediction with branch target buffer:** This builds on branch prediction that we mentioned earlier. It uses a hardware device called the *branch target buffer* (*BTB*)[10] to improve the prediction of branches. The BTB is essentially a table in which every entry contains three fields, as shown in Figure 5.18.

The BTB records the history of the branches encountered for a particular program during execution. The BTB may have some small number of entries (say, 100). Every time a branch instruction is encountered, the BTB is looked up by the hardware. Let us assume that the PC value of this branch instruction is not present in the BTB (because this is the first encounter). In that case, once the branch outcome is determined, a new BTB entry with the address of this branch instruction, the target address of the branch, and the direction of the branch (taken/not taken) is created. The next time that the same branch instruction is encountered, this history information helps in predicting the outcome of the branch. The BTB is looked up in the IF stage. Thus, if the lookup is successful (i.e., the BTB contains the address of the branch instruction currently being fetched and sent down the pipeline), then the IF stage starts fetching the target of the branch immediately. In this case, there will be no bubbles in the pipeline due to the branch instruction. Of course, there could be mispredictions. Typically, such mispredictions occur due to a branch instruction that is executed in either the first or the last iteration of a loop. The flush line in the datapath takes care of such mispredictions. We can make the history mechanism more robust by providing more than one bit of history.

---

10. We already introduced the idea of caches in Section 5.11. Chapter 9 contains a detailed discussion of caches. The BTB is essentially a cache of branch target addresses matched to addresses of branch instructions. The hardware needed to realize a BTB is similar to what would be found in a cache.

Summary of dealing with branches in a pipelined processor. Implementation detail of an ISA is commonly referred to as the *microarchitecture* of the processor. Dealing with branches in the microarchitecture is a key to achieving high performance, especially with the increased depth of the pipelines in modern processors. We already mentioned that the frequency of branches in compiled code could be as high as one in every three or four instructions. Thus, with a pipeline that has 20 stages, the instructions in partial execution in the various stages of the pipe are unlikely to be sequential instructions. Therefore, taking early decisions on the possible outcome of branches so that the pipeline can be filled with useful instructions is a key to achieving high performance in deeply pipelined processors. We will discuss the state of the art in pipelined processor design in Section 5.15. Table 5.5. summarizes the various techniques which we have discussed in this chapter for dealing with branches and processors that have used these techniques.

5.13.4 Summary of Hazards

We discussed structural, data, and control hazards and the most basic mechanisms for dealing with them in the microarchitecture. We presented mostly hardware assists for detecting and overcoming such hazards. When hazards are detected and enforced by the hardware, it is often referred to in the literature as *hardware interlocks*. However, it is perfectly feasible to shift this burden to the software, namely, the compiler. The trick is to expose the details of the microarchitecture to the compiler such that the compiler writer can ensure that either (a) these hazards are eliminated in the code as part of program optimization, or (b) by inserting NOPs into the code explicitly to overcome such hazards. For example, with the five-stage pipeline that we have been discussing, if the compiler always ensures that a register being written to is not used by at least the following three instructions, then there will be no RAW hazard. This can be done by either placing other useful instructions between the definition of a value and its subsequent use, or, in the absence of such useful instructions, by placing explicit NOP instructions.

The advantage of shifting the burden to the compiler is that the hardware is simplified, since it neither has to do hazard detection nor must incorporate techniques such as data forwarding. Early versions of the MIPS architecture eliminated hardware interlocks and depended on the compiler to resolve all such hazards. However, the problem is that it is not always possible to know such dependencies at compile time. For example, a load instruction may take more than two cycles to fetch the data, depending on the state of the memory system. The problem gets worse with deeper pipelines. Therefore, all modern processors use hardware interlocks to eliminate hazards. In the spirit of the partnership between hardware and software, the chip vendors publish the details of the microarchitecture to aid the compiler writer in using such details in writing efficient optimizers. Some microarchitectures even go one step further. Very large instruction word (VLIW) microarchitectures are designed in concert with the compiler; thus, the two are equal partners in determining the performance of the processor.

Table 5.6 summarizes the LC-2200 instructions that can cause potential stalls in the pipeline and the extent to which such stalls can be overcome with hardware solutions.

Table 5.5 Summary of Techniques for Handling Branches

Name	Pros	Cons	Use Cases
Stall the pipeline	Simple strategy, no hardware needed for flushing instructions	Loss of performance	Early pipelined machines such as IBM 360 series
Branch prediction (branch not taken)	Results in good performance with small additional hardware, since the instruction is being fetched from the sequential path already in IF stage	Needs ability to flush instructions in partial execution in the pipeline	Most modern processors, such as Intel Pentium, AMD Athlon, and PowerPC, use this technique. Typically, they also employ sophisticated branch target buffers; MIPS R4000 uses a combination one-delay slot plus a two-cycle branch-not-taken prediction.
Branch prediction (branch taken)	Results in good performance, but requires slightly more elaborate hardware design	Since the new PC value that points to the target of the branch is not available until the branch instruction is in the EX stage, this technique requires more elaborate hardware assists in order to be practical.	-
Delayed branch	No need for any additional hardware for either stalling or flushing instructions; it involves the compiler by exposing the pipeline delay slots and takes its help to achieve good performance.	With increase in depth of pipelines of modern processors, it becomes increasingly difficult to fill the delay slots by the compiler; limits microarchitecture evolution due to backward-compatibility restrictions; it makes the compiler not just ISA specific, but implementation specific.	Older RISC architectures such as MIPS, PA-RISC, SPARC

Table 5.6 Summary of Hazards in the LC-2200

Instruction	Type of Hazard	Potential Stalls	With Data Forwarding	With Branch Prediction (Branch Not Taken)
ADD, NAND	Data	0, 1, 2, or 3	0	Not Applicable
LW	Data	0, 1, 2, or 3	0 or 1	Not Applicable
BEQ	Control	1 or 2	Not Applicable	0 (success) or 2 (mispredict)

5.14 Dealing with Program Discontinuities in a Pipelined Processor

Earlier, when we discussed interrupts, we mentioned that we wait for the FSM to be in a clean state to entertain interrupts. In a nonpipelined processor, instruction completion offers such a clean state. In a pipelined processor, because several instructions are in flight (i.e., under partial execution) at any point in time, it is difficult to define such a clean state. This complicates dealing with interrupts and other sources of program discontinuities, such as exceptions and traps.

There is one of two possibilities for dealing with interrupts. One possibility is that, as soon as an external interrupt arrives, the processor can

1. stop sending new instructions into the pipeline (i.e., the logic in the IF stage starts manufacturing NOP instructions to send down the pipeline);

2. wait until the instructions that are in partial execution complete their execution (i.e., *drain* the pipe); and

3. go to the interrupt state, as we discussed in Chapter 4, and do what is needed to be done as detailed there. (See Example 5.17.)

The downside to draining the pipe is that the response time to external interrupts can be quite slow, especially with deep pipelining, as is the case with modern processors. The other possibility is to *flush* the pipeline. As soon as an interrupt arrives, send a signal to all the stages to abandon their respective instructions. This allows the processor to switch to the interrupt state immediately. Of course, in this case, the memory address of the last completed instruction will be used to record, in the PC, the address where the program needs to resume after interrupt servicing. There are subtle issues with implementing such a scheme, to ensure that no permanent program state has been changed (e.g., register values) by any instruction that was in partial execution in any of the pipeline stages.

In reality, processors do not use either of these two extremes. Interrupts are caught by a specific stage of the pipe. The program execution will restart at the instruction at that stage. The stages ahead are allowed to complete while the preceding stages are flushed. In each of these cases, one interesting question that comes up is, "What should happen implicitly in hardware to support interrupts in a pipelined processor?" The pipeline registers are part of the internal state of the processor. Each of the aforementioned approaches gets the processor to a clean state, so we have to worry only about saving a single value of the PC for the correct resumption of the interrupted program. The value of the PC to be saved depends on the approach chosen.

If we want to be simplistic and drain the pipe before going to the INT macro state (see Chapter 4), then it would be sufficient to freeze the PC value pointing to the next instruction in program order in the IF stage. Upon an interrupt, the hardware would communicate this PC value to the INT macro state for saving.

Example 5.17

Enumerate the steps taken in hardware from the time an interrupt occurs to the time the processor starts executing the handler code in a pipelined processor. Assume that the pipeline is drained upon an interrupt. (An English description is sufficient.)

Answer:

1. Allow instructions already in the pipeline (useful instructions) to complete execution.
2. Stop fetching new instructions.
3. Start sending NOPs from the fetch stage into the pipeline.
4. Once all the useful instructions have completed execution, record the address where the program needs to be resumed in the PC. (This will be the memory address of the last completed useful instruction plus 1).
5. The next three steps are interrupt state actions that we covered in Chapter 4.
6. Go to the INT state; sent INTA; receive vector; and disable interrupts.
7. Save the current mode in the system stack; change the mode to kernel mode.
8. Store the PC in $k0; retrieve the handler address by using vector; load the PC; and resume pipeline execution.

Flushing the instructions (either fully or partially) would require carrying the PC value of each instruction in the pipeline register, since we do not know when an external interrupt may occur.[11] Actually, carrying the PC value with each instruction is a necessity in a pipelined processor, because any instruction may cause an exception/trap. We need the PC value of the trapping instruction to enable program resumption at the point of trap/exception. Upon an interrupt, the hardware communicates the PC value of the first incomplete instruction (i.e., the instruction from which the program has to be resumed) to the INT macro state for saving. For example, if the interrupt is caught by the EX stage of the pipe, then the current instructions in the MEM and WB stages are

---

11. Recall that, in the earlier discussion of the pipeline registers, we mentioned that only the passage of the BEQ instruction needs the PC value to be carried with it.

allowed to complete, and the PC value corresponding to the instruction in the EX stage of the pipeline is the point of program resumption.

Example 5.18

A pipelined implementation of the LC-2200 allows interrupts to be caught in the EX stage of the five-stage pipeline, draining the instructions preceding it, and flushing the ones after it. Assume that there is register forwarding to address RAW hazards. Consider the following program:

```
Address
100    LW     R1, MEM[2000];    /* assume MEM[2000] contains
                                    value 2 */
101    LW     R2, MEM[2002];    /* assume MEM[2002] contains
                                    value 5 */
102    NOP                 ;    /* NOP for LW R2 */
103    ADD    R3, R1, R2;       /* addition R3 ← R1+R2 */
104    SW     R3, MEM[2004];    /* Store R3 into MEM[2004]
105    LW     R1, MEM[2006];    /* assume MEM[2006] contains
                                    value 3 */
```

An interrupt occurs when the NOP (at address 102) is in the MEM stage of the pipeline. Answer the following questions:

a. What are the values in R1, R2, R3, MEM[2000], MEM[2002], MEM[2004], and MEM[2006], when the INT state is entered?

b. What is the PC value passed to the INT state?

Answer:

When the interrupt occurs, the state of the pipeline is as follows:

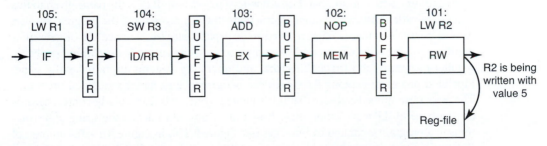

Therefore, instructions ahead of the EX stage (namely, MEM and RW) will complete, and the ones in the ID/RR and IF stages will be flushed. The program will restart execution at address `103: ADD R3, R1, R2`

a. R1 = 2; R2 = 5;
   R3 = unknown (since ADD instruction has been aborted due to the interrupt)

MEM[2000] = 2; MEM[2002] = 5;
MEM[2004] = unknown; (since ADD instruction has been aborted due to the interrupt)
MEM[2006] = 3

b. The PC value passed to the INT state is the address of the ADD instruction, namely, 103, which is where the program will resume after the interrupt service.

The preceding discussion concerns the program discontinuity that results upon an external interrupt. With traps and exceptions, we have no choice but to complete (i.e., drain) the preceding instructions, flush the succeeding instructions, and go to the INT state, passing the PC value of the instruction that caused the trap/exception.

5.15 Advanced Topics in Processor Design

Pipelined processor design had its beginnings in the era of high-performance mainframes and vector processors of the 1960s and 1970s. Many of the concepts invented in that era are still relevant in modern processor design. In this section, we will review some advanced concepts in processor design, including the state of the art in pipelined processor design.

5.15.1 Instruction-Level Parallelism

The beauty of pipelined processing is that it does not conceptually change the *sequential programming model*. That is, as far as the programmer is concerned, there is no perceived difference between the simple implementation of the processor presented in Chapter 3 and the pipelined implementation in this chapter. The instructions of the program *appear to execute* in exactly the same order as written by the programmer. The order in which instructions appear in the original program is called *program order*. A pipelined processor shrinks the execution time of the program by recognizing that adjacent instructions of the program are independent of each other and, therefore, their executions may be overlapped in time with one another. *Instruction-level parallelism (ILP)* is the name given to this potential overlap that exists among instructions. ILP is a property of the program and is a type of parallelism that is often referred to as *implicit parallelism*, since the original program is sequential. In Chapter 12, we will discuss techniques for developing explicitly parallel programs, and the architectural and operating systems support for the same. Pipelined processor exploits ILP to achieve performance gains for sequential programs. The reader can immediately see that ILP is limited by hazards. Particularly, control hazards are the bane of ILP exploitation. *Basic block* is a term used to define the string of instructions in a program separated by branches (see Figure 5.19). In Figure 5.19, the amount of ILP available for the first basic block is 4, and that for the second basic block is 3. The actual parallelism exploitable by the pipelined processor is limited further by other kinds of hazards (data and structural) that we discussed in this chapter.

We have only scratched the surface of the deep technical issues in processor design and implementation. For example, we presented very basic mechanisms for avoiding conflicts in shared resource requirements (such as register file and ALU) across stages of

```
BEQ  ⎫
LD   ⎪
LD   ⎬  Basic block, size = 4
ADD  ⎪
ADDI ⎭

BEQ  ⎫
LD   ⎪
NAND ⎬  Basic block, size = 3
ST   ⎪
BEQ  ⎭
```

Figure 5.19 Basic blocks and ILP.

the pipeline, so that the available ILP becomes fully exploitable by the processor implementation. Further, we also discussed simple mechanisms for overcoming control hazards so that ILP across multiple basic blocks becomes available for exploitation by the processor. Multiple-issue processors that have become industry standards pose a number of challenges to the architect.

5.15.2 Deeper Pipelines

The depth of pipelines in modern processors is much more than 5. For example, the Intel Pentium 4 has in excess of 20 pipeline stages. However, since the frequency of branches in compiled code can be quite high, the size of typical basic blocks may be quite small (in the range of 3 to 7). Therefore, it is imperative that clever techniques be invented to exploit ILP across basic blocks in order to make pipelined implementation worthwhile. The field of microarchitecture, which includes the myriad ways to improve the performance of the processor, is both fascinating and ever evolving. In Chapter 3, we mentioned *multiple issue* processors, with Superscalar and VLIW being specific instances of such processors. *Instruction issue* is the act of sending an instruction for execution through the processor pipeline. In the simple five-stage pipeline that we have considered thus far, exactly one in-struction is issued in every clock cycle. As the name suggests, multiple-issue processors *issue* multiple instructions in the same clock cycle. As a first order of approximation, let us assume that the hardware and/or the compiler would have ensured that the set of instruc-tions being issued in the same clock cycle do not have any of the hazards we discussed ear-lier, so that they can execute independently. Correspondingly, the processors have *multiple decode* units and *multiple functional units* (e.g., integer arithmetic unit, floating point arith-metic unit, load/store unit, etc.) to cater to the different needs of the instructions being issued in the same clock cycle (see Figure 5.20). The fetch unit would bring in multiple instructions from memory, to take advantage of the multiple decode units. A decode unit should be able to dispatch the decoded instruction to any of the functional units.

The effective throughput of such processors approaches the product of the depth of the pipelining and the degree of superscalarity of the processor. In other words, modern processors not only have deep pipelines, but also have several such pipelines executing in parallel. Deep pipelining and superscalarity introduce a number of interesting chal-lenges to both the architect and the developers of system software (in particular, com-piler writers).

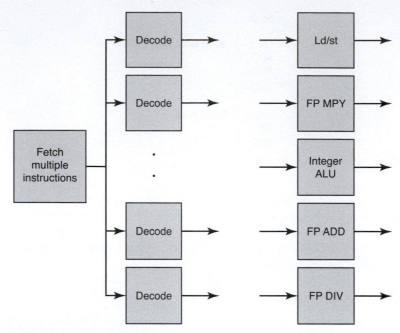

Figure 5.20   Multiple-issue processor pipeline.

You may be wondering about the necessity for deep pipelining. There are several reasons for adopting deep pipelining:

- **Relative increase in time to access storage:** In Chapter 3, we introduced the components of delays in a datapath. As feature sizes of transistors on the chip keep shrinking, wire delays (i.e., the cost of ferrying bits among the datapath elements), rather than logic operations, become the limiting factor for deciding the clock cycle time. However, the time to pull values out of registers and caches (which we will discuss in detail in Chapter 9) is still much greater than either the logic delays or the wire delays. Thus, with faster clock cycle times, it may become necessary to allow multiple cycles for the purpose of reading values out of caches. This increases the complexity to the unit that expects a value from the cache for performing its task, and increases the overall complexity of the processor. Breaking up the need for multiple cycles to carry out a specific operation into multiple stages is one way of dealing with the complexity.

- **Microcode ROM access:** In Chapter 3, we introduced the concept of microprogrammed implementation of instructions. Although this technique has its pitfalls, pipelined processors may still use it for implementing some selected complex instructions in the ISA. Accessing the microcode ROM could add a stage to the depth of the pipeline.

- **Multiple functional units:** Modern processors include both integer and floating-point arithmetic operations in their ISA. Typically, the microarchitecture includes specialized functional units for performing floating-point add, multiply, and division that are distinct from the integer ALU. The EX unit of the simple five-stage pipeline gets replaced by this collection of functional units (see Figure 5.20). There may be an additional stage to help schedule these multiple functional units.

- **Dedicated floating-point pipelines:** Floating-point instructions require more time to execute than their integer counterparts. With a simple five-stage pipeline, the slowest functional unit will dictate the clock cycle time. Therefore, it is natural to pipeline the functional units themselves so that we end up with a structure like the one shown in Figure 5.21, with different pipeline depth for different functional units. This differential pipelining facilitates supporting multiple outstanding long-latency operations (such as floating-point ADD), without stalling the pipeline due to structural hazards.

- **Out-of-order execution and reorder buffer:** Recall that the pipelined processor should preserve the appearance of a sequential execution of the program (i.e., the program order), despite the exploitation of ILP. With the potential for different instructions taking different paths through the pipeline, there is a complication in maintaining this appearance of sequentiality. For this reason, modern processors distinguish between *issue order* and *completion order*. The fetch unit issues the instructions *in order*. However, the instructions may execute and complete *out of order*, due to the different depths of the different pipelines and for other reasons (such as awaiting operands for executing the instruction). It turns out that this is fine so long as the instructions are *retired* from the processor in program order. In

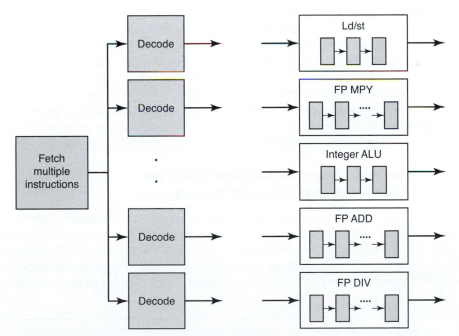

Figure 5.21   Different depths of pipelining for different functional units.

other words, an instruction is *not retired* from the processor, even though it has *completed execution,* until all the instructions preceding it in program order have also completed execution. To ensure this property, modern processors add additional logic that may be another stage in the pipeline. Specifically, the pipeline includes a *reorder buffer* (ROB) whose job it is to retire the completed instructions in program order. ROB ensures that the effect of an instruction completion (e.g., writing to an architecture-visible register, reading from or writing to memory, etc.) is not *committed* until all its predecessor instructions in program order have been committed. It does this by recording the program order of instructions at issue time and buffering addresses and data that need to be transmitted to the architecture-visible registers and memory. Reading from a register in the presence of a ROB respects the RAW dependency, as already discussed in Section 5.13.2.

• **Register renaming:** Earlier, we mentioned the program dependencies, in particular, anti and output dependencies caused primarily by the aggressive reuse of registers by the compiler (see Section 5.13.2). This in turn manifests as WAR and WAW hazards in a pipelined processor. To overcome these hazards, modern processors have several more physical registers than the architecture-visible general-purpose registers. The processor may use an additional stage to detect resource conflicts and take actions to disambiguate the usage of registers by a technique referred to as *register renaming.*[12] Register renaming is a one-level indirection between the architectural register named in an instruction and the actual physical register to be used by this instruction. We will discuss this in more detail later in this section, after introducing the Tomasulo algorithm.

• **Hardware-based speculation:** To overcome control hazards and fully exploit the multiple-issue capability, many modern processors use *hardware-based speculation,* an idea that extends branch prediction. The idea is to execute instructions in different basic blocks without waiting for the resolution of the branches and have mechanisms in place to *undo* the effects of the instructions that were executed incorrectly, due to the speculation, once the branches are resolved. Both ROB and register renaming (in hardware) help hardware-based speculation because the information in the physical registers or ROB, used in the speculation, can be discarded later when it is determined that the effects of a speculated instruction should not be committed.

5.15.3 Revisiting Program Discontinuities in the Presence of Out-Of-Order Processing

In Section 5.14, we discussed simple mechanisms for dealing with interrupts in a pipelined processor. Let's see the ramifications of handling interrupts in the presence of out-of-order processing. Several early processors, such as the CDC 6600 and the IBM 360/91, used out-of-order execution of instructions to overcome pipeline stalls due to data hazards and structural hazards. The basic idea is to issue instructions in order, but let the instructions

---

12. Note that register renaming could be done by the compiler as well, upon detection of data hazards, as part of program optimization, in which case such an extra stage would not be needed in the pipeline.

start their executions as soon as their source operands are available. This out-of-order execution, coupled with the fact that different instructions incur different execution time latencies, leads to instructions that could complete execution out of order and retire from the pipeline. That is, they not only complete execution, but also update processor state (architecture-visible registers and/or memory). Is this a problem? It would appear that it should not be, since these early pipelined processors did respect the program order at issue time, did honor the data dependencies among instructions, and never executed any instructions speculatively. External interrupts should not pose a problem with out-of-order processing, because we could adopt a very simple solution, namely, to stop issuing new instructions and to allow all the issued instructions to complete before taking the interrupt.

Exceptions and traps, however, do pose a problem, since some instructions that are subsequent to the one causing the exception could have completed their execution. This situation is defined as *imprecise exception,* to signify that the processor state, at the time that the exception happens, is not the same as it would have been in a purely sequential execution of the program. These early pipelined processors restored the precise exception state, either by software (i.e., in the exception handling routines) or by hardware techniques for the early detection of exceptions in long-latency operations (such as floating-point instructions).

As we saw in the previous subsection, modern processors retire the instructions in program order despite the out-of-order execution. This automatically eliminates the possibility of imprecise exception. Potential exceptions are buffered in the reorder buffer and will manifest strictly in program order.

Detailed discussion of interrupts in a pipelined processor is outside the scope of this book. The interested reader may want to refer to advanced textbooks on computer architecture [Hennessy, 2006].

5.15.4 Managing Shared Resources

With multiple functional units, managing the shared resources (such as register files) becomes even more challenging. One technique, popularized by the CDC 6600, is *scoreboard*, a mechanism for dealing with the different kinds of data hazards we discussed earlier in this chapter. The basic idea is to have a central facility, namely, a scoreboard that records the resources in use by an instruction at the time it enters the pipeline. A decision to either progress through the pipeline or stall an instruction depends on the current resource needs of that instruction. For example, if there is a RAW hazard, then the instruction that needs to read a register that is being currently written into by a preceding instruction is stalled until the scoreboard indicates that the register is available (which will be as soon as the preceding instruction completes writing into the register). Thus, the scoreboard keeps track of the resource needs of all the instructions in flight through the pipeline. Note that the busy bit and read-pending bit associated with individual registers of the register file (Section 5.13.2) implement such a scoreboard for the simple five-stage pipeline.

Robert Tomasulo of IBM came up with a clever algorithm (named after him), which is a distributed solution to the same resource-sharing and allocation problem in a pipelined processor. This solution was first used in the IBM 360/91, one of the earliest computers (in the 1960s) to incorporate principles of pipelining in its implementation. The basic idea is to associate storage (in the form of local registers) with each functional unit. At the time of instruction issue, the needed register values are transferred to these local registers,[13] thus avoiding the WAR hazard. If the register values are unavailable (due to RAW hazard), then the local registers remember the unit from which they should expect to get the value. Upon completing an instruction, a functional unit sends the new register value on a *common data bus (CDB)* to the register file. Other functional units (there could be more than one) that are waiting for this value grab it from the bus and start executing their respective instructions. Since the register file also works the same as any other functional unit, it remembers the peer unit that is generating a value for a given register, thus avoiding the WAW hazard. In this manner, the distributed solution avoids all the potential data hazards that we have discussed so far.

The core idea in the Tomasulo algorithm is the use of local registers that act as surrogates to the architecture-visible registers. Modern processors use this idea by consolidating all the distributed storage used in the Tomasulo algorithm into one large physical register file on the chip. The register renaming technique that we mentioned earlier creates a dynamic mapping between an architecture-visible register and a physical register at the time of instruction issue. For example, if register R1 is the architecture-visible source register for a store instruction, and the actual physical register assigned is, say, P12, then the value of R1 is transferred into P12 in the register-renaming stage. Thus, the register-renaming stage of the pipeline is responsible for the dynamic allocation of physical registers to the instructions. Essentially, register renaming removes the WAR and WAW data hazards. We already discussed, in Section 5.13.2, how data forwarding solves the RAW hazard in a pipelined processor. So, register renaming, combined with data forwarding, addresses all the data hazards in modern processors. The pipeline stage that is responsible for register renaming keeps track of which physical registers are in use at any point in time, and when they get freed (not unlike the scoreboarding technique of the CDC 6600) upon the retirement of an instruction.

The role of the reorder buffer (ROB) is to ensure that instructions retire in program order. The role of register renaming is to remove data hazards, as well as to support hardware-based speculative execution. Some processors eliminate the ROB altogether and incorporate its primary functionality (namely, retiring instructions in program order) into the register renaming mechanism itself.

Let us revisit WAW hazard. We saw that the techniques (such as scoreboarding and applying the Tomasulo algorithm) used in the early pipelined machines and the techniques (such as register renaming and ROB) now being used in modern processors eliminate WAW, despite the out-of-order execution of instructions. Does speculative execution lead to WAW hazard? The answer is no because, despite the speculation, the instructions are retired in program order. Any incorrect write to a register due to a mispredicted branch would have been removed from the ROB without being committed to any architecture-visible register.

---

13. These local registers in the Tomasulo algorithm perform the same function as the large physical register file in modern processors that support register renaming.

Despite multiple-issue processors, speculation, and out-of-order processing, the original question that we raised in Section 5.13.2 remains, namely, why would a compiler generate code with a WAW hazard? The answer lies in the fact that a compiler may have generated the first write to fill a delay slot (if the microarchitecture was using delayed branches) and the program took an unexpected branch wherein this first write was irrelevant. However, the out-of-order nature of the pipeline could mean that the second useful write may finish before the irrelevant first write. More generally, WAW hazard may manifest due to unexpected code sequences. Another example is the interaction between the currently executing program and a trap handler. Suppose that an instruction which would have written to a particular register (first write) if the execution had been normal traps for some reason. As part of handling the trap, the handler writes to the same register (second write in program order) and resumes the original program at the same instruction. The instruction continues and completes writing to the register (i.e., the first write in program order, which is now an irrelevant one due to the trap handling). If the writes do not occur in program order, then this first write would overwrite the second write by the trap handler. It is the hardware's responsibility to detect such hazards and eliminate them.

5.15.5 Power Consumption

Another interesting dimension in processor design is the concern about the power dissipation. Even in the present state of technology, current GHz microprocessors dissipate a lot of power, leading to a significant engineering challenge to keep the systems cool. As the processing power continues to increase, the energy consumption does, too. The challenge for the architect is to design techniques to keep the power consumption low while aspiring for higher performance.

The ability to pack more transistors on a single piece of silicon is a blessing, although it poses significant challenges to the architect. First of all, with the increase in density of transistors on the chip, all the delays (recall the width of the clock pulse discussed in Chapter 3) have shrunk. This includes the time to perform logic operations, wire delays, and access times to registers. This poses a challenge to the architect in the following way: In principle, the chip can be clocked at a higher rate because the delays have gone down. However, cranking up the clock increases power consumption. Figure 5.22 shows the growth in power consumption, with increasing clock rates, for several popular processors. You can see the high correlation between clock cycle time and the power consumption. A 3.2-GHz Intel P4 processor consumes 112 watts of power. In the chart, you will see some processors with lower clock rating incurring higher power consumption (e.g., compare the 1.8-GHz AMD K-8 with the 2.2-GHz Intel P4). The reason is that the power consumption also depends on other on-chip resources, such as the word width of the processor and the memory system, including on-chip caches. (We discuss the design of caches in Chapter 9.)

5.15.6 Multicore Processor Design

The reality is that, as technology keeps improving, if the processor is clocked at the maximum rate possible for that technology, pretty soon we will end up with a laptop whose

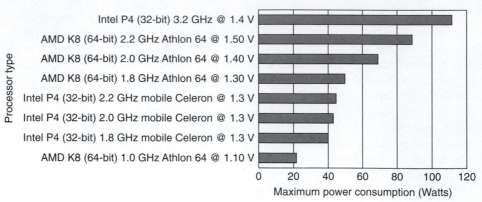

Figure 5.22   CPU power consumption.[14]

The power consumption in influenced significantly by the clocking frequency. Other factors, such as the processor word width and other on-chip resources (including caches), influence the power consumption as well.

power consumption equals that of a nuclear reactor! Of course, the solution is not to stop making chips with higher density and higher clock rates. Architects are turning to another avenue to increase performance of the processor, without increasing the clock rate, namely, *multiprocessing.* This new technology has already hit the market with the name *multicore* (the Intel Core 2 Duo, the AMD Opteron quad-core, etc.). Each chip holds multiple processors; when the processing to be done is divided among these multiple processors, the system throughput—that is, the performance—is increased. The architecture and hardware details underlying multicore processors (or *chip multiprocessors,* as they are often referred to) are beyond the scope of this textbook. However, multicore technology builds on the basic principles of parallel processing, which have been around as long as computer science has been around. We will discuss the hardware and software issues surrounding multiprocessors and parallel programming in much more detail in Chapter 12.

5.15.7 Intel Core[15] Microarchitecture: An Example Pipeline

It is instructive to understand the pipeline structure of modern processors. The Intel Pentium 4 Willamette and the Galatin use a 20-stage pipeline, whereas the Intel Pentium Prescott and the Irwindale use a 31-stage pipeline. One of the chief differentiators between the Intel and AMD product lines (though both support the same x86 ISA) is the depth of the pipeline. While Intel has taken the approach of supporting deeper pipelines for larger instruction throughput, AMD has taken the approach of a relatively shallower (14-stage) pipeline.

A family of Intel processors, including the Intel Core 2 Duo, Intel Core 2 Quad, and Intel Xeon, uses a common *core* microarchitecture, shown in Figure 5.23. It is

---

14. Source: The Intel data are from www.sandpile.org/impl/p4.htm. The AMD data are from www.sandpile. org/impl/k8.htm.

15. Intel Core is a registered trademark of Intel Corporation.

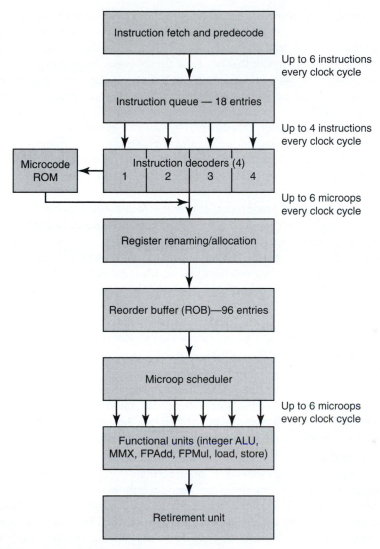

Figure 5.23 Intel Core microarchitecture pipeline functionality.

worth noting that this pipeline structure was first introduced in the Pentium "P6" microarchitecture back in the mid-1990s. Figure 5.23 is a much-simplified diagram intended to show the basic functionalities of a modern processor pipeline. The interested reader is referred to the Intel architecture manuals available for free on the Intel website.[16] At a highlevel, the microarchitecture has a *front end*, an *execution core*, and a *back end*. The role of the front end is to fetch instruction streams *in order* from memory,

---

16. Intel website: www.intel.com/products/processor/manuals/index.htm.

with four decoders to supply the decoded instructions (also referred to as *microops*) to the execution core. The front end comprises the fetch and predecode unit, the instruction queue, the decoders, and the microcode ROM. The middle section of the pipeline is an *out-of-order* execution core that can issue up to *six* microops every clock cycle as soon as the sources for the microops are ready (i.e., when there are no RAW hazards) and the corresponding execution units are available (i.e., when there are no structural hazards). This middle section incorporates register renaming, reorder buffer, reservation station, and an instruction scheduler. The back end is responsible for retiring the executed instructions in *program order*, and for updating the programmer-visible architecture-registers. The functionalities of the different functional units that feature in the pipeline microarchitecture of the Intel Core are as follows:

- **Instruction fetch and predecode:** This unit is responsible for two things: fetching the instructions that are most likely to be executed and predecoding the instructions recognizing variable-length instructions (since the x86 architecture supports it). Predecode helps the instruction fetcher to recognize a branch instruction long before the outcome of the branch will be decided. An elaborate branch prediction unit (BPU) is part of this stage that helps fetch the most-likely instruction stream. BPU has dedicated hardware for predicting the outcome of different types of branch instructions (conditional, direct, indirect, and call and return). The predecode unit can write up to six instructions, every clock cycle, into the instruction queue.

- **Instruction queue:** The instruction queue takes the place of an instruction register (IR) in a simple five-stage pipeline. Since it houses many more instructions (it has a depth of 18 instructions), the instruction queue can hold a snippet of the original program (e.g., a small loop) to accelerate the execution in the pipelined processor. Further, it also can help in saving power, because the rest of the front end (namely, the instruction fetch unit) can be shut down during the execution of the loop.

- **Decode and microcode ROM:** This unit contains four decoders and hence can decode up to four instructions in the instruction queue in every clock cycle. Depending on the instruction, the decode unit may expand it into several microops, with the help of the microcode ROM. The microcode ROM can emit three microops every cycle. The microcode ROM thus facilitates implementing complex instructions without slowing down the pipeline for the simple instructions. The decoders also support *macro-fusion,* fusing together two instructions into a single microop.

- **Register renaming/allocation:** This unit is responsible for allocating physical registers to the architectural registers named in the microop. It keeps the mapping created between the architectural registers and the actual physical registers in the microarchitecture. It supports hardware-based speculation and removes WAR and WAW hazards.

- **Reorder buffer:** This unit has 96 entries and is responsible for registering the original program order of the microops for later reconciliation. It holds the microops in various stages of execution. There can be up to 96 microops in flight (i.e., in various stages of execution), depending on the size of the ROB.

- **Scheduler:** This unit is responsible for scheduling the microops on the functional units. It includes a *reservation station* that queues all the microops until their respective sources are ready and the corresponding execution unit is available. It can schedule up to six microops every clock cycle, subject to their readiness for execution.

- **Functional units:** As the name suggests, these are the units that carry out the microops. They include execution units with single-cycle latency (such as integer add), pipelined execution units for frequently used longer latency microops, pipelined floating-point units, and memory load/store units.

- **Retirement unit:** This represents the back end of the microarchitecture and uses the reorder buffer to retire the microops in program order. In addition, it updates the architectural states, in program order, and manages the ordering of exceptions and traps that may arise during instruction execution. It also communicates with the reservation station to indicate the availability of sources that microops may be waiting on.

Summary

In this chapter, we have covered a lot of ground. Metrics for evaluating processor performance were covered in Sections 5.1 and 5.2. We introduced Amdahl's law and the notion of speedup in Section 5.5. The discussion of improving processor performance led to the introduction of pipelined processor design in Section 5.7. Datapath elements needed for supporting an instruction pipeline, as well as best practices for achieving a pipeline-conscious architecture and implementation, were discussed in Sections 5.11 and 5.12. The bane of pipelined design is hazards. Different kinds of hazards (structural, data, and control) encountered in a pipelined processor and solutions for overcoming hazards were discussed in Section 5.13. Another thorny issue in pipelined processor implementation is dealing with program discontinuities, which was discussed in Section 5.14. A flavor of advanced topics relating to pipelined processor implementation was presented in Section 5.15. We close this chapter with a discussion of how far we have come in processor implementation from the early days of computing.

Historical Perspective

Most of us have a tendency to take things for granted, depending on where we are in space and time and whether we are running water in faucets 24/7, driving high-speed cars, or holding and using high-performance computers in the palm of our hand. Of course, many of us realize quickly that we have come a long way in a fairly short period in terms of computer technology, due to the amazing pace of breakthrough development in chip integration.

It is instructive to look back at the road traversed. In the 1960s and the 1970s, pipelined processor design was reserved for high-end computers of the day. Researchers at Control Data Corporation and IBM pioneered fundamental work in pipelined processor design in the 1960s, which resulted in the design of systems such as the CDC 6600, the IBM 360 series, and the IBM 370 series of high-end computer systems. Such systems, dubbed *mainframes* perhaps because of their being packaged in a large metal chassis, were targeted primarily toward business applications. Gene Amdahl, who was the chief architect of the IBM 360 series and whose name is immortalized in *Amdahl's law*, discovered the principles of pipelining in the WISC computer, which are documented in his Ph.D. dissertation at the University of Wisconsin-Madison in 1952.[17] Seymour Cray, a pioneer in high-performance computers, founded Cray Research, which ushered in the age of *vector supercomputers* with the Cray series, starting with the Cray-1. Prior to founding Cray Research, Seymour Cray was the chief architect at Control Data Corporation, which was the leader in high-performance computing in the 1960s, with offerings such as the CDC 6600 (widely considered the first commercial supercomputer) and, shortly thereafter, the CDC 7600.

Simultaneous with the development of high-end computers, there was much interest in the development of *minicomputers*, DEC's PDP series leading the way with the PDP-8, followed by the PDP-11, and, later on, the VAX series. Such computers initially were targeted toward the scientific and engineering communities. Low cost was the primary focus, as opposed to high performance; hence, these processors were designed without employing pipelining techniques.

As we observed in Chapter 3, the advent of the "killer micros" in the 1980s, coupled with pioneering research in compiler technology and RISC architectures, paved the way for instruction pipelines to become the implementation norm for processor design, except for very low-end embedded processors. Today, even game consoles in the hands of toddlers use processors that employ principles of pipelining.

Just as a point of clarification of terminology, supercomputers were targeted toward solving challenging computational problems that arise in science and engineering. These *grand challenge problems* inspired the development of a research program by DARPA[18] to stimulate breakthrough computing technologies. Meanwhile, mainframes were targeted toward technical applications, for business, finance, and other entities. These days, it is normal to call such high-end computers *servers*. Also known as clusters, servers comprise a collection of computers interconnected by a high-speed network. Servers cater to both scientific applications (e.g., IBM's BlueGene massively parallel architecture) and technical applications (e.g., the IBM z series). The processor building blocks used in such servers are quite similar and adhere to the principles of pipelining that we discussed in this chapter.

Exercises

1. Answer True or False, with justification: For a given workload and a given ISA, reducing the CPI (clocks per instruction) of all the instructions will always improve the performance of the processor.

---

17. Source: http://en.wikipedia.org/wiki/Wisconsin_Integrally_Synchronized_Computer.
18. *DARPA* stands for a federal government entity, the *Defense Advanced Research Projects Agency*.

2. An architecture has three types of instructions that have the following CPI:

Type	CPI
A	2
B	5
C	3

An architect determines that he can reduce the CPI for B by some clever architectural trick, with no change to the CPIs of the other two instruction types. However, she determines that this change will increase the clock cycle time by 15%. What is the maximum permissible CPI of B (rounded up to the nearest integer) that will make this change worthwhile? Assume that all the workloads which execute on this processor use 40% of A, 10% of B, and 50% of C types of instructions.

3. What would be the execution time for a program containing 2,000,000 instructions if the processor clock were running at 8 MHz and each instruction took four clock cycles?

4. A smart architect reimplements a given instruction-set architecture, halving the CPI for 50% of the instructions, while increasing the clock cycle time of the processor by 10%. How much faster is the new implementation, compared with the original? Assume that all instructions are equally likely to be used in determining the execution time of any program.

5. A certain change is being considered in the nonpipelined (multicycle) MIPS CPU regarding the implementation of the ALU instructions. This change will enable you to perform an arithmetic operation and write the result into the register file, all in one clock cycle. However, doing so will increase the clock cycle time of the CPU. Specifically, the original CPU operates on a 500 MHz clock, but the new design will execute only on a 400 MHz clock.

   Will this change improve or degrade performance? How many times faster (or slower) will the new design be, compared with the original design? Assume that instructions are executed with the following frequency:

Instruction	Frequency
LW	25%
SW	15%
ALU	45%
BEQ	10%
JMP	5%

The CPI of the instructions in the original design is as follows:

Instruction	CPI
LW	5
SW	4
ALU	4
BEQ	3
JMP	3

6. Here are the CPIs of various instruction classes:

Class	CPI
R-type	2
I-type	10
J-type	3
S-type	4

And the instruction frequency for two different implementation of the same program is as follows:

Class	Implementation 1	Implementation 2
R	3	10
I	3	1
J	5	2
S	2	3

Which implementation will execute faster and why?

7. What is the difference between static and dynamic instruction frequency?

8. Given these instructions and their CPI, answer the question that follows:

Instruction	CPI
ADD	2
SHIFT	3
Others	2 (average for all instructions including ADD and SHIFT)
ADD/SHIFT	3

If the sequence ADD followed by Shift appears in 20% of the dynamic frequency of a program, what is the percentage improvement in the execution time of the program with all {ADD, SHIFT} replaced by the new instruction?

9. Compare and contrast structural, data, and control hazards. How are the potential negative effects on pipeline performance mitigated?

10. How can a read-after-write (RAW) hazard be minimized or eliminated?

11. What is a branch target buffer and how is it used?

12. Why is a second ALU needed in the execute stage of the pipeline for a five-stage pipeline implementation of the LC-2200?

13. In a processor with a five-stage pipeline, as shown in the picture that follows (with buffers between the stages), explain the problem posed by a branch instruction. Present a solution.

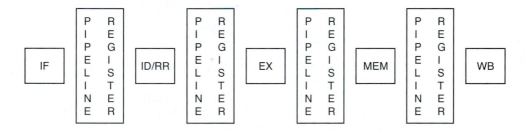

14. Regardless of whether we use a conservative approach or a branch prediction ("branch not taken"), explain why there is always a two-cycle delay if the branch is taken (i.e., two NOPs injected into the pipeline) before normal execution can resume in the five-stage pipeline presented in Section 5.13.3.

15. With reference to Figure 5.6(a), identify and explain the role of the datapath elements that deal with the BEQ instruction. Explain in detail what exactly happens, cycle by cycle, with respect to this datapath during the passage of a BEQ instruction. Assume a conservative approach to handling the control hazard. Your answer should include both cases: branch taken and branch not taken.

16. A smart engineer decides to reduce the two-cycle "branch taken" penalty in the five-stage pipeline down to one. Her idea is to directly use the branch target address computed in the EX cycle to fetch the instruction. (Note that the approach presented in Section 5.13.3 requires the target address to be saved in PC first.)

   a. Show the modification to the datapath in Figure 5.6(a) to implement this idea. [Hint: You have to simultaneously feed the target address to the PC and the instruction memory if the branch is taken.]

   b. Although this reduces the bubbles in the pipeline to one for branch taken, it may not be a good idea. Why? [Hint: Consider cycle-time effects.]

17. In a pipelined processor, where each instruction could be broken up into five stages and where each stage takes 1 ns, what is the best we could hope to do in terms of average time to execute 1,000,000,000 instructions?

18. Using the five-stage pipeline shown in Figure 5.6(b), answer the following two questions:

   a. Show the actions (similar to the material presented in Section 5.12.1) in each stage of the pipeline for the BEQ instruction of the LC-2200.

   b. Considering only the BEQ instruction, compute the sizes of the FBUF, DBUF, EBUF, and MBUF.

19. Repeat problem 18 for the SW instruction of the LC-2200.

20. Repeat problem 18 for the JALR instruction of the LC-2200.

21. You are given the pipelined datapath for a processor shown as follows:

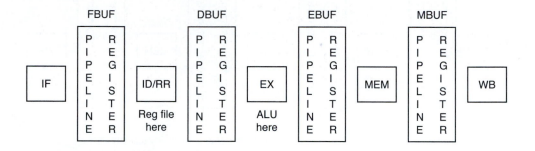

A load-word instruction has the following 32-bit format:

OPCode	A Reg	B Reg	Offset
8 bits	4 bits	4 bits	16 bits

The semantic of this instruction is

$$B \leftarrow Memory[A + offset].$$

Register B gets the data at the memory address given by the effective address generated by adding the contents of Register A to the 16-bit offset in the instruction. All data and addresses are 32-bit quantities.

   Show what is needed in the pipeline registers FBUF, DBUF, EBUF, and MBUF, between the stages of the pipeline, for the passage of this instruction. Clearly show the layout of each buffer. Show the width of each field in the buffer. For this problem, you do not have to concern yourself about the format or the requirements of other instructions in the architecture.

22. Consider the following two instructions:

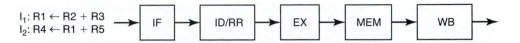

I_1: R1 ← R2 + R3
I_2: R4 ← R1 + R5

IF → ID/RR → EX → MEM → WB

If I_2 is immediately following I_1 in the pipeline, with no forwarding, how many bubbles (i.e., NOPs) will result in the foregoing execution? Explain your answer.

23. Consider the following program fragment:

Address	Instruction
1000	ADD
1001	NAND
1002	LW
1003	ADD
1004	NAND
1005	ADD
1006	SW
1007	LW
1008	ADD

Assume that there are no hazards in the preceding set of instructions. Currently, the IF stage is about to fetch the instruction at 1004.

a. Show the state of the five-stage pipeline.

b. Assuming that we use the *drain* approach to dealing with interrupts, how many cycles will elapse before we enter the INT macro state? What is the value of the PC that will be stored in the INT macro state into $k0?

c. Assuming that we use the *flush* approach to dealing with interrupts, how many cycles will elapse before we enter the INT macro state? What is the value of the PC that will be stored in the INT macro state into $k0?

Bibliographic Notes and Further Reading

It is inspiring to read the very first technical paper that proposed the basic principles of pipelining, written by Jim Thornton [Thornton, 1964], whose ideas were incorporated into the CDC 6600, the first supercomputer. The documentation from IBM [IBM

System/360, 1964; IBM System/370, 1978] is a good source to learn about the IBM architecture, which has been influential in the development of pipelined processor design. The Tomasulo algorithm, used in the IBM 360/91, first appeared in the public domain in a technical article [Tomasulo, 1967]. A good source for reading about the VAX 11 architecture is [Strecker, 1978]. The Berkeley RISC architecture was introduced in [Patterson, 1981]. The Stanford MIPS processor was introduced in [Hennessy, 1981]. The IBM 801 architecture was first discussed in the public domain in [Radin, 1982]. Yale Patt, winner of the Eckert-Mauchly award in 1996, has made deep contributions to instruction-level parallelism and superscalar processor design, particularly in the area of branch prediction [Yeh, 1992]. The Acorn RISC Machine (ARM) is a popular RISC architecture, especially for the embedded space [ARM, 1990]. The textbook by Hennessy and Patterson is a good source to learn about more advanced concepts with respect to pipelined processor design [Hennessy, 2006]. Premier conference venues in the area of computer architecture include ISCA,[19] Micro,[20] ASPLOS,[21] and HPCA.[22]

---

19. International Symposium on Computer Architecture (ISCA): http://isca2010.inria.fr/.

20. IEEE Micro: www.microarch.org/micro42/.

21. Architectural Support for Programming Languages and Operating Systems (ASPLOS): www.ece.cmu.edu/CALCM/asplos10/doku.php.

22. High Performance Computer Architecture (HPCA): www.cse.psu.edu/hpcl/hpca16.html.

Processor Scheduling

6.1 Introduction

Processor design and implementation is no longer a mystery to us. From the earlier chapters, we know how to design instruction sets, how to implement the instruction set by using an FSM, and how to improve upon the performance of a processor through techniques such as pipelining.

Fans of Google Earth have experienced the cool effect of looking at a country or a continent from a distance and then, if needed, zooming in to see every street name and the houses of a city that they are interested in exploring further.

We just did that for the processor. After understanding how a processor ISA is designed, we zoomed in to see the details of how to implement the processor by using the LC-2200 ISA, as a concrete example, and we got a good grasp of the details from a hardware perspective. Now it is time to zoom out and look at the processor as a black box, a precious and scarce resource. Several programs may have to run on this resource (Google Earth, e-mail, browser, IM, etc.), and the system software has to manage this resource effectively to cater to the needs of the end user.

Therefore, we turn our attention to a complementary topic, namely, how to manage the processor as a resource in a computer system. To do this, we do not need to know the internals of the processor. That is the power of abstraction. Viewing the processor as a black box, we will figure out the software abstractions that would be useful in managing this scarce resource. The portion of the operating system that deals with this functionality is *processor scheduling*, which is the topic of discussion in this chapter. Efficient implementation of this functionality may necessitate revisiting (i.e., zooming in to) the processor ISA and adding additional smarts to the ISA. We will revisit this issue toward the end of the chapter (see Section 6.11).

Let us consider a simple analogy. You have laundry to do. You have tests to prepare for. You have to get some food ready for dinner. You have to call Mom and wish her happy birthday. There is only one of you, and you have to get all of this done in a timely manner. You are going to prioritize these activities, but you also know that not all of them need your constant attention. For example, once you get the washing machine started, for the laundry, until it beeps at you at the end of the cycle you don't have to pay attention to it. Similarly, with our zapping culture, all you need to do to get dinner ready is to stick the "TV dinner" into the microwave and wait until that beeps. So, here is a plausible schedule to get all of this done:

1. Start the wash cycle.
2. Stick the food in the microwave and zap it.
3. Call Mom.
4. Prepare for tests.

Notice that your attention is needed for only a very short time for the first two tasks (relative to tasks 3 and 4). There is a problem, however. You have no idea how long tasks 3 and 4 are going to take. For example, Mom's call could go on and on. The washer may beep at you, and/or the microwave might beep at you, while Mom is still on the line. Well, if the washer beeps at you, you could politely tell your mom to hold for a minute, go transfer the load from the washer to the dryer, and come back to the phone call. Likewise, you could excuse yourself momentarily to take the food out of the microwave and keep it on the dinner table, ready to eat. Once you are done with Mom's call, you are going to eat dinner peacefully, then start preparing for the tests. You have a total of eight hours for studying, and you have four courses to prepare for. All the tests are equally important for your final course grades. In preparing for the tests, you have a choice to make. Either you could spend a little bit of time on each of the courses and cycle through all the courses to ensure that you are making progress on all of them, or you could study for the tests in the order in which you have to take them.

At this point, you may be scratching your head and asking yourself, "What does any of this have to do with processor scheduling?" Or, more than likely, you can already see what is going on here. You are the scarce resource. You are partitioning your time to allocate yourself to these various tasks. You have given higher priority to Mom's phone call relative to preparing for the test. You will see later, when we discuss processor scheduling algorithms, a similar notion of *priority*. You have given starting the wash cycle and the microwave higher priority, compared with the other two tasks. This is because you know that these require very little of your time. You will see a similar notion of *shortest job first* scheduling policy, for processors. When the washer beeps while you are still on the phone, you temporarily put your mom on hold while you attend to the washer. Later you will see a similar concept, namely, *preemption,* in the context of processor scheduling. In studying for the tests, the first choice you could make is akin to a processor scheduling policy we will see called *round robin*. The second choice is similar to the classic *first come first served* processor-scheduling policy.

6.2 Programs and Processes

Let's start the discussion of processor scheduling with a very basic understanding of what an operating system is. It is just a *program,* whose sole purpose is to supply the resources needed to execute users' programs.

To understand the resource requirements of a user program, let us review how we create programs in the first place. Figure 6.1 shows a plausible layout of the memory footprint of a program written in a high-level language such as C.

We use the term *program* in a variety of connotations. However, generally we use the term to denote a computer solution for a problem. The program may exist in several different forms.

Figure 6.2 shows the life cycle of program creation in a high-level language. First, we have a problem specification from which we develop an algorithm. We code the algorithm in some programming language (say, C), using an editor. Both the algorithm and the C code are different representations of the *program,* a means of codifying our solution to a problem. A compiler compiles the C code to produce a binary representation of the program. This representation is still not "executable" by a processor. This is because the program we write uses a number of facilities that we take for granted and are supplied to us by "someone else." For example, we make calls to do terminal I/O (such as *scanf* and *printf*) and calls to do mathematical operations (such as *sine* and *cosine*). Therefore, the next step is to *link* together our code with that of the libraries, provided by someone else, that fill in the facilities we have taken for granted. This is the work of the *linker.*[1] The output of the linker is, once again, a binary representation of the program, but now it is in a form that is ready for execution on the processor. These different representations of your program (English text, unlinked binary, and executable binary) ultimately, usually will end up on your hard drive. *Loader,* usually a part of the operating system, takes the disk representation and creates the memory footprint shown in Figure 6.1.

Each of the editor, compiler, and linker are themselves independent programs, and the loader is part of a larger program, namely, the operating system. Any program needs

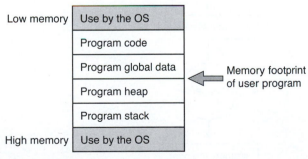

Figure 6.1 Memory footprint.

---

1. The linking step in generating an executable program is usually part of the compiler itself.

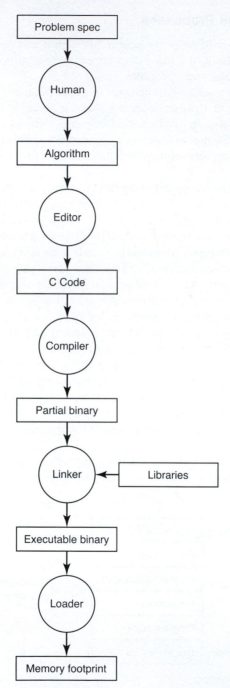

Figure 6.2 Life cycle of program creation.

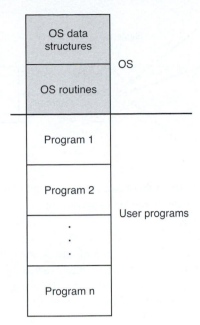

Figure 6.3　OS and user program in memory.

resources to execute. The resources are the processor, the memory, and any input/output devices. Suppose that you write a simple "Hello World" program. Let us enumerate the resources needed to run this simple program. You will need the processor and memory, of course; in addition, you will need the display to send your output. The operating system gives the resources needed by the programs.

As should be evident from the discussion so far, just like any other program, the operating system is also memory resident and has a footprint similar to any other program. Figure 6.3 shows the memory contents of user programs and the operating system.

In this chapter, we will focus on the operating system's functionality that deals with allocating the processor resource to the programs, namely, the *scheduler*.

A scheduler is a set of routines that is part of the operating system; just like any other program, the scheduler also needs the processor to do its work—that is, of selecting a program to run on the processor. The scheduler embodies an algorithm to determine a winner among the set of programs that need cycles on the processor.

You have heard the term *process*. Let us understand what a process is and how it differs from a program. *A process is a program in execution*. With reference to Figure 6.1, we define the *address space* of a process as the space occupied in memory by the program. Once a program starts executing on the processor, the contents of the memory occupied by the program may change due to manipulation of the data structures of the program. In addition, the program may use the processor registers as part of its execution. The current contents of the address space and the register values together constitute the *state* of a program in execution (i.e., the state of a process). We will shortly see how we can concisely represent the state of a process.

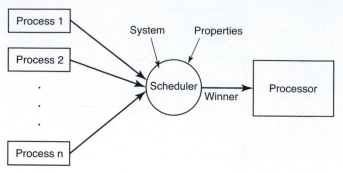

Figure 6.4   Scheduler—a program that takes the current set of ready processes as input and selects a winner to run on the processor, subject to the system state and program properties.

Quite often, a process may also be the unit of scheduling on the processor. The inputs to the scheduler are the set of processes that are ready to use the processor, and additional properties that help the scheduler to pick a winner from among the set of ready processes, as shown in Figure 6.4. The properties allow the scheduler to establish a sense of *priority* among the set of processes. For example, *expected running time, expected memory usage,* and *expected I/O requirements* are *static* properties associated with a program. Similarly, *available system memory, arrival time of a program,* and *instantaneous memory requirements of the program* are dynamic properties that are available to the scheduler as well. *Urgency* (either expressed as *deadlines*, and/or *importance*) may be other extraneous properties available to the scheduler. Some of these properties (such as urgency) are explicitly specified to the scheduler, whereas the scheduler may infer others (such as arrival time).

Quite often, terminologies such as *tasks* and *threads* denote units of work and/or units of scheduling. We should warn the reader that, although the definition of *process* is uniform in the literature, the same could not be said for either a task or a thread. In most literature, a *task* has the same connotation as a *process*. In this chapter, we will use the term *task* only to mean a unit of work. We will give a basic definition of *threads* that is useful for understanding the scheduling algorithms.

An analogy will be useful here, shown graphically in Figure 6.5(a)–(c). You get the morning newspaper. It is lying on the breakfast table. Nobody is reading it yet. That is like a program dormant in memory. You pick it up and start reading.

Now there is one active entity reading the paper, namely, you. Notice that, depending on your interest, you will read different sections of the paper. A process is similar.

(a)   (b)   (c)

Figure 6.5   You and your sibling reading the newspaper.

Table 6.1 Jobs, Processes, Threads, and Tasks

Name	Usual Connotation	Use in This Chapter
Job	Unit of scheduling	Synonymous with process
Process	Program in execution; unit of scheduling	Synonymous with job
Thread	Unit of scheduling and/or execution; contained within a process	Not used in the scheduling algorithms described in this chapter
Task	Unit of work; unit of scheduling	Not used in the scheduling algorithms described in this chapter, except in describing the scheduling algorithm of Linux

Depending on the input and the logic of the program, a process may traverse a particular path through the program. This path defines a *thread of control* for the process. Let us see why it makes sense to have multiple threads of control within the process by returning to our newspaper-reading analogy. Imagine now, as you are reading the paper, your sibling joins you at the breakfast table and starts reading the paper as well, as shown in Figure 6.5(c). Depending on his interests, perhaps he is going to start reading a different section of the paper. Now there are two activities (you and your sibling), or two threads of control, navigating the morning paper. Similarly, there could be multiple threads of control within a single process. We will elaborate on why having multiple threads in a process may be a good idea, and the precise differences between a thread and a process, later in the context of multiprocessors and multithreaded programs. At this point, it is sufficient to understand a thread as a unit of execution (and, perhaps, as a unit of scheduling as well) contained within a process. All the threads within a process execute in the same address space, sharing the code and data structures shown in the program's memory footprint (Figure 6.1). *In other words, a process is a program plus all the threads that are executing in that program.* This is analogous to the newspaper, your sibling, and you, all put together.

There could be multiple threads within a single process, but from the point of view of the scheduling algorithms discussed in this chapter, a process has a single thread of control. Scheduling literature uses the term *job* as a unit of scheduling, and to be consistent, we have chosen to use this term synonymously with *process* in this chapter. We summarize these terminologies and the connotations associated with them in Table 6.1.

6.3 Scheduling Environments

In general, a processor may be dedicated for a specific set of tasks. Take, for example, a processor inside an embedded device such as a cell phone. In this case, there may be a task to handle the ringing, one to initiate a call, etc. A scheduler for such a dedicated environment may simply cycle through the tasks to see if any one of them is ready to run.

In the age of large batch-oriented processing (spanning the 1960s, 1970s, and early 1980s), the scheduling environment was *multiprogrammed*; that is, multiple programs were loaded into memory from the disk, and the operating system cycled through them on the basis of their relative priorities. These were the days when you handed to a human operator punched cards containing a description of your program (on a disk) and its execution needs, in a language called *job control language (JCL)*. Typically, you would come back several hours later to collect your output. With the advent of data terminals and minicomputers, *interactive*, or *time-sharing*, environments became feasible. In this situation, the processor is time-shared among the set of interactive users sitting at terminals and accessing the computer. *It is important to note that a time-shared environment is necessarily multiprogrammed, whereas a multiprogrammed environment need not be time-shared.* These different environments gave rise to different kinds of schedulers as well (see Figure 6.6).

A *long-term scheduler*, typically used in batch-oriented multiprogrammed environments, balances the job mix in memory to optimize the use of resources in the system (processor, memory, disk, etc.). With the advent of personal computing and time-shared environments, long-term schedulers are, for all practical purposes, nonexistent

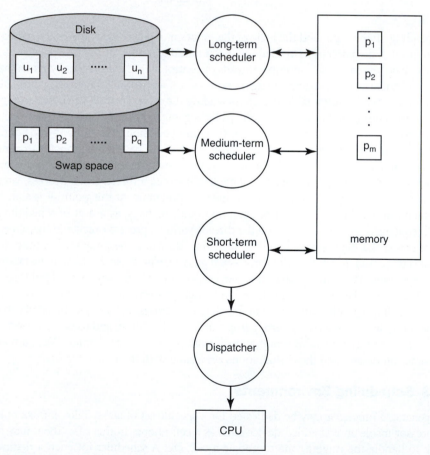

Figure 6.6 Types of schedulers (u_i represents user programs on the disk; p_i represents user processes in memory).

in most modern operating systems. Instead, a component of the operating system called a *loader* creates a memory footprint when the user starts a program that is resident on the disk (e.g., by clicking an icon on the laptop or typing a program name from a command line). The long-term scheduler (or the loader) is responsible for creating the memory resident processes (p_i) out of the disk resident user programs (u_i).

A *medium-term scheduler,* used in many environments including modern operating systems, closely monitors the dynamic memory usage of the processes currently executing on the CPU and makes decisions on whether or not to increase or decrease the *degree of multiprogramming*, defined as the number of processes coexisting in memory and competing for the CPU. This scheduler is primarily responsible for controlling a phenomenon called *thrashing, wherein the current memory requirements of the processes exceed the system capacity, resulting in the processes' not making much progress in their respective executions.* The medium-term scheduler moves programs back and forth between the disk (shown as *swap* space in Figure 6.6) and memory when the throughput of the system reduces. We will revisit the thrashing concept in much more detail in Chapter 8.

A *short-term scheduler*, found in most modern operating systems, made its first appearance in time-sharing systems. This scheduler is responsible for selecting a process to run, from among the current set of memory resident processes. The focus of this chapter, including the algorithms presented, mostly concerns the short-term scheduler. The last item is a *dispatcher,* an entity that takes the process selected by the short-term scheduler and sets up the processor registers in readiness for executing that process. Long-term scheduler, medium-term scheduler, short-term scheduler, and dispatcher are all components of the operating system and coordinate their activities with one another.

Table 6.2 summarizes the different types of schedulers found in different environments, and their respective roles.

Table 6.2 Types of Schedulers and Their Roles

Name	Environment	Role
Long-Term Scheduler	Batch-oriented OS	Control the job mix in memory to balance the use of system resources (CPU, memory, I/O)
Loader	In every OS	Load user program from disk into memory
Medium-Term Scheduler	Every modern OS (time-shared, interactive)	Balance the mix of processes in memory to avoid thrashing
Short-Term Scheduler	Every modern OS (time-shared, interactive)	Schedule the memory resident processes on the CPU
Dispatcher	In every OS	Populate the CPU registers with the state of the process selected for running by the short-term scheduler

6.4 Scheduling Basics

It is useful to understand program behavior before delving deep into the scheduler. Imagine a program that plays music on your computer from a CD player. The program repeatedly reads the tracks of the CD (I/O activity) and then renders the tracks (processor activity) read from the CD player to the speakers. It turns out that this is typical program behavior—cycling between bursts of activity on the processor and I/O devices (see Figure 6.7).

We will use the term *CPU burst* to denote the stretch of time a process would run without making an I/O call. Informally, we define *CPU burst* of a process as the time interval of continuous CPU activity by the process before it makes an I/O call. Using the analogy from the beginning of the chapter, CPU burst is similar to the stretch of time you would do continuous reading, while preparing for a test, before going to the fridge for a soda. Similarly, we will use the term *I/O burst* to denote the stretch of time a process would need to complete an I/O operation (such as reading a music file from the CD). It is important to note that during an I/O burst the process does not need to use the processor. In Chapter 4, we introduced the concept of interrupts and how they grab the attention of the processor for an external event such as I/O completion. In Chapter 10, we will discuss the actual mechanics of data transfer between the I/O devices and the processor. For now, to keep the discussion of processor scheduling simple, assume that, upon an I/O request by a process, the process is no longer in contention for the CPU resource until its I/O is complete.

Processor schedulers are divided into two broad categories: *nonpreemptive* and *preemptive*. A process either executes to completion or gives up the processor on its own accord—that is, voluntarily, to perform I/O—in a nonpreemptive scheduler. On the other hand, the scheduler yanks the processor away from the current process to give it to another process, in a preemptive scheduler. In either case, the steps involved in scheduling are the following:

1. Grab the attention of the processor.
2. Save the state of the currently running process.

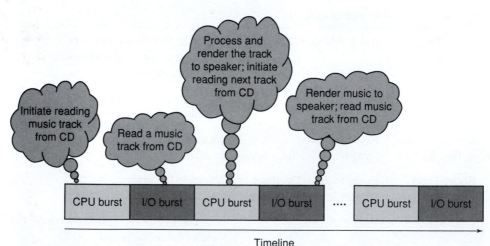

Figure 6.7 Music playing on your CD player.

```
enum state_type {new, ready, running, waiting, halted};

typedef struct control_block_type {
    enum state_type state;          /* current state */
    address PC;                     /* where to resume */
    int reg_file[NUMREGS];          /* contents of GPRs */
    struct control_block *next_pcb; /* list ptr */
    int priority;                   /* extrinsic property */
    address address_space;          /* where in memory */
          ....
          ....
} control_block;
```

Figure 6.8   Process control block (PCB).

3. Select a new process to run.

4. Dispatch the newly selected process to run on the processor.

The last step, *dispatch,* refers to loading the processor registers with the saved state of the selected process.

Let us understand the state of the running program, or process. It includes where we are currently executing in the program (PC value), what the contents of the processor registers are (assuming that one of these registers is also the stack pointer), and where in memory is the program's footprint. Besides, the process itself may be newly loaded into memory, ready to run on the processor or waiting for I/O, currently running, halted for some reason, or in some other state.

In addition, there are properties (intrinsic or extrinsic) that the scheduler may know about a process, such as process priority, arrival time of the program, and expected execution time. All this state information is aggregated into a data structure, *process control block (PCB),* shown in Figure 6.8. There is one PCB for each process, and the scheduler maintains all the PCBs in a linked list, the *ready queue,* as shown in Figure 6.9.

The PCB has all the information necessary to describe the process. It is a key data structure in the operating system. As we will see in later chapters that discuss memory systems and networking, the PCB is the aggregation of all the state information associated with a process (such as memory space occupied, open files, and network connections). Ready queue is the most important data structure in the

Figure 6.9   Ready queue of PCBs.

The PCB holds all the information regarding a process, and the ready queue is usually a linked list of the PCBs.

Figure 6.10   I/O queue of PCBs.

Upon a blocking I/O request made by a process, the PCB of the associated process moves to the I/O queue and awaits I/O completion.

scheduler. Efficient representation and manipulation of this data structure is a key to the performance of the scheduler. The role of the scheduler is to quickly make its scheduling decision and get out of the way, thus facilitating the use of the CPU for running user programs. Therefore, a key issue is identifying the right metrics for evaluating the *efficiency* of a scheduling algorithm. Intuitively, we would like the time spent in the scheduler to be a small percentage of the total CPU time. We will see in a case study (Section 6.12), how a Linux scheduler organizes its data structures to ensure high efficiency.

Note that we do not have the internal registers of the CPU datapath (see Chapters 3 and 5) as part of the process state. The reason for this will become clear toward the end of this subsection.

Similar to the ready queue of process control blocks, queues of PCBs of processes that are waiting on I/O are maintained by the operating system (see Figure 6.10).

For the purpose of this discussion, the PCBs go back and forth between the ready queue and the I/O queue, depending on whether a process needs the processor or I/O service. The CPU scheduler uses the ready queue for scheduling processes on the processor. Every one of the scheduling algorithms we discuss in this chapter assumes such a ready queue. The organization of the PCBs in the ready queue depends on the specifics of the scheduling algorithm. The PCB data structure simplifies the steps involved in scheduling, which we identified earlier in this section. The scheduler knows exactly which PCB corresponds to the currently running process. The state-saving step simply becomes a matter of copying the relevant information (identified in Figure 6.8) into the PCB of the currently running process. Similarly, once the scheduler chooses a process as the next candidate to run on the processor, dispatching it on the processor is simply a matter of populating the processor registers with the information contained in the PCB of the chosen process.

From Chapter 4, we know that system calls (such as an I/O operation) and interrupts are all different flavors of program discontinuities. The hardware treats all of these program discontinuities similarly, waiting for a clean state of the processor before dealing with the discontinuity. Completion of an instruction execution is such a clean state of the processor. Once the processor has reached such a clean state, the registers that are internal to the processor (i.e., not visible to the programmer) do not contain any information of relevance to the currently running program. Because the scheduler switches from one process to another, triggered by such well-defined program discontinuities, there is no need to save the internal registers of the processor (discussed in Chapters 3 and 5) that are not visible to the programmer through the instruction-set architecture.

Table 6.3 summarizes the terminologies that are central to scheduling algorithms.

Table 6.3 Scheduling Terminologies

Name	Description
CPU Burst	Continuous CPU activity by a process before requiring an I/O operation
I/O Burst	Activity initiated by the CPU on an I/O device
PCB	Process context block that holds the state of a process (i.e., program in execution)
Ready Queue	Queue of PCBs that represent the set of memory resident processes that are ready to run on the CPU
I/O Queue	Queue of PCBs that represent the set of memory resident processes that are waiting for some I/O operation either to be initiated or completed
Nonpreemptive Algorithm	Algorithm that allows the currently scheduled process on the CPU to voluntarily relinquish the processor (either by terminating or making an I/O system call)
Preemptive Algorithm	Algorithm that forcibly takes the processor away from the currently scheduled process in response to an external event (e.g., I/O completion interrupt, timer interrupt)
Thrashing	A phenomenon wherein the dynamic memory usage of the processes currently in the ready queue exceeds the total memory capacity of the system

6.5 Performance Metrics

In discussing scheduling algorithms, we use the terms *jobs* and *processes* synonymously. The scheduler, a part of the operating system, is also a program and needs to run on the processor. Ultimately, the goal of the scheduler is to run user programs. Therefore, the processor is put to good use when running user programs and not when running the operating system itself. The question then arises, however, What are the right metrics to use for evaluating the efficiency of a scheduling algorithm? *CPU utilization* refers to the percentage of time the processor is busy. Although this percentage is a useful metric, it does not tell us what the processor is doing. So let us try some other metrics. The metrics could be *user centric* or *system centric*. *Throughput* is a system-centric metric that measures the number of jobs executed per unit time. *Average turnaround time* is another system-centric metric that measures the average elapsed time for jobs entering and leaving the system. *Average waiting time* of jobs is another system-centric metric. *Response time* of a job is a user-centric metric that measures the elapsed time for a given job.

Figure 6.11 shows a timeline for scheduling three processes, P1, P2, and P3, on the processor. Assume that all the processes start at time 0. For the sake of this discussion,

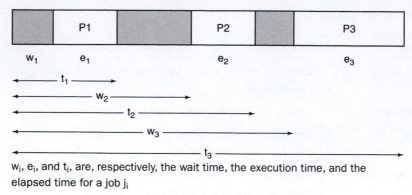

w_i, e_i, and t_i, are, respectively, the wait time, the execution time, and the elapsed time for a job j_i

Figure 6.11   Timeline of scheduling three processes, P1, P2, P3.

assume that in the shaded regions the processor is busy doing something else unrelated to running these processes.

With respect to Figure 6.11, we quantify the terms we just defined as follows:

> Throughput = $3/t_3$ jobs/sec
>
> Average turnaround time = $(t_1 + t_2 + t_3)/3$ secs
>
> Average wait time = $((t_1 - e_1) + (t_2 - e_2) + (t_3 - e_3))/3$ secs

Generalizing for n jobs, we see that

> Throughput = n/T jobs/sec, where T is the total elapsed time for all n jobs to complete,
>
> Average turnaround time = $(t_1 + t_2 + \cdots + t_n)/n$ secs
>
> Average wait time = $(w_1 + w_2 + \cdots + w_n)/n$ secs

Response time is the same as per-process turnaround time, resulting in the following equations:

> $R_{P1} = t1$
>
> $R_{p2} = t2$
>
> $R_{p3} = t3$
>
> . . . .
>
> $R_{pn} = tn$

Variance[2] in response time is a useful metric as well. In addition to these quantitative metrics, we should mention two *qualitative* metrics of importance to scheduling algorithms:

---

2. Variance in response time is the average of the squared distances of the possible values for response times from the expected value.

- **Starvation:** In any job mix, the scheduling policy should make sure that all the jobs make forward progress toward completion. We refer to the situation as *starvation* if, for some reason, a job does not make any forward progress. The quantitative manifestation of this situation is an unbounded response time for a particular job.

- **Convoy effect:** In any job mix, the scheduling policy should strive to prevent long-running jobs from dominating the CPU usage. We refer to the situation as *convoy effect* if, for some reason, the scheduling of jobs follows a fixed pattern (similar to a military convoy). The quantitative manifestation of this phenomenon is a high variance in the response times of jobs.

We will discuss several scheduling algorithms in the next few sections. Before we do that, note the following few caveats:

- In all the scheduling algorithms, we assume that the time to switch from one process to another is negligible, in order to make the timing diagrams for the schedules simple.

- We mentioned that a process might go back and forth between CPU and I/O requests during its lifetime. Naturally, the I/O requests may be to different devices at different times (output to the screen, read from the disk, input from the mouse, etc.). However, because the focus in this chapter is on CPU scheduling, for simplicity, we show just one I/O queue.

- Once again, to keep the focus on CPU scheduling, we assume a simple model (first-come-first-served) for scheduling I/O requests. In other words, intrinsic or extrinsic properties of a process that the CPU scheduler uses do not apply to I/O scheduling. The I/O requests are serviced in the order in which they are made by the processes.

Table 6.4 summarizes the performance metrics of interest from the point of view of scheduling.

6.6 Nonpreemptive Scheduling Algorithms

As we mentioned earlier, a nonpreemptive algorithm is one in which the scheduler has no control over the currently executing process once it has been scheduled on the CPU. The only way the scheduler can get back control is if the currently running process voluntarily relinquishes the CPU, either by terminating or by making a blocking system call (such as a file I/O request). In this section, we will consider three different algorithms that belong to this class: FCFS, SJF, and priority.

6.6.1 First-Come First-Served (FCFS)

The intrinsic property used in this algorithm is the *arrival time* of a process, which is the time that you launch an application program. For example, if you launched winamp at time t_0 and realplayer at a later time t_1, then winamp has an earlier arrival time, as far as

Table 6.4 Summary of Performance Metrics

Name	Notation	Units	Description
CPU Utilization	–	%	Percentage of time the CPU is busy
Throughput	n/T	Jobs/sec	System-centric metric quantifying the number of jobs n executed in time interval T
Average Turnaround Time (t_{avg})	$(t_1 + t_2 + \cdots + t_n)/n$	Seconds	System-centric metric quantifying the average time it takes for a job to complete
Average Waiting Time (w_{avg})	$((t_1 - e_1) + (t_2 - e_2) + \cdots + (t_n - e_n))/n$ or $(w_1 + w_2 + \cdots + w_n)/n$	Seconds	System-centric metric quantifying the average waiting time that a job experiences
Response Time/Turnaround Time	t_i	Seconds	User-centric metric quantifying the turnaround time for a specific job i
Variance in Response Time	$E[(t_i - e_i)^2]$	Seconds^2	User-centric metric quantifying the statistical variance of the actual response time (t_i) experienced by a process (P_i) from the expected value (t_{avg})
Starvation	-	-	User-centric qualitative metric that signifies denial of service to a particular process or a set of processes due to some intrinsic property of the scheduler
Convoy Effect	-	-	User-centric qualitative metric that results in a detrimental effect to some set of processes due to some intrinsic property of the scheduler

the scheduler is concerned. Thus, during the entire lifetime of the two programs, whenever both programs are ready to run, winamp will always get picked by the scheduler because it has an earlier arrival time. Remember that this "priority" enjoyed by winamp will continue even when it comes back into the ready queue after an I/O completion. Example 6.1 shows this advantage enjoyed by the early-bird process compared with other ready processes in the ready queue.

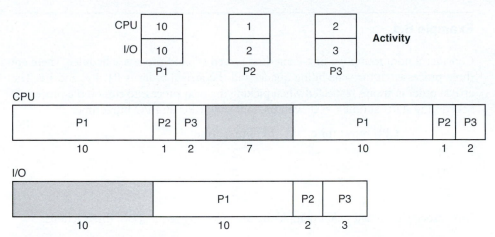

Figure 6.12 FCFS convoy effect.

Short jobs (P2, P3) get stuck behind a long job (P1) due to the nature of the FCFS schedule.

Figure 6.12 shows a set of processes and their activities at the top of the figure. Each process's activity alternates between CPU burst and I/O burst. For example, P2 does 1 unit of processing and 2 units of I/O, and repeats this behavior for its lifetime. The bottom of Figure 6.12 presents a timeline showing the FCFS scheduling of these processes on the CPU and I/O. At any point of time, there can be exactly one process executing on the CPU, and another process carrying out an I/O activity. Assume that each process has to do two bursts of CPU activity interspersed with one burst of I/O. All three processes are in the ready queue of the scheduler at the beginning of the timeline; however, P1 is the first to arrive, followed by P2 and P3. Thus, given a choice, the scheduler will always pick P1 over P2 or P3 for scheduling, due to the FCFS policy. The waiting times for the three jobs, P1, P2, and P3, are 0, 27, and 26, respectively.

The algorithm has the nice property that there will be no *starvation* for any process—that is, the algorithm has no inherent bias that results in denial of service for any process. We will see shortly that not all algorithms have this property. However, due to the very nature of the property, there can be a huge variation in the response time. For instance, if a short job arrives just after a long job, then the response time for the short job will be very bad. The algorithm also results in poor processor utilization due to the *convoy effect* depicted in Figure 6.12. The term *convoy effect* comes from the primarily military use of the word *convoy*, which signifies a group of vehicles traveling together. Of course, in the military sense, a convoy is a good thing because the vehicles act as support for one another in times of emergency. You may inadvertently become part of a convoy on a highway when you are stuck behind a slow-moving vehicle in single-lane traffic. The short jobs (P2 and P3) are stuck behind the long job (P1) for CPU. The convoy effect is unique to FCFS scheduling and is inherent in the nature of this scheduling discipline. Many of us have experienced being stuck behind a customer with a cartload of stuff at the checkout counter, when we ourselves have just a couple of items to check out. Unfortunately, the convoy effect is intrinsic to the FCFS scheduling discipline because, by its very nature, it does not give any preferential treatment to short jobs.

Example 6.1

Consider a nonpreemptive first-come-first-served (FCFS) process scheduler. There are three processes in the scheduling queue, and the arrival order is P1, P2, and P3. The arrival order is always respected when picking the next process to run on the processor. Scheduling starts at time t = 0, with the following CPU and I/O burst times:

	CPU burst time	I/O burst time
P1	8	2
P2	5	5
P3	1	5

Each process terminates after completing the following sequence of three actions:

1. CPU burst
2. I/O burst
3. CPU burst

   a. Show the CPU and I/O timelines that result with FCFS scheduling from t = 0, until all three processes complete.

   b. What is the response time for each process?

   c. What is the waiting time for each process?

Answer:

a.

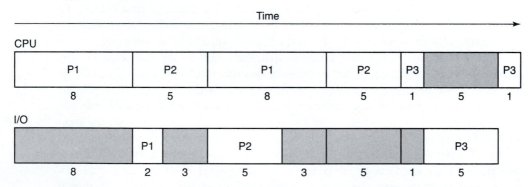

Notice that, at time t = 8, P2 and P3 are in the ready queue. P1 makes an I/O request and relinquishes the processor. The scheduler picks P2 to run on the processor due to its earlier arrival time, compared with P3. At time t = 10, P1 completes its I/O and rejoins the ready queue. P3 is already in the ready queue at this time. However, by virtue of its earlier arrival time, P1 gets ahead of P3 in the ready queue, which is why P1 gets picked by the scheduler at time t = 13.

b. We compute the response time for each process as the total time spent by the process in the system, from the time it enters to the time it departs.

$$\text{Response time (P1)} = 21$$
$$\text{Response time (P2)} = 26$$
$$\text{Response time (P3)} = 33$$

c. Each process does useful work when it is either executing on the CPU or performing its I/O operation. Thus, we compute the wait time for each process by subtracting the process's useful work done from its total turnaround time (or response time).

For example, the useful work done by P1

$$= \text{First CPU burst} + \text{I/O burst} + \text{Second CPU burst}$$
$$= 8 + 2 + 8$$
$$= 18.$$

Thus, the wait time for P1 is as follows:

$$\text{Wait-time (P1)} = (21 - 18) = 3.$$

Similarly,

$$\text{Wait-time (P2)} = (26 - 15) = 11; \text{ and}$$
$$\text{Wait-time (P3)} = (33 - 7) = 26.$$

As we mentioned earlier, the scheduler respects the arrival time of a process for its lifetime, when picking a winner to schedule on the CPU. Further, this intrinsic property is meaningful only for CPU scheduling and not for I/O. These two points are illustrated in the following example:

Example 6.2

Consider a FCFS process scheduler. Assume that there are three processes in the scheduling queue and that all three of them are ready to run. As the scheduling discipline suggests, the scheduler always respects the arrival time in selecting a winner. Assume that P1, P2, and P3 arrive in that order into the system. Scheduling starts at time t = 0. The CPU and I/O burst patterns of the three processes are as follows:

	CPU	I/O	CPU	I/O	CPU	
P1	5	5	5	3	5	P1 is done
P2	2	5	5			P2 is done
P3	3	2	2			P3 is done

Show the CPU and I/O timelines that result with FCFS scheduling from t = 0 until all three processes complete.

Answer:

Notes:

1. At time t = 15, both P3 and P1 need to perform I/O. However, P3 made the I/O request first (at time t = 10), while P1 made its request second (at time t = 15). As we mentioned earlier, the I/O requests are serviced in the order received. Thus, P3 gets serviced first, and then P1.

2. At time t = 20, both P3 and P1 are needing to get on the CPU. In fact, P3 finished its I/O at time t = 17, whereas P1 just finished its I/O, at time t = 20. Yet, P1 wins this race to get on the CPU because the CPU scheduler always respects the arrival time of processes in making its scheduling decision.

6.6.2 Shortest Job First (SJF)

The term *shortest job* comes from scheduling decisions taken in shop floors—for example, in a car mechanic shop. Unfortunately, this term can sometimes carry the wrong connotation when literally applied to CPU scheduling. Since the CPU scheduler does not know the exact behavior of a program, it works only with partial knowledge. In the case of the SJF scheduling algorithm, this knowledge is the *CPU burst time* needed, an intrinsic property of each process. As we know, each process goes through bursts of CPU and I/O activities. The SJF scheduler looks at the CPU burst times needed by the current set of processes that are ready to run and picks the one that needs the shortest CPU burst. Recalling the analogy at the beginning of the chapter, you started the washer and the microwave before you made your phone call to your mom. SJF scheduler uses the same principle of favoring short jobs. In reality, a scheduler does not know the CPU burst time for a program at program startup. However, it infers the expected burst time of a process from past CPU bursts.

The SJF algorithm results in a better response time for short jobs. Further, it does not suffer from the convoy effect of FCFS, because it gives preferential treatment to short jobs. It turns out that this algorithm also has been proved optimal for yielding the

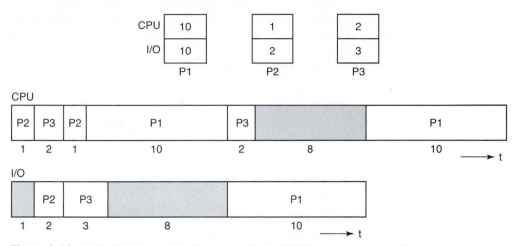

Figure 6.13   SJF schedule avoids the convoy effect of FCFS by giving preferential treatment to short jobs.

best average waiting time. Figure 6.13 shows the timeline for executing, by SJF, the same process activities shown in Figure 6.12 for FCFS. The waiting times for the three jobs P1, P2, and P3 are 4, 0, and 9, respectively.

Notice that the shortest job, P2, gets the best service with this schedule. At time t = 3, P2 has just completed its I/O burst; fortuitously, P3 has also just finished its CPU burst. At this time, although P1 and P2 are ready to be scheduled on the CPU, the scheduler gives preference to P2 over P1 due to P2's shorter CPU burst requirement. At time t = 4, P2 finishes its CPU burst. Since there is no other shorter job to schedule, P1 gets a chance to run on the CPU. At time t = 6, P3 has just completed its I/O burst and is ready to be scheduled on the CPU. However, P1 is currently executing on the processor. Since the scheduler is nonpreemptive, P3 has to wait for P1 to give up the processor on its own accord (which it does at t = 14).

There is a potential for starvation for long jobs in the SJF schedule. In the previous example, before P1 gets its turn to run, new, shorter jobs may enter the system. Thus, P1 could end up waiting a long time, perhaps even forever. To overcome this problem, a technique called *aging* gives preference—over other, short jobs—to a job that has been waiting in the ready queue for a long time. Basically, the idea is for the scheduler to add another predicate to each job, namely, the time it entered the scheduling mix. When the *age* of a job exceeds a threshold, the scheduler will override the SJF principle and give such a job preference for scheduling.

Example 6.3

Consider a nonpreemptive shortest job first (SJF) process scheduler. Assume that there are three processes in the scheduling queue and that all three of them are ready to run. As the scheduling discipline suggests, the shortest job that is ready to run is always given priority. Scheduling starts at time t = 0. The CPU and I/O burst patterns of the three processes are shown as follows:

	CPU	I/O	CPU	I/O	CPU	
P1	4	2	4	2	4	**P1 is done**
P2	5	2	5			**P2 is done**
P3	2	2	2	2	2	**P3 is done**

Each process exits the system once its CPU and I/O bursts, as just shown, are complete.

a. Show the CPU and I/O timelines that result with SJF scheduling from t = 0 until all three processes exit the system.

b. What is the waiting time for each process?

c. What is the average throughput of the system?

Answer:

a.

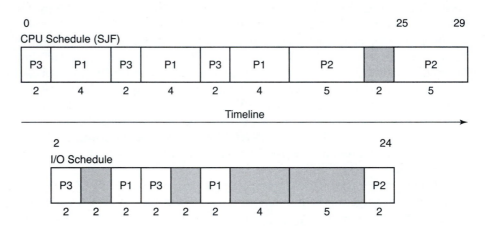

b. We compute the wait times for each process as we did in Example 6.1.

$$\text{Wait-time (P1)} = (18 - 16) = 2$$
$$\text{Wait-time (P2)} = (30 - 12) = 18$$
$$\text{Wait-time (P3)} = (14 - 10) = 4$$

c.   Total time = 30

Throughput = number of processes completed/total time

= 3/30

= 1/10 processes per unit time

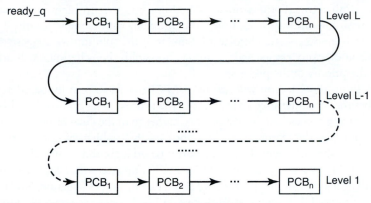

Figure 6.14   Multilevel ready queue for priority scheduler.
The scheduler may move processes among the different priority levels, over time.

6.6.3 Priority

For scheduling purposes, most operating systems associate an extrinsic property, *priority*, a small integer value, with each process to denote its relative importance, compared with other processes. For example, in the Unix operating system every user-level process starts with a certain default priority. The ready queue consists of several subqueues, one for each priority level, as shown in Figure 6.14.

The scheduling within each level is FCFS. New processes are placed in the queue commensurate with their priority levels. Since priority is an extrinsic property, the scheduler has complete control over the assignment of priorities to different processes. This scheduling discipline is highly flexible, compared with SJF or FCFS. For example, the scheduler may assign priorities on the basis of the class of users. This would be particularly attractive from the point of view of those who run data centers,[3] wherein different users may be willing to pay different rates for their respective jobs.

Priority is a very natural way of providing differential service guarantees for different users, not just in processor scheduling, but also in almost every walk of life. As an example, call centers operated by businesses that deal with customer service requests place different callers in different queues, according to their profiles. "High-maintenance" callers go into a slower queue with longer service times than those for preferred customers. Similarly, airlines use first class, business class, and economy class as a way of prioritizing service to its customers.

With a little bit of reflection, one could figure out that SJF is really a special case of priority scheduling wherein the priority level

$$L = 1/\text{CPU\_burst\_time}.$$

---

3. Data centers are becoming popular as a way of providing access to high-performance computing resources to users who do not own such resources. Companies such as Amazon, Microsoft, HP, and IBM are at the forefront of providing such services. *Cloud computing* is the industry buzzword for providing such services.

Thus, similar to SJF, the priority scheduler has the problem of starvation of processes with low priority. Countering this problem with explicit priority levels assigned to each process is straightforward. Similar to the solution we suggested for SJF, when the age of a process exceeds a preset threshold, the scheduler will artificially bump up the priority of the process.

If you think about it, you will realize that FCFS is also a priority-based algorithm. It is just that the scheduler uses arrival time of the process as its priority. For this reason, no newly arriving process can have a priority higher than the current set of processes in FCFS, which is also the reason FCFS does not have the problem of starvation.

Due to the similarity with FCFS, a priority-based algorithm could also exhibit the convoy effect. Let us see how this could happen. If a process with a higher priority also turns out to be a long-running process, we could end up with a situation similar to what we observed in the FCFS schedule. However, in FCFS, once assigned, the process priority never changes. This need not be the case in a priority-based scheduler; the same mechanism (bumping up the priority on the basis of age) used to overcome the starvation problem would also help to break the convoy effect.

6.7 Preemptive Scheduling Algorithms

This class of scheduling algorithms implies two things, simultaneously. First, the scheduler is able to assume control of the processor anytime, unbeknown to the currently running process. Second, the scheduler is able to save the state of the currently running process for proper resumption, from the point of preemption. Returning to our analogy from the beginning of the chapter, when the washer beeps while you are on the phone with Mom, you excuse yourself and make a mental note of where to resume the conversation when you get back on the phone again.

In principle, any of the algorithms discussed in the previous section could be made preemptive. To accomplish that, in the case of FCFS, whenever a process rejoins the ready queue after I/O completion, the scheduler can decide to preempt the currently running process (if its arrival time is later than that of the former process). Similarly, for SJF and priority, the scheduler reevaluates and makes a decision to preempt the currently running process whenever a new process joins the ready queue, or whenever an existing one rejoins the queue upon I/O completion.

Shortest remaining time first (SRTF) is a special case of the SJF scheduler, with preemption added in. The scheduler has an estimate of the running time of each process. When a process rejoins the ready queue, the scheduler computes the remaining processing time of the job. According to its calculation, the scheduler places this process at the correct spot in the ready queue. If the remaining time of this process is lower than that of the currently running process, then the scheduler preempts the latter in favor of the former.

Example 6.4

Consider the following four processes vying for the CPU. The scheduler uses **SRTF**. The table shows the arrival time of each process.

Process	Arrival Time	Execution Time
P1	T_0	4 ms
P2	$T_0 + 1$ ms	2 ms
P3	$T_0 + 2$ ms	2 ms
P4	$T_0 + 3$ ms	3 ms

a. Show the schedule, starting from time T_0.

Answer:

1. At T_0, P1 starts running, since there is no other process.
2. At $T_0 + 1$, P2 arrives. The following table shows the remaining/required running time for P1 and P2:

Process	Remaining Time
P1	3 ms
P2	2 ms

Scheduler switches to P2.

3. At $T_0 + 2$, P3 arrives. The following table shows the remaining/required running time for P1, P2, and P3:

Process	Remaining Time
P1	3 ms
P2	1 ms
P3	2 ms

Scheduler continues with P2.

4. At $T_0 + 3$, P4 arrives. P2 completes and leaves. The following table shows the remaining/required running for P1, P3, and P4:

Process	Remaining Time
P1	3 ms
P3	2 ms
P4	3 ms

Scheduler picks P3 as the winner and runs it to completion for the next 2 ms.

5. At $T_0 + 5$, P1 and P4 are the only two remaining processes, with remaining/required times as follows:

Process	Remaining Time
P1	3 ms
P4	3 ms

It is a tie, and the scheduler breaks the tie by scheduling P1 and P4 in the arrival order (P1 first and then P4), which would result in a lower average wait time.

The following table shows the schedule with SRTF.

Interval T_0+	0	1	2	3	4	5	6	7	8	9	10	11	12
Running	P1	P2	P2	P3	P3	P1	P1	P1	P4	P4	P4		

b. What is the waiting time for each process?

Answer:

Response time = completion time − arrival time

$R_{p1} = 8 - 0 = 8$ ms

$R_{p2} = 3 - 1 = 2$ ms

$R_{p3} = 5 - 2 = 3$ ms

$R_{p4} = 11 - 3 = 8$ ms

Wait time = response time − execution time

$W_{p1} = R_{p1} - E_{p1} = 8 - 4 = $ **4 ms**

$W_{p2} = R_{p2} - E_{p2} = 2 - 2 = $ **0 ms**

$W_{p3} = R_{p3} - E_{p3} = 3 - 2 = $ **1 ms**

$W_{p4} = R_{p4} - E_{p4} = 8 - 3 = $ **5 ms**

c. What is the average wait time with SRTF?

Answer:

Total waiting time = $W_{p1} + W_{p2} + W_{p3} + W_{p4} = $ **10 ms**

Average wait time = $10/4 = 2.5$ ms

d. What is the schedule for the same set of processes run with FCFS scheduling policy?

Answer:

Interval T_0+	0	1	2	3	4	5	6	7	8	9	10	11	12
Running	P1	P1	P1	P1	P2	P2	P3	P3	P4	P4	P4		

e. What is the average wait time with FCFS?

Answer:

Response time = completion time − arrival time

$R_{p1} = 4 - 0 = 4$ ms

$R_{p2} = 6 - 1 = 5$ ms

$R_{p3} = 8 - 2 = 6$ ms

$R_{p4} = 11 - 3 = 8$ ms

Wait time = response time − execution time

$W_{p1} = R_{p1} - E_{p1} = 4 - 4 = $ **0 ms**

$W_{p2} = R_{p2} - E_{p2} = 5 - 2 = $ **3 ms**

$W_{p3} = R_{p3} - E_{p3} = 6 - 2 = $ **4 ms**

$W_{p4} = R_{p4} - E_{p4} = 8 - 3 = $ **5 ms**

Total waiting time = $W_{p1} + W_{p2} + W_{p3} + W_{p4} = $ **12 ms**

Average wait time = 12/4 = 3 ms

Note: You can see that SRTF gives a lower-average wait time, compared with FCFS.

6.7.1 Round Robin Scheduler

Let us discern the characteristics of a scheduler that is appropriate for time-shared environments. As the name implies, in this environment every process should get its share of the processor. Therefore, a nonpreemptive scheduler is inappropriate for such an environment.

Time-shared environments are particularly well served by a round robin (RR) scheduler. Assume that there are n ready processes. The scheduler assigns the processor in time quantum units, q, usually referred to as *timeslice*, to each process (see Figure 6.15). You can see the connection between this type of scheduler and the first strategy we suggested at the beginning of the chapter in the analogy about test preparation. Switching among these ready processes in a round robin scheduler does not come for free. The *context switching time* has to be taken into account in determining a feasible value for the time quantum q.

Each process in the ready queue get its share of the processor for timeslice q. Once the timeslice is up, the currently scheduled process is placed at the end of the ready queue, and the next process in the ready queue is scheduled on the processor.

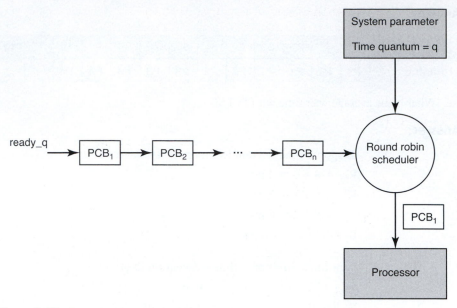

Figure 6.15 Round robin scheduler.

Each process gets a quantum of time to run on the processor before it is context-switched-out to make room for the next process.

We can draw a connection between the round robin scheduler and the FCFS scheduler. FCFS is a special case of the round robin scheduler, wherein the time quantum is *infinity*. *Processor sharing* is another special case of round robin, wherein each process gets 1 unit of time on the processor. Thus, each process gets the illusion of running on a dedicated processor with a speed of *1/n*. The processor-sharing concept is useful for proving theoretical results in scheduling.

Putting RR scheduler to work. Let us consider an example of round robin scheduling. Figure 6.16 gives three processes with CPU and I/O bursts. Let us assume that the order of arrival of the processes is P1, P2, and P3; and that the scheduler uses a timeslice of 2. Each process exits the system once its CPU and I/O bursts, as shown in the figure, are complete.

At time t = 0, the scheduling queue looks as shown in Figure 6.17. The key point to note is that this order at time t = 0 may not be preserved as the processes go back

	CPU	I/O	CPU	I/O	
P1	4	2	2		**P1 is done**
P2	3	2	2		**P2 is done**
P3	2	2	4	2	**P3 is done**

Figure 6.16 CPU and I/O bursts for round robin example.

Figure 6.17 Ready queue for example in Figure 6.16 at t = 0.

and forth between the CPU and I/O queues. When a process rejoins the CPU or the I/O queue, it is always at the end of the queue, because there is no inherent priority associated with any of the processes.

Figure 6.18 show a snapshot of the schedule for the first 17 time units (t = 0 to t = 16). Note that P2 uses only 1 unit of its timeslice the second time it is scheduled (at t = 6), because it makes an I/O burst after 3 units of CPU burst. In other words, in a round robin schedule, the timeslice is an upper bound for continuous CPU usage before a new scheduling decision. Also, at time t = 12, P2 has just completed its I/O burst and is ready to rejoin the CPU queue. At this time, P1 is in the middle of its CPU timeslice, and P3 is on the ready queue as well. Therefore, P2 joins the ready queue behind P3, as shown in Figure 6.19.

Example 6.5

What is the wait time for each of the three processes in Figure 6.16 with round robin schedule?

Answer:

As in Examples 6.1 and 6.3,

Wait time = (response time − useful work done either on the CPU or I/O)

Wait time for P1 = (13 − 8) = 5

Wait time for P2 = (17 − 7) = 10

Wait time for P3 = (17 − 10) = 7

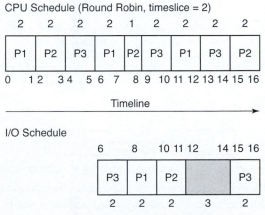

Figure 6.18 Round robin schedule for example in Figure 6.16.

Figure 6.19 Ready queue for example in Figure 6.16 at t = 12.

Details of round robin algorithm. Let us turn our attention to getting control of the processor for the scheduler. A hardware device, the *timer*, interrupts the processor when the time quantum q expires. The interrupt handler for the timer interrupt is an integral part of the round robin scheduler. Figure 6.20 shows the organization of the different layers of the system. At any point in time, the processor is hosting either the scheduler or one of the user programs. Consider that a user program is currently running on the processor. Upon an interrupt, the timer interrupt handler takes control of the processor. (Refer to the sequence of steps taken by an interrupt, as explained in Chapter 4). The handler saves the context of the currently running user program in the associated PCB and hands over control to the scheduler. This

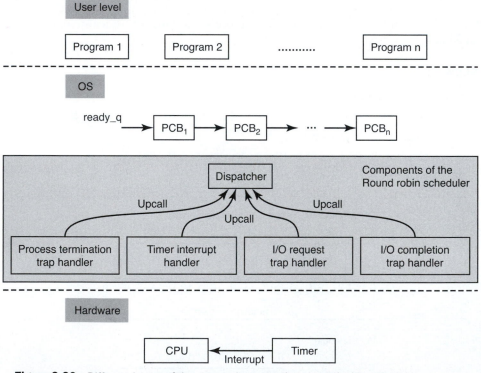

Figure 6.20 Different layers of the system incorporating a round-robin scheduler.

The different components of the round robin scheduler get invoked either due to the action of the currently running process or due to changes in the system state.

handoff, referred to as an *upcall*, allows the scheduler to run its algorithm to select the next process to be dispatched on the processor. In general, upcall refers to invoking a system function (i.e., a procedure call) from a lower level of the system software to the upper levels.

Figure 6.21 summarizes the round robin scheduling algorithm. The algorithm comprises five procedures: *dispatcher, timer interrupt handler, I/O request trap, I/O completion interrupt handler,* and *process termination trap handler.*

The dispatcher simply dispatches the process at the head of the ready queue on the processor, setting the timer to the time quantum q. The currently scheduled process may give up the processor in one of three ways: It makes an I/O call, or it terminates, or it completes its assigned time quantum on the processor. I/O request trap is the manifestation of the first option, for example, if the currently scheduled process makes a file read request from the disk. In this case, the I/O request trap procedure saves the state of the currently scheduled process in the PCB, moves it to the I/O queue, and upcalls the dispatcher. Timer interrupt handler is the manifestation of the time quantum for the current process expiring. The hardware timer interrupts the processor, resulting in the invocation of this handler. As can be seen in Figure 6.21, the timer interrupt handler saves the state in the PCB of the current process, moves the PCB to the end of the ready queue, and makes an upcall to the dispatcher. Upon completion of an I/O request, the processor will get an I/O completion interrupt. The interrupt

---

Dispatcher:
    get the PCB at the head of the ready queue;
    set timer;
    dispatch;

Timer interrupt handler:
    save context in PCB;
    move PCB to the end of the ready queue;
    upcall to dispatcher;

I/O request trap:
    save the context in PCB;
    move PCB to the I/O queue;
    upcall to dispatcher;

I/O completion interrupt handler:
    save context in PCB;
    move PCB of the I/O completed process to the ready queue;
    upcall to dispatcher;

Process termination trap handler:
    Free PCB;
    upcall to dispatcher;

Figure 6.21 Round robin scheduling algorithm.

will result in the invocation of the I/O completion handler. The role of this handler is tricky. Currently, some process is executing on the processor. This process's time quantum is not up, because it is still executing on the processor. The handler simply saves the state of the currently running process in the corresponding PCB. The I/O completion is on behalf of whichever process requested it in the first place. The handler moves the associated PCB of the process that requested the I/O to the end of the ready queue and upcalls the dispatcher. The dispatcher will do what is necessary to dispatch the original process that was interrupted by the I/O completion interrupt (since it still has time on the processor). The process termination handler simply frees up the PCB of the process, removing it from the ready queue, and upcalls the dispatcher.

6.8 Combining Priority and Preemption

General-purpose operating systems such as Unix and Microsoft Windows XP combine notions of priority and preemption in the CPU scheduling algorithms. Processes have priorities associated with them, determined at the time of creation by the operating system. They are organized into a multilevel ready queue, similar to the one shown in Figure 6.14. Additionally, the operating system employs a round robin scheduling with a fixed-time quantum for each process at a particular priority level. Lower-priority processes get service when there are no higher-priority processes to be serviced. To avoid starvation, the operating system may periodically boost the priority of processes that have not received service for a long time (i.e., aging). Further, an operating system may also give larger time quanta for higher-priority processes. The software system for such a scheduler has the structure depicted in Figure 6.20.

6.9 Meta-Schedulers

In some operating systems catering to multiple demands, the scheduling environment may consist of several ready queues, each having its own scheduling algorithm. For example, there may be a queue for foreground interactive jobs (with an associated scheduler) and a queue for background batch-oriented jobs (with an associated scheduler). The interactive jobs are scheduled in a round robin fashion, while the background jobs are scheduled by a priority-based FCFS scheduler. A meta-scheduler sits above these schedulers, timeslicing among the queues (see Figure 6.22). The parameter Q is the time quantum allocated by the meta-scheduler to each of the two schedulers at the next level. Often, the meta-scheduler provides for movement of jobs between the ready queues of the two lower-level schedulers, due to the dynamic changes in the application (represented by the different processes) requirements.

A generalization of this meta-scheduler idea is seen in *grid computing*, a somewhat nomadic Internet-based computing infrastructure that is gaining traction due to the

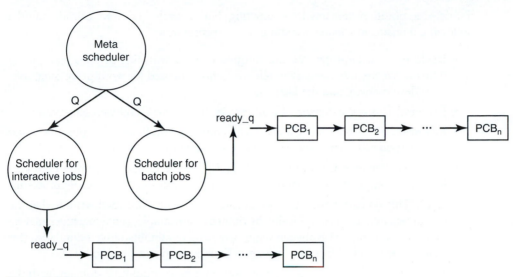

Figure 6.22   Meta-scheduler.

There is a scheduler for each class of jobs. The meta scheduler timeslices among these process level schedulers.

ability it offers to users to access *high-performance* computational resources without actually owning them. Grid computing harnesses computational resources that may be geographically distributed and crisscrossed over administrative boundaries. The term *grid* arises from the fact that the arrangement of these computational resources is analogous to the "power grid" that distributes electricity. Users of the grid submit jobs to this environment, that are executed by the distributed computational resources. The term *high-performance* refers to the fact that there may be hundreds or even thousands of computational resources working in concert to cater to the computational demands of the application. For example, an application for such an infrastructure may be global climate modeling. Computing environments designed for grid computing employ such meta-schedulers. The interested reader is referred to advanced books on the topic of grid computing [Foster, 2003].

6.10 Evaluation

How do we evaluate the efficiency of a scheduler? The key property of any OS entity is to quickly provide the requested resources to the user and get out of the way. Scheduling algorithms are evaluated with respect to the performance metrics that we mentioned earlier in the context of the specific environments in which they are to be deployed. We characterized different environments by attributes such as timeshared, batch-oriented, and multiprogrammed. These environments cater to different market forces or application domains for computing. For example, today we can identify the following domains in which computing plays a pivotal role:

- **Desktops and Laptops:** We are all quite familiar with this personal computing domain. We use this category to refer to computers used for word processing, software development, and the like.
- **Servers:** This is the domain of mail servers, files servers, and web servers.
- **Business:** This domain encompasses e-commerce and financial applications, and often is used synonymously with *enterprise computing*.
- **High-Performance Computing (HPC):** This is the domain requiring high-performance computational resources for solving scientific and engineering problems.
- **Grid:** This domain has all the elements of HPC, with the added wrinkle that the computers may be geographically distributed (for example, some machines may be in Tokyo and some in Bangalore) and may overlap administrative boundaries (for example, some machines may belong to Georgia Tech and some to MIT).
- **Embedded:** This is emerging as the most dominant computing domain, with the ubiquity of *personal digital assistants* (PDAs), including cellphones, iPODs, iPhones, and the like. This domain also encompasses dedicated computing systems found in automobiles, aircrafts, and space exploration.
- **Pervasive:** This emerging domain combines elements of HPC and embedded computing. Video-based surveillance in airports employing camera networks is an example of this domain.

We use the term *workload* to signify the nature of the applications that typify a particular domain. We can broadly classify workload as *I/O bound* or *compute bound*. However, the reader should note that this broad classification might not always be useful, especially in the case of I/O. This is because the nature of I/O can be vastly different, depending on the application domain. For example, one could say that both business applications and desktop/laptop computing are I/O intensive. Business applications manipulate large databases and, hence, involve a significant amount of I/O; desktop computing is also I/O bound, but differs from the business applications in that it is interactive I/O as opposed to I/O involving mass storage devices (such as disks). Applications in the server, HPC, and grid domains tend to be computationally intensive. Embedded and pervasive computing domains are quite different from the aforementioned domains. Such domains employ sensors and actuators (such as cameras, microphones, temperature sensors, and alarms) that need rapid response, similar to the interactive workloads; at the same time, analysis of sensor data (for example, camera images) tends to be computationally intensive.

Table 6.5 summarizes the characteristics of these different domains.

We can take one of three different approaches to evaluate a scheduler: *modeling, simulation,* and *implementation*. Each of these approaches has its pros and cons. *Modeling* refers to deriving a mathematical model (using techniques such as queuing theory) of the system. *Simulation* refers to developing a computer program that simulates the behavior of the system. Finally, *implementation* is the actual deployment of the algorithm in the operating system. Modeling, simulation, and implementation represent increasing

Table 6.5 Different Application Domains

Domains	Environment	Workload Characteristics	Types of Schedulers
Desktop	Timeshared, interactive, multiprogrammed	I/O bound	Medium-term, short-term, dispatcher
Servers	Timeshared, multiprogrammed	Computation bound	Medium-term, short-term, dispatcher
Business	Timeshared, multiprogrammed	I/O bound	Medium-term, short-term, dispatcher
HPC	Timeshared, multiprogrammed	Computation bound	Medium-term, short-term, dispatcher
Grid	Batch-oriented, timeshared, multiprogrammed	Computation bound	Long-term, medium-term, short-term, dispatcher
Embedded	Timeshared, interactive, multiprogrammed	I/O bounds	Medium-term, short-term, dispatcher
Pervasive	Timeshared, interactive, multiprogrammed	Combination of I/O bound and computation bound	Medium-term, short-term, dispatcher

amounts of effort, in that order. Correspondingly, there are payoffs from these approaches (in terms of understanding the performance potential of the system), commensurate with the effort. At the same time, modeling and simulation offer the ability to ask what-if questions, whereas the implementation freezes a particular algorithm, making it difficult to experiment with different design choices. In general, early estimates of system performance are obtained by modeling and simulation before the design is committed to an actual implementation.

6.11 Impact of Scheduling on Processor Architecture

Thus far, we have treated the processor as a black box. Having reviewed various processor-scheduling algorithms, it is natural to ponder whether this operating system functionality needs any special support from the processor architecture. Once a process is scheduled to run on the processor, the ISA has to cater to the needs of the running program, and we already know how that part is handled, from Chapter 2. Processor scheduling algorithms themselves are similar to any user-level programs, so there is nothing special about their needs insofar as the ISA is concerned. Therefore, it is during the transition—that is, context switching from one process to another—that the processor architecture may offer some special assists to the operating system.

Let us break it down so that we understand the opportunities for processor architecture to support scheduling. First, since modern operating systems support preemption, the processor architecture has to provide a way of *interrupting* the currently executing program so that the operating system can take control of the processor and run the scheduling algorithm instead of the user program. We already are familiar with this processor functionality from Chapter 4. Specifically, the processor architecture needs to provide a *timer* device for the scheduler to make its scheduling decisions and program in the time quantum for a process. Further, the ISA offers special instructions to turn on and off interrupts in order to ensure *atomicity*[4] for a group of instructions that an interrupt handler may have to execute. (See Chapter 4 for elaboration on this topic.)

Executing privileged instructions requires that the processor be in a privileged state—that is, to ensure that ordinary user programs are not allowed to execute these instructions. We saw in Chapter 4 that the processor offers *user/kernel mode* of operation precisely for this reason.

The scheduling algorithm modifies data structures (e.g., PCBs of processes) that are private to the operating system. There has to be *separation of the memory space* reserved for the operating system, from the user programs, to ensure the integrity of the operating system and to prevent either accidental or malicious corruption of the OS data structures by user programs. This is pictorially represented in Figure 6.20. In later chapters (see Chapters 7, 8, and 9), we will discuss, in much more detail, memory management and memory hierarchies that help achieve this isolation of user programs from kernel code. At this point, it is sufficient to say that providing kernel mode of operation is a convenient mechanism for achieving the separation from user programs and kernel code.

Finally, let us consider context switching—that is, saving the register values of the currently running process into its PCB—and populating the registers with the values contained in the PCB of the next process to be dispatched on the processor. We know that this has to be fast to make the OS efficient. Here is an opportunity for the processor ISA to offer some help. Some architectures (e.g., DEC VAX) offer a *single instruction* for loading *all* the processor registers from an area of the memory and, similarly, storing all the processor registers into memory. Whereas it is possible to be selective about saving/restoring registers for procedure call/return (see Chapter 2, Section 2.8), at the point of a context switch, the OS has to assume that every register of the currently running process is relevant to that process, warranting such new instructions in the ISA. Some architectures (e.g., Sun SPARC) offer *register windows* (see Chapter 2, Section 2.8) that may be used to maintain the context of the processes distinct, and thus eliminate the need for saving/restoring all the registers at the point of a context switch. In this case, it is sufficient for the scheduler to switch to the register window associated with the new process upon a context switch.

Summary and a Look Ahead

Table 6.6 summarizes the characteristics of the different scheduling algorithms discussed in this chapter. There are several advanced topics in scheduling, for the interested reader. The strategies discussed in this chapter do not guarantee any specific

---

4. We use the term atomicity, both here and elsewhere in this book to imply indivisibility of an action. The execution of a set of instructions without being interrupted is an example of an atomic action. We revisit this concept in the context of thread synchronization in Chapter 12.

Table 6.6 Comparison of Scheduling Algorithms

Name	Property	Scheduling Criterion	Pros	Cons
FCFS	Intrinsically nonpreemptive; could accommodate preemption at time of I/O completion events	Arrival time (intrinsic property)	Fair; no starvation	high variance in response time; convoy effect
SJF	Intrinsically nonpreemptive; could accommodate preemption at time of new job arrival and/or I/O completion events	Expected execution time of jobs (intrinsic property)	Preference for short jobs; has been proven to be optimal for response time; low variance in response times	Potential for starvation; bias against long-running computations
Priority	Could be either nonpreemptive or preemptive	Priority assigned to jobs (extrinsic property)	Highly flexible; since priority is not an intrinsic property, its assignment to jobs could be chosen commensurate with the needs of the scheduling environment	Potential for starvation
SRTF	Similar to SJF, but uses preemption	Expected remaining execution time of jobs	Similar to SJF	Similar to SJF
Round Robin	Preemptive, allowing equal share of the processor for all jobs	Time quantum	Equal opportunity for all jobs	Overhead for context-switching among jobs

quality of service. Several environments may demand such guarantees. Consider, for example, a rocket launcher, the control system onboard an aircraft, or a system that controls a nuclear reactor. Such systems, dubbed *real-time* systems, need deterministic guarantees; advanced topics in scheduling deal with providing such real-time guarantees. For example, *deadline scheduling* provides hints to the scheduler on the absolute time by which a task has to be completed. The scheduler will use these deadlines as a way of deciding process priorities for scheduling purposes.

As it turns out, many modern applications also demand real-time guarantees. You play music on your iPOD, play a game on your XBOX, or watch a movie on your laptop. These applications need real-time guarantees as well. However, the impact of missing deadlines may not be as serious as in a nuclear reactor. Such applications, often called *soft real-time* applications, have become part of the applications that run on general-purpose computers. Scheduling for such applications is an interesting topic for the reader to explore, as well.

Embedded computing is emerging as a dominant environment that is making quite a few inroads, exemplified by cell phones, iPODs, and iPhones. The interested reader should explore scheduling issues in such environments.

Moving beyond uniprocessor environments, scheduling in a multiprocessor environment brings its own set of challenges. We defer discussion of this topic to a later chapter in the book. Finally, scheduling in distributed systems is another exciting topic, which is outside the scope of this textbook.

Linux Scheduler—A Case Study

As we mentioned already, modern general-purpose operating systems use a combination of the techniques presented in this chapter. As a concrete example, let us review how scheduling works in Linux.

Linux is an *open source* operating-system project, which means that a community of developers has voluntarily contributed to the overall development of the operating system. New releases of the operating system appear with certain regularity. For example, circa December 2007, the release of the kernel had the number 2.6.13.12. The discussion in this section applies to the scheduling framework found in Linux release 2.6.x.

Linux offers an interesting case study because it is at once trying to please two different environments: (a) desktop computing and (b) servers. Desktop computing suggests an interactive environment wherein response time is important. This suggests that the scheduler may have to make frequent context switches to meet the interactive needs (mouse clicks, keyboard input, etc.). Servers, on the other hand, handle computationally intensive workload; thus, the less context switching there is, the more useful work can be done in a server. Linux sets out to meet the following goals in its scheduling algorithm:

- high efficiency, meaning spending as little time as possible in the scheduler itself, an important goal for the server environment;
- support for interactivity, which is important for the interactive workload of the desktop environment;
- avoiding starvation, to ensure that computational workloads do not suffer as a result of interactive workloads; and
- support for soft real-time scheduling, once again to meet the demands of interactive applications with real-time constraints.

Linux's connotations for the terms *process* and *threads* are a bit nonstandard from the traditional meanings associated with these terms. Therefore, we will simply use the term *task* as the unit of scheduling in describing the Linux scheduling algorithm.

Linux scheduler recognizes three classes of tasks:

- Real-time FCFS
- Real-time round robin
- Timeshared

The scheduler has 140 priority levels. It reserves levels 0–99 for real-time tasks, and the remaining levels for the timeshared tasks. A lower number implies a higher priority; thus, priority level 0 is the highest priority level in the system. The scheduler uses real-time FCFS and real-time round robin classes for interactive workloads, and the timeshared class for computational workloads. Real-time FCFS tasks enjoy the highest priority. The scheduler will not preempt a real-time FCFS task currently executing on the processor unless a new real-time FCFS task with a higher priority joins the ready queue. Real-time round robin tasks have lower priority compared with the real-time FCFS tasks. As the name suggests, the scheduler associates a time quantum with each round robin task. All the round robin tasks at a given priority level have the same time quantum associated with them; the higher the priority level is of a round robin task, the higher the time quantum associated with it will be. The timeshared tasks are similar to the real-time tasks except that they are at lower priority levels.

The main data structure (Figure 6.23) in the scheduler is a *runqueue*. The runqueue contains two *priority* arrays. One priority array is the active one, and the second is the expired one. Each priority array has 140 entries corresponding to the 140 priority levels. Each entry points to the first task at that level. The tasks at the same level are linked together through a doubly linked list.

The scheduling algorithm is straightforward:

- Pick the first task with the highest priority from the active array, and run it.
- If the task blocks (due to I/O), put it aside and pick the next highest one to run.
- If the time quantum runs out (does not apply to FCFS tasks) for the currently scheduled task, place it in the expired array.
- If a task completes its I/O, place it in the active array at the right priority level, adjusting its remaining time quantum.
- If there are no more tasks to schedule in the active array, simply flip the active and expired array pointers and continue with the scheduling algorithm (i.e., the expired array becomes the active array, and vice versa).

The first thing to note in the foregoing algorithm is that the priority arrays enable the scheduler to take a scheduling decision in a *constant* amount of time, independent of the number of tasks in the system. This meets the efficiency goal we mentioned earlier. For this reason, the scheduler is also called *O(1) scheduler,* implying that the scheduling decision is independent of the number of tasks in the system.

The second thing to note is that the scheduler gives preferential treatment to meeting soft real-time constraints of interactive tasks through the real-time FCFS and real-time round robin scheduling classes.

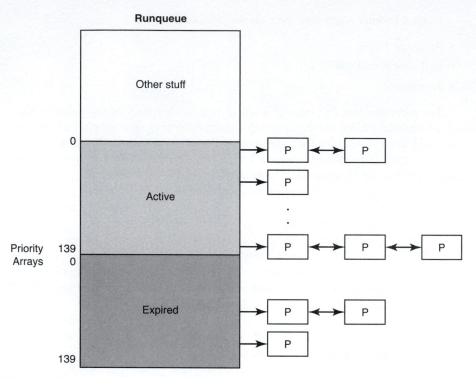

Figure 6.23 Linux scheduling data structures.

There is a doubly linked list for each of the 140 levels of scheduling priorities. The scheduler schedules the tasks in the active array in a time-sliced manner, moving them to the expired array when their time quantums run out. When the active array is empty, it makes the "expired" array the active one.

As we said earlier, but for the relative priority levels, there is not much difference, in terms of scheduling, between the real-time round robin and timeshared classes of tasks. In reality, the scheduler does not know which of these tasks are truly interactive. Therefore, it uses a heuristic to determine the nature of the tasks from execution history. The scheduler monitors the pattern of CPU usage of each task. If a task makes frequent blocking I/O calls, it is an interactive task (I/O bound); on the other hand, if a task does not do much I/O, it is a CPU intensive task (CPU bound).

Many us may be familiar with the phrase "carrot and stick" an idiom used to signify rewarding good behavior and punishing bad behavior. The scheduler does the same, rewarding tasks that are interactive by boosting their scheduling priority dynamically, and punishing tasks that are CPU-intensive by lowering their scheduling priority dynamically.[5] The scheduler boosts the priority level of an interactive task so that it will get a

---

5. A task has a static priority at the time of task creation. *Dynamic priority* is a temporary deviation from this static level, as either a reward or a punishment for good or bad behavior, respectively.

higher share of the CPU time, thus leading to good response times. Similarly, the scheduler lowers the priority of a compute-bound task so that it will get a lesser share of the CPU time compared with the interactive tasks.

Finally, for meeting the starvation goal, the scheduler has a starvation threshold. If a task has been deprived of CPU usage (due to interactive tasks getting higher priority) beyond this threshold, then the starved task gets CPU usage ahead of the interactive tasks.

Historical Perspective

Operating systems have a colorful history, just as CPUs do. Microsoft Windows, Mac OS, and Linux dominate the marketplace today. Let us take a journey through the history books to see how we got here.

The evolution of the operating system is inexorably tied to the evolution of the processor. Charles Babbage (1792–1871) built the first calculating machine (he called it the "analytical engine") out of purely mechanical parts: gears, pulleys, and wheels. Not much else happened in the evolution of computing until World War II. It is sad, but true, that wars spur technological innovations. John Mauchly and Presper Eckert at the University of Pennsylvania built ENIAC (Electronic Numerical Integrator and Calculator) in 1944, using vacuum tubes. Their work was funded by the U.S. Army to carry out the calculations needed to break the German secret codes. ENIAC and other early machines of this era (1944 to 1955) were primarily used in standalone mode and did not need any operating system. In fact, "programs" in these early days of computing were just wired-up circuits designed to repetitively perform specific computations.

The appearance in the late 1950s of mainframes using solid-state electronics gave birth to the first images of computing machinery as we know it today. IBM, the foremost player in the mainframe arena, introduced the FORTRAN programming language and, possibly, the first operating system to support it, called FMS (Fortran Monitoring System). IBM later introduced IBSYS, IBM's operating system for the IBM 7094 computer. This is the age of the *batch-oriented* operating system; users submitted their jobs as a deck of punched cards. The punched cards contained the resource needs of the program, in a language called the *job control language (JCL),* and the program itself in FORTRAN. The jobs were run one at a time on the computer, requiring quite a bit of manual work by the human operator to load the tapes and disks relevant to the resource requirements of each program. Users collected the results of the run of their program, on the computer at a later time.

Two distinct user communities were discernible in these early days of computing: scientific and business. In the mid-1960s, IBM introduced the 360 family of computers aimed at integrating the needs of both communities under one umbrella. It also introduced the OS/360 as the operating system for this family of machines. The most important innovation in this operating system was the *multiprogramming,* which ensured that the CPU was being used for some other process when the system was performing I/O for some users. Despite multiprogramming, the external appearance of the system was still a batch-oriented one, because the users submitted their jobs at one time and collected the results later.

The desire to get interactive response to the submitted jobs, from the point of view of analyzing the results for further refinement of the programs and/or for simple debugging, led to the next evolution in operating systems, namely, *timesharing*, which had its roots in CTSS (compatible time sharing system) developed, at MIT in 1962, to run on the IBM 7094. A follow-on project, at MIT, to CTSS was MULTICS (MULTiplexed Information and Computing Service), which was perhaps far ahead of its time in terms of concepts for information service and exchange, given the primitive nature of the computing base available at that time. MULTICS introduced several seminal operating-system ideas related to information organization, sharing, protection, security, and privacy that are relevant to this day.

MULTICS was the seed for the development of the UNIX operating system, at Bell Labs in 1974, by Dennis Ritchie and Ken Thompson, who named it UNIX to signify their intention to develop a stripped-down one-user version of MULTICS. UNIX[6] became instantly popular with educational institutions, government labs, and many companies such as DEC and HP. The emergence of Linux obliquely out of UNIX is an interesting story. With the popularity of UNIX and its adoption by widely varying entities, soon there were several incompatible versions of the operating system. In 1987, Andrew Tannenbaum[7] of Vrije University developed MINIX as a small clone of UNIX, for educational purposes. Linus Torvalds wrote Linux (starting from MINIX) as a free production version of UNIX and it soon took a life of its own due the open-software model promoted by the GNU foundation. Despite the interesting history behind the evolution of these different UNIX-based systems, one thing remained the same, namely, the operating-systems concepts embodied in these different flavors of UNICES.

All of the aforementioned operating systems evolved to support mainframes and minicomputers. In parallel with this evolution, microcomputers were hitting the market and slowly transforming both the computing base and the usage model. The computer was no longer necessarily a shared resource, the model suggested by the expensive mainframes and minicomputers. Rather, it was a *personal computer (PC)* intended for the exclusive use of a single user. There were a number of initial offerings of microcomputers built, using Intel 8080/8085 single-chip processors, in the 1970s. What should the operating system look like for such a personal computer? A simple operating system called CP/M (an acronym for *control program monitor*) was an industry standard for such microcomputers.

IBM developed the IBM PC in the early 1980s. A small company called Microsoft offered to IBM an operating system called MS-DOS for the IBM PC. Early versions of MS-DOS had striking similarities to CP/M, but had a simpler file system and delivered higher performance. With the blessing of an industry giant such as IBM, soon MS-DOS took over the PC market and sidelined CP/M. Initially, MS-DOS was quite primitive in its functionality, given the intended use of the PC, but it slowly started incorporating the ideas of multitasking and timesharing from the UNIX operating system. It is interesting to note that, whereas MS-DOS evolved from a small, lean operating system and

---

6. It was originally named UNICS (UNIplexed Information and Computing Service), and the name later was changed to UNIX.

7. Author of many famous textbooks in operating systems and architecture.

started incorporating ideas from the UNIX operating system, Apple's Mac OS X, also intended for PCs (Apple's Macintosh line), was a direct descendent of the UNIX operating system.

When Apple adopted the GUI (graphical user interface) in the Mac computers, Microsoft followed suit, offering Windows on top of MS-DOS as a way for users to interact with the PC. Initial offerings of Windows were wrappers on top of MS-DOS, until 1995, when Microsoft introduced Windows 95, which integrated the Windows GUI with the operating system. We have gone through several iterations of Windows operating systems since Windows 95, including Windows NT (*NT* stands for *new technology*), Windows NT 4.0, Windows 2000, Windows XP, Windows Vista, and Windows Version 7 (as of 2009). However, the basic concepts at the level of the core abstractions in the operating system have not changed much in these iterations. If anything, these concepts have matured to the point where they are indistinguishable from those found in the UNIX operating system. Similarly, UNIX-based systems have also absorbed and incorporated the GUI ideas that had their roots in the PC world.

Exercises

1. Compare and contrast process and program.

2. What items are considered to comprise the state of a process?

3. Which metric is the most user-centric in a timesharing environment?

4. Consider a preemptive priority processor scheduler. There are three processes, P1, P2, and P3, in the job mix, that have the following characteristics:

Process	Arrival Time	Priority	Activity
P1	0 sec	1	8 sec CPU burst followed by
			4 sec I/O burst followed by
			6 sec CPU burst and quit
P2	2 sec	3	64 sec CPU burst and quit
P3	4 sec	2	2 sec CPU burst followed by
			2 sec I/O burst followed by
			2 sec CPU burst followed by
			2 sec I/O burst followed by
			2 sec CPU burst followed by
			2 sec I/O burst followed by
			2 sec CPU burst and quit

What is the turnaround time for each of P1, P2, and P3?

What is the average waiting time for this job mix?

5. What are the deficiencies of FCFS CPU scheduling?

6. Explain the convoy effect in FCFS scheduling.

7. What are the merits of FCFS scheduling?

8. Discuss the different scheduling algorithms, with respect to the following criteria: (a) waiting time, (b) starvation, (c) turnaround time, and (d) variance in turnaround time. Which scheduling algorithm is noted as having a high variance in turnaround time?

9. Can any scheduling algorithm be made preemptive? What are the characteristics of the algorithm that lends itself to being preemptive? What support is needed from the processor architecture to allow preemption?

10. Summarize the enhancements to processor architecture warranted by processor scheduling.

11. Consider the following processes, which arrived in the order shown:

	CPU Burst Time	IO Burst Time
P1	3	2
P2	4	3
P3	8	4

Show the activity in the processor and the I/O area, using the FCFS, SJF, and round robin algorithms.

12. Redo Example 6.1 in Section 6.6 using SJF and round robin (timeslice = 2).

13. Redo Example 6.3 in Section 6.6 using FCFS and round robin (timeslice = 2).

Bibliographic Notes and Further Reading

A classic paper on time-shared operating systems by Bobrow et al. [Bobrow, 1972] had great influence on the design of early commercial operating systems such as Digital Equipment Corporation's TOPS-20. Other influential operating systems of years gone by include the VAX/VMS operating system from DEC, and the OS/360 from IBM. The original paper on Unix was published in 1974 [Ritchie, 1974]. The topic of processor scheduling is well covered in several textbooks [Silberschatz, 2008; Tanenbaum, 2007]. For details on CPU scheduling in Linux, the book by Bovet and Cesati is a good resource [Bovet, 2005]. Many operating-system textbooks [Silberschatz, 2008; Tanenbaum, 2007] include case studies of a few influential operating systems of yesteryears, as well as modern ones such as Linux, Windows XP, and Symbian OS. The book edited by Foster and Kesselman [Foster, 2003] is a good resource to learn about developments in grid computing.

Memory Management Techniques

Let us review what we have seen so far. On the hardware side, we have looked at the instruction set of the processor, interrupts, and the design of a processor. On the software side, we have seen how to use the processor as a resource and schedule it to run different programs. The software entities we have familiarized ourselves with include the *compiler* and *linker* that live above the operating system. We have also familiarized ourselves with the *loader* and *process scheduler* that are part of the operating system.

By now, we hope that we have demystified some of what may seem like the magic of what is inside a "box." In this chapter, we continue unraveling the box by looking at another important component of the computer system, namely, the memory.

More than any other subsystem, the memory system brings out the strong interrelationship between hardware and system software. Quite often, it is almost impossible to describe some software aspect of the memory system without mentioning the hardware support. We cover the memory system in three chapters, including this one. This chapter focuses on different strategies for memory management by the operating system, along with the necessary architectural support. In Chapter 8, we delve into the finer details of page-based memory system, in particular, page replacement policies. Finally, in Chapter 9, we discuss memory hierarchy—in particular, cache memories and main, or physical, memory.

7.1 Functionalities Provided by a Memory Manager

Let us understand what we mean by *memory management*. As a point of differentiation, we would like to disambiguate *memory management*, in terms of our meaning and our discussion in this textbook, from the concept of *automatic memory management* as used by programming languages such as Java and C#. The runtime systems of such languages automatically free up memory not currently used by the program. *Garbage collection (GC)* is another term used to describe this functionality. Some of the technical issues with GC are similar to those handled by the memory management component of an operating system. Discussion of the similarities and differences between the two are outside the scope of this textbook. The interested reader is referred to other sources to learn more about GC [Jones, 1996].

In this textbook, we focus on how the operating system manages memory. Just like the processor, memory is a precious resource, and the operating system ensures the best use of this resource. Memory management is an operating system entity that provides the following functionalities:

1. **Improved resource utilization:** Because the memory is a precious resource, it is best allocated on demand. The analogy is the use of office space. Each faculty member in the department may ask for a certain amount of space for his or her students and the lab. The chair of the department might not give all the space requested, all at once, but may allocate space, incrementally, as the faculty member's group grows. Similarly, even though the memory footprint[1] of the program includes the heap (Figure 6.1 in Chapter 6), there is no need to allocate this to a program at startup. It is sufficient to make the allocation if and when the program dynamically requests it. If a faculty member's group shrinks, he or she no longer needs all the space allocated. The chair of the department would reclaim that space and reallocate it to someone else who needs it more. In the same manner, if a process is not actively using the memory allocated to it, then perhaps it is best to release the memory from that process and use it for another process that needs it. Both these ideas, incremental allocation and dynamic reallocation, will lead to improved resource utilization of memory. The criticality of using this resource judiciously is best conveyed by a simple visual example. The left half of the figure that follows shows a screenshot of the task manager listing the actual applications running on a laptop. The right half of the figure shows a partial listing of the actual processes running on the laptop. There are four applications running, but there are 123 processes! We show this screenshot to point out that the operating system and other utilities spawn a number of background processes (often called *daemon* processes) in addition to the user processes. Thus, the demand placed on the memory system by the collection of processes running on the computer at any point in time is intense. The laptop shown in this example has 2 GB of memory, out of which 58% is in use despite the fact that only four applications are running.

---

1. In Chapters 5 and 6, we used the term *memory footprint* to denote the static space occupied by the program at load time. In Chapters 7 and 8, we expand the definition of *memory footprint* to include the memory dynamically allocated, in the heap, for the program during execution.

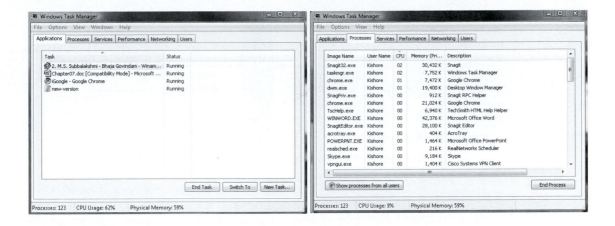

2. **Independence and protection:** We mentioned that several processes are coresident in memory at any point. A program may have a bug causing it to run amok, writing into areas of memory that are not part of its footprint. It would be prudent to protect a buggy process from itself and from other processes. Further, in these days of computer viruses and worms, a malicious program could be intentionally trying to corrupt the memories of other genuine programs. Therefore, the memory manager provides *independence* for each process, and *memory protection* from one another. Once again considering the space analogy, you probably can relate to the need for independence and protection if you grew up in a home with siblings. You either had or wished you had a room for yourself that you could lock when you wanted to keep the siblings (and the parents) out!

3. **Liberation from resource limitations:** When a faculty member is hired, the chair of the department may promise as much space as the new professor wants, perhaps even more than the total unoccupied space currently available in the department. This gives the faculty member the freedom to think "big" in terms of planning for establishing and growing his or her research agenda and student base. In a similar manner, it is ideal for the programmer not to worry about the amount of physical memory while developing his or her program. Imagine a faculty member with 10 students, but lab space for only 5. The students may have to work different shifts, sharing the same lab space. In the same vein, imagine having to write a multiplayer video game program, and your manager says that you have a total memory space of 10 KB. Let's say the code and data structures you need for your program require much more space than the given 10 KB of memory. Then you, as the programmer, will have to identify code and data structures that you will not need simultaneously and use the given memory space in a time-shared manner for storing them (in essence, overlaying these data structures in memory). The program can get ugly if you have to resort to such methods. To address this problem, the memory management software and the architecture work together to devise mechanisms that give the programmer an illusion of a large memory. The actual physical memory may be much smaller than that of which the programmer is given an illusion.

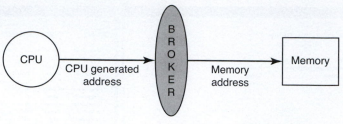

Figure 7.1   A generic schematic of a memory manager.

The memory manager acts as a broker between the address generated by the CPU and the memory.

4. **Sharing of memory by concurrent processes:** You may want to keep your siblings out most of the time, but there are times you will want to let them into your room, perhaps to play a video game. In a similar way, while memory protection among processes is necessary, processes sometimes may want to *share* memory, either implicitly or explicitly. For example, you may have multiple browser windows open on your desktop. Each of them may be accessing a different web page, but if all of them are running the same browser application, then they could share the code. This is an example of implicit sharing among processes. Copying and pasting an image from a presentation program into a word processor is an example of explicit data sharing. The memory manager facilitates memory sharing, as needed, among processes.

All of the foregoing functionalities come at a price. In particular, we are introducing a *broker* between the CPU and the memory, as shown in Figure 7.1. The broker is a piece of hardware that provides the mechanisms needed for implementing the memory management policies. In principle, it maps a CPU-generated (logical) memory address to the *real* memory address for accessing the memory. The level of sophistication of the broker depends on the functionalities provided by the memory manager.

So far, we have not introduced such functionality in the LC-2200. However, as we get ambitious and let the LC-2200 take over the world from game players to high-performance computers, such functionalities will become indispensable.

The overall goals of a good memory manager are three-fold. It should

1. require minimal hardware support;
2. keep the impact on memory accesses low; and
3. keep the memory-management overhead low (for allocation and deallocation of memory).

7.2 Simple Schemes for Memory Management

In this section, let us consider some simple schemes for memory management and the corresponding hardware support. This section is written in the spirit of shared discovery, to understand how to accomplish the aforementioned goals, while at the same time meeting the functionalities presented in the previous section. The first two schemes and the associated hardware support (fence registers and bounds registers) are for illustration purposes only. We do not know of any machine architecture that ever used such schemes. The third scheme (base and limit registers) was widely used in a number of architectures, including the CDC 6600 (the very first supercomputer) and the IBM 360 series. All three schemes have limitations in terms of meeting the functionalities identified in the previous section, and thus they set the stage for the sophisticated memory-management schemes, namely, paging and segmentation, found in modern architectures.

1. **Separation of user and kernel:** Let us consider a very simple memory-management scheme. As we have seen before, the operating system and the user programs share the total available memory space. The space used by the operating system is the *kernel space*, and the space occupied by the user programs is the *user space*. As a first order of approximation, we wish to ensure that there is a boundary between these two spaces, so that a user program does not straddle into the memory space of the operating system. Figure 7.2 shows a simple hardware scheme to accomplish this separation. The shaded area in the figure corresponds to the hardware portion of the work done by the broker in Figure 7.1. The scheme relies on three architectural elements: a *mode* bit that signifies whether the program is in user or kernel mode, a *privileged instruction* that allows flipping this bit, and a *fence* register. As you can imagine, the name for this register comes from the analogy of a physical fence built for property protection. The memory manager sets the fence register when the user program is scheduled. The hardware validates the processor-generated memory address by checking it against this fence register. This simple hardware scheme gives memory protection between the user program and the kernel.

    For example, let us assume that the fence register is set to 10000. This means that the kernel is occupying the memory region 0 through 10000. In user mode, if

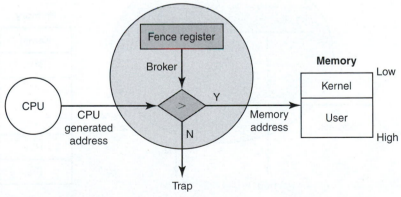

Figure 7.2   Fence register.

Allow the user program's memory access to proceed if the address is above a threshold specified by the fence register.

the CPU generates any address over 10000, the hardware considers it a valid user-program address. Anything less than or equal to 10000 is a kernel address and generates an access-violation trap. The CPU has to be in kernel mode to access the kernel memory region. To understand how the CPU gets into the kernel mode, recall that in Chapter 4 we introduced the notion of *traps,* a synchronous program discontinuity usually caused by a program wishing to make a system call (such as reading a file). Such traps result in the processor automatically entering the kernel mode as part of implementation of the trap instruction. Thus, the CPU implicitly gets into kernel mode on system calls and is now able to address the memory region reserved for the kernel. Once the operating system completes the system call, it can explicitly return to the user mode by way of the architecture-provided privileged instruction. It is a privileged instruction because its use is limited to kernel mode. Any attempt to execute this instruction in user mode will result in an *exception,* another synchronous program discontinuity (which we introduced in Chapter 4, as well) caused by an illegal action by a user program. As you may have already guessed, writing to the fence register is also a privileged instruction.

2. **Static relocation:** As previously discussed, we would like several user programs to be coresident in memory at the same time. Therefore, the memory manager should protect the coresident processes from one another. Figure 7.3 shows a hardware scheme to accomplish this protection. Once again, the shaded area in the figure corresponds to the hardware portion of the work done by the broker in Figure 7.1.

   Static relocation refers to the memory bounds, for a process, being set at the time of linking the program and creating an executable file. Once the executable is created, the memory addresses cannot be changed during the execution of the program. To support memory protection for processes, the architecture provides

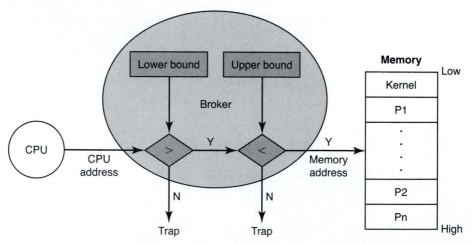

Figure 7.3   Bounds registers.

A user programs's memory access is allowed to proceed if it is in between the bounds specified in the lower-bound and upper-bound registers.

two registers: *upper bound* and *lower bound*. The *bounds* registers are part of the process control block (or PCB, which we introduced in Chapter 6). Writing to the bounds registers is a privileged instruction provided by the architecture. The memory manager sets the values from the PCB into the bounds registers at the time of dispatching the process. (Refer to Chapter 6 on scheduling a process on the CPU.) At link time, the linker allocates a particular region in memory for a particular process.[2] The loader fixes the lower and upper bound register values for this process at load time and never changes them for the life of the program. Let us assume that the linker has assigned P1 the address range 10001 to 14000. In this case, the scheduler will set the lower bound and upper bound registers to 10000 and 14001, respectively. Thus, while P1 is executing, if the CPU generates addresses in the range 10001 to 14000, the hardware permits them as valid memory accesses. Anything outside this range will result in an access violation trap.

A concept that we alluded to in Chapter 6 is *swapping*. *Swapping out* a process refers to the act of moving an inactive process (for example, if it is waiting on I/O completion) from the memory to the disk. The memory manager does this act to put the memory occupied by the inactive process to good use by assigning it to other active processes. Similarly, once a process becomes active again (for example, if its I/O request is complete), the memory manager would *swap in* the process from the disk to the memory (after making sure that the required memory is allocated to the process being swapped in).

Let us consider swapping in a process from the disk with static relocation support. Due to the fixed bounds, the memory manager brings a swapped-out process back to memory into exactly the same spot as before. If that memory space is in use by a different process, the swapped-out process cannot be brought back into memory just yet, which is the main limitation with static relocation.

In reality, compilers generate code, assuming some well-known address where the program will reside in memory.[3] Thus, if the operating system cannot somehow rectify this assumption, a process is essentially *nonrelocatable*. We define a process as nonrelocatable if the addresses in the program cannot be changed either during loading into memory or during execution. We define static relocation as the technique of locating a process at *load time* in a different region of memory than originally intended at compile time. That is, the addresses used in the program are bound (i.e., fixed) at the time the program is loaded into memory and do not change during execution. IBM used a version of this kind of static relocation in their early models of mainframes (in the early 1960s). At the time of loading a process into memory, the loader will look at unused space in memory and make a decision as to where to locate the new process. It will then "fix" up all the addresses in the executable so that the program will work correctly in its new home. For

---

2. Note that modern operating systems use dynamic linking, which allows deferring this decision of binding the addresses to a process until the time of loading the process into memory. Such a dynamic linker could take the current usage of memory into account when it assigns the bounds for a new process.

3. In most modern compilers, a program starts at address 0 and goes to some system-specified maximum address.

example, let us say that the original program occupied addresses 0 to 1000. The loader decides to locate this program between addresses 15000 and 16000. In this case, the loader will add 15000 to each address it finds in the executable as it loads it into memory. As you can imagine, this is a very cumbersome and arduous process. The loader has an intimate knowledge of the layout of the executable so that it can tell the difference between constant values and addresses to do this kind of fix-up.

3. **Dynamic relocation:** Static relocation constrains memory management and leads to poor memory utilization. This is because, once created, an executable occupies a fixed spot in memory. Two completely different programs that happen to have the same, or overlapping, memory bounds cannot coexist in memory simultaneously, even if there are other regions of memory currently unoccupied. This is similar to two kids wanting to play with the same toy, even though there are plenty of other toys to play with! This is not a desirable situation. *Dynamic relocation* refers to the ability to place an executable into any region of memory that can accommodate the memory needs of the process. Let us understand how this differs from static relocation. With dynamic relocation, the memory address generated by a program can be changed during the *execution* of the program. What this means is that, at the time of loading a program into memory, the operating system can decide where to place the program on the basis of the current usage of memory. From the previous discussion on static relocation, you might think that this is what a dynamic linker lets us do. However, the difference is that, with dynamic relocation, even if the process is swapped out, when it is later brought in it need not come to the same spot it occupied previously. Succinctly put, with static relocation, addresses generated by the program are fixed during execution; whereas with dynamic relocation, they can be changed during execution.

Now we need to figure out the architectural support for dynamic relocation. Let us try a slightly different hardware scheme, as shown in Figure 7.4. As before, the shaded area in the figure corresponds to the hardware portion of the work done by the broker in Figure 7.1. The architecture provides two registers: *base* and *limit*. A CPU-generated address is *always* shifted by the value in the base register. Since this shift necessarily happens during the execution of the program, such an architectural enhancement meets the criterion for dynamic relocation. As in the case of static relocation, these two registers are part of the PCB of every process. Every time a process is brought into memory (at either load time or swap time), the loader assigns the values for the base and bound registers for the process. The memory manager records these loader-assigned values into the corresponding fields of the PCB for that process. Similar to the bounds registers for static relocation, writing to the base and limit registers is a privileged instruction supported by the architecture. When the memory manager dispatches a particular process, it sets the values for the base and limit registers from the PCB for that process. Let us assume that P1's memory footprint is 4000. If the loader assigns the address range 10001 to 14000 for P1, then the memory manager sets the base register to 10001 and

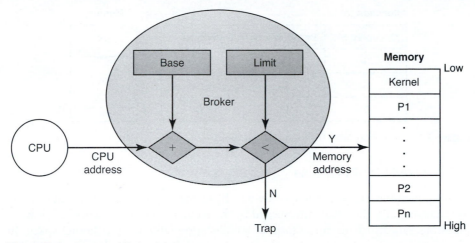

Figure 7.4   Base and limit registers.

> The CPU-generated address is shifted by a value specified in the base register before being sent to the memory. The limit register serves as the upper bound for allowable memory address for the current process.

the limit register 14001, in the PCB for P1. Thus, when P1 is executing, any CPU-generated address is automatically shifted up by 10000 by the hardware. So long as the shifted address is less than the value set in the limit register, the hardware permits it as a valid memory access. Anything that is beyond the limit results in an access violation trap. The reader should feel convinced that dynamic relocation will result in better memory utilization than static relocation.

The architectural enhancements we presented for both static and dynamic relocation required two additional registers in the processor. Let us review these two schemes, with respect to hardware implementation. Compare the datapath elements that you would need for Figures 7.3 and 7.4. For Figure 7.3, you need two comparison operations for bounds checking. For Figure 7.4, you need an addition, followed by a comparison operation. Thus, in both schemes you will need two arithmetic operations to generate the memory address from the CPU address. Therefore, both schemes come out even in terms of hardware complexity and delays. However, the advantage you get in terms of memory utilization is enormous with the base and limit register scheme. This is an example of how a little bit of human ingenuity can lead to enormous gains with little or no added cost.

7.3 Memory Allocation Schemes

We will assume that the *base plus limit register* scheme is used as the hardware support available to the memory manager, and discuss some policies for memory allocation. In each case, we will identify the data structures needed to carry out the memory management.

Allocation table

Occupied bit	Partition size	Process
0	5K	XXX
0	8K	XXX
0	1K	XXX

Memory

5K
8K
1K

Figure 7.5   Allocation table for fixed-size partitions

7.3.1 Fixed-Size Partitions

In this policy, the memory manager divides the memory into fixed-size partitions. Let us understand the data structure needed by the memory manager. Figure 7.5 shows a plausible data structure in the form of an allocation table kept in kernel space. In effect, the memory manager manages the portion of the memory that is available for use by user programs using this data structure. For this allocation policy, the table contains three fields, as shown in Figure 7.5. The *occupied bit* signifies whether the partition is in use or not. The bit is 1 if the partition has been allocated; 0 otherwise. When a process requests memory (either at load time or during execution), it is given one of the fixed partitions that is equal to or greater than the current request. For example, if the memory manager has partitions of sizes 1 KB, 5 KB, and 8 KB, and if a process P1 requests a 6 KB memory chunk, then it is given the 8 KB partition. The memory manager sets the corresponding bit in the table to 1, and resets the bit when the process returns the chunk. Upon allocating P1's request for 6 KB, the allocation table looks as shown in Figure 7.5(a). Note that there is wasted space of 2 KB within this 8 KB partition.

Unfortunately, it is not possible to grant a request for a 2 KB memory chunk from another process using this wasted space. This is because the allocation table maintains summary information on the basis of fixed-size partitions. This phenomenon, called *internal fragmentation*, refers to the wasted space internal to fixed-size partitions that leads to poor memory utilization. In general, internal fragmentation is the difference between the granularity of memory allocation and the actual request for memory.

$$\text{Internal fragmentation} = \text{Size of fixed partition} - \text{Actual memory request} \quad (1)$$

Allocation table

Occupied bit	Partition size	Process
0	5K	XXX
1	8K	P1
0	1K	XXX

Memory

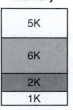

Figure 7.5(a)   Allocation table after P1's request satisfied.

Example 7.1

A memory manager allocates memory in fixed chunks of 4 KB. What is the maximum internal fragmentation possible?

Answer:

The smallest request for memory from a process is 1 byte. The memory manager allocates 4 KB to satisfy this request.

So, the maximum internal fragmentation possible

$$= 4 \text{ KB} - 1$$
$$= 4096 - 1 = 4095 \text{ bytes.}$$

Suppose that there is another memory allocation request, for 6 KB, while P1 has the 8 KB partition. Once again, this request also cannot be satisfied. Even though, cumulatively (between the 1 KB and 5 KB partitions), 6 KB memory space is available, it is not possible to satisfy this new request, because the two partitions are not contiguous (and a process's request is for a contiguous region of memory). This phenomenon, called *external fragmentation*, also results in poor memory utilization. In general, external fragmentation is the sum of all the noncontiguous memory chunks available to the memory system.

$$\text{External fragmentation} = \Sigma \text{ All noncontiguous memory partitions} \qquad (2)$$

7.3.2 Variable-Size Partitions

To overcome the problem of internal fragmentation, we will discuss a memory manager that allocates variable-size partitions commensurate with the memory requests. Let us assume that 13 KB is the total amount of memory that is available to the memory manager. Instead of having a static allocation table, as in the previous scheme, the memory manager dynamically builds the table, on the fly. Figure 7.6 shows the initial state of the allocation table before any allocation.

Figure 7.6(a) shows the table after the memory manager grants a series of memory requests. Note that the manager has 2 KB of free space left after satisfying the requests of P1, P2, and P3.

Allocation table

Start address	Size	Process
0	13K	FREE

Memory

13K

Figure 7.6 Allocation table for variable-size partitions.

Figure 7.6(b) shows the state upon P1's completion. The 2 KB partition occupied by P1 is marked FREE, as well.

Suppose that there is a new request for a 4 KB chunk of memory from a new process P4. Unfortunately, this request cannot be satisfied, because the space requested by P4 is contiguous in nature, but the available space is fragmented, as shown in Figure 7.6(b). Therefore, variable-size partition, while solving the internal fragmentation problem, does not solve the external fragmentation problem.

As processes complete, there will be *holes* created of available space in memory. The allocation table records these available spaces. If adjacent entries in the allocation table free up, the manager will be able to coalesce them into a larger chunk, as shown in the before–after Figures 7.6(c) and 7.6(d), respectively.

Allocation table

Start address	Size	Process
0	2K	P1
2K	6K	P2
8K	3K	P3
11K	2K	FREE

Memory

11K
2K

Figure 7.6(a)   State of the allocation table after a series of memory requests from P1 (2 KB), P2 (6 KB), and P3 (3 KB).

Allocation table

Start address	Size	Process
0	2K	FREE
2K	6K	P2
8K	3K	P3
11K	2K	FREE

Memory

2K
9K
2K

Figure 7.6(b)   State of allocation table after P1's completion.

Allocation table

Start address	Size	Process
0	2K	FREE
2K	6K	P2 → FREE
8K	3K	P3
11K	2K	FREE

Memory

2K
9K
2K

Figure 7.6(c)   Allocation table before P2 releases memory.

Allocation table

Start address	Size	Process
0	8K	FREE
8K	3K	P3
11K	2K	FREE

Memory

8K
3K
2K

Figure 7.6(d)   Allocation table after P2 releases memory (coalesced).

Example 7.2

What is the maximum external fragmentation represented by each of the Figures 7.6(b) and 7.6(d)?

Answer:

In Figure 7.6(b), 2 chunks of 2 KB each are available, but not contiguous.

External fragmentation = 4 KB

In Figure 7.6(d), 2 chunks of 8 KB and 2 KB are available, but not contiguous.

External fragmentation = 10 KB

Upon a new request for space, the memory manager has several options for ways to make the allocation. Here are two possibilities:

1. **Best fit:** The manager looks through the allocation table to find the best fit for the new request. For example, with reference to Figure 7.6(d), if the request is for 1 KB, the manager will make the allocation by splitting the 2 KB of free space rather than the 8 KB of free space.

2. **First fit:** The manager will allocate the request by finding the first free slot available in the allocation table that can satisfy the new request. For example, with reference to Figure 7.6(d), the memory manager will satisfy the same 1 KB request by splitting the 8 KB of free space.

The choice of the allocation algorithm has tradeoffs. The time complexity of the best-fit algorithm is high when the table size is large. However, the best-fit algorithm will lead to better memory utilization, since there will be less external fragmentation.

7.3.3 Compaction

The memory manager resorts to a technique called *compaction* when the level of external fragmentation goes beyond tolerable limits. For example, referring to Figure 7.6(d), the memory manager may relocate the memory for P3 to start from address 0, thus creating a

Allocation table

Start address	Size	Process
0	3K	P3
3K	10K	FREE

Memory

3K
10K

Figure 7.6(e)   Memory compacted to create a larger contiguous space.

contiguous space of 10 KB, as shown in Figure 7.6(e). Compaction is an expensive operation since all the embedded addresses in P3's allocation have to be adjusted to preserve the semantics. This is not only expensive, but also virtually impossible in most architectures. Remember that the early schemes for memory management date back to the 1960s. It is precisely for the allowing of dynamic relocation that the IBM 360 introduced the concept of a base register[4] (not unlike the scheme shown in Figure 7.4). The OS/360 would dynamically relocate a program at load time. However, even with this scheme, once a process is loaded in memory, compaction would require quite a few gyrations, such as stopping the execution of the processes to do the relocation. Further, the cost of compaction goes up with the number of processes requiring such relocation. For this reason, even in architectures where it is feasible to do memory compaction, memory managers rarely perform compaction. It is usual to combine compaction with swapping—that is, the memory manager will relocate the process as it is swapped back into memory.

7.4 Paged Virtual Memory

As the size of the memory keeps growing, external fragmentation becomes a very acute problem. We need to solve this problem.

Let us go back to basics. The user's view of the program is a contiguous footprint in memory. The hardware support for memory management that we have discussed until now at best relocates the program to a different range of addresses from that originally present in the user's view. We need to get around this inherent assumption of contiguous memory present in the user's view. The concept of *virtual memory* helps get around this assumption. *Paging* is a vehicle for implementing this concept.

The idea is to let the user preserve his view of contiguous memory for his program, which makes program development easy. The broker (in Figure 7.1) breaks up this contiguous view into equal *logical* entities called *pages*. Similarly, the physical memory consists of *page frames*, which we will refer to simply as *physical frames*. Both the logical page and the physical frame are of the same, fixed size, called *pagesize*. A physical frame *houses* a logical page.

Let us consider an analogy. The professor likes to get familiar with all the students in his large class. To help him in his quest to get familiar with all the students, he uses the

---

4. Source: See www.research.ibm.com/journal/rd/441/amdahl.pdf for Gene Andahl's original paper on IBM 360.

(a)   (b)   (c)

Figure 7.7   Picture frame analogy.

following ruse: He collects the photos of his students in the class. He has an empty picture frame in his office (Figure 7.7(a)). When a student comes to visit him during his office hours, he puts up the picture of the student in the frame (Figure 7.7(b)). When the next student comes to visit, he puts up the picture of that student in the frame (Figure 7.7(c)). The professor does not have a unique picture frame for each student, but simply reuses the same frame for the different students. He does not need a unique frame for each student also because he sees him or her, one at a time, during his office hours.

Allocation of physical memory divided into page frames bears a lot of similarity to this simple analogy. The picture frame can house any picture. Similarly, a given physical frame can be used to house any logical page. The broker maintains a *mapping* between a user's *logical page* and the physical memory's *physical frame*. As one would expect, it is the responsibility of the memory manager to create the mapping for each program. An entity called the *page table* holds the mapping of logical pages to physical frames. The page table effectively decouples the user's view of memory from the physical organization. For this reason, we refer to the user's view as *virtual memory* and to the logical pages as *virtual pages*, respectively. The CPU generates *virtual addresses* corresponding to the user's view. The broker *translates* this virtual address to a physical address by looking up the page table (shown in Figure 7.8). Since we have decoupled the user's view from the physical organization, the relative sizes of the virtual memory and physical memory do not matter. For example, it is perfectly reasonable for a user's view of the virtual memory to be much larger than the actual physical memory. In fact, this is the common situation in most memory systems today. The larger virtual memory removes any resource restriction arising out of limited physical memory and gives the illusion of a much larger memory to user programs.

The broker is required to maintain the contiguous memory assumption of the user only to addresses within a page. The distinct pages need not be contiguous in physical memory. Figure 7.9 shows a program with four virtual pages mapped, using the paging technique to four physical frames. Note that the paging technique circumvents external fragmentation. However, there can be internal fragmentation. Since the frame size is fixed, any request for memory that only partially fills a frame will lead to internal fragmentation.

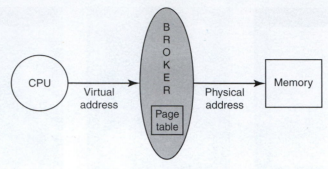

Figure 7.8   Page table.

The broker is able to shift the virtual address generated by a user program to a physical address on a per-page basis by using the page table.

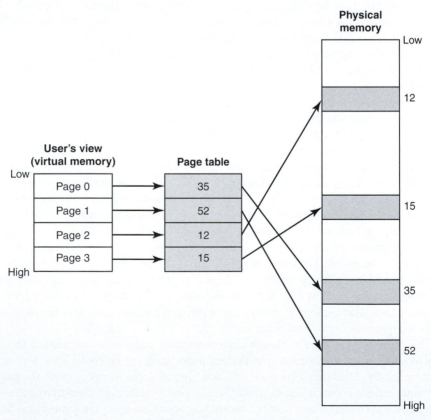

Figure 7.9   Breaking the user's contiguous view of virtual memory.

7.4.1 Page Table

Let us drill a little deeper into the paging concept. Given that a virtual page (or a physical frame) is of fixed size, and that addresses within a page are contiguous, we can view the virtual address generated by the CPU as consisting of two things: *virtual page number (VPN)* and *offset* within the page. For the sake of exposition, we will assume that the page size is an integral power of two. The hardware first breaks up the virtual address into these two pieces. This is a straightforward process. Remember that all the locations within a given page are contiguous. Therefore, the offset portion of the virtual address must come from the low-order bits. The number of bits needed for the offset is directly discernible from the page size. For example, if the page size is 8-KB, then there are 2^{13} distinct bytes in that page; so, we need 13 bits to address each byte uniquely, which will be the size of the offset. The remaining high-order bits of the virtual address form the virtual page number. In general, if the page size is N, then $\log_2 N$ low-order bits of the virtual address form the page offset.

Example 7.3

Consider a memory system with a 32-bit virtual address. Assume that the page size is 8 KB. Show the layout of the virtual address into VPN and page offset.

Answer:

Each page has 8 KB. We need 13 bits to uniquely address each byte within this page. Since the bytes are contiguous within a page, these 13 bits make up the least-significant bits of the virtual address (i.e., bit positions 0 through 12).

The remaining 19 high-order bits of the virtual address (i.e., bit positions 13 through 31) signify the virtual page number (VPN).

The translation of a virtual address to a physical address consists of looking up the page table to find the *physical frame number (PFN)* corresponding to the virtual page number (VPN) in the virtual address. Figure 7.10 shows this translation process. The shaded area in Figure 7.10 is the hardware portion of the work done by the broker. The hardware looks up the page table to translate the virtual address to a physical address. Let us investigate where to place the page table. Since the hardware has to look it up on every memory access in order to perform the translation, it seems fair to think that it should be part of the CPU datapath. Let us explore the feasibility of this idea. We need an entry for every VPN. In Example 7.3, we needed 2^{19} entries in the page table. Therefore, it is infeasible to implement the page table as a hardware device in the datapath of the processor. Moreover, there is not just one page table in the system. To provide memory protection, every process needs its own page table.

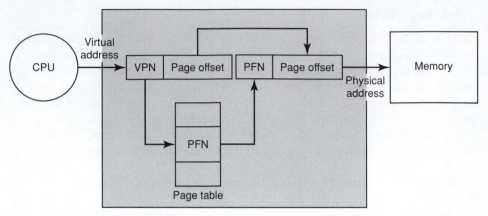

Figure 7.10 Address translation.

The page table is indexed by the VPN in the virtual address to get the PFN. The page offset in the virtual address is appended to the PFN to generate the physical address.

Therefore, the page table resides in memory, one per process, as shown in Figure 7.11. The CPU needs to know the location of the page table in memory in order to carry out address translation. For this purpose, we add a new register to the CPU datapath, *page table base register (PTBR),* which contains the base address of the page table for the currently running process. The PTBR is part of the process control block. At context switch time, this register value is loaded from the PCB of the newly dispatched process.

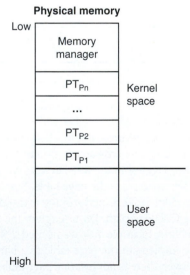

Figure 7.11 Page tables in physical memory.

Example 7.4

Consider a memory system with 32-bit virtual addresses and 24-bit physical memory addresses. Assume that the page size is 4 KB. (a) Show the layout of the virtual and physical addresses. (b) How big is the page table? How many page frames are there in this memory system?

Answer:

a. For a pagesize of 4 KB, the lower 12 bits of the 32-bit virtual address signify the page offset, and the remaining high-order bits (20 bits) signify the VPN.

Layout of the virtual address:

Since the physical address is 24 bits, the high-order bits, 12 bits $(24 - 12)$, of the physical address forms the PFN.

Layout of the physical address:

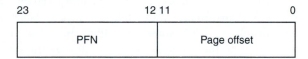

b. Number of page table entries $= 2^{(\text{Number of bits in VPN})} = 2^{20}$

Assuming each entry is 1 word of 32 bits (4 bytes),

The size of the page table $= 4 \times 2^{20}$ bytes $= 4$ MB

Number of page frames $= 2^{(\text{Number of bits in PFN})} = 2^{12} = 4096$

7.4.2 Hardware for Paging

The hardware for paging is straightforward. We add a new register, PTBR, to the datapath. On every memory access, the CPU computes the address of the *page table entry (PTE)* that corresponds to the VPN in the virtual address, using the contents of the PTBR. The PFN fetched from this entry, concatenated with the page offset, gives the physical address. This is the translation process for fetching either the instruction or the data in the FETCH and MEM stages of the pipelined processor, respectively. The new hardware added to the processor to handle paging is surprisingly minimal for the enormous flexibility achieved in memory management. Let us review the overhead for memory accesses with paging. In essence, the hardware makes two trips to the memory for each access: first to retrieve the PFN, and second to retrieve the memory content (instruction or data). This seems grossly inefficient and untenable from the point of view of sustaining a high-performance processor pipeline. Fortunately, it is possible to mitigate this inefficiency significantly and make paging actually viable. The trick lies in remembering the recent address translations (i.e., VPN to PFN mappings) that are stored for future use in a small hardware table inside the processor, because we are most likely to access many memory locations in the same physical page. The processor first consults this table, called a *translation lookaside buffer (TLB)*. Only on not finding this mapping does it retrieve the PFN from physical memory. More details on TLB will be forthcoming in the next chapter (see Section 8.6).

7.4.3 Page Table Setup

The memory manager sets up the page table on a process startup. In this sense, the page table does double duty. The hardware uses it for doing the address translation. It is also a data structure under the control of the memory manager. Upon setting up the page table, the memory manager records the PTBR value for this process in the associated PCB. Figure 7.12 shows the process control block with a new field for the PTBR.

7.4.4 Relative Sizes of Virtual and Physical Memories

From the discussion thus far, it would appear that the whole purpose of virtual memory is to liberate the programmer from the limitations of available physical memory. Naturally, this leads us to think that virtual memory should always be larger than physical memory. This is a perfectly logical way to think about virtual memory. Having said that, let us investigate whether it makes sense to have physical memory that is larger than the virtual memory. We can immediately see that it would not help an individual program, because the address space available to the program is constrained by the size of the virtual memory. For example, with a 32-bit virtual address space, a given program has access to 4 GB of memory. Even if the system has more physical memory than 4 GB, an individual

```
typedef struct control_block_type {
        enum state_type state;
        address PC;
        int reg_file[NUMREGS];
        struct control_block *next_pcb;
        int priority;
        address PTBR;
        ....
        ....
} control_block;
```

Figure 7.12   PCB with PTBR field.

This single field is enough for the operating system to determine the memory footprint of a process.

program cannot have a memory footprint larger than 4 GB. However, a larger physical memory can come in handy to enable the operating system to have more resident processes that are huge memory hogs. This is the reason for Intel architecture's *Physical Address Extension (PAE)* feature, which extends the physical address from 32 bits to 36 bits. As a result, this feature allows the system to have up to 64 GB of physical memory, and the operating system can map (using the page table) a given process's 4-GB virtual address space to live in different portions of the 64 GB physical memory.[5]

One could argue that, with the technological advances that allow larger than 32-bit physical addresses, the processor architecture should support a larger virtual address space as well. One would be right. In fact, vendors, including Intel, have already come out with 64-bit architectures. The reason Intel offers the PAE feature is simply to allow larger physical memories on 32-bit platforms that are still in use for supporting legacy applications.

7.5 Segmented Virtual Memory

Let us consider an analogy. Figure 7.13 shows a floor plan for a house. It may have a living room, a family room, a dining room, perhaps a study room, and one or more bedrooms. In other words, we have first logically organized the space in the house into

Figure 7.13 Floor plan for a house.[6]

---

5. For further information, the interested reader is referred to *Intel® 64 and IA-32 Architectures Software Developer's Manual, Volume 3A: System Programming Guide, Part 1*. [Intel System programming guide 3A, 2008].

6. Source: www.edenlanehomes.com/images/design/Typical-Floorplan.jpg.

functional units. We may then decide on the amount of actual physical space we would like to allocate, given the total space budget for the house. Thus, we may decide to have a guest bedroom that is slightly larger than, say, a kid's bedroom. We may have a breakfast area that is cozy, compared with the formal dining room, and so on. There are several advantages to this functional organization of the space. If you have visitors, you don't have to rearrange anything in your house. You can simply give them the guest bedroom. If you decide to bring a friend for a sleepover, you may simply share your bedroom with that friend without disturbing the other members of your family. Let us apply this analogy to program development.

In the previous chapter (see Section 6.2), we defined the address space of a process as the space occupied by the memory footprint of the program. In the previous section, we stressed the need to preserve the contiguous view of the memory footprint of a user's program. We will go a little further and underscore the importance of having the address space always start at 0 to some maximum value, so that it is convenient from the point of view of code generation by the compiler. Virtual memory helps with that view.

Let us investigate whether one address space is enough for a program. The analogy of the space planning in the house is useful here. We logically partitioned the space in the house into the different rooms, based on their intended use. These spaces are independent of each other and well protected from one another (doors, locks, etc.). This ensures that no one can invade the privacy of the other occupants without prior warning. At some level, constructing a program is similar to designing a house. Although we end up with a single program (*a.out,* as it is called in UNIX terminology), the source code has a logical structure. There are distinct data structures and procedures organized to provide specific functionality. If it is a group project, you may even develop your program as a team, with different team members contributing different functionalities of the total program. One can visualize the number of software engineers who would have participated in the development of a complex program such as MS Word at Microsoft. Therefore, the availability of multiple address spaces would help better organize the program logically. Especially with object-oriented programming, the utility of having multiple address spaces cannot be overemphasized.

Let us drill a little deeper and understand how multiple address spaces would help the developer. Even for the basic memory footprint (see Figure 6.1 in Chapter 6), we could have each of the distinct portions of the memory footprint—namely, code, global data, heap, and stack—in distinct address spaces. From a software engineering perspective, this organization gives us the ability to associate properties with these address spaces (for example, the code section is read only, etc.). Further, the ability to associate such properties with individual address spaces will be a great boon for program debugging.

Use of multiple address spaces becomes even more compelling in large-scale program development. Let us say that we are writing an application program for video-based surveillance. It may have several components, as shown in Figure 7.14. One can see the similarity between a program composed of multiple components, each in its dedicated address space, and the floor plan of Figure 7.13.

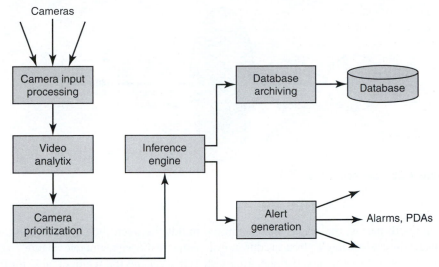

Figure 7.14   A esample application: Video-based surveillance.

A complex application such as this would be composed of several modules and, very likely, developed by a team of software engineers.

This is a complex enough application that there may be several of us working on this project together. The team members, using well-defined interfaces, may independently develop each of the boxes shown in Figure 7.14. It would greatly help both the development and debugging to have each of these components in separate address spaces, with the appropriate levels of protection and sharing among the components (similar to having doors and locks in the house floor plan). Further, it would be easy to maintain such an application. You don't move into a hotel if you want to retile just your kitchen. Similarly, you could rewrite specific functional modules of this application without affecting others.

Segmentation is a technique for fulfilling the aforementioned vision. As is always the case with any system-level mechanism, this technique is also a partnership between the operating system and the architecture.

The user's view of memory is not a single linear address space, but it is composed of several distinct address spaces. Each such address space is called a *segment*. A segment has two attributes:

- unique segment number
- size of the segment

Each segment starts at address 0 and goes up to (Segment size − 1). CPU generates addresses that have two parts, as shown in Figure 7.15.

Figure 7.15   A segmented address.

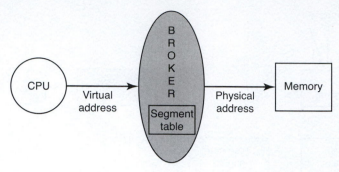

Figure 7.16 Segment table.

As with paging, the broker that sits in the middle between the CPU and memory converts this address into a physical address by looking up the segment table (Figure 7.16). As in the case of paging, it is the operating system that sets up the segment table for the currently running process.

Now, you are probably thinking that, but for the name change from *page* to *segment*, there appears to be not much difference between paging and segmentation. Before we delve into the differences between the two, let us return to the sample application in Figure 7.14. With segmentation, we could arrange the application as shown in Figure 7.17. Notice that each functional component is in its own segment and the segments are individually sized, depending on the functionality of that component. Figure 7.18 shows these segments housed in the physical memory.

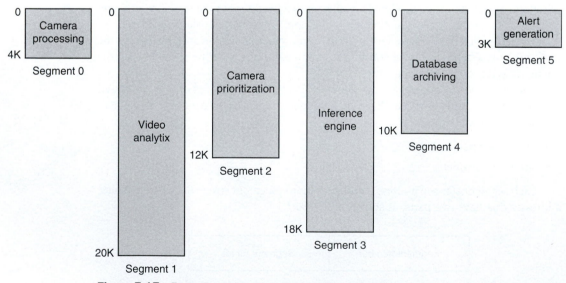

Figure 7.17 Example application organized into segments.

Address   Size

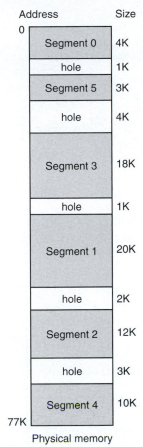

Physical memory

Figure 7.18   Segments of sample application in Figure 7.17 mapped into physical memory.

Example 7.5

A program has 10 KB code space and 3 KB global data space. It needs 5 KB of heap space and 3 KB of stack space. The compiler allocates individual segments for each of the preceding components of the program. The allocation of space in physical memory is as follows:

Code start address	1000
Global data start address	14000
Heap space start address	20000
Stack space start address	30000

a. Show the segment table for this program.

Answer:

Segment Number	Start Address	Size
0	1000	10 KB
1	14000	3 KB
2	20000	5 KB
3	30000	3 KB

b. Assuming byte-addressed memory, show the memory layout pictorially.

Answer:

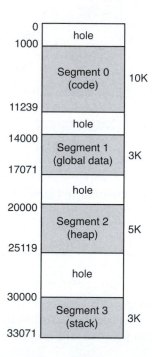

c. Give the physical memory address corresponding to the following virtual address:

0	299

Answer:

1. The offset 299 is within the size of segment 0 (10 KB).
2. The physical memory address

$$= \text{Start address of segment 0} + \text{offset}$$
$$= 1000 + 299$$
$$= \mathbf{1299}$$

7.5.1 Hardware for Segmentation

The hardware needed for supporting segmentation is fairly simple. The segment table is a data structure similar to the page table. Each entry in this table called a *segment descriptor*. The segment descriptor gives the start address for a segment and the size of the segment. Each process has its own segment table allocated by the operating system at the time of process creation. Similar to paging, this scheme also requires a special register in the CPU called *segment table base register (STBR)*. The hardware uses this register and the segment table to do address translation during the execution of the process (see Figure 7.19). The hardware performs a bounds check first, to ensure that the offset provided is within the size limit of the segment before allowing the memory access to proceed.

Segmentation should remind the reader of the memory allocation scheme from Section 7.3.2, variable-size partition. Segmentation suffers from the same problem that variable size partition does, namely, external fragmentation. This can be seen in Figure 7.18.

7.6 Paging versus Segmentation

Now we are ready to understand the difference between paging and segmentation. Both are techniques for implementing virtual memory, but differ greatly in detail. We summarize the similarities and differences between the two approaches in Table 7.1.

When you look at the table, you would conclude that segmentation has a lot going for it. Therefore, it is tempting to conclude that architectures should be using segmentation as the vehicle for implementing virtual memory. Unfortunately, the last row of the table is the real killer, namely, external fragmentation. There are other considerations as well. For example, with paging, the virtual address that the CPU generates occupies one memory word. However, with segmentation, it may be necessary to have two memory words to specify a virtual address. This is because we may want a segment to be as big as the total available address space in order to allow for maximum flexibility. This would mean that we would need one memory word for identifying the segment number and the second to identify the offset within the segment. Another serious system-level consideration has to do with balancing the system as a whole. Let us elaborate what we mean by this statement. It turns out that the hunger for memory of applications and system software keeps growing incessantly. The increase in memory footprint of desktop-publishing applications and web browsers from release to release is an attestation to this

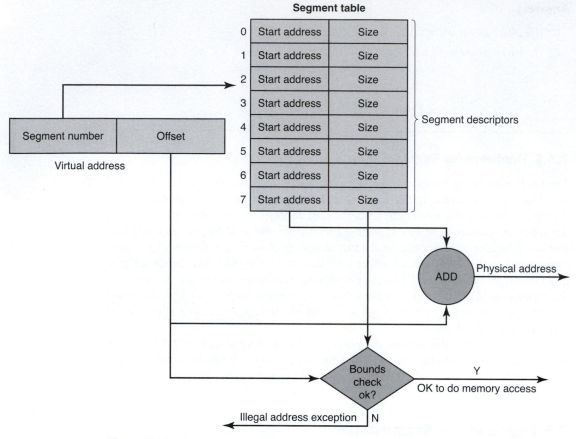

Figure 7.19   Address translation with segmentation.

The segment number from the virtual address serves as an index into the segment table to get the starting address of the segment. The offset from the virtual address is added to this starting address to generate the actual physical address to send to the memory.

growing appetite. The reason, of course, is the desire to offer increased functionality to the end user. The reality is that we will never be able to afford enough physical memory to satisfy our appetite for memory. Therefore, virtual memory will have to be far larger than physical memory. Pages or segments have to be brought in "on demand" from the hard drive into the physical memory. Virtual memory extends the memory system from the physical memory to the disk. Thus, the transfer of data from the disk to the memory system, on demand, has to be efficient in order for the whole system to work efficiently. This is what we mean by balancing the system as a whole. Because the pagesize is a system attribute, it is easier to optimize the system as a whole with paging. Since the user has control over defining the size of segments, it is more difficult to optimize the system as a whole with segmentation.

Table 7.1 Comparison of Paging and Segmentation

Attribute	Paging	Segmentation
User shielded from size limitation of physical memory	Yes	Yes
Relationship to physical memory	Physical memory may be less than or greater than virtual memory.	Physical memory may be less than or greater than virtual memory.
Address spaces per process	One	Several
Visibility to the user	User unaware of paging; user is given an illusion of a single linear address space.	User aware of multiple address spaces, each starting at address 0
Software engineering	No obvious benefit	Allows organization of the program components into individual segments at user discretion; enables modular design; increases maintainability
Program debugging	No obvious benefit	Aided by the modular design
Sharing and protection	User has no direct control; operating system can facilitate sharing and protection of pages across address spaces, but this has no meaning from the user's perspective.	User has direct control of orchestrating the sharing and protection of individual segments; especially useful for object-oriented programming and development of large software.
Size of page/segment	Fixed by the architecture	Variable chosen by the user for each individual segment
Internal fragmentation	Internal fragmentation possible for the portion of a page that is not used by the address space	None
External fragmentation	None	External fragmentation possible, since the variable-sized segments have to be allocated in the available physical memory, thus creating holes (see Figure 7.18)

For these reasons, true segmentation as described in this section is not a viable way to implement virtual memory. One way to solve the external fragmentation problem is as we described in Section 7.3.3, by using memory compaction. However, we observed in that section the difficulties in practically implementing compaction as well. A better approach is to have a combined technique, namely, *paged-segmentation*. The user is presented with a segmented view, as described in this section. Under the covers, the operating system and the hardware use paging, as described in the previous section, to eliminate the ill effects of external fragmentation.

A detailed description of such paged-segmentation techniques is beyond the scope of this textbook. We do present a historical perspective of paging and segmentation, as well as a commercial example of a paged-segmentation approach with an Intel Pentium architecture as a case study, later in this chapter.

7.6.1 Interpreting the CPU-Generated Address

The processor generates a simple linear address to address the memory.
CPU generated address:

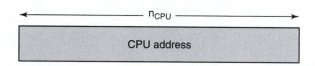

The number of bits in the CPU-generated address depends on the memory-addressing capability of the processor (usually tied to the word-width of the processor and the smallest granularity of access to memory operands). For example, for a 64-bit processor with byte-addressed memory, $n_{CPU} = 64$.

The number of bits in the physical address depends on the actual size of the physical memory.

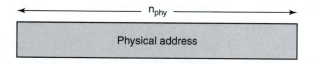

With byte-addressed memory,

$$n_{phy} = \log_2(\text{size of physical memory in bytes}) \qquad (3)$$

For example, for a physical memory size of 1 GB, $n_{phy} = 30$ bits.

The exact interpretation of the CPU-generated linear address as a virtual address depends on the memory system architecture (i.e., paging versus segmentation). Correspondingly, the computation of the physical address also changes. Table 7.2 summarizes the salient equations pertaining to paged and segmented memory systems.

Table 7.2 Address Computations in Paged and Segmented Memory Systems

Memory System	Virtual Address Computation	Physical Address Computation	Size of Tables
Segmentation	Segment number · Segment offset, with n_{seg} over Segment number and n_{off} over Segment offset. $n_{off} = \log_2(\text{segment-size})$ $n_{seg} = n_{cpu} - n_{off}$	Segment Start address[7] = SegmentTable[SegmentNumber] Physical address = Segment Start Address + Segment Offset	Segment table size = $2^{n_{seg}}$ entries
Paging	VPN · Page offset, with n_{VPN} over VPN and n_{off} over Page offset. $n_{off} = \log_2(\text{page-size})$ $n_{VPN} = n_{cpu} - n_{off}$	PFN[8] = PageTable[VPN] Physical address: PFN · Page offset, with n_{PFN} over PFN and n_{off} over Page offset. $n_{off} = \log_2(\text{page-size})$ $n_{PFN} = n_{phy} - n_{off}$	Page table size = $2^{n_{VPN}}$ entries

---

7. This is obtained by retrieving the contents of the Segment Table, indexed by the Segment Number.
8. This is similarly obtained by retrieving the contents of the Page Table, indexed by the VPN.

Summary

The importance of the memory system cannot be overemphasized. The performance of the system as a whole crucially depends on the efficiency of the memory system. The interplay between the hardware and the software of a memory system makes the study of memory systems fascinating. Thus far, we have reviewed several different memory-management schemes and the hardware requirement for those schemes. In the beginning of the chapter, we identified four criteria for memory management: improved resource utilization, independence and protection of processes' memory spaces, liberation from memory resource limitation, and sharing of memory by concurrent processes. These are all important criteria from the point of view of the efficiency of the operating system for managing memory, which is a precious resource. From the discussion on segmentation, we added another equally important criterion for memory management, namely, *facilitating good software engineering practices*. This criterion determines whether the memory management scheme, in addition to meeting the system-level criteria, helps in the development of software that is flexible, easy to maintain, and ever-evolving. Let us summarize these schemes with respect to the memory-management criteria. Table 7.3 gives such a qualitative comparison of these memory-management schemes.

Table 7.3 Qualitative Comparison of Memory Management Schemes

Memory Management Criterion	User/ Kernel Separation	Fixed Partition	Variable-Sized Partition	Paged Virtual Memory	Segmented Virtual Memory	Paged-Segmented Virtual Memory
Improved resource utilization	No	Internal fragmentation bounded by partition size; External fragmentation	External fragmentation	Internal fragmentation bounded by page size	External fragmentation	Internal fragmentation bounded by page size
Independence and protection	No	Yes	Yes	Yes	Yes	Yes
Liberation from resource limitation	No	No	No	Yes	Yes	Yes
Sharing by concurrent processes	No	No	No	Yes	Yes	Yes
Facilitates good software engineering practice	No	No	No	No	Yes	Yes

Table 7.4 Summary of Memory Management Schemes

Scheme	Hardware Support	Still in Use?
User/Kernel Separation	Fence register	No
Fixed Partition	Bounds registers	Not in any production operating system
Variable-Sized Partition	Base and limit registers	Not in any production operating system
Paged Virtual Memory	Page table and page table base register	Yes, in most modern operating systems
Segmented Virtual Memory	Segment table, and segment table base register	Segmentation in this pure form not supported in any commercially popular processors
Paged-Segmented Virtual Memory	Combination of the hardware for paging and segmentation	Yes, most modern operating systems based on Intel x86 use this scheme[9]

Only virtual memory with paged-segmentation meets all the criteria. It is instructive to review which one of these schemes is relevant with respect to the state-of-the-art in memory management. Table 7.4 summarizes the memory-management schemes covered in this chapter, along with the required hardware support and their applicability to modern operating systems.

Historical Perspective

Circa 1965, IBM introduced the System/360 series of mainframes. The architecture provided base and limit registers, thus paving the way for memory management that supports dynamic relocation. Any general-purpose register could be used as the base register. The compiler would designate a specific register as the base register so that any program written in high-level language could be dynamically relocated by the operating system OS/360. However, there was a slight problem. Programmers could find out which register was being used as the base register and could use this knowledge to "stash" away the base register value for assembly code that they wanted to insert into the high-level language program.[10] The upshot of doing this is that the program could no

---

9. It should be noted that Intel's segmentation is quite different from the pure form of segmentation presented in this chapter. We will shortly discuss Intel's paged-segmentation scheme.

10. Personal communication with James R. Goodman, University of Wisconsin-Madison.

longer be relocated, once it started executing, since programmers may have hard-coded addresses in the program. You may wonder why they would want to do such a thing. Well, it is not unusual for programmers who are after getting every ounce of performance from a system to lace in assembly code into a high-level language program. Some of us are guilty of that even in this day and age! For these reasons, dynamic relocation never really worked as well as IBM would have wanted it to work in OS/360. The main reason was the fact that the address shifting in the architecture used a general-purpose register that was visible to the programmer.

Circa 1970, IBM introduced virtual memory in their System/370 series of mainframes.[11] The fundamental way in which the System/370 differed from the System/360 was the architectural support for dynamic address translation, which eliminated the aforementioned problem with the System/360. The System/370 represents IBM's first offering of the virtual memory concept. Successive models of the System/370 series of machines refined the virtual memory model with expanded addressing capabilities. The architecture used paged virtual memory.

In this context, it is worth noting a difference in the use of the terms *static* and *dynamic*, depending on operating system or architecture orientation. Earlier (see Section 7.2), we defined what we mean by static and dynamic relocation, from the operating system's standpoint. With this definition, one would say that a program is dynamically relocatable if the hardware provides support for changing the virtual mapping to physical mapping of addresses at execution time. By this definition, the base and limit register method of the IBM 360 supports dynamic relocation.

Architects look at a much finer grain of individual memory accesses during program execution and use the term *address translation*. An architecture supports dynamic address translation if the mapping of virtual to physical can be altered at any time during the execution of the program. By this definition, the base and limit register method in the IBM 360 supports only static address translation, whereas paging supports dynamic address translation. The operating-system definition of *static* versus *dynamic* relocation is at the level of the whole program, whereas the architecture definition of *static* versus *dynamic* address translation is at the level of individual memory accesses.

Even prior to IBM's entry into the virtual memory scene, Burroughs Corporation introduced segmented virtual memory in their B5000 line of machines [Oliphint, 1987]. General Electric, in partnership with the MULTICS project at MIT, introduced paged-segmentation in their GE 600 line of machines in the mid 1960s [Schroeder, 1971]. IBM quickly sealed the victory in the mainframe war of the 1960s and 1970s, with the introduction of the VM/370 operating system to support virtual memory and the continuous refinement of paged virtual memory in their System/370 line of machines. This evolution has continued to this day, and one could see the connection to these early machines even in the IBM z series of mainframes[12] to support enterprise level applications.

---

11. For an authoritative paper that describes the System/360 and the System/370 architectures, refer to www.research.ibm.com/journal/rd/255/ibmrd2505D.pdf.

12. Source: www-03.ibm.com/systems/z/.

MULTICS

Some academic computing projects continue to have a profound impact on the evolution of the field for a very long time. The MULTICS project at MIT was one such. The project had its hey days in the 1960s, and one could very easily see that much of computer systems as we know them (UNIX, Linux, paging, segmentation, security, protection, etc.) had their birth in this project. In some sense, the operating systems concepts introduced in the MULTICS project were way ahead of their time, and the processor architectures of that time were not geared to support the advanced concepts of memory protection advocated by MULTICS. The MULTICS project is an excellent example of the basic theme of this textbook, namely, the connectedness of system software and machine architecture.

MULTICS introduced the concept of paged segmentation.[13] Figure 7.20 depicts the scheme implemented in MULTICS.

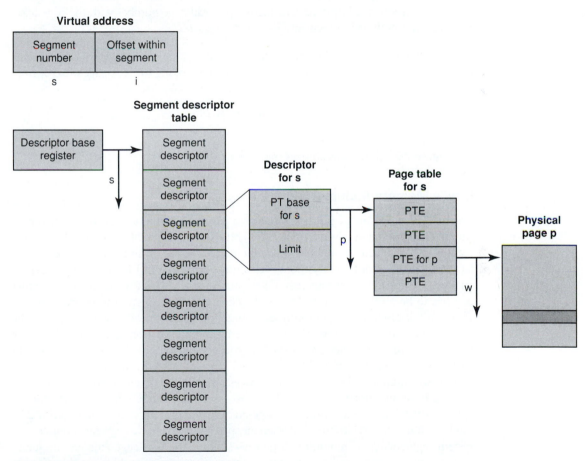

Figure 7.20   Address translation in MULTICS.

---

13. See the original MULTICS paper: www.multicians.org/multics-vm.html.

The 36-bit virtual address generated by the CPU consists of two parts: an 18-bit segment number (s) and an 18-bit offset (i) within that segment. Each segment can be arbitrary in size, bounded by the maximum segment size of $2^{18} - 1$. To avoid external fragmentation, a segment consists of pages (in MULTICS, the page-size is 1024 words, with 36 bits per word). Each segment has its own page table. Dynamic address translation in MULTICS is a two-step process:

- Locate the segment descriptor corresponding to the segment number: Hardware does this lookup by adding the segment number to the base address of the segment table contained in a CPU register called the descriptor base register.

- The segment descriptor contains the base address for the page table for that segment. Using the segment offset in the virtual address and the page-size, hardware computes the specific page-table entry corresponding to the virtual address. The physical address is obtained by concatenating the physical page number with the page offset (which is nothing but segment offset *mod* page-size).

If s is the segment number and i is the offset within the segment specified in the virtual address then, the specific memory word we are looking for is at page offset w from the beginning of the pth page of the segment, where:

$$w = i \bmod 1024$$
$$p = (i - w)/1024$$

Figure 7.20 shows this address translation.

Intel's Memory Architecture

The Intel Pentium line of processors also uses paged-segmentation. However, its organization is a lot more involved than the straightforward scheme of MULTICS. One of the realities of the debate between an academic project versus an industrial product is the fact that the latter has to worry about backward compatibility with its line of processors. Backward compatibility means that a new processor which is a successor to an earlier one has to be able to run, unchanged, the code that used to run on its predecessors. This is a tall order and significantly constrains the designers of a new processor. The current memory architecture of the Intel Pentium evolved from the early editions of Intel's x86 architectures such as the 80286; consequently, it has vestiges of the segmentation scheme found in such older processors, coupled with the aesthetic need for providing large numbers of virtual-address spaces for software development.

We have intentionally simplified the discussion in this section. As a first order of approximation, a virtual address is a segment selector plus an offset (see Figure 7.21). Intel's architecture divides the total segment space into two halves: *system* and *user*. The system segments are common to all processes, while the user segments are unique to each process. As you may have guessed, the system segments would be used by the operating system, since they are common to all the user processes. Correspondingly, there is one descriptor table, common to all processes, called the *global descriptor table (GDT)* and another, unique to each process, called the *local descriptor table (LDT)*. The segment

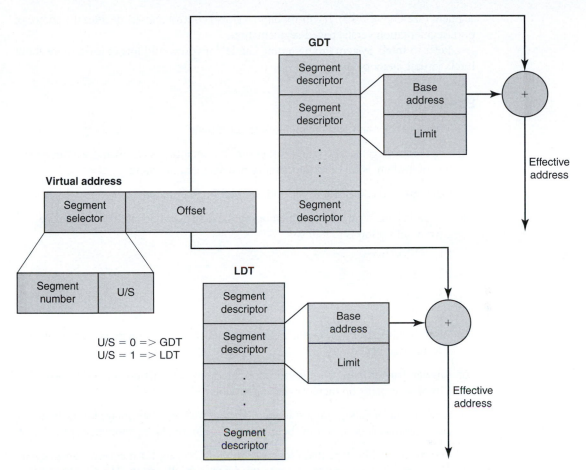

Figure 7.21 Address translation in Intel Pentium with pure segmentation.

selector in Intel is similar to the segment number in MULTICS, with one difference: A bit in the segment selector identifies whether the segment being named by the virtual address is a system or a user segment.

As in MULTICS, the segment descriptor for the selected segment contains the details for translating the offset specified in the virtual address, to a physical address. The difference is that there is a choice of using simple segmentation without any paging (to be compatible with the earlier line of processors) or using paged-segmentation. In the former case, the address translation would proceed as we described in Section 7.5 (i.e., without the need for any page table). This is shown in Figure 7.21. (The choice of GDT versus LDT for the translation is determined by the U/S bit in the selector.) The effective address computed is the physical address. In the case of paged-segmentation, the base address contained in the descriptor is the address of the page table base corresponding to this segment number. The rest of the address translation would proceed as we described earlier for MULTICS, going through the page table for the selected segment (see Figure 7.20). A control bit in a global control register decides the choice of pure segmentation versus paged-segmentation.

Refer to Intel's System Programming Guide[14] if you would like to learn more about Intel's virtual memory architecture.

Exercises

1. What are the main goals of memory management?

2. Argue for or against the statement: Given that memory is cheap and we can have lots of it, there is no need for memory management anymore.

3. Compare and contrast internal and external fragmentation.

4. A memory manager allocates memory in fixed-size chunks of 2048 bytes. The current allocation is as follows:

   P1   1200 bytes
   P2   2047 bytes
   P3   1300 bytes
   P4   1 byte

   With the allocation just given, what is the total amount of memory wasted due to internal fragmentation?

5. Answer True or False, with justification: Memory compaction is usually used with a fixed-size-partition memory-allocation scheme.

6. Answer True or False, with justification: There is no special advantage for the base and limit register solution, over the bounds register solution, for memory management.

7. Assume an architecture that uses base and limit register for memory management. The memory manager uses variable-sized partition allocation. The current memory allocation is as shown as follows:

Allocation table

Start address	Size	Process
0	8K	FREE
8K	3K	P3
11K	2K	FREE
13K	2K	P4

Memory

8K
3K (P3)
2K
2K (P4)

---

14. Intel® 64 and IA-32 Architectures Software Developer's Manual Volume 3A: System Programming Guide [Intel System programming guide 3A, 2008].

There is a new memory request for 9 KB. Can this allocation be satisfied? If not, why not? What is the amount of external fragmentation represented by the figure?

8. What is the relationship between page size and frame size in a paged memory system?

9. In terms of hardware resources needed (number of new processor registers and additional circuitry to generate the physical memory address, given a CPU-generated address), compare the base and limit register solution with a paged virtual memory solution.

10. How is a paged virtual memory system able to eliminate external fragmentation?

11. Derive a formula for the maximum internal fragmentation, with a page size of p, in a paged virtual memory system.

12. Consider a system where the virtual addresses are 20 bits and the page size is 1 KB. How many entries are in the page table?

13. Consider a system where the physical addresses are 24 bits and the page size is 8 KB. What is the maximum number of physical frames possible?

14. Distinguish between paged virtual memory and segmented virtual memory.

15. You are given the following segment table:

Segment Number	Start Address	Size
0	3000	3 KB
1	15000	3 KB
2	25000	5 KB
3	40000	8 KB

What is the physical address that corresponds to the virtual address shown here?

1	399

16. Compare the hardware resources needed (number of new processor registers and additional circuitry to generate the physical memory address, given a CPU-generated address) for paged and segmented virtual memory systems.

Bibliographic Notes and Further Reading

Elliot Organick's book [Organick, 1972] is a good historical reference for the MULTICS system, that had several pioneering ideas, including paged segmentation—ideas that have endured the test of time. IBM's role in the advance of memory systems is documented well in [IBM system/360, 1964] and in [IBM System/370, 1978]. Intel's memory architecture is well documented in [Intel System programming guide 3A, 2008].

Details of Page-Based Memory Management

In this chapter we will focus on page-based memory management. This is fundamental to most processors and operating systems that support virtual memory. As we mentioned already, even processors that support segmentation (such as the Intel Pentium) use paging to combat external fragmentation.

8.1 Demand Paging

As we mentioned in Chapter 7, the memory manager sets up the page table for a process, upon program startup. Let us first understand what fraction of the entire memory footprint of the program the memory manager should allocate at program startup. Production programs contain the functional or algorithmic logic part of the application, as well as the nonfunctional parts which deal with erroneous situations that may occasionally arise during program execution. Thus, it is a fair expectation that any well-behaved program will need only a significantly smaller portion of its entire memory footprint for proper execution. Therefore, it is prudent for the memory manager not to load the entire program into memory, upon startup. This requires some careful thinking, and understanding of what it means to execute a program that may not be completely in memory. The basic idea is to load parts of the program that are not in memory *on demand*. This technique, referred to as *demand paging,* results in better memory utilization.

Let us first understand what happens in hardware and in software to enable demand paging.

Figure 8.1 Page table entry.

Adding a valid bit to the PTE is needed to support demand paging.

8.1.1 Hardware for Demand Paging

In Chapter 7 (see Section 7.4.1), we mentioned that the hardware fetches the PFN from the page table as part of address translation. However, with demand paging, the page may not be in memory yet. Therefore, we need additional information in the page table to know whether the page is in memory. We add a *valid* bit to each page table entry. If the bit is 1, the PFN field in this entry is valid; if not, it is invalid, implying that the page is not in memory. Figure 8.1 shows the PTE to support demand paging. The role of the hardware is to recognize that a PTE is invalid and help the operating system take corrective action, namely, to load the missing page into memory. This condition (a PTE being invalid) is an unintended program interruption, since it is no fault of the original program. The operating system deliberately decided not to load this part of the program, in order to conserve memory resources. This kind of program interruption manifests as a *page fault exception* or *trap*.

The operating system handles this fault by bringing in the missing page from the disk. Once the page is in memory, the program is ready to resume execution where it left off. Therefore, to support demand paging, the processor has to be capable of restarting an instruction whose execution has been suspended in the middle due to a page fault.

Figure 8.2 shows the processor pipeline. The IF and MEM stages are susceptible to a page fault because they involve memory accesses.

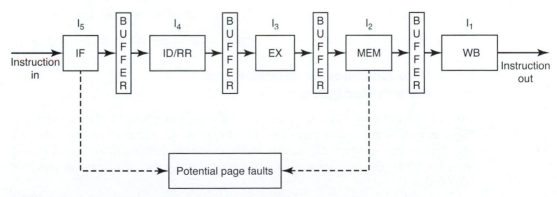

Figure 8.2 Potential page faults in a processor pipeline.

IF and MEM stages access memory operands and, hence, are liable to encounter a page fault.

Hardware for instruction restart. Let us first understand what should happen in the hardware. Consider that instruction I_2 in the MEM has a page fault. There are several instructions in partial execution in the pipeline. Before the processor goes to the INT state to handle the interrupt (refer to Chapter 4 for details on how interrupts are handled in hardware in the INT state), it has to take care of the instructions in partial execution already in the pipeline. In Chapter 5, we briefly mentioned the action that a pipelined processor may take to deal with interrupts. The page fault exception that I_2 experiences in the MEM stage is no different. The processor will let I_1 complete and squash the partial execution of instructions I_3–I_5 before entering the INT state. The INT state needs to save the PC value corresponding to instruction I_2 to restart the instruction after servicing the page fault. Note that there is no harm in squashing instructions I_3–I_5, since they have not modified the permanent state of the program (in processor registers and memory), so far. There is one interesting and important side effect manifesting from page faults (as well as from any type of exceptions): The pipeline registers (shown as buffers in Figure 8.2) contain the PC value of the instruction in the event there is an exception (arithmetic in the EX stage or page fault in the MEM stage) while this instruction is being executed. We discussed the hardware ramifications for dealing with traps and exceptions in a pipelined processor, in Chapter 5.

8.1.2 Page Fault Handler

The page fault handler is just like any other interrupt handler that we have discussed in earlier chapters. We know the basic steps that any handler has to take (saving/restoring state, etc.); we learned them in Chapter 4. Here, we will worry about the actual work that the handler does to service the page fault:

1. Find a free page frame.
2. Load the faulting virtual page from the disk into the free page frame.
3. Update the page table for the faulting process.
4. Place the PCB of the process back in the ready queue of the scheduler.

   We will explore the details of these steps in the next subsection.

8.1.3 Data Structures for Demand-Paged Memory Management

Now we will investigate the data structures and algorithms needed for demand paging. First, let us look at the data structures. We already mentioned that the page table is a per-process data structure maintained by the memory manager. In addition to using the page tables, the memory manager uses the following data structures for servicing page faults:

1. **Free-list of page frames:** This is a data structure which contains information about the currently unused page frames that a memory manager uses to service a page fault. The free-list does not contain the page frames themselves; each node of the free-list

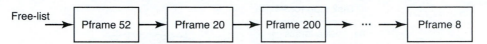

Figure 8.3 Free-list of page frames.

These are available frames for the memory manager to use for servicing a page fault.

simply contains the page frame number. For example (referring to Figure 8.3), page frames 52, 20, 200, . . ., 8 are currently unused. Therefore, the memory manager could use any page frame from this list to satisfy a page fault. Note that, to start with when a machine boots up, since there are no user processes, the free-list contains all the page frames of the user space. The free-list shrinks and grows as the memory manager allocates and releases memory to satisfy the page faults of processes.

2. **Frame table (FT):** This is a data structure that contains the reverse mapping. Given a frame number, it gives the Process ID (PID) and the virtual page number that currently occupies this page frame (Figure 8.4). For example, page frame 1 is currently unallocated while the virtual page 0 of Process 4 currently occupies page frame 6. It will become clear shortly how the memory manager uses this data structure.

3. **Disk map (DM):** This data structure maps the process virtual space to locations on the disk that contain the contents of the pages (Figure 8.5). This is the disk analog of the page table. There is one such data structure for each process.

For clarity of discussion, we have presented each of the given data structures as distinct from one another. Quite often, the memory manager may coalesce some of these data structures for efficiency or have common data structures, with multiple views into them, to simulate the behavior of the functionalities. This will become apparent when we discuss some of the page replacement policies (see Section 8.3).

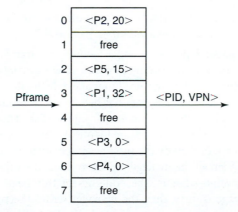

Figure 8.4 Frame table.

This is a data structure of the memory manager for reverse lookup, i.e., given a page frame, the process and the virtual page that is backed by this page frame.

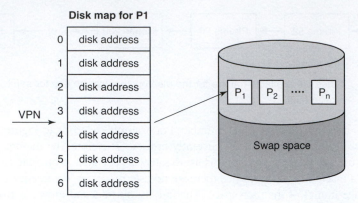

Figure 8.5   Disk map for process P1.

This data structure allows the memory manager to locate the disk blocks that back a process's virtual page.

8.1.4 Anatomy of a Page Fault

Let us revisit the work done by the page fault handler upon a page fault, using the given data structures.

1. **Find a free page frame:** The page fault handler (which is part of the memory manager) looks up the *free-list* of page frames. If the list is empty, we have a problem. This means that all the physical frames are in use. However, for the faulting process to continue execution, the memory manager has to bring the faulting page from the disk into physical memory. This implies that we have to make room in the physical memory to bring in the faulting page. Therefore, the manager selects some physical frame as a *victim* to make room for the faulting page. We will describe the policy for selecting a victim in Section 8.3.

2. **Pick the victim page:** Upon selecting a victim page frame, the manager determines the victim process that currently owns it. The *frame table* comes in handy to make this determination. Here, we need to make a distinction between a *clean* page and a *dirty* page. A clean page is one that has not been modified by the program from the time it was brought into memory from the disk. Therefore, the disk copy and the memory copy of a clean page are identical. On the other hand, a dirty page is one that has been modified by the program since it was brought from the disk. If the page is clean, then all the manager needs to do is to set the PTE corresponding to the page as *invalid*—that is, the contents of this page need not be saved. However, if the page is dirty, then the manager writes the page back to the disk (usually referred to as *flushing* to the disk), determining the disk location from the *disk map* for the victim process.

3. **Load the faulting page:** Using the *disk map* for the faulting process, the manager reads the page from the disk into the selected page frame.

4. **Update the page table for the faulting process and the frame table:** The manager sets the mapping for the PTE of the faulting process to point to the selected page frame, and makes the entry *valid*. It also updates the *frame table* to indicate the change in the mapping to the selected page frame.

5. **Restart faulting process:** The faulting process is ready to be restarted. The manager places the PCB of the faulting process in the scheduler's ready queue.

Example 8.1

Let us say that process P1 is currently executing, and it experiences a page fault at VPN = 20. The *free-list* is empty. The manager selects page frame PFN = 52 as the victim. This frame currently houses VPN = 33 of process P4. Figures 8.6(a) and 8.6(b) show the *before–after* pictures of the *page tables* for P1 and P2 and the *frame table* that resulted from the handling of the page fault.

Answer:

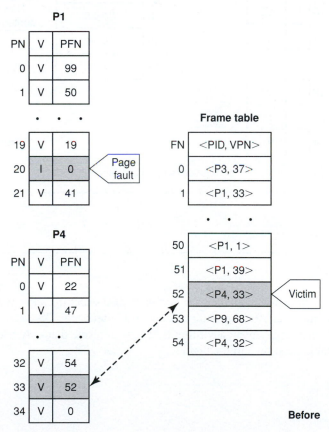

Figure 8.6(a)   Process P1 is executing and has a page fault on VPN 20.

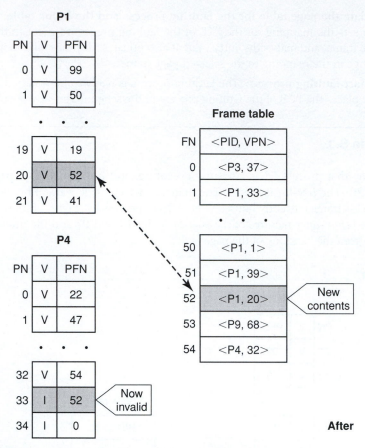

Figure 8.6(b)   Page fault service for process P1 is complete.

Example 8.2

Given next the before picture of the page manager's data structure, show the contents of the data structures after P1's page fault at VPN = 2 is serviced. The victim page frame chosen by the page replacement algorithm is PFN = 84. Note that only relevant entries of the frame table are shown in the figures.

BEFORE THE PAGE FAULT

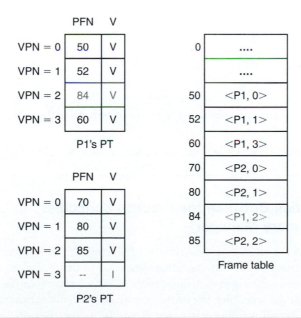

SHOW THE CONTENTS OF THE DATA STRUCTURES AFTER THE PAGE FAULT
FOR P1 at VPN = 2.

Answer:

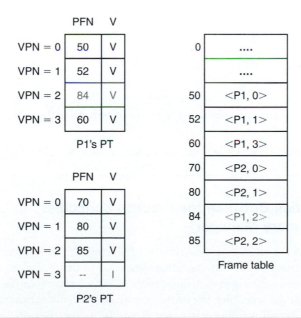

Remember that the page fault handler is also a piece of code just like any other user process. However, we cannot allow the page fault handler itself to page fault. The operating system ensures that certain parts of the operating system, such as the page fault handler, are always memory resident (i.e., never paged out of physical memory).

Example 8.3

Five of the following seven operations take place upon a page fault when there is no free frame in memory. Put the five correct operations in the right temporal order and identify the two incorrect operations.

a. Use the frame table to find the process that owns the faulting page.

b. Using the disk map of faulting process, load the faulting page from the disk into the victim frame.

c. Select a victim page for replacement (and the associated victim frame).

d. Update the page table of the faulting process and frame table to reflect the changed mapping for the victim frame.

e. Using the disk map of the victim process, copy the victim page to the disk (if dirty).

f. Look up the frame table to identify the victim process and invalidate the page table entry of the victim page in the victim page table.

g. Determine whether the faulting page is currently in physical memory.

Answer:

Step 1: c

Step 2: f

Step 3: e

Step 4: b

Step 5: d (Note: This may be shown as step 3 or 4, so long as the other steps remain in the same relative order.)

Operations (a) and (g) do not belong to page fault handling.

8.2 Interaction Between the Process Scheduler and Memory Manager

Figure 8.7 shows the interaction between the CPU scheduler and the memory manager. At any point in time, the CPU is executing either one of the user processes, one of the subsystems of the operating system such as the CPU scheduler, or the memory manager. The code for the scheduler, the memory manager, and all the associated data structures are in the kernel memory space (see Figure 8.7). The user processes live in the

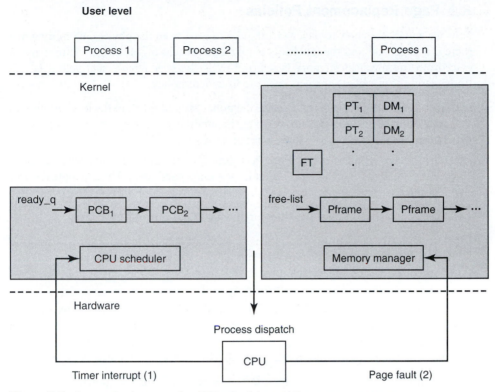

Figure 8.7 Interaction between the CPU scheduler and the memory manager.
In addition to the timer interrupt, the CPU may upcall to the operating system
upon detecting a page fault for the currently dispatched process.

user memory space. Once the CPU scheduler dispatches a process, it runs until one of
the following events happen:

1. The hardware timer interrupts the CPU, resulting in an upcall (indicated by 1 in the
   figure) to the CPU scheduler that may result in a process context switch. Recall that
   we defined an upcall (in Chapter 6) as a function call from the lower levels of the
   system software to the higher levels. The CPU scheduler takes the appropriate action
   to schedule the next process on the CPU.

2. The process incurs a page fault, resulting in an upcall (indicated by 2 in the figure) to
   the memory manager, which results in page fault handling, as described previously.

3. The process makes a system call (such as requesting an I/O operation), resulting in
   another subsystem's (not shown in the figure) getting an upcall to take the necessary action.

Whereas these three events exercise different sections of the operating system, all
of them share the PCB data structure, which aggregates the current state of the
process.

8.3 Page Replacement Policies

Now we will discuss how to pick a victim page to evict from the physical memory when there is a page fault and the free-list is empty. The process of selecting a victim page to evict from the physical memory is referred to as the *page replacement policy*. Let us understand the attributes of a good page replacement policy.

1. For a given string of page references, the policy should result in the least number of page faults. This attribute ensures that the amount of time spent in the operating system, dealing with page faults, is minimized.

2. Ideally, once a particular page has been brought into physical memory, the policy should strive not to incur a page fault for the same page again. This attribute ensures that the page fault handler respects the reference pattern of the user programs.

In selecting a victim page, the memory manager has one of two options:

- **Local victim selection:** The idea is to steal a physical frame, from the faulting process itself, to satisfy the request. Simplicity is the main attraction of this scheme. For example, this scheme eliminates the need for a *frame table*. However, local victim selection will lead to poor memory utilization.

- **Global victim selection:** The idea is to steal a physical frame from any process, not necessarily the faulting one. The exact heuristic used to determine the victim process and the victim page depends on the specifics of the algorithm. This scheme will result in good utilization due to the global selection of the victim page.

The norm is to use global victim selection to increase memory utilization. Ideally, if there are no page faults, the memory manager never needs to run and the processor executes user programs most of the time (except for context switching). Therefore, *reducing the page fault rate* is the goal of any memory manager. There are two reasons a memory manager strives to reduce the page fault rate: (1) The performance of a program incurring a page fault is adversely affected, because bringing in a page from secondary storage is slow, and (2) precious processor cycles should not be used too often in overhead activities such as page replacement.

In the rest of the discussion, the presumption is that the global page replacement policy is used, though the examples will focus on the paging behavior of a single process, to keep the discussion simple. The memory manager bases its victim selection on the paging activity of the processes. Therefore, whenever we refer to a page, we mean a virtual page. Once the memory manager identifies a virtual page as a victim, the physical frame that houses the virtual page becomes the candidate for replacement. For each page replacement policy, we will identify the hardware assist (if any) needed, the data structures needed, the details of the algorithm, and the expected performance in terms of number of page-faults.

8.3.1 Belady's Min

If we know the entire string of references, it is best if we replace the one that is not referenced for the *longest time in the future*. This replacement policy is not feasible to implement, because the memory manager does not know the future memory references of a process. However, in 1966, Laszlo Belady proposed the *optimal replacement algorithm,* called *Belady's Min,* to serve as the gold standard for evaluating the performance of any page replacement algorithm.

8.3.2 Random Replacement

The simplest policy is to replace a page randomly. At first glance, this may not seem like a good policy. The upside to this policy is that the memory manager does not need any hardware support, nor does it have to keep any bookkeeping information about the current set of pages (such as timestamp, and referential order). In the absence of knowledge about the future, it is worthwhile understanding how poorly or how well a random policy would perform for any string of references. Just as Belady's Min serves as an upper bound for performance of page replacement policies, a random replacement algorithm may serve as a lower bound for performance. In other words, if a page replacement policy requires hardware support and/or maintenance of bookkeeping information by the memory manager, it should perform better than a random policy, because, otherwise, it is not worth the trouble. In practice, memory managers may default to random replacement in the absence of bookkeeping information sufficient to make a decision (see Section 8.3.4).

8.3.3 First In First Out (FIFO)

This is one of the simplest page replacement policies. The FIFO algorithm works as follows:

- Affix a timestamp when a page is brought into physical memory.
- If a page has to be replaced, choose the *longest resident* page as the victim.

It is interesting to note that we do not need any hardware assist for this policy. As we will see shortly, the memory manager remembers the order of arrival of pages into physical memory, in its data structures.

Let us understand the data structure needed by the memory manager. The memory manager simulates the "timestamp," using a *queue* for recording the order of arrival of pages into physical memory. Let us use a circular queue (Figure 8.8) with a *head* and a *tail* pointer (initialized to the same value, say, 0). We insert at the tail of the queue. Therefore, the longest resident page is the one at the head of the queue. In addition to the queue, the memory manager uses a *full* flag (initialized to *false*) to indicate when the queue is full. The occupancy of the queue is the number of physical frames currently in use. Therefore, we will make the queue size equal the number of physical frames. Each index into the circular queue data structure corresponds to a unique physical frame. Initially, the queue is empty (*full* flag initialized to *false*), indicating that none of the physical frames are in use. As the memory manager demand-pages in the faulting pages, it allocates the physical frames to satisfy the page faults (incrementing the tail pointer after each allocation). The queue is full (*full* flag set to *true*) when there are no more page frames left for allocation (*head* and *tail* pointers are equal). This situation calls for page replacement on the next page fault. The memory manager replaces the page at the *head,* which is the longest

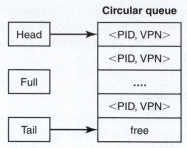

Figure 8.8 Circular queue for FIFO page replacement algorithm.

Tail points to first free physical frame index. Each queue entry corresponds to a physical page frame and contains the <PID, VPN> housed in that frame. The head contains the longest resident page.

resident page. The interesting point to note is that this one data structure, *circular queue*, simultaneously serves the purpose of the *free list* and the *frame table*.

Example 8.4

Consider a string of page references by a process:

Reference number:	1 2 3 4 5 6 7 8 9 10 11 12 13
Virtual page number:	9 0 3 4 0 5 0 6 4 5 0 5 4

Assume that there are 3 physical frames. Using a circular queue similar to Figure 8.8, show the state of the queue for the first 6 references.

Answer:

Initially, the circular queue looks as follows:

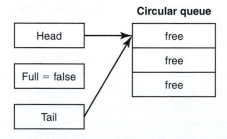

Upon a page fault, insertion of a new page happens at the entry pointed to by the tail. Similarly, the victim page is the one pointed to by the head, since the head always points to the FIFO page. Once selected, the head pointer moves to point to the next FIFO candidate. When the queue is full, both head and pointers move to satisfy a page fault. The following snapshots of the data structure show the state of the queue after each of the first six references (PF denotes page fault; HIT denotes that the reference is a hit—that is, there is no page fault):

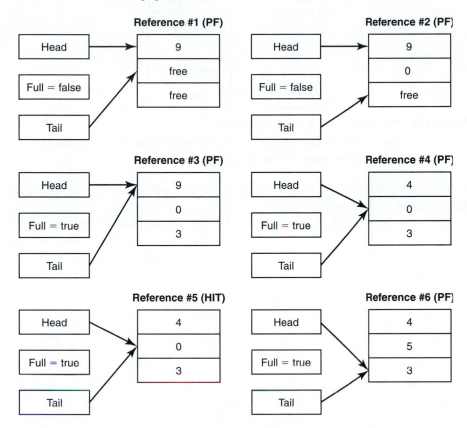

The given sequence shows the anomaly in the FIFO scheme. Reference #6 replaces page 0, since that is the longest resident one to make room for page 5. However, page 0 is the immediate next reference (Reference #7).

Looking at the sequence of memory accesses in the preceding example, we can conclude that page 0 is *hot*. An efficient page replacement policy should try not to replace page 0. Unfortunately, we know this fact postmortem. Let us see if we can do better than FIFO.

8.3.4 Least Recently Used (LRU)

Quite often, even in real life, we use the past as the predictor of the future. Therefore, even though we do not know the future memory accesses of a process, we do know the accesses made thus far by the process. Let us see how we use this information in page replacement. The *least recently used (LRU)* policy makes the assumption that if a page has not been referenced for a long time, there is a good chance it will not be referenced

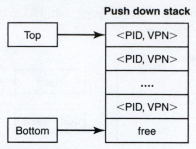

Figure 8.9 Push down stack for LRU replacement.

The most recently used page is at the top of the stack. The least recently used page is at the bottom of the stack.

in the future as well. Thus, the victim page in the LRU policy is the page that has not been used for the longest time.

Let us understand the hardware assist needed for the LRU policy. The hardware has to track every memory access from the CPU. Figure 8.9 shows a stack data structure. On every access, the CPU pushes the currently accessed page on the top of the stack; if that page currently exists anywhere else in the stack, the CPU removes it as well. Therefore, the bottom of the stack is the least recently used page and the candidate for replacement upon the event of a page fault. If we want to track the references made to every page frame, then the size of the stack should be as big as the number of frames.

Next, we will investigate the data structure for the LRU policy. The memory manager uses the hardware stack in Figure 8.9 to pick the page at the bottom of the stack as the victim. Of course, this requires some support from the instruction set for the software to read the bottom of the stack. The hardware stack, in addition to the page table, is necessary for the virtual-to-physical translation.

Notice that the memory manager has to maintain additional data structures, such as the *free-list* and *frame table,* to service page faults.

Example 8.5

We will consider the same string of page references by a process as in the FIFO example:

Reference number:	1 2 3 4 5 6 7 8 9 10 11 12 13
Virtual page number:	9 0 3 4 0 5 0 6 4 5 0 5 4

Assume that there are 3 physical frames. Initially, the stack looks as follows:

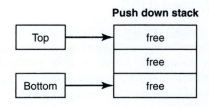

The following snapshots show the state of the stack after each of the first six references (PF denotes page fault; while HIT denotes that the reference is a hit, indicating that there is no page fault):

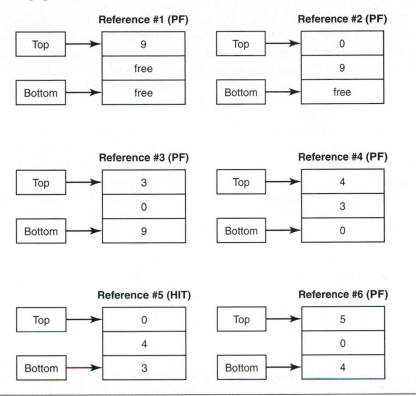

It is interesting to compare Examples 8.4 and 8.5. Both of them experience five page faults in the first six references. Unfortunately, we cannot do any better than that, since these pages (9, 0, 3, 4, and 5) are not in physical memory and, therefore, these are page faults, which are unavoidable with any policy. However, notice that Reference #6 replaces page 3 in the LRU scheme (not page 0, as in the FIFO example). Thus, Reference #7 results in a hit for the LRU scheme. In other words, LRU is able to avoid the anomalous situation that we encountered with the FIFO policy.

Approximate LRU #1: A small hardware stack. The LRU scheme, while conceptually appealing, is simply not viable from an implementation point of view, for a couple of reasons:

1. The stack has as many entries as the number of physical frames. For a physical memory size of 4 GB and a page size of 8 KB, the size of the stack is 0.5 MB. Such large hardware structures in the datapath of a pipelined processor add enormous latencies to the clock cycle time of the processor. For this reason, it is not viable to have such a huge hardware stack in the datapath of the processor.

2. On every access, the hardware has to modify the stack in order to place the current reference on the top of the stack. This expensive operation slows down the processor.

For these reasons, it is not feasible to implement a *true* LRU scheme. A more serious concern arises because true LRU, in fact, can be detrimental to performance in certain situations. For example, consider a program that loops over N+1 pages after accessing them in sequence. If the memory manager has a pool of N page frames to deal with this workload, there will be a page fault for every access, with the LRU scheme. This example, pathological as it sounds, is indeed quite realistic, because scientific programs manipulating large arrays are quite common.

It turns out that implementing an approximate LRU scheme is both feasible and less detrimental to performance. Instead of a stack equal in size to the physical memory size (in frames), its size can be some small number (say, 16). Thus, the stack maintains the history of the last 16 unique references made by the processor (older references fall off the bottom of the stack). The algorithm would pick a random page, that is not in the hardware stack, as the victim. Basically, the algorithm protects the most recent N referenced pages from replacement, where N is the size of the hardware stack.

In fact, some simulation studies have found that true LRU may even be worse than approximate LRU. This is because anything other than Belady's Min is simply guessing the page reference behavior of a process, and is therefore susceptible to failure. In this sense, a purely random replacement policy (see Section 8.3.2), which requires no sophisticated mechanisms in either hardware or software, has been shown to do well for certain workloads.

Approximate LRU #2: Reference bit per page frame. It turns out that tracking every memory access is just not feasible, from the point of view of implementing a high-speed pipelined CPU. Therefore, we have to resort to some other means to approximate the LRU scheme.

One possibility is to track references at the page level instead of individual accesses. The idea is to associate a *reference bit* per page frame. Hardware sets this bit when the CPU accesses any location in the page; software reads and resets it. The hardware orchestrates accesses to the physical memory through the page table. Therefore, we can have the reference bits in the page table.

Let us turn our attention to choosing a victim. Here is an algorithm using the reference bits:

1. The memory manager maintains a *bit vector* per page frame, called a *reference counter*.

2. Periodically, the memory manager reads the reference bits of all the page frames and dumps them in the *most significant bit (msb)* of the corresponding per-frame *reference counters*. The counters are right-shifted to accommodate the reference bits into their respective msb positions. Figure 8.10 shows this step, graphically. After reading the reference bits, the memory manager clears them. It repeats this step

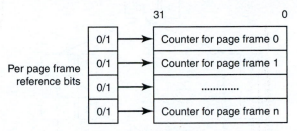

Figure 8.10 Page frame reference counters; the reference bit for each page may be 0 or 1.

every time quantum. Thus, each counter holds a snapshot of the references (or lack thereof) of the last n time quanta (n = 32 in Figure 8.10).

3. The reference counter with the largest absolute value is the most recently referenced page. The reference counter with the smallest absolute value is the least recently referenced page and, hence, a candidate for selection as a replacement victim.

A *paging daemon* is an entity which is part of the memory manager that wakes up periodically (as determined by the time quantum) to carry out the steps of the foregoing algorithm.

8.3.5 Second Chance Page Replacement Algorithm

This is a simple extension to the FIFO algorithm, using the reference bits. As the name suggests, this algorithm gives a second chance for a page *not* to be picked as a victim. The basic idea is to use the reference bit set by the hardware as an indication that the page deserves a second chance to stay in memory. The algorithm works as follows:

1. Initially, the operating system clears the reference bits of all the pages. As the program executes, the hardware sets the reference bits for the pages referenced by the program.

2. If a page has to be replaced, the memory manager chooses the replacement candidate in FIFO manner.

3. If the chosen victim's reference bit is set, then the manager clears the reference bit, gives it a *new arrival time,* and repeats step 1. In other words, this page is moved to the end of the FIFO queue.

4. The victim is the first candidate in FIFO order whose reference bit is not set.

Of course, in the pathological case where all the reference bits are set, the algorithm degenerates to a simple FIFO.

A simple way to visualize and implement this algorithm is to think of the pages forming a circular queue, with a pointer pointing to the FIFO candidate, as shown in Figure 8.11(a). When called upon to pick a victim, the pointer advances until it finds a

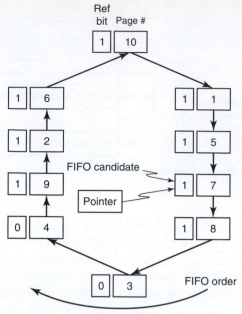

Figure 8.11(a) Second chance replacement—the memory manager keeps a software pointer that points to the FIFO candidate at the start of the algorithm.

Note the frames that have reference bits set and the ones that have their reference bits cleared. The ones that have their reference bits set to 1 are those that have been accessed by the program since the last sweep by the memory manager.

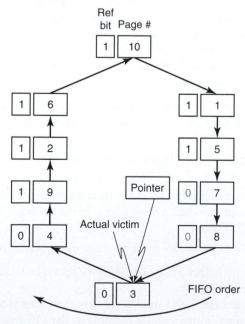

Figure 8.11(b) Second chance replacement—the algorithm passes over the frames whose reference bits are set to 1 (clearing them during the sweep) until it finds a frame that does not have its reference bit set, the actual victim frame.

page whose reference bit is not set. As it moves towards the eventual victim, the memory manager clears the reference bits of the pages that it encounters. As shown in Figure 8.11(a), the FIFO candidate is page 7. However, since its reference bit is set, the pointer moves until it gets to page 3, whose reference bit is not set (first such page in FIFO order), and chooses that page as the victim. The algorithm clears the reference bits for pages 7 and 8 as it sweeps in FIFO order. Note that the algorithm does not change the reference bits for the other pages not encountered during this sweep. It can be seen that the pointer sweep of the algorithm resembles the hand of a clock moving in a circle, and for the same reason, this algorithm is often referred to as the *clock* algorithm. After choosing page 3 as the victim, the pointer will move to the next FIFO candidate (page number 4 in Figure 8.11(b)).

Example 8.6

Suppose that we have only three physical frames and that we use the second-chance page replacement algorithm. Show the virtual page numbers that occupy these frames for the following sequence of page references:

Reference number:	1 2 3 4 5 6 7 8 9 10
Virtual page number:	0 1 2 3 1 4 5 3 6 4

Answer:

The next sequence of figures shows the state of the page frames and the associated reference bits *after* each reference is satisfied. The top entry is always the normal FIFO candidate. Note that the reference bit is set when the page is brought into the page frame.

To understand the choice of the victim in a particular reference, see the state of the pages shown after the previous reference.

References 1–3: no replacement

Reference 4: Page 0 is the victim (all have ref bits set, so FIFO candidate is the victim).

Reference 5: no replacement (page 1's reference bit set)

Reference 6: Page 2 is the victim (Page 1, the FIFO candidate, gets a second chance).

Reference 7: Page 1 is the victim (Page 3, the FIFO candidate, gets a second chance).

Reference 8: no replacement (page 3's reference bit set)

Reference 9: Page 4 is the victim (all have ref bits set, so FIFO candidate is the victim).

Reference 10: Page 3 is the victim (FIFO candidate; its ref bit is off).

Page in the frame	ref	Notation

Ref 1

0	1

Ref 2

0	1
1	1

Ref 3

0	1
1	1
2	1

Ref 4

1	0
2	0
3	1

Ref 5

1	1
2	0
3	1

Ref 6

3	1
1	0
4	1

Ref 7

4	1
3	0
5	1

Ref 8

4	1
3	1
5	1

Ref 9

3	0
5	0
6	1

Ref 10

5	0
6	1
4	1

8.3.6 Review of Page Replacement Algorithms

Table 8.1 summarizes the page replacement algorithms and the corresponding hardware assists needed. It turns out that approximate LRU algorithms using reference bits do quite well in reducing the page fault rate and perform almost as well as true LRU—a case in point for engineering ingenuity that gets you most of the benefits of an exact solution.

8.4 Optimizing Memory Management

In the previous sections, we presented rudimentary techniques for demand-paged virtual memory management. In this section, we will discuss some optimizations that memory managers employ to improve the system performance. It should be noted that the optimizations are not specific to any particular page replacement algorithm. They could be used on top of the basic page replacement techniques discussed in the preceding section.

8.4.1 Pool of Free Page Frames

It is not a good idea to wait until a page fault occurs to select a victim for replacement. Memory managers always keep a *minimum* number of page frames ready for allocation to satisfy page faults. The paging daemon wakes up periodically to check whether the pool of free frames on the *free-list* (Figure 8.3) is below this minimum threshold. If so, it will run the page replacement algorithm to free up more frames to meet this minimum threshold. It is possible that, occasionally, the number of page frames in the free list will be way over the minimum threshold. When a process terminates, all its page frames get on the free-list, leading to such a situation.

Table 8.1 Comparison of Page Replacement Algorithms

Page Replacement Algorithm	Hardware Assist Needed	Bookkeeping Information Needed	Comments
Belady's MIN	Oracle	None	Provably optimal performance; not realizable in hardware; useful as an upper bound for performance comparison
Random Replacement	None	None	Simplest scheme; useful as a lower bound for performance comparison
FIFO	None	Arrival time of a virtual page into physical memory	Could lead to anomalous behavior; often, performance worse than random
True LRU	Push down stack	Pointer to the bottom of the LRU stack	Expected performance close to optimal; infeasible for hardware implementation due to space and time complexity; worst-case performance may be similar to, or even worse than, FIFO
Approximate LRU #1	A small hardware stack	Pointer to the bottom of the LRU stack	Expected performance close to optimal; worst-case performance may be similar to, or even worse than, FIFO
Approximate LRU #2	Reference bit per page frame	Reference counter per page frame	Expected performance close to optimal; moderate hardware complexity; worst-case performance may be similar or even worse compared to FIFO
Second Chance Replacement	Reference bit per page frame	Arrival time of a virtual page into physical memory	Expected performance better than FIFO; memory manager implementation simplified compared with LRU schemes

Overlapping I/O with processing. In Section 8.1.4, we pointed out that, before the memory manager uses a page frame as a victim, the manager should save the current contents of the page that it houses to the disk if it is dirty. However, since the manager is simply adding the page frame to the *free-list*, there is no rush to do the saving right away. As we will see in a later chapter, high-speed I/O (such as to the disk) occurs concurrently with the CPU activity. Therefore, the memory manager simply schedules a write I/O for a dirty victim page frame before adding it to the *free-list*. Before the memory manager uses this dirty physical frame to house another virtual page, the write I/O must be complete. For this reason, the memory manager may skip over a dirty page on the *free-list* to satisfy a page fault (Figure 8.12(a)). This strategy helps to delay the necessity of waiting on a write I/O at the time of a page fault.

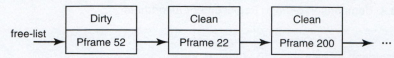

Figure 8.12(a)   Free-list—upon a page fault, the manager may choose pframe 22 over pframe 52 as the victim, because the former is clean, whereas the latter is dirty.

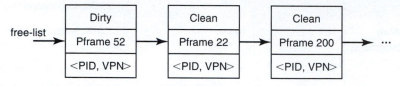

Figure 8.12(b)   Reverse mapping <PID, VPN> for the page frames on the free-list.

Reverse mapping to page tables.   To meet the minimum threshold requirement, the paging daemon may have to take away page frames currently mapped into running processes. Of course, the process that lost this page frame may fault on the associated page when it is scheduled to run. As it turns out, we can help this process with a little bit of additional machinery in each node of the free-list. If the memory manager has not yet reassigned the page frame to a different process, then we can retrieve it from the *free-list* and give it to the faulting process. To enable this optimization, we augment each node in the *free-list* with the reverse mapping (similar to the *frame table*), showing the virtual page it housed last (see Figure 8.12(b)).

Upon a page fault, the memory manager compares the <PID, VPN> of the faulting process with entries in the *free-list*. If there is a match, the manager simply reestablishes the original mapping in the page table for the faulting process by using the page frame of the matching entry to satisfy the page fault. This optimization removes the need for a read I/O from the disk to bring in the faulting page.

It is interesting to note that this enhancement, when used in tandem with the second change replacement algorithm, gives a *third* chance for a page before the page is kicked out of the system.

8.4.2 Thrashing

A term that we often come across with respect to computer system performance is *thrashing*, which is used to denote the situation that exists when the system is not getting useful work done. For example, let us assume that the degree of multiprogramming (which we defined in Chapter 6 as the number of processes coexisting in memory and competing for the CPU) is quite high, but still we observe low *processor utilization*. We may be tempted to increase the degree of multiprogramming to keep the processor busy. On the surface, this seems like a good idea, but let us dig a little deeper.

It is possible that all the currently executing programs are I/O bound (meaning that they do more I/O than processing on the CPU), in which case the decision to increase the degree of multiprogramming may be a good one. However, it is also possible that

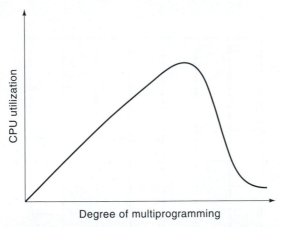

Figure 8.13 CPU thrashing phenomenon. The CPU utilization drops drastically beyond a certain degree of multiprogramming.

the programs are CPU bound. At first glance, it would appear odd that the processor utilization would be low with such CPU-bound jobs. The simple answer is, too much paging activity. Let us elaborate this point. With a demand-paged memory management, a process needs to have sufficient memory allocated to it in order to get useful work done. Otherwise, it will page fault frequently. Therefore, if there are too many processes coexisting in memory (i.e., a high degree of multiprogramming), then it is likely that the processes are continuously paging against one another to get physical memory. Thus, none of the processes is making forward progress. In this situation, it is incorrect to increase the degree of multiprogramming. In fact, we should reduce it. Figure 8.13 shows the expected behavior of CPU utilization as a function of the degree of multiprogramming. The CPU utilization drops rapidly after a certain point.

This phenomenon, called *thrashing*, occurs when processes spend more time paging than computing. Paging is *implicit I/O* done on behalf of a process by the operating system. Excessive paging could make a process, which is originally compute bound, into an I/O-bound process. An important lesson to take away from this discussion is that CPU scheduling should take into account memory usage by the processes. It is erroneous to have a CPU scheduling policy based solely on processor utilization. Fortunately, this situation can be corrected through cooperation between the CPU scheduling and memory management parts of the operating system.

Let us investigate how we can control thrashing. Of course, we can load the entire program into memory, but that would not be an efficient use of the resources. The trick is to ensure that each process has *sufficient* number of page frames allocated so that it does not page fault frequently. The *principle of locality* comes to our rescue. A process may have a huge memory footprint. However, if we look at a reasonably sized *window of time*, we will observe that the process accesses only a small portion of its entire memory footprint. This is the principle of locality. Of course, the locus of program activity may change over time, as shown in Figure 8.14. However, the change is gradual and not drastic. For example, the set of pages used by the program at time t1 is {p1, p2}; the set of pages at t2 is {p2, p3}; and so on.

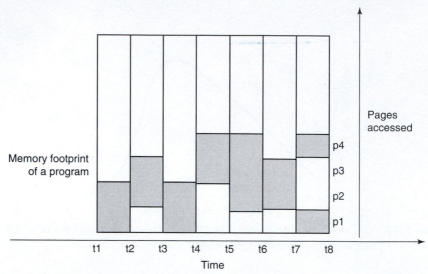

Figure 8.14 Changing loci of program activity as a function of time; the set of pages in use by the program is captured at times t1, t2, etc.; assume that the locus of program activity remains unchanged in the time intervals such as t1–t2, t2–t3, and so on.

We do not want the reader to conclude that the locus of activity of a program is always confined to consecutive pages. For example, at time t7, the set of pages used by the program is {p1, p4}. The point to take away is that the locus of activity is confined to a small subset of pages (see Example 8.7).

It is straightforward to use this principle to reduce page faults. If the current locus of program activity is in memory, the associated process will not page fault until the locus changes. For example, if the set of pages accessed by the program remains unchanged between t1 and t2, and if p1 and p2 are in physical memory, then the program will not experience any page fault between t1 and t2.

8.4.3 Working Set

To determine the locus of program activity, we define and use a concept called *working set*. The working set is the set of pages that defines the locus of activity of a program. Of course, the working set does not remain fixed, because the locus of program activity changes over time. For example, with reference to Figure 8.14,

Working set$_{t1-t2}$ = {p1, p2}

Working set$_{t2-t3}$ = {p2, p3}

Working set$_{t3-t4}$ = {p1, p2}

Working set$_{t4-t5}$ = {p3, p4}

Working set$_{t5-t6}$ = {p2, p3, p4}

....

The *working set size* (WSS) denotes the number of distinct pages touched by a process in a window of time. For example, the WSS for this process is 2 in the interval t1–t2, and 3 in the interval t5–t6.

The *memory pressure* exerted on the system is the summation of the WSS of all the processes currently competing for resources.

$$\text{Total memory pressure} = \sum_{i=1}^{i=n} WSSi \qquad (1)$$

Example 8.7

During the time interval t1–t2, the following virtual page accesses are recorded for the three processes P1, P2, and P3, respectively:

P1: 0, 10, 1, 0, 1, 2, 10, 2, 1, 1, 0

P2: 0, 100, 101, 102, 103, 0, 101, 102, 104

P3: 0, 1, 2, 3, 4, 5, 0, 1, 2, 3, 4, 5

a. What is the **working set** for each of the given three processes for this time interval?

b. What is the **cumulative memory pressure** on the system during this interval?

Answer:

a. P1's Working set = {0, 1, 2, 10}

P2's Working set = {0, 100, 101, 102, 103, 104}

P3's Working set = {0, 1, 2, 3, 4, 5}

b. Working set size of P1 = 4

Working set size of P2 = 6

Working set size of P3 = 6

Cumulative memory pressure = sum of the working sets of all processes

$$= 4 + 6 + 6$$

$$= 16 \text{ page frames}$$

8.4.4 Controlling Thrashing

1. If the total memory pressure exerted on the system is greater than the total available physical memory, the memory manager decreases the degree of multiprogramming. If the total memory pressure is less than the total available physical memory, the memory manager increases the degree of multiprogramming.

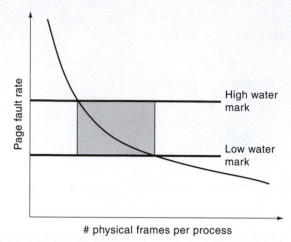

Figure 8.15   Page fault rate based control of thrashing.

The shaded area is the sweet spot for optimal system performance. Page fault rate lower than the low water mark is an opportunity to increase the degree of multiprogramming; page fault rate higher than the high water mark is an indication to decrease the degree of multiprogramming to avoid thrashing.

One approximate method for measuring the WSS of a process uses the reference bits associated with the physical frames. Periodically, say, every Δ time units, a daemon wakes up and samples the reference bits of the physical frames assigned to a process. The daemon records the page numbers that have their respective reference bits turned on; it then clears the reference bits for these pages. This recoding of the page numbers allows the memory manager to determine the working set and the WSS for a given process for any interval t and $t + \Delta$.

2. Another simple method of controlling thrashing is to use the observed page fault rate as a measure of thrashing. The memory manager sets two markers, a *low water mark*, and a *high water mark* for page faults (see Figure 8.15). An observed page fault rate that exceeds the high water mark implies excessive paging. In this case, the memory manager reduces the degree of multiprogramming, thus effectively increasing the number of page frames available for each process. On the other hand, an observed page fault rate that is lower than the low water mark presents an opportunity for the memory manager to increase the degree of multiprogramming, effectively reducing the number of page frames available to each process.

The shaded region in Figure 8.15 shows the preferred sweet spot of operation for the memory manager. The paging daemon kicks in to increase the pool of free physical frames when the page fault rate goes higher than the high water mark, decreasing the degree of multiprogramming, if necessary.

8.5 Other Considerations

The operating system takes a number of other measures to reduce page faults. For example, when the memory manager swaps out a process (to decrease the degree of multiprogramming), it remembers the current working set of the process. The memory manager brings in the corresponding working set at the point of swapping in a process. This optimization, referred to as *prepaging,* reduces disruption at process startup.

I/O activity in the system occurs simultaneously and concurrently with the CPU activity. This leads to interesting interaction between the memory and the I/O subsystems of the operating system. For example, the I/O subsystem may be initiating a transfer from a given physical frame to the disk. Simultaneously, the paging daemon may select the same physical frame as a potential victim, for servicing a page fault. Just as the CPU scheduler and memory manager work in concert, the I/O and the memory subsystems coordinate their activities. Typically, the I/O subsystem will *pin a page* in physical memory for the duration of the data transfer to prevent the paging daemon from selecting that page as a victim. The page table serves as a convenient communication area between the I/O subsystem and the memory manager for recording information such as the need to pin a page in physical memory. We will discuss I/O in much more detail in Chapter 10.

8.6 Translation Lookaside Buffer (TLB)

The discussion thus far should make one point very clear: Page faults are disruptive to system performance, and the memory manager strives hard to avoid them. To put things in perspective, the context switch time (from one process to another) approximates several tens of instructions; the page fault handling time (without disk I/O) also approximates several tens of instructions. On the other hand, the time spent in disk I/O is in the millisecond range that approximates to perhaps a million instructions on a GHz processor.

However, even if we reduce the number of page faults, with a variety of optimizations, it remains that every memory access involves two trips to the memory: one for the address translation and one for the actual instruction or data. This is undesirable. Fortunately, with a little bit engineering ingenuity, we can cut this down to one. The concept of paging removes the user's view of contiguous memory footprint for the program. However, it still is the case that, *within* a page, the memory locations are contiguous. Therefore, if we have performed the address translation for a page, then the same translation applies to *all* memory locations in that page. This suggests adding some hardware to the CPU to remember the address translations. However, we know that programs may have large memory footprints. The principle of locality that we introduced earlier comes to our rescue again. Referring to Figure 8.14, we may need to remember only a few translations *at a time* for a given program, irrespective of its total memory footprint. This is the idea behind the *translation look-aside buffer (TLB),* a small hardware table in which the CPU holds *recent* address translations (Figure 8.16). An address translation for a page needs to be done at least once. Therefore, none of the entries in the table is valid when the processor starts up. This is the reason for the *valid* bit in each entry. The *PFN* field gives the physical frame number corresponding to the *VPN* for that entry.

User/Kernel	VPN	PFN	Valid/Invalid
U	0	122	V
U	XX	XX	I
U	10	152	V
U	11	170	V
K	0	10	V
K	1	11	V
K	3	15	V
K	XX	XX	I

Figure 8.16   The translation look-aside buffer (TLB) stores the recent address translations carried out by the processor.

Notice how the TLB is split into two parts. One part holds the translations that correspond to the user address space. The other part holds the same for the kernel space. On a context switch, the operating system simply invalidates all the user space translations, schedules the new process, and builds up that part of the table. The kernel space translations are valid, independent of the user process currently executing on the processor. To facilitate TLB management, the instruction set provides *purge TLB*, a privileged instruction executable in kernel mode.

8.6.1 Address Translation with TLB

Figure 8.17(a) and Figure 8.17(b) show the CPU address translation in the presence of the TLB. The hardware first checks whether there is a valid translation in the TLB for

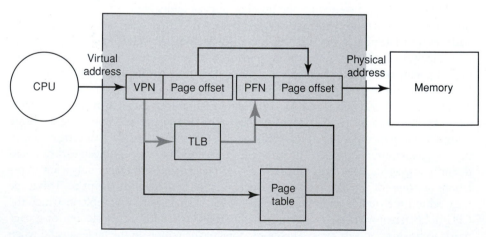

Figure 8.17(a)   Address translation (TLB hit).

The VPN to PFN mapping is currently in the TLB, obviating the need to refer to the page table.

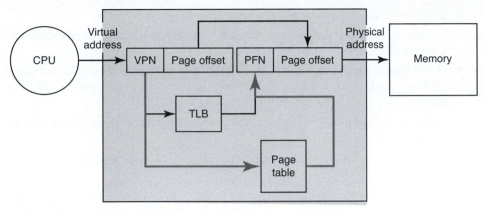

Figure 8.17(b)   Address translation (TLB miss).

The VPN to PFN mapping is currently not in the TLB, necessitating a page table lookup.

the CPU-generated address. We refer to such a successful lookup of the TLB as a *hit*. It is a *miss,* otherwise. On a hit, the PFN from the TLB helps in forming the physical address, thus avoiding a trip to the memory for address translation. On a miss, the page table in memory supplies the PFN. The hardware enters the resulting translation into the TLB for future accesses to the same page.

Of course, it is quite possible that the address translation is done entirely in software. You may be wondering how this would be possible. Basically, the hardware raises a "TLB fault" exception if it does not find the translation it needs in the TLB. At this point, the operating system takes over and handles the fault. The processing that the operating system needs to do to service this fault may escalate to a full-blown page fault if the page itself is not present in the memory. In any event, once it completes the TLB fault handling, the operating system will enter the translation into the TLB so that regular processing can resume. Architectures such as the MIPS and DEC Alpha take this approach of handling the TLB faults entirely in software. Naturally, the ISA for these architectures have special instructions for modifying the TLB entries. It is customary to call such a scheme *software managed TLB.*

The TLB is a special kind of memory, different from any hardware device that we have encountered thus far. The TLB is a hash table that contains VPN-PFN matches. The hardware has to look through the entire table to find a match for a given VPN. We refer to this kind of hardware device as *content addressable memory (CAM)* or *associative memory.* The exact details of the hardware implementation of the TLB depend on its organization.

It turns out that TLB is a special case of a general concept, namely, *caching,* which we deal with in much more detail, in Chapter 9, in the context of memory hierarchies. Suffice it to say at this point that caching refers to using a small table of items recently referred to by any subsystem. In this sense, the concept is exactly similar to the toolbox/tool-tray analogy we introduced in Chapter 2. The caching concept surfaces in several contexts. Here are a few concrete examples:

a. in processor design for keeping recently accessed memory locations in the processor in a hardware device called *processor cache,*

b. in processor design to keep recent address translations in the TLB,

c. in disk controller design to keep recently accessed disk blocks in memory (see Chapter 10),

d. in file system design to keep an in-memory data structure of recently accessed bookkeeping information regarding the physical location of files on the disk (see Chapter 11),

e. in file system design to keep an in-memory software cache of recently accessed files from the disk (see Chapter 11), and

f. in web browser design to keep an on-disk cache of recently accessed web pages.

In other words, *caching is a general concept of keeping a smaller stash of items nearer to the point of use than the permanent location of the information*. We will discuss the implementation choices for processor caches in more detail in the Chapter 9, which deals with memory hierarchy.

8.7 Advanced Topics in Memory Management

We mentioned that the memory manager's data structures include the process page tables. Let us do some math. Assuming a 40-bit byte-addressable virtual address and an 8 KB page size, we need 2^{27} page table entries for each process page table. This constitutes a whopping 128 million entries for each process page table. The entire physical memory of the machine may not be significantly more than the size of a single process page table.

We will present some preliminary ideas to get around this problem of managing the size of the page tables in physical memory. A more advanced course in operating systems would present a more detailed treatment of this topic.

8.7.1 Multi-Level Page Tables

The basic idea is to break a single page table into a multilevel page table. To make the discussion concrete, consider a 32-bit virtual address with a 4 KB page size. The page table has 2^{20} entries. Let us consider a two-level page table, as shown in Figure 8.18. The VPN of the virtual address has two parts. VPN1 picks out a unique entry in the first level page table that has 2^{10} entries. There is a second level page table (indexed by VPN2) corresponding to each unique entry in the first level. Thus, there are 2^{10} (i.e., 1024) second-level tables, each with 2^{10} entries. The second-level tables contain the PFN corresponding to the VPN in the virtual address.

What is the total space requirement for the page tables? With a single-level conventional structure, we will need a page table of size 2^{20} entries (1 M entries). With a two-level structure, we will need 2^{10} entries for the first level, plus 2^{10} second-level tables, each with 2^{10} entries. Thus, the total space requirement for a two-level page table is 1K entries (the size of the first-level table) more than the single-level structure.[1]

---

1. Note that the size of the page table entries in the two-level page table is different from that of the single-level structure. However, to keep the discussion simple, we do not get into this level of detail. Please refer to Exercise 11 for an elaboration of this point.

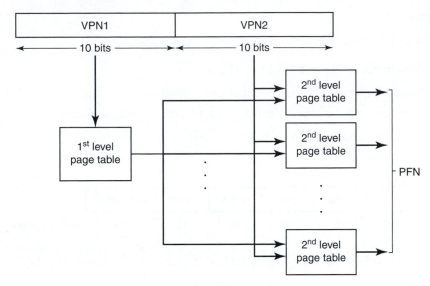

Figure 8.18 A two-level page table.

The top bits of the VPN (VPN1) index into the first-level page table to get the memory address for the second-level page table. Each second-level page table contains the mapping corresponding to virtual pages specified by the bottom bits of the VPN (VPN2).

What have we gained by this two-level structure? The requirement for kernel data structures that have to reside in physical memory all the time is drastically reduced by this structure. Let's see why. The first-level page table has 1 K entries per process. This is a reasonable sized data structure to have per process in physical memory. The second-level tables need not be in physical memory. The memory manager keeps them in virtual memory and demand-pages in the second-level tables on the basis of program locality.

Modern operating systems catering to 64-bit processor architectures implement multi-level page tables (i.e., more than two levels). Unfortunately, with multilevel page tables, a memory access potentially has to make multiple trips to the physical memory. Whereas this is true, fortunately, the TLB makes subsequent memory accesses to the same page, translation free.

Example 8.8

Consider a memory system with 64-bit virtual addresses and with an 8 KB page size. We use a five-level page table. The first-level page table keeps 2 K (2048) entries for each process. The remaining four levels each keep 1 K (1024) entries.

a. Show the layout of a virtual address in this system, with respect to this multilevel page table structure.

b. What is the total page table space requirement for each process (i.e., sum of all the levels of the page tables)?

Answer:

a. With 8 KB page size, the number of bits for page offset = 13.

Therefore, the VPN = 64 − 13 = 51 bits

Number of bits for the first level page table (2048 entries) = 11.
Number of bits for each of the remaining 4 levels (1024 entries each) = 10.

Layout of the virtual address is

63				13 12	0 bit positions
VPN1	VPN2	VPN3	VPN4	VPN5	Page offset
11	10	10	10	10	13 number of bits

b. Number of entries in the 1st level table = 2^{11}.

Number of entries in each 2nd level table = 2^{10}.

Similar to Figure 8.18, there are 2^{11} such second-level tables (one for each first-level table entry). So, the total number of entries at the second level = 2^{21}.

Number of entries in each 3rd level table = 2^{10}.

There are 2^{21} such third-level tables (one for each second-level table entry). So, the total number of entries at the third level = 2^{31}.

Number of entries in each fourth-level table = 2^{10}.

There are 2^{31} such fourth-level tables (one for each third-level table entry). So, the total number of entries at the fourth level = 2^{41}.

Number of entries in each fifth-level table = 2^{10}.

There are 2^{41} such fifth-level tables (one for each fourth-level table entry). So, the total number of entries at the fifth level = 2^{51}.

So, the total page table size for this virtual memory system

$$= 2^{11} + 2^{21} + 2^{31} + 2^{41} + 2^{51}.$$

A single-level page table for this virtual memory system would require a page table with 2^{51} entries.

8.7.2 Access Rights As Part of the Page Table Entry

A page table entry usually contains information in addition to the PFN and the valid bit. For example, it may contain access rights to the particular page, such as *read-only*, *read-write*, etc. This is extremely important from the viewpoint of meeting the expectations, laid out in Chapter 7, on the functionalities provided by the memory manager (see Section 7.1). In particular, we mentioned that the memory manager has to provide memory protection and isolation for processes from one another. Further, a process has to be protected against itself from erroneous behavior due to programming bugs (e.g., writing garbage unintentionally across the entire memory footprint due to a bug in the program). Lastly, processes have to be able to share memory with each other when needed. Access-rights information in a page table entry is another illustration of the cooperation between the hardware and software. The memory manager sets, in the page table, the access rights for the pages contained in the memory footprint of a program, at the time of process creation. For example, it will set the access rights for pages containing code to be read-only and data to be read-write. The hardware checks the access rights as part of the address translation process on every memory access. Upon detection of a violation of the access rights, the hardware takes corrective action. For example, if a process attempts to write to a read-only page, it will result in an *access violation trap,* giving the control to the operating system for any course correction.

The page table entry is also a convenient place for the operating system to place other information pertinent to each page. For example, the page table entry may contain the information needed to bring in a page from the disk, upon a page fault.

8.7.3 Inverted Page Tables

Since the virtual memory is usually much larger than the physical memory, some architectures (such as the IBM Power processors) use an *inverted page table,* which is essentially a frame table. The inverted page table alleviates the need for a per-process page table. Further, the size of the table is equal to the size of the physical memory (in frames) rather than the virtual memory. Unfortunately, inverted page tables complicate the logical-to-physical address translation done by the hardware. Therefore, in such processors the hardware handles address translations through the TLB mechanism. Upon a TLB miss, the hardware hands over control (through a trap) to the operating system to resolve the translation in software. The operating system is responsible for updating the TLB as well. The architecture usually provides special instructions for reading, writing, and purging the TLB entries in privileged mode.

Summary

The memory subsystem in modern operating systems comprises the *paging daemon, swapper, page fault handler,* and so on. The subsystem works in close concert with the CPU scheduler and the I/O subsystem. Here is a quick summary of the key concepts we learned in this chapter:

- demand paging basics, including hardware support, and data structures in the operating system for demand-paging;
- interaction between the CPU scheduler and the memory manager in dealing with page faults;
- page replacement policies, including FIFO, LRU, and second-chance replacement;

- techniques for reducing the penalty for page faults, including keeping a pool of page frames ready for allocation on page faults, lazily performing any necessary writes of replaced pages to disk, and reverse mapping of replaced page frames to the displaced pages;
- thrashing and the use of a working set of a process for controlling thrashing;
- translation look-aside buffer for speeding up address translation to keep the pipelined processor humming along; and
- advanced topics in memory management, including multilevel page tables and inverted page tables.

We observed in Chapter 7 that modern processors support page-based virtual memory. Correspondingly, operating systems on such modern processors such as Linux and Microsoft Windows (NT, XP, and Vista) implement page-based memory management. The second-chance page replacement policy, which we discussed in Section 8.3.5, is a popular one due to its simplicity and relative effectiveness, compared with the others.

Exercises

1. In a five-stage pipelined processor, upon a page fault, what needs to happen in hardware for instruction restart?

2. Describe the role of the frame table and the disk map data structures in a demand-paged memory manager.

3. Enumerate the steps in page fault handling.

4. Describe the interaction between the process scheduler and the memory manager.

5. What is the difference between a second change page replacement algorithm and a simple FIFO algorithm?

6. Consider an architecture wherein for each entry in the TLB there is
   - 1 reference bit (that is set by hardware when the associated TLB entry is referenced by the CPU for address translation), and
   - 1 dirty bit (that is set by hardware when the associated TLB entry is referenced by the CPU for a store access).

   These bits are in addition to the other fields of the TLB discussed in Section 8.6. The architecture provides three special instructions:
   - one for sampling the reference bit for a particular TLB entry
        (Sample_TLB(entry_num));
   - one for clearing the reference bit for a particular TLB entry
        (Clear_refbit_TLB(entry_num)); and
   - one for clearing the reference bits in all the TLB entries
        (Clear_all_refbits_TLB(ALL)).

Come up with a scheme to implement page replacement, using this additional help from the TLB. You should show data structures and pseudo-code that the algorithm maintains to implement page replacement.

7. A process has a memory reference pattern as follows:

$$1\ 3\ 1\ 2\ 3\ 4\ 2\ 3\ 1\ 2\ 3\ 4$$

The given pattern (which represents the virtual page numbers of the process) repeats throughout the execution of the process. Assume that there are three physical frames.

   Show the paging activity for a True LRU page replacement policy. Show an LRU stack and the page that is replaced (if any) for the first 12 accesses. Clearly indicate which accesses are hits and which are page faults.

8. A process has a memory reference pattern as follows:

$$4\ 3\ 1\ 2\ 3\ 4\ 1\ 4\ 1\ 2\ 3\ 4$$

The given pattern (which represents the virtual page numbers of the process) repeats throughout the execution of the process. What would be the paging activity for an optimal page replacement policy for the first 12 accesses? Indicate which accesses are hits and which are page faults.

9. A processor asks for the contents of virtual memory address 0x30020. The paging scheme in use breaks this into a VPN of 0x30 and an offset of 0x020.

   PTB (a CPU register that holds the address of the page table) has a value of 0x100, indicating that this process's page table starts at location 0x100.

   The machine uses word addressing, and the page table entries are each one word long:

   PTBR = 0x100

VPN	Offset
0x30	0x020

   The contents of selected memory locations are as follows:

Physical Address	Contents
0x00000	0x00000
0x00100	0x00010
0x00110	0x00000
0x00120	0x00045
0x00130	0x00022
0x10000	0x03333
0x10020	0x04444

0x22000	0x01111
0x22020	0x02222
0x45000	0x05555
0x45020	0x06666

What is the physical address calculated?

What are the contents of this address returned to the processor?

How many memory references would be required (worst case)?

10. During the time interval t1–t2, the following virtual page accesses are recorded for the three processes P1, P2, and P3, respectively:

    P1: 0, 0, 1, 2, 1, 2, 1, 1, 0

    P2: 0, 100, 101, 102, 103, 0, 1, 2, 3

    P3: 0, 1, 2, 3, 0, 1, 2, 3, 4, 5

    What is the working set for each of the given three processes for this time interval?

    What is the cumulative memory pressure on the system during this interval?

11. Consider a virtual memory system with a 20-bit page frame number. This exercise is to work out the details of the actual difference in page table sizes for a one-level and two-level page table arrangement. For a two-level page table, assume that the arrangement is similar to that shown in Figure 8.18. We are interested in only the page table that has to be memory resident always. For a two-level page table, this is only the first-level page table. For the single-level page table, the entire page table has to be memory resident. You will have to work out the details of the PTE for each organization (one-level and two-level) to compute the total page table requirement for each organization.

Bibliographic Notes and Further Reading

Peter Denning pioneered the research in the working set model and its impact on program performance [Denning, 1968]. The shortcoming of the FIFO replacement algorithm was first published by Belady et al. [Belady, 1969]. The optimal page replacement algorithm by Belady, which bears his name, "Belady's min," was first published in [Belady, 1966]. Carr and Hennessy [Carr, 1981] presented WSCLOCK, an enhanced version of the basic clock algorithm discussed in this chapter, that exploits the working set concept. The textbook by Silberschatz et al. [Silberschatz, 2008] has a lucid presentation of page replacement algorithms. The textbook by Bryant and O'Hallaron presents a nice treatment of virtual memory from the perspective of the programmer [Bryant, 2003].

Memory Hierarchy

Let us first understand what we mean by memory hierarchy. So far, we have treated the physical memory as a black box. In the implementation of the LC-2200 (Chapters 3 and 5), we treated memory as part of the datapath. There is an implicit assumption in such an arrangement, namely, that accessing the memory takes the same amount of time as performing any other datapath operation. Let us dig a little deeper into that assumption. Today, processor clock speeds have reached the GHz range. This means that the CPU clock cycle time is less than a nanosecond. We compare that to the state-of-the-art memory speeds (circa 2009). Physical memory, implemented by *dynamic random access memory (DRAM)* technology, has a cycle time in the range of 100 nanoseconds. We know that the slowest member determines the cycle time of the processor in a pipelined processor implementation. Given that IF and MEM stages of the pipeline access memory, we have to find ways to bridge the 100:1 speed disparity that exists between the CPU and the memory.

It is useful to define two terminologies frequently used in memory systems, namely, *access time* and *cycle time*. The delay between submitting a request to the memory and getting the data is called the access time. On the other hand, the time gap needed between two successive requests to the memory system is called the cycle time. A number of factors are responsible for the disparity between the access time and cycle time. For example, DRAM technology uses a single transistor to store a bit. Reading this bit depletes the charge and, therefore, requires a replenishment before the same bit is read again. This is why there is a disparity between cycle time and read access time in a DRAM. In addition to the specific technology used to realize the memory system, transmission delays on buses used to connect the processor to the memory system add to the disparity between access time and cycle time.

Let us revisit the processor datapath of the LC-2200. It contains a register file, which is also a kind of memory. The access time of a small 16-element register file is at the speed of the other datapath elements. There are two reasons why this is so. The first reason is that the register file uses a different technology, referred to as *static random access memory (SRAM)*. The virtue of this technology is speed. Succinctly put, SRAM gets its speed advantage over DRAM by using six transistors for storing each bit, arranged in a way that eliminates the need for replenishing the charge after a read. For the same reason, there is no disparity between cycle time and access time for SRAMs. As a rule of thumb, SRAM's cycle time can be 8 to 16 times faster than DRAM's. As you may have guessed, SRAMs are also bulkier than DRAMs since they use six transistors per bit (as opposed to the one per bit of DRAMs), and consume more power for the same reason. Not surprisingly, SRAMs are also considerably more expensive per bit (roughly 8 to 16 times) than DRAMs.

The second and more compelling reason that physical memory is slow compared with register file is the sheer *size*. We usually refer to a register file as a 16-, 32-, or 64-element entity. On the other hand, we usually specify the size of memory in quantities of KB, MB, or, these days, GB. In other words, even if we were to implement physical memory by using SRAM technology, the larger structure would result in slower access time, compared with a register file. A simple state of reality is that, independent of the implementation technology (i.e., SRAM or DRAM), you can have high speed or large size, but not both. You cannot have your cake and eat it, too!

Pragmatically speaking, SRAMs do not lend themselves to realizing large memory systems, due to a variety of reasons, including power consumption, die area, delays that are inevitable with large memories built out of SRAM, and, ultimately, the sheer cost of this technology for realizing large memories. On the other hand, DRAM technology is much more frugal with respect to power consumption, compared with its SRAM counterpart, and lends itself to very large-scale integration. For example, quoting 2007 numbers, a single DRAM chip may contain up to 256 Mbits and have an access time of 70 ns. The virtue of the DRAM technology is the size. Thus, it is economically feasible to realize large memory systems by using DRAM technology.

9.1 The Concept of a Cache

It is feasible to have a small amount of fast memory and/or a large amount of slow memory. Ideally, we would like to have the *size* advantage of a *large slow memory* and the *speed* advantage of a *fast small memory*. Given the earlier discussion regarding size and speed, we would choose to implement the small fast memory by using SRAM, and the large slow memory by using DRAM.

Memory hierarchy comes into play to achieve these twin goals. Figure 9.1 shows the basic idea behind memory hierarchy. *Main memory* is the physical memory that is visible to the instruction set of the computer. *Cache*, as the name suggests, is a hidden storage. We already introduced the general idea of caches and its application at various levels of the computer system, in Chapter 8 (see Section 8.6) when we discussed TLBs, which are a special case of caches used for holding address translations. Specifically, in the context of the memory accesses made by the processor, the idea is to stash information brought from the memory in the cache. It is much smaller than the main memory and, hence, much faster.

Our intent is as follows: The CPU looks in the cache for the data it seeks from the main memory. If the data are not there, it retrieves them from the main memory. If the

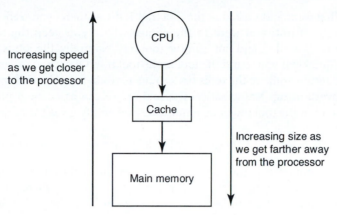

Figure 9.1 A basic memory hierarchy.

The figure shows a two-level hierarchy. Modern processors may have a deeper hierarchy (up to three levels of caches followed by the main memory).

cache is able to service most of the CPU requests, then we will be able to get the speed advantage of the cache.

9.2 Principle of Locality

Let us understand why a cache works in the first place. The answer is contained in the principles of locality that we introduced in the previous chapter (see Section 8.4.2).

Stated broadly, a program tends to access a relatively small region of memory, irrespective of its actual memory footprint in any given interval of time. Whereas the region of activity may change over time, such changes are gradual. The principle of locality zeroes in on this tendency of programs.

The principle of locality has two dimensions, namely, *spatial* and *temporal*. Spatial locality refers to the high probability of a program accessing *adjacent* memory locations . . ., $i-3, i-2, i-1, i+1, i+2, i+3, . . .$, if it accesses a location i. This observation is intuitive. A program's instructions occupy contiguous memory locations. Similarly, data structures such as arrays and records occupy contiguous memory locations. *Temporal locality* refers to the high probability of a program accessing, in the near future, the *same* memory location i that it is accessing currently. This observation is intuitive as well, considering that a program may be executing a looping construct and thus revisiting the same instructions repeatedly and/or updating the same data structures repeatedly in an iterative algorithm. We will shortly find ways to exploit these locality properties in the cache design.

9.3 Basic Terminologies

We will now introduce some intuitive definitions of terms commonly used to describe the performance of memory hierarchies. Before we do that, it would be helpful to remind ourselves of the toolbox and tool tray analogy from Chapter 2. If you needed a tool, you first went and looked in the tool tray. If it was there, you were saved a trip to the toolbox; if not, you went to the garage where you keep the toolbox and brought the tool, used it, and put it in the tool tray. Naturally, the job is going to go much more quickly if you found the tool in the tool tray. Of course, occasionally, you may have to return some of the tools back to the toolbox from the tool tray when the tray starts overflowing. Mathematically speaking, we can associate a probability of finding the tool in the tool tray; one minus this probability gives the odds of going to the toolbox.

Now we are ready to use this analogy for defining some basic terminologies.

- **Hit:** This term refers to the CPU finding the contents of the memory address in the cache, thus saving a trip to the deeper levels of the memory hierarchy, and analogous to finding the tool in the tool tray. The *hit rate (h)* is the probability of such a *successful lookup* of the cache by the CPU.

- **Miss:** This term refers to the CPU *failing* to find what it wants in the cache, thus incurring a trip to the deeper levels of the memory hierarchy, and analogous to taking a trip to the toolbox; the *miss rate (m)* is the probability of *missing* in the cache and is equal to $1 - h$.

- **Miss penalty:** This is the time penalty associated with servicing a miss at any particular level of the memory hierarchy, and analogous to the time required to go to the garage to fetch the missing tool from the tool box.

- **Effective memory access time (EMAT):** This is the effective access time experienced by the CPU.

  EMAT has two components:

  a. time to lookup the cache to see whether the memory location that the CPU is looking for is already there, defined as the *cache access time* or *hit time*, and

  b. upon a miss in the cache, the time to go to the deeper levels of the memory hierarchy to fetch the missing memory location, defined as the *miss penalty*.

The CPU is always going to incur the first component on every memory access. The second component, namely, *miss penalty*, is governed by the access time to the deeper levels of the memory hierarchy, and is measured in terms of the number of CPU clock cycles that the processor has to be idle while waiting for the miss to be serviced. The miss penalty depends on a number of factors, including the organization of the cache and the details of the main memory system design. These factors will become more apparent in later sections of this chapter. Since the CPU incurs this penalty only on a miss, to compute the second component, we need to condition the miss penalty with the probability (quantified by the miss rate m) that the memory location which the CPU is looking for is not presently in the cache.

Thus, if m, Tc, and Tm are the cache miss rate, the cache access time, and the miss penalty, respectively, then

$$\boxed{\text{EMAT} = Tc + m * T_m} \qquad (1)$$

9.4 Multilevel Memory Hierarchy

As it turns out, modern processors employ multiple levels of caches. For example, a state-of-the-art processor (circa 2009) has at least two levels of caches on chip, referred to as *first-level (L1), second-level (L2) caches*. You may be wondering, if both the first-level and second-level caches are on-chip, why not make it a single big cache? The answer lies in the fact that we are trying to take care of two different concerns, simultaneously: fast access time to the cache (i.e., hit time), and lower miss rate. On the one hand, we want the hit time to be as small as possible to keep pace with the clock cycle time of the processor. Since the size of the cache has a direct impact on the access time, this suggests that the cache should be small. On the other hand, the growing gap between the processor cycle time and main memory access time suggests that the cache should be large. Addressing these twin concerns leads to multilevel caches. The first-level cache is optimized for speed, to keep pace with the clock cycle time of the processor, and hence, is small. The speed of the second-level cache affects only the miss penalty incurred by the first level cache and does not directly affect the clock cycle time of the processor. Therefore, the second-level cache design focuses on reducing the miss rate and, hence, is large. The processor sits in an integrated circuit board, referred to as a *motherboard*, which houses the main (physical) memory.[1] High-end CPUs intended for enterprise class machines (database and web servers) even have a large off-chip *third-level cache (L3)*. For considerations of speed of access time, these multiple levels of the caches are usually implemented with SRAM technology.

For reasons outlined previously, the sizes of the caches become bigger as we move away from the processor. If S_i is the size of the cache at level i, then

$$S_{i+n} > S_{i+n-1} > \ldots > S_2 > S_1$$

Correspondingly, the access times also increase as we move from the processor. If T_i is the access time at level i, then

$$T_{i+n} > T_{i+n-1} > \ldots > T_2 > T_1$$

Generalizing the EMAT terminology to the memory hierarchy as a whole, let T_i and m_i be the access time and miss rate for any level of the memory hierarchy, respectively. The effective memory access time for any level i of the memory hierarchy is given by the recursive formula:

$$\text{EMAT}_i = T_i + m_i * \text{EMAT}_{i+1} \qquad (2)$$

We are now ready to generalize the concept of memory hierarchy:

> Memory hierarchy is defined as all the storage containing either instructions and/or data that a processor accesses either directly or indirectly.

---

1. The typical access times and sizes for these different levels of the cache hierarchy change with advances in technology.

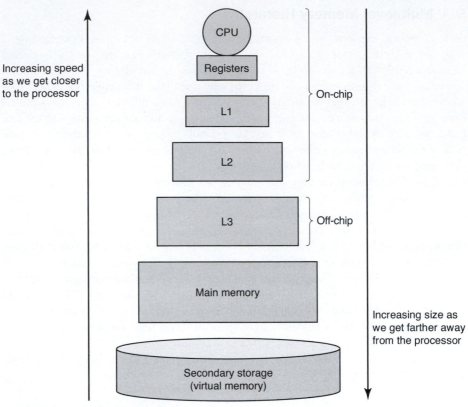

Figure 9.2   The entire memory hierarchy stretching from processor registers to the virtual memory.

By *direct access*, we mean that the storage is visible to the ISA. By *indirect access*, we mean that it is not visible to the ISA. Figure 9.2 illustrates this definition. In Chapter 2, we introduced registers, which are the fastest and closest data storage available to the processor for direct access from the ISA. Typically, load/store instructions and arithmetic/logic instructions in the ISA access the registers. L1, L2, and L3 are different levels of caches that a processor (usually) implicitly accesses every time it accesses the main memory to bring in an instruction or data. Usually, L1 and L2 are on chip, whereas L3 is off chip.[2] The main memory serves as the storage for the instructions and data of the program. The processor explicitly accesses the main memory for instructions (via the program counter) and for data (via load/store instructions, and other instructions that use memory operands). It should be noted that some architectures also allow direct access to the cache from the ISA by the processor (e.g., for flushing the contents of the cache). The secondary storage serves as the home for the entire memory footprint of the program, a part of which is resident in the main memory, consistent with the working set principle that we discussed in Chapter 8. In other words, the secondary storage serves as the home for the

---

2. Newer designs incorporate L3 cache on chip also. (See Chapter summary for an example.)

virtual memory. The processor accesses the virtual memory implicitly upon a page fault in order to bring the faulting virtual page into the main (i.e., physical) memory.

This chapter focuses only on the portion of the memory hierarchy that includes the caches and main memory. We already have a pretty good understanding of the registers, from earlier chapters (Chapters 2, 3, and 5). Similarly, we have a good understanding of the virtual memory from Chapters 7 and 8. In this chapter, we focus only on the caches and main memory. Consequently, we use the terms *cache hierarchy* and *memory hierarchy* interchangeably, to mean the same thing, in the rest of the chapter.

Example 9.1

Consider a three-level memory hierarchy, as shown in Figure 9.3. Compute the effective memory access time.

Answer:

$$EMAT_{L2} = T_{L2} + (1 - h_2) * T_m$$
$$= 10 + (1 - 0.8) * 100$$
$$= 30 \text{ ns}$$
$$EMAT_{L1} = T_{L1} + (1 - h_1) * EMAT_{L2}$$
$$= 2 + (1 - 0.95) * 30$$
$$= 2 + 1,5$$
$$= 3.5 \text{ ns}$$
$$EMAT = EMAT_{L1} = \textbf{3.5 ns}$$

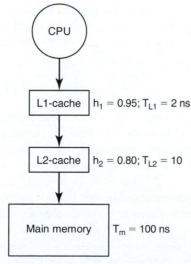

Figure 9.3 Three-level memory hierarchy.

9.5 Cache Organization

There are three facets to the organization of the cache: *placement, algorithm for lookup,* and *validity*.

These three facets deal with the following questions, respectively:

1. Where do we place in the cache the data read from the memory?

2. How do we find something that we have placed in the cache?

3. How do we know whether the data in the cache is valid?

A mapping function that takes a given memory address to a cache index is the key to answering the first question. In addition to the mapping function, the second question concerns the additional metadata in each cache entry that help identify the cache contents, unambiguously. The third question brings out the necessity of providing a valid bit in each cache entry, to assist the lookup algorithm.

We will look at these three facets specifically in the context of a simple cache organization, namely, a *direct-mapped* cache. In Section 9.11, we will look at other cache organizations, namely, *fully associative* and *set-associative*.

9.6 Direct-Mapped Cache Organization

A direct-mapped cache has a one-to-one correspondence between a memory location and a cache location.[3] That is, given a memory address, there is exactly one place to put its contents in the cache. To understand how direct-mapping works, let us consider a very simple example, a memory with 16 words and a cache with 8 words (Figure 9.4). The shading in the figure shows the mapping of memory locations 0 to 7 to locations 0 to 7 of the cache, respectively; and similarly, locations 8 to 16 of the memory map to locations 0 to 7 of the cache, respectively.

Before we explore the questions of lookup and validity, let us first understand the placement of memory locations in the cache, with this direct mapping. To make the discussion concrete, let us assume that the cache is empty and consider the following sequence of memory references:

$$0, 1, 2, 3, 1, 3, 0, 8, 0, 9, 10 \text{ (all decimal addresses)}$$

Since the cache is initially empty, the first four references (addresses 0, 1, 2, 3) *miss* in the cache and the CPU retrieves the data from the memory and stashes them in the cache. Figure 9.5 shows the cache after servicing the first four memory references. These are inevitable misses, referred to as *compulsory misses*, since the cache is initially empty.

The next three CPU references (addresses 1, 3, 0) *hit* in the cache, thus avoiding trips to the memory. Let us see what happens on the next CPU reference (address 8).

---

3. Of course, since the cache is necessarily smaller than the memory, there is a many-to-one relationship between a set of memory locations and a given cache location.

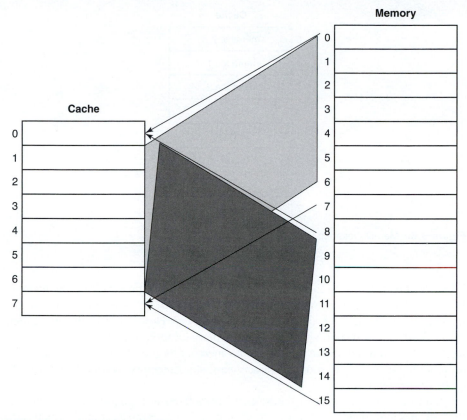

Figure 9.4   Direct-mapped cache.

There is a one-to-one mapping between a memory location and a cache location.

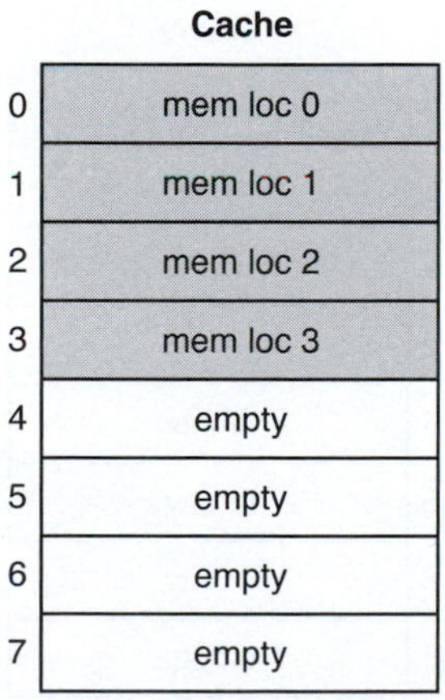

Figure 9.5   Content of the cache after the first four references.

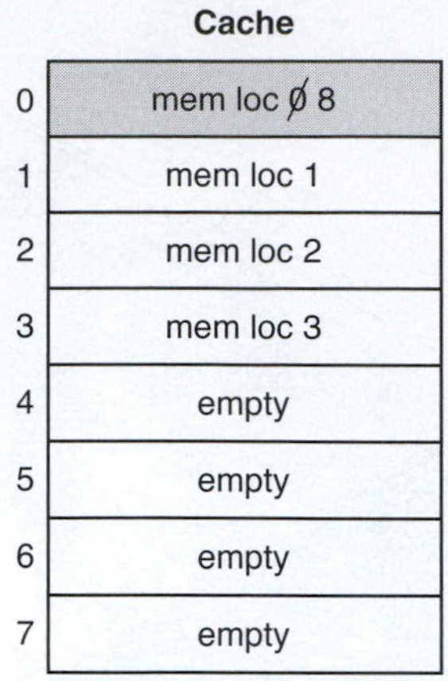

Cache

0	mem loc ~~0~~ 8
1	mem loc 1
2	mem loc 2
3	mem loc 3
4	empty
5	empty
6	empty
7	empty

Figure 9.6   Memory location 0 replaced by 8.

This reference will *miss* in the cache, and the CPU retrieves the data from the memory. Now we have to figure out where in the cache the system will stash the data from this memory location. The cache has space in locations 4–7. However, with direct-mapping cache location, 0 is the only spot for storing memory location 8. Therefore, the cache has to evict memory location 0 to make room for memory location 8. Figure 9.6 shows this state of the cache. This is also a *compulsory miss,* since memory location 8 is not in the cache to start with.

Consider the next reference (address 0). This reference also *misses* in the cache, and the CPU has to retrieve it from the memory and stash it in cache location 0, which is the only spot for memory location 0. Figure 9.7 shows the new contents of the cache. This miss occurs due to the *conflict* between memory locations 0 and 8 for a spot in the

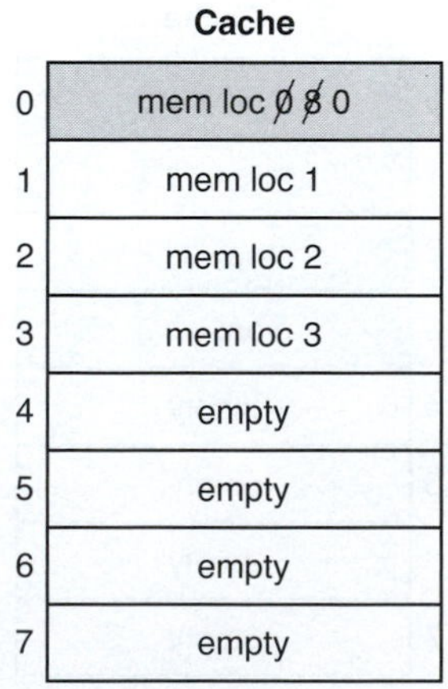

Cache

0	mem loc ~~0~~ ~~8~~ 0
1	mem loc 1
2	mem loc 2
3	mem loc 3
4	empty
5	empty
6	empty
7	empty

Figure 9.7   Memory location 8 replaced by 0 (conflict miss).

cache, and hence is referred to as a *conflict miss*. A conflict miss occurs due to direct mapping, despite the fact that there are unused locations available in the cache. Note that the previous miss (location 8 in Figure 9.6) also caused a conflict, because location 0 was already present in that cache entry. Regardless of this situation, first access to a memory location will always result in a miss, which is why we categorized the miss in Figure 9.6 as a compulsory miss. We will revisit the different types of misses in more detail in Section 9.15.

9.6.1 Cache Lookup

By now, we know the information exchange, or the *handshake,* between the CPU and the memory: The CPU supplies the address and the command (e.g., read) and gets back the data from the memory. The introduction of the cache (Figure 9.1) changes this simple setup. The CPU looks up the cache first to see whether the data it is looking for are in the cache. Only upon a miss does the CPU resort to its normal CPU–memory handshake.

Let us understand how the CPU *looks up* the cache for the memory location of interest. Specifically, we need to figure out what *index* the CPU has to present to the cache, with a direct-mapped organization. Looking back at Figure 9.4, we can see how the CPU addresses map to their corresponding cache *indices*.

We can compute the numerical value of the cache index as follows:

$$\text{Memory-address } mod \text{ cache-size}$$

For example, given the memory address 15, the cache index is

$$15 \bmod 8 = 7.$$

Similarly, the cache index for memory address 7 is

$$7 \bmod 8 = 7.$$

Essentially, to construct the cache index, we simply take the least significant bits of the memory address, commensurate with the cache size. In our previous example, since the cache has eight entries, we would need three bits for the cache index (the least significant three bits of the memory address).

Suppose that the CPU needs to get data from memory address 8; 1000 is the memory address in binary; the cache index is 000. The CPU looks up the cache location at index 000. We need some way of knowing whether the contents of this cache entry are from memory location 0 or 8. Therefore, in addition to the data, we need information in each entry of the cache to distinguish between multiple memory addresses that may map to the same cache entry. The bits of the memory address that were "dropped" to generate the cache index are exactly the information needed for this purpose. We refer to this additional information (which will be stored in the cache) as the *tag*. For example, the most significant bits of the memory address 0000 and 1000 are 0 and 1, respectively. Therefore, our simple cache needs a 1-bit tag with

	Tag	Data
0	1	mem loc Ø 8
1	0	mem loc 1
2	0	mem loc 2
3	0	mem loc 3
4		empty
5		empty
6		empty
7		empty

Figure 9.8   Direct-mapped cache with a tag field and a data field in each entry.

The tag field uniquely identifies the actual memory location currently in a given cache location.

each cache entry (Figure 9.8). If the CPU wants to access memory location 11, it looks up location 11 mod 8 in the cache—that is, location 3 in the cache. This location contains a tag value of 0. Therefore, the data contained in this cache entry correspond to memory location 3 (binary address 0011) and not memory location 11 (binary address 1011).

Suppose that the CPU generates memory address 0110 (memory address 6). Let us assume that this is the first time memory address 6 is being referenced by the CPU. So, we know it cannot be in the cache. Let us see the sequence of events here as the CPU tries to read memory location 6. The CPU will first look up location 6 (6 mod 8)

	Valid	Tag	Data
0	1	1	loc 8
1	1	0	loc 1
2	1	0	loc 2
3	1	0	loc 3
4	0	X	empty
5	0	X	empty
6	0	X	empty
7	0	X	empty

Figure 9.9   Direct-mapped cache with valid field, tag field, and data field in each entry.

A value of "X" in the tag field indicates a "don't care" condition.

Figure 9.10   Fields of each cache entry.

in the cache. If the tag happens to be 0, then the CPU will assume that the data correspond to memory location 6. Well, the CPU never has fetched that location from memory, so far, in our example; it is by chance that the tag is 0. Therefore, the data contained in this cache entry do not correspond to the actual memory location 6. We can see that this is erroneous, and it points to the need for additional information in each cache entry in order to avoid this error. The tag is useful for disambiguation of the memory location currently in the cache, but it does not help in knowing whether the entry is *valid*. To fix this problem, we add a *valid* field to each entry in the cache (Figure 9.9).

9.6.2 Fields of a Cache Entry

To summarize, each cache entry contains three fields (Figure 9.10). Thus, the memory address generated by the CPU has two parts, from the point of view of looking up the cache: *tag* and *index*. The *index* is the specific cache location that could contain the memory address generated by the CPU; the *tag* is the portion of the address that helps to disambiguate the contents of the specific cache entry (Figure 9.11). We use the least significant (i.e., the right-most) bits of the memory address as cache index to take advantage of the principle of spatial locality. For example, in our simple cache, if we use the most significant three bits of the memory address to index the cache, then memory locations 0 and 1 will be competing for the same spot in the cache.

Consider the access sequence for memory addresses 0, 1, 0, 1, with the eight-entry direct-mapped cache shown in Figure 9.4. Assume that the most significant three bits of the memory address are used as the cache index and the least significant bit (since the memory address is only four bits for this example) is used as the tag. Figure 9.12 shows the contents of the cache after each access. Notice how the same cache entry (first row of the cache) is reused for the sequence of memory accesses, even though the rest of the cache is empty. Every access results in a miss, replacing what previously was in the cache due to the access pattern.

The situation shown in Figure 9.12 is undesirable. Recall the locality properties (spatial and temporal), which we mentioned in Section 9.2. It is imperative that sequential access to memory falls into different cache locations. This is the reason for choosing to interpret the memory address as shown in Figure 9.11.

Figure 9.11   Interpreting the memory address generated by the CPU for cache lookup.

	Valid	Tag	Data
0	1	0	loc 0
1	0	X	empty
2	0	X	empty
3	0	X	empty
4	0	X	empty
5	0	X	empty
6	0	X	empty
7	0	X	empty

Access location 0

	Valid	Tag	Data
0	1	1	loc ~~0~~ 1
1	0	X	empty
2	0	X	empty
3	0	X	empty
4	0	X	empty
5	0	X	empty
6	0	X	empty
7	0	X	empty

Access location 1

	Valid	Tag	Data
0	1	0	loc ~~0~~ ~~1~~ 0
1	0	X	empty
2	0	X	empty
3	0	X	empty
4	0	X	empty
5	0	X	empty
6	0	X	empty
7	0	X	empty

Access location 0

	Valid	Tag	Data
0	1	1	loc ~~0~~ ~~1~~ ~~0~~ 1
1	0	X	empty
2	0	X	empty
3	0	X	empty
4	0	X	empty
5	0	X	empty
6	0	X	empty
7	0	X	empty

Access location 1

Figure 9.12   Sequence of memory accesses if the cache index is chosen as the most significant bits of the memory address.

9.6.3 Hardware for a Direct-Mapped Cache

Let us put together the ideas we have discussed thus far. Figure 9.13 shows the hardware organization for a direct-mapped cache.

The index part of the memory address picks out a unique entry in the cache (the textured cache entry in Figure 9.13). The comparator shown in Figure 9.13 compares the tag field of this entry against the tag part of the memory address. If there is a *match* and if the entry is *valid*, then it signals a *hit*. The cache supplies the data field of the selected entry (also referred to as *cache line*) to the CPU, upon a hit. *Cache block* is another term used synonymously with *cache line*. We have used three terms synonymously thus far: *cache entry, cache line,* and *cache block.* Whereas it is unfortunate to

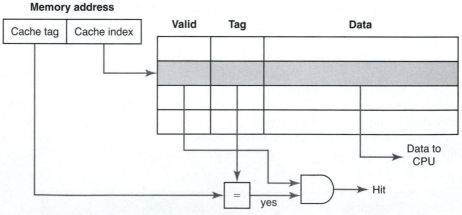

Figure 9.13   Hardware for direct-mapped cache.

The shaded entry is the cache location picked out by the cache index.

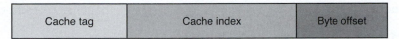

| Cache tag | Cache index | Byte offset |

Figure 9.14 Interpreting the memory address generated by the CPU when a single cache block contains multiple bytes.

have so many terms that mean the same thing, it is important for the reader to develop this vocabulary, since computer architecture textbooks tend to use these terms interchangeably.

Note that the actual amount of storage space needed in the cache is more than that needed simply for the *data* part of the cache. The *valid* bits and *tag* fields, called *metadata*, are for managing the actual data contained in the cache, and represent a *space overhead*.

Thus far, we have treated the data field of the cache to hold one memory location. The size of the memory location depends on the granularity of memory access allowed by the instruction set. For example, if the architecture is byte addressable, then a byte is the smallest possible size of a memory operand. Usually, in such an architecture, the word-width is some integral number of bytes. We could place each byte in a separate cache line, but from Section 9.2, we know that the principle of spatial locality suggests that if we access a byte of a word there is a good chance that we would access other bytes of the same word. Therefore, it would make sense to design the cache to contain a complete word in each cache line, even if the architecture is byte addressable. Thus, the memory address generated by the CPU would be interpreted as consisting of three fields, as shown in Figure 9.14: cache tag, cache index, and *byte offset*. The last term, byte offset, is defined as the bits of the address that specify the byte within the word. For example, if the word-width is 32 bits and the architecture is byte addressable, then the bottom 2 bits of the address form the byte offset.

Example 9.2

Let us consider the design of a direct-mapped cache for a realistic memory system. Assume that the CPU generates a 32-bit byte-addressable memory address. Each memory word contains 4 bytes. A memory access brings a full word into the cache. The direct-mapped cache is 64 K bytes in size (this is the amount of data that can be stored in the cache), with each cache entry containing one word of data. Compute the additional storage space needed for the valid bits and the tag fields of the cache.

Answer:

Assuming little-endian notation, 0 is the least significant bit of the address. With this notation, the least significant two bits of the address, namely, bits 1 and 0, specify the byte within a word address. A cache entry holds a full word of four bytes. Therefore, the least significant two bits of the address, while necessary for uniquely identifying a byte within a word, are not needed to uniquely identify the particular cache entry. Therefore, these bits do not form part of the index for cache lookup.

The ratio of the cache size to the data stored in each entry gives the number of cache entries:

64 K bytes/(4 bytes/word) = 16 K entries

16 K entries require 14 bits to enumerate; thus, bits 2–15 form the cache index, leaving bits 16–31 to form the tag. Thus, each cache entry has a 16-bit tag.

The metadata per entry totals 16 bits for the tag + 1 bit for valid bit = 17 bits.

Thus, the additional storage space needed for the metadata is

17 bits × 16 K entries = 17 × 16,384 = **278,528 bits**.

The following figure shows the layout of the cache for this problem:

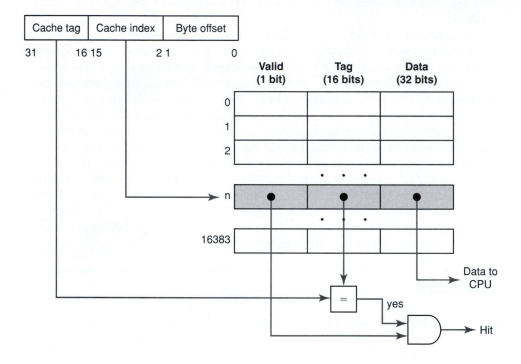

Total space needed for the cache (actual data + metadata)

$$= 64 \text{ K bytes} + 278{,}528$$
$$= 524{,}288 + 278{,}528$$
$$= 802{,}816.$$

The space overhead = metadata/total space = 278,528/802,816 = **35%**.

Let us see how we can reduce the space overhead. In Example 9.2, each cache line holds one memory word. One way of reducing the space overhead is to modify the design such that each cache line holds multiple contiguous memory words. For example, consider each cache line holding four contiguous memory words in Example 9.2. This would reduce the number of cache lines to 4 K. *Block size* is the term used to refer to the amount of contiguous data in one cache line. Block size in Example 9.2 is 4 bytes. If each cache line were to contain 4 words, then the block size would be 16 bytes. Why would we want to have a larger block size? Moreover, how would it help in reducing the space overhead? Would it help in improving the performance of the memory system as a whole? We will let the reader ponder these questions for awhile. We will revisit them in much more detail in Section 9.10, where we discuss the impact of block size on cache design.

9.7 Repercussion on Pipelined Processor Design

With the cache memory introduced between the processor and the memory, we can return to our pipelined processor design and reexamine instruction execution in the presence of caches. Figure 9.15 is a reproduction of the pipelined processor from Chapter 6 (see Figure 6.6).

Notice that we have replaced the memories, I-MEM and D-MEM in the IF and MEM stages, by caches I-cache and D-cache, respectively. The caches make it possible for the IF and MEM stages to have comparable cycle times to the other stages of the pipeline, assuming that the references result in hits in the respective caches. Let us see what would happen if the references miss in the caches.

- **Miss in the IF stage:** Upon a miss in the I-cache, the IF stage sends the reference to the memory to retrieve the instruction. As we know, the memory access time may be several 10's of CPU cycles. Until the instruction arrives from the memory, the IF stage sends NOPs (bubbles) to the next stage.

- **Miss in the MEM stage:** Of course, misses in the D-cache are relevant only for memory reference instructions (load/store). Similar to the IF stage, a miss in the MEM stage results in NOPs to the WB stage until the memory reference completes. It also *freezes* the preceding stages from advancing past the instructions they are currently working on.

We define *memory stall* as the processor cycles wasted due to waiting for a memory operation to complete. Memory stalls come in two flavors: *read stall* may be incurred due to read access from the processor to the cache; *write stall* may be incurred during write access from the processor to the cache. We will define and elaborate on these stalls in the next section, together with discussing mechanisms to avoid them, since they are detrimental to processor pipeline performance.

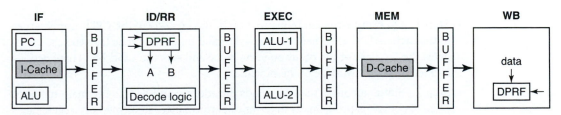

Figure 9.15 Pipelined processor with caches.

9.8 Cache Read/Write Algorithms

In this section, we discuss policies and mechanisms for reading and writing the caches. Different levels of the cache hierarchy may choose different policies.

9.8.1 Read Access to the Cache from the CPU

A processor needs to access the cache to read a memory location for either instructions or data. In our five-stage pipeline for implementing the LC-2200 ISA, this could happen either for instruction fetch in the IF stage, or for operand fetch in response to a load instruction in the MEM stage. The basic actions taken by the processor and the cache are as follows:

- **Step 1:** The CPU sends the index part of the memory address (Figure 9.16) to the cache. The cache does a lookup, and if successful (a cache *hit*), it supplies the data to the CPU. If the cache signals a miss, then the CPU sends the address on the memory bus to the main memory. In principle, all of these actions happen in the same cycle (either the IF or the MEM stage of the pipeline).

- **Step 2:** Upon sending the address to the memory, the CPU sends NOPs down to the subsequent stage until it receives the data from the memory. *Read stall* is defined as the number of processor clock cycles wasted to service a read-miss. As we observed earlier, this could take several CPU cycles, depending on the memory speed. The cache allocates a cache block to receive the memory block. Eventually, the main memory delivers the data to the CPU and simultaneously updates the allocated cache block with the data. The cache modifies the tag field of this cache entry appropriately and sets the valid bit.

9.8.2 Write Access to the Cache from the CPU

Write requests to the cache from the processor are the result of an instruction that wishes to write to a memory location. In our five-stage pipeline for implementing the LC-2200 ISA, this could happen for storing a memory operand in the MEM stage. There are a couple of choices for handling processor write access to the cache: *write through* and *write back*.

Write-through policy. The idea is to update the cache and the main memory on each CPU write operation. The basic actions taken by the processor and the cache are as follows:

- **Step 1:** On every write (store instruction in the LC-2200), the CPU simply writes to the cache. There is no need to check the valid bit or the cache tag. The cache updates the tag field of the corresponding entry and sets the valid bit. These actions happen in the MEM stage of the pipeline.

- **Step 2:** Simultaneously, the CPU sends the address and data to the main memory. This, of course, is problematic in terms of performance, since memory access takes several CPU cycles to complete. To alleviate this performance bottleneck, it is

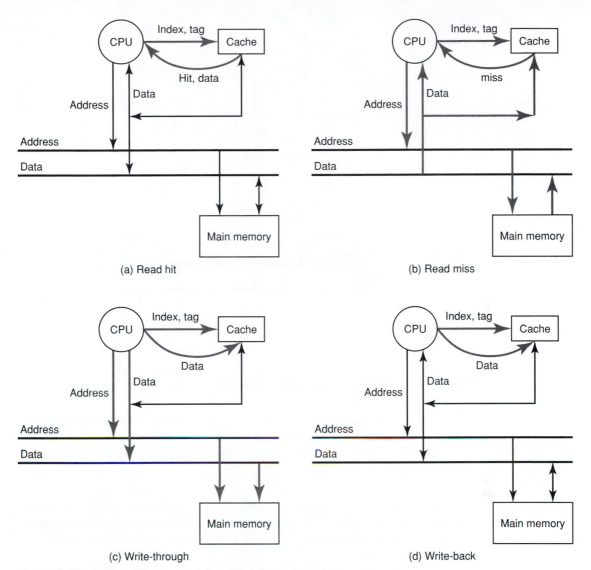

Figure 9.16 CPU, cache, memory interactions for reads and writes.

customary to include a *write buffer* in the datapath between the CPU and the memory bus (as shown in Figure 9.17). The write buffer is a small hardware store (similar to a register file) designed to smoothen out the speed disparity between the CPU and the memory. As far as the CPU is concerned, the write operation is complete as soon as it places the address and data in the write buffer. Thus, this action also happens in the MEM stage of the pipeline, without stalling the pipeline.

- **Step 3:** The write buffer completes the write to the main memory, independent of the CPU. Note that, if the write buffer is full at the time the processor attempts

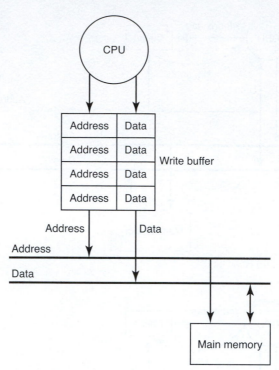

Figure 9.17 A four-element write buffer to bridge the CPU and main memory speeds for a write-through policy.

The processor write is complete, and the pipeline can resume as soon as the write has been placed in the write buffer. It will be sent out to the memory, in the background, in parallel with the pipeline operation. The pipeline will freeze if the write buffer is full.

to write to it, then the pipeline will stall until one of the entries from the write buffer has been sent to the memory. *Write stall* is defined as the number of processor clock cycles wasted due to a write operation (regardless of a hit or a miss in the cache).

With the write-through policy, write stall is a function of the cache block allocation strategy upon a write miss. There are two choices:

- **Write allocate:** This is the usual way to handle write misses. The intuition is that the data being written to will be needed by the program in the near future. Therefore, it is judicious to put it in the cache as well. However, since the block is missing from the cache, we have to allocate a cache block and bring the missing memory block into it. In this sense, a write-miss is treated exactly the same as a read-miss. With a direct-mapped cache, the cache block to receive the memory block is predetermined. However, as we will see later with flexible placement (see Section 9.11), the allocation depends on the other design considerations.

- **No-write allocate:** This is an unusual way of handling a write miss. The argument for this strategy is that the write access can complete quickly since the processor does not need the data. The processor simply places the write in the write buffer to complete the operation needed in the MEM stage of the pipeline. Thus, there are write stalls incurred because the missing memory block need not be brought from the memory.

Write-back policy. The idea here is to update only the cache upon a CPU write operation. The basic actions taken by the processor and the cache are as follows:

- **Step 1:** The CPU–cache interaction is exactly the same as the write-through policy. Let us assume that the memory location is already present in the cache (i.e., a write hit). The CPU writes to the cache. The cache updates the tag field of the corresponding entry and sets the valid bit. These actions happen in the MEM stage of the pipeline.

- **Step 2:** The contents of this chosen cache entry and the corresponding memory location are inconsistent with each other. As far as the CPU is concerned, this is not a problem, because it first checks the cache before going to memory on a read operation. Thus, the CPU always gets the latest value from the cache.

- **Step 3:** Let us see when we have to update the main memory. By design, the cache is much smaller than the main memory. Thus, at some point, it may become necessary to replace an existing cache entry to make room for a memory location not currently present in the cache. (We will discuss cache replacement policies in Section 9.14). At the time of replacement, if the CPU had written into the cache entry chosen for replacement, then the corresponding memory location would have to be updated with the latest data for this cache entry.

The processor treats a write-miss exactly like a read-miss. After taking the steps necessary to deal with a read-miss, it completes the write action as detailed previously.

We need some mechanism by which the cache can determine that the data in a cache entry is more up to date than the data in the corresponding memory location. The *metadata* in each cache entry (valid bit and tag field) do not provide the necessary information for the cache to make this decision. Therefore, we add a new *metadata* to each cache entry, a *dirty bit* (see Figure 9.18).

The cache uses the dirty bit in the following manner:

- The cache *clears* the bit upon processing a miss that brings a memory location into this cache entry.

- The cache *sets* the bit upon a CPU write operation.

- The cache *writes back* the data in the cache into the corresponding memory location upon replacement. Note that this action is similar to writing back a physical page frame to the disk in the virtual memory system (see Chapter 8).

We introduced the concept of a write buffer in the context of write-through policy. It turns out that the write buffer is useful for the write-back policy as well. Note that the focus is on keeping the processor happy. This means that the missing memory block

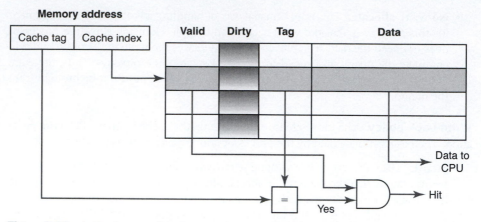

Figure 9.18 A direct-mapped cache organization with write-back policy.

Each entry has an additional field (dirty bit) to indicate whether the block is dirty or clean. The horizontally shaded block is the one selected by the cache index.

should be brought into the cache as quickly as possible. In other words, servicing the miss is more important than writing back the dirty block that is being replaced. The write buffer comes in handy to give preferential treatment to reading from the memory over writing to memory. The block that has to be replaced (if dirty) is placed in the write buffer. It will eventually be written back. But the immediate request that is sent to the memory is to service the current miss (be it a read or a write miss). The write requests from the write buffer can be sent to the memory when there are no read or write misses to be serviced from the CPU. This should be reminiscent of the optimization that the memory manager practices to give preferential treatment for reading in missing pages from the disk over writing out dirty victim pages to the disk (see Section 8.4.1).

Comparison of the write policies. Which write policy should a cache use? The answer to this depends on several factors. On the one hand, write through ensures that the main memory is always up to date. However, this comes at the price of sending every write to memory. Some optimizations are possible. For example, if it is a repeated write to the same memory location that is already in the write buffer (i.e., it has not yet been sent to the memory), then it can be replaced by the new write. However, the chance of this occurring in real programs is quite small. Another optimization, referred to as *write merging*, merges independent writes to different parts of the same memory block. Write back has the advantage that it is faster, and more importantly, does not use the memory bus for every write access from the CPU. Thus, repeated writes to the same memory location do not result in creating undue traffic on the memory bus. Only upon a replacement does the cache update the memory with the latest content for that memory location. In this context, note that the write buffer is useful for the write-back policy as well, to hold the replacement candidate needing a write-back to the main memory.

Another advantage enjoyed by the write through policy is the fact that the cache is always clean. In other words, upon a cache block replacement to make room for a missing block, the cache never has to write the replaced block to the lower levels of the memory hierarchy. This leads to a simpler design for a write through cache and, hence, higher speed than a write-back cache. Consequently, if a processor has multilevel cache hierarchy, then it is customary to use write through for the level closer to the processor. For example, most modern processors use a write-through policy for the L1 D-cache, and a write-back policy for the L2 and L3 levels.

As we will see in Chapters 10 and 12, the choice of write policy has an impact on the design of I/O and multiprocessor systems. The design of these systems could benefit from the reduced memory bus traffic of the write-back policy; at the same time, they would also benefit from the write-through policy keeping the memory always up to date.

9.9 Dealing with Cache Misses in the Processor Pipeline

Memory accesses disrupt the smooth operation of the processor pipeline. Therefore, we need to mitigate the ill effect of misses in the processor pipeline. It is not possible to mask a miss in the IF stage of the pipeline. However, it may be possible to *hide* a miss in the MEM stage.

- **Read miss in the MEM stage:** Consider the following sequence of instructions:

  ```
  I1: lw      r1, a        ;   r1 ← memory location a
  I2: add     r3, r4, r5   ;   r3 ← r4 + r5
  I3: nand    r6, r7, r8   ;   r6 ← r7 NAND r8
  I4: add     r2, r4, r5   ;   r2 ← r4 + r5
  I5: add     r2, r1, r2   ;   r2 ← r1 + r2
  ```

  Suppose that the `lw` instruction results in a miss in the D-cache; the CPU has to stall this load instruction in the MEM stage (freezing the preceding stages and sending NOPs to the WB stage) until the memory responds with the data. However, I5 is the instruction that uses the value loaded into `r1`. Let us understand how we can use this knowledge to prevent stalling the instructions I2, I3, and I4.

  In Chapter 5, we introduced the idea of a *busy* bit with each register in the register file for dealing with hazards. For instructions that modify a register value, the bit is set in the ID/RR stage (see Figure 9.15) and cleared, once the write is complete. This idea is extensible to dealing with memory loads, as well.

- **Write miss in the MEM stage:** This could be problematic, depending on the write policy, as well as the cache allocation policy. First, let us consider the situation with write-through policy. If the cache block allocation policy is no-write allocate, then the pipeline will not incur any stalls, thanks to the write buffer. The processor simply places the write in the write buffer to complete the actions needed in the MEM stage. However, if the cache block allocation policy is write-allocate, then it has to be handled exactly the same as a read-miss. Therefore, the processor pipeline will incur write stalls in the MEM stage. The missing data block has to be brought into the cache before the write operation can complete, despite the presence of the write buffer. For a write-back policy, write stalls in the MEM stage are inevitable, since a write-miss has to be treated exactly the same as a read-miss.

9.9.1 Effect of Memory Stalls Due to Cache Misses on Pipeline Performance

Let us revisit the program execution time. In Chapter 5, we defined it as follows:

$$\text{Execution time} = \text{Number of instructions executed} * \text{CPI}_{\text{Avg}} * \text{clock cycle time}$$

A pipelined processor attempts to make the CPI_{Avg} equal 1 since it tries to complete an instruction in every cycle. However, structural, data, and control hazards induce bubbles in the pipeline, thus inflating the CPI_{Avg} to be higher than 1.

Memory hierarchy exacerbates this problem even more. Every instruction has at least one memory access, namely, to fetch the instruction. In addition, there may be additional accesses for memory reference instructions. If these references result in *misses,* they force bubbles in the pipeline. We refer to these additional bubbles caused by the memory hierarchy as the *memory stall cycles.*

Thus, a more accurate expression for the execution time is

$$\text{Execution time} = (\text{Number of instructions executed} * \\ (\text{CPI}_{\text{Avg}} + \text{Memory-stalls}_{\text{Avg}})) * \text{clock cycle time} \qquad (3)$$

We can define an effective CPI of the processor as

$$\text{Effective CPI} = \text{CPI}_{\text{Avg}} + \text{Memory-stalls}_{\text{Avg}} \qquad (4)$$

The total memory stalls experienced by a program is

$$\text{Total memory stalls} = \text{Number of instructions} * \text{Memory-stalls}_{\text{Avg}} \qquad (5)$$

The average number of memory stalls per instruction is

$$\text{Memory-stalls}_{\text{Avg}} = \text{misses per instruction}_{\text{Avg}} * \text{miss-penalty}_{\text{Avg}} \qquad (6)$$

Of course, if reads and writes incur different miss penalties, we may have to account for them differently (see Example 9.3).

Example 9.3

Consider a pipelined processor that has an average CPI of 1.8 without accounting for memory stalls. The I-cache has a hit rate of 95%, and the D-cache has a hit rate of 98%.

Assume that memory reference instructions account for 30% of all the instructions executed. Out of these, 80% are loads and 20% are stores. On average, the read-miss penalty is 20 cycles, and the write-miss penalty is 5 cycles. Compute the effective CPI of the processor, accounting for the memory stalls.

Answer:

The solution to this problem uses the preceding equations (4) and (6).

Cost of instruction misses = I-cache miss rate * read miss penalty

$$= (1 - 0.95) * 20$$

$$= 1 \text{ cycle per instruction}$$

Cost of data read misses = fraction of memory reference instructions in the program * fraction of memory reference instructions that are loads * D-cache miss rate * read miss penalty

$$= 0.3 * 0.8 * (1 - 0.98) * 20$$

$$= 0.096 \text{ cycles per instruction}$$

Cost of data write misses = fraction of memory reference instructions in the program * fraction of memory reference instructions that are stores * D-cache miss rate * write miss penalty

$$= 0.3 * 0.2 * (1 - 0.98) * 5$$

$$= 0.006 \text{ cycles per instruction}$$

Effective CPI = base CPI + Effect of I-cache on CPI + Effect of D-cache on CPI

$$= 1.8 + 1 + 0.096 + 0.006 = \textbf{2.902}$$

Reducing the *miss rate* and reducing the *miss penalty* are the keys to reducing the memory stalls, and thereby increase the efficiency of a pipelined processor.

There are two avenues available for reducing the miss rate, and we will cover them in Sections 9.10 and 9.11. In Section 9.12, we will discuss ways to decrease the miss penalty.

9.10 Exploiting Spatial Locality to Improve Cache Performance

The first avenue to reducing the miss rate exploits the principle of spatial locality. The basic idea is to bring adjacent memory locations into the cache upon a miss for a memory location i. Thus far, each entry in the cache corresponds to the unit of memory access architected in the instruction set. To exploit spatial locality in the cache design, we decouple the *unit of memory access* by an instruction from the *unit of memory transfer* between the memory and the cache. The instruction-set architecture of the processor decides the unit of memory access. For example, if an architecture has instructions that manipulate individual bytes, then the unit of memory access for such a processor would

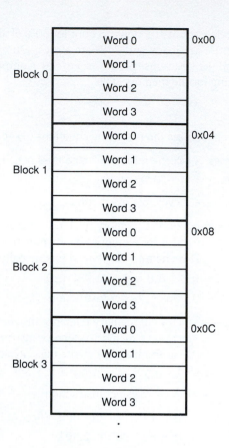

Figure 9.19   Main memory organized as blocks of contiguous locations to
enable block transfer between memory and cache upon a miss.

be a byte. On the other hand, the unit of memory transfer is a design parameter of the memory hierarchy. In particular, this parameter is always some integral multiple of the unit of memory access to exploit spatial locality. We refer to the unit of transfer between the cache and the memory as the *block size*. Upon a miss, the cache brings an entire *block* of *block size* bytes that contains the missing memory reference.

Figure 9.19 shows an example of such an organization and a view of the memory. In this example, the block size is four words, where a word is the unit of memory access by a CPU instruction. The memory addresses for a block start on a block boundary, as shown in the figure. For example, if the CPU misses on a reference to a memory location `0x01`, then the cache brings in four memory words that make up *block 0* (starting at address `0x00`), and contain the location `0x01`.

With each entry in the cache organized as blocks of contiguous words, the address generated by the CPU has *three* parts: *tag, index,* and *block-offset,* as shown in Figure 9.20.

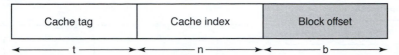

Figure 9.20 Interpreting the memory address generated by the CPU for a cache block containing multiple words.

Note that the block offset is the number of bits necessary to enumerate the set of contiguous memory locations contained in a cache block. For example, if the block size is 64 bytes, then the block offset is 6 bits. All the data of a given block are contained in one cache entry. The tag and index fields have the same meaning as before. We will present general expressions for computing the number of bits needed for the different fields shown in Figure 9.20.

Let a be the number of bits in the memory address, S be the total size of the cache in bytes, and B the block size.

We have the following expressions for the fields shown in Figure 9.20:

$$b = log_2B \qquad (7)$$
$$L = S/B \qquad (8)$$
$$n = log_2L \qquad (9)$$
$$t = a - (b + n) \qquad (10)$$

L is the number of lines in a direct-mapped cache of size S and B bytes per block. Field b represents the least significant bits of the memory address; field t represents the most significant bits of the memory address; and field n represents the middle bits as shown in Figure 9.20. (See Example 9.4 for a numerical calculation of these fields.)

Now let us revisit the basic cache algorithms (lookup, read, write) in the context of a multiword block size. Figure 9.21 shows the organization of such a direct-mapped cache.

1. **Lookup:** The index for cache lookup comes from the middle part of the memory address, as shown in Figure 9.20. The entry contains an entire block (if it is a hit as determined by the cache tag in the address and the tag stored in the specific entry). The least significant b bits of the address specify the specific word (or byte) within that block requested by the processor. A multiplexer selects the specific word (or byte) from the block, using these b bits, and sends it to the CPU (see Figure 9.21).

2. **Read:** Upon a read, the cache brings out the entire block corresponding to the cache index. If the tag comparison results in a hit, the multiplexer selects the specific word (or byte) within the block and sends it to the CPU. If it is a miss, the CPU initiates a block transfer from the memory.

3. **Write:** We have to modify the write algorithm, because there is only one valid bit for the entire cache line. Similar to the read-miss, the CPU initiates a block transfer from the memory upon a write-miss (see Figure 9.22).

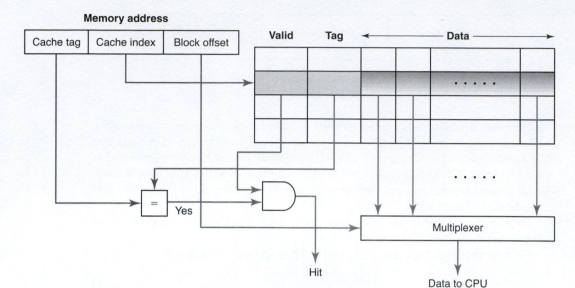

Figure 9.21 A multiword direct-mapped cache organization.

The block offset chooses the particular word to send to the CPU from the selected block, using the multiplexer. The horizontally shaded block is the one selected by the cache index.

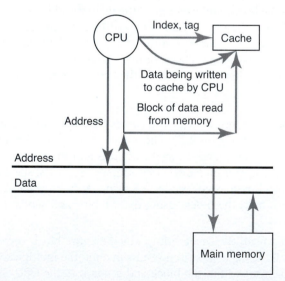

Figure 9.22 CPU, cache, and memory interactions for handling a write-miss.

The missing block is first transferred from the memory into the cache, and then the specific location being written to by the CPU is updated in the cache block.

Upon a hit, the CPU writes the specific word (or byte) into the cache. Depending on the write policy, the implementation may require additional metadata (in the form of dirty bits) and may take additional actions (such as writing the modified word or byte to memory) to complete a write operation (see Example 9.4).

Example 9.4

Consider a multiword direct-mapped cache with a data size of 64 KB. The CPU generates a 32-bit byte-addressable memory address. Each memory word contains four bytes. The block size is 16 bytes. The cache uses a write-back policy with one dirty bit per word. The cache has one valid bit per data block.

  a. How does the CPU interpret the memory address?

Answer:

Referring to formula (7),

Block size

$$B = 16 \text{ bytes};$$

therefore,

$$b = log_2 16 = 4 \text{ bits}.$$

We need 4 bits (bits 3–0 of the memory address) for the block offset.

Referring to formula (8), number of cache lines

$$L = 64 \text{ KB}/16 \text{ bytes} = 4096.$$

Referring to formula (9), number of index bits

$$n = log_2 L = log_2 4096 = 12.$$

Referring to formula (10), number of tag bits

$$t = a - (n + b) = 32 - (12 + 4) = 16.$$

Therefore, we need 12 bits (bits 15-4 of the memory address) for the index. The remaining 16 bits (bits 31-16 of the memory address) constitute the tag. The following figure shows how the CPU interprets the memory address:

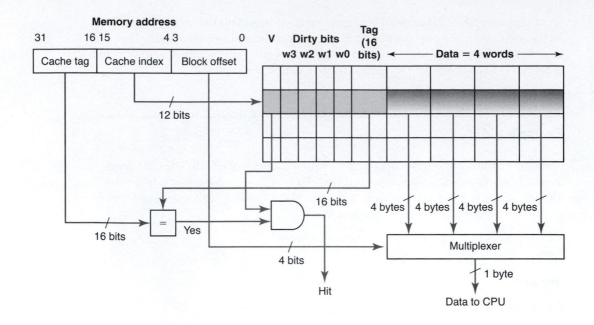

b. Compute the total amount of storage for implementing the cache (i.e., actual data plus the metadata).

Answer:

Each cache line will have

Data	16 bytes × 8 bits/byte = 128 bits
Valid bit	1 bit
Dirty bits	4 bits (1 for each word)
Tag	16 bits
	149 bits.

Total amount of space for the cache = 149 × 4096 cache lines = **610,304 bits**.

The space requirement for the metadata = total space − actual data

$$= 610,304 - 64 \text{ KB}.$$
$$= 610,304 - 524,288$$
$$= 86,016$$

The space overhead = metadata/total space = 86,016/610,304 = **14%**.

Recall from Example 9.2 that the space overhead for the same cache size, but with a block size of 4 bytes, was 35%. In other words, increased block size decreases the metadata requirement and, hence, reduces the space overhead.

9.10.1 Performance Implications of Increased Block Size

It is instructive to understand the impact of increasing the block size on cache perform-ance. Exploiting spatial locality is the main intent in having an increased block size. Therefore, for a *given total size of the cache,* we would expect the miss rate to decrease with increasing block size. In the limit, we can simply have one cache block whose size is equal to the total size of the cache. Thus, it is interesting to ask two questions related to the block size:

1. Will the miss rate keep decreasing forever?
2. Will the overall performance of the processor go up as we increase the block size?

The answer is no for the first question. In fact, the miss rate may decrease up to an inflection point and start increasing thereafter. The *working set* notion that we introduced in Chapter 8 is the reason for this behavior. Recall that the working set of a program changes over time. A cache block contains a contiguous set of memory locations. However, if the working set of the program changes, the large block size results in increasing the miss rate (see Figure 9.23).

The answer to the second question is a little more complicated. As is seen in Figure 9.23, the miss rate does decrease with increasing block size up to an inflection point for a given cache size. This would translate to the processor incurring fewer memory stalls and thus would improve the performance. However, beyond the inflection point, the proces-sor starts incurring more memory stalls, thus degrading the performance. However, as it turns out, the downturn in processor performance may start happening much sooner than the inflection point shown in Figure 9.23. While the miss rate decreases with in-creasing block size up to an inflection point for a given cache size, the increased block size

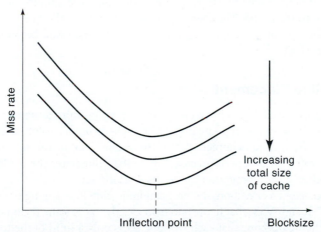

Figure 9.23 Expected behavior of miss rate as a function of block size.

The miss rate will decrease as we increase the block size, but for a given total cache size, we will reach a point of diminishing returns, after which the miss rate will go up.

could negatively interact with the miss penalty. Recall that reducing the execution time of a program is the primary objective. This objective translates to reducing the number of stalls introduced in the pipeline by the memory hierarchy. The larger the block size, the larger the time penalty will be for the transfer from the memory to the cache on misses, thus increasing the memory stalls. We will discuss techniques to reduce the miss penalty shortly. The main point to note is that, since the design parameters (block size and miss penalty) are interrelated, optimizing for one may not always result in the best overall performance. Put another way, just focusing on the miss rate as the output metric to optimize may lead to erroneous cache design decisions.

In pipelined processor design (Chapter 5), we understood the difference between the latency of individual instructions and the throughput of the processor as a whole. Analogously, in cache design, the choice of block size affects the balance between latency for a single instruction (that incurred the miss) and throughput for the program as a whole, by reducing the potential misses for other later instructions that might benefit from the exploitation of spatial locality. A real-life analogy is income tax. An individual incurs a personal loss of revenue by the taxes (akin to latency), but helps the society as a whole to become better (akin to throughput). Of course, beyond a point, the balance tips. Depending on your political orientation, the tipping point may be sooner than later.

Modern-day processors have much more going on that compounds these issues. The microarchitecture of the processor—that is, the implementation details of an ISA— is both complex and fascinating. Instructions do not have to execute in program order, so long as the semantics of the program is preserved. A cache miss does not necessarily block the processor; such caches are referred to as lock-up free caches. These and other microlevel optimizations interact with one another in unpredictable ways, and are, of course, sensitive to the workload executing on the processor as well. The simple fact is that a doubling of the cache block size requires doubling the amount of data that need to be moved into the cache. The memory system cannot usually keep up with this requirement. The upshot is that we see a dip in performance well before the inflection point in Figure 9.23.

9.11 Flexible Placement

In a direct-mapped cache, there is a one-to-one mapping from a memory address to a cache index. Because of this rigid mapping, the cache is unable to place a new memory location in a currently unoccupied slot in the cache. Due to the nature of program behavior, this rigidity hurts performance. Figure 9.24 illustrates the inefficient use of a direct-mapped cache as a program changes its working set.

In the course of its execution, the program frequently flips among the three working sets (WS1, WS2, and WS3) that happen to map exactly to the same region of the cache as shown in the figure. Assume that each working set is only a third of the total cache size. Therefore, in principle, there is sufficient space in the cache to hold all three working sets. Yet, due to the rigid mapping, the working sets displace one another from the cache, resulting in poor performance. Ideally, we would want all three working sets of the program to reside in the cache so that there will be no more misses beyond the compulsory ones.

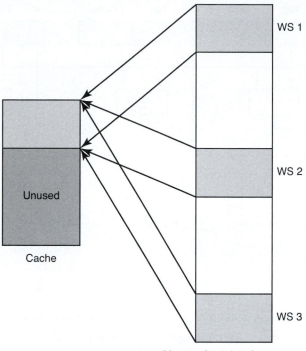

Figure 9.24 Different working sets of a program occupying the same portion of a direct-mapped cache.

Let us investigate how we can work toward achieving this ideal. The design of the cache should take into account that the locality of a program may change over time. We will first discuss an extremely flexible placement that avoids this problem altogether.

9.11.1 Fully Associative Cache

In this setup, there is no unique mapping from a memory block to a cache block. Thus, a cache block can host any memory block. Therefore, by design, *compulsory* and *capacity misses* are the only kind of misses encountered with this organization. The cache interprets a memory address presented by the CPU, as shown in Figure 9.25. Note that there is no cache index in this interpretation.

This is because, in the absence of a unique mapping, a memory block could reside in any of the cache blocks. Thus, with this organization, to perform a lookup, the cache has to search through all the entries to see whether there is a match between the cache tag in

Figure 9.25 Memory address interpretation for a fully associative cache.

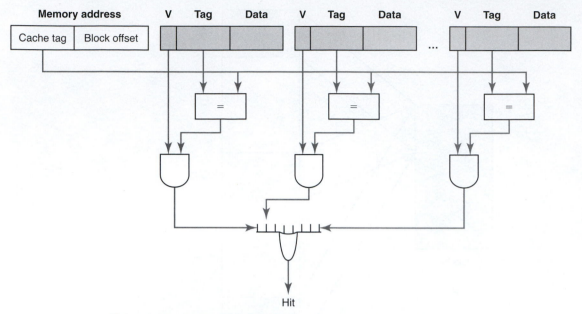

Figure 9.26 Parallel tag matching hardware for a fully associative cache.

Each block of the cache represents an independent cache. Tag matching has to happen in parallel for all the caches to determine a hit or a miss. Thus, a given memory block could be present in any of the cache blocks (shown by the shading). Upon a hit, the data from the block that successfully matched the memory address are sent to the CPU.

the memory address and the tags in any of the valid entries. One possibility is to search through each of the cache entries, sequentially. This is untenable from the point of view of processor performance. Therefore, the hardware contains replicated comparators, one for each entry, so that all the tag comparisons happen in parallel to determine a hit (Figure 9.26).

The complexity of the parallel tag matching hardware makes a fully associative cache infeasible for any reasonably sized cache. At first glance, due to its flexibility, it might appear that a fully associative cache could serve as the gold standard for the best possible miss rate for a given workload and a given cache size. Unfortunately, such is not the case. A cache, being a high-speed precious resource, will be mostly operating at near full utilization. Thus, misses in the cache will inevitably result in replacement of something that is already present in the cache. The choice of a replacement candidate has a huge impact on the miss rates experienced in a cache (since we don't know what memory accesses will be made in the future), and may overshadow the flexibility advantage of a fully associative cache for placement of the missing cache line. We will shortly see more details on cache replacement (see Section 9.14). Suffice it to say at this point that, for all of these reasons, a fully associative cache is seldom used in practice, except in very special circumstances. Translation look-aside buffer (TLB), introduced in

Chapter 8, lends itself to an implementation as a fully associative organization due to its small size. *Fully associative* derives its name from the fact that a memory block can be *associated* with *any* cache block.

9.11.2 Set Associative Cache

An intermediate organization between direct-mapped and fully associative is a *set associative cache*. This organization derives its name from the fact that a memory block can be *associated* with a *set* of cache blocks. For example, a two-way set associative cache gives a memory block two possible homes in the cache. Similarly, a four-way set associative cache gives a memory block one of four possible homes in the cache. The *degree of associativity* is defined as the number of homes that a given memory block has in the cache. It is two for a two-way set associative cache, four for a four-way set associative cache, and so on.

One simple way to visualize a set associative cache is as multiple direct-mapped caches. To make this discussion concrete, consider a cache with a total size of 16 data blocks. We can organize these 16 blocks as a direct-mapped cache (Figure 9.27(a)), as a two-way set associative cache (Figure 9.27(b)), or as a four-way set associative cache (Figure 9.27(c)). Of course, with each data block there will be associated metadata.

In a direct-mapped cache, given an index (say, 3) there is exactly one spot in the cache that corresponds to this index value. A two-way set associative cache has two spots in the cache (shaded spots in Figure 9.27(b)) that correspond to the same index. A four-way has four spots that correspond to the same index (shaded spots in Figure 9.27(c)). With 16 data blocks total, the first organization requires a four-bit index to look up the cache, while the second organization requires a three-bit index, and the third a two-bit index. Given a memory address, the cache simultaneously looks up all possible spots, referred to as a *set*, corresponding to that index value in the address for a match. The amount of tag matching hardware required for a set associative cache equals the degree of associativity.

Figure 9.28 shows the complete organization of a four-way set associative cache, with a block size of 4 bytes.

The cache interprets the memory address from the CPU as consisting of *tag*, *index*, and *block offset*, similar to a direct-mapped organization (see Figure 9.29).

Let us understand how to break up the memory address into index and tag for cache lookup. The total size of the cache determines the number of index bits for a direct-mapped organization $log_2(S/B)$, where S is the cache size and B the block size in bytes, respectively). For a set associative cache with the same total cache size, $log_2(S/pB)$ determines the number of index bits, where p is the degree of associativity. For example, a four-way set associative cache with a total cache size of 16 data blocks requires $log_2(16/4) = 2$ *bits* (Figure 9.27(c)).

9.11.3 Extremes of Set Associativity

Both direct-mapped and fully associative caches are special cases of the set associative cache. Consider a cache with a total size S bytes and block size B bytes. N, the total number of data blocks in the cache, is given by S/B. Let us organize the data blocks into

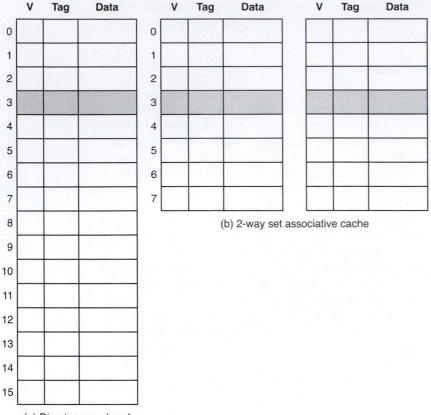

(a) Direct-mapped cache

(b) 2-way set associative cache

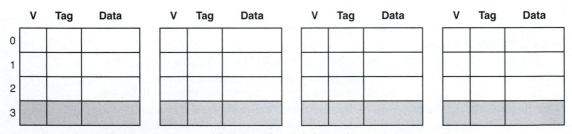

(c) 4-way set associative cache

Figure 9.27 Three different organizations of 16 cache blocks.

A given memory block could be present in one of several cache blocks, depending on the degree of associativity. The shaded blocks in each of the three figures represent the possible homes for a given memory block.

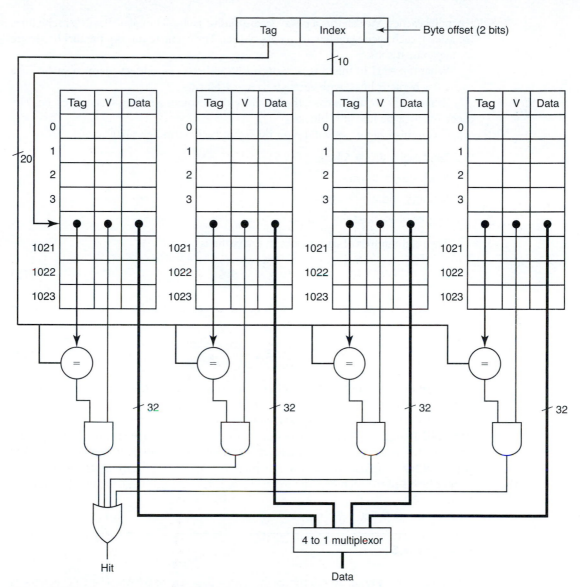

Figure 9.28   Four-way set associative cache organization.

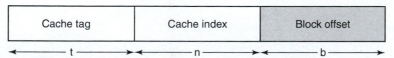

Figure 9.29   Interpreting the memory address generated by the CPU for a set associative cache is no different from that for a direct-mapped cache.

p parallel caches. We call this a *p-way set associative* cache. The cache has N/p cache lines (or sets[4]), each cache line having p data blocks. The cache requires p parallel hardware for tag comparisons.

What if $p = 1$? In this case, the organization becomes a direct-mapped cache. The cache has N cache lines, with each set having 1 block.

What if $p = N$? In this case, the organization becomes a fully associative cache. The cache has 1 cache line of N blocks.

Given this insight, we will revisit the formulae (7) through (10):

Total cache size $= S$ bytes

Block size $= B$ bytes

Memory address $= a$ bits

Degree of associativity $= p$

The total number of data blocks in the cache is

$$N = S/B \qquad \qquad (11)$$

We replace equation (8) for the number or cache lines by the following general equation:

$$L = S/pB = N/p \qquad \qquad (12)$$

Equation (8) is a special case of (12) when $p = 1$. The number of index bits n is computed as $log_2 L$ (given by equation (9)).

As we said earlier, a fully associative cache is primarily used for TLBs. The degree of associativity usually depends on the level of the cache in the memory hierarchy. Either a direct-mapped cache or a two-way set associative cache is typically preferred for L1 (close to the CPU). A higher degree of associativity is the norm for deeper levels of the memory hierarchy. We will revisit these design considerations in Section 9.19.

Example 9.5

Consider a four-way set associative cache with a data size of 64 KB. The CPU generates a 32-bit byte-addressable memory address. Each memory word contains 4 bytes. The block size is 16 bytes. The cache uses a write-through policy. The cache has one valid bit per data block.

a. How does the CPU interpret the memory address?

b. Compute the total amount of storage for implementing the cache (i.e., actual data plus the metadata).

---

4. So now we have four terms that refer to the same thing: *cache line, cache block, cache entry,* and *set*.

Answer:

a. Number of bits in the memory address is

$a = 32\ bits.$

Since the block size is 16 bytes, using equation (7), the block offset

$b = 4$ bits (bits 0−3 of the memory address).

Since the cache is four-way set associative (Figure 9.27(c)),

$p = 4.$

Number of cache lines (equation (12))

$L = S/pB = 64\ K\ bytes/(4 * 16)\ bytes = 1\ K.$

Number of index bits (equation (9))

$n = log_2L = log_21024 = 10\ bits.$

Number of tag bits (equation (10))

$t = a − (n + b) = 32 − (10 + 4) = 18\ bits.$

Thus, the memory address with 31 as msb, and 0 as the lsb is interpreted as

Tag	**18 bits (31 to 114)**
Index	**10 bits (13 to 4)**
Block offset	**4 bits (3 to 0)**

b. A block in each of the 4 parallel caches contains (data plus metadata):

Data: 16 × 8 bits	=	128 bits (16 bytes in one cache block)
Valid bit	=	1 bit (1 valid bit per block)
Tag	=	18 bits
Total	=	147 bits

Each line of the cache contains 4 of these blocks = 147 * 4 = 588 bits.

With 1 K such cache lines in the entire cache, **the total size of the cache =**

588 bits/cache line * 1024 cache lines = **602,112 bits**.

Example 9.6

Consider a four-way set-associative cache.

- Total data size of cache = 256 KB.
- CPU generates 32-bit byte-addressable memory addresses.

- Each memory word consists of 4 bytes.
- The cache block size is 32 bytes.
- The cache has one valid bit per cache line.
- The cache uses write-back policy with one dirty bit per word.

a. Show how the CPU interprets the memory address. (Which bits are used as the cache index, which bits are used as the tag, and which bits are used as the offset into the block?)

b. Compute the total size of the cache (including data and metadata).

Answer:

a. Using reasoning similar to Example 9.5,

Tag	**16 bits (31 to 16)**
Index	**11 bits (15 to 5)**
Block offset	**5 bits (0 to 4)**

b. A block in each of the four parallel caches contains the following:

Data: 32 × 8 bits	= 256 bits	(32 bytes in one cache block)
Valid bit	= 1 bit	(1 valid bit per block)
Dirty bits: 8 × 1 bit =	8 bits	(1 dirty bit per word of 4 bytes)
Tag	= 16 bits	
Total	= 281 bits	

Each cache line contains four of these blocks = 281 * 4 = 1124 bits.

With 2 K such cache lines in the entire cache, **the total size of the cache =**

1124 bits/cache line * 2048 cache lines = **281 KB**.

9.12 Instruction and Data Caches

In the processor pipeline (see Figure 9.15), we show two caches, one in the IF stage and one in the MEM stage. Ostensibly, the former is for instructions and the latter is for data. Some programs may benefit from a larger instruction cache, while other programs may benefit from a larger data cache.

It is tempting to combine the two caches and make one single, large, *unified* cache. Certainly, that will increase the hit rate for most programs for a given cache size, irrespective of their access patterns for instructions and data.

However, there is a downside to combining. We know that the IF stage accesses the I-cache in every cycle. The D-cache comes into play only for memory reference instructions (loads/stores). The contention for a unified cache could result in a structural hazard and reduce the pipeline efficiency. Empirical studies have shown that the detrimental effect of the structural hazard posed by a unified cache reduces the overall pipeline efficiency, despite the increase in hit rate.

There are hardware techniques (such as multiple read ports to the caches) to get around the structural hazard posed by a unified I-cache and D-cache. However, these techniques increase the complexity of the processor, which in turn would affect the clock cycle time of the pipeline. Recall that caches cater to the twin requirements of speed of access and reduced miss rate. As we mentioned right at the outset (see Section 9.4), the primary design consideration for the L1 cache is matching the hit time to the processor clock cycle time. This suggests avoiding unnecessary design complexity for the L1 cache in order to keep the hit time low. In addition, due to the differences in access patterns for instructions and data, the design considerations such as associativity may be different for I- and D-caches. Further, thanks to the increased chip density, it is now possible to have separate I- and D-caches large enough that the increase in miss rate due to splitting the caches is negligible. Finally, the I-cache does not have to support writes, which makes them simpler and faster. For these reasons, it is usual to have split I- and D-caches on-chip. However, since the primary design consideration for the L2 cache is reducing the miss rate, it is usual to have a unified L2 cache.

9.13 Reducing the Miss Penalty

The miss penalty is the service time for the data transfer from memory to cache on misses. As we observed earlier, the penalty may be different for reads and writes, and the penalty depends on other hardware in the datapath, such as *write buffers* that allow overlapping computation with the memory transfer.

Usually, the main memory system design accounts for the cache organization. In particular, the design supports block transfer, to and from the CPU, to populate the cache. The memory bus that connects the main memory to the CPU plays a crucial role in determining the miss penalty. We refer to *bus cycle time* as the time taken for each data transfer between the processor and memory. The amount of data transfer in each cycle between the processor and memory is referred to as the *memory bandwidth*. Memory bandwidth is a measure of the throughput available for information transfer between processor and memory. The bandwidth depends on the number of data wires connecting the processor and memory. Depending on the width of the bus, the memory system may need multiple bus cycles to transfer a cache block. For example, if the block size is four words and the memory bus width is only one word, then it takes four bus cycles to complete the block transfer. As a first order, we may define the miss penalty as the total time (measured in CPU clock cycles) for transferring a cache block from the memory to the cache. However, the actual latency experienced by the processor for an individual miss may be less than this block transfer time. This is because the memory system may respond to a miss by providing the specific data that the processor missed on before sending the rest of the memory block that contains the missed reference.

Despite such block transfer support in the memory system, increasing the block size beyond a certain point has other adverse effects. For example, if the processor incurs a read-miss on a location x, the cache subsystem initiates bringing in the whole block containing x, perhaps ensuring that the processor is served with x first. Depending on the bandwidth available between the processor and memory, the memory system may be busy transferring the rest of the block for several subsequent bus cycles. In the meanwhile, the processor may incur a second miss for another memory location y in a different cache block. Now the memory system cannot service the miss immediately, since it is busy completing the block transfer for the earlier miss on x. This is the reason, which we observed earlier in Section 9.10, that it is not sufficient to focus just on the miss-rate as the output metric to decide on cache block size. This is the classic tension between latency and throughput that surfaces in the design of every computer subsystem. We saw it in the context of processor in Chapter 5; we see it now in the context of memory system; later (in Chapter 13), we will see it in the context of networks.

9.14 Cache Replacement Policy

In a direct-mapped cache, the placement policy predetermines the candidate for replacement. Hence, there is no choice.

There is a possibility to exercise a choice in the case of a set-associative or a fully associative cache. Recall that a temporal locality consideration suggests using an LRU policy. For a fully associative cache, the cache chooses the replacement candidate, applying the LRU policy across all the blocks. For a set-associative cache, the cache's choice for a replacement candidate is limited to the set that will house the currently missing memory reference.

To keep track of LRU information, the cache needs additional metadata. Figure 9.30 shows the hardware for keeping track of the LRU information for a two-way set associative cache. Each set (or cache line) has one LRU bit associated with it.

On each reference, the hardware sets the LRU bit for the set containing the currently accessed memory block. Assuming valid entries in both the blocks of a given set, the hardware sets the LRU bit to 0 or 1, depending on whether a reference hits in cache

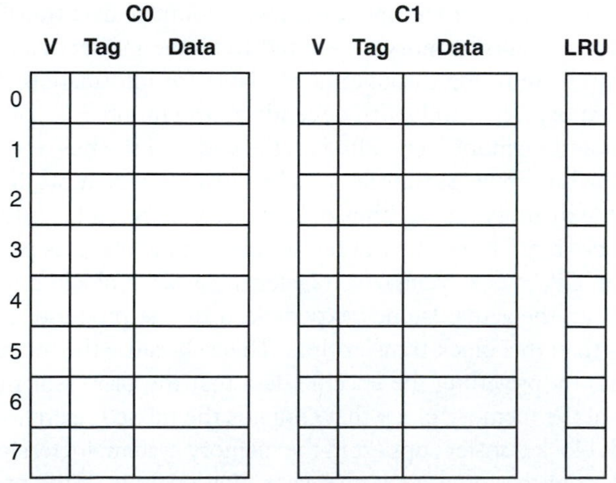

Figure 9.30   1-bit LRU per set in a two-way set associative cache.

For a given row, the associated LRU bit tells which cache (C0 or C1) was recently referenced.

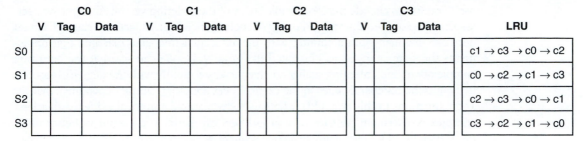

Figure 9.31 LRU information for a four-way set-associative cache.

C0 or C1, respectively. The candidate for replacement is the block in C0 if the LRU bit is 1; it is the block in C1 if the LRU bit is 0.

The hardware needed for a two-way set-associative cache is rather minimal, but there is a time penalty because the hardware updates the LRU bit on every memory reference (affects the IF and MEM stages of the pipelined design).

The LRU hardware for higher degrees of associativity quickly becomes more complex. Suppose that we label the four parallel caches C0, C1, C2, and C3, as shown in Figure 9.31. Building on the two-way set-associative cache, we could have a 2-bit field with each set. The encoding of the 2-bit field gives the block accessed most recently. Unfortunately, whereas this tells us the most recently used block, it does not tell us which block in a set is the least recently used. What we really need is an ordering vector, as shown in Figure 9.31, for each set. For example, the ordering for set S0 shows that C2 was the least recently used, and C1 the most recently used. That is, the decreasing time order of access to the blocks in S0 is this: C1, followed by C3, followed by C0, followed by C2. Thus, at this time, if a block has to be replaced from S0, the LRU victim is the memory block in C2. On each reference, the CPU updates the ordering for the currently accessed set. Figure 9.32 shows the change in the LRU ordering vector to set S0 on a sequence of references that map to this set. Each row shows how the candidate for replacement changes, according to the currently accessed block.

What does it take to implement this scheme in hardware? The number of possibilities for the ordering vector with four parallel caches is $4! = 24$. Therefore, we need a

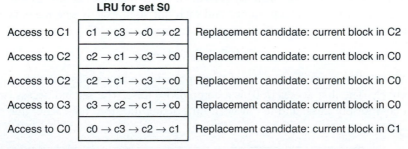

Figure 9.32 Change in the LRU vector for set S0 on a sequence of references that map to that set.

5-bit counter to encode the 24 possible states of the ordering vector. An eight-way set-associative cache requires a counter big enough to encode eight factorial states. Each set needs to maintain such a counter with the associated fine-state machine that implements the state changes, as illustrated in Figure 9.32. We can see that the hardware complexity of implementing such a scheme increases rapidly with the degree of associativity and the number of lines in the cache. There are other, simpler encodings that are approximations to this true LRU scheme. There is ample empirical evidence that less-complex replacement policies may in fact perform better (i.e., result in better miss-rates) than true LRU, for many real code sequences.

9.15 Recapping Types of Misses

We identified three categories of misses in the cache: *compulsory*, *capacity*, and *conflict*. As the name suggests, compulsory misses result because the program is accessing a given memory location, for the first time during execution. Naturally, the location is not in the cache, and a miss is inevitable. Using the analogy of an automobile engine being cold or warm (at the time of starting), we customarily refer to such misses as *cold misses*.

On the other hand, consider the situation wherein the CPU incurs a miss on a memory location X that used to be in the cache, previously.[5] This can be due to one of two reasons: The cache is full at the time of the miss, so there is no choice except to evict some memory location to make room for X. This is what is referred to as a *capacity miss*. Or, it is conceivable that the cache is not full, but the mapping strategy forces X to be brought into a cache line that is currently occupied by some other memory location. This is what is referred to as a *conflict miss*. By definition, we cannot have a conflict miss in a fully associative cache, because a memory location can be placed anywhere. Therefore, in a fully associative cache the only kinds of misses that are possible are compulsory and capacity.

Sometimes, it can be confusing to decide how to categorize the misses. Consider a fully associative cache. Let us say that the CPU accesses a memory location X for the first time. Let the cache be full at this time. We have a cache miss on X. Is this a capacity or a compulsory miss? We can safely say it is both. Therefore, it is fair to categorize this miss as either compulsory or capacity, or as both.

Note that a capacity miss can happen in any of direct-mapped, set-associative, or fully associative caches. For example, consider a direct-mapped cache with four cache lines. Let the cache be initially empty, and each line hold exactly one memory word. Consider the following sequence of memory accesses by the CPU:

$$0, 4, 0, 1, 2, 3, 5, 4$$

We will denote the memory word at the preceding addresses as m0, m1, . . ., m5, respectively. The first access (m0) is a compulsory miss. The second access (m4) is also a compulsory miss, and it will result in evicting m0 from the cache, due to the

---

5. We do not know why X was evicted in the first place, but it is immaterial from the point of view of characterizing the current miss.

direct-mapped organization. The next access is once again to m0, which will be a miss. This is definitely a conflict miss because m0 was evicted earlier by bringing in m4, in spite of the fact that the cache had other empty lines. Continuing with the accesses, m1, m2, and m3 all incur compulsory misses.

Next, we come to memory access for m5. This was never in the cache earlier, so the resulting miss for m5 may be considered a compulsory miss. However, the cache is also full at this time with m0, m1, m2, and m3. Therefore, we could argue that this miss is a capacity miss. Thus, it is fair to categorize this miss as either a compulsory miss or a capacity miss, or as both.

Finally, we come to the memory access for m4 again. This could be considered a conflict miss, since m4 used to be in the cache earlier. However, at this point the cache is full with m0, m5, m2, and m3. Therefore, we could also argue that this miss is a capacity miss. Thus, it is fair to categorize this miss as either a conflict miss or a capacity miss, or as both.

Compulsory misses are unavoidable. Therefore, this type of a miss dominates the other kinds of misses. In other words, if a miss can be characterized as either compulsory or something else, we will choose compulsory as its characterization. Once the cache is full, independent of the organization, we will incur a miss on a memory location that is not currently in the cache. Therefore, a capacity miss dominates a conflict miss. In other words, if a miss can be characterized as either conflict or capacity, we will choose capacity as its characterization.

Example 9.7

Assume the following:

- Total number of blocks in a two-way set associative cache = 8;
- LRU replacement policy.

C1	C2
0	
1	
2	
3	

The processor makes the following 18 accesses to memory locations in the order shown:

$$0, 1, 8, 0, 1, 16, 8, 8, 0, 5, 2, 1, 10, 3, 11, 10, 16, 8$$

With respect to the two-way set-associative cache given, show in a tabular form the cache that will host the memory location; the specific cache index where it will be hosted; and in case of a miss, the type of miss (cold/compulsory, capacity, conflict).

Memory location	C1	C2	Hit/miss	Type of miss

Note:

- The caches are initially empty.
- Upon a miss, if both the spots (C1 and C2) are free, the missing memory location will be brought into C1.
- Capacity miss dominates over conflict miss.
- Cold/compulsory miss dominates over capacity miss.

Answer:

Memory Location	C1	C2	Hit/Miss	Type of Miss
0	Index = 0		Miss	Cold/compulsory
1	Index = 1		Miss	Cold/compulsory
8		Index = 0	Miss	Cold/compulsory
0	Index = 0		Hit	
1	Index = 1		Hit	
16		Index = 0	Miss	Cold/compulsory
8	Index = 0		Miss	Conflict
8	Index = 0		Hit	
0		Index = 0	Miss	Conflict
5		Index = 1	Miss	Cold/compulsory
2	Index = 2		Miss	Cold/compulsory
1	Index = 1		Hit	
10		Index = 2	Miss	Cold/compulsory
3	Index = 3		Miss	Cold/compulsory
11		Index = 3	Miss	Cold/compulsory
10		Index = 2	Hit	
16	Index = 0		Miss	Capacity
8		Index = 0	Miss	Capacity

9.16 Integrating TLB and Caches

In Chapter 8, we introduced TLB, which is nothing but a cache of addresses. Recall that, given a virtual page number (VPN), the TLB returns the physical frame number (PFN) if it exists in the TLB. The TLB is usually quite small for considerations of speed of access, and the space of virtual pages is quite large. Similar to the processor caches, there is the need for a mapping function to look up the TLB, given a VPN. The design considerations for a TLB are quite similar to those of processor caches—that is, the TLB may be organized as a direct-mapped or a set-associative structure. Depending on the specifics of the organization, the VPN is broken up into tag and index fields to enable the TLB lookup. The following example brings home this point:

Example 9.8

Assume the following:

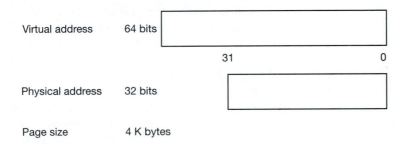

Virtual address   64 bits

Physical address   32 bits

Page size   4 K bytes

A direct mapped TLB with 512 entries

a. How many tag bits per entry are there in the TLB?

b. How many bits are needed to store the page frame number in the TLB?

Answer:

a. With a page size of 4 KB, the number of bits needed for page offset $= 12$.

Therefore, the number of bits for VPN $= 64 - 12 = 52$.

Number of index bits for looking up a direct mapped TLB of size 512 $= 9$.

So, the number of tag in the TLB $= 52 - 9 =$ **43 bits**.

b. The number of bits needed to store the PFN in the TLB equals the size of the PFN.

With a page size of 4 KB, the PFN is $32 - 12 =$ **20 bits**.

Now we can put the TLB and the memory hierarchies together to get a total picture. Figure 9.33 shows the path of a memory access from the CPU (in either the IF or the MEM stage) that proceeds as follows:

- The CPU (IF or MEM stage of the pipeline) generates a virtual address (VA).

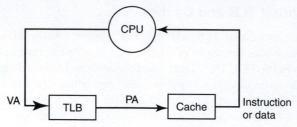

Figure 9.33 Path of a memory access.

The CPU virtual address has to be translated first to a physical address, via TLB lookup, before the cache lookup can happen.

- The TLB does a virtual-to-physical-address (PA) translation. If it is a hit in the TLB, then the pipeline continues without a hiccup. If it is a miss, then the pipeline freezes until the completion of the miss service.
- The stage uses the PA to look up the cache (the I-cache or the D-cache, respectively). If it is a hit in the cache, then the pipeline continues without a hiccup. If it is a miss, then the pipeline freezes until the completion of the miss service.

Note that the IF and MEM stages of the pipeline may access the TLB, simultaneously. For this reason, most processors implement split TLB for instructions and data (I-TLB and D-TLB), respectively, so that two address translations can proceed in parallel. As shown in Figure 9.33, the TLB is in the critical path of determining the processor clock cycle time, since every memory access has to go first through the TLB and then through the cache. Therefore, the TLB is small in size—typically, 64 to 256 entries for each of the I- and D-TLBs.

9.17 Cache Controller

This hardware interfaces the processor to the cache internals and the rest of the memory system and is responsible for taking care of the following functions:

- Upon a request from the processor, it looks up the cache to determine hit or miss, serving the data up to the processor in case of a hit.
- Upon a miss, it initiates a bus transaction to read the missing block from the deeper levels of the memory hierarchy.
- Depending on the details of the memory bus, the requested data block may arrive asynchronously with respect to the request. In this case, the cache controller receives the block and places it in the appropriate spot in the cache.
- As we will see in the next chapter, the controller provides the ability for the processor to specify certain regions of the memory as "uncachable." The need for this will become apparent when we deal with interfacing I/O devices to the processor (see Chapter 10).

Example 9.9

Consider the following memory hierarchy:

- A 128-entry fully associative TLB is split into two halves: one-half for user processes and the other half for the kernel. The TLB has an access time of one cycle. The hit rate for the TLB is 95%. A miss results in a main memory access to complete the address translation.
- An L1 cache has a one-cycle access time and 99% hit rate.
- An L2 cache has a four-cycle access time and a 90% hit rate.
- An L3 cache has a 10-cycle access time and a 70% hit rate.
- A physical memory has a 100-cycle access time.

Compute the average memory access time for this memory hierarchy. Note that the page-table entry may itself be in the cache.

Answer:

Recall the following from Section 9.4:

$$\text{EMAT}_i = T_i + m_i * \text{EMAT}_{i+1}$$

$$\text{EMAT}_{\text{physical memory}} = 100 \text{ cycles}.$$

$$\text{EMAT}_{L3} = 10 + (1 - 0.7) * 100 = 40 \text{ cycles}$$

$$\text{EMAT}_{L2} = (4) + (1 - 0.9) * (40) = 8 \text{ cycles}$$

$$\text{EMAT}_{L1} = (1) + (1 - 0.99) * (8) = 1.08 \text{ cycles}$$

$$\text{EMAT}_{TLB} = (1) + (1 - 0.95) * (1.08) = 1.054 \text{ cycles}$$

$$\text{EMAT}_{\text{Hierarchy}} = \text{EMAT}_{TLB} + \text{EMAT}_{L1} = 1.054 + 1.08 = 2.134 \text{ cycles}.$$

9.18 Virtually Indexed Physically Tagged Cache

Looking at Figure 9.33, we see that every memory access goes through the TLB and then through the cache. The TLB helps in avoiding a trip to the main memory for address translation. However, TLB lookup is in the critical path of the CPU. What this means is that the virtual-to-physical-address translation has to be done first, before we can look up the cache to see whether the memory location is present in the cache. In other words, due to the sequential nature of the TLB lookup followed by the cache lookup, the CPU incurs a significant delay before a determination can be made of whether a memory access is a hit or a miss in the cache. It would be nice if accessing the TLB for address translation and looking up the cache for the memory word could be done in parallel. In other words, we would like to get the address translation "out of the way" of the CPU access to the cache. That is, we want to take the CPU address and look up the cache,

VPN	Page offset

Figure 9.34   Virtual address.

bypassing the TLB. At first, it seems as though this is impossible because we need the physical address to look up the cache.

Let us reexamine the virtual address in Figure 9.34. The VPN changes to PFN because of the address translation. However, the page offset part of the virtual address remains unchanged.

A direct-mapped or set-associative cache derives the index for the lookup from the least-significant bits of the physical address (see Figure 9.11).

This gives us an idea. If we derive the cache index from the unchanging part of the virtual address (i.e., the page offset part), then we can lookup the cache in parallel with the TLB lookup. We refer to such an organization as a *virtually indexed physically tagged* cache (see Figure 9.35). The cache uses virtual index, but derives the tag from the physical address.

With a little bit of thought, it is not difficult to figure out the limitation with this scheme. The unchanging part of the virtual address limits the size of the cache. For example, if the page size is 8 KB, then the cache index is at most 13 bits, and typically less, since part of the least-significant bits specifies the block offset. Increasing the set associativity allows for increasing the size of the cache, despite this restriction. However, we know there is a limit to increasing the associativity, due to the corresponding increase in hardware complexity.

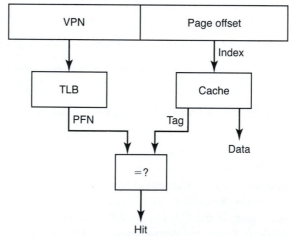

Figure 9.35   A virtually indexed, physically tagged cache.

Using the bits of the virtual address (page offset) that is expected to remain unchanged during the address translation, the cache lookup can proceed in parallel with the TLB lookup.

A partnership between software and hardware helps to eliminate this restriction. Although the hardware does the address translation, the memory manager is the software entity that sets up the VPN-to-PFN mapping. The memory manager uses a technique called *page coloring* to guarantee that more of the virtual address bits will remain unchanged, by the translation process, by choosing the VPN to PFN mapping, carefully (see Example 9.7). Page coloring allows the processor to have a larger, virtually indexed, physically tagged cache, independent of the page size.

Another way to get the translation out of the way is to use *virtually tagged* caches. In this case, the cache uses virtual index and tag. The reader should ponder on the challenges such an organization introduces. A discussion of these caches, however, is beyond the scope of this book.[6]

Example 9.10

Consider a virtually indexed physically tagged cache:

1. Virtual address is 32 bits.
2. Page size is 8 KB.
3. Details of the cache are as follows:
   - four-way set associative;
   - Total size = 512 KB;
   - Block size = 64 bytes.

The memory manager uses page coloring to allow the large cache size.

1. How many bits of the virtual address should remain unchanged for this memory hierarchy to work?
2. Pictorially show the address translation and cache lookup, labeling the parts of the virtual and physical addresses used in them.

Answer:

An 8-KB page size means that the page offset will be 13 bits, leaving 19 bits for the VPN.

The cache has 4 blocks/set × 64 bytes/block = 256 bytes/set, and 512-KB total cache size/256 bytes/set = 2-K sets, which implies 11 bits for the index.

Therefore, the cache breakdown of a memory reference is

Tag, 15 bits; Index, 11 bits; Offset 6 bits.

Thus, the memory management software must assign frames to pages in such a way that the least-significant 4 bits of the VPN must be equal to the least-significant 4 bits of the PFN.

---

6. See advanced computer architecture textbooks (such as [Hennessy, 2006]) for a more complete treatment of this topic.

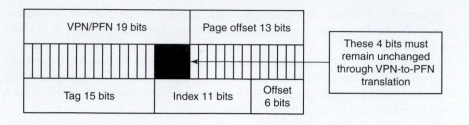

9.19 Recap of Cache Design Considerations

Thus far, we have introduced several concepts, and it will be useful to enumerate them before we look at main memory:

1. principles of spatial and temporal locality (Section 9.2)
2. hit, miss, hit rate, miss rate, cycle time, hit time, miss penalty (Section 9.3)
3. multilevel caches and design considerations thereof (Section 9.4)
4. direct-mapped caches (Section 9.6)
5. cache read/write algorithms (Section 9.8)
6. spatial locality and block size (Section 9.10)
7. fully associative and set-associative caches (Section 9.11)
8. considerations for I- and D-caches (Section 9.12)
9. cache replacement policy (Section 9.14)
10. types of misses (Section 9.15)
11. TLB and caches (Section 9.16)
12. cache controller (Section 9.17)
13. virtually indexed, physically tagged caches (Section 9.18)

Modern processors have on-chip TLB, L1, and L2 caches. The primary design considera-tion for TLB and L1 is reducing the hit time. Both use a simple design consistent with this design consideration. TLB is, quite often, a small fully associative cache of address transla-tions, with sizes in the range of 64 to 256 entries. It is usually split into a system portion that survives context switches and a user portion that is flushed upon a context switch. Some processors provide process tags in the TLB entries to avoid flushing at context switch time. L1 is optimized for speed of access. Usually, it is split into I- and D-caches, employ-ing a small degree of associativity (usually, 2), and the size is relatively small compared with the higher levels of the memory hierarchy (typically less than 64 KB for each of I- and D-caches in processors developed circa 2008). L2 is optimized for reducing the miss rate. Usually, it is a unified I-D cache employing a larger associativity (4-way and 8-way are quite common; some are even 16-way). They may even employ a larger block size than L1, to reduce the miss rate. L2 cache size for processors designed circa 2008 is in the range of several hundreds of kilobytes to a few megabytes. Most modern processors also provide a larger off-chip L3 cache, which may have similar design considerations as L2, but may be even larger in size (several tens of megabytes in processors introduced circa 2008).

9.20 Main Memory Design Considerations

The design of the processor-memory bus and the organization of the physical memory play a crucial part in the performance of the memory hierarchy. As we mentioned earlier, the implementation of the physical memory uses DRAM technology that has nearly a 100:1 speed differential, compared with the CPU. The design may warrant several trips to the physical memory on a cache miss, depending on the width of the processor-memory bus and the cache block size.

In the spirit of the textbook in undertaking joint discovery of interesting concepts, we will start out by presenting very simple ideas for organizing the main memory system. At the outset, we want the reader to understand that these ideas are far removed from the sophisticated memory system that one might see inside a modern box today. We will end this discussion with a look at the state-of-the-art in memory system design.

First, let us consider three different memory bus organizations and the corresponding miss penalties. For the purposes of this discussion, we will assume that the CPU generates 32-bit addresses and data; the cache block size is four words of 32 bits each.

9.20.1 Simple Main Memory

Figure 9.36 shows the organization of a simple memory system. It entertains a block read request to service cache misses. The CPU simply sends the block address to the physical memory. The physical memory internally computes the successive addresses of the block, retrieves the corresponding words from the DRAM, and sends them, one after the other, back to the CPU.

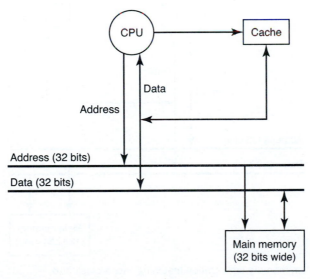

Figure 9.36 A simple memory system.

> The maximum unit of memory access from the CPU and the unit of transfer from the memory are the same (32 bits of data).

Example 9.11

Assume that the DRAM access time is 70 cycles. Assume that the bus cycle time for address or data transfer from/to the CPU/memory is 4 cycles. Compute the block transfer time for a block size of 4 words. Assume that all 4 words are first retrieved from the DRAM before the data transfer to the CPU.

Answer:

Address from CPU to memory = 4 cycles.

DRAM access time = 70 * 4 = 280 cycles (4 successive words).

Data transfer from memory to CPU = 4 * 4 = 16 cycles (4 words).

Total block transfer time = **300 cycles**.

9.20.2 Main Memory and Bus to Match Cache Block Size

To cut down on the miss penalty, we could organize the processor-memory bus and the physical memory to match the block size. Figure 9.37 shows such an organization. This organization transfers the block from the memory to the CPU in a single bus cycle and a single access to the DRAM. All 4 words of a block form a single row of the DRAM and thus are accessed with a single block address. However, this comes at a price of significant hardware complexity, since we need a 128-bit-wide data bus.

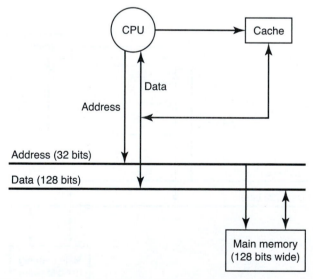

Figure 9.37 Main memory organization matching cache block size.

The memory is organized into blocks, and upon a miss, the entire block containing the missing memory word is transferred, using the wider data bus (128 bits).

Example 9.12

Assume that the DRAM access time is 70 cycles. Assume that the bus cycle time for address or data transfer from/to the CPU/memory is 4 cycles. Compute the block transfer time with the memory system, wherein the bus width and the memory organization match the block size of 4 words.

Answer:

Address from CPU to memory = 4 cycles.

DRAM access time = 70 cycles (all 4 words retrieved with a single DRAM access).

Data transfer from memory to CPU = 4 cycles.

Total block transfer time = **78 cycles**.

9.20.3 Interleaved Memory

The increased bus width makes the previous design infeasible from a hardware standpoint. Fortunately, there is a way to achieve the performance advantage of the previous design, with a little engineering ingenuity called *memory interleaving*. Figure 9.38 shows the organization of an interleaved memory system. The idea is to have multiple *banks* of memory. Each bank is responsible for providing a specific word of the cache block. For example, with a 4-word cache block size, we will have 4 banks labeled M0, M1, M2, and M3. M0 supplies word 0, M1 supplies word 1, M2 supplies word 2, and M3 supplies word 3. The CPU sends the block address, which is simultaneously received

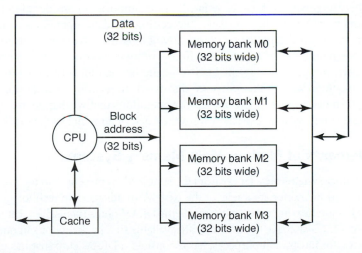

Figure 9.38 An interleaved main memory.

Each memory bank takes a turn transferring the word of the block (that it hosts), upon receiving the block address.

by all 4 banks. The banks work in parallel, each retrieving the word of the block that it is responsible for, from their respective DRAM arrays. Once the words are retrieved, the banks take turns sending the data back to the CPU, using a standard bus similar to the first simple main memory organization.

The interleaved memory system focuses on the fact that DRAM access is the most time-intensive part of the processor–memory interaction. Thus, interleaved memory achieves most of the performance of the wide memory design without having to deal with its hardware complexity.

Example 9.13

Assume that the DRAM access time is 70 cycles. Assume that the bus cycle time for address or data transfer from/to the CPU/memory is 4 cycles. Compute the block transfer time with an interleaved memory system as shown in Figure 9.38.

Answer:

Address from CPU to memory = 4 cycles (all four memory banks receive the address simultaneously).

DRAM access time = 70 cycles (all 4 words retrieved in parallel by the 4 banks).

Data transfer from memory to CPU = 4 * 4 cycles (the memory banks take turns sending their respective data back to the CPU).

Total block transfer time = **90 cycles**.

Keeping the processor busy is by far the most important consideration in the design of memory systems. This translates into getting the data, upon a cache read miss, from the memory to the processor as quickly as possible. Writing to an interleaved memory system need not be any different from writing to a normal memory system. For the most part, the processor is shielded from the latency for writing to memory, by techniques such as write-buffers that we discussed in Section 9.8.2. However, many processor–memory buses support block write operations that work quite nicely with an interleaved memory system, especially for write-back of an entire cache block.

9.21 Elements of Modern Main Memory Systems

Modern memory systems are a far cry from the simple ideas presented in the previous section. Interleaved memories are a relic of the past. With advances in technology, the conceptual idea of interleaving now resides inside the DRAM chips themselves. Let us explain how this works. Circa 2010, DRAM chips are available that pack 4 G-bits in one chip.

However, for illustration purposes, let us consider a DRAM chip that has 64×1 bit capacity. That is, if we supply this chip with a 6-bit address, it will emit 1 bit of data. Each bit of the DRAM storage is called a *cell*. In reality, the DRAM cells are arranged in a rectangular array, as shown in Figure 9.39. The 6-bit address is split into a row address i (3 bits)

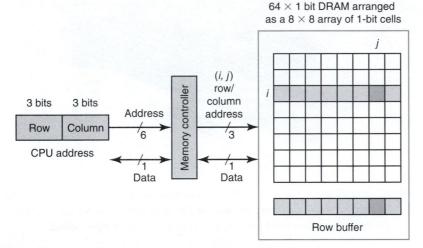

Figure 9.39 Accessing a 64 × 1 bit DRAM.

The row address pulls a whole row from the DRAM; the column address picks out the specific bit in the row.

and a column address j (3 bits), as shown in the figure. To access one bit out of this DRAM chip, you would first supply the 3-bit row address i (called a *row access strobe, or RAS,* request). The DRAM chip pulls the whole row corresponding to i, as shown in the figure. Then, you would supply the 3-bit column address j (called a *column access strobe, or CAS,* request). This selects the unique bit (the purple bit in the row buffer) given by the 6-bit address and sends it to the memory controller, which in turn sends it to the CPU.

For a 1 G-bit chip,[7] we will need a 32 K × 32 K array of cells. The size of the row buffer in this case would be 32 K-bits. It is instructive to understand what constitutes the *cycle time* of a DRAM. As we have said before, each cell in the DRAM is a capacitive charge. There is circuitry (not shown in the figure) that senses this capacitive charge for every cell in the chosen row and buffers the values as 0's and 1's in the corresponding bit positions of the row buffer. In this sense, reading a DRAM is a destructive operation. Naturally, after reading the chosen row, the DRAM circuitry has to recharge the row so that it is back to what it originally contained. This destructive read, followed by the recharge, combined with the row and column address decode, times add up to determine the cycle time of a DRAM. Reading a row out of the array into the buffer is the most time-consuming component of the whole operation. You can quickly see that, after all this work, only 1 bit, corresponding to the column address, is being used, and all the other bits are discarded. We will shortly see (Section 9.21.1) how we may be able to use more of the data in the row buffer without discarding all of them.

We can generalize the DRAM structure so that each cell (i, j), instead of emitting 1 bit, emits some k bits. For example, a 1 M × 8-bit DRAM will have a 1 K × 1 K array

---

7. Recall that 1 G-bit is 2^{30} bits.

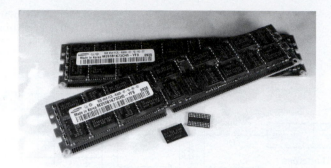

Figure 9.40   Samsung's 2 Gbit DDR3 DRAM chip. An individual 2 Gb DDR3 chip (top and bottom view) is shown; the printed circuit boards show an assembly of these chips and associated circuitry to realize an 8 GB memory module.

of cells, with each cell of the array containing 8 bits. Address and data are communicated to the DRAM chip via *pins* on the chip (see Figure 9.40). One of the key considerations in chip design is reducing the number of such input/output pins. It turns out that the electrical current needed to actuate logic elements within a chip is quite small. However, to communicate logic signals in and out of the chip requires much larger currents. This means having bulky signal-driving circuitry at the edges of the chip, which eats into the real estate available on the chip for other uses (such as logic and memory). For this reason, the cells within a DRAM are arranged as a square array, rather than a linear array, so that the same set of pins can be time-multiplexed to send the row and column addresses to the DRAM chip. This is where the *RAS* (*row address strobe*) and *CAS* (*column address strobe*) terms come from in the DRAM chip parlance. The downside to sharing the pins for row and column addresses is that they have to be sent to the DRAM chip in sequence, thus increasing the cycle time of the DRAM chip.

The following example illustrates how to design a main memory system out of these basic DRAM chips:

Example 9.14

Design a main memory system, given the following:

- Processor to memory bus
  - Address lines = 20.
  - Data lines = 32.
- Each processor-to-memory access returns a 32-bit word specified by the address lines.
- DRAM chip details: 1 M × 8 bits.

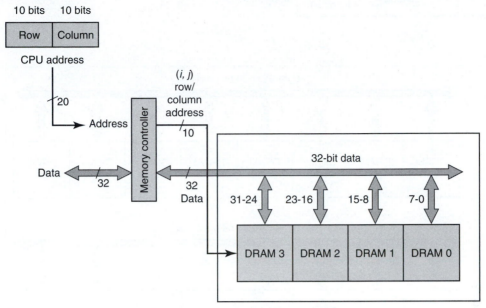

Figure 9.41   32 M-bits memory system using 1 M × 8 bits DRAM chips.

The memory controller supplies the 10-bit row address and column address in sequence to all four DRAM chips. Each of them uses the 10-bit row address to pull out 1024 * 8 bits from their respective arrays into their respective row buffers (row buffer size = 8,192 bits). The 10-bit column address allows each DRAM to select the unique 8-bit byte from its respective row buffers to put out on the data bus.

Answer:

Total size of the main memory system = 2^{20} words × 32 bits/word = 1 M words

$$= 32 \text{ M-bits.}$$

Therefore, we need 4 DRAM chips, each of 1 M × 8 bits, arranged as shown in Figure 9.41.

It is straightforward to extend the design to a byte-addressed memory system. The following example shows how to build a 4-GB memory system, using 1 G-bit DRAM chips.

Example 9.15

Design a 4-GB main memory system, given the following:

- Processor to memory bus
  - Address lines = 32
  - Data lines = 32

15-bit row/column
address from
memory controller

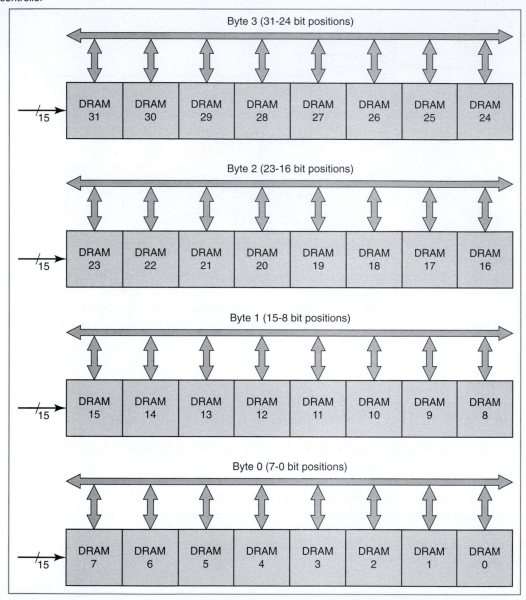

Figure 9.42 A 4-GB memory system using a 1 G-bit DRAM chip (This is a companion figure for Example 9.15).

For reading a 32-bit word, the memory controller sends the 15-bit RAS and CAS in sequence, simultaneously to all 4 rows. Each DRAM chip in a row pulls out a unique bit from its respective arrays, using the RAS and CAS addresses. Thus, each row supplies 8 bits of the required 32-bit word in response to an address received by the memory controller from the CPU).

- Each CPU word is 32 bits made up of 4 bytes.
- CPU supports byte addressing.
- The least-significant 2 bits of the address lines specify the byte in the 32-bit word.
- Each processor-to-memory access returns a 32-bit word specified by the word address.
- DRAM chip details: 1 G-bit (organized as $2^{30} \times 1$ bit).

Answer:

In the 32-bit address, the most significant 30 bits specify the word address.

$$\text{Total size of the main memory system} = 2^{30} \text{ words} \times 4 \text{ bytes/word} = 4 \text{ GB}$$
$$= 32 \text{ G-bits.}$$

Therefore, we need 32 DRAM chips, each of 1 G-bit, arranged for convenience in a two-dimensional array, as shown in Figure 9.42. For writing individual bytes in a word, the memory controller (not shown in the figure) will select the appropriate row in this two-dimensional array and send the 15-bit RAS and CAS requests to that row, along with other control signals (not shown in the figure). For reading a 32-bit word, it will send the 15-bit RAS and CAS requests to all the DRAMs so that a full 32-bit word will be returned to the controller.

Manufacturers package DRAM chips in what are called *dual in-line memory modules* (DIMMs). Figure 9.43 shows a picture of a DIMM. Typically, a DIMM is a small printed circuit board containing 4–16 DRAM chips organized in an 8-byte wide datapath. These days, the DIMM is the basic building block for memory systems.

9.21.1 Page Mode DRAM

Recall what happens within a DRAM upon reading a cell. The memory controller first supplies the DRAM with a row address. DRAM reads the entire selected row into a row buffer. Then the memory controller supplies the column address, and the DRAM selects the particular column out of the row buffer and sends the data to the memory controller. These two components constitute the *access time* of the DRAM and represent the bulk of a DRAM cycle time. As we mentioned earlier in this section, the rest of the row buffer is discarded once the selected column data are sent to the controller. As we can see from Figures 9.41 and 9.42, consecutive column addresses within the same row map to contiguous memory addresses generated by the CPU. Therefore, getting a block of data from memory translates to getting successive columns of the *same row* from a DRAM. Recall the trick involved in building interleaved memory (see Section 9.20.3). Each memory bank stored a different word of the same block and sent it on the memory bus, to the CPU, in successive bus cycles. DRAMs support the same functionality through a technique referred to as *fast page mode (FPM)*. This technique

Figure 9.43   Dual in-line memory module (DIMM).

allows different portions of the row buffer to be accessed in successive CAS cycles, without the need for additional RAS requests. This concept is elaborated on in the following example:

Example 9.16

The memory system in Example 9.15 is augmented with a processor cache that has a block size of 16 bytes. Explain how the memory controller delivers the requested block to the CPU, upon a cache miss.

Answer:

The top part of Figure 9.44 shows the address generated by the CPU. The memory controller's interpretation of the CPU address is shown in the bottom part of the figure. Note that the bottom two bits of the column address are the top two bits of the block offset in the CPU address. The block size is 16 bytes, or 4 words. The successive words of the requested cache block are given by the 4 successive columns of row i, with the column address changing only in the last two bits.

For example, assume that the CPU address for the block is (i, j), where $j = 010000011000101$.

Let us denote

> j by $j_{13}xy$, where j_{13} represents the top 13 bits of the column address j.

To fetch the entire block from the DRAM array, the memory controller does the following:

1. Send RAS/CAS request to DRAM array for address (i, j).
2. Send 3 more CAS requests with addresses $j_{13}xy$, where $xy = 00, 10, 11$.

Each of the CAS requests will result in the DRAM array sending 4 words successively. (The first word returned will be the actual address that incurred a miss.) The memory controller will pipeline these 4 words in responses back to the CPU, in four successive memory bus cycles.

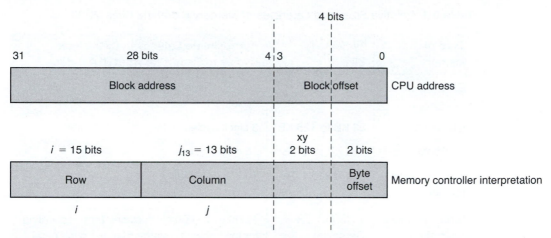

Figure 9.44   Memory controller's interpretation of a 32-bit CPU address.

The **xy** address bits denote the word within a block. In Figure 9.42, each row of DRAM chips provides one byte of a word. The RAS request from the memory controller pulls out the spatially adjacent words of a memory block and puts them into the row buffers of the DRAMs. To get the consecutive words of a given memory block, the memory controller has to send CAS requests, corresponding to the different binary combinations of **xy**, to the DRAM banks so that the successive words of the block can be read out from the row buffers of the DRAMs.

Over the years, there have been numerous enhancements to the DRAM technology. We have given a flavor of this technology in this section. Perhaps we have stimulated enough interest for the reader to look beyond this textbook at more advanced topics in this area.

9.22 Performance Implications of Memory Hierarchy

There is a hierarchy of memory that the CPU interacts with, either explicitly or implicitly: processor registers, cache (several levels), main memory (in DRAM), and virtual memory (on the disk). The farther the memory is from the processor, the larger the size and slower the speed. The cost per byte decreases, as well, as we move down the memory hierarchy away from the processor.

As we already mentioned, the actual sizes and speeds continue to improve yearly, though the relative speeds and sizes remain roughly the same. As a concrete example, Table 9.1 summarizes the relative latencies and sizes of the different levels of the memory hierarchy, circa 2006. The clock cycle time circa 2006 for a 2 GHz Pentium processor was 0.5 ns.

Table 9.1 Relative Sizes and Latencies of Memory Hierarchy, Circa 2006

Type of Memory	Typical Size	Approximate Latency in CPU Clock Cycles to Read One Word of 4 Bytes
CPU registers	8 to 32	Usually, immediate access (0 to 1 clock cycles)
L1 Cache	32 KB to 128 KB	3 clock cycles
L2 Cache	128 KB to 4 MB	10 clock cycles
Main (Physical) Memory	256 MB to 4 GB	100 clock cycles
Virtual Memory (on disk)	1 GB to 1 TB (Terabyte)	1,000 to 10,000 clock cycles (not accounting for the software overhead of handling page faults)

Memory hierarchy plays a crucial role in system performance. We can see that the miss penalty affects the pipeline processor performance for the currently executing program. More importantly, the design of the memory system and the CPU scheduler has to be cognizant of the memory hierarchy while making design decisions. For example, page replacement by the memory manager wipes out the contents of the corresponding physical frame from all the levels of the memory hierarchy. Therefore, a process that page faulted may experience a significant loss of performance immediately after the faulting is brought into physical memory from the disk. This performance loss continues until the contents of the page fill up the nearer levels of the memory hierarchy.

CPU scheduling has a similar effect on system performance. A *direct* cost of context switch includes saving and loading the process control blocks (PCBs) of the descheduled and newly scheduled processes, respectively. Flushing the TLB of the descheduled process forms part of this direct cost. There is an *indirect* cost of context switching due to the memory hierarchy. This cost manifests as misses at the various levels of the memory hierarchy, all the way from the caches to the physical memory. Once the working set of the newly scheduled process gets into the nearer levels of the memory hierarchy, the process performance reaches the true potential of the processor. Thus, it is important that the *time quantum* used by the CPU scheduler take into account the true cost of context switching as determined by the effects of the memory hierarchy.

Summary

Table 9.2 provides a glossary of the important terms and concepts introduced in this chapter.

Table 9.2 Summary of Concepts Relating to Memory Hierarchy

Category	Vocabulary	Details
Principle of locality (Section 9.2)	Spatial	Access to contiguous memory locations
	Temporal	Reuse of memory locations already accessed
Cache organization	Direct-mapped	One-to-one mapping (Section 9.6)
	Fully associative	One-to-any mapping (Section 9.11.1)
	Set associative	One-to-many mapping (Section 9.11.2)
Cache reading/ writing (Section 9.8)	Read hit/Write hit	Memory location being accessed by the CPU is present in the cache
	Read miss/Write miss	Memory location being accessed by the CPU is not present in the cache
Cache write policy (Section 9.8)	Write through	CPU writes to cache and memory
	Write back	CPU writes only to cache; memory updated on replacement
Cache parameters	Total cache size (S)	Total data size of cache in bytes
	Block Size (B)	Size of contiguous data in one data block
	Degree of associativity (p)	Number of homes in a cache in which a given memory block can reside
	Number of cache lines (L)	S/pB
	Cache access time	Time in CPU clock cycles to check hit/miss in cache
	Unit of CPU access	Size of data exchange between CPU and cache
	Unit of memory transfer	Size of data exchange between cache and memory
	Miss penalty	Time in CPU clock cycles to handle a cache miss
Memory address interpretation	Index (n)	$log_2 L$ bits, used to look up a particular cache line
	Block offset (b)	$log_2 B$ bits, used to select a specific byte within a block
	Tag (t)	$a - (n + b)$ bits, where a is number of bits in memory address; used for matching with tag stored in the cache

(continued)

Table 9.2 Summary of Concepts Relating to Memory Hierarchy *(continued)*

Category	Vocabulary	Details
Cache entry/cache block/cache line/set	Valid bit	Signifies data block is valid
	Dirty bits	For write-back, signifies whether the data block is more up-to-date than memory
	Tag	Used for tag matching with memory address for hit/miss
	Data	Actual data block
Performance metrics	Hit rate (h)	Percentage of CPU accesses served from the cache
	Miss rate (m)	$1 - h$
	Avg. Memory stall	Misses-per-instruction$_{Avg}$ * miss-penalty$_{Avg}$
	Effective memory access time (EMAT$_i$) at level i	$EMAT_i = T_i + m_i * EMAT_{i+1}$
	Effective CPI	CPI_{Avg} + Memory-stalls$_{Avg}$
Types of misses	Compulsory miss	Memory location accessed for the first time by CPU
	Conflict miss	Miss incurred due to limited associativity, even though the cache is not full
	Capacity miss	Miss incurred when the cache is full
Replacement policy	FIFO	First-in–first-out
	LRU	Least-recently used
Memory technologies	SRAM	Static RAM with each bit realized by using 6 transistors
	DRAM	Dynamic RAM with each bit realized by using a single transistor
Main memory	DRAM access time	DRAM read access time
	DRAM cycle time	DRAM read and refresh time
	Bus cycle time	Data transfer time between CPU and memory
	Simulated interleaving, using DRAM	Using page mode bits of DRAM

Memory Hierarchy of Modern Processors—An Example

Modern processors employ several levels of caches. It is not unusual for the processor to have on-chip an L1 cache (separate for instructions and data), and a combined L2 cache for instructions and data. Outside the processor, there may be an L3 cache followed by

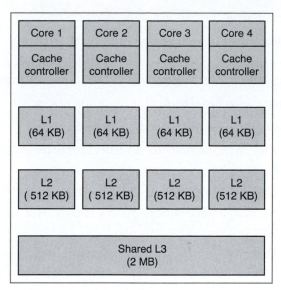

Figure 9.45 AMD's Barcelona chip.

The quad-core chip has three levels of cache memory on-chip.

the main memory. With multicore technology, the memory system is becoming even more sophisticated. For example, AMD introduced the Barcelona[8] chip in 2006.[9] This chip, which has quad-core, has a per core L1 (split I and D) cache and an L2 cache. This is followed by an L3 cache that is shared by all the cores. Figure 9.45 shows the memory hierarchy of the Barcelona chip. The L1 cache is two-way set-associative (64 KB for instructions and 64 KB for data). The L2 cache is 16-way set-associative (512 KB combined for instructions and data). The L3 cache is 32-way set-associative (2 MB shared among all the cores).

Exercises

1. Compare and contrast spatial locality with temporal locality.

2. Compare and contrast direct-mapped, set-associative, and fully associative cache designs.

3. A fellow student has designed a cache with the most-significant bits containing the index and the least-significant bits containing the tag. How well do you suppose this cache will perform? Why?

4. In a direct-mapped cache with a t-bit-long tag, how many tag comparators would you expect to find and how many bits would they compare at a time?

---

8. Phenom is the brand name under which AMD markets this chip on desktops.

9. AMD Phenom processor data sheet: http://www.amd.com/us-en/assets/content_type/white_papers_and_tech_docs/44109.pdf.

5. Explain the purpose of dirty bits in a cache.

6. Give compelling reasons for using a multilevel-cache hierarchy.

7. What are the primary design considerations of caches? Discuss how these considerations influence the different levels of the memory hierarchy.

8. What is the motivation for increasing the block size of a cache?

9. What is the motivation for a set-associative cache design?

10. Answer True/False, with justification: L1 caches usually have higher associativity, compared with L2 caches.

11. Give three reasons for having a split I- and D-cache at the L1 level.

12. Give compelling reasons for a unified I-cache and D-cache at deeper levels of the cache hierarchy.

13. Answer True/False, with justification: As long as there is an L2 cache, the L1 cache design can focus exclusively on matching its speed of access to the processor clock cycle time.

14. Your engineering team tells you that you can have a total of 2 MB of on-chip cache. You have a choice of making it one big L1 cache, two level L1 and L2 caches, split I- and D-caches at several levels, etc. What would be your choice and why? Consider hit time, miss rate, associativity, and pipeline structure in making your design decisions. For this problem, it is sufficient for you to give a qualitative explanation for your design decisions.

15. How big a counter do you need to implement a true LRU replacement policy for a four-way set associative cache?

16. Consider the following memory hierarchy:

    - L1 cache: Access time = 2 ns;   hit rate = 99%
    - L2 cache: Access time = 5 ns;   hit rate = 95%
    - L3 cache: Access time = 10 ns;   hit rate = 80%
    - Main memory: Access time = 100 ns

    Compute the effective memory access time.

17. A memory hierarchy has the following resources:

    | L1 cache | 2 ns access time | 98% hit rate |
    | L2 cache | 10 ns access time | ?? |
    | Memory | 60 ns access time | |

    Assume that, for each of L1 and L2 caches, a lookup is necessary to determine whether a reference is a hit or miss. What should be the hit rate of L2 cache to ensure that the effective memory access time is no more than 3 ns?

18. You are designing a cache for a 32-bit processor. Memory is organized into words, but byte addressing is used. You have been told to make the cache 2-way set associative with 64 words (256 bytes) per block. You are allowed to use a total of 64 K words (256 K bytes) for the data (excluding tags, status bits, etc.)

    Sketch the layout of the cache.

    Show how a CPU-generated address is interpreted for cache lookup into block offset, index, and tag.

19. From the following statements regarding cache memory, select the ones that are true:

    • It can usually be manipulated just like registers from the instruction-set architecture of a processor.

    • It cannot usually be directly manipulated from the instruction-set architecture of a processor.

    • It is usually implemented with the same technology as the main memory.

    • It is usually much larger than a register file, but much smaller than the main memory.

20. Distinguish between cold miss, capacity miss, and conflict miss.

21. Redo Example 9.7, with the following changes:

    • 4-way set associative cache with 16 blocks total

    • LRU replacement policy

    • reference string:

        0, 1, 8, 0, 1, 16, 24, 32, 8, 8, 0, 5, 6, 2, 1, 7, 10, 0, 1, 3, 11, 10, 0, 1, 16, 8

22. Redo Example 9.8, with the following changes:

    • 32-bit virtual address, 24-bit physical address, page size 8 KB, and direct mapped TLB with 64 entries

23. Explain the term *virtually indexed, physically tagged cache*. What is the advantage of such a design? What are the limitations of such a design?

24. Explain the term *page coloring*. What problem is this technique aimed to solve? How does it work?

25. Redo Example 9.10, with the following changes:

    • virtual address is 64 bits

    • page size is 8 KB

    • cache parameters: 2-way set associative, 512 KB total size, and block size of 32 bytes

26. Redo Example 9.15, with the following changes:
    - 64-bit address and data lines
    - 64-bit CPU word
    - use a 1 G-bit DRAM chip

27. Explain the term *page mode DRAM*.

Bibliographic Notes and Further Reading

Memory hierarchy has been a fertile area of intellectual endeavor ever since the caches were invented in the early 1960s. Maurice Wilkes, a computer pioneer, wrote the first technical paper that described the idea of cache memory [Wilkes, 1971]. For an in-depth survey article on cache memories, we refer the reader to the paper by Alan Jay Smith [Smith, 1982]. Hennessy and Patterson [Hennessy, 2006] cover many advanced optimization techniques to enhance cache performance. Bryant and O'Hallaron [Bryant, 2003] cover the fundamentals of cache memory design and the impact of cache memories on program performance. Memory technology is a continuously moving target. There is a DRAM growth rule that states, "DRAM capacity quadruples every three years." Given this reality, the best sources from which to find the latest in memory technology are the manufacturer's web pages. Companies such as Samsung, Kingston technology, Hynix, and Micron lead the DRAM market, so those vendors' web pages would be a good place to start in finding the latest developments in memory technology.

Input/Output and Stable Storage

The next step in demystifying what is inside a box is understanding the I/O subsystem. In Chapter 4, we discussed interrupts, a mechanism for I/O devices to grab the attention of the processor. In this chapter, we will present more details on the interaction between processor and I/O devices, as well as different methods of transferring data among the processor, memory, and I/O devices.

We start out by discussing the basic paradigms that describe the CPU's communication with I/O devices. We then identify the hardware mechanisms needed to carry out such communication in hardware, as well as the details of the buses that serve as the conduits for transferring data between the CPU and I/O. Complementary to the hardware mechanisms is the operating system entity called a device driver that carries out the actual dialogue between the CPU and each specific I/O device. Stable storage, provided in most computer systems by the *hard disk*, is unquestionably one of the most important and intricate members of the I/O devices found inside a box. We will discuss the details of the hard disk, including scheduling algorithms for orchestrating the I/O activities.

10.1 Communication Between the CPU and the I/O Devices

Although we started our exploration of the computer system with a discussion of the processor, most users of computers may not even be aware of the processor that is inside the gadget they are using. Take, for example, the cell phone or the iPod. It is the functionality provided by the iPod that attracts a user to it. An iPod or a cell phone gets its utility from the input/output devices that each provides for interacting with it. Thus, knowing how I/O devices interact with the rest of the computer system is a key

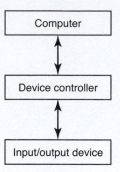

Figure 10.1 Relationship of the device controller to other components.

component to unraveling mystery within the "box." (See Figure 10.1.) Although there are a wide variety of I/O devices, their connection to the rest of the system is quite similar. As we have seen so far, the processor executes instructions in its instruction set repertoire. The LC-2200 has no special instruction that would make it directly communicate with a CD player or a speaker. Let's understand how a device such an iPod plays music.

A special piece of hardware known as a *device controller* acts as an intermediary between an I/O device and the computer. This controller knows how to communicate with both the I/O device and with the computer.

10.1.1 Device Controller

To make this discussion concrete, let us consider a very simple device, the *keyboard*. The device itself has circuitry inside it to map the mechanical action of tapping on a key to a binary encoding of the character that the key represents. This binary encoding, usually in a format called ASCII *(American standard code for information interchange),* has to be conveyed to the computer. For this information exchange to happen, two things are necessary. First, we need temporary space to hold the character that was typed. Second, we have to grab the attention of the processor to give it this character. This is where the device controller comes in. Let us consider the minimal smarts needed in the keyboard device controller. It has two registers: *data* register, and *status* register. The data register is the storage space for the character typed on the keyboard. As the name suggests, the status register is an aggregation of the current state of information exchange of the device with the computer.

With respect to the keyboard, the state includes

- a bit, called a *ready* bit, that represents the answer to the question, "Is the character in the data register new (i.e., not seen by the processor yet)?";
- a bit, called *interrupt enable (IE),* that represents the answer to the question, "Is the processor allowing the device to interrupt it?"; and
- a bit, called *interrupt flag (IF),* that serves to answer the question, "Is the controller ready to interrupt the processor?"

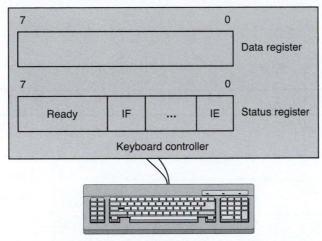

Figure 10.2 The keyboard controller houses a data register that holds the last character sent from the keyboard and a status register that contains the current state of the interaction between the CPU and the device.

Figure 10.2 shows such a minimal keyboard controller. Depending on the sophistication of the device, additional status information may need to be included. For example, if the input rate of the device exceeds the rate of information transfer to the processor, a *data overrun flag* may record this status on the controller.

Sometimes, it may be a good idea to separate the *status* that comes from the device from the *command* that comes from the processor. The keyboard is a simple enough device that the only command from the processor is to turn on or off the interrupt enable bit. A more sophisticated device (for example, a camera) may require additional commands (take picture, pan, tilt, etc.). In general, a device controller may have a set of registers through which it interacts with the processor.

10.1.2 Memory Mapped I/O

Next, we investigate how to connect the device controller to the computer. Somehow, we have to make the registers in the controller visible to the processor. A simple way to accomplish this is via the processor–memory bus, as shown in Figure 10.3. The processor reads and writes to memory, using load/store instructions. If the registers in the controller (data and status) appear as memory locations to the CPU, the processor can simply use the same load/store instructions to manipulate these registers. This technique, referred to as *memory mapped I/O,* allows interaction between the processor and the device controller without any change to the processor.

It is a very simple trick to make the device registers appear as memory locations. We give the device registers unique memory addresses. For example, let us arbitrarily give the data register the memory address 5000 and the status register the memory address 5002. The keyboard controller has smarts (i.e., circuitry) in it to react to these

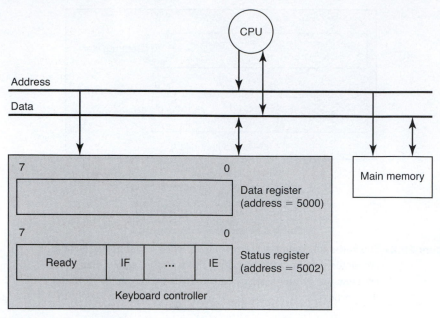

Figure 10.3 Connecting the device controller to the processor-memory bus.

The registers in the controller are made to appear as memory locations to the CPU by giving them unique memory addresses.

two addresses appearing on the address bus. For example, suppose that the processor executes the following instruction:

```
LW r1, Mem[5000]
```

The controller recognizes that address 5000 corresponds to the data register, and puts the contents of the data register on the data bus. The processor has no idea that the contents are coming from a special register on the controller. It simply takes the value appearing on the data bus and stores it into register `r1`.

This is the power of memory mapped I/O. Without adding any new instructions to the instruction set, we have now integrated the device controller into the computer system. You may be wondering whether this technique causes confusion between the memory that also reacts to addresses appearing on the bus and the device controllers. The basic idea is to reserve a portion of the address space for such device controllers. Assume that we have a 32-bit processor and that we wish to reserve 64 KB for I/O device addresses. We could arbitrarily designate addresses in the range of `0xFFFF0000` through `0xFFFFFFFF` for I/O devices and assign addresses within this range to the devices we wish to connect to the bus. For example, we may assign `0xFFFF0000` as the data register, and `0xFFFF0002` as the status register, for the keyboard controller. The design of the keyboard device controller considers this assignment and reacts to these addresses. What this means is that every device controller has circuitry to decode an address appearing on the bus. If an address appearing on the bus corresponds to one assigned to this controller, it behaves as "memory" for the associated command on the bus (read or write). Correspondingly, the design of the memory system will make it ignore addresses in the range designated for I/O. Of course, it is a matter of convention as to the range of addresses reserved for I/O. The usual convention is to reserve high addresses for I/O device registers.

You are perhaps wondering how to reconcile this information with the details of the memory hierarchy that we just finished learning about in Chapter 9. If a memory address assigned to a device register were present in the cache, wouldn't the processor get a stale value from the cache, instead of the contents of the device register? This is a genuine concern, and it is precisely for this reason that cache controllers provide the ability to treat certain regions of memory as "uncachable." Even though the processor reads a device register as if it were a memory location, the cache controller has been set *a priori* to not encache such locations, but read them afresh every time the processor accesses them.

The advantage of memory mapped I/O is that no special I/O instructions are required; but the disadvantage is that a portion of the memory address space is lost to device registers, and hence not available to users or the operating system for code and data. Some processors provide special I/O instructions and connect I/O devices to a separate I/O bus. Such designs (called *I/O mapped I/O*) are especially popular in the domain of embedded systems, where memory space is limited. However, with modern general-purpose processors with a 64-bit address space, reserving a small portion of this large address space for I/O seems a reasonable design choice. Thus, memory mapped I/O is the design of choice for modern processors, especially because it integrates easily into the processor architecture, without the need for new instructions.

10.2 Programmed I/O

Now that we know how to interface a device via a device controller to the processor, let us turn our attention to moving data back and forth between a device and the processor. *Programmed I/O (PIO)* refers to writing a computer program that accomplishes such data transfer. To make the discussion concrete, we will use the keyboard controller example we introduced earlier.

Let us summarize the actions of the keyboard controller:

1. It sets the ready bit in the status register when a new character gets into the data register.

2. Upon the CPU reading the data register, the controller clears the ready bit.

With the given semantics of the keyboard controller, we can write a simple program to move data from the keyboard to the processor (shown pictorially in Figure 10.4):

Step 1. Check the ready bit (see Figure 10.4).

Step 2. If the ready bit is not set, go to Step 1.

Step 3. Read the contents of the data register (see Figure 10.4). Note that reading this register automatically clears the ready bit.

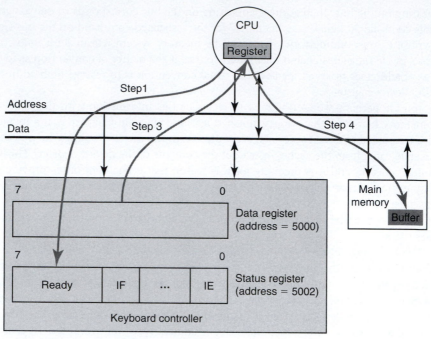

Figure 10.4 An example of PIO data transfer.

The controller sets the ready bit to indicate to the CPU that the data register has new data. The CPU transfers the data from the data register to the memory buffer, using simple load/store instructions.

Step 4. Store the character read into memory (see Figure 10.4).

Step 5. Go to Step 1.

Steps 1 and 2 constitute the handshake between the processor and the device controller. The processor continuously checks whether the device has new data through these two steps. In other words, the processor *polls* the device for new data. Consider the speed differential between the processor and a device such as a keyboard. A 1 GHz processor executes an instruction in roughly 1 ns. Even if one were to type at an amazing speed, say, of 300 characters a minute, the controller inputs a character only once every 200 ms. The processor would have been polling the ready bit of the status register several million times before it gets to input a character. This is an inefficient use of the processor resource. Instead of polling, the processor could enable the interrupt bit for a device and, upon an interrupt, execute the instructions, as given previously, to complete the data transfer. The operating system schedules other programs to run on the CPU and context switches to handle the interrupts, as we described in Chapter 4.

Programmed data transfer, accomplished either by polling or interrupt, works for slow-speed devices (for example, a keyboard and a mouse) that typically produce data *asynchronously*. That is, the data production is not rhythmic with any clock pulse. However, high-speed devices such as disks produce data *synchronously*. That is, the data production follows a rhythmic clock pulse. If the processor fails to pick up the data when the device has them ready, then the device may likely overwrite it with new data, leading to data loss. The memory bus bandwidth of state-of-the-art processors is around 200 MB/sec. All the entities on the bus—processor and device controllers—share this bandwidth. A state-of-the-art disk drive produces data at the rate of 150 MB/sec. Given the limited margin between the production rate of data and the available memory bus bandwidth, it is just not feasible to orchestrate the data transfer, between the memory and a synchronous high-speed device such as a disk, through programmed I/O.

Further, even for slow-speed devices, using the processor to orchestrate the data transfer through programmed I/O is an inefficient use of the processor resource. In the next subsection, we introduce a different technique for accomplishing this data transfer.

10.3 DMA

Direct memory access (DMA), as the name suggests, is a technique by which the device controller has the capability to transfer data between itself and the memory, without the intervention of the processor.

The transfer itself is initiated by the processor, but once it is initiated, the device carries out the transfer. Let us try to understand the smarts needed in the DMA controller. We will consider that the controller is interfacing a synchronous high-speed device such as a disk. We refer to such devices as *streaming devices*: Once data transfer starts in either direction (from or to the device), data move in or out of the device continuously until completion of the transfer.

As an analogy, suppose that you are cooking. You need to fill a large cooking vessel, on the stove, with water. You are using a small cup, catching water from the kitchen faucet, pouring it into the vessel, going back to refill the cup, and repeating this process until the vessel is full. Now you know that if you keep the faucet open, water will continue to stream. Therefore, you use the cup as a *buffer* between the faucet that runs continuously and the vessel, turning the faucet on and off as needed.

A streaming device is like a water faucet. To read from the device, the device controller turns on the device, gets a stream of bits, turns it off, transfers the bits to memory, and repeats the process until it has completed the entire data transfer. It does the reverse to write to the device. Let us focus on reading from the device into memory. What is involved in transferring the bits to memory? The controller acquires the bus and sends one byte (or whatever the granularity of the bus transfer is) at a time to memory. Recall that the bus is a shared resource. There are other contenders for the bus, including the processor. Therefore, the data transfer between the device controller and the memory is asynchronous; worse yet, the controller may not get the bus for quite a while if there are other higher-priority requests for the bus. To smooth out this dichotomy of a synchronous device and an asynchronous bus, the controller needs a *hardware buffer* similar to the cup in the cooking analogy. It is fairly intuitive for us to reason that the buffer should be as big as the *unit of synchronous transfer* between the device and device controller. For example, if the device is a camcorder, then the size of a single image frame (e.g., 100 K pixels) may be the smallest unit of synchronous data transfer between the device and the controller. Thus, in the case of a device controller for a camcorder, the size of the hardware buffer should be at least as big as one image frame.

To initiate a transfer, the processor needs to convey four pieces of information to the device controller: *command*, *address on the device*, *memory buffer address*, and *amount of data transfer*. Note that the data transfer is between contiguous regions of the device space and memory space. In addition, the controller has a status register to record the device status. As in the case of the keyboard controller, we can assign five memory-mapped registers in the controller: *command, status, device address, memory buffer address,* and *count*. All of these registers have unique memory addresses assigned to them. Figure 10.5 shows a simplified block diagram for a DMA controller for such a streaming device.

For example, to transfer *N bytes* of data from a memory buffer at address *M* to the device at address *D,* the CPU executes the following instructions:

Step 1. Store *N* into the *Count* register.

Step 2. Store *M* into the *Memory buffer address* register.

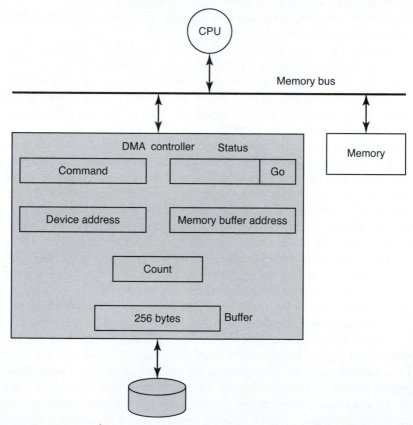

Figure 10.5   DMA controller.

All the registers in the controller are assigned unique memory addresses so that the CPU can manipulate them with load/store instructions.

Step 3. Store *D* into the *Device address* register.

Step 4. Store *write to the device* command into the *Command* register.

Step 5. Set the *Go* bit in the *Status* register.

Note that all of the steps are simple *memory store* instructions (so far as the CPU is concerned), since these registers are memory mapped.

The device controller is like a CPU. Internally, it has the data path and control to implement each of a set of instructions that it gets from the processor. For instance, to complete the preceding transfer (see Figure 10.6), the controller will access the memory bus repeatedly to move into its buffer, *N* contiguous bytes starting from the memory address *M*. Once the buffer is ready, the controller will initiate the transfer of the buffer contents into the device at the specified device address. If the processor had enabled interrupt for the controller, then the controller will interrupt the processor upon completion of the transfer.

The device controller competes with the processor for memory bus cycles, a phenomenon commonly referred to as *cycle stealing*. This is an archaic term and stems from the fact that the processor is usually the bus master. The devices *steal* bus cycles when the processor does not need them. From the discussion on memory hierarchies in Chapter 9, we know that the processor mostly works out of the cache for both instructions and data. Therefore, devices stealing bus cycles from the processor do not pose a problem with a well-balanced design that accounts for the size of the aggregate bandwidth of the memory bus being greater than the cumulative needs of the devices (including the processor) connected to it.

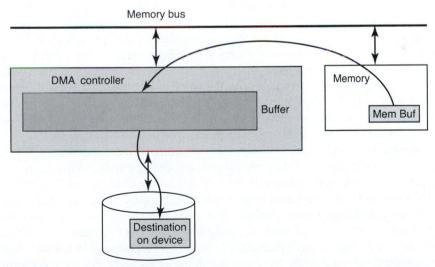

Figure 10.6 An example of DMA data transfer.

Once the CPU initiates the DMA by setting the registers in the controller with all the needed information, the controller autonomously completes the required data transfer without bothering the CPU.

10.4 Buses

The system bus (or memory bus) is a key resource in the entire design. Functionally, the bus has the following components:

- Address lines
- Data lines
- Command lines
- Interrupt lines
- Interrupt acknowledge lines
- Bus arbitration lines

Electrically, high-performance systems run these wires in parallel to constitute the system bus. For example, a processor with 32-bit addressability will have 32 address lines. The number of data lines on the bus depends on the command set supported on the bus. As we have seen in the discussion in, Chapter 9, on memory hierarchy, it is conceivable that the data bus is wider than the word width of the processor, to support large cache block size. The command lines encode the specific command to the memory system (read, write, block read, block write, etc.), and hence should be sufficient in number to carry the binary encoding of the command set. We saw, in Chapter 4, details of the interrupt handshake between the processor and I/O devices. The number of interrupt lines (and acknowledgment lines) corresponds to the number of interrupt levels supported. In Chapter 9, we emphasized the importance of the memory system. In a sense, the performance of the system depends crucially on the performance of the memory system. Therefore, it is essential that the system bus, the porthole for accessing the memory, be used to its fullest potential. Normally, during the current bus cycle, devices compete to acquire the bus for the next cycle. Choosing the winner for the next bus cycle happens before the current cycle completes. A variety of techniques exists for *bus arbitration*, from a centralized scheme (at the processor) to more distributed schemes. A detailed discussion of bus arbitration schemes is beyond the scope of this textbook. Some older textbooks tend to cover this topic in more detail (e.g., [Patterson, 1998]). It is instructive to look at advanced architecture textbooks (e.g., [Hennessy, 2006]) to understand how system buses work in modern high-speed processors such as the Intel Pentium.

Over the years, there have been a number of efforts to standardize buses. The purpose of standardization is to allow third-party vendors to interface with the buses to develop I/O devices. Standardization poses an interesting challenge to "box makers." On the one hand, standardization helps a box maker because it increases the range of peripherals available on a given platform, from third-party sources. On the other hand, to keep the competitive edge, most box makers resist such standardization. In the real world, we see a compromise. System buses tend to be proprietary and not adherent to any published, open standards. I/O buses to connect peripherals do tend to conform to standards, however. For example, *peripheral component interchange (PCI)* is an open standard for I/O buses. Most box makers will support PCI buses and provide internal *bridges* to connect the PCI bus to the system bus (see Figure 10.7).

Some bus designs may electrically share the lines for multiple functions. For example, the PCI bus uses the same 32 wires for both addresses and data. The Command lines

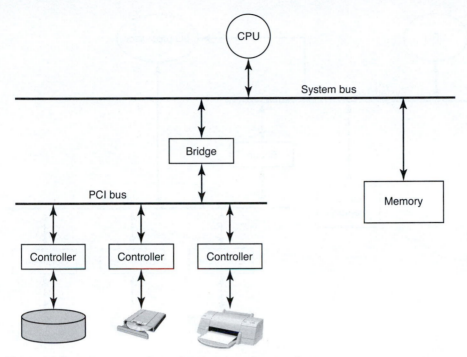

Figure 10.7   Coexistence of standard buses and system buses.

The bridge connects the internal system bus of the CPU to standard buses like PCI.

and the details of the protocol determine whether these wires carry data or addresses at any point in time.

An important consideration in the design of buses is the control regime. Buses may operate in a *synchronous* fashion. In this case, a common *bus clock* line (similar to the CPU clock) orchestrates the protocol action on individual devices. Buses may also operate in an *asynchronous* fashion. Here, the bus *master* initiates a bus action; the bus action completes when the *slave* responds with a reply. This *master–slave* relationship obviates the need for a bus clock. To increase bus utilization, high-performance computer systems use *split transaction buses*. In this scenario, several independent conversations can simultaneously proceed. This complicates the design considerably in the interest of increasing the bus throughput. Such topics are the purview of more advanced courses in computer architecture.

10.5 I/O Processor

In very high-performance systems used in enterprise-level applications such as web servers and database servers, *I/O processors* decouple the I/O chores from the main processor. An I/O processor takes a *chain* of commands for a set of devices and carries them out without intervention from or to the main processor. The I/O processor reduces the number of interruptions that the main processor has to endure. The main processor sets up an I/O program in shared memory (see Figure 10.8) and starts up the I/O processor. The I/O processor completes the program and then interrupts the main processor.

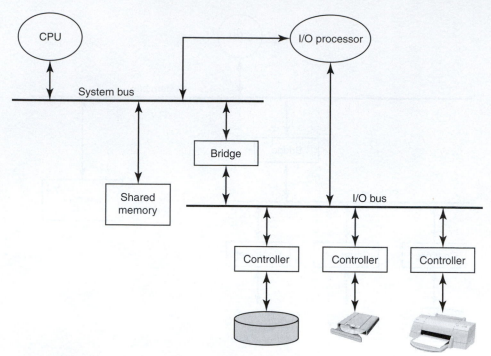

Figure 10.8 The I/O processor absorbs the management chores associated with I/O to ensure minimum disruption of the main processor's computational work.

IBM popularized I/O processors in the era of mainframes. As it turns out, even today mainframes are popular for large enterprise servers. IBM gave these I/O processors the name *channels*. A *multiplexer channel* controls slow-speed character-oriented devices such as a bank of terminals or displays. A *block multiplexer channel* controls several medium-speed block-oriented devices (*stream-oriented devices*, as we refer to them in this chapter) such as tape drives. A *selector channel* services a single high-speed stream-oriented device such as a disk.

An I/O processor is functionally similar to a DMA controller. However, it is at a higher level because it can execute a series of commands (via an I/O program) from the CPU. On the other hand, the DMA controller works in *slave* mode, handling one command at a time from the CPU.

10.6 Device Driver

The device driver is a part of the operating system, and there is a device driver for controlling each device in the computer system. Figure 10.9 shows the structure of the system software—specifically, the relationship between the device drivers and the rest of the operating system, such as the CPU scheduler, the I/O scheduler, and the memory manager.

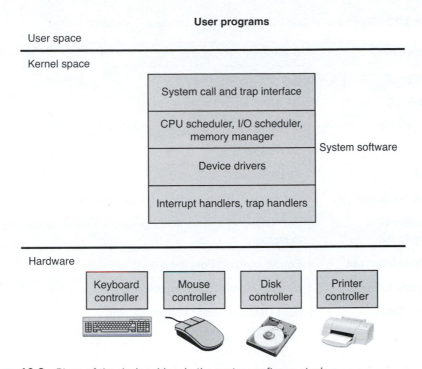

Figure 10.9   Place of the device driver in the system software stack.

The device driver interfaces with the I/O scheduler as part of the operating system.

The specifics of the device driver software depend on the characteristics of the device that the software controls. For example, a keyboard driver may use interrupt-driven programmed I/O for data transfer between the keyboard controller and the CPU. On the other hand, the device driver for the hard drive (disk) would set up the descriptors for a DMA transfer between the disk controller and the memory and await an interrupt that indicates completion of the data transfer. You can see the power of abstraction at work here. It does not really matter what the details of the device are, as far as the device driver is concerned. For example, the device could be some slow-speed device such as a keyboard or a mouse. As far as the device driver is concerned, it is simply executing code similar to the pseudo-code we discussed, in Section 10.2, for moving the data from the device register in the controller to the CPU. Similarly, the high-speed device may be a disk, a scanner, or a video camera. As for the data movement, the device driver for such high-speed devices does pretty much the same thing as the pseudo-code we discussed in Section 10.3, namely, set up the descriptor for the DMA transfer and let the DMA controller associated with the device take charge. Of course, the device driver needs to take care of control functions specific to each device. As should be evident by now, there is an intimate relationship between the device controller and the device driver.

Table 10.1 Summary of Commands for a PTZ Camera Controller

Command	Controller Action
Pan (± □)	Pan the camera view by ± □
Tilt (± □)	Tilt camera position by ± □
Zoom (±z)	Zoom camera focus by ±z
Start	Start camera
Stop	Stop camera
Memory buffer (M)	Set memory buffer address for data transfer to M
Number of frames (N)	Set number of frames (N) to be captured and transferred to memory
Enable interrupt	Enable interrupt from the device
Disable interrupt	Disable interrupt from the device
Start DMA	Start DMA data transfer from camera

10.6.1 An Example

As a concrete example, consider a device driver for a pan-tilt-zoom (PTZ) camera. The device controller may provide a memory-mapped command register for the CPU to specify the control functions, such as the zoom level, tilt level, and x-y coordinates of the space in front of the camera, for focusing the camera view. Similarly, the controller may provide commands to start and stop the camera. In addition to possessing these commands for carrying out such control functions, the controller may implement a DMA facility for the data transfer. Table 10.1 summarizes the capabilities of the device controller for a PTZ camera.

A device driver for such a device may consist of the following modules, shown as pseudo-code:

```
// device driver: camera
// The device driver performs several functions:
//    control_camera_position;
//    convey_DMA_parameters;
//    start/stop data transfer;
//    interrupt_handler;
//    error handling and reporting;
// Control camera position
camera_position_control(angle pan_angle; angle tilt_angle; int z)
{
    pan(pan_angle);
```

```
        tilt(tilt_angle);
        zoom(z);
}

// Set up DMA parameters for data transfer
camera_DMA_parameters(address mem_buffer;int num_frames)
{
        memory_buffer(mem_buffer);
        capture_frames(num_frames);
}

// Start DMA transfer
camera_start_data_transfer()
{
        start_camera();
        start_DMA();
}

// Stop DMA transfer
camera_stop_data_transfer();
{
        // automatically aborts data transfer
        // if camera is stopped;
        stop_camera();
}

// Enable interrupts from the device
camera_enable_interrupt()
{
        enable_interrupt();
}


// Disable interrupts from the device
camera_disable_interrupt()
{
        disable_interrupt();
}

// Device interrupt handler
camera_interrupt_handler()
{
        // This will be coded similar to any
        // interrupt handler we have seen in
        // Chapter 4.
        //
        // The upshot of interrupt handling may be
        // to deliver "events" to the upper layers
        // of the system software (see Figure 10.9)
```

```
        // which may be one of the following:
        //          - normal I/O request completion
        //          - device errors for the I/O request
        //
    }
```

This simplistic treatment of a device driver is meant to give you the confidence that writing such a piece of software is a straightforward exercise similar to any programming assignment. We should point out that modern devices might be much more sophisticated. For example, a modern PTZ camera may incorporate the device controller in the camera itself so that the level of interface presented to the computer is much higher. Similarly, the camera may plug directly into the local area network (we cover more on networking in Chapter 13), so communicating with the device may be similar to communicating with a peer computer on a local area network, using the network protocol stack.

The main point to take away from this pseudo-code is that the code for a device driver is straightforward. From your programming experience, you already know that writing any program requires taking care of corner cases (such as checking array bounds) and dealing with exceptions (such as checking the return codes on system calls). Device driver code is no different. What makes device driver code more interesting—or more challenging, depending on your point of view—is that a number of things could happen that may have nothing to do with the logic of the device driver code. It is possible to plan for some of these situations in the device driver code. Examples include the following:

1. The parameters specified in the command to the controller are illegal (such as illegal values for pan, tilt, zoom, and illegal memory address for data transfer).

2. The device is already in use by some other program.

3. The device is not responding due to some reason (e.g., device is not powered on, device is malfunctioning, etc.).

Some of the situations may be totally unplanned for and could occur simply because of "human in the loop." Examples include these:

1. The device is unplugged from the computer while data transfer is going on.

2. The power cord for the device is unplugged while the data transfer is going on.

3. The device starts malfunctioning during data transfer (e.g., someone accidentally knocks the camera off its moorings, etc.).

10.7 Peripheral Devices

Historically, I/O devices have been grouped into *character-oriented*[1] and *block-oriented* devices. Dot matrix printers, cathode ray terminals (CRT), and teletypewriters are examples of the former. The input/output from these devices happen a character at a time. Due to the relative slowness of these devices, programmed I/O (PIO) is a viable

---

1. We introduced the terms *character-oriented* and *block-oriented* earlier, in Section 10.5, without formally defining these terms.

method of data transfer to/from such devices from/to the computer system. A hard drive (disk), a CD-RW, and an MP3 player are examples of block-oriented devices. As the name suggests, such devices move a block of data to/from the device from/to the computer system. For example, once a laser printer starts printing a page, it continually needs the data for that page, since there is no way to pause the laser printer in the middle of printing a page. The same is true of a magnetic tape drive. It reads or writes a block of data at a time from the magnetic tape. Data transfers from such devices are subject to the data overrun problem that we mentioned in Section 10.1.1. Therefore, DMA is the only viable way of effecting data transfers between such devices and the computer system.

Table 10.2 summarizes the devices typically found in a modern computer system, their data rates (circa 2008), and the efficacy of programmed I/O versus DMA. The

Table 10.2 A Snapshot of Data Rates of Computer Peripherals[7]

Device	Input/Output	Human in the Loop	Data Rate (Circa 2008)	PIO	DMA
Keyboard	Input	Yes	5–10 bytes/sec	X	
Mouse	Input	Yes	80–200 bytes/sec	X	
Graphics display	Output	No	200–350 MB/sec		X
Disk (hard drive)	Input/output	No	100–200 MB/sec		X
Network (LAN)	Input/output	No	1 G-bit/sec		X
Modem[2]	Input/output	No	1–8 M-bit/sec		X
Inkjet printer[3]	Output	No	20–40 KB/sec	X[4]	X
Laser printer[5]	Output	No	200–400 KB/sec		X
Voice (microphone/speaker)[6]	Input/output	Yes	10 bytes/sec	X	
Audio (music)	Output	No	4–500 KB/sec		X
Flash memory	Input/output	No	10–50 MB/sec		X
CD-RW	Input/output	No	10–20 MB/sec		X
DVD-R	Input	No	10–20 MB/sec		X

2. Slow-speed modems of yesteryears, with data rates of 2400 bits/sec, may have been amenable to PIO with interrupts. However, modern cable modems that support upstream data rates in excess of 1 M-bits/sec, and downstream bandwidth in excess of 8 M-bits/sec, require DMA transfer to avoid data loss.

3. This assumes an Inkjet print speed of 20 pages per min (ppm) for text and 2–4 ppm for graphics.

4. Inkjet technology allows pausing printing while awaiting data from the computer. Since the data rate is slow enough, it is conceivable to use PIO for this device.

5. This assumes a laser print speed of 40 ppm for text and about 4–8 ppm for graphics.

6. Typically, speakers are in the range of outputting 120 words/minute.

7. Many thanks to Yale Patt, UT-Austin, and his colleague, for shedding light on the speed of peripheral devices.

second column signifies whether a "human in the loop" influences the data rate from the device. Devices such as a keyboard and a mouse work at human speeds. For example, a typical typewriting speed of 300–600 characters/minute translates to a keyboard input rate of 5–10 bytes/second. Similarly, moving a mouse generating 10–20 events/second translates to an input rate of 80–200 bytes/second. A processor could easily handle such data rates without data loss by using programmed I/O (with either polling or interrupt). A graphics display found in most modern computer systems has a frame buffer in the device controller that is updated by the device driver using DMA transfer. For a graphics display, (1) a screen resolution of 1600 × 1200, (2) a screen refresh rate of 60 Hz, and (3) 24 bits per pixel together yield a data rate of over 300 MB/sec. A music CD holds over 600 MB of data with a playtime of 1 hour. A movie DVD holds over 4 GB of data with a playtime of 2 hours. Both these technologies allow faster-than-real-time reading of data from the media. For example, a CD allows reading at 50 × real time, whereas a DVD allows reading at 20 × real time, resulting in the data rates shown. It should be noted that technology changes continuously. Therefore, this table should be taken as a snapshot of technology, circa 2008, just as a way of understanding how computer peripherals may be interfaced with the CPU.

10.8 Disk Storage

We will study the disk as a concrete example of an important peripheral device. Disk drives are the result of a progression of technology that started with magnetically recording analog data onto wire. This led to recording data onto a magnetic coating applied to Mylar tape. Tapes allowed only sequential access to the recorded data. To increase the data transfer rate, as well as to allow random access, magnetic recording transitioned to a rotating drum. The next step in the evolution of magnetic recording was the disk.

Modern disk drives typically consist of some number of *platters* of a lightweight nonferromagnetic metal coated with a ferromagnetic material on both the top and bottom *surfaces* (see Figure 10.10), thus providing both surfaces for storing data. A central spindle gangs these platters together and rotates them at a very high speed (~15,000 RPM in state-of-the-art high-capacity drives). There is an array of magnetic *read/write heads*, one per surface. The heads do not touch the surfaces. A microscopic air gap (measured in nanometers and tinier than a smoke or dust particle) between the head and the surface allows the movement of the head over the surface, without physical contact with the surface. An *arm* connects each head to a common *shaft,* as shown in the figure. The shaft, the arms, and the attached heads form the *head assembly*. The arms are mechanically fused together to the shaft to form a single aligned structure, such that all the heads can be moved, in unison (like a swing door), in and out of the disk. Thus, all the heads simultaneously line up on their respective surfaces at the *same* radial position.

Depending on the granularity of the *actuator* that controls the motion of the head assembly, and the *recording density* allowed by the technology, this arrangement leads to configuring each recording surface into *tracks,* where each track is at a certain predefined radial distance from the center of the disk. As the name suggests, a *track* is a circular band of magnetic recording material on the platter. Further, each track consists of

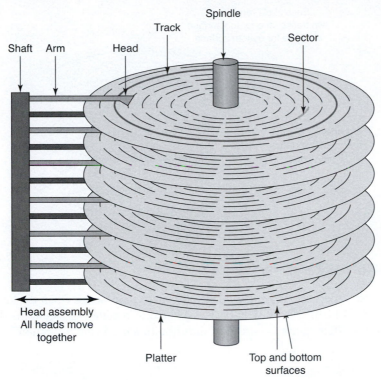

Figure 10.10 Magnetic disk.

sectors. A sector is a contiguous recording of bytes of information, fixed in size, and forms the basic *unit of recording* on the disk. In other words, a sector is the smallest unit of information that can be read or written to the disk. Sensors around the periphery of the disk platters demarcate the sectors. The set of corresponding tracks on all the surfaces form a *logical cylinder* (see Figure 10.11). The cylinder is an aggregation of the corresponding tracks on all the surfaces. The reason for identifying cylinder as a logical entity will become evident shortly when we discuss the latencies involved in accessing the disk and performing I/O operations. The entire disk (platters, head assembly, and sensors) is vacuum-sealed because even the tiniest of dust particles on the surface of the platters will cause the disk to fail.

Tracks are concentric bands on the surface of the disk platters. Naturally, the outer track has a larger circumference, compared with the inner track. Therefore, the outer sectors have a larger footprint, compared with the inner ones (see Figure 10.12(a)). As we mentioned, a sector has a fixed size in terms of recorded information. To reconcile the larger sector footprint and the fixed sector size in the outer tracks, earlier disk technology took the approach of reducing the recording density in the outer tracks. This resulted in underutilizing the available space on the disk.

To overcome this problem of underutilization, modern disk drives use a technology called *zoned bit recording* (ZBR) that keeps the footprint of the sectors roughly constant

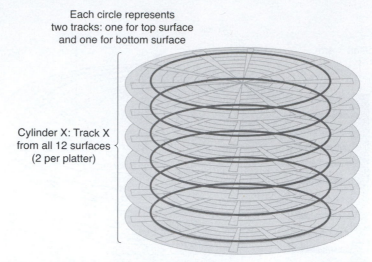

Each circle represents
two tracks: one for top surface
and one for bottom surface

Cylinder X: Track X
from all 12 surfaces
(2 per platter)

Figure 10.11   A logical cylinder for a disk with 6 platters.

on the entire surface. However, the outer tracks have more sectors than the inner ones (see Figure 10.12(b)). The disk surface is divided into zones; tracks in the different zones have different numbers of sectors, thus resulting in a better utilization.

Let

p – number of platters,

n – number of surfaces per platter (1 or 2),

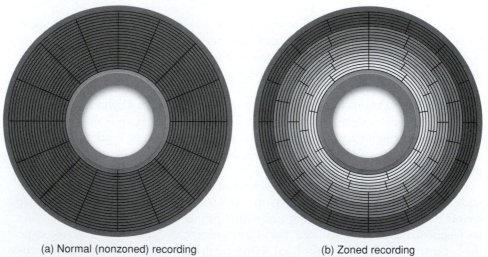

(a) Normal (nonzoned) recording   (b) Zoned recording

Figure 10.12   Difference between nonzoned and zoned recording.[8]

---

8. Picture source: http://www.pcguide.com/ref/hdd/geom/tracksZBR-c.html. © Charles M. Kozierok/ The PC Guide, PCGuide.com.

t – number of tracks per surface,

s – number of sectors per track, and

b – number of bytes per sector.

The total capacity of the disk, assuming nonzoned recording, is

$$\text{Capacity} = (p * n * t * s * b) \text{ bytes} \qquad (1)$$

With zoned recording,

z – number of zones,

t_{zi} – number of tracks at zone z_i, and

s_{zi} – number of sectors per track at zone z_i.

The total capacity of the disk with zoned recording is

$$\text{Capacity} = (p * n * (\Sigma (t_{zi} * s_{zi}), \text{ for } 1 \leq i \leq z) * b) \text{ bytes} \qquad (2)$$

Example 10.1

Assume the following specifications for a disk drive:

- 256 bytes per sector
- 12 sectors per track
- 20 tracks per surface
- 3 platters

a. What is the total capacity of such a drive in bytes, assuming normal recording?

b. Assume a zoned bit recording with the following specifications:

- 3 zones
  - Zone 3 (outermost): 8 tracks, 18 sectors per track
  - Zone 2: 7 tracks, 14 sectors per track
  - Zone 1: 5 tracks, 12 sectors per track

What is the total capacity of this drive with the zoned-bit recording?

Answer:

a. Total capacity

= number of platters * surfaces/platter * tracks/surface * sectors/track * bytes/sector

= 3 * 2 * 20 * 12 * 256 bytes

= **360 KB (where K = 1024)**.

b. Capacity of Zone 3 =

= number of platters * surfaces/platter * tracks in zone 3 * sectors/track * bytes/sector

= 3 * 2 * 8 * 18 * 256

= 216 KB.

Capacity of Zone 2 =

= number of platters * surfaces/platter * tracks in zone 2 * sectors/track * bytes/sector

= 3 * 2 * 7 * 14 * 256

= 147 KB.

Capacity of Zone 1 =

= number of platters * surfaces/platter * tracks in zone 1 * sectors/track * bytes/sector

= 3 * 2 * 5 * 12 * 256

= 90 KB.

Total capacity = sum of all zonal capacities = 216 + 147 + 90

= 453 KB (where K = 1024).

An important side effect of ZBR is the difference in transfer rates between outer and inner tracks. The outer track has more sectors, compared with the inner ones; and the angular velocity of the disk is the same, independent of the track being read. Therefore, the head reads more sectors per revolution of the disk when it is over an outer track, compared with an inner track. In allocating space on the disk, there is a tendency to use the outer tracks first, before using the inner tracks.

The address of a particular data block on the disk is a triple: {*cylinder#, surface#, sector#*}. Reading or writing information to or from the disk requires several steps. First, the head assembly has to move to the specific cylinder. The time to accomplish this movement is the *seek time*. We can see that seeking to a particular cylinder is the same as seeking to any specific track in that cylinder, since a cylinder is just a logical aggregation of the corresponding tracks on all the surfaces (see Figure 10.11). Second, the disk must spin to bring the required sector under the head. This time spent spinning is the *rotational latency*. Third, data from the selected surface are read and transferred to the controller as the sector moves under the head. This period is the *data transfer time*.

Of the three components to the total time for reading or writing to a disk, the seek time is the most expensive, followed by the rotational latency, and last, the data transfer time. Typical values for seek time and average rotational latency are 8 ms and 4 ms, respectively. These times are high, due to the electromechanical nature of the disk subsystem.

Let us understand how to compute the data transfer time. Note that the disk does not stop for reading or writing. Just as in a VCR, the tape is continuously moving while the head is reading and displaying the video on the TV, the disk is continually spinning and the head is reading (or writing) the bits off the surface as they pass under the head. The data transfer time is derivable from the rotational latency and the recording density of the media. You are perhaps wondering whether reading or writing the media itself does not cost anything. The answer is, it does; however, this time is purely electromagnetic and is negligible in comparison with the electromechanical delay caused by the disk's spinning to enable all the bits of a given sector to be read.

We refer to the *data transfer rate* as the amount of data transferred per unit time, once the desired sector is under the magnetic reading head. Circa 2008, data transfer rates were in the range of 200–300 MB/sec.

Let

r – rotational speed of the disk in Revolutions Per Minute (RPM),

s – number of sectors per track, and

b – number of bytes per sector.

Time for one revolution = $60/r$ seconds.

Amount of data read in one revolution = $s * b$ bytes.

The data transfer rate of the disk is

(Amount of data in track)/(time for one revolution) = $(s * b)/(60/r)$.

$$\text{Data transfer rate} = (s * b * r)/60 \text{ bytes/second} \qquad (3)$$

Example 10.2

Assume the following specifications for a disk drive:

- 512 bytes per sector
- 400 sectors per track
- 6000 tracks per surface
- 3 platters
- Rotational speed 15000 RPM
- Normal recording

What is the transfer rate of the disk?

Answer:

Time for one rotation = 1/15000 minutes
                      = 4 ms.

The amount of data in track = sectors per track * bytes per sector

$$= 400 * 512$$

$$= 204{,}800 \text{ bytes}.$$

Since the head reads one track in one revolution of the disk, the transfer rate

$$= \text{data in one track/time per revolution}$$

$$= (204{,}800/4) * 1000 \text{ bytes/sec}$$

$$= \mathbf{51{,}200{,}000 \text{ bytes/sec}}.$$

The seek time and rotational latency experienced by a specific request depend on the exact location of the data on the disk. Once the head is positioned on the desired sector, the time to read/write the data is deterministic, governed by the rotational speed of the disk. It is often convenient to think of *average seek time* and *average rotational latency* in performance estimation of disk drives, to satisfy requests. Assuming a uniform distribution of requests over all the tracks, the average seek time is the mean of the observed times to seek to the first track and the last track of the disk. Similarly, assuming a uniform distribution of requests over all the sectors in a given track, the average rotational latency is the mean of the access times to each sector in the track. This is half the rotational latency of the disk.[9]

Let

a – average seek time in seconds,

r – rotational speed of the disk in revolutions per minute (RPM), and

s – number of sectors per track.

$$\text{Rotational latency} = 60/r \text{ seconds} \qquad\qquad (4)$$

$$\text{Average rotational latency} = (60/(r * 2)) \text{ seconds} \qquad\qquad (5)$$

Once the read head is over the desired sector, then the time to read that sector is entirely decided by the RPM of the disk.

Sector read time = rotational latency/number of sectors per track.

$$\text{Sector read time} = (60/(r * s)) \text{ seconds} \qquad\qquad (6)$$

To read a random sector on the disk, the head has to seek to that particular sector, and then the head has to wait for the desired sector to appear under it before it can read the sector. Thus, there are three components to the time to read a random sector:

• Time to get to the desired track

$$= \text{Average seek time}$$

$$= a \text{ seconds}.$$

---

9. In the best case, the desired sector is already under the head when the desired track is reached; in the worst case, the head just missed the desired sector and waits for an entire revolution.

- Time to get the head over the desired sector

$$= \text{Average rotational latency}$$
$$= (60/(r * 2)) \text{ seconds.}$$

- Time to read a sector

$$= \text{Sector read time}$$
$$= (60/(r * s)) \text{ seconds.}$$

> Time to read a random sector on the disk
> $$= \text{Time to get to the desired track}$$
> $$+ \text{ Time to get the head over the desired sector} \qquad (7)$$
> $$+ \text{ Time to read a sector}$$
> $$= a + (60/(r * 2)) + (60/(r * s)) \text{ seconds}$$

Example 10.3

Assume the following specifications for a disk drive:

- 256 bytes per sector
- 12 sectors per track
- 20 tracks per surface
- 3 platters
- Average seek time of 20 ms
- Rotational speed 3600 RPM
- Normal recording

a. What would be the time to read 6 contiguous sectors from the same track?
b. What would be the time to read 6 sectors at random?

Answer:

a. Average seek time = 20 ms

Rotational latency of the disk

$$= 1/3600 \text{ minutes}$$
$$= 16.66 \text{ ms.}$$

Average rotational latency

$$= \text{rotational latency}/2$$
$$= 16.66/2.$$

Time to read 1 sector

$$= \text{rotational latency/number of sectors per track}$$
$$= 16.66/12 \text{ ms}.$$

To read 6 contiguous sectors on the same track, the time taken

$$= 6 * (16.66/12)$$
$$= 16.66/2.$$

Time to read 6 contiguous sectors from the disk

$$= \text{average seek time} + \text{average rotational latency} + \text{time to read 6 sectors}$$
$$= 20 \text{ ms} + 16.66/2 + 16.66/2$$
$$= \mathbf{36.66 \text{ ms}}.$$

b. For the second case, we will have to seek and read each sector separately. Therefore, each sector read will take

$$= \text{average seek time} + \text{average rotational latency} + \text{time to read 1 sector}$$
$$= 20 + 16.66/2 + 16.66/12.$$

Thus, the total time to read 6 random sectors

$$= 6 * (20 + 16.66/2 + 16.66/12)$$
$$= \mathbf{178.31 \text{ ms}}.$$

10.8.1 The Saga of Disk Technology

The discussion until now has been kept simple for the sake of understanding the basic terminologies in disk subsystems. The disk technology has seen an exponential growth in recording densities, for the past two decades. For example, circa 1980, 20 MB was considered significant disk storage capacity. Such disks had about 10 platters and were bulky. The drive itself looked like a clothes washer (see Figure 10.13), and the media were usually removable from the drive itself.

Circa 2008, a desktop PC came with several-hundred gigabytes of storage capacity. Such drives had the media integrated into them. Also circa 2008, small disks for the desktop PC market (capacity roughly 100 GB to 1 TB, 3.5″ diameter) had two to four platters, rotation speed in the range of 7200 RPM, 5000 to 10000 tracks per surface, several hundred sectors per track, and 256 to 512 bytes per sector (see Figure 10.14).

Whereas we have presented fairly simple ways to compute the transfer rates of disks and a model of accessing the disk based on the cylinder-track-sector concept, modern technology has thrown all these models out of whack. The reason for this is fairly simple. Internally, the disk remains the same as pictured in Figure 10.14. Sure, the recording densities and the RPM have increased; and consequently, the size of the platter, as well as the number of platters in a drive, have dramatically decreased. But

(a) Removable media   (b) Disk drive

Figure 10.13   Magnetic media and disk drive.[10]

Figure 10.14   PC hard drive (circa 2008).[11]

---

10. Picture source: Fig. 10.13(a)–© Barry Demchak; 10.13(b)–Photograph courtesy of the Charles Babbage Institute, University of Minnesota, Minneapolis.

11. Picture of a Western Digital Hard Drive: variable RPM, 1 TB capacity, source: http://www.wdc.com. Courtesy Western Digital Corporation.

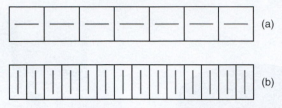

Figure 10.15   Disk recording: (a) longitudinal recording; (b) PMR.

these changes in themselves do not change the basic model of disk access and account-ing for transfer times. The real changes are in three areas of advancement: the drive electronics, the recording technology, and interfaces.

The first advance is in the internal drive electronics. The simple model assumes that the disk rotates at a constant speed. The head moves to the desired track and waits for the desired sector to appear under it. This is a waste of power. Therefore, modern drives vary the RPM, depending on the sector that needs to be read, ensuring that the sector appears under the head just as the head assembly reaches the desired track.

Another advance is in the recording strategy. Figure 10.15 shows a cross section of the magnetic surface, to illustrate this advance in recording technology. Traditionally, the medium records the data bits by magnetizing the medium horizontally parallel to the magnetic surface. This technique is sometimes referred to as *longitudinal* recording (Figure 10.15(a)). A recent innovation in the recording technology is the *perpendicular magnetic recording* (PMR), which, as the name suggests, records the data bits by mag-netizing the medium perpendicular to the magnetic surface (Figure 10.15(b)). Delving into the electromagnetic properties of these two recording techniques is beyond the scope of this book. The intent here is to get across the point that this new technology greatly enhances the recording density achievable per unit area of the magnetic surface on the disk. Figure 10.15 illustrates this. It can be seen that PMR results in doubling the recording density and, hence, achieves larger storage capacity than longitudinal record-ing for a given disk specification.

The third change is in the computational capacity that has been designed into modern drives. Today, a hard drive provides much more intelligent interfaces for con-necting to the rest of the system. Gone are the days when a disk controller sits outside the drive. Today the drive is integrated into the controller. You may have heard terms such as *IDE (integrated drive electronics)*, *ATA (advanced technology attachment)*, *SATA (serial advanced technology attachment)*, and *SCSI (small computer systems interface)*. These are some of the names for modern intelligent interfaces.

The concept is that these advanced interfaces reduce the amount of work the CPU has to do in ordering its requests for data from the disk. Internal to the drive is a micro-processor that decides how logically contiguous blocks (which would be physically contiguous, as well, in the old world order) may be physically laid out to provide the best access time to the data on the disk. In addition to the microprocessors, the drives include data buffers into which disk sectors may be preread in readiness for serving re-quests from the CPU. The microprocessor maintains an internal queue of requests from the CPU and may decide to reorder the requests in order to maximize performance.

Much of the latency in a disk drive arises from the mechanical motions involved in reading and writing. A discussion of the electromechanical aspects of disk technology is beyond the scope of this book. Our focus is on how the system software uses the disk drive for storing information. The storage allocation schemes should try to reduce the seek time and the rotational latency for accessing information. Since we know that seek time is the most expensive component of disk transfer latency, we can now elaborate on the concept of a logical cylinder. If we need to store a large file that may span several tracks, should we allocate the file to *adjacent tracks on the same surface* or to *corresponding (same) tracks of a given cylinder*? The answer to this question has become quite complex with modern disk technology. As a first order, we will observe that the former will result in multiple seeks to access different parts of the given file, whereas the latter will result in a single seek to access any part of a given file. We can easily see that the latter allocation would be preferred. This is the reason for recognizing a logical cylinder in the context of the disk subsystem. Having said that, we should observe that, because the number of platters in a disk has been reducing and is typically one or two, the importance of the cylinder concept is diminishing.

File systems is the topic of the next chapter, wherein we elaborate on storage allocation schemes.

From the system throughput point of view, the operating system should schedule operations on the disk in such a manner as to reduce the overall mechanical motion of the disk. In modern drives, this kind of reordering of requests happens within the drive itself. Disk scheduling is the topic of discussion in the next section.

10.9 Disk Scheduling Algorithms

A device driver for a disk embodies algorithms for efficiently scheduling the disk to satisfy the requests that it receives from the operating system. As we saw in Chapters 7 and 8, the memory manager component of the operating system may make its own requests for disk I/O to handle demand paging. As we will see in Chapter 11, disk drives host file systems for end users. Thus, the operating system (via system calls) may issue disk I/O requests in response to users' requests for opening, closing, and reading/writing files. Thus, at any point in time, the device driver for a disk may be entertaining a number of I/O requests from the operating system (see Figure 10.16). The operating system queues these requests in the order of generation. The device driver schedules these requests, commensurate with the disk-scheduling algorithm in use. Each request will name, among other things, the specific track in which the data resides on the disk. Since seek time is the most expensive component of I/O to or from the disk, the primary objective of disk scheduling is to minimize seek time.

We will assume for this discussion that we are dealing with a single disk that has received a number of requests and must determine the most efficient algorithm to process

Figure 10.16   Disk request queue in the order of arrival.

those requests. We will further assume that there is a single head and that seek time is proportional to the number of tracks crossed. Finally, we will assume a random distribution of data on the disk, and that reads and writes take equal amounts of time.

The typical measures of how well the different algorithms stack up against one another are the *average waiting time* for a request, *the variance in wait time,* and the overall *throughput. Average wait time* and *throughput* are self-explanatory terms, which you may recall from our discussion on CPU scheduling in Chapter 6. They are system-centric measures of performance. From an individual-request point of view, variance in waiting time is more meaningful. This measure tells us how much an individual request's waiting time can deviate from the average. Similar to CPU scheduling, the *response time, or turnaround time,* is a useful metric from the point of view of an individual request.

In Table 10.3, t_i, w_i, and e_i, are the turnaround time, wait time, and actual I/O service time, for an I/O request i, respectively. Most of these metrics and their mathematical notation are similar to the ones given in Chapter 6 for CPU scheduling.

Table 10.3 Summary of Performance Metrics

Name	Notation	Units	Description
Throughput	n/T	Jobs/sec	System-centric metric quantifying the number of I/O requests n executed in time interval T
Avg. Turnaround time (t_{avg})	$(t_1 + t_2 + \cdots + t_n)/n$	Seconds	System-centric metric quantifying the average time it takes for a job to complete
Avg. Waiting time (w_{avg})	$((t_1 - e_1) + (t_2 - e_2) + \cdots + (t_n - e_n))/n$ or $(w_1 + w_2 + \cdots + w_n)/n$	Seconds	System-centric metric quantifying the average waiting time that an I/O request experiences
Response time/ turnaround time	t_i	Seconds	User-centric metric quantifying the turnaround time for a specific I/O request i
Variance in Response time	$E[(t_i - t_{avg})^2]$	Seconds^2	User-centric metric that quantifies the statistical variance of the actual response time (t_i) experienced by an I/O request i from the expected value (t_{avg})
Variance in Wait time	$E[(w_i - w_{avg})^2]$	Seconds^2	User-centric metric that quantifies the statistical variance of the actual wait time (w_i) experienced by an I/O request i from the expected value (w_{avg})
Starvation	-	-	User-centric qualitative metric that signifies denial of service to a particular I/O request or a set of I/O requests due to some intrinsic property of the I/O scheduler

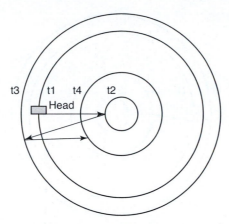

Figure 10.17   Movement of disk head with FCFS.

We review five different algorithms for disk scheduling. To make the discussion simple and concrete, we will assume that the disk has 200 tracks numbered 0 to 199 (with 0 being the outermost and 199 being the innermost). The head in its fully retracted position is on track 0. The head assembly extends to its maximum span from its resting position when it is on track 199.

You will see a similarity between these disk-scheduling algorithms and some of the CPU scheduling algorithms we saw in Chapter 6.

10.9.1 First-Come-First-Served (FCFS)

As the name suggests, this algorithm services the requests by the order of arrival. In this sense, it is similar to the FCFS algorithm for CPU scheduling. The algorithm has the nice property that a request incurs the least variance in waiting time, regardless of the track from which it requests I/O. However, that is the only good news. From the system's perspective, this algorithm will result in poor throughput for most common workloads. Figure 10.17 illustrates how the disk head may have to swing back and forth across the disk surface to satisfy the requests in an FCFS schedule, especially when the FCFS requests are to tracks that are far apart.

10.9.2 Shortest Seek Time First (SSTF)

This scheduling policy is similar to the SJF processor scheduling. The basic idea is to service the tracks that lead to minimizing the head movement (see Figure 10.18). As with SJF for processor scheduling, SSTF minimizes the average wait time for a given set of requests and results in good throughput. However, also similar to SJF, it has the potential of starving requests that happen to be far away from the current cluster of requests. Compared with FCFS, this schedule has high variance.

10.9.3 SCAN (Elevator Algorithm)

This algorithm is in tune with the electromechanical properties of the head assembly. The basic idea is as follows: The head moves from its position of rest (track 0) toward

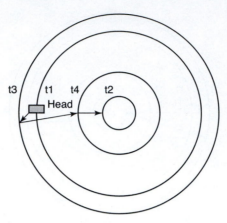

Figure 10.18   Movement of disk head with SSTF.

the innermost track (track 199). As the head moves, the algorithm services the requests that are *en route,* from outermost to innermost track, regardless of the arrival order. Once the head reaches the innermost track, it reverses direction and moves toward the outermost track, once again servicing requests en route. As long as the request queue is not empty, the algorithm continuously repeats this process. Figure 10.19 captures the spirit of this algorithm.

The requests t1, t2, t3, and t4 existed during the forward movement of the head (as in Figure 10.16). Requests t5 and t6 (in that order) appeared after the head reached the innermost track. The algorithm services these requests on the reverse traversal of the head. This algorithm should remind you of what happens when you wait for an

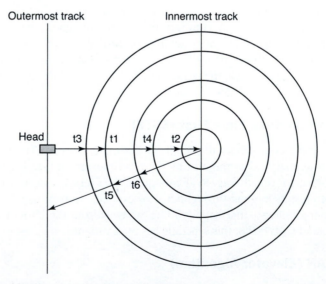

Figure 10.19   Movement of disk head with SCAN.

elevator, which uses a similar algorithm for servicing requests. Hence, the SCAN algorithm is often referred to as the elevator algorithm. SCAN has lower variance in wait time, compared with SSTF, and overall, has an average wait time that is similar to SSTF. Similar to SSTF, SCAN does not preserve the arrival order of the requests. However, SCAN differs from SSTF in one fundamental way. SSTF may starve a given request, arbitrarily. On the other hand, there is an upper bound for SCAN's violation of the first-come-first-served fairness property. The upper bound is the traversal time of the head from one end to the other. Hence, SCAN avoids starvation of requests.

10.9.4 C-SCAN (Circular Scan)

This is a variant of SCAN. The algorithm views the disk surface as logically circular. Hence, once the head reaches the innermost track, the algorithm retracts the head assembly to the position of rest, and the traversal starts all over again. In other words, the algorithm does not service any requests during the traversal of the head in the reverse direction. This is pictorially shown, for the same requests serviced in the SCAN algorithm, in Figure 10.20.

By ignoring requests in the reverse direction, C-SCAN removes the bias that the SCAN algorithm has for requests clustered around the middle tracks of the disk. This algorithm reduces unfairness in servicing requests (notice how it preserves the order of arrival for t5 and t6), and overall, leads to lowering the variance in waiting time, compared with SCAN.

10.9.5 LOOK and C-LOOK

These two policies are similar to SCAN and C-SCAN, respectively, with the exception that if there are no more requests in the direction of head traversal, the head assembly

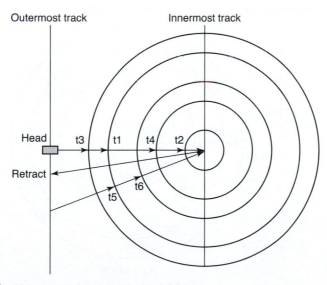

Figure 10.20   Movement of disk head with C-SCAN.

immediately reverses direction. That is, the head assembly does not unnecessarily traverse all the way to the end (in either direction). One can see the similarity to how an elevator works. Because they avoid unnecessary mechanical movement, these policies tend to be even better performers than the SCAN and C-SCAN policies. Even though, historically, SCAN is referred to as the elevator algorithm, LOOK is closer to the servicing pattern observed in most modern-day elevator systems. Figure 10.21 shows the same sequence of requests as in the SCAN and C-SCAN algorithms, for LOOK and C-LOOK

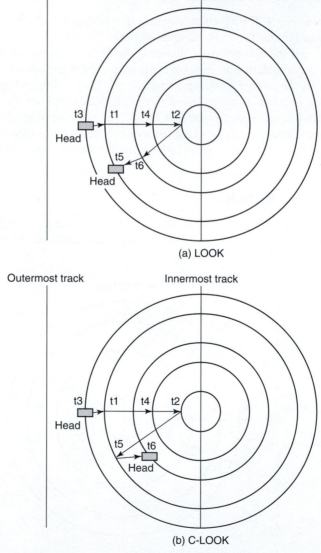

Figure 10.21   Movement of disk head with LOOK and C-LOOK.

algorithms. Note the position of the head at the end of servicing the outstanding requests. The head stops at the last serviced request if there are no further requests. This is the main difference between LOOK and SCAN, and C-LOOK and C-SCAN, respectively.

10.9.6 Disk Scheduling Summary

The choice of the scheduling algorithm depends on a number of factors, including expected layout, the storage allocation policy, and the electromechanical capabilities of the disk drive. Typically, some variant of LOOK or C-LOOK is used for disk scheduling. We covered the other algorithms more for the purpose of presenting a complete discussion than as recommendations of viable choices for implementation in a real system.

As we mentioned in Section 10.8.1, modern disk drives provide very sophisticated interface to the CPU. Thus, the internal layout of the blocks on the drive may not even be visible to the disk device driver, which is part of the operating system. Assuming that the interface allows multiple outstanding requests from the device driver, the disk scheduling algorithms discussed in this section are in the controller itself.

Example 10.4 illustrates the difference in schedule of the various algorithms.

Example 10.4

Assume the following:

Total number of cylinders in the disk	=	200 (numbered 0 to 199)
Current head position	=	cylinder 23
Current requests in order of arrival	=	20, 17, 55, 35, 25, 78, 99

Show the schedule for the various disk scheduling algorithms for the given set of requests.

Answer:

a. Show the schedule for C-LOOK for the given requests:

   25, 35, 55, 78, 99, 17, 20

b. Show the schedule for SSTF:

   25, 20, 17, 35, 55, 78, 99

c. Show the schedule for LOOK:

   25, 35, 55, 78, 99, 20, 17

   d. Show the schedule for SCAN:

      `25, 35, 55, 78, 99, 199, 20, 17, 0`

   e. Show the schedule for FCFS:

      `20, 17, 55, 35, 25, 78, 99`

   f. Show the schedule for C-SCAN:

      `25, 35, 55, 78, 99, 199, 0, 17, 20`

10.9.7 Comparison of the Algorithms

Let us analyze the different algorithms, using the request pattern in Example 10.4. In the order of arrival, we have seven requests: R1 (cylinder 20), R2 (cylinder 17), R3 (cylinder 55), R4 (cylinder 35), R5 (cylinder 25), R6 (cylinder 78), and R7 (cylinder 99).

Let us focus on request R1. We will use the number of tracks traversed as the unit of response time for this comparative analysis. Since the starting position of the head in this example is 23, the response time for R1 for the different algorithms is

- $T_1^{FCFS} = 3$ (R1 gets serviced first);
- $T_1^{SSTF} = 7$ (service R5 first, and then R1);
- $T_1^{SCAN} = 355$ (sum up the head traversal for (d) in the example);
- $T_1^{C-SCAN} = 395$ (sum up the head traversal for (f) in the example);
- $T_1^{LOOK} = 155$ (sum up the head traversal for (c) in the example); and
- $T_1^{C-LOOK} = 161$ (sum up the head traversal for (a) in the example).

Table 10.4 shows a comparison of the response times (in units of head traversal) with respect to the request pattern in Example 10.4, for some chosen disk scheduling algorithms (FCFS, SSTF, and LOOK).

The throughput is computed as the ratio of the number of requests completed to the total number of tracks traversed by the algorithm to complete all the requests.

- FCFS = $7/148 = 0.047$ requests/track-traversal
- SSTF = $7/92 = 0.076$ requests/track-traversal
- LOOK = $7/158 = 0.044$ requests/track-traversal

From the preceding analysis, it would appear that SSTF does the best in terms of average response time and throughput. But this comes at the cost of fairness. (Compare the response times for R5 with respect to earlier request R1–R4 in the column under SSTF). Further, as we observed earlier, SSTF has the potential for starvation. At first glance, it would appear that LOOK has the worst response time of the three in the table. However, there are a few points to note. First, the response times are sensitive to the initial head position and the distribution of requests. Second, it is possible to come up

Table 10.4 Quantitative Comparison of Scheduling Algorithms for Example 10.4

Requests	Response Time		
	FCFS	SSFT	LOOK
R1 (cyl 20)	3	7	155
R2 (cyl 17)	6	10	158
R3 (cyl 55)	44	48	32
R4 (cyl 35)	64	28	12
R5 (cyl 25)	74	2	2
R6 (cyl 78)	127	71	55
R7 (cyl 99)	148	92	76
Average	66.4	36	70

with a pathological example that may be particularly well suited (or by the same token, ill-suited) for a particular algorithm. Third, in this contrived example we started with a request sequence that did not change during the processing of this sequence. In reality, new requests may join the queue that would have an impact on the observed through-put as well as the response time (see Exercise 13).

In general, with uniform distribution of requests on the disk, the average response time of LOOK will be closer to that of SSTF. More important, something that is not apparent from the table is both the time and energy, needed to change the direction of motion of the head assembly, that is inherent in both FCFS and SSTF. This is perhaps the single most important consideration that makes LOOK a more favorable choice for disk scheduling.

Using Example 10.4, it would be a useful exercise for the reader to compare all the disk scheduling algorithms with respect to the other performance metrics that are summarized in Table 10.3.

Over the years, disk-scheduling algorithms have been studied extensively. As we observed earlier (Section 10.8.1), disk drive technology has been advancing rapidly. Due to such advances, it becomes imperative to reevaluate the disk-scheduling algorithms with every new generation of disks.[12] So far, some variant of LOOK has proven to perform the best among all the candidates.

10.10 Solid State Drive

One of the fundamental limitations of the hard disk technology is its electromechanical nature. Over the years, several new storage technologies have threatened to force disk, as the storage unit of choice, into extinction; but they have not succeeded in doing so,

---

12. See for example, http://www.ece.cmu.edu/~ganger/papers/sigmetrics94.pdf.

Figure 10.22   A railroad switch.

primarily due to the low cost per byte of disk storage, compared with these other, newer, and more expensive technologies.

A technology that is threatening the relative monopoly of the hard disk is the *solid state drive (SSD)*. Origins of this technology can be traced back to the *electrically erasable programmable read-only memory (EEPROM)*. In Chapter 3, we introduced ROM as a kind of solid state memory whose contents are *nonvolatile*, i.e., the contents remain unchanged across power cycling. It will be easier to understand this technology with a simple analogy. You have seen a railroad switch, as shown in Figure 10.22. Once the switch is thrown, the incoming track (bottom part of the figure) remains connected to the chosen fork. A ROM works in exactly the same manner.

Figure 10.23 pictures a simple electrical analogy of the railroad switch. If the switch in the middle of the figure is opened, the output is a 1; otherwise, the output is a 0. This is the basic building block of a ROM. The switches are realized by basic logic

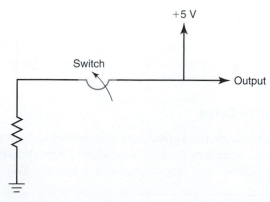

Figure 10.23   An electrical switch.

gates (NAND or NOR). A collection of such switches, packed inside an integrated circuit, is the ROM. Depending on the desired output, a switch can be "programmed" so that the output is a 0 or a 1. This is the reason that such a circuit is referred to as *programmable read-only memory (PROM)*.

A further evolution in this technology allows the bit patterns in the ROM to be electrically erased and reprogrammed to contain a different bit pattern. This is the EEPROM technology. Whereas this technology appears to be very similar to the capability found in a RAM, there is an important difference. The granularity of read/write in a RAM can be whatever we choose it to be. However, due to the electrical properties of the EEPROM technology, erasure in an EEPROM needs to happen a block of bits at a time. Further, such writes take several orders of magnitude more time, compared with reading and writing a RAM. Thus, EEPROM technology cannot be used in place of the DRAM technology. However, this technology, popularized as *flash memory*, has found a place in portable memory cards, and for storage inside embedded devices such as cell phones and iPods.

A reasonable question that may perplex you is why flash memory has not replaced the disk as permanent storage in desktops and laptops. After all, being entirely solid state, this technology does not have the inherent problems of the disk technology (slower access time for data due to the electromechanical nature of the disk).

Three areas where the hard disk still has an edge are density of storage (leading to lower cost per byte), higher read/write bandwidth, and longer life. The last area needs some elaboration. SSD, due to the nature of the technology, has an inherent limitation: Any given area of the storage can be rewritten only a finite number of times. This means that frequent writes to the same block would lead to uneven wear, thus shortening the lifespan of the storage as a whole. Typically, manufacturers of SSD adopt *wear leveling* to avoid this problem. The purpose of wear leveling is to redistribute frequently written blocks to different sections of the storage. This necessitates additional read/write cycles over and beyond the normal workload of the storage system.

Technological advances in SSD are continually challenging these gaps. For example, since 2008, SSD devices with a capacity of 100 GB and transfer rates of 100 MB/second have hit the market place. Several box makers have introduced laptops with SSD as the mass storage for low-end storage needs. However, circa 2010, the cost of SSD-based mass storage is still significantly higher than a comparable disk-based mass storage.

Only time will tell whether the hard drive technology will continue its unique long run as the ultimate answer for massive data storage.

10.11 Evolution of I/O Buses and Device Drivers

With the advent of the PC, connecting peripherals to the computer has taken on a life of its own. While the data rates in Table 10.4 suggest how the devices could be interfaced to the CPU, it is seldom the case that devices are directly interfaced to the CPU. This is because peripherals are made by *third party vendors*[13] a term used in the computer industry to distinguish "box makers" such as IBM, Dell, and Apple from the vendors (e.g., Seagate for disks, Axis for cameras, etc.) who make peripheral devices and device drivers

---

13. We already introduced this term, without defining it, in Section 10.4.

that go with such devices. Such third party vendors are not privy to the internal details of the boxes and, therefore, have to assume that their wares could be interfaced to any box, regardless of the manufacturer. You have heard the term *plug and play*. This refers to a feature that allows any peripheral device to be connected to a computer system without needing any change to the internal organization of the box. This feature has been the primary impetus for the development of standards such as PCI, introduced in Section 10.4.

It is impossible for a modern computer enthusiast not to have heard of such terms as *USB* and *Firewire*. Let us understand what these terms mean. As we mentioned in Section 10.4, the PCI bus uses a 32-bit parallel bus that it multiplexes for address, data, and command. *USB,* which stands for *universal serial bus*, and *Firewire* are two competing standards for *serial* interface of peripherals to the computer. You may wonder why you would want a serial interface to the computer, since a parallel interface would be faster. In fact, if we look back in time, we see that only slow-speed character-oriented devices (such as cathode ray terminal, or CRT, usually referred to as *dumb terminals*) used a serial connection to the computer system.

Well, you know that the speed of the signals on a single wire ultimately is limited by the *speed of light*. The actual data rates, as you can see from Table 10.2, are nowhere near that. Latency of electronic circuitry has been the limiting factor in pumping the bits faster on a single wire. Parallelism helps overcome this limitation and boosts the overall throughput by pumping the bits on parallel wires. However, as technology has been improving, the latency of the circuitry has been reducing as well, allowing signaling to occur at higher frequencies. Under such circumstances, the serial interface offer several advantages over the parallel interface. First, it is smaller and cheaper due to the reduced number of wires and connectors. Second, parallel interfaces suffer from cross talk, at higher speeds, without careful shielding of the parallel wires. On the other hand, with careful wave-shaping and filtering techniques, it is easier to operate serial signaling at higher frequencies. This has led to the situation now where serial interfaces are actually faster than parallel ones.

Thus, it has become the norm to connect high-speed devices serially to the computer system. This was the reason for the development of standards such as USB and Firewire for serially interfacing the peripherals to the computer system. Consequently, you may notice that most modern laptops do not support any parallel ports. Even the parallel printer port has disappeared from laptops, post 2007. Serial interface standards have enhanced the plug-and-play" nature of modern peripheral devices.

You may wonder why there are two competing standards for serial interfaces. This again is indicative of the box makers wanting to capture market share. Microsoft and Intel promoted USB, while Firewire came out of Apple. Today, both these serial interfaces have become industry standards for connecting both slow-speed and high-speed peripherals. USB 1.0 could handle transfer rates up to 1.5 MB/sec and was typically used for aggregating the I/O of slow-speed devices such as the keyboard and mouse. Firewire could support data transfers at speeds up to a 100 MB/sec and was typically used for multimedia consumer electronics devices such as digital camcorders. USB 2.0 supports data rates up to 60 MB/sec, and thus, the distinction between Firewire and USB is getting a bit blurred.

To complete the discussion of I/O buses, we should mention two more enhancements to the I/O architecture that are specific to the PC industry. *AGP,* which stands for *advanced graphics port*, is a specialized, dedicated channel for connecting the 3-D graphics controller card to the motherboard. Sharing the bandwidth available on the PCI bus with other devices was found inadequate for 3-D graphics, especially for supporting interactive games. The demand for higher bandwidth for 3-D graphics led to the evolution of the AGP channel. In recent times, AGP has been largely replaced by *PCI Express* (*PCI-e*), which is a new standard that also provides a dedicated connection between the motherboard and graphics controller. Detailed discussions of the electrical properties of these standards and the finer differences among them are beyond the scope of this book.

10.11.1 Dynamic Loading of Device Drivers

Just as the devices are plug and play, so are the device drivers for controlling them. Consider for a moment the device driver for a digital camera. The driver for this device need not be part of your system software (see Figure 10.9) all the time. In modern operating systems such as Linux and Microsoft Vista, the device drivers get "dynamically" linked into the system software when the corresponding device comes online. The operating system recognizes (via device interrupt) a new device when it comes online (e.g., when you plug your camera or flash memory stick into a USB port). The operating system looks through its list of device drivers and identifies the one that corresponds to the hardware that came online. (Most likely, the device vendor in cooperation with the operating system vendor developed the device driver.) It then dynamically links and loads the device driver into the memory for controlling the device. Of course, if the device plugged in does not have a matching driver, then the operating system cannot do much except to ask the user to provide a driver for the new hardware device plugged into the system.

10.11.2 Putting it All Together

With the advent of such high-level interfaces to the computer system, the devices—be they slow speed or high speed—are getting farther and farther away from the CPU itself. Thus, programmed I/O is almost a thing of the past. In Section 10.5, we mentioned the IBM innovation, in terms of I/O processors, in the context of mainframes of the 1960s and 1970s. Now such concepts have made their way into your PC.

Motherboard is a term coined in the PC era to signify the circuitry that is central to the computer system. It is a single, printed circuit board consisting of the processor, memory system (including the memory controller), and the I/O controller for connecting the peripheral devices to the CPU. The name comes from the fact that the printed circuit board contains slots into which expansion boards (usually referred to as *daughter* cards) may be plugged in to expand the capabilities of the computer system. For example, the expansion of physical memory is accomplished in this manner. Figure 10.24 shows a picture of a modern motherboard. The picture is self-explanatory in terms of the components and their capabilities. You can see the slots into which daughter cards for peripheral controllers and DIMMS (see Chapter 9 for a discussion of DIMMS) may be plugged in.

Figure 10.25 shows the block diagram of the important circuit elements inside a modern motherboard. It is worth understanding some of these elements. Every computer system needs some low-level code that executes automatically upon power-up. As

Figure 10.24   Picture of a motherboard (ASRock K7VT4A Pro).[14]

we already know, the processor simply executes instructions. The trick is to bring the computer system to the state such that the operating system is in control of all the resources. You have heard the term *booting up* the operating system. The term is short for *bootstrapping*, an allusion to picking yourself up by the straps of your own boots. Upon power-up, the processor automatically starts executing a bootstrapping code that is in a well-known fixed location in read-only memory (ROM). This code does all the initialization of the system, including recognizing the peripheral devices, before transferring the control to the upper layers of the system software shown in Figure 10.9. In the world of PCs, this bootstrapping code is called *BIOS*, which stands for *basic input/output system*.

The following additional points are worth noting, with respect to Figure 10.25:

- The box labeled *Northbridge* is a chip that serves as the *hub* for orchestrating the communication between the CPU and the memory system, as well as the I/O controllers.

- Similarly, the box labeled *Southbridge* is a chip that serves as the I/O controller hub. It connects to the standard I/O buses that we discussed in this section, including PCI and USB, and arbitrates among the devices—among the buses and their needs for direct access to the memory via the Northbridge, as well as for interrupt service by the CPU. It embodies many of the functions that we discussed in the context of an I/O processor, in Section 10.5.

- PCI Express is another bus standard that supports the high-transfer-rate and response-time needs of devices such as a high-resolution graphics display.

14. Picture source: http://en.wikibooks.org/wiki/File:ASRock_K7VT4A_Pro_Mainboard_Labeled_English.svg.

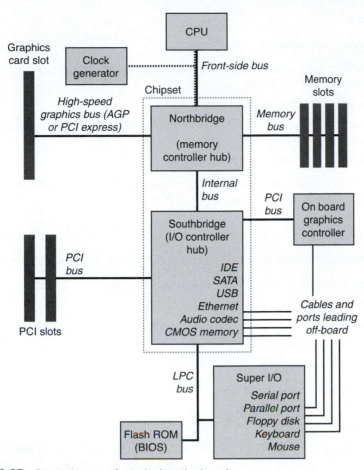

Figure 10.25 Block diagram of a typical motherboard.

- LPC, which stands for *low pin count,* bus is another standard for connecting low bandwidth devices (such as the keyboard and mouse) to the CPU.

- The box labeled *Super I/O* is a chip that serves the I/O controller for a number of slow-speed devices, including the keyboard, mouse, and printer.

As can be seen from this discussion, the hardware inside the computer system is quite fascinating. Whereas we have used the PC as a concrete example in this section, the functionalities embodied in the elements shown in Figure 10.25 generalize to any computer system. There was a time when the inside of a computer system would be drastically different, depending on the class of machine, ranging from a personal computer such as an IBM PC to a Vector Supercomputer such as a Cray-1. With advances in single chip microprocessor technology, which we discussed in Chapter 5, and the level of integration made possible by Moore's law (see Chapter 3), there now is a commonality in the building blocks used to assemble computer systems, ranging from PCs to desktops to servers to supercomputers.

Summary

In this chapter, we covered the following topics:

1. mechanisms for communication between the processor and I/O devices, including programmed I/O and DMA;
2. device controllers and device drivers;
3. buses in general, and the evolution of I/O buses in particular, found in modern computer systems; and
4. disk storage and disk-scheduling algorithms.

In the next chapter, we will study the file system, which is the software subsystem built on top of stable storage in general, hard disk in particular.

Exercises

1. Compare and contrast program-controlled I/O with direct memory access (DMA).

2. Assume a disk drive with the following characteristics:
   - Number of surfaces = 200.
   - Number of tracks per surface = 100.
   - Number of sectors per track = 50.
   - Bytes per sector = 256.
   - Speed = 2400 RPM.

   What is the total disk capacity?

   What is the average rotational latency?

3. A disk has 20 surfaces (i.e., 10 double-sided platters). Each surface has 1000 tracks. Each track has 128 sectors. Each sector can hold 64 bytes. The disk space allocation policy allocates an integral number of contiguous cylinders to each file.

   How many bytes are contained in one cylinder?

   How many cylinders are needed to accommodate a 5-MB file on the disk?

   How much space is wasted in allocating this 5-MB file?

4. A disk has the following configuration:

   The disk has 310 MB.

   Track size: 4096 bytes

   Sector Size: 64 bytes

   A programmer has 96 objects, each being 50 bytes in size. He decides to save each object as an individual file. How many bytes (in total) are actually written to disk?

5. Describe in detail the sequence of operations involved in a DMA data transfer.

6. What are the mechanical operations that must take place before a disk drive can read data?

7. A disk drive has 3 double-sided platters. The drive has 300 cylinders. How many tracks are there per surface?

8. Assume the following specifications for a disk drive:
   - 512 bytes per sector
   - 30 tracks per surface
   - 2 platters
   - zoned bit recording with the following specifications:
     - 3 Zones

       Zone 3 (outermost): 12 tracks, 200 sectors per track

       Zone 2: 12 tracks, 150 sectors per track

       Zone 1: 6 tracks, 50 sectors per track

   What is the total capacity of this drive with the zoned-bit recording?

9. Assume the following specifications for a disk drive:
   - 256 bytes per sector
   - 200 sectors per track
   - 1000 tracks per surface
   - 2 platters
   - Rotational speed 7500 RPM
   - Normal recording

   What is the transfer rate of the disk?

10. Assume the following specifications for a disk drive:
    - 256 bytes per sector
    - 100 sectors per track
    - 1000 tracks per surface
    - 3 platters
    - Average seek time of 8 ms
    - Rotational speed 15000 RPM
    - Normal recording

    a. What would be the time to read 10 contiguous sectors from the same track?

    b. What would be the time to read 10 sectors at random?

11. What are the objectives of a disk scheduling algorithm?

12. Using the number of tracks traversed as a measure of the time, compare all the disk scheduling algorithms for the specifics of the disk and the request pattern given in Example 10.4, with respect to the different performance metrics summarized in Table 10.3.

13. Assume the same details about the disk as in Example 10.4. The request queue does not remain the same, but changes as new requests are added to the queue. At any point in time, the algorithm uses the current requests to make its decision as to the next request to be serviced. Consider the following request sequence:

   • Initially (at time 0), the queue contains requests for cylinders 99, 3, 25.
   • At the time the next decision has to be taken by the algorithm, one new request has joined the queue: 46.
   • Next decision point, one more request has joined the queue: 75.
   • Next decision point, one more request has joined the queue: 55.
   • Next decision point, one more request has joined the queue: 85.
   • Next decision point, one more request has joined the queue: 73.
   • Next decision point, one more request has joined the queue: 50.

   Assume that the disk head at time 0 is just completing a request at track 55.

   a. Show the schedule for FCFS, SSTF, SCAN, C-SCAN, LOOK, and C-LOOK.

   b. Compute the response time (in units of head traversal) for each of the preceding requests.

   c. What is the average response time and throughput observed for each of the algorithms?

Bibliographic Notes and Further Reading

To learn about the latest advances in storage technology, it is best to visit the web pages of leading companies. IBM, MAXTOR, and Seagate are some of the leading disk manufacturers. Companies such as Samsung and Intel are leading the flash-based SSD market today, and their web pages are good indicators of the latest advances in SSD storage technology. To get an insight into the design considerations for a disk cache, we refer the reader to a seminal paper by Alan Jay Smith [Smith, 1985]. Several textbooks cover different aspects of I/O, to varying extents. Hennessy and Patterson [Hennessy, 2006] present advanced topics in storage system design. Tanenbaum [Tanenbaum, 2007] covers I/O from the point of managing them (i.e., programming them) from the operating system. Bryant and O'Hallaron [Bryant, 2003] cover I/O from the point of user-level programming. Silberschatz et al. [Silberchatz, 2008] give a good overview of the structure of mass storage devices (including disk scheduling algorithms), as well as software design alternatives, for managing the I/O devices in the operating system.

## CHAPTER 1

File System

In this chapter, we will discuss issues related to mass storage systems. In particular, we will discuss the choices available in designing a file system, and its implementation on the disk (or *hard drive*, as it is popularly referred to in personal computer parlance). Let us understand the role of the file system with respect to the overall mission of this textbook to "demystify the box." Appreciating the capabilities of the computer system is inextricably tied to getting a grip on the way information is stored and manipulated inside the box. Therefore, getting our teeth into how the file system works is an important aspect of demystifying the box.

We all are familiar with physical filing cabinets and manila file folders with papers in them. Typically, tags on the folders identify the contents, for easy retrieval (see Figure 11.1). Usually, there may be a directory folder that identifies the organization of the files in the filing cabinet.

A computer file system is similar to a physical filing cabinet. Each file (similar to a manila file folder) is a collection of information, with attributes associated with the information. Process is the software abstraction for the processor; data structure is the software abstraction for memory. Similarly, a file is the software abstraction for an input/output device, since a device serves as either a source or sink of information. This abstraction allows a user program to interact with I/O in a device-independent manner.

First, we will discuss the attributes associated with a file and the design choices therein. Then we will consider the design choices in the implementation of a file system on a mass storage device.

11.1 Attributes

We refer to the attributes associated with a file as *metadata*. The metadata represent *space overhead* and therefore require careful analysis as to their utility.

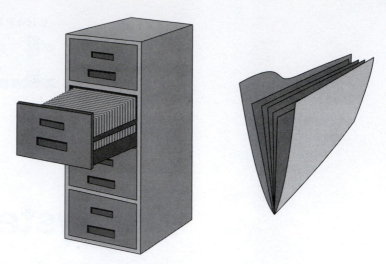

Figure 11.1   File cabinet and file folder.

Let us understand the attributes we may want to associate with a file.

- **Name:** This attribute allows the logical identification of the contents of the file. For example, if we are storing music files, we may want to give a *unique name* to each recording. To enable easy lookup, we may keep a *single* directory file that contains the names of all the music recordings. We can easily see that such a *single level* naming scheme, used in early storage systems such as the Univac Exec 8 computer systems (in the 1970s), is restrictive. Later systems such as the DEC TOPS-10 (in the early 1980s) used a two-level naming scheme. A top-level directory allows access to an individual user or a project (e.g., recordings of Billy Joel). The second level identifies a specific file for that user/project (e.g., a specific song).

    However, as systems grew in size, it became evident that we need a more hierarchical structure to naming files (e.g., each user may want to have his/her own music collection of different artists). In other words, we may need a multilevel directory, as shown in Figure 11.2.

    Most modern operating systems, such as Windows XP, UNIX, and MacOS, implement a multipart hierarchical name. Each part of the name is *unique* only with respect to the previous parts of the name. This gives a tree structure to the organization of the files in a file system, as shown in Figure 11.3. Each node in the tree is a name that is unique with respect to its parent node. Directories are files as well. In the tree structure shown in Figure 11.3, the intermediate nodes are *directory files,* and the leaf nodes are *data files.* The contents of a directory file are information about the files in the next level of the subtree, rooted at that directory file (e.g., the contents of directory **users** are {**students, staff, faculty**}; the contents of directory **faculty** are members of the faculty such as **rama**).

    Some operating systems make extensions (in the form of suffixes) to a file name mandatory. For instance, in the DEC TOPS-10 operating system, text files automatically get the .TXT suffix appended to the user-supplied name. In UNIX and Windows

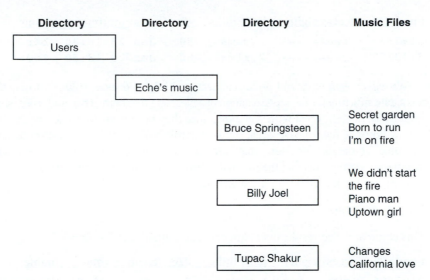

Figure 11.2 A multilevel directory. A hierarchical organization is a natural way to organize information.

operating systems, such file name extensions are optional. The system uses the suffix to guess the contents of the file and launch the appropriate application program to manipulate the file (such as the C compiler, document editor, and photo editor).

Some operating systems allow *aliases* to a file. Aliases may be at the level of the actual content of the file. Alternatively, the alias may simply be at the level of the names and not the actual contents. For example, the **ln** command (stands for *link*) in UNIX creates an alias to an existing file. The command

```
ln foo bar
```

results in creating an alias **bar** to access the contents of an existing file named **foo**. Such an alias, referred to as a *hard link*, gives status to the new name **bar** that is equal to the original name **foo**. Even if we delete the file **foo**, the contents of the file are still accessible through the name **bar**.

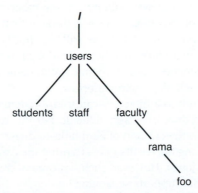

Figure 11.3 A tree structure for the file name/users/faculty/rama/foo.

i-node	access rights	hard links	size	creation time	name
3193357	-rw-------	2 rama	80	Jan 23 18:30	bar
3193357	-rw-------	2 rama	80	Jan 23 18:30	foo

We will explain what an i-node is in Section 11.3.1. For now, suffice it to say that it is a data structure for the representation of a file. Note that both **foo** and **bar** share exactly the same internal representation, since they both have the same i-node. This is how both the names have equal status, regardless of the order of creation of **foo** and **bar**. This is also the reason that both names are the same size and have the same timestamp, despite that fact that the name **bar** was created later than **foo**.

Contrast the foregoing situation with the UNIX command

```
ln -s foo bar
```

This command also results in creating an alias named **bar** for **foo**.

i-node	access rights	hard links	size	creation time	name
3193495	lrwxrwxrwx	1 rama	3	Jan 23 18:52	bar → foo
3193357	-rw-------	1 rama	80	Jan 23 18:30	foo

However, the difference is in the fact that **bar** is *name equivalence* to **foo** and does not directly point to the file contents. Note that the i-nodes for the two names are different. Thus, the time of creation of **bar** reflects the time when the **ln** command was actually executed to create an alias. Also, the size of the files are different. The size of **foo** depicts the actual size of the file (80 bytes), whereas the size of **bar** is just the size of the name string **foo** (3 bytes). Such an alias is referred to as a *soft link*. It is possible to manipulate the contents of the file with equal privilege, with either name. However, the difference arises in file deletion. Deletion of **foo** results in the removal of the file contents. The name **bar** still exists, but its alias **foo** and the file contents do not. Trying to access the file named **bar** results in an access error.

You may wonder why the operating system may want to support two different aliasing mechanisms, namely, hard and soft links. The tradeoff is one of efficiency and usability. A file name that is a soft link immediately tells you the original file name, whereas a hard link obfuscates this important detail.

Therefore, soft links increase usability. On the other hand, every time the file system encounters a soft link it has to resolve the alias by traversing its internal data structures (namely, i-nodes in UNIX). We will see shortly how this is done in the UNIX file system. The hard link directly points to the internal representation of the original file name. Therefore, there is no time lost in name resolution, and this benefit can lead to improved file system performance.

However, a hard link to a directory can lead to circular lists, which can make deletion operations of directories very difficult. For this reason, operating systems such as UNIX disallow the creation of hard links to directories.

Writing to an existing file results in overwriting the contents, in most operating systems (UNIX, Windows). However, such writes may create a new version of the file, in a file system that supports versioning.

- **Access rights:** This attribute specifies *who* has access to a particular file and *what* kind of privilege each allowed user enjoys. The privileges generally provided on a file include *read, write, execute, change ownership,* and *change privileges*. Certain privileges exist at the individual user level (e.g., either the creator or the users of a file), while some other privileges exist only for the system administrator (**root** in UNIX and **administrator** in Windows). For example, in UNIX the owner of a file may execute the "change the permission mode of a file" command

```
chmod u+w foo      /* u stands for user;
                    * w stands for write;
                    * essentially this command
                    * says add write access
                    * to the user;
                    */
```

that gives write permission, to the owner, to a file named **foo**. On the other hand, only the system administrator may execute the "change ownership" command

```
chown rama foo
```

that makes **rama** the new owner of the file **foo**.

An interesting question that arises for a file system designer is deciding on the granularity of access rights. Ideally, we may want to give individual access rights to *each* user in the system, to *each* file in the system. This choice results in an O (*n*) metadata space overhead per file, where *n* is the number of users in the system. Operating systems exercise different design choices in order to limit space overhead. For example, UNIX divides the world into three categories: *user, group,* and *all*. *User* is an authorized user of the system; *group* is a set of authorized users; and *all* refers to all authorized users on the system. The system administrator maintains the membership of different group names. For example, students in a CS2200 class may all belong to a group name cs2200. UNIX supports the notion of individual ownership and group ownership to any file. The owner of a file may change the group ownership for a file by using the command

```
chgrp cs2200 foo
```

that makes **cs2200** the group owner of the file **foo**.

With the world divided into three categories, as noted, UNIX provides *read, write,* and *execute* privileges for each category. Therefore, 3 bits encode the access rights for each category (1 each for read, write, and execute). The execute privilege allows a file to be treated as an executable program. For example, the compiled and linked output of a compiler is a binary executable file. The following example shows all the visible metadata associated with a file in UNIX:

```
rwxrw-r-- 1 rama fac 2364 Apr 18 19:13 foo
```

The file `foo` is owned by rama, group-owned by fac. The first field gives the access rights for the three categories. The first three bits (rwx) give read, write, and execute privileges to the user (rama). The next three bits (rw-) give read and write privileges (no execute privilege) to the group (fac). The last three bits (r--) give the read privilege (no write or execute privilege) to all users. The "1" after the access rights states the number of hard links that exists to this file. The file is of size 2364 bytes, and the modification timestamp of the contents of the file is April 18 at 19:13 hours.

The Windows operating system and some flavors of the UNIX operating systems allow a finer granularity of access rights by maintaining an *access control list (ACL)* for each file. This flexibility comes at the expense of increased metadata for each file.

Table 11.1 summarizes common file system attributes and their meaning. Table 11.2 gives a summary of common commands available in most UNIX file systems. All the commands are with respect to the current working directory. Of course, an exception to this rule is if the command specifies an absolute UNIX path-name (e.g., /users/r/rama).

Table 11.1 File System Attributes

Attribute	Meaning	Elaboration
Name	Name of the file	Attribute set at the time of creation or renaming.
Alias	Other names that exist for the same physical file	Attribute gets set when an alias is created; systems such as UNIX provide explicit commands for creating aliases for a given file; UNIX supports aliasing at two different levels (physical or hard, and symbolic or soft).
Owner	Usually, the user who created the file	Attribute gets set at the time of creation of a file; systems such as UNIX provide a mechanism for the file's ownership to be changed by the superuser.
Creation time	Time when the file was created first	Attribute gets set at the time a file is created or copied from some other place.
Last write time	Time when the file was last written to	Attribute gets set at the time the file is written to or copied; in most file systems the creation time attribute is the same as the last write time attribute. Note that moving a file from one location to another preserves the creation time of the file.
Privileges • **Read** • **Write** • **Execute**	The permissions or access rights to the file specifies who can do what to the file	Attribute gets set to default values at the time of creation of the file; usually, file systems provide commands to modify the privileges by the owner of the file; modern file systems such as NTFS provide an access control list (ACL) to give different levels of access to different users.
Size	Total space occupied on the file system	Attribute gets set every time the size changes due to modification to the file.

Table 11.2 Summary of Common UNIX File System Commands

UNIX Command	Semantics	Elaboration
touch \<name\>	Create a file with the name \<name\>	Creates a zero byte file with the name \<name\> and a creation time equal to the current wall clock time.
mkdir \<sub-dir\>	Create a subdirectory \<sub-dir\>	The user must have write privilege to the current working directory (if \<sub-dir\> is a relative name) to be able to successfully execute this command.
rm \<name\>	Remove (or delete) the file named \<name\>	Only the owner of the file (and/or superuser) can delete a file.
rmdir \<sub-dir\>	Remove (or delete) the sub-directory named \<sub-dir\>	Only the owner of the \<sub-dir\> (and/or the superuser) can remove the named subdirectory.
ln –s \<orig\> \<new\>	Create a name \<new\> and make it symbolically equivalent to the file \<orig\>	This is name equivalence only; so if the file \<orig\> is deleted, the storage associated with \<orig\> is reclaimed, and hence, \<new\> will be a dangling reference to a nonexistent file.
ln \<orig\> \<new\>	Create a name \<new\> and make it physically equivalent to the file \<orig\>	Even if the file \<orig\> is deleted, the physical file remains accessible via the name \<new\>.
chmod \<rights\> \<name\>	Change the access rights for the file \<name\> as specified in the mask \<rights\>	Only the owner of the file (and/or the superuser) can change the access rights.
chown \<user\> \<name\>	Change the owner of the file \<name\> to be \<user\>	Only the superuser can change the ownership of a file.
chgrp \<group\> \<name\>	Change the group associated with the file \<name\> to be \<group\>	Only the owner of the file (and/or the superuser) can change the group associated with a file.
cp \<orig\> \<new\>	Create a new file \<new\> that is a copy of the file \<orig\>	The copy is created in the same directory if \<new\> is a file name; if \<new\> is a directory name, then a copy with the same name \<orig\> is created in the directory \<new\>.
mv \<orig\> \<new\>	Rename the file \<orig\> with the name \<new\>	Renaming happens in the same directory if \<new\> is a file name; if \<new\> is a directory name, then the file \<orig\> is moved into the directory \<new\> preserving its name \<orig\>.
cat/more/less \<name\>	View the file contents	

11.2 Design Choices in Implementing a File System on a Disk Subsystem

We started our discussion on file systems by presenting a file as a software abstraction for an input/output device. An equally important reason for file systems arises from the need to keep information around, beyond the lifetime of a program execution. A file serves as a convenient abstraction for meeting this need. Permanent read/write storage is the right answer for keeping such persistent information around. The file system is another important software subsystem of the operating system. Using disk as the permanent storage, we will discuss the design choices in implementing a file system.

As we saw in Chapter 10, a disk physically consists of platters, tracks, and sectors. A given disk has specific fixed values for these hardware parameters. Logically, the corresponding tracks on the various platters form a cylinder. There are four components to the latency for doing input/output from/to a disk:

- seek time to a specific cylinder;
- rotational latency to get the specific sector under the read/write head of the disk;
- transfer time from/to the disk controller buffer; and
- DMA transfer from/to the controller buffer to/from the system memory.

We know that a file is of arbitrary size, commensurate with the needs of the program. For example, files that contain simple ASCII text may be a few kilobytes in size. On the other hand, a movie that you may download and store digitally on the computer can occupy several hundreds of megabytes. The file system has to bridge the mismatch between the user's view of a file as a storage abstraction, and physical details of the hard drive. Depending on its size, a file potentially may occupy several sectors, several tracks, or even several cylinders.

Therefore, one of the fundamental design issues in file system is the physical representation of a file on the disk. Choice of a design point should take into consideration both end users' needs and system performance. Let us understand these issues. From a user's perspective, there may be two requirements. One, the user may want to view the contents of a file sequentially (e.g., the UNIX `more`, `less`, and `cat` commands). Two, the user may want to search for something in a file (e.g., the UNIX `tail` command). The former implies that the physical representation should lend itself to efficient *sequential access;* and the latter, to *random access.* From the system performance point of view, the file system design should lend itself to easily *growing* a file when needed and to *efficient allocation* of space on the disk for new files or the growth of existing files.

Therefore the *figures of merit*[1] for a file system design are

- fast sequential access;
- fast random access;

---

1. A figure of merit is a criterion used to judge the performance of the system.

- ability to grow the file;
- easy allocation of storage; and
- efficiency of space utilization on the disk.

In the next few paragraphs, we will identify several file allocation schemes on a hard drive. For each scheme, we will discuss the data structures needed in the file system, and the impact of the scheme on the figures of merit. We will establish some common terminology for the rest of the discussion. An *address* on the disk is a triple {*cylinder#, surface#, sector#*}. The file system views the disk as consisting of *disk blocks*, a design parameter of the file system. Each disk block is a physically contiguous region of the disk (usually, a set of sectors, tracks, or cylinders, depending on the specific allocation scheme), and is the smallest granularity of disk space managed by the file system. For simplicity of discussion, we will use *disk block address* as nickname for the disk address (the 4-tuple, {*cylinder#, surface#, sector#, size of disk block*}) corresponding to a particular disk block, and designate it by a unique integer.

11.2.1 Contiguous Allocation

This disk allocation scheme has similarities to both the fixed- and variable-size partition-based memory-allocation schemes discussed in Chapter 8. At file creation time, the file system preallocates a fixed amount of space to the file. The amount of space allocated depends on the type of file (e.g., a text file versus a media file). Further, the amount of space allocated is the maximum size that the file can grow to. Figure 11.4 shows the data structures needed for this scheme. Each entry in the *directory* data structure contains a mapping of the file name to the disk block address, and the number of blocks allocated to this file.

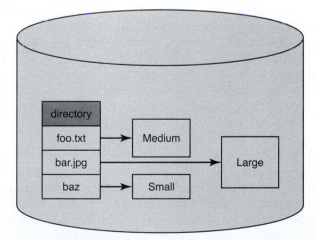

Figure 11.4   A disk with a directory that maps file name to a disk block address, for contiguous allocation.

The size of contiguous allocation matches the size of the file.

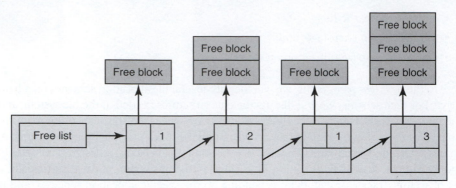

Figure 11.5   A free list, with each node containing {pointer to the starting disk block address, number of blocks} for contiguous allocation.

The file system maintains a *free list* of available disk blocks (Figure 11.5). A free list is a data structure that enables the file system to keep track of the currently unallocated disk blocks. In Chapter 8, we discussed how the memory manager uses the free list of physical frames to make memory allocation upon a page fault; similarly, the file system uses the free list of disk blocks to make disk block allocation for the creation of new files. As we will see, the details of this free list depend on the specific allocation strategy in use by the file system.

For contiguous allocation, each node in this free list gives the starting disk block address and the number of available blocks. Allocation of disk blocks to a new file may follow one of *first fit* or *best fit* policy. Upon file deletion, the released disk blocks return to the free list. The file system combines adjacent nodes to form bigger, contiguous, disk block partitions. Of course, the file system does such *compaction* infrequently due to the overhead it represents. Alternatively, the file system may choose to do such compaction upon an explicit request from the user. Much of this description should sound similar to the issues discussed, in Chapter 8, for variable-size memory partitions. Similar to that memory management scheme, this disk allocation strategy also suffers from *external fragmentation*. Further, since the file system commits a fixed-size chunk of disk blocks (to allow for the maximum expected growth size of that file) at file creation time, this scheme suffers from *internal fragmentation* (similar to the fixed-size partition memory allocation scheme discussed in Chapter 8).

The file system could keep these data structures in memory or on the disk. The data structures have to be in persistent store (i.e., some disk blocks are used to implement these data structures), since the files are persistent. Therefore, these data structures reside on the disk itself. However, the file system caches this data structure in memory to enable quick allocation decisions, as well as to speed up file access.

Let us analyze this scheme qualitatively with respect to the figures of merit. Allocation can be expensive, depending on the algorithm used (first fit or best fit). Since a file occupies a fixed partition (a physically contiguous region on the disk), both sequential access and random access to a file are efficient. Upon positioning the disk head at the starting disk block address for a particular file, the scheme incurs very little additional time for seeking different parts of the file, due to the nature of the allocation. There are two downsides to the allocation scheme:

1. The file cannot grow in place beyond the size of the fixed partition allocated at the time of file creation. One possibility to get around this problem is to find a free list node with a bigger partition and copy the file over to the new partition. This is an expensive choice; besides, such a larger partition has to be available. The file system may resort to compaction to create such a larger partition.

2. As we said already, there is potential for significant wastage due to internal and external fragmentation.

Example 11.1

Assume the following:

Number of cylinders on the disk	= 10,000
Number of platters	= 10
Number of surfaces per platter	= 2
Number of sectors per track	= 128
Number of bytes per sector	= 256
Disk allocation policy	= contiguous cylinders

a. How many cylinders should be allocated to store a file of size 3 MB?

b. How much internal fragmentation is caused by this allocation?

Answer:

a. Number of tracks in a cylinder = number of platters * number of surfaces per platter
$$= 10 * 2 = 20.$$

Size of track = number of sectors in track * size of sector
$$= 128 * 256$$
$$= 2^{15} \text{ bytes.}$$

Capacity in 1 cylinder = number of tracks in cylinder * size of track
$$= 20 * 2^{15}.$$
$$= 10 * 2^{16} \text{ bytes.}$$

Number of cylinders to host a 3 MB file = CEIL $((3 * 2^{20})/(10 * 2^{16}))$ = **5**.

b. Internal fragmentation = 5 cylinders − 3 MB

$$= 3276800 - 3145728 = \textbf{131072 bytes}.$$

11.2.2 Contiguous Allocation with Overflow Area

This strategy is the same as the previous one, with the difference that the file system sets aside an *overflow* region that allows spillover of large files that do not fit within the fixed partition. The overflow region also consists of physically contiguous regions allocated to accommodate such spillover of large files. The file system needs an additional data structure to manage the overflow region. This scheme fares exactly the same, with respect to the figures of merit, as the previous scheme. However, on the plus side, this scheme allows file growth limited only by the maximum amount of space available in the overflow region, without the need for any other expensive operation, as described previously. Also on the minus side, random access suffers slightly for large files due to the spill into the overflow region (resulting in additional seek time).

Despite some of the limitations, contiguous allocation has been used quite extensively in systems such as the IBM VM/CMS, due to the significant performance advantage for file access times.

11.2.3 Linked Allocation

In this scheme, the file system deals with allocation at the level of individual disk blocks. The file system maintains a *free list* of all available disk blocks. A file occupies as many disk blocks as it takes to store it on the disk. The file system allocates the disk blocks from the free list as the file grows. The free list may actually be a linked list of the disk blocks, with each block pointing to the next free block on the disk. The file system has the head of this list cached in memory so that it can quickly allocate a disk block to satisfy a new allocation request. Upon deletion of a file, the file system adds its disk blocks to the free list. In general, having such a linked list implemented via disk blocks leads to expensive traversal times for free-list maintenance. An alternative is to implement the free list as a bit vector, one bit for each disk block. The block is free if the corresponding bit is 0, and busy if it is 1.

Note that the free list changes over time, as applications produce and delete files, and as files grow and shrink. Thus, there is no guarantee that a file will occupy contiguous disk blocks. Therefore, a file is physically stored as a linked list of the disk blocks assigned to it, as shown in Figure 11.6. As in the previous allocation schemes, some disk blocks hold the persistent data structures (free list and directory) of the file system.

On the plus side, the allocation is quick, since it is performed one disk block at a time. Further, the scheme accommodates the easy growth of files. There is no external fragmentation due to on-demand allocation. Consequently, the scheme never requires disk compaction. On the minus side, since the disk blocks of a file may not be contiguous, the scheme performs poorly for file access, compared with contiguous allocation, especially for random access, due to the need for retrieving the next block pointers from the disk blocks. Even for sequential access, the scheme may be inefficient due to the

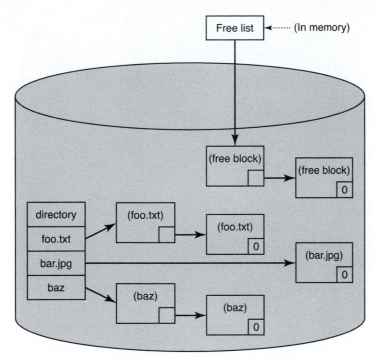

Figure 11.6   Linked allocation.

The disk blocks form a linked list data structure.

variable seek time for the disk blocks that make up the list. The error-prone nature of this scheme is another downside: Any bug in the list maintenance code leads to a complete breakdown of the file system.

11.2.4 File Allocation Table (FAT)

This is a variation of the linked allocation. A table on the disk, the *file allocation table (FAT)*, contains the linked list of the files currently populating the disk (see Figure 11.7). The scheme divides the disk logically into partitions. Each partition has a FAT, in which each entry corresponds to a particular disk block. The *free/busy* field indicates the availability of that disk block (0 for free; 1 for busy). The *next* field gives the next disk block of the linked list, that represents a file. A distinguished value (−1) indicates that this entry is the last disk block for that file. A single *directory* for the entire partition contains the *file name* to *FAT index* mapping, as shown in Figure 11.7. Similar to the linked allocation, the file system allocates a disk block on demand to a file.

For example, */foo* occupies two disk blocks: 30 and 70. The *next* field of entry 30 contains the value 70, the address of the next disk block. The next field of entry 70 contains −1, indicating that this is the last block for */foo*. Similarly, */bar* occupies one disk block (50). If */foo* or */bar* were to grow, the scheme would allocate a free disk block and fix up the FAT accordingly.

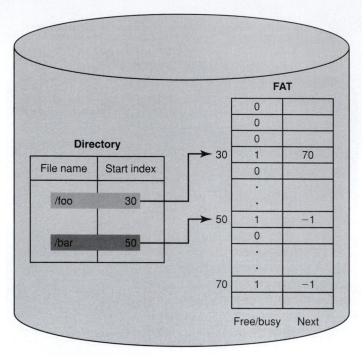

Figure 11.7 File allocation table (FAT).

The linked list representing each individual file is maintained as an array.

Let us analyze the pros and cons of this scheme. Since FAT captures the linked list structure of the disk in a tabular data structure, there is less chance of errors, compared with the linked allocation. By caching FAT in the memory, the scheme leads to efficient allocation times compared with linked allocation. The scheme performs in a way similar to linked allocation for sequential file access. It performs better than linked allocation, for random access, because the FAT contains the next block pointers for a given file.

One of the biggest downsides to this scheme is the logical partitioning of a disk. This leads to a level of management of the space on the disk that is not pleasant for the end user. It creates an artificial scarcity of space on the disk in a particular partition even when there is plenty of physical space on the disk. However, due to its simplicity (centralized data structures in the directory and FAT), this allocation scheme was popular in early personal computer operating systems such as MS-DOS and IBM OS/2.

Example 11.2

This question concerns the disk space allocation strategy referred to as FAT. Assume that there are 20 data blocks, numbered 1 through 20.

There are three files currently on the disk:

foo occupies disk blocks 1, 2 and 3;

bar occupies disk blocks 10, 13, 15, 17, 18 and 19; and

gag occupies disk blocks 4, 5, 7 and 9.

Show the contents of the FAT. (Show the free blocks and allocated blocks per convention used in this section.)

Answer:

1	2
2	3
3	−1
4	5
5	7
6	0
7	9
8	0
9	−1
10	13
11	0
12	0
13	15
14	0
15	17
16	0
17	18
18	19
19	−1
20	0

11.2.5 Indexed Allocation

This scheme allocates an *index* disk block for each file. The index block for a file is a fixed-size data structure that contains addresses for data blocks that are part of that file. This scheme aggregates data block pointers for a file, scattered all over the FAT data structure (in the previous scheme), into one table per file, as shown in Figure 11.8. This table, called *index node* or *i-node*, occupies a disk block. The *directory* (also on the disk) contains the *file name* to *index node* mapping for each file. Similar to the linked allocation, this scheme maintains the *free list* as a bit vector of disk blocks (0 for free, 1 for busy).

Compared with FAT, this scheme performs better for random access, since the i-node aggregates all the disk block pointers into one concise data structure. The downside to this scheme is the limitation on the maximum size of a file, since i-node is a fixed-size data

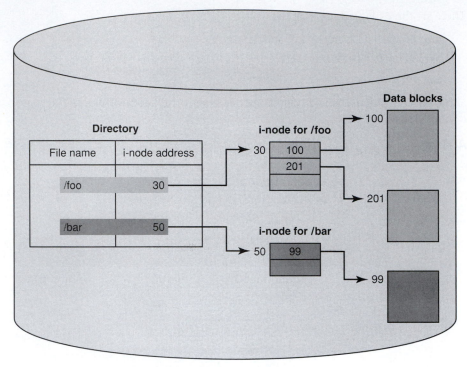

Figure 11.8 Indexed allocation.

Rather than a single table for all the files, as in FAT, there is an individual table (the index block) for each file.

structure per file, with direct pointers to data blocks. The number of data block pointers in an i-node bounds the maximum size of the file.

We will explore other schemes that remove this restriction on maximum file size, in the subsections that follow.

Example 11.3

Consider an indexed allocation scheme on a disk:

- The disk has 10 platters (2 surfaces per platter).
- There are 1000 tracks in each surface.
- Each track has 400 sectors.
- There are 512 bytes per sector.
- Each i-node is a fixed size data structure occupying one sector.
- A data block (unit of allocation) is a contiguous set of 2 cylinders.
- A pointer to a disk data block is represented by an 8-byte data structure.

a. What is the minimum amount of space used for a file on this system?

b. What is the maximum file size with this allocation scheme?

Answer:

Size of a track = number of sectors per track * size of sector

$$= 400 * 512 \text{ bytes} = 200 \text{ KBs} (K = 1024).$$

Number of tracks in a cylinder = number of platters * number of surfaces per platter

$$= 10 * 2 = 20.$$

Size of a cylinder = number of tracks in a cylinder * size of track

$$= 20 * 200 \text{ KB}$$
$$= 4000 \text{ Kbytes}.$$

Unit of allocation (data block) = 2 cylinders

$$= 2 * 4000 \text{ KB}$$
$$= 8000 \text{ KB}.$$

Size of i-node = size of sector = 512 bytes.

a. Minimum amount of space for a file = size of i-node + size of data block

$$= 512 + (8000 * 1024) \text{ bytes}$$
$$= \textbf{8,192,512 bytes}.$$

Number of data block pointers in an i-node = size of i-node/
size of data block pointer

$$= 512/8 = 64.$$

b. Maximum size of file = number of data block pointers in i-node * size of data block

$$= 64 * 8000 \text{ KB} (K = 1024)$$
$$= \textbf{5,24,288,000 bytes}.$$

11.2.6 Multilevel Indexed Allocation

This scheme fixes the limitation in the indexed allocation by making the i-node for a file an indirection table. For example, with one-level indirection, each i-node entry points to a first-level table, which in turn points to the data blocks, as shown in Figure 11.9. In this figure, the i-node for foo contains pointers to a first-level indirection index block. The number of first-level indirection tables equals the number of pointers that an i-node can hold. These first-level indirection tables hold pointers to the data blocks of the file.

The scheme can be extended to make an i-node a two-level (or even higher-level) indirection table, depending on the size of the files that need to be supported by the file system. The downside to this scheme is that even small files that may fit in a few data blocks have to go through extra levels of indirection.

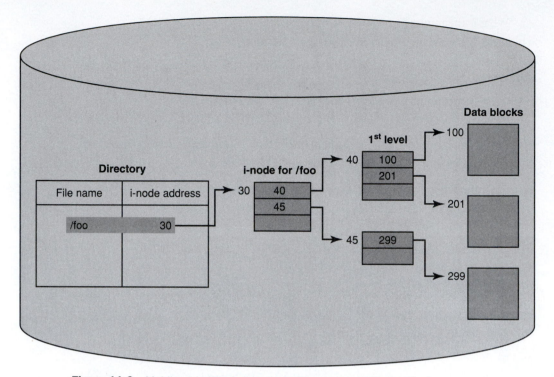

Figure 11.9   Multilevel indexed allocation (with one level of indirection).

Compared with the single-level indexed allocation, this scheme is more flexible with respect to the growth of a file.

11.2.7 Hybrid Indexed Allocation

This scheme combines the ideas in the previous two schemes to form a hybrid scheme. Every file has an i-node, as shown in Figure 11.10. The scheme accommodates all the data blocks for a small file with direct pointers. If the file size exceeds the capacity of the direct blocks, then the scheme uses a single level, or more levels, of indirection for the additional data blocks. Figure 11.10 shows */foo* using direct, single indirect, and double indirect pointers. The i-node for */foo* is a complex data structure, as shown in the figure. It has pointers to two direct data blocks (100 and 201); one pointer to an indirect index block (40); one pointer to a double indirect index block (45), which in turn has pointers to single indirect index blocks (60 and 70); and one pointer to a triple indirect index block (currently unassigned). The scheme overcomes the disadvantages of the previous two schemes while maintaining their good points. When a file is created with this scheme, only the i-node is allocated for it. That is, the single, double, and triple indirect pointers are initially null. If the file size does not exceed the amount of space available in the direct blocks, there is no need to create additional index blocks. However, as the file grows and exceeds the capacity of the direct data blocks, space is allocated on an as-needed basis for the first-level index block, second-level index block, and third-level index block.

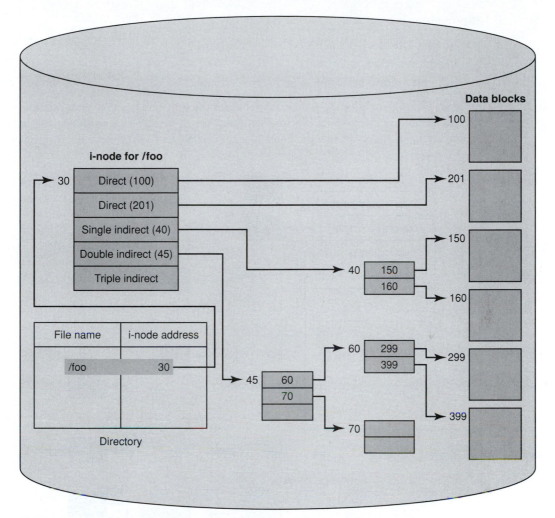

Figure 11.10 Hybrid indexed allocation.

This scheme is a compromise between the single-level and multilevel indexed allocations, allowing for file growth while ensuring fast access to small files.

Example 11.4

Assume the following:

- Size of index block = 512 bytes.
- Size of data block = 2048 bytes.
- Size of pointer = 8 bytes (to index or data blocks).

The i-node consists of

- 2 direct data block pointers,
- 1 single indirect pointer, and
- 1 double indirect pointer.

An index block is used for the i-node as well as for the index blocks that store pointers to other index blocks and data blocks. Pictorially, the organization is as shown in the accompanying figure. Note that the index blocks and data blocks are allocated on an as-needed basis.

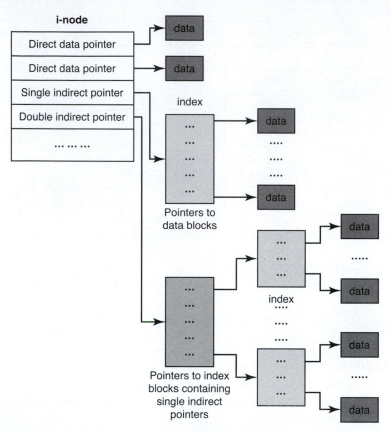

a. What is the maximum size (in bytes) of a file that can be stored in this file system?

b. How many data blocks are needed for storing a data file of 266 KB?

c. How many index blocks are needed for storing the same data file of size 266 KB?

Answer:

a. Number of single indirect or double indirect pointers in an index block

$$= 512/8$$

$$= 64.$$

Number of direct data blocks = 2.

An i-node contains 1 single indirect pointer that points to an index block (we call this *single indirect index block*) containing pointers to data blocks.

Number of data blocks with one level of indirection

> = number of data block pointers in an index block
>
> = 64.

An i-node contains 1 double indirect pointer that points to an index block (we call this *double indirect index block*) containing 64 single indirect pointers. Each such pointer points to a single indirect index block that, in turn, contains 64 pointers to data blocks. This is shown in the figure.

Number of data block with two levels of indirection

> = number of single indirect pointers in an index block *
>   number of data block pointers index node
>
> = 64 * 64.

Max file size in blocks

> = number of direct data blocks
> + number of data blocks with one level of indirection
> + number of data blocks with two levels of indirection
>
> = 2 + 64 + 64 * 64 = 4162 data blocks.

Max file size = Max file size in blocks * size of data block

> = 4162 * 2048 bytes
>
> = **8,523,776 bytes.**

b. Number of data blocks needed

> = size of file/size of data block
>
> = $226 * 2^{10}/2048$
>
> = **133**.

c. To get 133 data blocks we need

1 i-node	(gets us 2 direct data blocks)
1 single indirect index block	(gets us 64 data blocks)
1 double indirect index block	
2 single indirect index blocks off the double indirect index block	(gets us the remaining 64 + 3 data blocks)
Therefore, in total, we need	**5 index blocks**.

11.2.8 Comparison of the Allocation Strategies

Table 11.3 summarizes the relative advantages and disadvantages of the various allocation strategies.

Table 11.3 Comparison of Allocation Strategies

Allocation Strategy	File Representation	Free List Maintenance	Sequential Access	Random Access	File Growth	Allocation Overhead	Space Efficiency
Contiguous	Contiguous blocks	Complex	Very good	Very good	Messy	Medium to high	Internal and external fragmentation
Contiguous With Overflow	Contiguous blocks for small files	Complex	Very good for small files	Very good for small files	OK	Medium to high	Internal and external fragmentation
Linked List	Noncontiguous blocks	Bit vector	Good, but dependent on seek time	Not good	Very good	Small to medium	Excellent
FAT	Noncontiguous blocks	FAT	Good, but dependent on seek time	Good but dependent on seek time	Very good	Small	Excellent
Indexed	Noncontiguous blocks	Bit vector	Good, but dependent on seek time	Good but dependent on seek time	Limited	Small	Excellent
Multilevel Indexed	Noncontiguous blocks	Bit vector	Good, but dependent on seek time	Good but dependent on seek time	Good	Small	Excellent
Hybrid	Noncontiguous blocks	Bit vector	Good, but dependent on seek time	Good but dependent on seek time	Good	Small	Excellent

For the integrity of the file system across power failures, the persistent data structures of the file system (e.g., i-nodes, free list, directories, FAT, etc.) have to reside on the disk itself. The number of disk blocks devoted to holding these data structures represents space overhead of the particular allocation strategy. There is a time penalty, as well, for accessing these data structures. File systems routinely cache these critical data structures in the main memory to avoid the time penalty.

11.3 Putting It All Together

As a concrete example, the UNIX operating system uses a hybrid allocation approach with hierarchical naming. With hierarchical naming, the directory structure is no longer centralized. Each i-node represents a part of the multipart hierarchical name. Except for the leaf nodes, which are data files, all the intermediate nodes are directory nodes. The type field in the i-node identifies whether this node is a directory or a data file. The i-node data structure includes fields for the other file attributes that we discussed earlier, such as access rights, timestamp, size, and ownership. In addition, to allow for aliasing, the i-node also includes a *reference count* field.

Figure 11.11 shows the complete i-node structure for a file */users/faculty/rama/foo*. For the sake of simplicity, we do not show the data blocks.

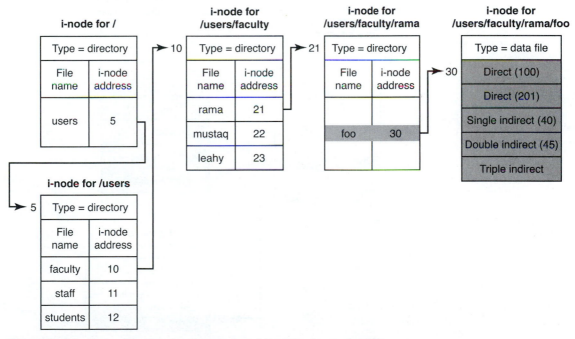

Figure 11.11 A simplified i-node structure for a hierarchical name in UNIX. (A sequence of commands has resulted in creating the file /users/faculty/rama/foo.)

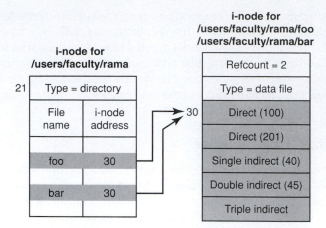

Figure 11.12   Two files, foo and bar, share an i-node, since they are hard links to each other. (The command "ln foo bar" results in this structure.)

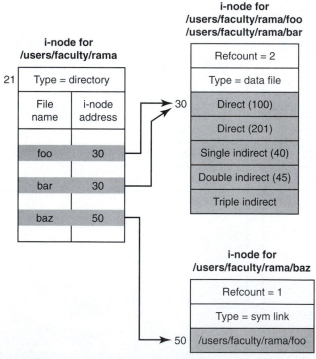

Figure 11.13   File baz is a symbolic link to /users/faculty/rama/foo. (The command "ln–s /users/faculty/rama/foo baz" results in this structure.)

Figure 11.12 shows the i-node structure with *bar* as a hard link to *foo*. Both files share the same i-node. Hence, the *reference count* field in the i-node is 2. Figure 11.13 shows the i-node structure when a third file *baz* is symbolically linked to the name */users/faculty/rama/foo*. The i-node for *baz* denotes it as a symbolic link and contains the name */users/faculty/rama/foo*. The file system starts traversing the i-node structure given by the symbolic name (i.e., in this case, upon accessing *baz*, the traversal will start from the i-node for */*).

Example 11.5

Current directory	/tmp
I-node for /tmp	20

The following UNIX commands are executed in the current directory:

```
touch foo          /* creates a zero byte file
                      in the current directory */
ln foo bar         /* create a hard link */
ln -s /tmp/foo baz /* create a soft link */
ln baz gag         /* create a hard link */
```

Note:

- Type of i-node can be one of directory-file, data-file, sym-link.

- If the type is sym-link, you have to give the name associated with that sym-link; otherwise, the name field in the i-node is blank.

- Reference count is a nonzero positive integer.

In the accompanying graphic, fill in all the blanks to complete the contents of the various i-nodes.

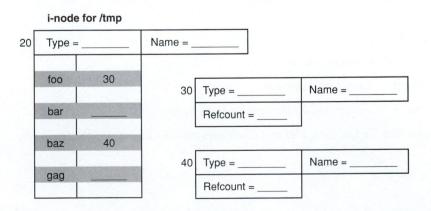

Answer:

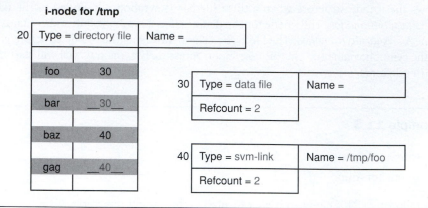

i-node for /tmp

Example 11.6

Given the commands that follow, pictorially show the i-nodes and their contents. You can fabricate disk block addresses for the i-nodes to make the pictures simpler. Where it's relevant, show the reference count for the i-nodes.

```
touch /tmp/foo
mkdir /tmp/bar
mkdir /tmp/bar/gag
ln /tmp/foo /tmp/bar/foo2
ln -s /tmp/foo /tmp/bar/foo
ln /tmp/foo /tmp/bar/gag/foo
ln -s /tmp/bar /tmp/bar/gag/bar
ln -s /tmp /tmp/bar/gag/tmp
```

Note:

- "mkdir" creates a directory

- "touch" creates a zero byte file

- "ln" is link command (-s denotes symbolic link)

Assume that the foregoing files and directories are the only ones in the file system.

Answer:

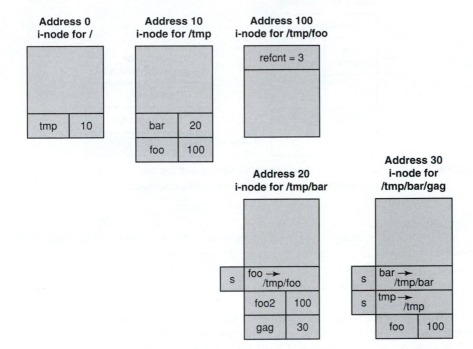

Now execute the following command:

```
rm /tmp/bar/foo
```

Show the new contents of the i-nodes. (Show only the affected i-nodes.)

Answer:

Only i-node for /tmp/bar changes as shown below. The symbolic link entry is removed from the i-node.

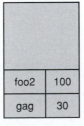

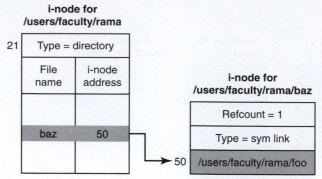

Figure 11.14   State of i-node structure after both foo and bar are deleted. (The command "rm foo bar" results in this structure.)

With reference to Figure 11.13, first let us understand what would happen to the i-node structure if the file *bar* were deleted. The entry bar would be removed from the i-node for */user/faculty/rama,* and the *reference count* field in the i-node for */users/faculty/rama/foo* (block 30) would be decremented by 1 (i.e., the new *refcount* would be 1).

Next, let us see what would happen to the i-node structure once both *bar* and *foo* are deleted. Figure 11.14 depicts this situation. Since the *refcount* for i-node at block 30 goes to 0 with the deletion of both *foo* and *bar*, the file system returns the disk block 30 to the free list. Notice that *baz* still exists as a file in */users/faculty/rama*. This is because the file system checks only the validity of the name being aliased at the time of creation of the symbolic link. However, notice that no information about the symbolic link is kept in the i-node of the name ("foo" in this case). Therefore, there is no way for the file system to check for the existence of symbolic links to a name at the time of deleting a name ("foo" in this case). However, any attempt to examine the contents of *baz* results in an error, since the name */users/faculty/rama/foo* is nonexistent, so far as the file system is concerned. This illustrates the need for exercising care when using symbolic links.

Example 11.7

Consider the following:

```
touch foo;          /* creates a zero byte file */
ln foo bar;         /* creates a hard link called bar
                       to foo */
ln -s foo baz;      /* creates a soft link called baz
                       to foo */
rm foo;             /* removes the file foo */
```

Discuss what would happen if we now execute the command

```
cat baz;              /* attempt to view the content of baz
                      */
```

Answer:

Let the current directory be tmp, where all the action previously shown takes place. In this case, foo, bar, and baz are names created in the i-node for tmp.

Let the i-node for foo be 20. When we create the hard link bar, the refcount for i-node 20 goes up to 2. When foo is removed, the refcount for i-node drops to 1, but the i-node is not removed, because bar has a hard link to it; however, the name foo is removed from the i-node of the current directory.

Therefore, when we attempt to view the contents of baz by using the cat command, the file system flags an error, since the name foo does not exist in the current directory anymore. This is shown in the accompanying figure:

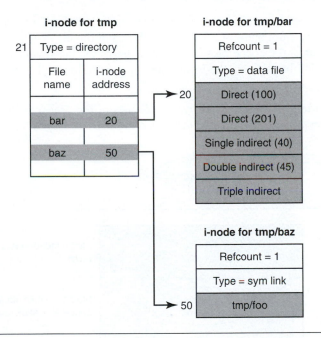

11.3.1 i-node

In UNIX, every file has a *unique* number associated with it, called the *i-node* number. You may think of this number as an *index* into a table that has all the information associated with the file (owner, size, name, etc.). As UNIX systems evolved, the complexity of the information associated with each file increased as well. (The name itself can be arbitrarily long, etc.) Thus, in modern UNIX systems, each file is represented by a unique i-node data structure that occupies an entire disk block. The collection of i-nodes thus forms a logical table, and the i-node number is simply the unique disk block address that indexes into this logical table and contains the information about that particular file. For the sake of convenience in implementing the file system, all the i-nodes occupy spatially adjacent disk blocks in the layout of the file system on the physical media. Typically, the file system reserves a sufficiently large number of disk blocks as i-nodes. This implicitly becomes the limit of the maximum number of files in a given file system. It is customary for the storage allocation algorithm to maintain a bit vector (one bit for each i-node) that indicates whether a particular i-node is currently in use or not. This allows for efficient allocation of i-nodes upon file creation requests. Similarly, the storage manager may implement the free list of data blocks on the disk as a bit vector (one bit to signify whether a particular data block is presently in use or not on the media) for efficient storage allocation.

11.4 Components of the File System

Whereas it is possible to implement a file system at the user level, typically, it is part of the operating system. Figure 11.15 shows the layers of the file system for the disk. We refer to the part of the operating system that manages the file system as the *file system (FS) manager*. We break down the FS manager into the following layers, for the sake of exposition:

- **Media independent layer:** This layer consists of the user interface—that is, the *application program interface (API)* provided to the users. The API module gives the

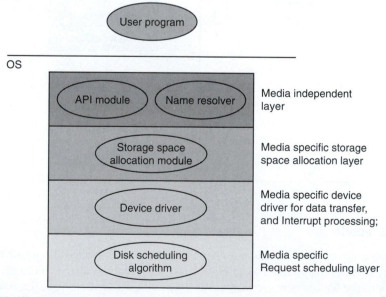

Figure 11.15   Layers of a disk-specific file system manager.

file system commands for the user program to open and close files, read and write files, etc. This layer also consists of the *name resolver* module which translates the user-supplied name into an internal representation that is meaningful to the file system. For instance, the name resolver will be able to map the user-specific name (e.g., E:\myphotos) to the specific device on which the file exists (such as the disk, CD, and flash drive).

- **Media specific storage space allocation layer:** This layer embodies the space allocation (on file creation), space reclamation (on file deletion), free-list mainte-nance, and other functions associated with managing the space on the physical device. For instance, if the file system exists on a disk, the data structures and algo-rithms will use the allocation schemes discussed in Section 11.2.

- **Device driver:** This is the part that deals with communicating the command to the device and effecting the data transfer between the device and the operating system buffers. The device driver details (see Chapter 10 for a general description of device drivers) depend on the specifics of the mass storage that hosts the file system.

- **Media specific requests scheduling layer:** This layer is responsible for schedul-ing the requests from the OS, commensurate with the physical properties of the device. For example, in the case of a disk, this layer may embody the disk-scheduling algorithms that we learned in Chapter 10. As we observed in Chapter 10, even in the case of a disk, the scheduling algorithms may in fact be part of the device controller that is part of the drive itself. The scheduling algorithm may be quite dif-ferent, depending on the nature of the mass storage device.

There will be distinct instances of the bottom three layers of the software stack shown in Figure 11.15, for each mass storage device that provides a file system interface to the user. Thus, the file is a powerful abstraction for hiding the details of the actual physical storage on which the data pertaining to the file is kept.

11.4.1 Anatomy of Creating and Writing Files

As a concrete example, let us say that your program makes an I/O call to create a file on the hard disk. The following steps trace the path of such an I/O call through the soft-ware layers shown in Figure 11.15:

1. The API routine for creating a file call validates the call by checking the permis-sions, access rights, and other related information for the call. After validation, it calls the name resolver.

2. The name resolver contacts the storage allocation module to allocate an i-node for the new file.

3. The storage allocation module gets a disk block from the free list and returns it to the name resolver. The storage allocation module fills in the i-node commen-surate with the allocation scheme (see Section 11.2). Let us assume that the allocation in effect is the hybrid scheme (Section 11.2.7). Since the file has been

created without any data as yet, no data blocks would have been allocated to the file.

4. The name resolver creates a directory entry and records the name to i-node, mapping information for the new file in the directory.

Notice that these steps do not involve actually making a trip to the device, because the data structures accessed by the file system (directory and free list) are all in memory.

Now suppose that your program writes to the file just created. Let us trace the steps through the software layers for this operation.

1. As before, the API routine for file write does its part in terms of validating the request.

2. The name resolver passes the memory buffer to the storage allocation module, along with the i-node information for the file.

3. The storage allocation module allocates data blocks from the free list, commensurate with the size of the file write. It then creates a request for disk write and hands the request to the device driver.

4. The device driver adds the request to its request queue. In concert with the disk-scheduling algorithm, the device driver completes the write of the file to the disk.

5. Upon completion of the file write, the device driver gets an interrupt from the disk controller that is passed back up to the file system, which in turn communicates with the CPU scheduler to continue the execution of your program from the point of file write.

It should be noted that, as far as the OS is concerned, the file write call is complete as soon as the request is handed to the device driver. The success or failure of the actual call will be known later when the controller interrupts. The file system interacts with the CPU scheduler in exactly the same manner as did the memory manager. (See Section 8.2 in Chapter 8.) The memory manager, in order to handle a page fault, makes an I/O request on behalf of the faulting process. The memory manager gets notified when the I/O completes so that it can tell the CPU scheduler to resume execution of the faulting process. This is exactly what happens with the file system as well.

11.5 Interaction Among the Various Subsystems

It is interesting to review the various software subsystems that we have come across within the operating system so far: CPU scheduler, VM manager, file system (FS) manager, and device drivers for the various I/O devices.

All of these subsystems are working for the user programs, of course. For example, the VM manager is servicing page faults that a user program incurs, implicitly performing I/O on behalf of the faulting process. The FS manager explicitly performs I/O catering to the requests of a user program to read and write files. In both cases, some mass storage device (hard disk, flash memory, CD, DVD, etc.) is the target of the I/O operation. The device driver pertinent to the specific I/O request performs the I/O request and reports the result of the I/O operation back to the requestor.

The device driver has to figure out, somehow, whose I/O request was completed upon an I/O completion interrupt from the device controller. One simple and unifying method is to use the PCB data structure that we introduced in Chapter 6 (Section 6.4), as a communication vehicle among the subsystems.

For example, the top layer of the FS manager passes the file I/O request to the device driver, via the PCB of the process. This is straightforward and similar to a procedure call, except that the procedure call is across layers of the software stack shown in Figure 11.15. This information flow is shown in Figure 11.16(a). Let PCB_1 represent the PCB of the process that makes the file system call. Once the call has been handed over to the device driver, the process is no longer runnable; this is depicted in Figure 11.16(b). PCB_1 is now in the Disk_IO_q while being serviced by the device driver.

The device driver has to notify the upper layers of the system software stack, upon completion of the I/O. In Chapter 6 (see Section 6.7.1), we introduced the concept of

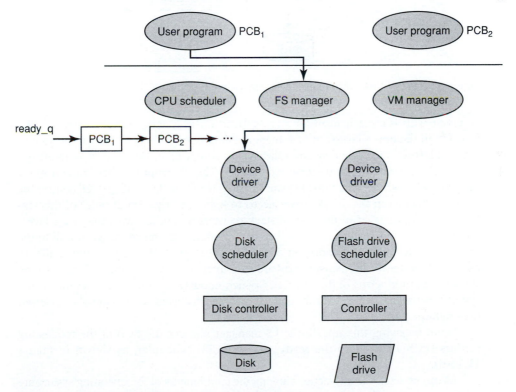

Figure 11.16(a)　Information flow on a file system call.

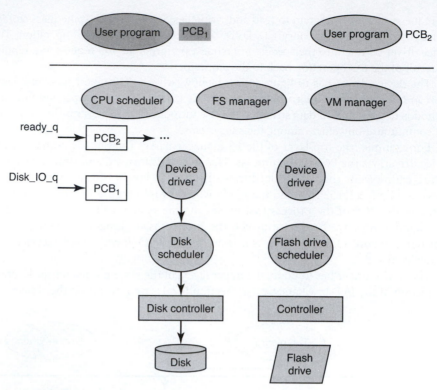

Figure 11.16(b) Disk driver handling the file system call from PCB$_1$.

an *upcall*. This is a mechanism for a lower layer in the system software stack to call a function in the upper layers. In fact, there is a continuum of upcalls, as can be seen in Figure 11.16(c). First, the disk controller makes an upcall, in the form of an interrupt, to the interrupt handler in the device controller. The interrupt handler knows exactly the process on whose behalf this I/O was initiated (from the Disk_IO_q). Of course, the interrupt handler in the device driver needs to know exactly who to call. For this reason, every upper layer in the system stack registers a handler, with the lower layers for enabling such upcalls. Using this handler, the device driver makes an upcall to the FS manager to indicate completion of the file I/O request. We can see the similarity between this upcall mechanism and hardware interrupts (see Chapter 4). Due to the similarity both in terms of the function (asynchronously communicating events to the system), as well as the mechanism used to convey such events, upcalls are often referred to as *software interrupts*.

Upon receiving this upcall, the FS manager restores the PCB of the requesting process (PCB$_1$) back into the ready_q of the CPU scheduler, as shown in Figure 11.16(d).

As can be seen, the interactions among the components of the operating system are enabled smoothly, through the abstraction of the executing program in the form of a PCB. This is the power of the PCB abstraction.

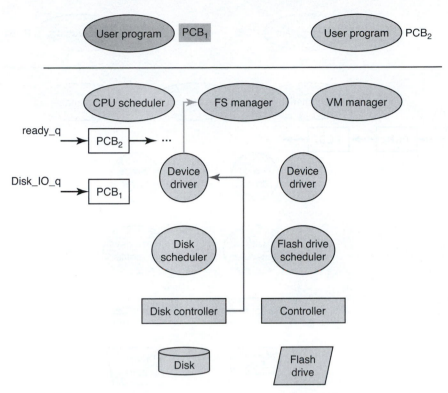

Figure 11.16(c)   A series of upcalls upon completion of the file I/O request. (The up arrow from the disk controller to the device driver is in hardware; the up arrow from the device driver to the FS manager is in software.)

A similar sequence of events would take place upon a page fault by a process; the only difference is that the VM Manager would be the initiator of the actions up and down the software stack shown in Figures 11.16(a)–(d).

11.6 Layout of the File System on the Physical Media

Let us now understand how the operating system takes control of the resources in the system on power-up.

In Chapter 10, we mentioned the basic idea behind booting up an operating system. We described how the BIOS performs the basic initialization of the devices and hands over control to the higher layers of the system software. Well, actually, the process of booting up the operating system is a bit more involved. The image of the operating system is in the mass storage device. In fact, the BIOS does not even know what operating system needs to be booted up. Therefore, the BIOS has to have a clear idea as to where and how the information is kept in the mass storage device so that it

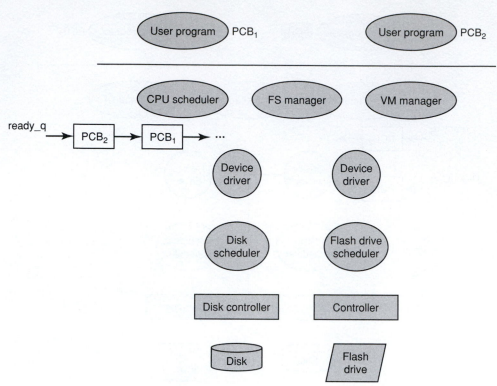

Figure 11.16(d)   The FS manager puts the process (PCB$_1$) that made the I/O
call back in the CPU ready_q.

can read in the operating system and hand over control to it. In other words, the layout
of the information on the mass storage device becomes a *contract* between the BIOS and
the operating system, be it Windows, Linux, or whatever else.

To make this discussion concrete, let us assume that the mass storage device is a
disk. At the very beginning of the storage space on the disk, let's say that {*platter 0, track
0, sector 0*} is a special record called the *master boot record (MBR)*. Recall that when you
create an executable through the compilation process, it lives on the disk until loaded
into memory by the loader. In the same manner, MBR is just a program at this well-
defined location on the disk. BIOS is serving as a loader to load this program into
memory, and it will transfer control to MBR.

The MBR program knows the layout of the rest of the disk and knows the exact
location of the operating system on the disk. The physical disk itself may be made up of
several partitions. For example, on your desktop or laptop, you may have seen several
"drives" with distinct names. (Microsoft Windows gives them names such as C, D, etc.)
These may be distinct physical drives, but they may also be logical drives, each of which
corresponds to a distinct partition on the same physical drive. Let us say you have a
single disk, but have a dual-boot capability that allows either Linux or Windows to be
your operating system, depending on your choice. The file systems for each of these

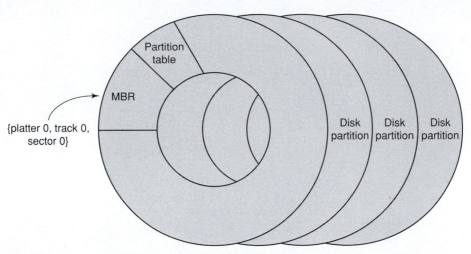

Figure 11.17   Conceptual layout of information on the disk.

There could be one or more partitions on each platter of the disk.

operating systems necessarily have to be distinct. This is where the partitions come into play.

Figure 11.17 shows a conceptual layout of the disk. For the sake of clarity, we have shown each partition on a different disk platter. However, it should be emphasized that several partitions may live on the same platter, depending on the disk capacity. The key data structure of the MBR program is the partition table. This table gives the start and end device address (i.e., the triple {*platter, track, sector*}) of each partition on the disk (see Table 11.4). MBR uses the partition table to decide which partition has to be activated, depending on the choice exercised by the user at boot time. Of course, in some systems there may be no choice (e.g., there is a single partition, or only one partition has an operating system associated with it).

Table 11.4 shows several partitions. Depending on the OS to be booted up, the MBR program will activate the appropriate partition (in this case, either partition 1 or 2).

Table 11.4 Partition Table Data Structure

Partition	Start Address {Platter, Track, Sector}	End Address {Platter, Track, Sector}	OS
1	{1, 10, 0}	{1, 600, 0}	Linux
2	{1, 601, 0}	{1, 2000, 0}	MS Vista
3	{1, 2001, 0}	{1, 5000, 0}	None
4	{2, 10, 0}	{2, 2000, 0}	None
5	{2, 2001, 0}	{2, 3000, 0}	None

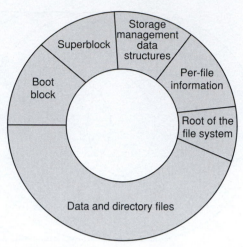

Figure 11.18 Layout of each partition.

The various entries in the partition are simply the data structures used by the storage manager to organize the information on the disk.

Note that partitions 3–5 do not have any OS associated with them. They may simply be logical "drives" for one or the other operating system.

Figure 11.18 shows the layout of information in each partition. Other than the very first entry (boot block), the actual layout of information in the partition varies from file system to file system. However, to keep the discussion concrete, we will assume a particular layout and describe the functionality of each entry. The chosen layout of information in Figure 11.18 is close to that of traditional UNIX file systems.

Let us review each entry in the partition:

- *Boot block* is the very first item in every partition. MBR reads in the boot block of the partition being activated. The boot block is simply a program (just like MBR) that is responsible for loading in the operating system associated with this partition. For uniformity, every partition starts with a boot block even if there is no OS associated with a particular partition. (See entries 3–5 in Table 11.4.)

- *Superblock* contains all the information pertinent to the file system contained in this partition. This is the key to understanding the layout of the rest of this partition. The boot program (in addition to loading the operating system, or in lieu thereof) reads the superblock into memory. Typically, it contains a *code,* usually referred to as the *magic number,* that identifies the type of file system housed in this partition; the number of disk blocks; and other administrative information pertaining to the file system.

- The next entry in the partition contains the *data structures for storage management* in this partition. The data structures will be commensurate with the specific allocation strategy being employed by the file system (see Section 11.2). For example, it may contain a bit map to represent all the available disk data blocks (i.e., the free list). As another example, this entry may contain the FAT data structure that we mentioned earlier (see Section 11.2.4).

- The next entry in the partition corresponds to the *per-file information* maintained by the file system. This data structure is unique to the specifics of the file system. For example, as we mentioned in Section 11.3.1, in a UNIX file system, every file has a unique number associated with it, called the i-node number. In such a system, this entry may simply be a collection of all the i-nodes in the file system.

- Modern-day file systems are all hierarchical in nature. The next entry in the partition points to the *root directory* of the hierarchical tree-structured file system. For example, in UNIX this would correspond to the information pertaining to the file named "/."

- The last entry in the partition is just the collection of disk blocks that serve as containers for *data and directory files*. The data structures in the storage management entry of the partition are responsible for allocating and deallocating these disk blocks. The disk blocks may be used to hold data (e.g., a JPEG image) or a directory containing other files (i.e., data files and/or other directories).

As should be evident, the superblock is a critical data structure of the file system. If it is corrupted for some reason, it is very difficult to recover the contents of the file system.

11.6.1 In Memory Data Structures

For efficiency, a file system would read in the critical data structures (the superblock, free list of i-nodes, and free list of data blocks) from the disk at the time of booting. The file system manipulates these in-memory data structures as user programs create and delete files. In fact, the file system does not even immediately write the data files created to the mass storage device. The reason for the procrastination is twofold. First, many files, especially in a program development environment, have a short lifetime (less than 30 seconds). Consider the lifetime of intermediate files created during a program compilation and linking process. The programs (such as the compiler and linker) that create such files will delete them upon creation of the executable file. Thus, waiting for awhile to write to the mass storage device is advantageous, because such procrastination will help reduce the amount of I/O traffic. The second reason is simply a matter of convenience and efficiency. The file system may batch the I/O requests both to reduce the overhead of making individual requests and to deal with interrupts from the device signaling I/O completion.

There is a downside to this tactic, however. The in-memory data structures may be inconsistent with their counterparts on the disk. We may have noticed the message on the computer screen that says, "It is not safe to remove the device," when we try to unplug a memory stick from the computer. This is because the OS has not committed the changes it has made to the in-memory data structures (and, perhaps, even to the data themselves) to the mass storage device. Many operating systems offer commands to help you force the issue. For example, the UNIX command *sync* forces a write of all the in-memory buffers to the mass storage device.

11.7 Dealing with System Crashes

Let us understand what exactly is meant by an operating system crash. As we have said often, an operating system is simply a program. It is as prone to bugs as any other piece of software that you may write. A user program may be terminated by the operating system if it does something it should not do (e.g., tries to access a portion of memory beyond its bounds), or it may simply hang because it is expecting some event that might never occur. An operating system may have such bugs, as well, and could terminate abruptly. In addition, a power failure may force an abnormal termination of the operating system. This is what is referred to as a *system crash*.

The file system is a crucial component of the computer system. Since it houses persistent data, the health of the file system is paramount to productivity in any enterprise. Therefore, it is very important that the file system survive machine crashes. Operating systems take tremendous care to keep the integrity of the file system. If a system crashes unexpectedly, there may be inconsistencies between the in-memory data structures, at the time of the crash, and on-disk versions.

For this reason, as a last-ditch effort, the operating system will dump the contents of the memory onto the mass storage device at a well-known location before terminating (whether the crash is due to a bug in the OS or due to power failure). On system boot, one of the first things that the boot program will do is to see whether such a crash image exists. If so, it will try to reconstruct the in-memory data structures and reconcile them with the on-disk versions. One of the reasons your desktop takes time when you boot up your machine is due to the consistency check that the operating system performs to ensure file system integrity. The UNIX operating system automatically runs *file system consistency check (fsck)* on boot-up. Only if the system passes the consistency check will the boot process continue. Any enterprise does periodic backup of the disk onto tapes to ward off failures.

11.8 File Systems for Other Physical Media

Thus far, we have assumed the physical media to be the disk. We know that a file system may be hosted on a variety of physical media. Let us understand to what extent some of the discussion we have had thus far changes if the physical media for the mass storage is different. A file system for a CD-ROM and a CD-R (a recordable CD) are perhaps the simplest. Once recorded, the files can never be erased in such media, which significantly reduces the complexity of the file system. For example, in the former case, there is no question of a free list of space on the CD; by contrast, in the latter all the free space is at the end of the CD, where the media may be appended with new files. The file system for a CD-RW (rewritable CD) is a tad more complex in that the space of the deleted files need to be added to the free space on the media. File systems for DVD are similar.

As we mentioned in Chapter 10, solid-state drives (SSD) are competing with disk as mass storage media. Since SSD allows random access, seek time to disk blocks—a primary concern in disk-based file systems—is less of a concern in SSD-based file systems. Therefore, there is an opportunity to simplify the allocation strategies. However, there are considerations specific to SSD with respect to file system implementation. For example, a given area of an SSD (usually referred to as a *block*) may be written to only a finite number of times before it becomes unusable. This is due to the nature of the SSD technology. Consequently, file systems for SSD adopt a *wear leveling* allocation policy to ensure that all the areas of the storage are equally used over the lifetime of the SSD.

11.9 A Glimpse of Modern File Systems

In this section, we will study some of the exciting new developments in the evolution of modern file systems. In Chapter 6, we gave a historical perspective of the evolution of the UNIX system and how it paved the way for both Mac OS X and Linux. Today, of course, Mac OS X, Linux, and Microsoft Windows rule the marketplace for a variety of application domains. Here, we limit our discussion of modern file systems to the Linux and Microsoft families of operating systems.

11.9.1 Linux

The file system interface (i.e., API) provided by Linux has not changed from the days of early UNIX systems. However, internally, the implementation of the file system has been undergoing enormous changes. This is akin to the architecture-versus-implementation dichotomy that we discussed in Chapters 2 and 3, in the context of processor design.

Most of the evolutionary changes are designed to accommodate multiple file system partitions, longer file names, and larger files, and to hide the distinction between files present on local media and those on the network.

One important change in the evolution of UNIX file systems is the introduction of the *virtual file system (VFS)*. This abstraction allows multiple, potentially different, file systems to coexist "under the covers." The file system may be on a local device, an external device accessible through the network, and/or on different media types. VFS does not impact you as a user. You open, read, or write a file just the same way as you do in a traditional UNIX file system. Abstractions in VFS know exactly which file system is responsible for your file and, through one level of indirection (function pointers stored in the VFS abstraction layer), redirect your call to the specific file system that can service your request.

Now let us take a quick look at the evolution of file system implementation in Linux itself. In Chapter 6, we mentioned how MINIX served as a starting point for Linux. The very first file system for Linux used the MINIX file system. It had its limitation in the length of file names and maximum size of individual files. So, this was quickly replaced by *ext* (which stands for *extended file system*), which circumvented those limitations. However, ext had several performance inefficiencies giving rise to the *ext2*, a second version of ext, which is still in widespread use in the Linux community.

ext2. The disk layout of an ext2 file system partition is not remarkably different from the generic description we gave in Section 11.6. A few things are useful to mention regarding ext2.

- **Directory file:** The first is the contents of an i-node structure for a directory file. A directory file is made up of an integral number of contiguous disk blocks intended to facilitate writing the directory file to the disk, in one I/O operation. Each entry in the directory names a file or another subdirectory. Since a name can be of arbitrary length, the size of each entry is variable. Figure 11.19(a) shows the format of an entry in the directory.

  Each entry is composed of the following items:

  - **i-node number:** a fixed-length field that gives the i-node number for the associated entry;
  - **length of entry:** a fixed-length field that gives the length of the entry, in bytes (i.e., the total amount of space occupied by the entry on the disk)—this is needed to identify where in the directory structure the next entry begins;
  - **type of entry:** a fixed-length field that specifies whether the entry is a data file (f) or a directory file (d);
  - **length of name:** a fixed-length field that specifies the length of the file name;
  - **name:** a variable-length field that gives the name of the file in ASCII; and
  - **padding:** an optional variable-length field that is sometimes used to make the total size of an entry a multiple of a binary power; as we will see shortly, such padding space also may be created or expanded upon file deletions.

Figure 11.19(b) shows an example entry for a file named "i_like_my_file_names_long" with the values filled in. The size of each field, in bytes, is shown below the graphic part of the figure.

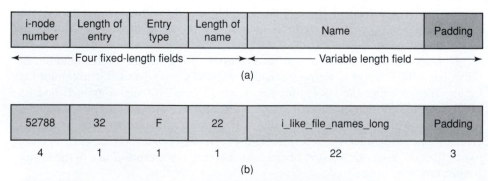

Figure 11.19 Format of each individual entry in a directory file.

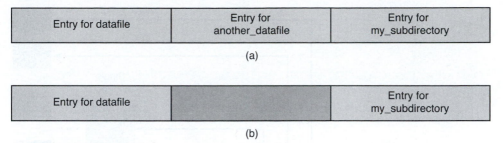

Figure 11.20 Layout of multiple entries in a directory file.

Entries in the directory are laid out contiguously in the textual order of creation of the files. For example, you might create the files "datafile," "another_datafile," and a "my_subdirectory," in that order in a directory, the first two being data files, and the third a directory file. The directory entries will be as shown in Figure 11.20(a). Suppose that you delete one of the files, say, "another_datafile." In this case, there will simply be an empty space in the directory layout, as shown in Figure 11.20(b). The space occupied by the deleted file entry will become part of the padding of the previous entry. This space can be used for the creation of a new file entry in the directory.

- **Data file:** The second point of interest is the i-node structure for a data file. As we said earlier, ext2 removes the limitation of MINIX with respect to the maximum size of files. The i-node structure for a data file reflects this enhancement. The scheme used is the hybrid allocation scheme we discussed in Section 11.2.7. An i-node for a data file contains the following fields:
  - **12 data block addresses:** The first 12 blocks of a data file can be directly reached from the i-node. This is very convenient for small files. The file system will also try to contiguously allocate these 12 data blocks so that the performance can be optimized.
  - **1 single indirect pointer:** This points to a disk block that serves as a container for pointers to data blocks. For example, with a disk block size of 512 bytes, and a data block pointer size of 4 bytes, this first-level indirection allows expanding the file size by an additional 128 data blocks.
  - **1 double indirect pointer:** This points to a disk block that serves as a container for pointers to tables that contain single-level indirect pointers. Continuing the same example, this second-level indirection allows expanding the file size by an additional 128 * 128 (i.e., 2^{14}) data blocks.
  - **1 triple indirect pointer:** This adds one more level of indirection over the double indirect pointer, allowing a file to be expanded by an additional 128 *128 * 128 (i.e., 2^{21}) data blocks.

Figure 11.21 pictorially shows such an i-node with all the important fields filled in.

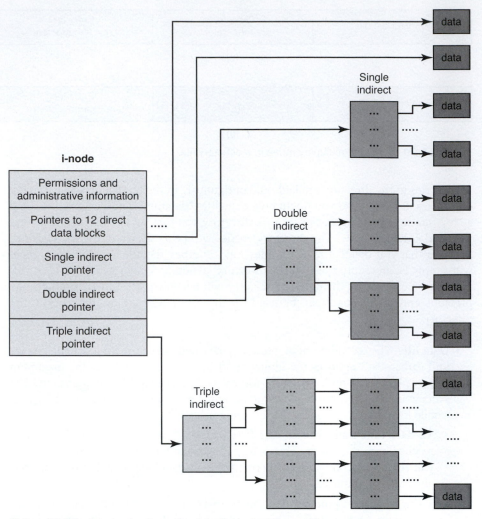

Figure 11.21   i-node structure of a data file in the Linux ext2.

Example 11.8

What is the maximum possible file size in bytes in the ext2 system? Assume that a disk block is 1 KB and pointers to disk blocks are 4 bytes.

Answer:

<u>Direct data blocks</u>

Number of direct data blocks = number of direct pointers in an i-node

$$= 12. \tag{1}$$

Data blocks via the single indirect pointer

Next, let us count the number of data blocks available to a file via the single indirect pointer in an i-node. The single indirect pointer points to a single indirect table that contains pointers to data blocks.

Number of data blocks via the single indirect pointer in an i-node

$$= \text{Number of pointers in a single indirect table}$$
$$= \text{Number of pointers in a disk block}$$
$$= \text{size of disk block/size of pointer} \qquad (2)$$
$$= 1 \text{ KB/4 bytes}$$
$$= 256.$$

Data blocks via double indirect pointer

Next, let us count the number of data blocks available to a file via the double indirect pointer in an i-node. The double indirect pointer points to a disk block that contains pointers to tables of single indirect pointers.

Number of single indirect tables via the double indirect pointer

$$= \text{Number of pointers in a disk block}$$
$$= \text{size of disk block/size of pointer}$$
$$= 1 \text{ KB/4 bytes} \qquad (3)$$
$$= 256.$$

Number of data blocks via each of these single indirect tables (from Equation (2))

$$= 256. \qquad (4)$$

From Equations (3) and (4), the number of data blocks via the double indirect pointer in an i-node

$$= 256 * 256. \qquad (5)$$

Data blocks via triple indirect pointer

By a similar analysis, the number of data blocks via the triple indirect pointer in an i-node

$$= 256 * 256 * 256. \qquad (6)$$

Putting Equations (1), (2), (5), and (6) together, the total number of disk blocks available to a file

$$= 12 + 256 + 256 * 256 + 256 * 256 * 256$$
$$= 12 + 2^8 + 2^{16} + 2^{24}.$$

The maximum file size in bytes for a data file (assuming that the data block is of size 1 KB)

$$= (12 + 2^8 + 2^{16} + 2^{24}) \text{ KB}$$
$$> 16 \text{ GB}.$$

Journaling file systems. Most modern file systems for Linux are *journaling* file systems. Normally, you think of writing to a file as writing to the data block of the file. Logically, this is correct. However, practically, there are issues with this approach. For example, if the file size is too small, then there is both space and—more important— time overhead in writing such small files to the disk. Of course, operating systems buffer writes to files in memory and write to disk opportunistically. Despite such optimizations, ultimately, these files have to be written to disk. Small files not only waste space on the disk (due to internal fragmentation), but also result in time overhead (seek time, rotational latency, and metadata management).

Another complication is system crashes. If the system crashes in the middle of writing to a file, the file system will be left in an inconsistent state. We alluded to this problem already (see Section 11.7).

Both to address the problem of overcoming the inefficiency of writing small files and to aid in the recovery from system crashes, modern file systems use a journaling approach. The idea is simple and intuitive and applies the metaphor of keeping a personal journal or a diary. One's personal diary is a time-ordered record of events of importance in one's everyday activities. The *journal* serves the same purpose for the file system. Upon file writes, instead of writing to the file and/or creating a small file, the file system creates a log record (similar to a database record) that would contain the information corresponding to the file write (i.e., metadata modifications to i-node and superblock, as well as modifications to the data blocks of the file). Thus, the journal is a *time-ordered* record of all the changes to the file system. The nice thing about this approach is that the journal is distinct from the file system itself and allows the operating system to optimize its implementation to best suit the file system needs. For example, the journal may be implemented as a sequential data structure. Every entry in this sequential data structure represents a particular file system operation.

For example, let us say that you modified specific data blocks of three files (X, Y, and Z), that are scattered all over the disk, in that order. The journal entries corresponding to these changes will appear as shown in Figure 11.22. Note that each log record may be of a different size, depending on the number of data blocks of a file that are modified at a time by the corresponding write operation.

The journal data structure is a composite of several *log segments*. Each log segment is of finite size (for example, 1 MB). As soon as a log segment fills up, the file system writes this out to a contiguous portion of the disk and starts a new log segment for the subsequent writes to the file system. Note that the files X, Y, and Z do not reflect yet the changes made to them. Every once in awhile, the file system may *commit* the changes to the actual files by reading the log segment (in the order in which they were generated)

File name = X	File name = Y	File name = Z
Data block = d_x	Data block = d_y	Data block = d_z
New contents = c_x	New contents = c_y	New contents = c_z
Log record for changes to file X	Log record for changes to file Y	Log record for changes to file Z

Figure 11.22   Journal entries of changes to the file system.

and applying the log entries to the corresponding files. Once the changes have been committed, the log segments may be discarded. If the file X is read before the changes have been applied to it, the file system is smart enough to apply the changes from the log segment to the file before allowing the read to proceed.

As should be evident, the log segment serves to aggregate small writes (to either small files or small parts of a large file) into coarser-grain operations (i.e., larger writes to contiguous portion of the disk) to the journal.

Journaling overcomes the small write problem. As a bonus, journaling also helps the system cope with crashes. Remember that, as a last ditch effort (see Section 11.7), the operating system stores everything in memory to the disk at the time of the crash or power failure. Upon restart, the operating system will recover the in-memory log segments. The file system will recognize that the changes in the log segments (both the ones on the disk as well as the in-memory log segments that were recovered from the crash) were not committed successfully. It will simply reapply the log records to the file system to make the file system consistent.

Ext3 is the next iteration of the Linux file system. Compared with the ext2, the main extension in the ext3 file system is support for journaling. In this sense, a file partition built with ext2 may be accessed by using the ext3 file system, since the data structures and internal abstractions are identical in both. Because creating a journal of all file system operations may be expensive in terms of space and time, ext3 may be configured to journal only the changes to the metadata (i.e., i-nodes, superblock, etc.). This optimization will lead to better performance in the absence of system crashes, but cannot make guarantees against file data corruption in the event of a crash.

There are a number of new UNIX file systems. *ReiserFS* is another file system with only metadata journaling for Linux. *jFS* is a journaling file system from IBM for use with IBM's AIX (a version of UNIX) and with Linux. *xFS* is a journaling file system primarily designed for SGI Irix operating system. *zFS* is a high-performance file system for high-end enterprise systems, built for the Sun Solaris operating system. Discussion of such file systems is beyond the scope of this textbook.

11.9.2 Microsoft Windows

Microsoft file systems have an interesting history. As you may recall, MS-DOS started out as an operating system for the PC. Because disks in the early stages of PC evolution had fairly small capacity (on the order of 20–40 MB), the file systems for such computers were limited as well. For example, the FAT-16 (a specific instance of the allocation scheme discussed in Section 11.2.4) uses 16-bit disk addresses, with a limit of 2 GB per file partition. FAT-32, by virtue of its use of 32-bit disk addresses, extends the limit of a file partition to 2 TB. These two file systems have mostly been phased out, with the advent of Microsoft XP and Vista operating systems. Currently (circa 2010), the NT file system (referred to as NTFS), which was first introduced with the Microsoft NT operating system, has been the *de facto* standard Microsoft file system. FAT-16 may still be in use for removable media such as the floppy disk. FAT-32 also still finds use, especially for interoperability with older versions of Windows such as 95/98.

NTFS supports most of the features that we discussed in the context of UNIX file systems earlier. It is a complex modern file system using 64-bit disk address, and thus can support very large disk partitions. *Volume* is the fundamental unit of structuring the file system. A volume may occupy a part of the disk, the whole disk, or even multiple disks.

API and System Features. A fundamental difference between NTFS and UNIX is the view of a file. In NTFS, a file is an *object* composed of *typed attributes,* rather than a stream of bytes, as in UNIX. This view of a file offers some significant flexibility at the user level. Each typed attribute is an independent byte stream. It is possible to create, read, write, and/or delete each attributed part without affecting the other parts of the same file. Some attribute types are standard for all files (e.g., name, creation time, and access control). As an example, you may have an image file with multiple attributes: raw image, thumbnail, etc. Attributes for a file may be created and deleted at will.

NTFS supports long file names (up to 255 characters in length), using Unicode character encoding to allow non-English file names. It is a hierarchical file system similar to UNIX, although the hierarchy separator in UNIX, namely, "/", is replaced by "\" in NTFS. Aliasing a file through hard and soft links, which we discussed in Section 11.1, is a fairly recent addition to the NTFS file system.

Some of the interesting features of NTFS include on-the-fly compression and decompression of files as they are written and read, respectively; an optional encryption feature; and support for small writes and system crashes via journaling.

Implementation. Similar to the i-node table in UNIX (see Section 11.3.1), the main data structure in NTFS is the *master file table (MFT)*. This is also stored on the disk and contains important metadata for the rest of the file system. A file is represented by one or more records in the MFT, depending on both the number of attributes and the size of the file. A bit map specifies which MFT records are free. The collection of MFT records describing a file is similar in functionality to an i-node in the UNIX world, but the similarity stops there. An MFT record (or records) for a file contains the following attributes:

- file name;
- timestamp;
- security information (for access control to the file);
- data or pointers to disk blocks containing data; and
- an optional pointer to other MFT records if the file size is too large to be contained in one record or if the file has multiple attributes, all of which do not fit in one MFT record.

File name and other standard attributes	File size = 13	Cluster address = 64 Size = 4	Cluster address = 256 Size = 8	Cluster address = 408 Size = 1

Figure 11.23   An MFT record for a file with 13 data blocks.

Each file in NTFS has a unique ID called an *object reference*, a 64-bit quantity. The ID is an index into the MFT for this file and serves a function similar to that of the i-node number in UNIX.

The storage allocation scheme tries, to the extent possible, to allocate contiguous disk blocks to the data blocks of the file. For this purpose, the storage allocation scheme maintains available disk blocks in *clusters*, where each cluster represents a number of contiguous disk blocks. The cluster size is a parameter chosen at the time of formatting the drive. Of course, it may not always be possible to allocate all the data blocks of a file to contiguous disk blocks. For example, consider a file that has 13 data blocks. Let us say that the cluster size is 4 blocks, and the free list contains clusters starting at disk block addresses 64, 256, 260, and 408. In this case, there will be three noncontiguous allocations made for this file, as shown in Figure 11.23.

Note that internal fragmentation is possible with this allocation, since the remaining three disk blocks in cluster 408 are unused.

An MFT record is usually 1 KB to 4 KB in size. Thus, if the file size is small, the data for the file are contained in the MFT record itself, thereby solving the small write problem. Further, the clustered disk allocation ensures good sequential access to files.

Summary

In this chapter, we studied perhaps one of the most important components of your system, namely, the file system. The coverage included

- attributes associated with a file,
- allocation strategies and associated data structure for storage management on the disk,
- metadata managed by the file system,
- implementation details of a file system,
- interaction among the various subsystems of the operating system,
- layout of the files on the disk,
- data structures of the file system and their efficient management,
- dealing with system crashes, and
- file system for other physical media.

We also studied some modern file systems currently in use (circa 2010).

File systems is a fertile ground for research and development. In file systems, we can see an analogy to processor architecture versus implementation. Whereas the file system API remains mostly unchanged across versions of operating systems (be they UNIX,

Microsoft, or anything else), the implementation of the file system continually evolves. Some of the changes are due to the evolution in disk technology, and some are due to the changes in the types of files used in applications. For example, modern workloads generate multimedia files (audio, graphics, photos, video, etc.), and the file system implementation has to adapt in order to efficiently support such diverse file types.

In this chapter, we have only scratched the surface of the intricacies involved in implementing a file system. We hope that we have stimulated your interest enough to get you to take a more advanced course in operating systems.

Exercises

1. Where can the attribute data for a file be stored? Discuss the pros and cons of each choice.

2. Examine the following directory entry in UNIX:

$$-rwxrwxrwx \quad 3\ rama \qquad 0\ Apr\ 27\ 21{:}01\ foo$$

   After the following commands are executed

$$chmod\ u-w\ foo$$
$$chmod\ g-w\ foo$$

   what are the access rights of the file "foo"?

3. Select all that apply:

   Linked allocation results in

   - good sequential access
   - good random access
   - ability to grow the file easily
   - poor disk utilization
   - good disk utilization

4. Select all that apply:

   Fixed contiguous allocation of disk space results in

   - good sequential access
   - good random access
   - ability to grow the file easily
   - poor disk utilization
   - good disk utilization

5. Consider the following:

   Number of cylinders on the disk   = 6000

Number of platters	= 3
Number of surfaces per platter	= 2
Number of sectors per track	= 400
Number of bytes per sector	= 512
Disk allocation policy	= contiguous cylinders

a. How many cylinders should be allocated to store a file of size 1 GB?

b. How much is the internal fragmentation caused by this allocation?

6. What are the problems with FAT allocation policy?

7. Compare linked allocation policy with FAT.

8. How does indexed allocation overcome the problem of FAT and linked allocation?

9. Consider an indexed allocation scheme on a disk

- The disk has 3 platters (2 surfaces per platter).
- There are 4000 tracks in each surface.
- Each track has 400 sectors.
- There are 512 bytes per sector.
- Each i-node is a fixed size data structure occupying one sector.
- A data block (unit of allocation) is a contiguous set of 4 cylinders.
- A pointer to a disk data block is represented by an 8-byte data structure.

a. What is the minimum amount of space used for a file on this system?

b. What is the maximum file size with this allocation scheme?

10. Consider the following for a hybrid allocation scheme:

- size of index block = 256 bytes
- size of data block = 8 KB
- size of disk block pointer = 8 bytes (to either index or data block)
- An i-node consists of 2 direct block pointers, 1 single indirect pointer, 1 double indirect pointer, and 1 triple indirect pointer.

a. What is the maximum size (in bytes) of a file that can be stored in this file system?

b. How many data blocks are needed for storing a data file of 1 GB?

c. How many index blocks are needed for storing the same data file of size 1 GB?

11. What is the difference between hard and soft links?

12. Consider the following:

```
touch f1              /* create a file f1 */
ln -s f1 f2           /* sym link */
ln -s f2 f3
ln f1 f4              /* hard link */
ln f4 f5
```

   a. How many i-nodes will be created by the previous set of commands?

   b. What is the reference count on each node thus created?

13. For ext2 file system with a disk block size of 8 KB and a pointer to disk blocks of 4 bytes, what is the largest file that can be stored on the system? Sketch the structure of an i-node and show the calculations to arrive at the maximum file size (see Example 11.8).

Bibliographic Notes and Further Reading

In systems, the microarchitecture of the processor, cache memories, and file systems are perhaps the three most well-studied topics. The fixation on these three topics is perhaps understandable, since they have the biggest impact on application performance. Whereas UNIX was invented in Bell labs by Ritchie and Thompson, much of the credit for popularizing UNIX, especially in the academic world, goes to the efforts of the researchers at UC-Berkeley, in particular Bill Joy, the co-founder of Sun Microsystems. For a seminal paper that gives an overview of the design principles underlying the Berkeley UNIX file system, the reader is referred to [McKusick, 1984]. McKusick et al. [McKusick, 1996] present a detailed description on the design and implementation of the Berkeley UNIX operating system. This is an excellent resource for any student who wishes to write an operating system. The article by Prabhakaran et al. [Prabhakaran, 2005] is an excellent resource to understand the evolution of journaling file systems such as Linux ext3, ReiserFS, and Microsoft NTFS. Linux, being an open-source project, evolves continually. Therefore, the best source of information to learn about Linux is online resources.[2] The books on Linux by Love [Love, 2003] and Bovet and Cesati [Bovet, 2005] are additional good resources for the Linux enthusiast. For details on Microsoft file systems, the reader is referred to [Russinovich, 2005].

---

2. www.linux.org.

CHAPTER

12

Multithreaded Programming and Multiprocessors

Multithreading is a technique for a program to do multiple tasks, possibly concurrently. Since the early stages of computing, exploiting parallelism has been a quest of computer scientists. As early as the 1970s, languages such as *Concurrent Pascal* and *Ada* have proposed features for expressing program-level concurrency. Humans think and do things in parallel all the time. For example, you may be reading this book while you are listening to some favorite music in the background. Often, we may have an intense conversation with someone on some important topic while working on something with our hands, fixing a car, or folding our laundry. Given that computers extend the human capacity to compute, it is only natural to provide the opportunity for humans to express concurrency in the tasks that they want the computer to do on their behalf. Sequential programming forces us to express our computing needs in a sequential manner. This is unfortunate, since humans think in parallel, but end up coding their thoughts sequentially. For example, let us consider an application such as video surveillance. We want the computer to continually gather images from 10 different cameras, analyze each image individually for any suspicious activity, and raise an alarm in case of a threat. There is nothing sequential in this description. If anything, the opposite is true. Yet, if we want to write a computer program in C to carry out this task, we end up coding it sequentially.

The intent of this chapter is to introduce concepts in developing multithreaded programs, the operating system support needed for these concepts, and the architectural support required to realize the operating system mechanisms. It is imperative for students to learn parallel programming and the related system issues, because single chip processors today incorporate multiple processor cores. Therefore, parallel processing is the norm these days in all computing systems, from low-end to high-end machines. The important point we want to convey in this chapter is that the threading concept and the system support for threading are simple and straightforward.

12.1 Why Multithreading?

Multithreading allows the expression of the inherent parallelism in the algorithm. A *thread* is similar to a process in that it represents an active unit of processing. Later in this chapter, we will discuss the semantic differences between a thread and a process. Suffice it at this point to say that a user-level process may comprise multiple threads.

Let us understand how multithreading helps at the programming level. First, it allows the user program to express its intent for concurrent activities in a modular fashion, just as the procedure abstraction helps organize a sequential program in a modular fashion. Second, it helps in overlapping computation with inherent I/O activities in the program. We know from Chapter 10 that DMA allows a high-speed I/O device to communicate directly with the memory, without the intervention of the processor. Figure 12.1 shows this situation for a program that periodically does I/O, but does not need the result of the I/O immediately. Expressing the I/O activity as a separate thread helps in overlapping computation with communication.

Next, let us see how multithreading helps at the system level. It is common these days to have multiple processors in the same computer or even in a single chip. This is another important reason for multithreading, since any expression of concurrency at the user level can serve to exploit the inherent hardware parallelism that may exist in the computer. Imagine what the program does in a video surveillance application. Figure 12.2 shows the processing associated with a single stream of video in such an

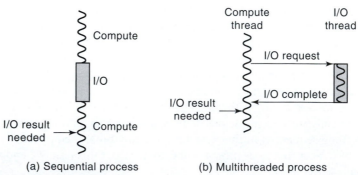

(a) Sequential process   (b) Multithreaded process

Figure 12.1   Overlapping computation with I/O, using threads.

The compute thread in (b) can continue to do useful computation that does not immediately depend on the I/O activity being carried out by the I/O thread.

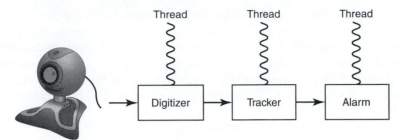

Figure 12.2 Video processing pipeline.

A continuous application wherein camera frames are captured and digitized by the digitizer, and analyzed by the tracker, triggering control actions by the alarm module.

application. The digitizer component of the program continually converts the video into a sequence of frames of pixels. The tracker component analyzes each frame for any content that needs flagging. The alarm component takes control action based on the tracking. The application pipeline resembles the processor pipeline, albeit at a much coarser level. Thus, if we have multiple processors in the computer that work autonomously, they could be executing the program components in parallel, leading to increased performance for the application.

Thus, multithreading is attractive from the point of view of program modularity, opportunity for overlapping computation with I/O, and the potential for increased performance due to parallel processing.

We will use the application shown in Figure 12.2 as a running example to illustrate the programming concepts for multithreading, to be developed in this chapter.

12.2 Programming Support for Threads

Now that we appreciate the utility of threads as a way of expressing concurrency, let us understand what it takes to support threads as a programming abstraction. We want to be able to dynamically *create* threads, *terminate* threads, *communicate* among the threads, and *synchronize* the activities of the threads.

Just as the system provides a math library for common functions that programmers may need, the system likewise provides a library of functions to support the threads abstraction. We will explore the facilities provided by such a library in the next few subsections. It should be understood that, in the discussion, the syntax used for data types and library functions are for illustration purposes only. The actual syntax and supported data types may be different in different actual implementations of thread libraries.

12.2.1 Thread Creation and Termination

A thread executes some program component. Consider the relationship between a process and the program. A process starts executing a program at the *entry* point of the program, the *main* procedure in the case of a C program. In contrast, we want to be able to express concurrency, using threads, at *any* point in the program, *dynamically*. This suggests that the entry point of a thread is *any user-defined procedure*. We define *top-level* procedure as a procedure name that is visible (through the visibility rules of the programming language) wherever this procedure has to be used as a target of thread creation. The top-level procedure may take a number of arguments to be passed in.

Thus, a typical thread creation call may look as follows:

```
thread_create (top-level procedure, args);
```

The thread creation call names the top-level procedure and passes the arguments (packaged as args) to initiate the execution of a thread in that procedure. From the user program's perspective, this call results in the creation of a *unit of execution* (namely, a *thread*), concurrent with the current thread that made the call. (See the before/after picture in Figure 12.3.)

Thus, a **thread_create** function *instantiates* a new and independent entity called a *thread* that has a life of its own.

This is analogous to parents giving birth to children. Once a child is born and learns to walk, he or she roams around the house doing his or her own thing (within the limits set by the parents), independent of the parents. This is exactly what happens with a thread. Recall that a program in execution is a process. In a sequential program there is only one *thread of control*, namely, the process. By a thread of control, we mean an active entity that is roaming around the memory footprint of the program, carrying out the intent of the programmer. Now that it has a life of its own, a thread can do its own thing (within the limits set by the parent process). For example, in Figure 12.3, once created, "child" can make its own procedure calls programmed into the body of its code, independent of what "main" is doing in its code body, past the thread creation point.

Let us understand the limits set for the child thread. In the human analogy, a parent may place a gate near the stairs to prevent the child from going up the stairs, install child-proof cabinets, and so on. For a thread, there are similar limits, imposed by both the programming language and the operating system. A thread starts executing in a top-level procedure. In other words, the starting point for a threaded program is a normal sequential program. Therefore, the visibility and scoping rules of

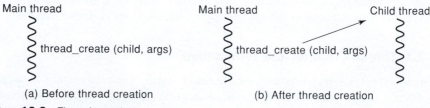

(a) Before thread creation   (b) After thread creation

Figure 12.3   Thread creation.

the programming language apply to constrain the data structures that a thread can manipulate during its lifetime. The operating system creates a unique and distinct memory footprint for the program, called an *address space*, when it instantiates the program as a process. As we saw in earlier chapters, the address space contains the code, global data, stack, and heap sections specific to each program. A process plays in this "sandbox." This is exactly the same sandbox that children of this process play in, as well.

The reader may be puzzled as to the difference between a *process* and a *thread*. We will elaborate on this difference more when we get to Section 12.7 on operating system support for threads. Suffice it to say at this point that the amount of state associated with a process is much greater than that associated with a thread. On the other hand, a thread shares the parent process's address space, and in general has less state information associated with it than a process does. This makes a process heavier in weight than a thread is. However, both the process and the thread are independent threads of control within the process's address space and have lives of their own.

One fundamental difference between a process and a thread is memory protection. The operating system turns each program into a process, each with its own address space that acts as a wall around each process. However, threads execute within a single address space. Thus, they are not protected from each other. In human terms, one does not walk into a neighbor's house and start scribbling on the walls. However, one's children (if not supervised) happily go about scribbling with their crayons on the walls of their own house. They might also get into fistfights with one another. We will see shortly how we can enforce some discipline among the threads in order to maintain a sense of decorum while they are executing within the same address space.

A thread automatically terminates when it exits the top-level procedure that it started in. Additionally, the library may provide an explicit call for terminating a thread in the same process:

```
thread_terminate (tid);
```

Here, **tid** is the system-supplied identifier of the thread that we wish to terminate.

Example 12.1

Show the code fragment to instantiate the digitizer and tracker parts of the application shown in Figure 12.2.

Answer:

See Figure 12.4(a).

```
digitizer()
{
    /* code for grabbing images from camera
     * and share the images with the tracker
     */
}

tracker()
{
    /* code for getting images produced by the digitizer
     * and analyzing an image
     */
}

main()
{
    /* thread ids */
    thread_type digitizer_tid, tracker_tid;

    /* create digitizer thread */
    digitizer_tid = thread_create(digitizer, NULL);

    /* create tracker thread */
    tracker_tid = thread_create(tracker, NULL);

    /* rest of the code of main including
     * termination conditions of the program
     */
}
```

Figure 12.4(a)   Code fragment for thread creation.

Note that the shaded box (in Figure 12.4(a)) is all that is needed to create the required structure.

12.2.2 Communication Among Threads

Threads may need to share data. For example, the digitizer in Figure 12.2 shares the buffer of frames that it creates with the tracker.

Let us see how the system facilitates this sharing. As it turns out, this is straightforward. We already mentioned that a threaded program is created out of a sequential program by turning the top-level procedures into threads. Therefore, the data structures that are visible to multiple threads (i.e., top-level procedures) within the scoping rules of the original program become shared data structures for the threads. Concretely, in a programming language such as C, the global data structures become shared data structures for the threads.

Of course, if the computer is a multiprocessor, there are system issues (at both the operating system and hardware levels) that need to be dealt with in order to facilitate this sharing. We will revisit these issues in Section 12.9.

Example 12.2

Show the data structure definition for the digitizer and tracker threads of Figure 12.2, to share images.

Answer:

See Figure 12.4(b).

```
#define MAX 100                  /* maximum number of images */

    image_type frame_buf[MAX];   /* data structure for
                                  * sharing images between
                                  * digitizer and tracker
                                  */

digitizer()
{
  loop {
    /* code for putting images into frame_buf */
  }
}


tracker()
{
  loop {
    /* code for getting images from frame_buf
     * and analyzing them
     */
  }
}
```

Figure 12.4(b)   Shared data structure between the digitizer and the tracker.

Note: The shaded box (in Figure 12.4(b)) shows the data structure created at the global level to allow both the tracker and digitizer threads to share.

12.2.3 Read-Write Conflict, Race Condition, and Nondeterminism

In a sequential program, we never had to worry about the integrity of data structures, because, by definition, there are no concurrent activities in the program. However, with multiple threads working concurrently within a single address space, it becomes essential to ensure that the threads do not step on one another. We define *read–write conflict* as a condition in which multiple concurrent threads simultaneously try to access a shared variable while at least one of the threads tries to write to the shared variable. A *race* condition occurs when a read–write conflict exists in a program, without an intervening synchronization operation separating the conflict. Race conditions in a program may be intended or unintended. For example, if a shared variable is used for synchronization among threads, there will be an intended race condition.

Consider the following code fragment:

```
Scenario #1:

int flag = 0;  /* shared variable initialized to zero */

Thread 1                            Thread 2
while (flag == 0) {                   .
   /* do nothing */                   .
}                                     .
                                    if (flag == 0) flag = 1;
                                      .
                                      .
```

Threads 1 and 2 are part of the same process. Per definition, threads 1 and 2 are in a read–write conflict. Thread 1 is in a loop, continuously reading shared variable flag, while thread 2 is writing to it in the course of its execution. On the surface, this setup might appear to be a problem, since there is a race between the two threads. However, this is an intentional race (sometimes referred to as *synchronization race*), wherein thread 1 is awaiting the value of flag to be changed by thread 2. Thus, a race condition does not always imply that the code is erroneous.

Next, we will define a particular kind of race condition that could lead to erroneous program behavior. A *data race* is defined as a read–write conflict without an intervening synchronization operation, wherein the variable being accessed by the threads is *not* a synchronization variable. That is, a data race occurs in a parallel program when there is unsynchronized access to arbitrary shared variables.

Consider, the following code fragment:

```
Scenario #2:

int count = 0; /* shared variable initialized to zero */

Thread 1 (T1)       Thread 2 (T2)       Thread 3 (T3)
      .                   .                   .
      .                   .                   .
      .                   .                   .
```

```
count = count+1;     count = count+1;     count = count+1;
  .                      .                      .
  .                      .                      .
```

Thread 4 (T4)
```
  .

  .
printf("count = %d\n", count);
  .

  .
```

There is a data race (for the variable **count**) among all the four threads. What value will thread 4 print? Each of the threads 1, 2, and 3 are adding 1 to the current value of count. However, what is the current value of count seen by each of these threads? Depending on the order of execution of the increment statement (**count = count+1**), the printf statement in thread 4 will result in different values being printed.

This is illustrated in Figure 12.5, wherein four different orders of execution are captured, to illustrate the point.

The first question that should arise in the mind of the reader is, Why are there many different possible executions of the code shown in Scenario #2? The answer is straightforward. The threads are concurrent and execute asynchronously with respect to each other. Therefore, once these threads are created, the order of their execution is simply a function of the available number of processors in the computer, any

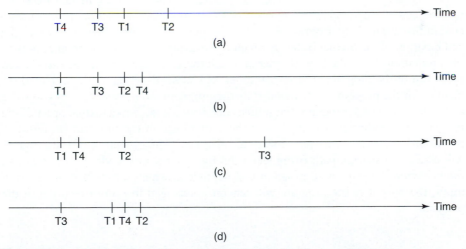

Figure 12.5   Examples of possible executions of Scenario #2 on a uniprocessor using nonpreemptive scheduling of threads.

Nondeterminism in the execution order of the threads will lead to nondeterminism in the output generated by T4.

dependency among the threads, and the scheduling algorithm used by the operating system.

The timeline of execution shown in Figure 12.5 for Scenario #2 assumes that there is a single processor to schedule the threads and that there is no dependency among the threads. That is, once spawned, the threads may execute in any order. Further, a non-preemptive scheduling discipline is assumed. The following example illustrates that there are more than four possible executions for these threads:

Example 12.3

Assume that there are four threads in a process. Assume that the threads are scheduled on a uniprocessor. Once spawned, each thread prints its thread-id and terminates. Assuming a nonpreemptive thread scheduler, how many different executions are possible?

Answer:

As stated in the problem, the threads are independent of one another. Therefore, the operating system may schedule them in any order.

The number of possible executions of the 4 threads = **4!**.

Thus, the execution of a parallel program is a fundamental departure from the sequential execution of a program in a uniprocessor. The execution model presented to a sequential program is very simple: The instructions of a sequential program execute in the *program* order of the sequential program.[1] We define *program order* as the combination of the textual order in which the instructions of the program appear to the programmer, and the logical order in which these instructions will be executed in every run of the program. The logical order, of course, depends on the intended semantics for the program, as envisioned by the programmer. For example, if you write a high-level language program, the source code listing gives you a textual order of the program. Depending on the input and the actual logic in the program (in terms of conditional statements, loops, procedure calls, etc.), the execution of the program will result in a specific path being taken through your source code. In other words, the behavior of a sequential program is *deterministic*, which means that, for a given input, the output of the program will remain unchanged in every execution of the program.

---

1. Note that, as we mentioned in Chapter 5 (Section 5.13.2), processor implementation might choose to reorder the execution of the instructions; this is fine, so long as the appearance of program order to the programmer is preserved despite such reordering.

It is instructive to understand the execution model for a parallel program that comprises several threads. The individual threads of a process experience the same execution model as a sequential program. However, there is no guarantee as to the order of execution of the different threads of the same process. That is, the behavior of a parallel program is *nondeterministic*. We define a *nondeterministic execution* as one in which the output of the program, for a given input, may change from one execution of the program to the next.

Let us return to Scenario #2 and the four possible nonpreemptive executions of the program shown in Figure 12.5. What are the values that would be printed by T4 in each of the four executions?

Look at Figure 12.5(a). Thread T4 is the first one to complete execution. Therefore, the value it would print for count is zero. On the other hand, in Figure 12.5(b), thread T4 is the last to execute. Therefore, the value printed by T4 would be 3. (Each of the executions of T1, T2, and T3 would have incremented count by 1.) In Figures 12.5(c) and 12.5(d), T4 would print 1 and 2, respectively.

Further, if the scheduler is preemptive, many more interleavings of the threads of an application are possible. Worse yet, a statement such as

```
count = count + 1
```

would get compiled into a sequence of machine instructions. For example, compilation of this statement would result in a series of instructions that includes a load from memory, increment, and a store to memory. The thread could be preempted after the load instructions before the store. This has serious implications on the expected program behavior and the actual execution of a program that has such data races.

In Chapter 4 (Section 4.3.4), we introduced the basic concept of what it means for an action to be *atomic*—that is, indivisible. As we saw in Chapter 5, the execution of every instruction in an ISA is designed to be atomic by construction. A processor will entertain external interrupts only upon the completion of an instruction execution to guarantee atomicity for individual instructions. With a multithreaded program, the atomicity of individual instructions is insufficient to achieve the expected program behavior in the presence of data races. We will revisit these issues in Section 12.2.6 and demonstrate the need for atomicity of a group of instructions, in the context of a programming example.

Figure 12.6 demonstrates how, due to the nondeterminism inherent in the parallel programming model, instructions of threads of the same program may get arbitrarily interleaved in an actual run of the program on a uniprocessor.

There are a few points to take away from Figure 12.6. Instructions of the *same* thread execute in program order (e.g., $T_1{:}I_1$, $T_2{:}I_2$, $T_3{:}I_3$, $T_4{:}I_4$, . . .). However, instructions of different threads may get arbitrarily interleaved (see Figure 12.6(b)), while preserving the program order of the individual threads. For example, if you observe the instructions of thread 2 (T_2), you will see that they are in the program order for T_2.

			$T_3:I_1$
			$T_2:I_1$
			$T_3:I_2$
			$T_3:I_3$
			$T_1:I_1$
			$T_2:I_2$
			$T_1:I_2$
			$T_1:I_3$
			$T_1:I_4$
Thread 1 (T_1)	Thread 2 (T_2)	Thread 3 (T_3)	$T_2:I_3$
I_1	I_1	I_1	$T_3:I_4$
I_2	I_2	I_2	$T_2:I_4$
I_3	I_3	I_3	$T_2:I_5$
I_4	I_4	I_4	$T_2:I_6$
I_5	I_5	I_5	$T_1:I_5$
I_6	I_6	I_6	$T_1:I_6$
I_7	I_7	I_7	$T_1:I_7$
I_8	I_8	I_8	$T_3:I_5$
I_9	I_9	I_9	$T_3:I_6$

(a) A parallel program with three threads   (b) An arbitrary interleaving of the instructions from the three threads

Figure 12.6 A parallel program and a possible trace of its execution on a uniprocessor.

The interleaving of the instructions from the three threads depends on how they are scheduled to run on the uniprocessor.

Example 12.4

Given the threads shown here, and their execution history, what is the final value in memory location x? Assume that the execution of each instruction is atomic. Assume that Mem[x] = 0 initially.

Thread 1 (T1)	Thread 2 (T2)
Time 0: R1 ← Mem[x]	Time 1: R2 ← Mem[x]
Time 2: R1 ← R1+2	Time 3: R2 ← R2+1
Time 4: Mem[x] ← R1	Time 5: Mem[x] ← R2

Answer:

Each of the threads T1 and T2 load a memory location, add a value to it, and write it back. With the presence of data race and preemptive scheduling, unfortunately, x will contain the value written to it by the last store operation.

Since T2 is the last to complete its store operation, the final value in x is **1**.

To summarize, nondeterminism is at the core of the execution model for a parallel program. For the application programmer, it is important to understand and come to terms with this concept in order to be able to write correct parallel programs. Table 12.1 summarizes the execution models of sequential and parallel programs.

12.2.4 Synchronization Among Threads

How could a programmer expect a deterministic behavior for her program, given that the execution model for a parallel program is nondeterministic? The answer is quite simple: Deterministic behavior is accomplished by synchronization among the threads. We will elaborate what we mean by *synchronization among the threads* in the rest of this subsection. Specifically, we will discuss two types of synchronization: *mutual exclusion* and *rendezvous*.

Mutual exclusion. As an analogy, let us watch some children at play, as shown in Figure 12.7. There are activities that they can do independently and concurrently (Figure 12.7(a)), without stepping on each other. However, if they are sharing a toy, we tell them to take turns so that each child gets a chance (Figure 12.7(b)).

Similarly, if there are two threads, one a *producer* and the other a *consumer*, it is essential that the producer not modify the shared buffer while the consumer is reading

Table 12.1 Execution Models of Sequential and Parallel Programs

	Execution Model
Sequential program	The program execution is deterministic, i.e., instructions execute in program order. The hardware implementation of the processor may reorder instructions for efficiency of pipelined execution, so long as the appearance of program order is preserved despite such reordering.
Parallel program	The program execution is nondeterministic, i.e., instructions of each individual thread execute in program order. However, the instructions of the different threads of the same program may be arbitrarily interleaved.

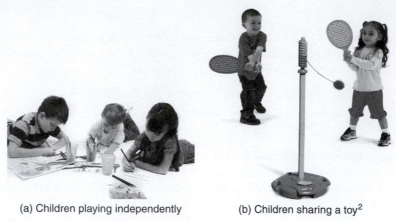

(a) Children playing independently   (b) Children sharing a toy[2]

Figure 12.7   Children playing in a shared "sandbox."

it (see Figure 12.8). We refer to this requirement as *mutual exclusion*. The producer and consumer work concurrently, except when either or both have to modify or inspect shared data structures. In that case, it is necessary that they execute sequentially to ensure data integrity.

The library provides a *mutual exclusion lock* for this purpose. A *lock* is a data abstraction that has the semantics shown here. A program can declare any number of these locks just as it declared variables of any other data type. The reader can see the analogy to a physical lock. Only one thread can hold a particular lock at a time. Once a thread *acquires* a lock, other threads cannot get that same lock until the first thread *releases* the lock. The following declaration creates a variable of type lock:

```
mutex_lock_type mylock;
```

The following calls allow a thread to acquire and release a particular lock:

```
thread_mutex_lock (mylock);
thread_mutex_unlock(mylock);
```

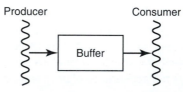

Figure 12.8   Shared buffer between threads.

The producer thread places items in the buffer, and the consumer picks them up for processing.

---

2. Picture source: http://www.liveandlearn.com/toys/tetherball.html.

Successful return from the first function given is an indication to the calling thread that it has successfully acquired the lock. If another thread currently holds the lock, the calling thread *blocks* until the lock becomes free. In general, we define the *blocked* state of a thread as one in which the thread cannot proceed in its execution until some condition is satisfied. The second function releases the named lock.

Sometimes, a thread may not want to block, but may choose to go on to do other things if the lock is unavailable. The library provides a nonblocking version of the lock acquisition call:

```
{success, failure} ← thread_mutex_trylock (mylock);
```

This call returns a success or failure indication for the named lock acquisition request.

Example 12.5

Show the code fragment to allow the producer and consumer threads in Figure 12.8 to access the buffer, in a mutually exclusive manner, to place an item and retrieve an item, respectively.

Answer:

```
item_type buffer;
mutex_lock_type buflock;
int producer()                        int consumer()
{                                     {
  item_type item;                       item_type item;

  /* code to produce item */            . . . . . . . . . .
  . . . . . . . . .                     . . . . . . . . .
  thread_mutex_lock(buflock);           thread_mutex_lock(buflock);
    buffer = item;                        item = buffer;
  thread_mutex_unlock(buflock);         thread_mutex_unlock(buflock);

  . . . . . . . .                       . . . . . . . . .
  . . . . . . . .                       /* code to consume item */
}                                     }
```

Note: Only buffer and buflock are shared data structures. "item" is a local variable within each thread.

In Example 12.5, the producer and consumer execute concurrently, for the most part. When either the producer or the consumer executes code in its respective shaded box, what is the other thread doing? The answer to this question depends on where the other thread is in its execution. Let us say that the producer is executing within its shaded box. Then the consumer is in one of two situations:

- Consumer is also actively executing if it is outside its shaded box.
- If the consumer is trying to get into its shaded box, then it has to *wait* until the producer is out of its shaded box; similarly, the producer has to wait until the consumer is already in the shaded box.

That is, the execution of the producer and that of the consumer in their respective shaded boxes are *mutually exclusive* of each other. Code that is executed in such a mutually exclusive manner is referred to as *critical section*. We define *critical section* as a region of the program in which the execution of the threads is serialized. That is, exactly one thread at a time can be executing the code *inside* a critical section. If multiple threads arrive at a critical section at the same time, one of them will succeed in entering and executing the code inside the critical section, while the others wait at the entry point. Many of us have encountered a similar situation at a busy ATM machine, where we have to wait for our turn to withdraw cash or deposit a check.

As an example of a critical section, we present the code for implementing updates to a shared counter:

```
mutex_lock_type lock;
int counter; /* shared counter */

int increment_counter()
{
            /* critical section for
             * updating a shared counter
             */
            thread_mutex_lock(lock);
                  counter = counter + 1;
            thread_mutex_unlock(lock);
            return 0;

}
```

Any number of threads may simultaneously call increment_counter. Due to the mutually exclusive nature of thread_mutex_lock, exactly one thread can be inside the critical section, updating the shared counter.

Example 12.6

Given the points of execution of the threads (indicated by the arrows) in the figure that follows, state which ones are active and which ones are blocked, and why. Assume that the critical sections are mutually exclusive (i.e., they are governed by the same lock). T1–T4 are threads of the same process.

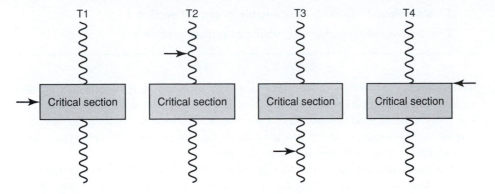

Answer:

T1 is **active** and executing code **inside** its **critical section**.

T2 is **active** and executing code **outside** its **critical section**.

T3 is **active** and executing code **outside** its **critical section**.

T4 is **blocked** and **waiting** to get into its **critical section**. (It will get in once the lock is released by T1).

Example 12.7

Given the points of execution of the threads (indicated by the arrows) in the figure that follows, state which ones are active and which ones are blocked, and why. Note that distinct locks govern each of critical sections 1 and 2.

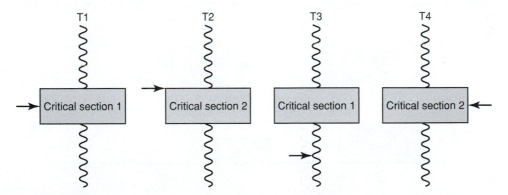

Answer:

T1 is **active** and executing code **inside** its **critical section 1**.

T2 is **blocked** and **waiting** to get into its **critical section 2**. (It will get in once the lock is released by T4).

T3 is **active** and executing code **outside** its **critical section 1**.

T4 is **active** and executing code **inside** its **critical section 2**.

Rendezvous. To motivate the second type of synchronization, let us consider another analogy. You and your friend decide to go to a movie. You arrive at the movie house first. You wait for your friend to arrive so that you can then go into the movie house together. You are synchronizing your action with your friend, but this is a different type of synchronization, one we will refer to as a *rendezvous*.

Similar to this analogy, a thread may want to wait for another thread in the same process. The most common usage of such a mechanism is for a parent to wait for the children that it spawns. Consider, for example, that a thread is spawned to read a file from the disk while main has some other, concurrent activity to perform. Once main completes this concurrent activity, it cannot proceed further until the spawned thread completes its file read. This is a good example of main's waiting for its child to terminate, which would be an indication that the file read is complete.

The library provides such a *rendezvous* mechanism through the function call:

```
thread_join (peer_thread_id);
```

The function blocks the caller until the named peer thread terminates. Upon the peer thread's termination, the calling thread resumes execution.

More formally, we define *rendezvous* as a meeting point between threads of the same program. A rendezvous requires a minimum of two threads, but in the limit may include all the threads of a given program. Threads participating in a rendezvous continue with their respective executions once all the other threads have also arrived at the rendezvous point. Figure 12.9 shows an example of a rendezvous among threads.

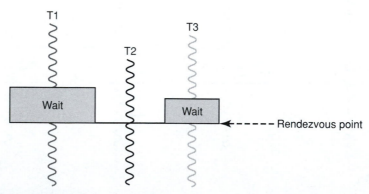

Figure 12.9 Rendezvous among threads.

Threads may arrive at different times to the rendezvous point, but they all wait until everyone has arrived before proceeding.

T1, the first to arrive at the rendezvous point, awaits the arrival of the other two threads. T3 arrives next; finally, once T2 arrives, the rendezvous is complete, and the three threads proceed with their respective executions. As should be evident, rendezvous is a convenient way for threads of a parallel program to coordinate their activities with respect to one another in the presence of the nondeterministic execution model. Further, any subset of the threads of a process may decide to rendezvous amongst them. The most general form of rendezvous mechanism is often referred to in the literature as *barrier synchronization*. This mechanism is extremely useful in parallel programming of scientific applications. *All* the threads of a given application that would like to participate in the rendezvous execute the barrier synchronization call. Once all the threads have arrived at the barrier, the threads are allowed to proceed with their respective executions.

The thread_join call is a special case of the general rendezvous mechanism. It is a one-sided rendezvous. Only the thread that executes this call may experience any waiting (if the peer thread has not already terminated). The peer thread is completely oblivious of the fact that another thread is waiting on it. Note that this call allows the calling thread to wait on the termination of exactly one thread. For example, if a main thread spawns a set of children threads and would like to be alive until all of them have terminated, it has to execute multiple thread_join calls, one after the other, one call for each of its children. In Section 12.2.8 (see Example 12.10), we will show a symmetric rendezvous between two threads, using conditional variables.

There is one way in which the real-life analogy breaks down in the context of threads. A child usually outlives the parent in real life. This is not necessarily true in the context of threads. In particular, recall that all the threads execute within an address space. As it turns out, not all threads are equal in status. There is a distinction between a parent thread and a child thread. As shown in Figure 12.4(a) (Example 12.1), when the process is instantiated, there is only one thread within the address space, namely, "main." Once "main" spawns the "digitizer" and "tracker" threads, the address space has three active threads: "main," "digitizer," and "tracker." What happens when "main" exits? This is the parent thread and is **synonymous** with the process itself. According to the usual semantics implemented by most operating systems, when the parent thread in a process terminates, the entire process terminates. However, note that if a child spawns its own children, the immediate parent does not determine these children's life expectancy; the main thread that is synonymous with the process determines it. This is another reason that the thread_join call comes in handy, wherein the parent thread can wait on the children before exiting.

Example 12.8

"main" spawns a top-level procedure "foo." Show how we can ensure that "main" does not terminate prematurely.

Answer:

```
int foo(int n)
{

  .  .  .  .  .

  return 0;
}

int main()
{
        int f;
        thread_type child_tid;

        .  .  .  .  .

        child_tid = thread_create (foo, &f);

        .  .  .  .  .

        thread_join(child_tid);

}
```

Note: "main" by executing **thread_join** on the child_tid waits for the child to be finished before itself terminating.

12.2.5 Internal Representation of Data Types Provided by the Threads Library

We mentioned that a thread blocks when a lock it wants is currently being used by another thread. Let us understand the exact meaning of this statement. As should be evident by now, in contrast to data types (such as "int" and "float") supported by a programming language such as C, the threads library supports the data types we have been introducing in this chapter.

The **thread_type** and the **mutex_lock_type** are opaque data types, meaning that the user has no direct access to the internal representation of these data types. Internally, the threads library may have some accounting information associated with a variable of the **thread_type** data type. The **mutex_lock_type** data type is interesting and worth knowing more about, from the programmer's perspective. The internal representation for a variable of this data type will have a minimum of two things:

- the thread (if any) that is currently holding the lock; and
- a queue of waiting requestors (if any) for this lock.

Thus, if we have a lock variable **L**; currently, a thread **T1** has it; and there are two other threads **T2** and **T3** waiting to get the lock, then the internal representation in the threads library for this variable L will look as follows:

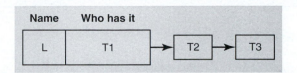

When **T1** releases the lock, **T2** gets the lock, because **T2** is the first thread in the waiting queue for this lock. Note that every lock variable has a distinct waiting queue associated with it. A thread can be on exactly one waiting queue at any point in time.

Example 12.9

Assume that the following events happen in the order shown (T1–T5 are threads of the same process):

T1 executes `thread_mutex_lock(L1);`

T2 executes `thread_mutex_lock(L1);`

T3 executes `thread_mutex_lock(L2);`

T4 executes `thread_mutex_lock(L2);`

T5 executes `thread_mutex_lock(L1);`

Assuming that there have been no other calls to the threads library prior to this, show the state of the internal queues in the threads library after the given five calls.

Answer:

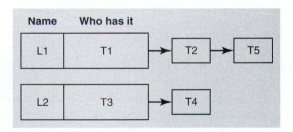

12.2.6 Simple Programming Examples

Basic code with no synchronization. First, let us understand why we need the synchronization constructs. Consider the sample program which follows (Sample Program #1) that shows the interaction between the digitizer and the tracker threads of Figure 12.2. Here, we will progressively refine this sample program to ensure that it delivers the desired semantics for this application. For the benefit of advanced readers, Sample Program #5, which appears a little later in the text, delivers the desired semantics (see Section 12.2.9).

```
/*
 * Sample program #1:
 */
#define MAX 100

int bufavail = MAX;
image_type frame_buf[MAX];
```

```
digitizer()                          tracker()
{                                    {
  image_type dig_image;                image_type track_image;
  int tail = 0;                        int head = 0;

  loop { /* begin loop */              loop { /* begin loop */
    if (bufavail > 0) {                  if (bufavail < MAX) {

      grab(dig_image);
      frame_buf[tail mod MAX] =            track_image =
          dig_image;                         frame_buf[head mod MAX];
      bufavail = bufavail - 1;            bufavail = bufavail + 1;

      tail = tail + 1;                     head = head + 1;
    }                                      analyze(track_image);
  } /* end loop */                       }
}                                      } /* end loop */
                                     }
```

In this sample program, `bufavail` and `frame_buf` are the shared data structures between the digitizer and the tracker threads. The sample program shows an implementation of the `frame_buf` as a circular queue, with a `head` and a `tail` pointer and insertion at the tail and deletion at the head. (See Figure 12.10; the shaded region contains valid items in `frame_buf`.) The availability of space in the buffer is indicated by the `bufavail` variable.

The `head` and `tail` pointers themselves are local variables inside the digitizer and tracker, respectively. The digitizer code continuously loops, grabbing an image from the camera, putting it in the frame buffer, and advancing its `tail` pointer to point to the next open slot in `frame_buf`. Availability of space in the frame buffer (`bufavail > 0`) predicates this execution within the loop. Similarly, the tracker code continuously loops, getting an image from the frame buffer (if one is available), advancing its `head` pointer to the next valid frame in `frame_buf`, and then analyzing the frame for items of interest. The two threads are independent of one another except for the interaction that happens in the shaded boxes in the two threads shown in Sample Program #1. The

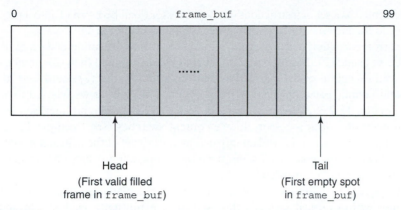

Figure 12.10   frame_buf implemented as a circular queue, with head and tail pointers.

The shaded areas are new items as yet unprocessed by the tracker.

code in the shaded boxes manipulates the shared variables, namely, **frame_buf** and **bufavail**.

Need for atomicity for a group of instructions. The problem with the previous code fragment is that the digitizer and the tracker are concurrent threads, and they could be reading and writing to the shared data structures *simultaneously,* if they are each executing on a distinct processor. Figure 12.11 captures this situation, wherein both the digitizer and the tracker are modifying **bufavail** at the same time.

Let us drill down into this situation a little more. The statement

$$\text{bufavail} = \text{bufavail} - 1; \qquad\qquad (1)$$

is implemented as a set of instructions on the processor (load **bufavail** into a processor register; do the decrement; store the register back into **bufavail**).

Similarly, the statement

$$\text{bufavail} = \text{bufavail} + 1; \qquad\qquad (2)$$

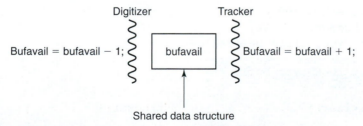

Figure 12.11   Problem with unsynchronized access to shared data.

Both the digitizer and the tracker are simultaneously updating the same memory location (bufavail).

is implemented as a set of instructions on the processor (load `bufavail` into a processor register; do the increment; store the register back into `bufavail`).

A correct execution of the program requires the *atomic* execution of each of the two statements (1) and (2). That is, either statement (1) executes and then (2), or vice versa. Interleaved execution of the instruction sequences for (1) and (2) could lead to erroneous and unanticipated behavior of the program. This is what we referred to as *data race* in Section 12.2.3. As we mentioned in Section 12.2.3, such an interleaving could happen even on a uniprocessor, due to context switches (see Example 12.4). The processor guarantees atomicity of an instruction at the level of the instruction-set architecture. However, the system software (namely, the operating system) has to guarantee atomicity for a group of instructions.

Therefore, to ensure atomicity, we need to encapsulate accesses to shared data structures within *critical sections;* this will ensure mutually exclusive execution. However, we have to be careful in deciding how and when to use synchronization constructs. Indiscriminate use of these constructs, while ensuring atomicity, could lead to restricting concurrency and, worse yet, could introduce incorrect program behavior.

Code refinement with coarse-grain critical sections. We will now proceed to use the synchronization constructs `thread_mutex_lock` and `thread_mutex_unlock` in the sample program to achieve the desired mutual exclusion.

Sample Program #2 is another attempt at writing a threaded sample program for the example given in Figure 12.2. This program illustrates the use of mutual exclusion lock. The difference from Sample Program #1 is the addition of the synchronization constructs inside the shaded boxes in Sample Program #2. In each of the digitizer and tracker, the code between lock and unlock is the work done by the respective threads to access shared data structures. Note that the use of synchronization constructs ensures atomicity of the entire code block between lock and unlock calls for the digitizer and tracker, respectively. This program is "correct" in terms of the desired semantics, but has a serious performance problem that we will elaborate on next.

```
/*
 * Sample program #2:
 */
#define MAX 100
int bufavail = MAX;
image_type frame_buf[MAX];

mutex_lock_type buflock;

digitizer()                        tracker()
{                                  {
  image_type dig_image;              image_type track_image;
  int tail = 0;                      int head = 0;
```

```
    loop { /* begin loop */           loop { /* begin loop */
      thread_mutex_lock(buflock);       thread_mutex_lock(buflock);

      if (bufavail > 0) {               if (bufavail < MAX) {
        grab(dig_image);                  track_image =
        frame_buf[tail mod MAX] =           frame_buf[head mod MAX];
          dig_image;                      head = head + 1;
        tail = tail + 1;                  bufavail = bufavail + 1;
        bufavail = bufavail - 1;          analyze(track_image);
      }                                 }

      thread_mutex_unlock(buflock);     thread_mutex_unlock(buflock);

    } /* end loop */                  } /* end loop */
  }                                 }
```

Code refinement with fine-grain critical sections. A close inspection of Sample Program #2 will reveal that it has no synchronization problem, but there is no concurrency in the execution of the digitizer and the tracker. Let us analyze what needs mutual exclusion in this sample program. There is no need for mutual exclusion for either grabbing the image by the digitizer or for analyzing the image by the tracker. Similarly, once the threads have ascertained the validity of operating on **frame_buf** by checking **bufavail**, insertion or deletion of the item can proceed concurrently. That is, although **frame_buf** is a shared data structure, the way it is used in the program obviates the need for serializing access to it. Therefore, we modify the program as shown in Sample Program #3 to increase the amount of concurrency between the tracker and the digitizer. We limit the mutual exclusion to the checks and modifications done to **bufavail**. Unfortunately, the resulting code has a serious problem that we will explain next.

```
/*
 * Sample program #3:
 */
#define MAX 100
int bufavail = MAX;
image_type frame_buf[MAX];
mutex_lock_type buflock;
```

```
digitizer()                          tracker()
{                                    {
  image_type dig_image;                image_type track_image;
  int tail = 0;                        int head = 0;

  loop { /* begin loop */              loop { /* begin loop */
    grab(dig_image);
                                         thread_mutex_lock(buflock);
    thread_mutex_lock(buflock);            while (bufavail == MAX)
      while (bufavail == 0)                  do nothing;
        do nothing;                      thread_mutex_unlock(buflock);
    thread_mutex_unlock(buflock);
                                         track_image =
    frame_buf[tail mod MAX] =              frame_buf[head mod MAX];
      dig_image;                         head = head + 1;
    tail = tail + 1;
                                         thread_mutex_lock(buflock);
    thread_mutex_lock(buflock);            bufavail = bufavail + 1;
      bufavail = bufavail - 1;          thread_mutex_unlock(buflock);
    thread_mutex_unlock(buflock);
                                         analyze(track_image);
  } /* end loop */                     } /* end loop */
}                                    }
```

12.2.7 Deadlocks and Livelocks

Let us dissect Sample Program #3 to identify and understand its problem. Consider the while statement in the digitizer code. It is checking bufavail for an empty spot in the frame_buf. Let us assume that frame_buf is full. In this case, the digitizer is continuously executing the while statement, waiting for space to free up in frame_buf. The tracker has to make space in the frame_buf by removing an image and incrementing bufavail. However, the digitizer has buflock, and hence the tracker is stuck trying to acquire buflock. A similar situation arises when frame_buf is empty (the while statement in the tracker code).

The problem we have just described, called *deadlock,* is the bane of all concurrent programs. Deadlock is a situation wherein a thread is waiting for an event that will never happen. For example, the digitizer is waiting for bufavail to become nonzero in the while statement, but that event will not happen because the tracker cannot get the lock. The situation captured in the foregoing description is a special case of deadlock, often referred to as a *livelock.* A thread involved in a deadlock may be waiting actively or passively. Livelock is the situation in which a thread is actively checking for an event that will never happen. Let us say that, in this case, the digitizer is holding the buflock and checking for bufavail to become nonzero. This is a livelock, since it is wasting processor resource to check for an event that will never happen. On the other hand, the tracker is waiting for the lock to be released by the digitizer. Tracker's waiting is passive, because it is blocked in the operating system for the lock release. Regardless of whether the waiting is passive or active, the threads involved in a dead-lock are stuck forever. It should be evident to the reader that deadlocks and livelocks are yet another manifestation of the basic nondeterministic nature of a parallel program execution.

We could make a case that the **while** statements in the previous code do not need mutual exclusion, because they are only inspecting buffer availability. In fact, removing mutual exclusion around the **while** statements will remove the *deadlock* problem. Sample Program #4 takes this approach. The difference from Sample Program #3 is that the lock around the **while** statement has been removed for both the digitizer and the tracker.

```
/*
 * Sample program #4:
 */
#define MAX 100

int bufavail = MAX;
image_type frame_buf[MAX];
mutex_lock_type buflock;

digitizer()                        tracker()
{                                  {
  image_type dig_image;              image_type track_image;
  int tail = 0;                      int head = 0;

  loop {/* begin loop */             loop {/* begin loop */
    grab(dig_image);
                                       while (bufavail == MAX)
    while (bufavail == 0)                 do nothing;
      do nothing;
                                       track_image =
    frame_buf[tail mod MAX] =            frame_buf[head mod MAX];
      dig_image;                       head = head + 1;
    tail = tail + 1;
                                       thread_mutex_lock(buflock);
    thread_mutex_lock(buflock);        bufavail = bufavail + 1;
    bufavail = bufavail - 1;         thread_mutex_unlock(buflock);
    thread_mutex_unlock(buflock);
                                       analyze(track_image);
  } /* end loop */                   } /* end loop */
}                                  }
```

This solution is correct and has concurrency as well for the digitizer and the tracker. However, the solution is grossly inefficient due to the nature of waiting. We refer to the kind of waiting that either the digitizer or the tracker does in the while statement as *busy waiting*. The processor is busy doing nothing. This is inefficient, since the processor could have been doing something more useful for some other thread or process.

12.2.8 Condition Variables

Ideally, we would like the system to recognize that the condition that the digitizer is waiting for, (**bufavail > 0**), is not satisfied, and therefore release the lock on behalf of the digitizer, and reschedule it later when the condition is satisfied.

This is exactly the semantics of another data abstraction commonly provided by the library, called a *condition variable*.

The following declaration creates a variable of type *condition variable*:

```
cond_var_type buf_not_empty;
```

The library provides calls to allow threads to *wait* and *signal* one another by using these condition variables:

```
thread_cond_wait(buf_not_empty, buflock);
thread_cond_signal(buf_not_empty);
```

The first call allows a thread (tracker, in our example) to wait on a condition variable. *Waiting* on a condition variable amounts to the library descheduling the thread that made that call. Notice that the second argument to this call is a mutual exclusion lock variable. Implicitly, the library performs **unlock** on the named lock variable before descheduling the calling thread. The second call *signals* any thread that may be waiting on the named condition variable. A *signal*, as the name suggests, is an indication to the waiting thread

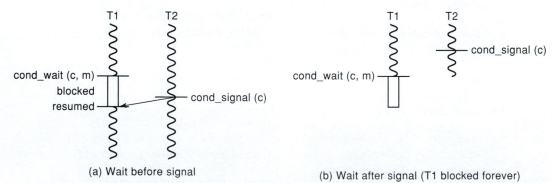

(a) Wait before signal   (b) Wait after signal (T1 blocked forever)

Figure 12.12   Wait and signal, with condition variable: "c" is a condition variable, and "m" is a mutex lock with which "c" is associated through the cond_wait call.

In (a), T1 receives the signal, since it is already waiting; in (b), the signal is lost, since T1 is not yet waiting.

that it may resume execution. The library knows the specific lock variable associated with the *wait* call. Therefore, the library performs an implicit **lock** on that variable, prior to scheduling the waiting thread. Of course, the library treats as a NOP any signal on a condition variable for which there is no waiting thread. Multiple threads may wait on the same condition variable. The library picks one of them (usually, on a first-come-first-served basis) among the waiting threads to deliver the signal. One has to be very careful in using wait and signal for synchronization among threads. Figure 12.12(a) shows a correct use of the primitives. Figure 12.12(b) shows an incorrect use, creating a situation in which T1 starts waiting after T2 has signaled, leading to a deadlock.

Figure 12.12(b) illustrates that a signal sent prematurely will land a peer in a deadlock. Example 12.10 shows how one can devise a rendezvous mechanism between two peers, independent of the order of arrival.

Example 12.10

Write a function **wait_for_buddy()** to be used by *exactly* 2 threads to rendezvous with each other, as shown in the accompanying figure. The order of arrival of the two threads should be immaterial. Note that this is a general example of accomplishing a rendezvous (described in Section 12.2.4) among independent threads of the same process.

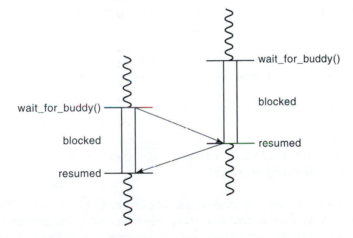

Answer:

The solution uses a Boolean (buddy_waiting), a mutex lock (mtx), and a condition variable (cond). The basic idea is the following:

- Whichever thread arrives first (the "if" section of the code shown next), sets the buddy_waiting flag to be true and waits.
- The second arriving thread (the "else" section of the code shown next), sets the buddy_waiting to be false, signals the first thread, and waits.
- The first arriving thread is unblocked from its conditional wait, signals the second thread, unlocks the mutex, and leaves the procedure.

- The second arriving thread is unblocked from its conditional wait, unlocks the mutex, and leaves the procedure.
- It is important to observe the wait–signal ordering in the "if" and "else" code blocks; not following the order shown will result in deadlock.

```
boolean buddy_waiting = FALSE;
mutex_lock_type mtx; /* assume this has been initialized
                            properly */
cond_var_type cond;  /* assume this has been initialized
                            properly */
wait_for_buddy()
{
  /* both buddies execute the lock statement */
  thread_mutex_lock(mtx);

  if (buddy_waiting == FALSE) {
    /* first arriving thread executes this code block */
    buddy_waiting = TRUE;

    /* the following order is important */
    /* the first arriving thread will execute a wait statement */
    thread_cond_wait (cond, mtx);

    /* the first thread wakes up due to the signal from the second
     * thread, and immediately signals the second arriving thread
     */
    thread_cond_signal(cond);
  }
  else {
    /* second arriving thread executes this code block */
    buddy_waiting = FALSE;

    /* the following order is important */
    /* signal the first arriving thread and then execute a wait
     * statement awaiting a corresponding signal from the
     * first thread
     */
    thread_cond_signal (cond);
    thread_cond_wait (cond, mtx);
  }

  /* both buddies execute the unlock statement */
  thread_mutex_unlock (mtx);
}
```

Internal representation of the condition variable data type. It is instructive from a programming standpoint to understand the internal representation within the threads library of the `cond_var_type` data type. A variable of this data type has, at a minimum, the following:

- a queue of threads (if any) waiting for signal on this variable; and
- for each thread waiting for a signal, the associated mutex lock.

A thread that calls `thread_cond_wait` names a mutex lock. The threads library unlocks this lock on behalf of this thread before placing it on the waiting queue. Similarly, when a signal is received on this condition variable and when a thread is unblocked from the waiting queue, it is the responsibility of the threads library to reacquire the lock on behalf of the thread before resuming the thread. This is why the threads library remembers the lock associated with a thread on the waiting queue.

Thus, for instance, suppose that two threads T3 and T4 execute conditional wait calls on a condition variable C. Let T3's call be

```
thread_cond_wait (C, L1)
```

and let T4's call be

```
thread_cond_wait (C, L2)
```

The internal representation of C after the preceding two calls will look as follows:

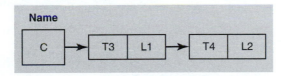

Note that it is not necessary that all wait calls on a given condition variable name the same lock variable.

Example 12.11

Assume that the following events happen in the order shown (T1–T7 are threads of the same process):

T1 executes `thread_mutex_lock(L1);`

T2 executes `thread_cond_wait(C1, L1);`

T3 executes `thread_mutex_lock(L2);`

T4 executes `thread_cond_wait(C2, L2);`

T5 executes `thread_cond_wait(C1, L2);`

a. Assuming that there have been no other calls to the threads library prior to this, show the state of the internal queues in the threads library after the preceding five calls.

b. Subsequently, the following event happens:

T6 executes `thread_cond_signal(C1);`

T7 executes `thread_cond_signal(C2);`

Show the state of the internal queues in the threads library after these two calls.

Answer:

a.

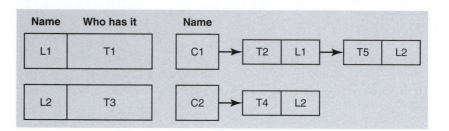

b.

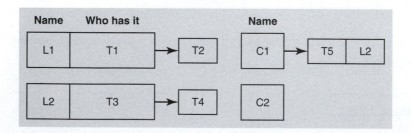

The library moves T2 to the waiting queue of L1, and T4 to the waiting queue of L2, upon receiving the signals on C1 and C2, respectively.

12.2.9 A Complete Solution for the Video Processing Example

Now we will return to our original video processing example of Figure 12.2. Shown next is a program sample that uses wait and signal semantics for the same example. Note that each thread waits after checking a condition which currently is not true; the other thread enables this condition, eventually ensuring that there will not be a deadlock. Note also that each thread performs the signaling while holding the mutual exclusion lock. Whereas this is strictly not necessary, it is nevertheless a good programming practice and results in fewer erroneous parallel programs.

```
/*
 * Sample program #5:  This solution delivers the expected
 *                     semantics for the video processing
 *                     pipeline shown in Figure 12.2, both
 *                     in terms of performance and
 *                     correctness for a single digitizer
 *                     feeding images to a single tracker.
 */
#define MAX 100

int bufavail = MAX;
image_type frame_buf[MAX];
mutex_lock_type buflock;

cond_var_type buf_not_full;
cond_var_type buf_not_empty;
```

```
digitizer()                      tracker()
{                                {
  image_type dig_image;            image_type track_image;
  int tail = 0;                    int head = 0;

  loop { /* begin loop */          loop { /* begin loop */
    grab(dig_image);
                                     thread_mutex_lock(buflock);
    thread_mutex_lock(buflock);        if (bufavail == MAX)
      if (bufavail == 0)                 thread_cond_wait(buf_       (3)
        thread_cond_wait(buf_            not_empty, buflock);
(1)       not_full, buflock);      thread_mutex_unlock(buflock);
    thread_mutex_unlock(buflock);

                                     track_image = frame_buf
    frame_buf[tail mod MAX] =          [head mod MAX];
      dig_image;                     head = head + 1;
    tail = tail + 1;
```

(2)
```
thread_mutex_lock(buflock);
  bufavail = bufavail - 1;
   thread_cond_signal
    (buf_not_empty);
thread_mutex_unlock(buflock);
```

```
    } /* end loop */
}
```

(4)
```
thread_mutex_lock(buflock);
  bufavail = bufavail + 1;
   thread_cond_signal
    (buf_not_full);
thread_mutex_unlock(buflock);
```

```
    analyze(track_image);
  } /* end loop */
}
```

The key point to note in this program sample is the *invariant* maintained by the library on behalf of each thread. An invariant is some indisputable truth about the state of the program. At the point of making the **thread_cond_wait** call, the invariant is the indisputable truth that the calling thread is holding a lock. The library implicitly releases the lock on behalf of the calling thread. When the thread resumes, it is necessary to reestablish the invariant. The library reestablishes the invariant on behalf of the blocked thread, prior to resumption, by implicitly reacquiring the lock.

12.2.10 Discussion of the Solution

Concurrency. Let us analyze the solution presented in Program Sample #5 and convince ourselves that there is no lack of concurrency.

- First, notice that code blocks (1) and (3) hold the lock only for checking the value in **bufavail**. If the checking results in a favorable outcome, then release the lock and go on to either putting an image or getting an image, respectively. What if the checking results in an unfavorable outcome? In that case, the code blocks execute a conditional wait statement on **buf_not_full** and **buf_not_empty**, respectively. In either case, the library immediately releases the associated lock.

- Second, notice that code blocks (2) and (4) hold the lock only for updating the **bufavail** variable, and signaling to unblock the other thread (if it is waiting).

Given these two points, we see that there is **no lack of concurrency**, since the lock is never held for any extended period by either thread.

Example 12.12

Assume that the digitizer is in code block (2) and is about to signal on the **buf_not_empty** condition variable in Sample Program #5.

State whether the following statement is **True** or **False**, and give justification:

```
The tracker is guaranteed to be waiting for a signal on
buf_not_empty inside code block (3).
```

Answer:

False. The tracker could be waiting, but not always. Note that the signaling in code block (2) is unconditional. Therefore, we do not know what the value of `bufavail` is. The only way for the tracker to be blocked inside code block (2) is if `bufavail = MAX`. We know it is nonzero, since the digitizer is able to put a frame in, but we do not know that it is = MAX.

Absence of deadlock. Next, let us convince ourselves that the solution is correct and does not result in deadlock. First, we will informally show that, at any point in time, **both** the threads do not block, leading to a deadlock.

- Let the digitizer be waiting inside code block (1) for a signal. Given this, we will show that the tracker will not also block, leading to a deadlock. Since the digitizer is blocked, we know the following to be true:
  - `bufavail = 0`
  - digitizer is blocked, waiting for a signal on `buf_not_full`
  - `buflock` has been implicitly released by the thread library on behalf of the digitizer.

  There are three possible places for the tracker to block:
  - Entry to code block (3): Since the digitizer does not hold `buflock`, tracker will not block at the entry point.
  - Entry to code block (4): Since the digitizer does not hold `buflock`, tracker will not block at the entry point.
  - Conditional wait statement inside code block (3): The digitizer is blocked, waiting for a signal inside code block (1). Therefore, `bufavail = 0`; hence, the "if" statement inside code block (3) will return a favorable result, and the tracker is guaranteed not to block.
- With a similar line of argument as the foregoing, we can establish that if the tracker is waiting inside code block (3) for a signal, the digitizer will not also block, leading to a deadlock.

Next, we will show that if one thread is blocked, it will eventually unblock, thanks to the other.

- Let us say that the digitizer is blocked, waiting for a signal inside code block (1). As we argued earlier, the tracker will be able to execute its code without blocking.

Therefore, eventually, it will get to the signal statement inside code block (4). Upon receiving this signal, the digitizer waits for reacquiring the lock (currently held by the tracker inside code block (4)). Note that the thread library does this lock reacquisition implicitly for the digitizer. Tracker leaves code block (4), releasing the lock; digitizer reacquires the lock and moves out of code block (1), releasing the lock on its way out.

- With a similar line of argument as we used previously, we can establish that if the tracker is waiting inside code block (3) for a signal, the digitizer will issue the signal that will unblock the tracker.

Thus, we have shown informally that the solution is correct and does not suffer from lack of concurrency.

12.2.11 Rechecking the Predicate

The Program Sample #5 works correctly for the specific example where there is one tracker and one digitizer. However, in general, programming with condition variables needs more care to avoid synchronization errors. Consider the program fragment shown next for using a shared resource. Any number of threads can execute the procedure **use_shared_resource**.

```
/*
 * Sample program #6:
 */
enum state_t {BUSY, NOT_BUSY} res_state = NOT_BUSY;
mutex_lock_type cs_mutex;
cond_var_type res_not_busy;

/* helper procedure for acquiring the resource */
acquire_shared_resource()
{
    thread_mutex_lock(cs_mutex);                    T3 is here

    if (res_state == BUSY)

        thread_cond_wait (res_not_busy, cs_mutex);   T2 is here

    res_state = BUSY;
    thread_mutex_unlock(cs_mutex);
}

/* helper procedure for releasing the resource */
release_shared_resource()
{
    thread_mutex_lock(cs_mutex);
```

```
    res_state = NOT_BUSY;                              T1 is here

      thread_cond_signal(res_not_busy);
    thread_mutex_unlock(cs_mutex);
  }


  /* top level procedure called by all the threads */
  use_shared_resource()
  {
    acquire_shared_resouce();
      resource_specific_function();
    release_shared_resource();
  }
```

As just shown,

- T1 has just finished using the resource and has set the **res_state** as **NOT_BUSY**;

- T2 is in conditional wait; and

- T3 is waiting to acquire the **cs_mutex**.

Figure 12.13 shows the state of the waiting queues in the library for **cs_mutex** and **res_not_busy**:

- T2 is in the **res_not_busy** queue, while T3 is in the **cs_mutex** queue, respectively (Figure 12.13(a)).

- T1 signals on the condition variable **res_not_busy**, which results in the library moving T2 to the **cs_mutex** queue, since the library has to reacquire the **cs_mutex** before resuming T2 (Figure 12.13(b)).

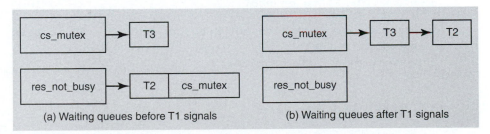

(a) Waiting queues before T1 signals   (b) Waiting queues after T1 signals

Figure 12.13   State of the waiting queues.

Once T1 signals, T2 is out of the conditional wait; however, cs_mutex has to be reacquired on T2's behalf to satisfy the invariant, mentioned in Section 12.2.9. For this reason, T2 moves into the waiting queue for cs_mutex in (b).

When T1 releases **cs_mutex**, the following things happen:

- The lock is given to T3, the first thread in the waiting queue for **cs_mutex**.
- T3 tests **res_state** to be **NOT_BUSY**, releases **cs_mutex**, and goes on to use the resource.
- T2 resumes from the **thread_cond_wait** (since **cs_mutex** is now available for it), releases **cs_mutex**, and goes on to use the resource as well.

Now we have violated the mutual exclusion condition for using the shared resource. Let us investigate what led to this situation. T1 enables the condition that T2 is waiting on prior to signaling, but T3 negates it before T2 resumes execution. Therefore, rechecking the predicate (i.e., the condition that needs to be satisfied in the program) upon resumption is a defensive coding technique designed to avoid such synchronization errors.

The program fragment shown next fixes the previous problem by changing the **if** statement associated with the **thread_cond_wait** to a **while** statement. This ensures that a thread tests the predicate again upon resumption and blocks again on **thread_cond_wait** call if necessary.

```
/*
 * Sample program #7:
 */
enum state_t {BUSY, NOT_BUSY} res_state = NOT_BUSY;
mutex_lock_type cs_mutex;
cond_var_type res_not_busy;

acquire_shared_resource()
{
  thread_mutex_lock(cs_mutex);                        T3 is here

  while (res_state == BUSY)

     thread_cond_wait (res_not_busy, cs_mutex);  T2 is here
   res_state = BUSY;
  thread_mutex_unlock(cs_mutex);
}

release_shared_resource()
{
  thread_mutex_lock(cs_mutex);
   res_state = NOT_BUSY;                              T1 is here
   thread_cond_signal(res_not_buys);
  thread_mutex_unlock(cs_mutex);
}
```

```
use_shared_resource()
{
  acquire_shared_resouce();
    resource_specific_function();
  release_shared_resource();
}
```

Example 12.13

Rewrite Sample Program #5 to allow multiple digitizers and multiple trackers to work together. This is left as an exercise for the reader.

[Hint: Rechecking the predicate after it awakens from a conditional wait becomes important. In addition, now the instances of digitizers share the head pointer and instances of trackers share the tail pointer. Therefore, modifications of these pointers require mutual exclusion among the digitizer instances and tracker instances, respectively. To ensure concurrency and reduce unnecessary contention among the threads, use distinct locks to provide mutual exclusion for the head and tail pointers, respectively.]

12.3 Summary of Thread Function Calls and Threaded Programming Concepts

Let us summarize the basic function calls, that we proposed in the earlier sections, for programming multithreaded applications. Note that this is just an illustrative set of basic calls and not meant to be comprehensive. In Section 12.6, we give a comprehensive set of function calls proposed as an IEEE POSIX[3] standard thread library.

- `thread_create (top-level procedure, args);`
  This creates a new thread that starts execution in the top-level procedure, with the supplied args as actual parameters for the formal parameters specified in the procedure prototype.

- `thread_terminate (tid);`
  This terminates the thread with id given by **tid**.

- `thread_mutex_lock (mylock);`
  When the thread returns it has **mylock**; the calling thread blocks if the lock is in use currently by some other thread.

- `thread_mutex_trylock (mylock);`
  The call does not block the calling thread; instead it returns **success** if the thread gets **mylock**; **failure** if the lock is currently in use by some other thread.

---

3. IEEE is an international society and stands for **Institute of Electrical and Electronics Engineers, Inc.**; and *POSIX* stands for portable operating system interface (**POSIX®**).

Table 12.2 Summary of Concepts Relating to Threads

Concept	Definition and/or Use
Top-level procedure	The starting point for execution of a thread of a parallel program.
Program order	This is the execution model for a sequential program that combines the textual order of the program together with the program logic (conditional statements, loops, procedures, etc.) enforced by the intended semantics of the programmer.
Execution model for a parallel program	The execution model for a parallel program preserves the program order for individual threads, but allows arbitrary interleaving of the individual instructions of the different threads.
Deterministic execution	Every run of a given program results in the same output for a given set of inputs. The execution model presented to a sequential program has this property.
Nondeterministic execution	Different runs of the same program for the same set of inputs could result in different outputs. The execution model presented to a parallel program has this property.
Data race	Multiple threads of the same program are simultaneously accessing an arbitrary shared variable, without any synchronization, with at least one of the accesses being a write to the variable.
Mutual exclusion	Signifies a requirement to ensure that threads of the same program execute serially (i.e., not concurrently). This requirement needs to be satisfied in order to avoid data races in a parallel program.
Critical section	A region of a program wherein the activities of the threads are serialized to ensure mutual exclusion.
Blocked	Signifies the state of a thread in which it is simply waiting in a queue for some condition to be satisfied to make it runnable.
Busy waiting	Signifies the state of a thread in which it is continuously checking for a condition to be satisfied before it can proceed further in its execution.
Deadlock	One or more threads of the same program are blocked, awaiting a condition that will never be satisfied.
Livelock	One or more threads of the same program are busy, waiting for a condition that will never be satisfied.
Rendezvous	Multiple threads of a parallel program use this mechanism to coordinate their activities. The most general kind of rendezvous is barrier synchronization. A special case of rendezvous is the thread_join call.

- `thread_mutex_unlock(mylock);`
  If the calling thread currently has **mylock**, it is released; error results otherwise.
- `thread_join (peer_thread_tid);`
  The calling thread blocks until the thread given by **peer_thread_tid** terminates.
- `thread_cond_wait(buf_not_empty, buflock);`
  The calling thread blocks on the condition variable **buf_not_empty**; the library implicitly releases the lock **buflock**; error results if the lock is not currently held by the calling thread.
- `thread_cond_signal(buf_not_empty);`
  A thread (if any) waiting on the condition variable **buf_not_empty** is woken up; the awakened thread is ready for execution if the lock associated with it (in the wait call) is currently available; if not, the thread is moved from the queue for the condition variable to the appropriate lock queue.

Table 12.2 summarizes, for quick reference, the important concepts we have introduced in the context of multithreaded programming.

12.4 Points to Remember in Programming with Threads

There are several important points to keep in mind while programming with threads:

1. Design the data structures in such a way as to enhance concurrency among threads.
2. Minimize both the granularity of data structures that need to be locked in a mutually exclusive manner, and the duration for which such locks need to be held.
3. Avoid busy waiting, since it is wasteful of the processor resource.
4. Take care to understand the invariant that is true for each critical section in the program, and ensure that this invariant is preserved while in the critical section.
5. Make the critical section code as simple and concise as possible to enable manual verification that there are no deadlocks or livelocks.

12.5 Using Threads as Software Structuring Abstraction

Figure 12.14 shows some of the models for using threads as a structuring mechanism for system software.

Software entities such as file servers, mail servers, and web servers typically execute on multiprocessors. Figure 12.14(a) shows a dispatcher model for such servers. A *dispatcher* thread dispatches requests as they come in to one of a pool of *worker* threads. Upon completion of the request, the worker thread returns to the free pool. The *request queue* serves to smooth the traffic when the burst of requests exceeds server capacity. The dispatcher serves as a workload manager as well, shrinking and growing the number of worker threads to meet the demand. Figure 12.14(b) shows a *team* model in which all the members of the team directly access the request queue for work. Figure 12.14(c)

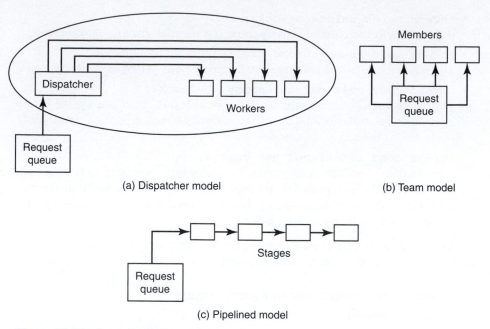

(a) Dispatcher model   (b) Team model

(c) Pipelined model

Figure 12.14   Structuring servers using threads.

shows a pipelined model, which is more appropriate for continuous applications such as video surveillance that we discussed earlier in the chapter. Each stage of the pipeline handles a specific task (e.g., digitizer, tracker, etc.).

Client programs benefit from multithreading as well. Threads increase modularity and simplicity of client programs. For example, a client program may use threads to deal with exceptions, to handle signals, and for terminal input/output.

12.6 POSIX pthreads Library Calls Summary

IEEE has standardized the application programming interface (API) for threads with the POSIX *pthreads* library. Every flavor of the UNIX operating system implements this standard. Program portability is the main intent of such standardization efforts. Microsoft Windows does not follow the POSIX standard for its thread library.[4] Summarized next are some of the most commonly used pthread library calls, with a brief description of their purpose. For more information, see appropriate documentation sources (e.g., man pages on any flavor of UNIX systems[5]).

```
int pthread_mutex_init (pthread_mutex_t *mutex,
                const pthread_mutex-attr_t *mutexattr);
```

---

4. Although Microsoft does not directly support the POSIX standard, the thread library available in WIN32 platforms for developing multithreaded applications in C have, for the most part, a semantically equivalent function call for each of the POSIX standard thread calls presented in this section.

5. For example, see http://linux.die.net/man/.

Arguments

mutex   address of the mutex variable to be initialized

mutexattr   address of the attribute variable used to initialize the mutex. see pthread_mutexattr_init for more information

Semantics   Each mutex variable must be declared (pthread_mutex_t) and initialized.

```
int pthread_cond_init(pthread_cond_t *cond,
               pthread_condattr_t *cond_attr);
```

Arguments

cond   address of the condition variable being initialized

cond_attr   address of the attribute variable used to initialize the condition variable. Not used in Linux.

Semantics   Each condition variable must be declared (pthread_cond_t) and initialized.

```
int pthread_create(pthread_t *thread,
          pthread_attr_t *attr,
          void *(*start_routine)(void *),
          void *arg);
```

Arguments

thread   Address of the thread identifier (tid)

attr   Address of the attributes to be applied to the new thread

start_routine   Function that new thread will start executing

arg   address of first argument passed to start_routine

Semantics   This function will create a new thread, establish the starting address (passed as the name of a function), and pass arguments to be passed to the function where the thread starts. The thread id (*tid*) of the newly created thread will be placed in the location pointed to by the thread.

```
int pthread_kill(pthread_t thread,
          int signo);
```

Arguments

thread   thread id of the thread to which the signal will be sent

signo   signal number to send to thread

Semantics   Used to send a signal to a thread whose *tid* is known.

```
int pthread_join(pthread_t th,
          void **thread_return);[6]
```

---

6. The pthreads library also supports general barrier synchronization, which is especially useful in parallel scientific applications. The interested reader is referred to a UNIX reference source such as http://linux.die.net/man/.

Arguments

th   tid of thread to wait for

thread_return   If thread_return is not NULL, the return value of th is stored in the location pointed to by thread_return. The return value of th is either the argument it gave to pthread_exit(3), or PTHREAD_CANCELED if th was cancelled.

Semantics   pthread_join suspends the execution of the calling thread until the thread identified by th terminates, either by calling pthread_exit(3) or by being cancelled.

```
pthread_t pthread_self(void);
```

Arguments   None

Semantics   pthread_self returns the thread identifier for the calling thread.

```
int pthread_mutex_lock(pthread_mutex_t *mutex);
```

Arguments

mutex   address of mutex variable to be locked

Semantics   Waits until the specified mutex is unlocked and then locks it and returns.

```
int pthread_mutex_unlock(pthread_mutex_t *mutex);
```

Arguments

mutex   address of mutex variable to be unlocked

Semantics   Unlocks the specified mutex if the caller is the thread that locked the mutex.

```
int pthread_cond_wait(pthread_cond_t *cond,
          pthread_mutex_t *mutex);
```

Arguments

cond   address of condition variable to wait upon

mutex   address of mutex variable associated with cond

Semantics   pthread_cond_wait atomically unlocks the mutex (as per pthread_unlock_mutex) and waits for the condition variable cond to be signaled. The thread execution is suspended and does not consume any CPU time until the condition variable is signaled. The mutex must be locked by the calling thread on entrance to pthread_cond_wait. Before returning to the calling thread, pthread_cond_wait reacquires mutex (as per pthread_lock_mutex).

```
int pthread_cond_signal(pthread_cond_t *cond);
```

Arguments

cond   address of condition variable

Semantics   Wakes up one thread waiting for a signal on the specified condition variable.

```
int pthread_cond_broadcast(pthread_cond_t *cond);
```

Arguments

cond   address of condition variable

Semantics   Variant of the previous call, wherein the signal wakes up *all* threads waiting for a signal on the specified condition variable.

```
void pthread_exit(void *retval);
```

Arguments

retval   address of the return value of the thread

Semantics   Terminates the execution of the calling thread.

12.7 OS Support for Threads

In operating systems such as MS-DOS, an early bare-bones OS for the PC, there is no separation between the user program and the kernel (Figure 12.15). Thus, the line between the user program and the kernel is imaginary; hence, it costs very little (in terms of time, it is equivalent to a procedure call) to go between user and kernel spaces. The downside to this structure is the fact that there is no memory protection among user programs, and an errant or malicious program can easily corrupt the memory space of the kernel.

Modern operating systems such as MS Windows® XP, Linux, Mac OS X, and UNIX provide true memory protection through virtual memory mechanisms, which we have

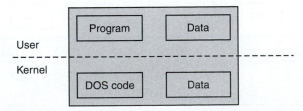

Figure 12.15   MS-DOS user-kernel boundary.

MS-DOS was an early OS for the PC. The shading indicates that there is no enforced separation between user and kernel.

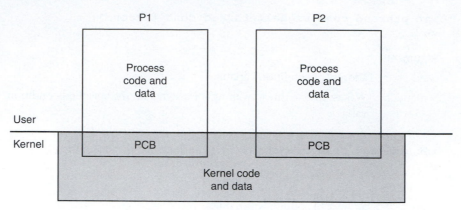

Figure 12.16 Memory protection in traditional operating systems.

There is an enforced separation between the user and the kernel.

discussed in earlier chapters. Figure 12.16 shows the memory spaces of user processes, and the kernel, in such operating systems.

Every process is in its own address space. There is a clear dividing line between the user space and the kernel space. System calls result in a change of protection domain. Now that we are familiar with memory hierarchy, we can see that the working set (which affects all the levels of the memory hierarchy, from virtual memory to processor caches) changes on each such address-space crossing. Consequently, frequent crossing of the boundary is detrimental to performance. A process control block (PCB) defines a particular process. In previous chapters, we have seen how the various components of the operating system, such as the scheduler, the memory system, and the I/O subsystem, use the PCB. In a traditional operating system (i.e. one that is not multithreaded), the process is single-threaded. Hence, the PCB contains information for fully specifying the activity of

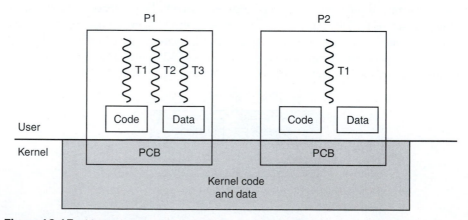

Figure 12.17 Memory protection in modern operating systems.

A process may encompass multiple threads. All the threads in the same process share the process address space.

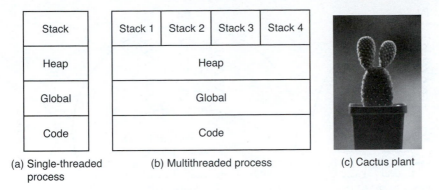

Figure 12.18   Memory layout of single threaded and multithreaded processes.

Each thread of the multithreaded process (b) has its own stack.

this single thread on the processor (current PC value, stack pointer value, general-purpose register values, etc.). If a process makes a system call that blocks the process (e.g., read a file from the disk), then the program as a whole does not make any progress.

Most modern operating systems (Windows XP, Sun Solaris, HP Tru64, etc.) are multithreaded. That is, the operating system recognizes that the state of a running program is a composite of the states of all of its constituent threads. Figure 12.17 shows the distribution of memory spaces in modern operating systems supporting both single-threaded as well as multithreaded programs. All threads of a given process share the address space of the process.

A given process may have multiple threads, but since all the threads share the same address space, they share a common page table in memory. Let us elaborate on the computational state of a thread. A *thread control block (TCB)* contains all the state information pertaining to a thread. However, the information contained in a TCB is minimal compared with a PCB. In particular, the TCB contains the PC value, the stack pointer value, and the GPR contents.

It is interesting to contrast the memory layout of multithreaded processes and single-threaded processes (Figure 12.18). As we mentioned earlier, all the threads of a given process share the code, the global data, and the heap. Thus, the stack is the only portion of the memory that is unique for a particular thread. Due to the visual similarity of the stack layout of a multithreaded process to the cactus plant (Figure 12.18(c)), we refer to this stack as a *cactus stack*.

Next, we will see what it takes to implement a threads library—first at the user level and then at the kernel level.

12.7.1 User Level Threads

First, we will consider the implementation to be entirely at the user level. That is, the operating system knows only the existence of processes (which are single threaded).

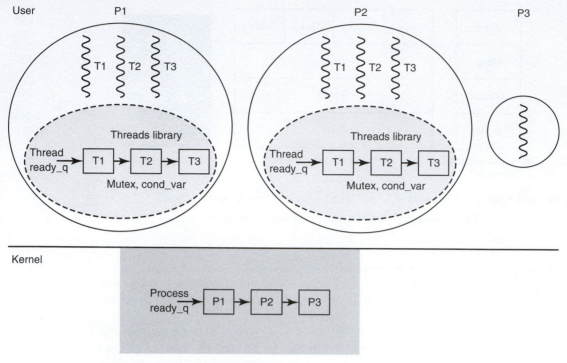

Figure 12.19 User-level threads.

The threads library is part of the application process's address space. In this sense, there is no enforced memory protection between the application logic and the threads library functionalities. On the other hand, there is an enforced separation between the user and the kernel.

However, we could still have threads implemented at the user level. That is, the threads library exists as functionality above the operating system, just as you have math libraries available for use in any program. The library provides thread creation calls, which we discussed earlier, and supports data types such as **mutex** and **cond_var** and operations on them. A program that wishes to make calls to the threads library links in that library, which then becomes part of the program, as shown in Figure 12.19.

The operating system maintains the traditional ready queue with the set of schedulable processes, which is the unit of scheduling at the operating system level. The threads library maintains a list of ready-to-run *threads* in each process, with information about them in their respective *thread control blocks (TCBs)*. A TCB contains minimal information about each thread (PC value, SP value, and GPR values). Processes at the user level may be single threaded (e.g., P3) or multithreaded (P1 and P2).

The reader may wonder about the utility of user-level threads if process is the unit of scheduling by the operating system. Even if the underlying platform is a multiprocessor, the threads at the user level in a given process cannot execute concurrently. Recall that a thread is a structuring mechanism for constructing software. This is the primary purpose served by the user-level threads. They operate as *co-routines*; that is, when one thread makes a thread synchronization call that blocks it, the thread scheduler picks some other thread, within the same process, to run. The operating system is oblivious to such thread level-context switching that the thread scheduler performs by using the TCBs. It is cheap to switch threads at the user level, since the switching does not involve the operating system. The cost of a context switch approximates making a procedure call in a program. Thus, user-level threads provide a structuring mechanism without the high cost of a context switch involving the operating system. User-level threads incur minimal direct and indirect costs for context switching. (See Chapter 9, Section 9.22 for details on direct and indirect costs.) Further, thread-level scheduler is customizable for a specific application.

It is interesting to understand what happens when one of the threads in a multithreaded process makes a blocking system call. In this case, the operating system blocks the whole process, since it has no knowledge of other threads within the same process that are ready to run. This is one of the fundamental problems with user-level threads. There are a number of different approaches to solving this problem:

1. One possibility is to wrap all OS calls with an envelope (e.g., *fopen* becomes *thread_fopen*) that forces all the calls to go through the thread library. Then, when some thread (e.g., T1 of P1 in Figure 12.19) makes such a call, the thread library recognizes that issuing this call to the OS will block the whole process. Therefore, it defers making the call until all the threads in the process are unable to run anymore. At that point, the library issues the blocking call to the OS on behalf of the thread.

2. A second approach is for an *upcall* mechanism (see Figure 12.20) from the operating system to warn the thread scheduler that a thread in that process is about to make a blocking system call. This warning allows the thread scheduler (in the library) to perform a thread switch and/or defer the blocking call by the thread, to a later more-opportune time. Of course, this approach requires an extension to the operating system for supporting such upcalls.

In Chapter 6, we explored different CPU scheduling policies. Given that background, let us see how the thread scheduler switches among user-level threads. Of course, when a thread makes a synchronization call into the threads library, that is an opportune moment for the threads scheduler to switch among the threads of this process. Similarly, the threads library may provide a *thread_yield* call to let a thread voluntarily give up the processor to give a chance for other threads in the same process to execute. One of the scheduling disciplines we studied in Chapter 6 is preemptive scheduling. If it is necessary to implement a preemptive thread scheduler at the user level, the thread scheduler can request a timer interrupt from the kernel and use that as a trigger to perform preemptive scheduling among the threads.

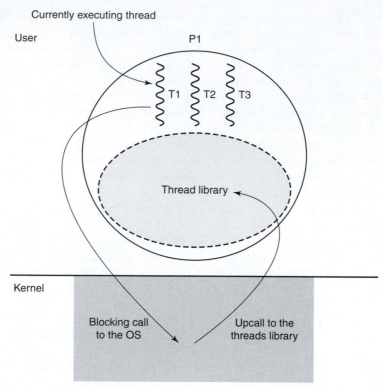

Figure 12.20 Upcall mechanism.

The thread library registers a handler with the kernel. The thread makes a blocking call to the OS. The OS makes an upcall to the handler, thus alerting the threads library of the blocking system call made by a thread in that process.

12.7.2 Kernel-Level Threads

Let us understand the operating system support needed for implementing threads at the kernel level:

1. All the threads of a process live in a single address space. Therefore, the operating system should ensure that the threads of a process share the same page table.
2. Each thread needs its own stack, but shares other portions of the memory footprint.
3. The operating system should support the thread-level synchronization constructs discussed earlier.

First, let us consider a simple extension to the process-level scheduler to support threads in the kernel. The operating system may implement a two-level scheduler, as shown in Figure 12.21. A process-level scheduler manages PCBs with information that

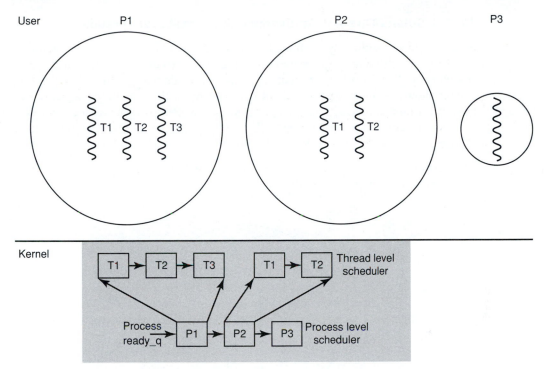

Figure 12.21   Kernel-level threads.

The process-level scheduler uses the process ready_q. Even if a thread in the currently scheduled process makes a blocking system call, the OS uses the thread-level scheduler to pick a ready thread from the currently running process to run for the remainder of the time quantum.

is common to all the threads in that process (page table, accounting information, etc.). A thread-level scheduler manages TCBs. The process-level scheduler allocates *time quanta* for processes, and performs preemptive scheduling among processes. Within a time quantum, the thread-level scheduler schedules the threads of that process either in a round-robin fashion or in a co-routine mode. In the latter case, a thread voluntarily yields the processor, to allow other threads in the same process to be scheduled by the thread-level scheduler. Since the operating system recognizes threads, it can switch among the threads of a process when the currently executing thread makes a blocking system call for I/O or thread synchronization.

With computers and chips these days becoming multiprocessors, it is a serious limitation if the threads of a process cannot take advantage of the available hardware concurrency. The structure shown in Figure 12.21 allows threads of a given process to overlap I/O with processing—a definite step forward from user-level threads. However, to fully exploit available hardware concurrency in a multiprocessor, the thread should be the unit of scheduling in the operating system. Next, we will discuss Sun Solaris threads as a concrete example of kernel-level threads.

12.7.3 Solaris Threads: An Example of Kernel-Level Threads

Figure 12.22 shows the organization of threads in the Sun Solaris operating system.

A process is the entity that represents a program in execution. A process may create any number of user-level threads that are contained within that process. The operating system allows the creator of threads to have control of the scheduling semantics of threads within that process. For example, threads may be truly concurrent or may execute in a coroutine manner. To support these different semantics, the operating system recognizes three kinds of threads: *user, lightweight process (lwp),* and *kernel.*

1. **Kernel:** The kernel threads are the unit of scheduling. We will see shortly their relation to the lwp and user threads.

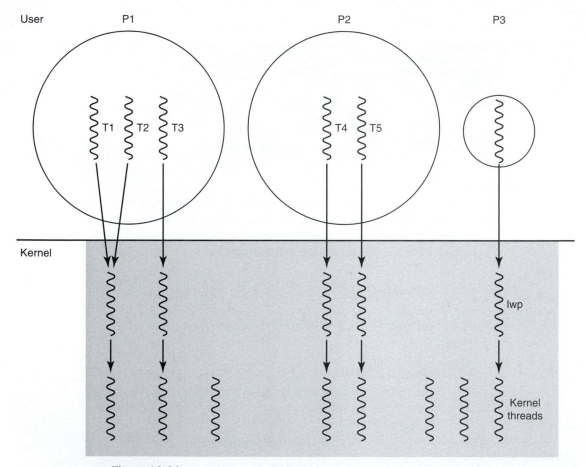

Figure 12.22 Sun Solaris threads structure.

A thread in a process is bound to a light-weight process (lwp). Multiple threads of the same process may be bound to the same lwp. There is a one-to-one mapping between an lwp and a kernel thread. The unit of processor scheduling is the kernel thread.

2. **lwp:** An lwp (light-weight process) is the representation of a process within the kernel. Every process, upon startup, is associated with a distinct lwp. There is a one-to-one association between an lwp and a kernel thread, as shown in Figure 12.22. On the other hand, a kernel thread may be unattached to any lwp. The operating system uses such threads for functions that it has to carry out independent of user-level processes. For example, kernel threads serve as vehicles for executing device-specific functions.

3. **User:** As the name suggests, these threads are at the user level.

Thread creation calls supported by the operating system result in the creation of user-level threads. The thread creation call specifies whether the newly created thread should be attached to an existing lwp of the process or allocated to a new lwp. See, for example, the threads T1 and T2 in process P1, in Figure 12.22. They both execute in a coroutine manner because they are bound to the same lwp. Any number of user-level threads may bind themselves to an lwp. On the other hand, thread T3 of P1 executes concurrently with one of T1 or T2. Threads T4 and T5 of P2 execute concurrently, as well.

The ready queue of the scheduler is the set of kernel threads that are ready to run. Some of them, due to their binding to an lwp, result in the execution of a user thread or a process. If a kernel thread blocks, the associated lwp and, therefore, the user level thread, block as well. Since the unit of scheduling is the kernel thread, the operating system has the ability to schedule these threads concurrently on parallel processors if the underlying platform is a multiprocessor.

It is interesting to understand the inherent cost of a thread switch, given this structure. Remember that every context switch is from one kernel thread to another. However, the cost of the switch changes dramatically, depending on what is bound to a kernel thread. The cheapest form of context switch is between two user-level threads bound to the same lwp (T1 and T2, in Figure 12.22). Presumably, the process has a thread library available at the user level. Thus, the thread switch is entirely at the user level (similar to user level-threads we discussed earlier). Switching between lwps in the same process (for example, T1 and T3 in Figure 12.22) is the next-higher-cost context switch. In this case, the direct cost (in terms of saving and loading TCBs) is a trip through the kernel that performs the switch. There are no hidden costs in the switch due to memory hierarchy effects, since both the threads are in the same process. The most expensive context switch is between two lwps that are in different processes (for example, T3 and T4 in Figure 12.22). In this case, there are both direct and indirect costs involved, since the threads are in different processes.

12.7.4 Threads and Libraries

Irrespective of the choice of implementing threads at the user level or the kernel level, it is imperative to ensure the safety of libraries that multithreaded programs use. For example, all the threads of a process share the heap. Therefore, the library

```
/* original version */        | /* thread safe version */
                              |
                              | mutex_lock_type cs_mutex;
void *malloc(size_t size)     | void *malloc(size_t size)
{                             | {
                              |    thread_mutex_lock(cs_mutex);
                              |
 . . . . . .                  |    . . . . . .
 . . . . . .                  |    . . . . . .
                              |
                              |    thread_mutex_unlock(cs_mutex);
                              |
   return(memory_pointer);    |    return (memory_pointer);
}                             | }
```

Figure 12.23   Thread-safe wrapper for library calls.

The entire function is wrapped up between a mutex lock and unlock, ensuring atomicity.

that supports dynamic memory allocation needs to recognize that threads may simultaneously request memory from the heap. It is usual to have *thread-safe* wrappers around such library calls to ensure atomicity for such calls, in anticipation of concurrent calls from the threads. Figure 12.23 shows an example. The library call implicitly acquires a mutual exclusion lock on behalf of the thread that makes that call.

12.8 Hardware Support for Multithreading in a Uniprocessor

Let us understand what is required in hardware for supporting multithreading. There are three things to consider:

1. thread creation and termination;

2. communication among threads; and

3. synchronization among threads.

12.8.1 Thread Creation, Termination, and Communication Among Threads

First, let us consider a uniprocessor. Threads of a process share the same page table. In a uniprocessor each process has a unique page table. On a thread context switch, within the same process, there is no change to the TLB or the caches, since all the memory mapping and contents of the caches remain relevant for the new thread. Thus, creation and termination of threads, or communications among the threads, do not require any special hardware support.

12.8.2 Inter-Thread Synchronization

Let us consider what it takes to implement the *mutual exclusion lock*. We will use a memory location `mem_lock` initialized to zero. The semantics are as follows: If `mem_lock` is zero, then the lock is available. If `mem_lock` is 1, then some thread currently has the lock. Here are the algorithms for `lock` and `unlock`:

```
Lock:
        if (mem_lock == 0)
                mem_lock = 1;
        else
                block the thread;

Unlock:
        mem_lock = 0;
```

The lock and unlock algorithms have to be *atomic*. Let us examine these algorithms. Unlock algorithm is a single memory store instruction of the processor. Given that each execution of an instruction is atomic, we can declare that unlock is atomic.

The datapath actions necessary to implement the lock algorithm are as follows:

- Read a memory location.
- Test whether the value read is 0.
- Set the memory location to 1.

12.8.3 An Atomic Test-and-Set Instruction

We know that the LC-2200 (see Chapter 2) ISA does not provide any single instruction that would atomically perform the foregoing datapath actions. Therefore, to make the lock algorithm atomic, we introduce a new instruction:

```
Test-And-Set memory-location
```

The semantics of this instruction is as follows:

- Read the current value of memory-location into some processor register.
- Set the memory location to a 1.

The key point of this instruction is that if a thread executes this instruction, the previous two actions (getting the current value of the memory location and setting the new value to 1) happen *atomically;* that is, no other instruction (by any other thread) intervenes the execution of `Test-and-set`.

Example 12.14

Consider the following procedure called `binary-semaphore`:

```
static        int shared-lock = 0; /* global variable to
                                       both T1 and T2 */
/* shared procedure for T1 and T2 */
int binary-semaphore(int L)
{
  int X;

  X = test-and-set (L);

  /* X = 0 for successful return */
  return(X);
}
```

Two threads **T1** and **T2** simultaneously execute the following statement:

```
MyX = binary_semaphore(shared-lock);
```

where **MyX** is a local variable in each of **T1** and **T2**.

What are the possible values returned to T1 and T2?

Answer:

Note that the instruction `test-and-set` is atomic. Therefore, although T1 and T2 execute the procedure simultaneously, the semantics of this instruction ensures that one or the other (whichever happens to be the winner) gets to execute the instruction first.

So, possible outcomes are as follows:

1. T1 is the winner.
   T1's **MyX** = 0; T2's **MyX** = 1
2. T2 is the winner.
   T1's **MyX** = 1; T2's **MyX** = 0

Note that it will never be the case that **both** T1 and T2 will get a 0 or 1 as the return value.

You may have seen and heard of the *semaphore* signaling system used extensively in railroads. In olden times (and even to this day in some developing countries), mechanical arms (see Figure 12.24) on a high pole cautioned an engine driver in a train to either stop or proceed with caution when approaching shared railroad tracks.

Computer scientists have borrowed the term *semaphore* for computer science parlance. The procedure shown in Example 12.14 is a *binary semaphore;* that is, it signals one among many threads that it is safe to proceed into a critical section.

Edsger Dijkstra, a well-known computer scientist of Dutch origin, was the proponent of the semaphore as a synchronization mechanism for coordinating the activities of

Figure 12.24   Railroad semaphore.

concurrent threads. He proposed two versions of this semaphore. *Binary semaphore* is the one we just saw, wherein the semaphore grants or denies access to a single resource to a set of competing threads. *Counting semaphore* is a more general version, wherein there are *n* instances of a given resource; the semaphore grants or denies access to **an** instance of these *n* resources to competing threads. At most, *n* threads can enjoy these resources **simultaneously** at any point in time.

12.8.4 Lock Algorithm with Test-and-Set Instruction

Having introduced the atomic **test-and-set** instruction, we are now ready to review the implementation of the mutual exclusion lock primitive, which is at the core of programming support for multithreaded applications. As it turns out, we can implement the lock-and-unlock algorithm by building on the binary semaphore, as follows:

```
#define SUCCESS 0
#define FAILURE 1

int lock(int L)
{
    int X;
    while ( (X = test-and-set (L)) == FAILURE ) {
            /* current value of L is 1
             * implying that the lock is
             * currently in use
             */
            block the thread;
```

```
                        /* the threads library puts the
                         * the thread in a queue; when
                         * lock is released it allows
                         * this thread to check the
                         * availability of the lock again
                         */
        }

        /* falling out of the while loop implies that
         * the lock attempt was successful
         */

        return(SUCCESS);

}

int unlock(int L)
{
    L = 0;
    return(SUCCESS);
}
```

By design, a thread calling the lock algorithm has the lock when it returns. Using this basic lock-and-unlock algorithm, we can build the synchronization mechanisms (such as mutex locks and condition variables) that we discussed in Section 12.2 and the POSIX thread library calls summarized in Section 12.6.

Therefore, the minimal hardware support for multithreading is an atomic **test-and-set**(**TAS**, for short) instruction. The key property of this instruction is that it *atomically reads, modifies,* and *writes* a memory location. There are other instructions that implement the same property. The point is that most modern processor architectures include in their repertoires one or more instructions that have this property.

Note that if the operating system deals with threads directly, it can simply turn off interrupts while executing the lock algorithm, to ensure atomicity. The **TAS** instruction allows implementing locks at the **user** level.

12.9 Multiprocessors

As the name suggests, a multiprocessor consists of multiple processors in a single computer, sharing all the resources such as memory, bus, and input/output devices (see Figure 12.25). This is a *symmetric multiprocessor (SMP),* so named because all the processors have an identical view of the system resources. An SMP is a cost-effective approach to increasing the system performance at a nominal increase in total system cost. Many servers that we use on an everyday basis (web server, file server, mail server) run on four-way or eight-way SMPs.

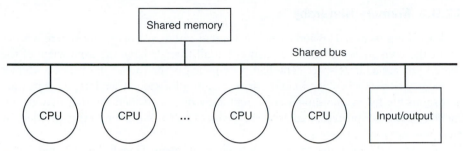

Figure 12.25 A symmetric multiprocessor (SMP).

All processors have a symmetric view of the system resources.

Complication arises at the system level when the program is running on a multi-processor. In this case, the threads of a given program may be on different physical processors. Thus, the system software (meaning the operating system and runtime libraries) and the hardware have to work in partnership to provide the semantics expected, at the user-program level, for data structures shared by the threads.

We have seen that there are several intricacies associated with preserving the semantics of a sequential program, with the hardware and software entities, even in a single processor: TLB, page tables, caches, and memory manager, to name just a few. The reader can envision the complications that arise when the system software and hardware have to preserve the semantics of a multithreaded program. We will discuss these issues in this section.

The system (hardware and the operating system together) has to ensure three things:

1. Threads of the same process share the same page table.

2. Threads of the same process have identical views of the memory hierarchy despite being on different physical processors.

3. Threads are guaranteed atomicity for synchronization operations while executing concurrently.

12.9.1 Page Tables

The processors share physical memory, as shown in Figure 12.25. Therefore, the operating system satisfies the first requirement by ensuring that the page table in shared memory is the same for all the threads of a given process. However, there are a number of issues associated with an operating system for a multiprocessor. In principle, each processor *independently* executes the *same* operating system. However, they coordinate some of their decisions for overall system integrity. In particular, they take specific, coordinated actions to preserve the semantics of multithreaded programs. These include simultaneously scheduling threads of the same process, on different processors; page replacement; and maintaining the consistency of the TLB entries in each CPU. Such issues are beyond the scope of this discussion. Suffice it to say that these are fascinating issues, and the reader is encouraged to take advanced courses in operating systems to study them.

12.9.2 Memory Hierarchy

Each CPU has its own TLB and cache. As we said earlier, the operating system worries about the consistency of TLBs to ensure that all threads have the same view of the shared process address space. The hardware manages the caches. Each per-processor cache may currently be encaching the same memory location. Therefore, the hardware is responsible for maintaining a consistent view of shared memory that may be en-cached in the per-processor caches (see Figure 12.26). We refer to this problem as *multiprocessor cache coherence*.

Figure 12.27 illustrates the cache-coherence problem. Threads T1, T2, and T3 (of the same process) execute on processors P1, P2, and P3, respectively. All three of them currently have location X cached in their respective caches (Figure 12.27(a)). T1 writes to X. At this point, the hardware has one of two choices:

- It can *invalidate* copies of X in the peer caches, as shown in Figure 12.27(b). This requires enhancement to the shared bus in the form of an *invalidation line*. Correspondingly, the caches *monitor* the bus by *snooping* on it to watch out for invalidation requests from peer caches. Upon such a request on the bus, every cache checks whether this location is cached locally; if it is, the cache invalidates that location. Subsequent misses for the same location are either satisfied by the cache that has the most up-to-date copy (for example, P1 in this example) or by the memory, depending on the write policy used. We refer to this solution as the *write-invalidate* protocol.

- It can *update* copies of X in the peer caches, as shown in Figure 12.27(c). This may manifest simply as a memory write on the bus. The peer caches that *observe* this bus request update their copies of X (if present in the cache). We refer to this solution as the *write-update* protocol.

Snoopy caches is a popular term used for bus-based cache-coherence protocols. In this section, we have presented a very basic, intuitive solution to the multi-processor cache-coherence problem and snoopy cache solution approaches to the

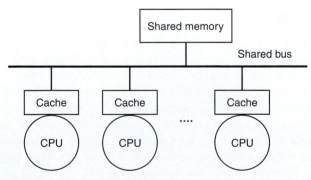

Figure 12.26   SMP with per-processor caches.

The hardware ensures that the per-processor caches are consistent.

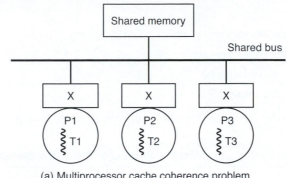

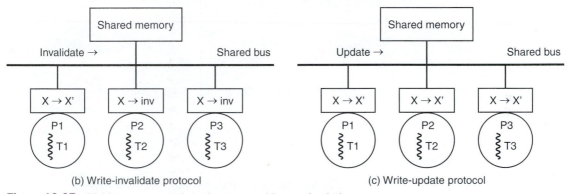

Figure 12.27 Multiprocessor cache-coherence problem and solutions.

In (b), the writing processor P1 forces the peers to invalidate their local copies before writing; in (c), the writing processor P1 places the new value on the bus, allowing the peers to update their local copies.

problem. Snoopy caches do not work if the processors do not have a shared bus (a broadcast medium) to snoop on. In Section 12.10.2, we will discuss a different solution approach, called a *directory-based scheme,* that does not rely on a shared bus for communication among the processors. The investigation of scalable solution approaches to the cache-coherence problem was a fertile area of research in the mid- to late 1980s and produced several doctoral dissertations. The reader is encouraged to take advanced courses in computer architecture to learn more on this topic.

Example 12.15

Consider the following details about an SMP (symmetric multiprocessor):

    Cache coherence protocol: **write-invalidate**
    Cache to memory policy: **write-back**

Initially,

the caches are empty; and

memory locations are

A contains 10

B contains 5.

Consider the following timeline of memory accesses from processors P1, P2, and P3:

Time (In Increasing Order)	Processor P1	Processor P2	Processor P3
T1	Load A		
T2		Load A	
T3			Load A
T4		Store #40, A	
T5	Store #30, B		

Using the table that follows, summarize the activities and the values in the caches.

Answer:

(I indicates that the cache location is invalid. NP indicates not present.)

Time	Variables	Cache of P1	Cache of P2	Cache of P3	Memory
T1	A	10	NP	NP	10
T2	A	10	10	NP	10
T3	A	10	10	10	10
T4	A	I	40	I	10
T5	A	I	40	I	10
	B	30	NP	NP	5

12.9.3 Ensuring Atomicity

By design, the CPUs share memory in an SMP; consequently, the lock and unlock algorithms (presented in Section 12.8) work fine in a multiprocessor. The key requirement is ensuring atomicity of these algorithms in the presence of concurrent execution of the threads on different processors. An instruction such as TAS (introduced in Section 12.8) that has the ability to atomically *read-modify-write* a shared-memory location serves this purpose.

12.10 Advanced Topics

We will introduce the reader to some advanced topics of special relevance in the context of multiprocessors and multithreading.

12.10.1 OS Topics

Deadlocks. In Section 12.2.7, we introduced the concept of deadlocks and live-locks. Here, we will generalize and expand on the concept of deadlocks. We gave a very simple and intuitive definition of deadlock as a situation in which a thread is waiting for an event that will never happen. There are several reasons that deadlocks occur in a computer system. One reason is that there are concurrent activities in the system, and there are finite resources, be they hardware or software. For example, let us consider a uniprocessor running multiple applications. If the scheduler uses a nonpreemptive algorithm, and the application currently running on the processor goes into an infinite loop, all the other applications are deadlocked. In this case, the processes are all waiting for a physical resource, namely, a processor. This kind of deadlock is usually referred to as a *resource deadlock*. The conditions that led to the deadlock are twofold: the need for *mutual exclusion* for accessing the shared resource (i.e., the processor), and the *lack of preemption* for yanking the resource away from the current user.

A similar situation arises because locks govern different data structures of a complex application. Let us first consider a fun analogy. Nick and his partner arrive in the recreation center to play squash. There are only one court and exactly two rackets available in the recreation center. There is one service desk to check out rackets and another to claim the court. Nick and his partner go first to the former and check out the rackets. Alex and his partner have similar plans. However, they first claim the court and then go to the service desk to check out the rackets. Now Nick and Alex are deadlocked. This is also a resource deadlock. In addition to the two conditions we identified earlier, there are two conditions that led to the deadlock in this case: *circular wait* (Alex is waiting for Nick to give up the rackets, and Nick is waiting for Alex to give up the court), and the fact that each of them can *hold one resource and wait for another one*. Complex software systems use fine-grain locking to enhance the opportunity for concurrent execution of threads. For example, consider payroll processing. A check-issuing process may lock the records of all the employees in order to generate the paychecks, whereas a merit-raise process may sweep through the database, locking all the employee records to add raises to all the employees at the same time. *Hold and wait* and *circular wait* by each of these processes, respectively, will lead to a deadlock.

To sum up, there are four conditions that *must hold simultaneously* for processes to be involved in resource deadlock in a computer system:

- **Mutual exclusion:** A resource can be used only in a mutually exclusive manner.
- **No preemption:** The process holding a resource has to give it up voluntarily.
- **Hold and wait:** A process is allowed to hold a resource while waiting for other resources.

- **Circular wait:** There is a cyclic dependency among the processes waiting for resources (A is waiting for a resource held by B; B is waiting for a resource held by C; C. . . . X; X is waiting for a resource held by A).

These are called *necessary* conditions for a deadlock. There are three strategies for dealing with deadlocks: deadlock *avoidance, prevention*, and *detection*. A reader interested in detailed treatment of these strategies is referred to advanced textbooks in operating systems (such as [Tanenbaum, 2007; Silberschatz, 2008]). Here we will give the basic intuition behind these strategies. The deadlock avoidance algorithm is ultra-conservative. It basically assumes that the request pattern for resources are all known *a priori*. With this global knowledge, the algorithm will make resource allocation decisions that are guaranteed never to result in a deadlock. For example, if you have $100 in your hand, and you know that in the worst-case scenario you will need a maximum of $80 to see you through the rest of the month, you will be able to loan $20 to help out a friend. If your friend needs $30, you will say no because you could potentially get into a situation in which you don't have enough money for the rest of the month. However, it could turn out that this month you get some free lunches and dinners and may end up not needing $80. So, you are making a conservative decision as to how much you can loan a friend, based on the worst-case scenario. As you probably guessed, deadlock avoidance leads to poor resource utilization due to its inherent conservatism.

More important, deadlock avoidance is simply not practical because it requires prior knowledge of future resource requests. A better strategy is deadlock prevention, which goes after each of the four *necessary* conditions for deadlock. The basic idea is to break one of the necessary conditions and thus *prevent* the system from deadlocking. Using the same monthly finances analogy, you could loan your friend $30. However, if it turns out that this month you do need $80 to survive, you go to your friend and get back $10 out of the $30 you loaned him. This strategy breaks the necessary condition "no preemption." Of course, the same prevention strategy may not be applicable for all types of resources. For example, if processes need to access a single shared physical resource in a mutually exclusive manner, then one way to avoid deadlock is to pretend that there are as many instances of that shared resource as the number of requestors. This may seem like a crazy idea, but if you think about it, this is precisely how a departmental printer is shared. Basically, we spool our print jobs, which are then buffered, awaiting the physical printer. "Spooling," or "buffering," is a way to break the necessary condition "mutual exclusion." Similarly, to break the necessary condition "hold and wait," we can mandate that all resources need to be obtained simultaneously before starting the process. Returning to our squash player analogy, Nick (or Alex) would have to get both the court and the rackets together, not one after another. Finally, to break the necessary condition "circular wait," we could order the resources and mandate that the requests be made *in order*. For example, we could mandate that you first have to claim the squash court (resource #1) before you request the rackets (resource #2). This would ensure that there would not be any circular wait.

Deadlock prevention leads to better resource utilization than avoidance does. However, it is still conservative. For example, consider a mandate that a process get all the resources *a priori* before it starts. This certainly prevents deadlock. However, if the process does not need all the resources for the entire duration, then the resources are being underutilized. Therefore, a more liberal policy is deadlock detection and recovery. The idea is to be liberal with resource requests and grants. However, if a deadlock does occur, have a mechanism for detecting it and recovering from it. Returning to our squash players analogy, when the desk clerk at the court-claim counter notices the deadlock, she takes the rackets from Nick, calls up her cohort at the racket-claim counter, and tells her to send Alex over to her counter to resolve the deadlock.

Example 12.16

Consider a system with three resources:

> 1 display, 1 KBD, 1 printer.

There are four processes:

> P1 needs all three resources.
>
> P2 needs KBD.
>
> P3 needs display.
>
> P4 need KBD and display.

Explain how deadlock avoidance, prevention, and detection will work to cater to the needs of the four processes, respectively.

Answer:

Let us consider solutions for each strategy.

Avoidance: Allocate all needed resources as a bundle at the start of a process. This amounts to not starting P2, P3, or P4 if P1 is running; not starting P1 if any of the others are running.

Prevention: Have an artificial ordering of the resources—say, KBD, display, printer. Make the processes always request the three resources in the preceding order and release all the resources that a process is holding, at the same time, upon completion. This ensures no circular wait (P4 cannot hold display and ask for a KBD; P1 cannot ask for printer without already having the display, etc).

Detection: Allow resources to be requested individually and in any order. We will assume that all processes are restartable. If a process P2 requests a resource (say, KBD), which is currently assigned to another process P4, and if P4 is waiting for another resource, then force a release of KBD by aborting P4, assign the KBD to P2, and restart P4.

A topic closely related to deadlocks in the context of resource allocation is *starvation*. This is the situation in which some process is indefinitely blocked while awaiting a resource. For example, if the resources are allocated by some sort of a priority scheme, lower-priority processes may be starved if there is a steady stream of higher-priority processes requesting the same resource. Returning to our squash court example, consider the situation in which faculty members are given priority over students. This could lead to the "starvation" of students. We will give another example of starvation when we discuss classic problems in synchronization later in this subsection.

Beyond resource deadlocks, computer systems are susceptible to other kinds of deadlocks as well. Specifically, the kinds of deadlocks we discussed earlier in this chapter have to do with errors in writing a correct parallel program—errors that could lead to deadlocks and livelocks. This problem gets exacerbated in distributed systems (see Chapter 13), where messages may be lost in transit due to a variety of reasons, leading to deadlocks. All of these situations can be lumped under the heading of *communication deadlocks*.

Advanced synchronization algorithms. In this chapter, we have studied basic synchronization constructs. Such constructs have been incorporated into IEEE standards such as a POSIX threading library. As we observed earlier, the libraries or their variants have been incorporated into almost all modern operating systems. Most application software for parallel systems is built with such multithreading libraries.

Programming mutual exclusion locks and condition variables is difficult and error-prone. The primary reason is that the logic of synchronized access to shared data structures is strewn all over the program, and this makes such programming hard, from a software-engineering point of view. This difficulty has implications on the design, development, and maintenance of large, complex, parallel programs.

We can boil down the needs of concurrent programming to three things:

1. an ability for a thread to execute some sections of the program (which we called critical sections, in Section 12.2.4) in a mutually exclusive manner (i.e., serially),

2. an ability for a thread to wait if some condition is not satisfied, and

3. an ability for a thread to notify a peer thread who may be waiting for some condition to become true.

Monitor is a programming construct, proposed by Brinch Hansen and Tony Hoare in the 1970s, that meet the aforementioned needs. A monitor is an abstract data type that contains the data structures and procedures for manipulating these data structures. In terms of modern programming languages such as Java or C++, we can think of the monitor as syntactically similar to an object. Let us understand the difference between a Java object and a monitor. The principal difference is that there can be exactly one active thread inside a monitor at any point in time. In other words, if you have a need for a critical section in your program, you will write that portion of the program as a monitor. A program structure that requires multiple, independent, critical sections (as we saw in Example 12.7) will be constructed with multiple monitors, each with a distinct name for each of the critical sections. A thread inside the monitor may have to block for a resource. For this purpose, the monitor provides *condition variables*, with two operations, *wait* and *notify*, on the variables. The reader can see an immediate parallel to the condition variable inside a monitor and the condition variable available in the pthreads library. The monitor construct meets all the three needs for writing concurrent programs that we laid out previously. To verify that this is true, we will present an example.

Example 12.17

Write a solution, using monitors for the video processing example developed in this chapter.

Answer:

The digitizer and tracker codes are written, assuming the existence of a monitor called FrameBuffer. The procedures grab and analyze used by the digitizer and tracker, respectively, are outside the monitor.

```
digitizer()
{
  image_type dig_image;

  loop {
    grab(dig_image);
    FrameBuffer.insert(dig_image);
  }
}

tracker()
{
  image_type track_image;

  loop {
    FrameBuffer.remove_image(&track_image);
    analyze(track_image);
  }
}

monitor FrameBuffer
{

#define MAX 100

image_type frame_buf[MAX];
int bufavail = MAX;
int head = 0, tail = 0;

condition not_full, not_empty;
```

```
    void insert_image(image_type image)
    {
      if (bufavail == 0)
          wait(not_full);
      frame_buf[tail mod MAX] = image;
      tail = tail + 1;
      bufavail = bufavail — 1;
      if (bufavail == (MAX-1)) {
        /* tracker could be waiting */
        notify(not_empty);
      }
    }

    void remove_image(image_type *image)
    {
      if (bufavail == MAX)
          wait(not_empty);
      *image = frame_buf[head mod MAX];
      head = head + 1;
      bufavail = bufavail + 1;
      if (bufavail == 1) {
        /* digitizer could be waiting */
        notify(not_full);
      }
    }

} /* end monitor */
```

A number of things are worth commenting on in the solution presented in Example 12.17. The most important point to note is that all the details of synchronization and buffer management that were originally strewn about in the digitizer and tracker procedures in the pthreads version are now nicely tucked away inside the monitor named **FrameBuffer**. This simplifies the tracker and digitizer procedures to be just what is needed for those functions. This also ensures that the resulting program will be less error-prone compared with sprinkling synchronization constructs all over the program. Another elegant aspect of this solution is that there can be any number of digitizer and tracker threads in the application. Due to the semantics of the monitor construct (mutual exclusion), all the calls into the monitor from these various threads get serialized. Overall, the monitor construct adds significantly to the effective software engineering of parallel programs.

The reader may be wondering, If the monitor is such a nice construct, why are we not using it? The main catch is that it is a programming construct. In the Example 12.17, we write the monitor, using a C-style syntax, to be compatible with the earlier solutions of the video-processing-application problem developed in this chapter. However, C does not support the monitor construct. We could, of course, "simulate" the monitor construct by writing the monitor with the facilities available in the operating system (e.g., pthreads library; see Exercise 21).

Some programming languages have adopted the essence of the monitor idea. For example, Java is an object-oriented programming language. It supports user-level threads and allows methods (i.e., procedures) to be grouped together into what are called classes. By prefixing a method with the keyword "synchronized," Java ensures that, in its runtime, exactly one user-level thread is able to execute a synchronized method at any time in a given object. In other words, as soon as a thread starts executing a synchronized method, no other thread will be allowed to execute another synchronized method within the same object. Other methods that do not have the keyword "synchronized" may, of course, be executed concurrently, with the single execution of a synchronized method. Whereas Java does not have an in-built data type similar to the monitor's condition variable, it does provide wait and notify functions that allow blocking and resumption of a thread inside a synchronized method (see Exercise 22).

Scheduling in a multiprocessor. In Chapter 6, we covered several processor scheduling algorithms. All of these apply to parallel systems as well. However, with multiple processors, the scheduler has an opportunity to run either multiple threads of the same application or threads of different applications. This gives rise to some interesting options.

The simplest way to coordinate the scheduling of the threads on the different processors is to have a single data structure (a run queue) that is shared by the scheduler on each of the processors (Figure 12.28). This also ensures that all the processors equally share the computational load (in terms of the runnable threads).

There are some downsides to this approach. The first issue is pollution of the memory hierarchy. On modern processors with multiple levels of caches, there is a significant time penalty for reaching into levels that are farther away from the processor (see Chapter 9 for more details). Consider a thread T1 that was running on processor P2. Its time quantum ran out, and it was context switched out. With a central queue, T1 may be picked up by some other processor, say, P5, the next time around. Let us understand

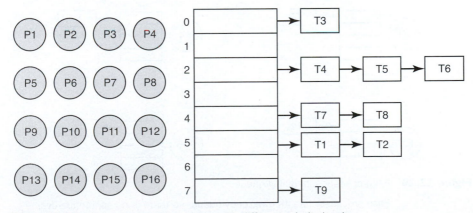

Figure 12.28   Shared scheduling queue with different priority levels.
The processors on the left share a common ready queue.

why this may not be a desirable situation. Perhaps most of the memory footprint of T1 is still in the nearer levels of processor P2's memory hierarchy. Therefore, T1 would have incurred fewer cache misses if it had been run on P2 the second time around. In other words, T1 has an *affinity* for processor P2. Thus, one embellishment to the basic scheduling algorithm, when applied to multiprocessors, is to use cache affinity, a technique first proposed by Vaswani and Zahorjan. A per-processor scheduling queue (shown in Figure 12.29) would help in managing the threads and their affinity for specific processors better than a shared queue. For load balancing, processors that find themselves out of work (due to their queues' being empty) may do what is usually referred to as *work stealing* from the scheduling queues of other processors. Another embellishment is to *lengthen the time quantum* for a thread that is currently holding a mutual exclusion lock. The intuition behind this arises from the fact that other threads of the same application cannot really run until this thread relinquishes the lock. Zahorjan proposed this technique, as well. Figure 12.29 shows a conceptual picture of a per-processor scheduling queue.

We will introduce the reader to two additional techniques for making multiprocessor scheduling more effective, especially for multithreaded applications. The first one is called *space sharing*. The idea here is to dedicate a set of processors for an application, for its lifetime. At application startup, as many processors as there are threads in the application are allocated to this application. The scheduler will delay starting the application until such time as that many idle processors are available. Since a processor is dedicated to a thread, there is no context-switching overhead (and affinity is preserved, as well). If a thread is blocked on synchronization or I/O, then the processor cycles are simply wasted. This technique provides excellent service to applications, but at the risk of wasting resources. One modification to this basic idea of space sharing is for the application to have the ability to scale up or down its requirements for CPUs, depending on the load on the system. For example, a web server may be able to shrink the number of threads to 10 down from 20 if the system can provide only 10 processors. Later on, if the system has more processors available, the web server can claim them and create additional threads to run on those processors.

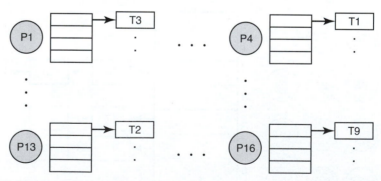

Figure 12.29   Per-processor scheduling queue.

Each processor has its own ready queue, so there is no contention over accessing the ready queue by the scheduler on each processor.

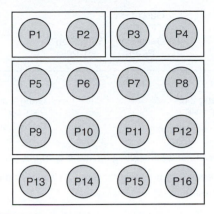

Figure 12.30   The scheduler has created four partitions to enable space sharing.

There are two 2-processor partitions; and one each of a 4-processor and an 8-processor partition.

A space-sharing scheduler would divide the total number of processors in the system into different-sized partitions (see Figure 12.30) and allocate partitions, one at a time, to applications instead of to individual processors. This reduces the number of bookkeeping data structures that the scheduler needs to keep. This should remind the reader of fixed-sized-partition memory allocation that we studied in Chapter 7. Similar to that memory-management scheme, space sharing may result in internal fragmentation. For example, if an application requires six processors, it would get a partition with eight processors. Two of the eight processors would remain idle for the duration of the application.

The last technique we introduce is *gang scheduling*. It is a technique complementary to space sharing. Consider the following: Thread T1 is holding a lock; T2 is waiting for it. T1 releases the lock, but T2 currently is not scheduled to take advantage of the lock that just became available. The application may have been designed to use fine-grain locks such that a thread holds a lock for only a very short amount of time. In such a situation, there is tremendous loss of productivity for this application, due to the fact that the scheduler is unaware of the close coupling that exists among the threads of the application. Gang scheduling alleviates this situation. Related threads of an application are scheduled as a group, hence the name *gang scheduling*. Each thread runs on a different CPU. However, in contrast to space sharing, a CPU is not dedicated to a single thread. Instead, each CPU is time-shared.

Gang scheduling works as follows:

- Time is divided into fixed-size quanta.
- All the CPUs are scheduled at the beginning of each time quantum.
- The scheduler uses the principle of gangs to allocate the processors to the threads of a given application.
- Different gangs may use the same set of processors in different time quanta.

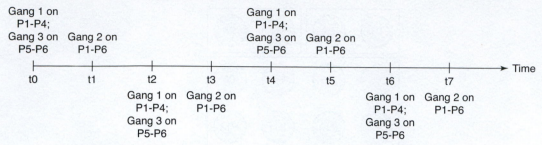

Figure 12.31 A timeline of gang scheduling for three different gangs.

Gang 1 needs four processors; Gang 2 needs six processors; Gang 3 needs two processors.

- Multiple gangs may be scheduled at the same time, depending on the availability of the processors.
- Once scheduled, the association of a thread to a processor remains until the next time quantum, even if the thread blocks (i.e., the processor will remain idle).

Gang scheduling may incorporate cache affinity in its scheduling decision. Figure 12.31 shows how three gangs may share six CPUs, both in space and time, using the gang scheduling principle.

To summarize, we introduced the reader to four techniques that are used to increase the efficiency of CPU scheduling in a multiprocessor:

- cache affinity scheduling;
- lock-based time quantum extension;
- space sharing; and
- gang scheduling.

A multiprocessor scheduler might use a combination of these techniques to maximize efficiency, depending on the workload for which the system is intended. Finally, these techniques are on top of and work in concert with the short-term scheduling algorithm that is used in each processor. (See Chapter 6 for coverage of short-term scheduling algorithms).

Classic problems in concurrency. We will conclude this discussion by mentioning some classic problems in concurrency that have been used as a way of motivating the synchronization developments in parallel systems.

1. **Producer–consumer problem:** This is also referred to as the bounded-buffer problem. The video processing application that has been used as a running example in this chapter is an instance of the producer–consumer problem. Producers keep putting stuff into a shared data structure, and consumers keep taking stuff out of it. This is a common communication paradigm that occurs in

several applications. Any application that can be modeled as a pipeline applies this communication paradigm.

2. **Readers–writers problem:** Let us say that you are trying to get tickets to a ball game. You go to a website such as Ticketmaster.com. You pull up the specific date for which you want to get the tickets and check the availability of seats. You may look at different options, in terms of pricing and seating, before you finally decide to lock in on a specific set of seats and purchase the tickets. While you are doing this, there are probably hundreds of other sports fans who are also looking to purchase tickets for the same game on the same day. Until you actually purchase the seats you want, those seats are up for grabs by anyone. A database contains all the information concerning the availability of seats on different dates, etc. Looking for the availability of seats is a read operation on the database. Any number of concurrent readers may browse the database for availability. Purchasing tickets is a write operation on the database. This requires exclusive access to the database (or at least part of the database), implying that there should be no readers present during the writing.

The preceding example is an instance of the classic readers–writers problem first formulated in 1971 by Courtois, et al. A simpleminded solution to the problem would be as follows: So long as readers are in the database, allow new readers to come in, since none of them needs exclusive access. When a writer comes along, make him wait if there are readers currently active in the database. As soon as all the readers have exited the database, let the writer in exclusively. Conversely, if a writer in the database, block the readers until the writer exists the database. This solution, using mutual exclusion locks, is shown in Figure 12.32.

Pondering on this simple solution, we can immediately see some of its shortcomings. Since readers do not need exclusive access, so long as at least one reader is currently in the database, new readers will continue to be let in. This will lead to the starvation of writers. The solution can be fixed by checking whether there are waiting writers when a new reader wants to join the party, and simply enqueueing the new reader behind the waiting writer (see Exercises 23–26).

3. **Dining philosophers problem:** This is a famous synchronization problem attributed to Dijkstra (1965). Ever since then, any new synchronization construct proposal has used this problem as a litmus test to see how efficiently the proposed synchronization construct solves it. Five philosophers are sitting around a round table. They alternate between eating and thinking. There is a bowl of spaghetti in the middle of the table. Each philosopher has his individual plate. There are a total of five forks, one in between every pair of philosophers, as shown in Figure 12.33. When a philosopher wants to eat, he picks up the two forks nearest to him on either side, serves some spaghetti from the bowl onto his plate, and eats. Once finished eating, he puts down his forks and continues thinking.[7]

---

7. It would appear that these philosophers did not care much about personal hygiene, reusing forks used by neighbors!

```
mutex_lock_type readers_count_lock, database_lock;
int readers_count = 0;

void readers()
{
  lock(read_count_lock); /* get exclusive lock
                           * for updating readers
                           * count
                           */
    if (readers_count == 0) {
      /* first reader in a new group,
       * obtain lock to the database
       */
      lock(database_lock);
      /* note only first reader does this,
       * so in effect this lock is shared by
       * all the readers in this current set
       */
    }
    readers_count = readers_count + 1;
  unlock(read_count_lock);
  read_dabatase();
  lock(read_count_lock); /* get exclusive lock
                           * for updating readers
                           * count
                           */
    readers_count = readers_count - 1;
    if (readers_count == 0) {
      /* last reader in current group,
       * release lock to the database
       */
      unlock(database_lock);
    }
  unlock(read_count_lock);
}

void writer()
{
  lock(database_lock);    /* get exclusive lock */
  write_dabatase();
  unlock(database_lock); /* release exclusive lock */
}
```

Figure 12.32 Solution to readers–writers problem, using mutual exclusion locks.

Figure 12.33   Dining Philosophers.[8]

A hungry philosopher picks up two forks, one on either side of him, and puts them down when finished eating.

The problem is to make sure that each philosopher does his bit of eating and thinking without bothering anyone else. In other words, we want each philosopher to be an independent thread of execution with maximal concurrency for the two tasks that each has to do, namely, eating and thinking. Thinking requires no coordination, since it is an individual effort. On the other hand, eating requires coordination, since there is a shared fork between every two philosophers.

A simple solution is for each philosopher to agree ahead of time to pick up one fork first (say, the left fork), and then pick up the right fork, and finally, start eating. The problem with this solution is that it does not work. If every philosopher simultaneously picks up his left fork, each one will be waiting for the right fork, which is held by his right neighbor. This would lead to the circular wait condition of deadlock.

---

8. Picture source: http://commons.wikimedia.org/wiki/File:Dining_philosophers.png.

Let us sketch a possible correct solution. We will introduce an intermediate state between *thinking* and *eating*, namely, *hungry*. In the hungry state, a philosopher will try to pick up both forks. If successful, he will proceed to the eating state. If he cannot get both forks simultaneously, he will keep trying until he succeeds in getting both forks. What would allow a philosopher to pick up both forks, simultaneously? Both his immediate neighbors *should not be* in the *eating* state. Further, he will want to ensure that his neighbors do not change states while he is testing whether he can pick up the forks. Once finished eating, he will change his state to thinking, and simply notify his immediate neighbors so that they may attempt to eat if they are hungry. Figure 12.34 gives a solution to the dining philosophers' problem, using monitors. Note that when a philosopher tries to get the forks by using `take_forks`, the monitor—thanks to its guarantee that there is only one active thread in it at any point in time—ensures that no other philosopher can change his state.

12.10.2 Architecture Topics

In Section 12.9, we introduced multiprocessors. We will delve a little deeper into advanced topics relating to parallel architectures.

Hardware multithreading. A pipelined processor exploits instruction-level parallelism (ILP). However, as we discussed in Chapters 5 and 9, there are limits to exploiting instruction-level parallelism set by a variety of factors, including branches, limited functional units, and the growing gap between processor cycle time and memory cycle time. For example, cache misses result in pipeline stalls, and the severity grows with the level at which cache misses occur. A cache miss that requires off-chip servicing could result in the CPU waiting for several tens of clock cycles. With multithreaded programs, there is another way to use the processor resources efficiently, namely, across all the active threads that are ready to run. This is referred to as *thread level parallelism (TLP)*. *Multithreading* at the hardware level comes in handy to help reduce the ill effects of pipeline stalls due to ILP limitations, by exploiting TLP.

```
void philosopher(int i)
{
  loop {/* forever */
    do_some_thinking();
    DiningPhilosphers.take_forks(i);
    eat();
    DiningPhilosphers.put_down_forks(i);
  }
}
```

Figure 12.34(a)   Code that each philosopher thread executes.

```
monitor DiningPhilosophers
{
#define N 5
#define THINKING 0
#define HUNGRY 1
#define EATING 2
#define LEFT ((i+N-1) mod N)
#define RIGHT ((i+1) mod N)

condition phil_waiting[N]; /* one for each philosopher */
int phil_state[N]; /* state of each philosopher */

        void take_forks (int i)
        {
          phil_state[i] = HUNGRY;
          repeat
            if ( (phil_state[LEFT] != EATING) &&
                 (phil_state[RIGHT] != EATING) )
               phil_state[i] = EATING;
            else
               wait(phil_waiting[i]);
          until (phil_state[i] == EATING);
        }

        void put_down_forks (int i)
        {
          phil_state[i] = THINKING;
          notify(phil_waiting[LEFT]);  /* left neighbor
                                          notified */
          notify(phil_waiting[RIGHT]); /* right neighbor
                                          notified */
        }

        /* monitor initialization code */
        init:
        {
          int i;
          for (i = 1; i < N; i++) {
                phil_state[i] = THINKING;
          }
        }

} /* end monitor */
```

Figure 12.34(b) Monitor for dining philosophers problem.

A simple analogy will help here. Imagine a queue of people awaiting service in front of a single bank teller. A customer walks up to the teller. The teller finds that the customer needs to fill out a form before the transaction can be completed. The teller is smart. She asks the customer to step aside and fill out the form, and she then starts dealing with the next customer. When the first customer is ready again, the teller will attend to him to finish the original transaction. The teller may temporarily sideline multiple customers who need to fill out forms, and thus keep the waiting line moving efficiently.

Hardware multithreading is very much like this real-life example. The uniprocessor is the teller. The customers are the independent threads. A long latency operation that could stall the processor is the filling out of the form by the customer. Upon a thread stall on a long latency operation (e.g., a cache miss that forces main memory access), the processor picks the next instruction to execute from another ready thread, and so on. Thus, just like the bank teller, the processor utilizes its resources efficiently, even if one or more ready threads are stalled on long latency operations. Naturally, this raises several questions. How does the processor know there are multiple threads ready to run? How does the operating system know that it can simultaneously schedule multiple threads to run on the same physical processor? How does the processor keep the *state* (PC, register file, etc.) of each thread distinct from the other? Does this technique work only for speeding up multithreaded applications, or does it also work for sequential applications? We will answer these questions in the next couple of paragraphs.

Multithreading in hardware is yet another example of a contract between hardware and system software. The processor architecture specifies how many concurrent threads it can handle in hardware. In the Intel architecture, this is referred to as the number of *logical processors*. This represents the level of *duplication* of the hardware resources needed to keep the states of the threads distinct. Each logical processor has its own distinct PC, and register file. The operating system allows an application to bind a thread to a logical processor. In Section 12.7 we discussed the operating system support for thread-level scheduling. With multiple logical processors at its disposal, the operating system can simultaneously schedule multiple ready threads for execution on the processor. The physical processor maintains distinct persona for each logical processor, through duplicate sets of register files, PC, page tables, etc. Thus, when an instruction corresponding to a particular logical processor goes through the pipeline, the processor knows the thread-specific hardware resources that have to be accessed for the instruction execution.

A multithreaded application stands to gain efficiency with hardware support for multithreading, since even if one thread is blocked due to limitations of ILP, some other thread in the same application may be able to make forward progress. Unfortunately, if an application is single-threaded, it cannot benefit from hardware multithreading to speed up its execution. However, hardware multithreading would still help improve the *throughput* of the system as a whole. This is because hardware multithreading is agnostic as to whether the threads it is pushing through the pipeline belong to independent processes or are part of the same process.

This discussion begs another question: Can exploitation of ILP by the processor using superscalar design coexist with exploitation of TLP? The answer is yes, and this is precisely what most modern processors do to enhance performance. The basic fact is that modern multiple-issue processors have more functional units than can be gainfully used up by a single thread. Therefore, it makes perfect sense to combine ILP exploitation using multiple-issue with TLP exploitation using the logical processors.

Each vendor gives a different name for this integrated approach to exploiting ILP and TLP. Intel's *hyperthreading* is pretty much a standard feature on most Intel processors. IBM calls it *simultaneous multithreading (SMT)* and uses it in the IBM Power5 processor.

Interconnection networks. Before we look at different types of parallel architectures, it is useful to get a basic understanding of how to interconnect the elements inside a computer system. In the case of a uniprocessor, we already learned, in Chapters 4, 9, and 10, the concept of buses that enable the processor, memory, and peripherals to be connected to one another. The simplest form of interconnection network for a parallel machine is a shared bus (Section 12.9). However, large-scale parallel machines may have on the order of thousands of processors. We call each node in such a parallel machine a *processing element, or PE* for short. A shared bus would become a communication bottleneck among the PEs in such a large-scale machine. Therefore, large-scale machines use more sophisticated interconnection networks, such as a *mesh* (in which each processor is connected to its four neighbors, north, south, east, and west) or a *tree*. Such sophisticated interconnection networks allow for simultaneous communication among different PEs. Figure 12.35 shows

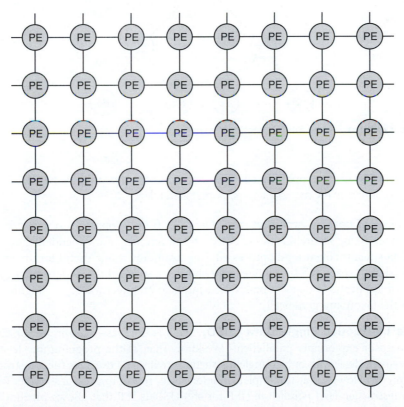

Figure 12.35(a)   A mesh interconnection network.

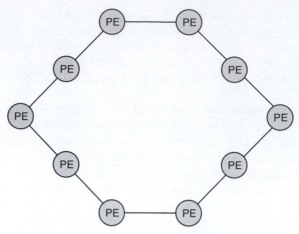

Figure 12.35(b)   A ring interconnection network.

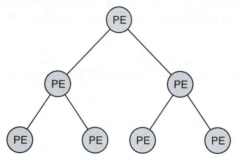

Figure 12.35(c)   A tree interconnection network.

some examples of such sophisticated interconnection networks. Each PE may locally have buses to connect to the memory and other peripheral devices.

Taxonomy of parallel architectures. Flynn, in 1966, proposed a simple taxonomy for characterizing all architectures, based on the number of independent instruction and data streams concurrently processed. The taxonomy, while useful for understanding the design space and the architectural choices, also aided the understanding of the kinds of applications that are best suited for each architectural style. Figure 12.36 shows the taxonomy, graphically.

Single Instruction Single Data (SISD). This is the classic uniprocessor. Does a uniprocessor exploit any parallelism? We know that, at the programming level, the uniprocessor deals with only a single instruction stream and executes these instructions sequentially. However, at the implementation level, the uniprocessor exploits what is called *instruction-level parallelism* (*ILP* for short). It is ILP that allows pipelined and superscalar implementation of an instruction-set architecture (see Chapter 5).

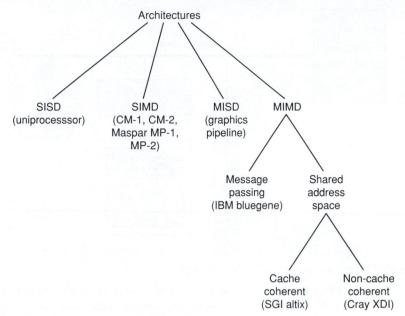

Figure 12.36 A taxonomy of parallel architectures.

Single Instruction Multiple Data (SIMD). All the processors execute the same instruction in a lock-step fashion, on independent data streams. Before the killer micros (the powerful single-chip microprocessors of the 1990s) made this style of architecture commercially noncompetitive, several machines were built to cater to this architecture style. Examples include Thinking Machine Corporation's Connection Machine, CM-1 and CM-2; and Maspar MP-1 and MP-2. This style of architecture was particularly well suited to image-processing applications (for example, applying the same operation to each pixel of a large image). Figure 12.37 shows a typical organization of an SIMD machine. Each processor of the SIMD machine is called a *processing element (PE)*, and has its own data memory that is preloaded with a distinct data stream. There is a single instruction memory contained in the control unit that fetches and broadcasts the instructions to the PE array. The instruction memory is also preloaded with the program to be executed on the PE array. Each PE executes the instructions with the distinct data streams from the respective data memories. The SIMD model promotes parallelism at a very *fine granularity*. For example, a **for** loop may be executed in parallel, with each iteration running on a different PE. We define *fine-grained parallelism* as one in which each processor executes a small number of instructions (say, less than 10) before communicating with other processors.

An SIMD machine is a workhorse designed to carry out some fine-grained compute-intensive task. Program development for the SIMD machine is usually via a front-end processor (a workstation-class machine). The front-end is also responsible for preloading the data memories of the PEs and the instruction memory of the array control unit. All I/O is orchestrated through the front-end processor, as well. The PEs

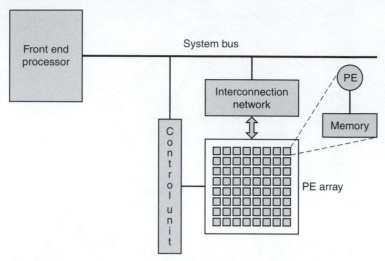

Figure 12.37   Organization of an SIMD machine.

A front-end processor is typically a powerful workstation running some flavor of UNIX. *PE* stands for *processing element* and is the basic building block of an SIMD machine.

communicate with one another via an interconnection network. Since SIMD machines may have on the order of thousands of processors, they use sophisticated interconnection networks (e.g., a mesh or a tree), as discussed earlier in this section. Although no commercial machines of this flavor are on the market today, the Intel MMX instructions are inspired by the parallelism exploited by this architectural style. There has been a resurgence in this style of computation, as exemplified by stream accelerators such as the nVidia graphics card (referred to as a *graphics processing unit* or *GPU* for short). Further, as stream-oriented processing (audio, video, etc.) is becoming more common, the traditional processor architecture and the stream accelerators are converging. For example, Intel's Larrabee *general purpose GPU (GPGPU)* architecture represents one such integrated architecture, meant to serve as the platform for future supercomputers.

Multiple Instructions Single Data (MISD).   At an algorithm level, we could see a use for this style of architecture. Let us say that we want to run several different face-detection algorithms on the same image stream. Each algorithm represents a different instruction stream working on the same data stream (i.e., the image stream). Whereas MISD serves to round out the classification of parallel architecture styles, there is not a compelling argument for this style. It turns out that most computations map more readily to the MIMD or the SIMD style. Consequently, no known architecture exactly matches this computation style. Systolic arrays[9] may be considered a form of MISD architecture.

---

9. The article by Kung and Leiserson on systolic arrays [Kung, 1978] is a seminal work in this area.

Each cell of a systolic array works on the data stream and passes the transformed data to the next cell in the array. Although it is a stretch, one could say that a classic instruction processing pipeline represents an MISD style at a very fine grain if you consider each instruction as "data" and what happens to the instruction as it moves from stage to stage.

Multiple Instructions Multiple Data (MIMD). This is the most general architectural style, and most modern parallel architectures fall into it. Each processor has its own instruction and data stream, and work asynchronously with respect to one another. The processors themselves may be off-the-shelf processors. The programs running on each processor may be completely independent, or may be part of a complex application. If the program is of the latter kind, then the threads of the same application executing on the different processors need to synchronize explicitly with one another due to the inherent asynchrony of the architectural model. This architectural style is best suited to supporting applications that exhibit medium- and coarse-grained parallelism. We define *medium-grained parallelism* as one in which each processor executes approximately 10–100 instructions before communicating with other processors. We define *coarse-grained parallelism* as one in which each processor executes on the order of thousands of instructions before communicating with other processors.

Early multiprocessors were of the SIMD style. Therefore, it was necessary for each processor of an SIMD machine to be specially designed for that machine. This was fine so long as general-purpose processors were built out of discrete circuits. However, as we said already, the arrival of the killer micros made custom-built processors increasingly unviable in the marketplace. On the other hand, the basic building block in an MIMD machine is the general-purpose processor. Therefore, such architectures benefit from the technology advances of off-the-shelf commercial processors. Further, the architectural style can use such a parallel machine for running several independent sequential applications, threads of a parallel application, or some combination thereof. It should be mentioned that with the advent of stream accelerators (such as the nVidia GeForce family of GPUs), hybrids of the parallel machine models are emerging.

Message-passing versus shared address space multiprocessors. MIMD machines may be subdivided into two broad categories: message-passing and shared address space. Figure 12.38 shows a picture of a message-passing multiprocessor. Each

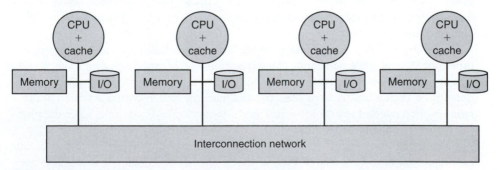

Figure 12.38   Message passing multiprocessor.

processor has its private memory, and processors communicate with each other via messages sent over an interconnection network. There is no shared memory among the processors. For this reason, such architectures are also referred to as *distributed memory* multiprocessors.

IBM's Bluegene series is an example of a modern-day message-passing machine that fits this model. Several examples of message-passing machines of yesteryears include TMC's CM-5, the Intel Paragon, and the IBM SP-2. The previous generation of parallel machines relied on special interconnection network technologies to provide low-latency communication among the processors. However, with advances in computer networking (see Chapter 13), local area networking technology is offering viable low-latency high-bandwidth communication among the processors in a message-passing multicomputer. Consequently, a *cluster parallel machine*, a collection of computers interconnected by local area networking gear such as gigabit ethernet (see Section 13.8) has become a popular platform for parallel computing. Just as `pthreads` library offers a vehicle for parallel programming in a shared-memory environment, *message-passing interface* (*MPI* for short) is a programming library for the message-passing computing environment.

Shared address space multiprocessor is the second category of MIMD machines, which, as the name suggests, provides address equivalence for a memory location, irrespective of which processor is accessing that location. In other words, a given memory address (say, 0x2000) refers to the same physical memory location in whichever processor that address is generated. As we have seen, a processor has several levels of caches. Naturally, upon access to a memory location, data in that location will be brought into the processor cache. As we saw in Section 12.9, this gives rise to the cache-coherence problem in a multiprocessor. Shared address space machines may be further subdivided into two broad categories, according to whether this problem is addressed in hardware or software. Noncache coherent (NCC) multiprocessors provide shared address space, but no cache coherence in hardware. Examples of such machines from yesteryears include the BBN Butterfly, the Cray T3D, and the Cray T3E. A more recent example is the Cray XDI.

Cache coherent (CC) multiprocessors provide shared address space, as well as hardware cache coherence. Examples of this class of machines from yesteryears include the KSR-1, the Sequent Symmetry, and the SGI Origin 2000. Modern machines of this class include the SGI Altix. Further, the individual nodes of any high-performance cluster system (such as the IBM Bluegene) is usually a cache-coherent multiprocessor.

In Section 12.9, we introduced the reader to a bus-based shared-memory multiprocessor. A large-scale parallel machine (regardless of whether it is a message-passing or a shared address space machine) would need an interconnection network more sophisticated than a bus. A large-scale parallel machine that provides a shared address space is often referred to as a *distributed shared-memory* (*DSM*) machine, since the physical memory is distributed and associated with each individual processor.

The cache-coherence mechanisms we discussed in Section 12.9 assume a broadcast medium, namely, a shared bus, so that a change to a memory location is seen simultaneously by all the caches of the respective processors. With an arbitrary interconnection network such as a tree, a ring, or a mesh (see Figure 12.35), there is no longer a broadcast medium. The communication is point to point. Therefore, some other mechanism is needed to implement cache coherence. Such large-scale shared-memory multiprocessors use a *directory-based scheme* to implement cache coherence. The idea is quite simple. Shared memory is already physically distributed; simply associate a directory along with each piece of the shared memory. There is a directory entry for each memory location. This entry contains the processors that currently have this memory location encached. The cache-coherence algorithm may be invalidation or update based. The directory has the bookkeeping information for sending either the invalidations or updates.

Figure 12.39 shows a directory-based DSM organization. Location X is currently encached in P2, P3, and P4. If P4 wishes to write to location X, the directory associated with X sends an invalidation to P2 and P3, before P4 is allowed to write to X. In a nutshell, the distributed directories orchestrate the fulfillment of the memory access

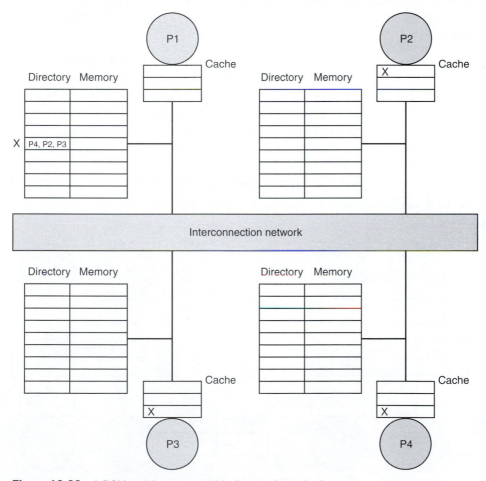

Figure 12.39 A DSM multiprocessor with directory-based coherence.

requests from the different processors to ensure that the data values returned to the processors in response to those requests are coherent. Each directory services the memory access requests in the order received, for the portion of the shared memory for which this directory is responsible, thereby ensuring the coherence property for the data values returned to the processors.

Example 12.18

In a four-processor DSM similar to that shown in Figure 12.39, memory location Y is in the physical memory of P3. Currently, P1, P2, and P4 have a copy of Y in their respective caches. The current value in Y is 101. P1 wishes to write the value 108 to Y. Explain the sequence of steps that happen before the value of Y changes to 108. Assume that the cache write policy is write-back.

Answer:

a. Since memory location Y is in P3, P1 sends a request through the interconnection network to P3 and asks write permission for Y (see Figure 12.40(a)).

b. P3 notices that P2 and P4 have copies of Y in their caches, by looking up directory entry for Y. It sends invalidation request for Y to P2 and P4 (Figure 12.40(b)).

c. P2 and P4 invalidate their respective cache entries for Y and send back acknowledgements to P3 via the interconnection network. P3 removes P2 and P4 from the directory entry for Y (Figure 12.40(c)).

d. P3 sends write permission to P1 (Figure 12.40(d)).

e. P1 writes 108 in the cache entry for Y (Figure 12.40(e)).

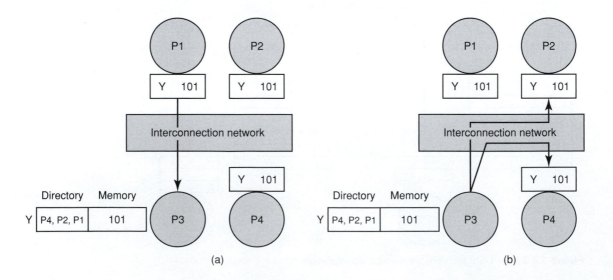

(a)   (b)

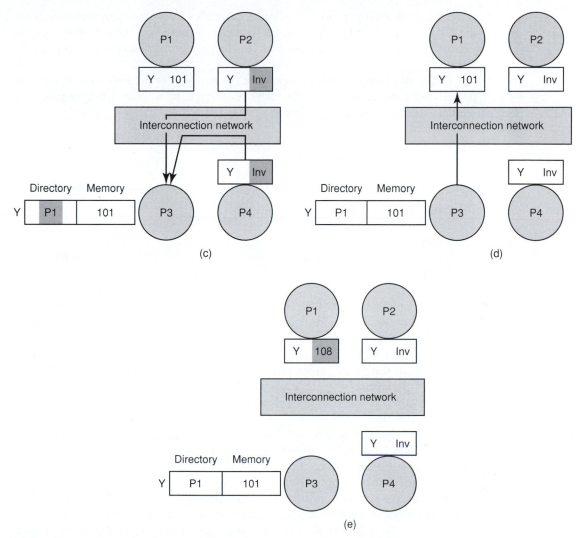

Figure 12.40 Sequence of steps for Example 12.18.

Memory consistency model and cache coherence. A cache-coherent multiprocessor ensures that once a memory location (which may be currently cached) is modified, the value will propagate to all the cached copies and the memory as well. We would expect that there would be some delay before all the cached copies have been updated with the new value that has just been written. This begs the question, What is the view from the programmer's perspective? The *memory consistency model* is the contract between the programmer and the memory system for defining this view. We have seen repeatedly in this textbook that system design is all about establishing a contract between the hardware and the software. For example, ISA is a contract between the compiler writer and the processor architect. Once the ISA is set, the implementer of the ISA can exercise his or her choice in the hardware realization of the ISA. Memory consistency model is a similar contract between the programmer and the memory system architect.

Let us illustrate this with an example. Given next is the execution history on processors P1 and P2 of an SMP. The memory is shared, by definition, but the processor registers are private to each processor.

Initially,

$$Mem[X] = 0$$

	Processor P1	Processor P2
Time 0:	R1 ← 1	
Time 1:	Mem[X] ← R1	R2 ← 0
Time 2:	. . . .	. . . .
Time 3:	. . . .	R2 ← Mem[X]
Time 4:	. . . .	. . . .

What would you expect the contents of R2 on P2 to be at time 4? The intuitive answer is 1. However, this really depends on the implementation of the memory system. Let us say that each of the instructions shown in the execution history is atomic with respect to that processor. Thus, at time 1, processor P1 has written a value of 1 into Mem[X]. What this means, as far as P1 is concerned, is that if it tries to read Mem[X] after time 1, the memory system guarantees that it will see the value 1 in it. However, what guarantee does the memory system give for values to the same memory location when accessed from other processors? Is it legal for the memory system to return a value 0 for the access at time 3 on P2? The cache-coherence mechanism guarantees that both the caches on P1 and P2, as well as the memory, will *eventually* contain the value 1 for Mem[x]. But it does not specify *when* the values will become consistent. The memory consistency model answers the *when* question.

An intuitive memory consistency model proposed by Leslie Lamport is called *sequential consistency (SC)*. In this model, memory reads and writes are atomic with respect to the *entire system*. Thus, if we say that P1 has written to Mem[X] at time 1, then the new value for this memory location henceforth is *visible* to *all* the processors. Thus, when P2 reads Mem[X] at time 3, it is also guaranteed by the memory system that it will see the value 1. As far as the programmer is concerned, this is all the detail about the memory system that he or she needs to write correct programs. The implementation of the memory system with caches and the details of the cache-coherence mechanisms are irrelevant to the programmer. This is akin to the separation between architecture and implementation that we saw in the context of processor ISA design.

Let us give a more precise definition of the SC memory model. The effects of the memory accesses from an individual processor will be exactly the same as if there are no other processors accessing the memory. That is, each memory access (read or write) will be atomic. We would expect this behavior from a uniprocessor, and therefore it is natural to expect this from a multiprocessor as well. As for memory accesses from different processors, the model says that the observed effect will be an arbitrary interleaving of these individually atomic memory accesses emanating from the different processors.

One way to visualize the SC memory model is to think of memory accesses from different processors as the cards dealt to a number of players in a card game. You may have seen a card shark take two splits of a card deck and do a shuffle merge, as shown in the accompanying picture, while preserving the original order of the cards in the two splits. The SC memory model does an *n-way* shuffle merge of all the memory accesses coming from the *n* processors that the multiprocessor comprises.

Returning to the previous example, we showed a particular postmortem execution history in which the access to Mem[X] from P2 *happened after* the access to Mem[X] from P1. The processors are asynchronous with respect to each other. Therefore, another run of the same program could have an execution in which the accesses are reversed. In this case, the access by P2 to Mem[X] would return a value of 0. In other words, for the previous program, the SC model would allow the memory system to return a 0 or a 1 for the access by P2 to Mem[X].

We can see that the SC memory model could result in parallel programs that have data races. (See Section 12.2.3 for a discussion of data races.) Fortunately, this does not affect correct parallel program development, as long as the programmer uses synchronization primitives, as discussed in earlier sections, to coordinate the activities of the threads that an application comprises. In fact, as we have seen in earlier sections, the application programmer is completely oblivious to the memory consistency model, since he or she is programming by using libraries such as *pthreads*. Just as the ISA is a contract between the compiler writer and the architect, the memory consistency model is a contract between the library writer and the system architect.

The SC memory model says nothing about how the processors may coordinate their activities by using synchronization primitives to eliminate such data races. As we have discussed in earlier sections, the system may provide synchronization primitives in hardware or software for the purposes of coordination among the threads. Therefore, it is possible to include such synchronization primitives, along with the normal memory accesses, to specify the contract between hardware and software. This would give more implementation choices for the system architect to optimize the performance of the memory system. The area of memory consistency models for shared-memory systems was a fertile area of research in the late 1980s and early 1990s, resulting in several doctoral dissertations. Detailed treatment of this topic is beyond the scope of this textbook. (We provide suggestions for further reading at the end of this chapter.)

12.10.3 The Road Ahead: Multicore and Many-Core Architectures

The road ahead is exciting for parallel computing. The new millennium has ushered in the age of multicore processors. The name *multicore* comes from the simple fact that the chip now consists of several independently clocked processing cores that constitute the processor. Moore's law fundamentally predicts an increase in chip density over time. Thus far, this increase in chip density has been exploited to increase processor performance. Several modern processors, including the AMD Phenom II, the IBM Power5, the Intel Pentium D, the Xeon-MP, and the Sun T1 have embraced multicore technology.

However, with the increase in processor performance, the power consumption of single-chip processors has also been increasing steadily (see Section 5.15.5). The power consumption is directly proportional to the clock frequency of the processor. This trend is forcing processor architects to focus attention on ways to reduce power consumption while increasing chip density. The answer is to have multiple processing cores on a single chip, each of which may be clocked at a lower clock frequency. The basic strategy for conserving power would then involve selectively turning off the power to parts of the chip. In other words, power-consumption consideration is forcing us to choose parallelism over faster uniprocessors. With single-chip processors now containing multiple independent processing cores, parallel computing is no longer an option, but a must, as we move forward. The next step in the evolution of single-chip processors is *many-core* processors, wherein a single-chip may contain hundreds or even thousands of cores. Each of these processing cores will likely be a very simple processor, not that different from the basic pipelined processor we discussed in Chapter 5. Thus, even though in the earlier chapters we did not get into the micro-architectural intricacies of modern processors, the simple implementations we did discuss may become more relevant with the many-core processors of tomorrow.

We might be tempted to think that a multicore architecture is no different from shrink-wrapping an SMP into a single chip; and that a many-core architecture is, similarly, a shrink-wrapped version of a large-scale multiprocessor with hundreds or thousands of PEs. However, it is not business as usual, considering the range of issues that requires a radical rethinking, including electrical engineering, programming paradigm, and resource management at the system level.

At the electrical engineering level, we already mentioned the need for reducing the power dissipation. The reason for conserving power is a pragmatic matter. It is just impossible to cool a processor that is smaller than the size of a penny, but consumes several hundred watts of power. Another concern is distribution of electrical signals, especially the clock, on the chip. Normally, one would think that placing a 1 or 0 on a wire would result in this signal being propagated, as is, to the recipients.

This is a safe assumption as long as there is sufficient time—referred to as the *wire delay*—for the signal to travel to the recipient on the wire. We saw in Chapter 3 that the wire delay is a function of the resistance and capacitance of the electrical wire. As clock speed increases, the wire delay may approach the clock cycle time, causing a wire inside a chip to behave like a transmission line, in which the signal strength deteriorates with distance. The upshot is that a 1 may appear as a 0 at the destination, and vice versa, leading to erroneous operation. Consequently, chip designers have to reevaluate some basic assumptions about digital signals, as the chip density increases in the multicore and many-core era. This is giving rise to new trends in integrated circuit (IC) design, namely, three-dimensional design popularly referred to as *3D ICs*. In brief, in order to reduce the wire length, the chips are being designed with active elements (transistors) in several parallel planes in the z-dimension. Wires, which hitherto were confined to two dimensions, will now be run in three dimensions, thus giving an opportunity to reduce the wire delay between active elements. Developing a 3D chip is akin to building skyscrapers! Mainstream general-purpose processors are yet to embrace this new technology, but it is just a matter of time before it will be the norm.

At the architecture level, there are several differences between an SMP and a multicore processor. In an SMP, at the hardware level, the only shared hardware resource is the bus. On the other hand, in a multicore processor, several hardware resources may be common to all the cores. For example, we showed the memory hierarchy of the AMD Barcelona chip in Chapter 9 (see Figure 9.45). The on-chip L3 cache is shared across all the four cores on the chip. There could be other shared resources such as I/O and memory buses coming out of the chip. It is an architectural issue to schedule the efficient use of such shared resources.

At the programming level, there are important differences in the way we think about a parallel program running on a multicore versus on an SMP. A good rule of thumb in designing parallel programs is to ensure that there is a good balance between computation and communication. In an SMP, threads should be assigned a significant amount of work before they are required to communicate with other threads that are running on other processors. That is, the computations have to be *coarse-grained* to amortize for the cost of interprocessor communication. Due to the proximity of the PEs in a multicore processor, it is conceivable to achieve *finer-grain* parallelism than would be feasible in an SMP.

At the operating system level, there is a fundamental difference between an SMP and a multicore processor. Scheduling threads of a multithreaded application on a multicore versus an SMP requires rethinking to take full advantage of the shared hardware resources between the cores. In an SMP, each processor has an independent image of the operating system. In a multicore processor, it is advantageous for the cores to share the same image of the operating system. The OS designers have to rethink which operating systems data structures should be shared across the cores, and which ones should be kept independent.

Many-core processors may bring forth a whole new set of problems at all of these levels, and add new ones, such as coping with partial software and hardware failures.

Summary

In this chapter, we covered key concepts in parallel programming with threads, the operating system support for threads, and the architectural assists for threads. We also reviewed advanced topics in operating systems and parallel architectures.

The three things that an application programmer has to worry about in writing threaded parallel programs are thread creation/termination, data sharing among threads, and synchronization among threads. Section 12.3 gives a summary of the thread function calls, and Table 12.2 gives the vocabulary that the reader should be familiar with in the context of developing threaded programs. Section 12.6 gives a summary of the important thread programming API calls supported by the *pthreads* library.

In discussing the implementation of threads, in Section , we covered the possibility of threads being implemented above the operating system, as a user-level library, with minimal support from the operating system itself. Most modern operating systems, such as Linux, Microsoft XP, and Vista, support threads as the basic unit of CPU scheduling. In this case, the operating system implements the functionality expected at the programming level. We covered kernel-level threads in Section 12.7.2, as well as an example of how threads are managed in the Sun Solaris operating system, in Section 12.7.3.

The fundamental architectural assist needed for supporting threads is an atomic read-modify-write memory operation. We introduced test-and-set instruction in Section 12.8, and showed how, by using this instruction, it is possible to implement higher-level synchronization support in the operating system. In order to support data sharing among the processors, the cache-coherence problem needs to be solved, which we discussed in Section 12.9.

We considered advanced topics in operating systems and architecture as they pertain to multiprocessors, in Section 12.10. In particular, we introduced the reader to a formal treatment of deadlocks, sophisticated synchronization constructs such as monitor, advanced scheduling techniques, and classic problems in concurrency and synchronization (see Section 12.10.1). In Section 12.10.2, we presented a taxonomy of parallel architectures (SISD, SIMD, MISD, and MIMD) and discussed in depth the difference between message-passing style and shared-memory style MIMD architectures.

The hardware and software issues associated with multiprocessors and multithreaded programs are intriguing and deep. We have introduced the reader to a number of exciting topics in this area. However, we have barely scratched the surface of some these issues in this chapter. We hope that we have raised the reader's curiosity level enough for the reader to undertake further exploration of these issues in more advanced courses. A more in-depth treatment of some of the topics covered in this chapter may be found in advanced textbooks on parallel systems, such as [Almasi, 1993; Culler, 1999].

Historical Perspective

Parallel computing and multiprocessors have been of interest to computer scientists and electrical engineers from the very early days of computing.

In Chapter 5, we saw that pipelined processor design exploits instruction-level parallelism, or ILP. In contrast, multiprocessors exploit a different kind of parallelism, namely, thread-level parallelism, or TLP. Exploitation of ILP does not require the end user to do anything different; the user continues to write sequential programs. The compiler, in concert with the architect, does all the magic to exploit the ILP in the sequential program. However, exploitation of TLP requires more work. Either the program has to be written as an explicitly parallel program that uses multiple threads (as developed in this chapter), or the sequential program has to be converted automatically into a multithreaded parallel program. For the latter approach, a sequential programming language such as FORTRAN is extended, with directives that the programmer inserts to indicate opportunities for automatic parallelization. The compiler exploits such directives to parallelize the original sequential program. This approach was quite popular in the early days of parallel computing, but eventually met with diminishing returns, since its applicability is restricted usually to exploiting loop-level parallelism and not function parallelism. Just as a point of clarification, loop-level parallelism notices that successive iterations of a "for" loop in a program are independent of one another and turns every iteration or groups of iterations into a parallel thread. Function parallelism, or task parallelism, deals with conceptual units of work that the programmer has deemed to be parallel (similar to the video surveillance example used in developing the thread-programming constructs in this chapter).

We can easily understand the lure of harnessing parallel resources to get more work done. It would appear that an application that achieves a given single-processor performance could, in theory, achieve an N-fold improvement in performance if parallelized. However, we know from Chapter 5 that Amdahl's law limits this linear increase in performance due to the inherent serial component in the application (see Exercise 16). Further, there is usually a lag between the performance of a single processor and that of the individual processors that a parallel machine comprises. This is because constructing a parallel machine is not simply a matter of replacing the existing processors with faster ones as soon as they become available. Moore's law (see Chapter 3, Section 3.1) has been giving us increased single-processor performance almost continuously for the past 30 years. Thus, a parallel machine quickly becomes outdated as the next generation of higher-performance microprocessors hit the market. For example, a modern-day notebook computer costing a few thousand dollars has more processing power than a multimillion-dollar Cray machine of the 1970s and 1980s. The obsolescence factor has been the main reason that software for parallel machines has not seen the same rapid growth as software for uniprocessors.

Parallel architectures were a high-end niche market reserved for applications that demanded such high performance, mainly from the scientific and engineering domains. Examples of companies and the parallel machines marketed by them include TMC (connection machine line of parallel machines, starting with CM-1 and culminating in CM-5); Maspar (MP-1 and MP-2); Sequent (Symmetry); BBN (Butterfly); Kendall Square Research (KSR-1 and KSR-2); SGI (Origin line of machines and, currently, Altix); and IBM (SP line of machines). Typical characteristics of such machines include either an off-the-shelf processor (e.g., TMC's CM-5 used Sun SPARC, and SGI's Origin series used MIPS), or a custom-built processor (e.g., KSR-1, CM-1, CM-2, MP-1, and MP-2); a proprietary interconnection network; and glue logic relevant to the taxonomical style of the architecture. The interconnection network was a key component of such architectures, since efficient data sharing and synchronization among the processors were dependent on capabilities in the interconnection network.

The advent of the powerful single-chip microprocessors of the 1990s (dubbed *killer micros*) is an example of the introduction of a "disruptive technology" that shook up the high-performance computing market. Once the single-chip microprocessor performance surpassed that of a custom-crafted processor, for a parallel machine, the economic viability of constructing such parallel machines came into question. While a few have survived by reinventing themselves, many parallel computing vendors that thrived in the niche market disappeared (for example, TMC and Maspar).

Alongside the single-chip microprocessor performance, local area network technology was advancing at a rapid pace as well. We will visit the evolution of local area networks (LAN) in Chapter 13, but suffice it to say here that, with the advent of switched gigabit Ethernet (see Section 13.8), the need for proprietary interconnection networks to connect processors of a parallel machine became less relevant. This breakthrough in LAN technology spurred a new class of parallel machines, namely, clusters. A cluster is a set of compute nodes interconnected by off-the-shelf LAN technology. This has been the workhorse for high-performance computing from the mid- to late 1990s to the present day. Clusters promote a message-passing style of programming, and as we said earlier, the MPI communication library has become the *de facto* standard for programming on clusters. What is inside a computing node changes, of course, with advances in technology. For example, at present it is not uncommon to have each computing node as an *n*-way SMP, where *n* may be 2, 4, 8, or 16, depending on the vendor. Further, each processor inside an SMP may be a hardware multithreaded multicore processor. This gives rise to a mixed parallel programming model: shared-memory style programming within a node and message-passing style programming across the nodes.

Exercises

1. Compare and contrast processes and threads.

2. Where does a thread start executing?

3. When does a thread terminate?

4. How many threads can acquire a mutex lock at the same time?

5. Does a condition variable allow a thread to wait conditionally or unconditionally?

6. Define *deadlock*. Explain how it can happen and how it can be prevented.

7. Describe the problems that could be encountered with the following construct:

```
if(state == BUSY)
   pthread_cond_wait(c, m);
   state = BUSY;
```

8. Compare and contrast the contents of a PCB and a TCB.

9. Is there any point to using user threads on a system that is scheduling only processes and not threads? Will the performance be improved?

10. Select one from the items that follow to complete the sentence:

    User-level thread synchronization in a uniprocessor

    - needs no special hardware support, since turning off interrupts will suffice.
    - needs some flavor of a *read-modify-write* instruction.
    - can be implemented simply by using load/store instruction.

11. Select one from the items that follow to complete the sentence:

    Ensuring that all the threads of a given process share an address space in an SMP is

    - impossible.
    - trivially achieved, since the page table is in shared memory.
    - achieved by careful replication of the page table by the operating system for each thread.
    - achieved by the hardware providing cache coherence.

12. Select one from the items that follow to complete the sentence:

    Keeping the TLBs consistent in an SMP

    - is the responsibility of the user program.
    - is the responsibility of the hardware.
    - is the responsibility of the operating system.
    - is impossible.

13. Select all choices that apply regarding threads created in the same address space:

    - They share code.
    - They share global data.
    - They share the stack.
    - They share the heap.

14. From the following sentences regarding threads, select the ones that are True.

    - An operating system that provides no support for threads will block the entire process if one of the (user-level) threads in that process makes a blocking system call.
    - In pthreads, a thread that does a pthreadcondwait will always block.
    - In pthreads, a thread that does a pthreadmutexlock will always block.
    - In Solaris, all user-level threads in the same process compete equally for CPU resources.
    - All the threads within a single process in Solaris share the same page table.

15. Discuss the advantages of kernel threads in Sun Solaris.

16. Consider a multiprocessor that has 100,000 cores. It is being used for simulating jet-airplane wings. The program is 80% parallel. What speedup is expected by running the program on the multiprocessor with 100,000 cores?

17. Distinguish between write-invalidate and write-update cache-coherence policies.

18. Consider the following details about an SMP (symmetric multiprocessor):

    Cache coherence protocol: **write-invalidate**

    Cache to memory policy: **write-back**

    Initially, the situation is as follows:

    The caches are empty.

    Memory locations:

    C contains 31

    D contains 42

Consider the following timeline of memory accesses from processors P1, P2, and P3:

Time (In Increasing Order)	Processor P1	Processor P2	Processor P3
T1		Load C	Store #50, D
T2	Load D	Load D	Load C
T3			
T4		Store #40, C	
T5	Store #55, D		

Fill in the table that follows, showing the contents of the caches after each timestep. We have started it off by showing the contents after time T1.

(I indicates that the cache location is invalid. NP indicates not present.)

Time	Variables	Cache of P1	Cache of P2	Cache of P3	Memory
T1	C	NP	31	NP	31
	D	NP	NP	50	42
T2	C				
	D				
T3	C				
	D				
T4	C				
	D				
T5	C				
	D				

19. Why is it considered a good programming practice to do a `pthread_cond_signal` while still holding the `mutex lock` associated with the corresponding `pthread_cond_wait`?

20. Why is it considered a good programming practice to retest the predicate upon resuming from a `pthread_cond_wait` call?

21. Implement the monitor solution shown in Example 12.17, in C, using pthreads library.

22. Implement the monitor solution shown in Example 12.17, using Java.

23. Write a solution to the readers–writers problem, using mutual exclusion locks, that gives priority to writers.

24. Write a solution to the readers–writers problem, using mutual exclusion locks, that is fair to both readers and writers. (Hint: Use an FCFS discipline in the solution.)

25. Repeat Exercises 23 and 24 using monitors.

26. Repeat Exercises 23 and 24 using Java.

27. Write a solution to the readers-writers problem using counting semaphores, allowing, at most, n simultaneous readers or 1 writer into the database at any time.

28. Figure 12.34 gives a monitor solution for the dining philosophers problem. Reimplement the solution, using mutual exclusion locks.

Bibliographic Notes and Further Reading

It is fascinating to read about early attempts at building parallel machines. The Illiac IV (a University of Illinois project that started in the 1960s and took a decade to complete) [Hord, 1982], C.mmp (Carnegie Mellon, early 1970s) [Wulf, 1972], and Cm* (Carnegie Mellon, late 1970s) [Swan, 1977] are early attempts at building a parallel machine. The Illiac IV was patterned as an SIMD-style parallel machine, while both C.mmp and Cm* were patterned as MIMD-style parallel machines. Reading papers and books from these projects will be inspirational to students.

A seminal paper by Michael Flynn presented a taxonomy for parallel machines [Flynn, 1966]. H. T. Kung [Kung, 1979] classified parallel algorithms into different classes with a view to identifying the types of parallel machines that are most suitable to executing them. The ISA serves as a well-defined interface between the hardware and software in a uniprocessor. Leslie Lamport's seminal paper [Lamport, 1979] defined sequential consistency as the memory-consistency model to serve as a contract between the software and the hardware in a shared-memory multiprocessor.

The 1980s and the early 1990s saw a flurry of research activity in understanding how to build memory hierarchies for shared-memory multiprocessors. This resulted in defining new cache-coherence protocols (see [Archibald, 1986] for a comparative study of bus-based snoopy cache-coherence protocols). Researchers also engaged in defining new memory-consistency models to serve as a contract between hardware and software (see [Adve, 1996] for a tutorial on memory consistency models). Several bus-based commercial machines appeared on the market.

The early 1980s also saw a wave of research in attempts to build large-scale multiprocessors. Prominent examples from this era include the IBM RP3 [Pfister, 1985], the NYU Ultracomputer [Edler, 1985], University of Illinois' Cedar project [Gajski, 1983], and the BBN Butterfly [BBN Buterly, 1986].

The next wave of parallel-machine building extended the multiprocessor cache-coherence schemes to work for large-scale shared-memory machines. (See [Lilja, 1993] for a survey of issues in building large-scale cache-coherent shared-memory machines.) Prominent examples from the 1990s include Kendall Square Research KSR-1 [Burkhardt, 1992], Stanford DASH [Lenoski, 1992], and MIT Alewife [Agarwal, 1995].

In recent times, the action in building large-scale parallel machines is mostly in industries. The best way to keep up with the fascinating technology development is to follow the industry leaders in parallel supercomputers (such as IBM and Cray) by visiting their web pages. Another useful resource is a site that periodically publishes the "Top 500" supercomputers in the world, their configurations, their physical location, and their relative performance.[10]

System software for parallel systems has been evolving along two fronts. The first front has been compilers, languages, and programming libraries. Researchers tried to understand how to construct high-performing parallel software by focusing primarily on compiler technology [Kuck, 1976; Padua, 1980; Allen, 1987]. This led to the definition of parallel extensions to sequential programming languages (such as FORTRAN-D [Fox, 1990], and IBM Parallel FORTRAN [Toomey, 1988]), as well as parallel programming libraries (such as POSIX pthreads [Nichols, 1996], MPI [MPI, 2009; Snir, 1998], OpenMP [OpenMP, 2010; Chapman, 2007], PVM [Sunderam, 1990], CMU's Cthreads [Cooper, 1988], IVY [Li, 1988], Treadmarks [Keleher, 1994], Shasta [Scales, 1996], Cashmere [Kontothanassis, 2005], and CRL [Johnson, 1995]).

In recent times, much of the focus has been on reducing the complexity of parallel programming for the end user by providing higher-level programming abstractions. (See, for example, the Intel web pages on *Concurrent Collections*) [Intel CnC, 2009]; and Google's *Map-Reduce* programming [Dean, 2004].) Another focus is efficient parallel programming runtime systems for multicore and many-core architectures. The best way to track such developments is by following leading conferences in the area of programming languages and compilers (such as PPoPP[11] and PLDI[12]).

The second front has been on operating system mechanisms for efficient resource management of a parallel machine. Multiprocessor scheduling is a well-researched topic and well covered in most operating systems textbooks. Mellor-Crummey and Scott [Mellor-Crummey, 1991] give a good overview of different synchronization algorithms

---

10. http://www.top500.org/.

11. Principles and Practice of Parallel Programming (PPoPP) is a leading conference venue in this space: http://polaris.cs.uiuc.edu/ppopp10/.

12. PLDI is another leading conferences venue in this space: http://cs.stanford.edu/pldi10/.

for use in a multiprocessor. The focus on the operating system structure to take advantage of locality in a multiprocessor has garnered quite a bit of attention in the past and continues to do so to this day. Sun's Spring kernel [Mitchell, 1994] and IBM's K42 project [Krieger, 2006] are examples.

In recent times, a significant focus in both academia and industries has been on virtualization technologies to make efficient use of resources, provide isolation among distinct users, and effect recovery from both hardware and software failures. For a representative paper on the basics of resource virtualization, see [Barham, 2003]; also, visit the web pages of companies such as VMware[13] and open-source projects such as Xen[14] to keep up with latest developments in this space. Premier conference venues to track scholarly publications include SOSP,[15] OSDI,[16] and Usenix Annual Technical Conference.[17]

---

13. http://www.vmware.com/.

14. http://xen.org/.

15. Symposium on Operating Systems Principles (SOSP): http://www.sigops.org/sosp/sosp09/.

16. Operating System Design and Implementation (OSDI): http://www.usenix.org/event/osdi10/.

17. Usenix Annual Technical Conference: http://www.usenix.org/event/atc10/.

13

Fundamentals of Networking and Network Protocols

Imagine that your computer has no connectivity to the Internet. Would we consider such a computer fully functional? Probably not. Although we take the Internet and network connectivity for granted, it is a revelation to learn how we got to this point in the first place. We will do such a historical review at the end of this chapter. First, we will understand the basic elements of networking that allow computers to talk to one another, be they in the same building or halfway across the globe from each other.

13.1 Preliminaries

As we mentioned in Chapter 10, peripheral devices interface with the rest of the computer system in one of two ways: *programmed I/O* or *direct memory access (DMA)*. The former is appropriate for slow-speed devices and, the latter for high-speed devices. The network, a high-speed device, uses DMA for interfacing with the system.

Up until now, everything we have learned from the previous chapters regarding the computer is in our control, be it the hardware inside the box or the operating system abstractions for dealing with the hardware. Whereas connecting our computer to the network requires a simple piece of DMA hardware, the implications of such a connection are profound. As opposed to using a peripheral device such as a disk, which is still part of our "box," connecting our computer to the network opens up our computer to the whole world. On the one hand, connecting the computer to the network gives us the ability to browse the web, electronically chat with our friends anywhere in the world, and act as both a user and a contributor to information available via the network. On the other hand, we cannot control everything that happens on the network, and it is unpredictable how our computer may be affected by such vagaries of the network. It is like a roller-coaster ride—you want the adrenaline rush, but with an assurance of safety.

The number of topics worthy of discussion in the context of networks is plenty and includes network protocols, network security, network management, network services, and so on. Suffice it to say that each of these topics deserves its own textbook, and we list several good ones in the references.

The intent in this chapter is to stick to the theme of this textbook, namely, hardware and operating system issues as they pertain to your box. With this goal in mind, Chapter 13 takes you on a specific journey into computer networking, focusing on the fundamentals of networking from both the hardware and operating system's points of view. The aim is not to delve into the depths, but to give you enough of an exposure to networking that it will pique your interest to pursue more advanced courses on this topic. We do not cover topics relating to network security or network management in this chapter.

We take a top-down approach to exploring the fascinating area of computer networking. There are three touch points for the operating system to facilitate the box to hook up to the network. Just as the *pthreads* library provides an API for developing multithreaded programs, the `socket` library provides an API for developing network applications. Defining and implementing this API is the first touch point for the operating system to facilitate network programming. Messages generated by an application program have to reach their destination. This involves a myriad of issues, as we will see shortly. The abstraction that addresses all these issues is referred to as the `protocol stack` and is the second touch point for the operating system to facilitate network programming. The box itself connects to the network via a *network interface card (NIC)*. The `network device driver` that interacts with the NIC is the third touch point for the operating system to facilitate network programming.

13.2 Basic Terminologies

We will start our journey with some basic terminologies. In network parlance, our computer that hooks onto the network is called a *host*. To hook up our computer to the network, we need a peripheral controller. This is called a *network interface card,* or *NIC* for short. Figure 13.1 shows a number of hosts connected to the network.

Figure 13.1 shows the network as one big cloud. However, what is *the network*? It really is a composite of several networks, as we will see shortly. This collection of networks is given the name *Internet*.

What is the Internet? Open any book on computer networks, and each will answer this question in a unique way. In this book, let us try to do this from *your* perspective. Consider the postal service as an analogy. Vasanthi wants to send a letter to her grandmother in Mailpatti, Tamilnadu, India, from Atlanta, Georgia. She writes the address of her grandma on the envelope and places the letter in her mailbox (see Figure 13.2). The postal carrier picks up the letter. Of course, she does not know how to get the letter to Vasanthi's grandma; all she knows is her route—the houses to which she has to deliver mail and from which she has to pick up mail to be sent out. But she knows for sure that if the mail is submitted to the regional post office, the postal workers there will take care

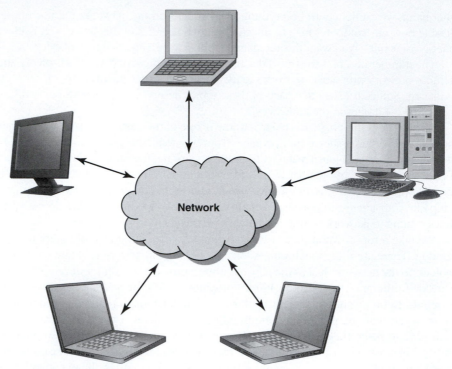

Figure 13.1   Hosts connected to the network.

of the rest of the journey for that piece of mail. Let us carry this story forward some more, since it will serve as a close parallel to how the Internet works. In the post office, the letters get sorted, and the letters meant for the state of Tamilnadu, India, get placed in a specific bin. Eventually, this bin rides a plane to Chennai, India. From the main post office in Chennai, the letter gets routed to the post office in Mailpatti. Since there are no roads to reach grandma's house, the last mile is covered by a bullock cart from the regional post office in Mailpatti. Grandma is happy

There is a striking resemblance between the journey undertaken by Vasanthi's letter and the passage of an e-mail from Charlie to his mom in Yuba City, California. Charlie lives in Atlanta and gets his Internet connectivity via cable. His computer plugs into a *cable modem*. The cable modem connects him to an *Internet service provider (ISP)*, which in this case is the local cable company. Since this ISP serves as Charlie's access point into the Internet, it represents an *access network*. One's access to the Internet could be by any means, of course, cable, phone line, satellite, and so on. One chooses an appropriate ISP, depending on one's circumstances and preference. The access network is like the postal carrier. It knows how to get stuff to a given computer and stuff from a given computer, but does not know how to get Charlie's e-mail all the way to his mom in California. However, the access network knows how to hand it over to a regional ISP, quite similar in functionality to the regional post office. The regional ISP knows how to talk to other regional ISPs across the country and across the globe. Charlie's e-mail from

Figure 13.2 Postal delivery from Atlanta, Georgia, USA, to Mailpatti, Tamilnadu, India.

the Atlanta regional ISP is sent to the Bay Area ISP in California. There are a lot more messages flying between Atlanta and the Bay Area than just Charlie's e-mail. Therefore, the *core* of the network is capable of handling much larger traffic, which is akin to sending all the U.S. mail destined for Tamilnadu, India, in a U.S. Postal Service airplane. From the regional ISP in the Bay Area, the message reaches the access network in Yuba

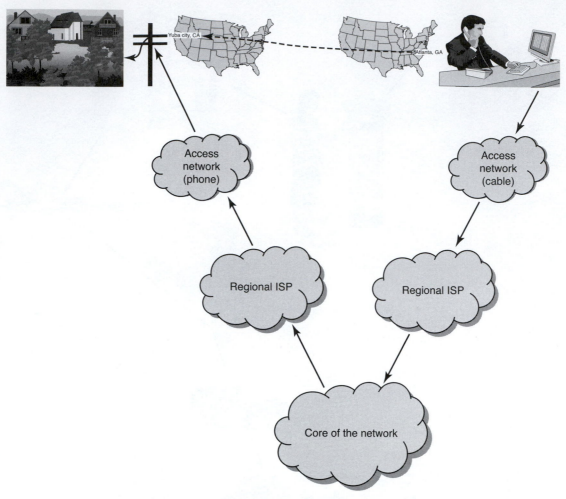

Figure 13.3 Passage of Charlie's e-mail from Atlanta, Georgia to Yuba City, California.

City. Charlie's mom is not much of a computer user. She uses her phone line to dial up a connection to the Internet via a modem attached to her computer. The local phone company in Yuba City is the access network for Charlie's mom. The slow-speed dial-up connection that delivers the e-mail to Charlie's mom's computer is akin to the bullock cart that finally delivers Vasanthi's letter to her grandma.

Each of the ISP clouds in Figure 13.3 represents computer systems of the respective ISPs. These ISP systems are not directly connected to one another. Entities called *routers* sit in the core of the network and route messages between the various ISPs across the globe. The regional ISPs know one another and route messages destined for one another through the core of the network. This might seem like magic at first glance, but it is not. How does the regional post office in Atlanta, Georgia, know that Vasanthi's letter to her grandma has to be put on a plane to Chennai, India? The U.S. Postal Service has universally adopted the *ZIP code* as a way of uniquely identifying any particular postal region in the entire world. In the same manner, the Internet has adopted a universal addressing system for every device that may be connected to the Internet. This is the familiar *Internet protocol address,* or *IP address* for short. Charlie's computer has a globally unique IP address, and so does his mom's computer. The collection of access networks, ISPs, and the core of the network together form what we commonly refer to as the Internet. In short, the Internet is a network of networks.

The key point to understand about the packet flow on the Internet is that a packet traverses through a series of *queues* that reside at the input of the routers *en route* from source to destination. In the absence of any contention, the queues are empty and Charlie's e-mail will sail through these routers to his mom. However, in the presence of other traffic (i.e., *network congestion;* see Section 13.6.3), a packet may experience *queuing delays* as it makes its way through the routers toward the destination. Due to its finite size, if a queue associated with a router is full, packets may be dropped, leading to *packet loss.* Thus, queuing delays and packet loss are problems inherent to the nature of packet traffic on the Internet. We will discuss these aspects in more detail in Sections 13.3, 13.6, and 13.12.

At an abstract level, the postal service delivers letters from person A to person B. Let us look at the supporting infrastructure for the global postal service. It includes human mail carriers on foot, on bikes, in vans, in boats, and, yes, even on bullock carts. It further includes postal trucks, freight carriers, and airplanes. Similarly, a whole host of gadgetry supports the Internet. Let us take a bird's eye view of this networking landscape before delving into the details in the rest of the chapter.

We will expand the earlier definition of a *host* to include computers that we come into contact with directly in everyday life (our laptops, PDAs, servers such as our web server and mail server). These computers represent the *edge* of the network. Quite often, we hear the terms *client* and *server* machines. Basically, these terms refer to the role played by a given host. For example, when we do a Google search, our machine is a client; the machine that takes on the role of the search engine at the other end is a server. The edge of the network is distinguished from the *core* of the network. The machines that sit in the bowels of the network, routing packets from source to destination, constitute the core of the network.

Today, you connect to your computer to a *local area network (LAN)* if you are in school, in your office, or in your dorm room. Even at home, especially in the Western world, many may have a LAN connecting all the machines in the home. As we mentioned already, at home you connect to an *Internet service provider (ISP)*, which may be a cable company, a phone company, or a satellite company. The ISPs have a way of communicating with one another so that, independent of which ISP is used by the edges of the network, Charlie from Atlanta, Georgia, is always able to send an e-mail to his mom in Yuba City, California. There are a number of other types of gadgetry that complete the nuts and bolts of the Internet infrastructure. These include the physical medium itself for ferrying the bits, as well as the electronic circuitry for connecting the hosts to the physical medium. Such circuitry include *hubs/repeaters, bridges, switches,* and *routers.* We will discuss these hardware elements and their functionalities in Section 13.9, after we discuss the networking software.

13.3 Networking Software

The networking software is a crucial part of any modern operating system. We usually refer to this part of the operating system as the *protocol stack*. Let us understand what is meant by *network protocol*. It is a *language* that defines the *syntax* and *semantics* of messages for computers to talk to one another. As the reader may have already guessed from the use of the term in this chapter, a *protocol* refers to any agreed-upon convention for two entities to interact with each other. For example, even inside the box, the processor and the memory follow a protocol for interaction on the memory bus. The software convention for register save/restore that we discussed in Chapter 2 (Section 2.8) is also a protocol between the caller and the callee.

However, the protocol for computers to communicate with one another gets complicated due to a variety of reasons. For example, we will shortly review Ethernet, a protocol used on LANs (Section 13.8.1). Ethernet uses a maximum packet size of 1518 bytes, referred to as a *frame,* which contains data, the destination address, and other necessary information to assure the integrity of data transmission. The maximum packet-size limit for a given network technology is set primarily according to the details of the protocol design constraints. An orthogonal issue is the maximum transmission rate on the medium for a given network technology. Just as the processor clock speed is a function of the delay properties of the logic used in the implementation, the maximum transmission rate limit for any network technology also arises due to the signaling properties of the physical layer and the delay properties of the logic used to drive the medium.

Consider usage of the network. You may be sending an image you took in class, over the network, from your dorm room to your family. The image may be several megabytes in size. You can immediately see the problem. Your image is not going to fit in one network packet. Thus, your notion of a message (arbitrary in size) has to be *broken into several smaller-sized packets* commensurate with the physical limitations of the network medium. Breaking a message into packets immediately introduces another problem. Referring to Figure 13.3, we see that the packets originating in Charlie's computer may have to go over several different networks before they get to his mom's home computer. There are other traffic flows on the network, in addition to Charlie's e-mail. Consequently, there is no predicting how many *queuing delays* his e-mail will experience along the way, both in the presence of and in the absence of other competing network flows. There is no way to guarantee that the packets of the message will arrive *in order* at the destination. That is, consider that a message consists of three packets: 0, 1, and 2. The packets are sent, in that order, at the sender. However, since there may be multiple paths between the sender and the receiver, the network is free to route the packets along different paths. Thus, the receiver may get the packet in the order 0, 2, and 1. Still, the receiver has to be able to assemble these packets correctly to form the original message. Thus, *out-of-order delivery* of packets is a second issue in data transport. A third problem arises due to the very nature of the network architecture—that is, a fully decentralized network with local autonomy over how packets are buffered, forwarded, and/or ignored. Consequently, a packet may get *lost* on the network. Such packet loss happens due to insufficient resources (for example, inadequate buffer capacity in an intermediate router) as a packet moves through the network. A fourth problem involves transient failures along the way that may *mangle* the contents of a packet. That is, there can be *bit errors* in the transmission of the packet through the network.

We summarize the **set of problems** associated with message traversal through the network from source to destination:

1. **arbitrary message size** and physical limitations of network packets;
2. **out-of-order delivery** of packets;
3. **packet loss** in the network;
4. **bit errors** in transmission; and
5. **queuing delays** en route to the destination.

Of course, we can let the application program take care of all these problems. However, since any network application will need to worry about these problems, it makes sense to solve them as part of the operating system. The portion of the operating system that addresses these problems is the *protocol stack*. Soon it will become clear why this piece of software is called a protocol *stack*.

Just as the system software (compiler and operating system) takes an arbitrary application data structure and houses it into rigidly structured physical memory, the protocol stack takes an arbitrary-sized application message, transports it across the network, and reconstructs the message in its entirety at the destination. Figure 13.4 shows this message exchange between two processes P1 and P2, on two different hosts.

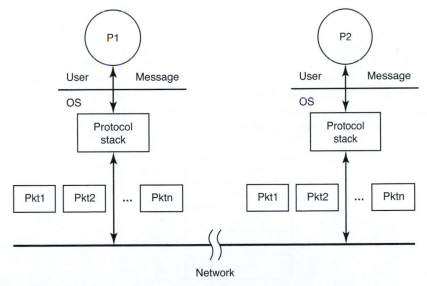

Figure 13.4 Message exchange between two network-connected nodes.

Message is broken into packets and sent over the physical medium connecting the nodes.

13.4 Protocol Stack

How should we structure the protocol stack? One possibility is to implement the protocol stack as one big monolith subsuming all the functions that we have discussed so far, to ensure the reliable transport of the message from source to destination. The downside to this approach is that it unnecessarily bundles the details of the physical network into this stack. For example, if the physical network changes, the entire stack is affected.

Protocol layering addresses this problem, precisely. Rather than bundle all the functionalities into one stack, protocol layering uses the power of abstraction to separate the concerns. This is why we call this piece of the operating system a protocol *stack*. Outgoing messages are *pushed* down the layers of the stack, from the application to the physical medium; similarly, incoming messages are *popped* up the layers of the stack, from the wire to the application.

13.4.1 Internet Protocol Stack

Next, we need to understand the concerns that the protocol stack has to address. This has been the focus of networking research that had its origins in the late 1960s. Networking luminaries such as Vinton Cerf and Robert Kahn, envisioning that islands of smaller networks might have to be networked together to form larger networks, coined the term *Internetting*. Of course, today *Internet* is a household term. By the end of the 1970s, many of the protocols that are considered ubiquitous today, such as TCP, UDP, and IP, were in place conceptually in the Internet protocol architecture.

Figure 13.5 shows the five-layer Internet protocol stack. We will quickly summarize the role performed by each layer. In later sections of this chapter, we will go into much more depth on each of the transport, network, and link layers.

Application layer. As the name suggests, this layer is responsible for supporting network-based applications such as an instant messenger (IM), multiplayer video games, P2P music/video sharing, web browser, electronic mail, and file transfer. A variety of protocols may be employed in this layer, including HTTP for web applications, SMTP for electronic mail, and FTP for file transfer. Essentially, the role of such protocols is to provide a common language for application-level entities (clients, servers, and peers) to use for communicating with each other.

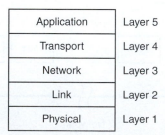

Application	Layer 5
Transport	Layer 4
Network	Layer 3
Link	Layer 2
Physical	Layer 1

Figure 13.5   Internet protocol stack.

This structure, solidified by the end of the 1970s, continues to be the five-layer protocol stack in use today.

Transport layer. This layer is responsible for taking an application-layer message and ferrying it between the ends of communication. Naturally, this layer has to worry about all the vagaries of the network we discussed earlier (such as breaking a message into packets, and out-of-order delivery of packets). TCP and UDP are the two dominant transport protocols in use on the Internet today. TCP (which stands for *transmission control protocol*) provides a *reliable* and *in-order delivery* of application data in the form of a *byte-stream* between two endpoints. TCP is a connection-oriented protocol; that is, there is a logical connection established[1] between the two endpoints, much like a telephone call, before the actual data transmission takes place. Once the conversation is over, the connection is closed—usually referred to as connection *teardown,* in network parlance. On the other hand, UDP (which stands for *user datagram protocol*) is analogous to sending a postcard through U.S. mail. It deals with *messages* that have *strict boundaries*; that is, there is no relationship at the protocol level between successive messages sent using UDP. Succinctly put, TCP gives stream semantics for data transport, whereas UDP gives datagram semantics. UDP does not involve any connection establishment before sending the message, nor any teardown after sending the message. With UDP, the messages may arrive out of order, since the protocol makes no guarantees regarding ordered delivery. In short, the salient difference between these two dominant transport protocols on the Internet is that TCP gives end-to-end reliability for in-order data delivery, while UDP does not.

Network layer. The transport layer has no knowledge as to how to *route* a packet from source to destination. Routing is the responsibility of the network layer of the protocol stack. The role of the network layer is simple: On the sending side, given a packet from the transport layer, the network layer finds a way to get the packet to the intended destination address. At the receiving end, the network layer passes the packet up to the transport layer, which is responsible for collating this packet into the message to be delivered to the application layer. In this sense, the role of the network layer is much like the postal service. Drop your letter in the postbox and hope that it gets to the destination. Of course, in the case of the postal service, a human is reading the address you have scribbled on the envelope and determining how best to route the letter. In the case of the network packet, which is processed by the network layer, we need a precise format of the information in the packet (address, data, etc.). In Internet parlance, the protocol for this layer has the generic name *Internet protocol* (IP for short), and subsumes both the formatting of the packet and the identification of the route that a packet has to take toward the destination.

Link layer. Consider the postal service analogy. Vasanthi's letter went by airplane from Atlanta, Georgia, to Chennai, India. However, to cover the last mile, a bullock cart carried the letter from the post office in Mailpatti to grandma's house. The airplane and the

---

1. Telephone infrastructure establishes a real connection, called circuit switching (see Section 13.7.3), between the two endpoints by preallocating physical resources. On the other hand, TCP is "connection oriented," since it provides only an appearance of a connection between the two endpoints, without preallocating physical resources (see Section 13.6.5).

bullock cart serve as different conduits for the postal service for transporting Vasanthi's letter between different hops of the postal system. The *link layer* performs a similar role for ferrying the IP packets between nodes on the Internet, through which a packet has to be routed from source to destination. Ethernet, Token Ring, and IEEE 802.11 are all examples of link-layer protocols. The network layer hands the IP packet to the appropriate link layer, depending on the next hop to be taken by the packet (if necessary, breaking up the IP packet into *fragments* at the network layer, commensurate with the characteristics of the link layer). The link layer delivers the fragments to the next hop, where they are passed up to the network layer. This process is repeated until the packet (possibly, fragmented) reaches the destination. As should be evident, a given IP packet may be handled by divers link-layer protocols in its journey from source to destination. At the destination, the network layer *reassembles* the fragments to reconstruct the original IP packet.

Physical layer.   This layer is responsible for physically (electrically, optically, etc.) moving the *bits* of the packet from one node to the next. In this sense, this layer is intimately tied to the link layer. A given link-layer protocol may use multiple physical media to ferry the bits. And for each such physical medium, there may be a distinct physical-layer protocol. For example, Ethernet may use a different physical-layer protocol for a twisted pair of copper wires, a coaxial cable, an optical fiber, etc.

Figure 13.6 shows the passage of a message from source to destination through the layers of the protocol stack and through multiple network hops.

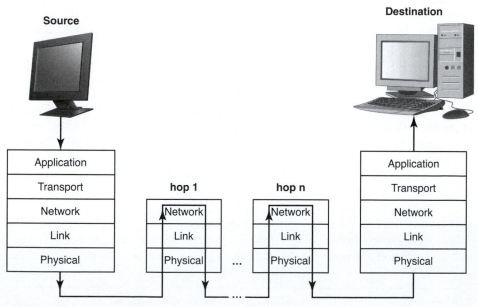

Figure 13.6   Passage of a packet through the network.

The intermediate nodes serve as "relays" to pass the packets of the message along toward the destination.

There are well-defined interfaces between any two layers of the protocol stack. Layering provides the modularity for each layer to make its own implementation decisions, independent of the other layers.

Layering is a structuring tool for combating the complexity of the protocol stack. It allows for partitioning of the total responsibility for both message transmission and reception among various layers. The modularity allows integration of a new module at a particular layer, with minimal changes to the other layers. For example, the appearance of a new physical layer in the stack affects the link layer and, in principle, should not affect the network and transport layers. At first glance, it would seem that a potential downside to layering might be a performance penalty, as the message has to traverse several layers. However, judicious definition of interfaces between the layers can prevent such inefficiencies.

There is no hard-and-fast rule as to the number of layers that a protocol stack should have. In reality, it depends on the functionality provided by the protocol stack.

13.4.2 OSI Model

The International Standards Organization (ISO) has come up with a seven-layer model of the protocol stack, the *Open Systems Interconnection (OSI)* suite. The OSI seven-layer model is an abstract reference model for describing the functionalities that are part of the protocol stack and for suggesting how to apportion them among the various layers. Figure 13.7 shows this reference model.

Comparing Figures 13.5 and 13.7, we can see that the latter has two more layers than the former: *presentation and session*. The *session* layer, as the name suggests, is the manager of a *specific* communication session between two end points. For example, imagine that you are having several simultaneous *instant messaging (IM)* sessions with friends across the network. The session layer maintains process-level information specific to each of such pairs of communication sessions. The transport layer worries about getting the message reliably across *any* pair of end points. The session layer abstracts out the details of the transport from the application, and presents a higher-level interface to the application (for example, the UNIX *socket* abstraction). The *presentation* layer subsumes some functionality that may be common across several applications. For example, formatting the textual output on your display window is independent of the specific client program (AOL, MSN,

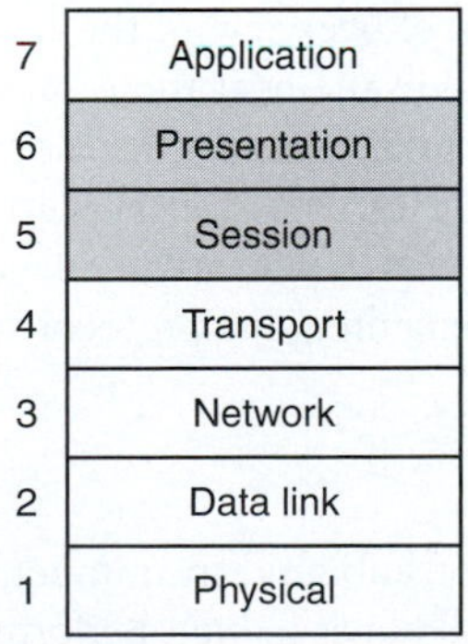

7	Application
6	Presentation
5	Session
4	Transport
3	Network
2	Data link
1	Physical

Figure 13.7   The OSI reference model is an abstract reference model developed by the standards body ISO.

etc.) that you may be using for IM. Thus, presentation functions (such as locally echoing text characters, formatting, and character conversion) that are not dependent on the internal details of the application itself belong in the presentation layer.

13.4.3 Practical Issues with Layering

The OSI model serves as a useful reference checklist to ensure that an implementation covers all the necessary functionalities of the protocol stack. However, real implementations of the stack seldom stick to the strict layering discipline prescribed by the model. As a practical matter, the Internet evolved simultaneous with the definition of the OSI model in the 1980s. As we have mentioned already, TCP/IP protocol is the *de facto* standard for the transport and network layers for communication on the Internet. The main observation to take away is that, with the evolution of the Internet, standard protocols such as TCP and IP have led to the collapsing of the layers embodied in the OSI model. For example, protocols such as HTTP, FTP, and SMTP subsume layers 7–5 of the OSI model. TCP and UDP are at the level of layer 4 of the OSI model. IP subsumes layer 3 of the OSI model functionality. Network interfaces (such as an Ethernet card on your computer) assume the role of layer 2 of the OSI model.

We have given a high-level description of the five-layer Internet protocol stack. There are several excellent textbooks devoted to covering the details of each of these layers. As we have said at the outset, the intent in this chapter is to expose the reader to network as an important I/O device, both from the point of view of the system architecture and the operating system.

We will take a top-down approach in exploring the layers of the protocol stack and the design considerations therein. We start with a discussion of the application layer, to set the context for the rest of the chapter. We place particular emphasis on the transport layer, since that is the strongest touch point to the operating system. We then work our way down the stack, to cover the networking layer, which is also part of the operating system. Finally, we will review the link layer, which represents the strongest touch point to the system architecture.

A note on the organization of the rest of the chapter is in order. We explore the transport, the network, and the link layers in some depth in the next three subsections. This level of detail may not be necessary, depending on the reader's perspective. Since we have already given a high-level overview of the functionalities of these layers, it is perfectly fine for the reader to skip the next three subsections if such detailed discussions of the transport, network, and link layers are not necessary. Section 13.9 gives an overview of the networking hardware used in modern computer systems. In Section 13.10, we discuss the relationship between these layers, and then go on to explore operating system issues in implementing the protocol stack.

13.5 Application Layer

As we know, Internet applications abound in number, with the ubiquity of network-connected gadgets ranging from iPhones to high-performance computing clusters. In this context, it is important to differentiate between *applications* and *application-layer protocols*.

Generally speaking, any network application has two parts:

- **Client:** This is the part that sits on end devices such as handhelds, cellphones, laptops, and desktops.
- **Server:** This is the part that provides the expected functionality of some network service (e.g., a search engine).

Examples of network applications include the World Wide Web (WWW), electronic mail, and network file systems. For instance, the client side of the WWW is a web browser such as FireFox or Internet Explorer. The server side of WWW is referred to as a *web server* and includes Apache[2] (an open-source web server platform for constructing generic services such as web proxy) and portals for a host of specialized services such as Google and Yahoo!. As another instance, on the client side of electronic mail are programs such as Microsoft Outlook and UNIX Pine. The server side is a mail server such as Microsoft Exchange.

A network application is much more than the application-layer protocol. For example, the web browser has to maintain a history of URLs accessed, a cache of web pages downloaded, etc. These details make one particular application different from another. On the other hand, since the message exchanges between the client and the server of a network application are well defined, they are embodied in application-layer protocols.

Application-layer protocols may be tailored for different classes of network applications. For example, web applications use **HTTP** (which stands for hyper-text transfer protocol) for specifying the interactions between the web clients and the servers. Similarly, electronic mail uses **SMTP** (which stands for simple mail transfer protocol) for specifying the interactions between the mail clients and the servers.

Many network applications, such as WWW and e-mail, often transcend the hardware architecture of the box and the operating systems. This is why you can read your e-mail or access a popular website such as CNN or BBC from your cellphone and/or public terminals at airports and Internet cafés. Thus, application-layer protocols such as HTTP and SMTP are *standards,* independent of the *platform* (defined as the combination of the hardware architecture and the operating system) that hosts either the client or the server for such applications.

On the other hand, operating systems provide their own unique network services. For example, you may be accessing a file from a departmental UNIX file system. Alternatively, you may be printing from a UNIX terminal to a network printer. These are also examples of client–server applications that enhance the functionality of an operating system. To enable the development of such applications, operating systems provide network communication libraries. These libraries provide APIs for client–server interaction across the network, similar to the way pthreads provide APIs for the interactions of threads within an address space. Such a communication library represents an application-layer protocol, as well. For example, the UNIX operating system provides the **socket**

---

2. See http://www.apache.org/.

library as the API for building network applications. Other popular operating systems, such as Microsoft Vista and Apple Mac OS, also provide a similar API for enabling the development of network applications on their platforms. Similar to implementing a thread library (see Chapter 12), there are specific operating system issues involved in implementing the socket library API. Such issues are outside the scope of this textbook. The interested reader is referred to other books that deal with the details of these issues [Wright, 1995; McKusick, 2004]. We will discuss the basics of network programming with socket API in Section 13.15.

13.6 Transport Layer

Let us assume that the transport layer provides a set of calls, *application program interface (API)*, so that the application layer can send and receive data on the network:

- **send (destination-address, data)**
- **receive (source-address, data)**

Let us enumerate the expected functionality of the transport layer of the protocol stack:

1. Support arbitrary data size at the application level.
2. Support in-order delivery of data.
3. Shield the application from loss of data.
4. Shield the application from bit errors in transmission.

The transport layer may view the data from the application layer either as a *byte stream* or as a *message*. Correspondingly, the transport may be either *stream* or *connection-oriented* (e.g., *TCP*, short for *transmission control protocol*), in which case the application data are considered as a continuous stream of bytes. The transport layer chunks the data into predefined units called *segments* and sends these segments to its peer at the destination. Alternatively, the transport layer may be *message* or *datagram oriented* (e.g., *UDP*, short for *User Datagram Protocol*), in which case the application data are treated similarly to the way a postcard is sent through the postal mail system. To keep the discussion simple, we will simply refer to the unit of transfer at the transport level as a *message*.

The transport layer at the source has to break up the data into *packets*, commensurate with the hardware limitations of the network. Correspondingly, the peer transport layer at the destination has to assemble the packets into the original message for delivery to the recipient of the message. We refer to this combined functionality as *scatter/gather*.[3] Recall that the packets may arrive out of order at the destination. Therefore, the transport layer at the source gives a unique *sequence number* for each packet of a message. The sequence number helps in the reconstruction of the original

---

3. Referred to as *segmenting* the stream of data into packets, in TCP parlance.

message at the receiving end despite the order of arrival of the individual packets. Thus, attaching a unique sequence number to each packet takes care of the first two problems with network communication, namely, arbitrary message size and out-of-order delivery.

The source needs confirmation that the destination did receive the packets. Recall that there could be packet loss and packet corruption *en route*. In either case, the upshot, as far as the transport layer is concerned, is that the packet did not make it to the intended destination. There is nothing mysterious about packet loss or packet corruption. Surely, you have experienced sometimes that two hands are not enough to carry all the grocery bags from shopping. Occasionally, you may have even dropped an item or two without even realizing it, until a friendly shopper points that out to you. We are dealing with physical resources in the network, and as we will see when we discuss the network layer, we may run into capacity limits of these resources during peak load, leading to packet loss. Similarly, electrical interference could result in bit errors during transmission. It should be mentioned that such bit errors do not always make the packet completely unusable. As we will see toward the end of this section, it is possible to do error correction on packets, usually referred to as *forward error correction (FEC),* when such bit errors occur. However, when the errors are beyond the fixing capabilities of FEC algorithms, the packet is as good as lost. The protocol should have a facility for recognizing such packet loss. One possibility is to use *positive acknowledgement,* as shown in Figure 13.8. You may have used, on occasion, the postal service's

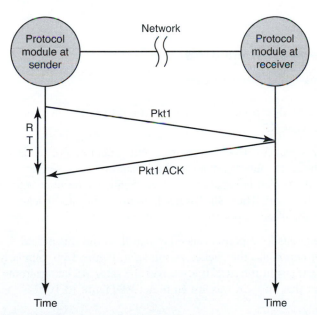

Figure 13.8 Packet-level positive acknowledgement.

The receiver sends an ACK packet in response to receiving a valid data packet.

feature "delivery confirmation" when sending mail. The postal service returns to the sender a signed receipt serving as proof that her mail was successfully delivered to the recipient. To disambiguate the acknowledgements from one another, the postal service gives a *unique id* to each such mail item, for tracking purposes. Positive acknowledgement in the transport layer is akin to this service. In this context, it is important to mention an important parameter of the transport layer, namely, *round trip time (RTT* for short). We define *round trip time (RTT)* as the time taken for a small (say, zero-byte) message to be sent from the sender to the receiver, and back again to the sender (see Figure 13.8). RTT serves as an estimation of the cumulative time delay experienced at the sender for sending a packet and receiving an acknowledgment, and is used in selecting timeout values for retransmission as we will see in Section 13.6.1. RTT depends on a number of factors, including the distance between the sender and receiver, queuing delays in the network en route, and message-processing overheads at the sender and receiver.

However, there are some important differences. First, the post office delivers the acknowledgement (in the form of delivery confirmation) to the end user. The entity analogous to the post office is the transport layer, where the acknowledgement stops; it does not go up to the application. Second, in the case of the postal service, the message is delivered in its entirety, and there is just one acknowledgement for the entire message. In the case of a network message, the transport layer breaks up the message into several packets. There are a number of choices on how the transport layer deals with acknowledgements, and these choices give rise to a plethora of transport protocols.

13.6.1 Stop-and-Wait Protocols

A simple approach is to do the following:

1. The sender sends a packet and waits for a positive acknowledgement, commonly referred to as ACK.

2. As soon as a packet is received, the recipient generates and sends an ACK for that packet. The ACK should contain the information for the sender to discern unambiguously the packet being acknowledged. Sequence number is the unique signature of each packet. Thus, all that needs to be in the ACK packet is the sequence number of the received packet.

3. The sender waits for a period called *timeout*. If within this period, it does not hear an ACK, it *retransmits* the packet, as shown in Figure 13.9. Similarly, the destination may retransmit the ACK if it receives the same packet again (an indication to the receiver that his ACK was lost en route; see Figure 13.10).

We refer to such a protocol as *stop-and-wait*, since the sender *stops* transmission after sending one packet and *waits* for an ACK before proceeding to send the next packet.

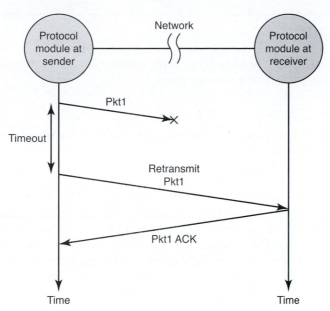

Figure 13.9 Timeout-based retransmission.

Source retransmits if acknowledgement is not received within a timeout period.

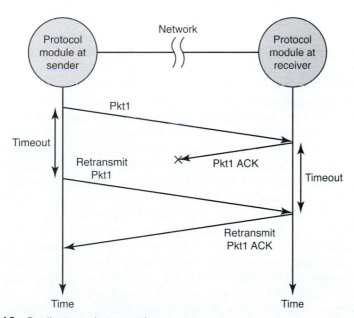

Figure 13.10 Duplicate packet reception.

Destination retransmits the acknowledgement for the previous packet if it receives the same packet.

Example 13.1

How many packets need to be buffered in the protocol stack of the sender for reliable transport in a stop-and-wait protocol regime?

Answer:

The answer is 1. The sender-side protocol stack sends one packet at a time and waits for an ACK.

Why do we need sequence numbers in the first place? After all, the sender will not proceed to send the next packet until it hears an ACK for the current packet that it has already sent. The reason is quite simple and intuitive. Packet loss can happen for the data and ACK packets. Therefore, both the sender and the receiver have the mechanics in the protocol for retransmitting the data or an ACK packet after a certain timeout period. How will the sender know whether a received ACK is for the current packet or a duplicate ACK for the previous packet? This is the role of the sequence number. By giving a monotonically increasing sequence number, the sender can determine whether an incoming ACK is for the current packet or a duplicate ACK.

Let us see whether we can simplify the sequence number associated with each packet for this protocol. At any point in time, there is exactly *one* packet that is in transit from the source to the destination. Given this protocol property, do we really need a monotonically increasing sequence number for the packets? Not really, since the packets, by design of the protocol, arrive in order from source to destination. The purpose of the sequence number is simply to eliminate duplicates. Therefore, it is sufficient if we represent the sequence number by a *single bit*. The protocol sends a packet with the sequence number 0 and waits for an ACK with the sequence number 0. Upon receiving an ACK with the sequence number 0, it will proceed to send the next packet with the sequence number 1 and wait for an ACK with the sequence number 1. For this reason, the stop-and-wait protocol is also often referred to as the *alternating bit protocol*.

Let us see how we can choose the timeout parameter. From our commuting experience, we know that the time it takes to come to school may be different from the time it takes to go home from school. We may take a different route each way, the traffic conditions may be different, and so on. The same is true of message transmission. The path taken by a message from the sender to the receiver may be different from that taken in the opposite direction. Further, the queuing delays experienced in the network may be different in the two directions, as well. All of this may lead to asymmetry in the measured times for message traversal, in the forward and backward directions, between two hosts on the network. This is the reason RTT (round-trip time) is more useful than one-way message transmission time. We will discuss message transmission time in more detail in Section 13.12. At this point, we just note that the timeout parameter has to have a value larger than the expected RTT.

Figure 13.11 shows the flow of data and ACK packets between the sender and the receiver for the stop-and-wait protocol. In this figure, RTT is the round-trip time for a

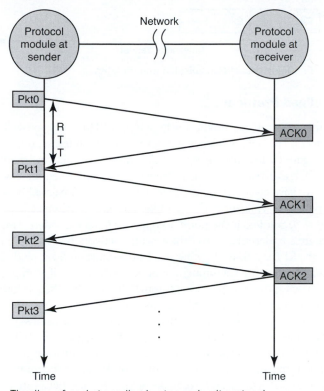

Figure 13.11 Timeline of packet-sending in stop-and-wait protocol.

Every packet is individually acknowledged. The sender transmits the next data packet only after receiving the ACK for the previous one.

message. The sender has to wait for RTT units of time after transmitting a packet, in order to receive an ACK. Then it is ready to send the next packet, and so on.

Example 13.2

A message has 10 packets, and the RTT for a packet is 2 msec. Assuming that the time to send the packet and receive the ACK are negligible compared with the propagation time on the medium, and given no packet loss, how much time is required to complete the transmission with the stop-and-wait protocol?

Answer:

In this example, **RTT** = 2 msec.

Therefore, the total time for the message transmission = 10 * RTT

$$= 10 * 2 \text{ msec}$$

$$= \textbf{20 msec.}$$

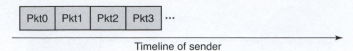

Timeline of sender

Figure 13.12 Pipelining packet transmission with no ACKs.

13.6.2 Pipelined Protocols

The virtue of the stop-and-wait protocol is its simplicity. However, you will not be happy with this protocol if you are downloading a movie over the Internet, from your buddy in India. Look at Figure 13.11. There is so much *dead time* on the network while the sender is waiting for the ACK to arrive. *Dead time* is defined as the time when there is no activity on the network. If we have gigabit connectivity to our computer, we could be sending 1 gigabit of data every second while the network is idle. The flaw in the preceding protocol is the presumption that packet loss is the norm, as opposed to an exception. This presumption could lead to a gross underutilization of the available network bandwidth. For instance, in Example 13.2, the RTT is 2 msec. In other words, the transport layer sends 1 packet every 2 msec, yielding a transport-level throughput of 500 packets/sec. If each packet has a data payload of 1000 bytes, the transport level throughput is 4 Mbits/sec. In other words, the gigabit connectivity is heavily under-utilized, since we are using only 0.4% of the available network bandwidth. If the network is reliable (i.e., there is no packet loss), we will blast all the packets of the message, one after another, without waiting for any ACKs.

For example, if the network is reliable (i.e., there is no packet loss), then we can *pipeline* the packet transmission, without waiting for ACKs, as shown in Figure 13.12.

It is important at this point to make a distinction between *bandwidth* and *propagation time*. The bandwidth determines the amount of time it would take the host to place a packet on the wire. The propagation time pertains to the end-to-end delay for a packet to reach the destination, which is a cumulative function of the propagation delays and queuing delays en route to the destination. We will revisit this subject and have a more precise definition of these terms in Section 13.12.

Example 13.3

A message has 10 packets, and the time to send a packet from source to destination is 1 msec. Assuming that the time to send/receive the packet is negligible compared with the propagation time on the medium, and given no packet loss, how much time is required to complete the transmission with the pipelining with a no-ACKs protocols?

Answer:

This is similar to the earlier example, with a difference: The packets are pipelined, as shown in Figure 13.12. Time to form the packets and place them on the wire is negligible, so the time for all the packets to reach the destination is just the source-to-destination end-to-end delay.

Total time for transmission = **1 msec.**

This extreme example, though unrealistic, shows the importance of pipelining the packets, especially when there is a huge latency from source to destination. Figure 13.13 shows pictorially the difference between stop-and-wait and pipelined protocols. In Figure 13.13(a), only one data packet is in transit at any point in time, whereas in Figure 13.13(b) multiple data packets are in transit.

Figure 13.12 begs the question, Do we even need ACKs? The answer to this question really depends on the service guarantee needed by the application from the transport layer. For example, some applications may not need reliable delivery. As we will see shortly (Section 13.6.5), UDP is a transport protocol that does not use ACKs, and it would be suitable for such applications. However, as we mentioned before, some applications may need a reliable transport, just as one would use

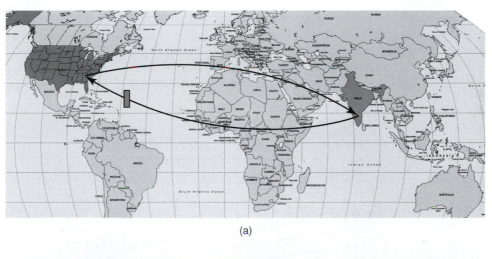

(a)

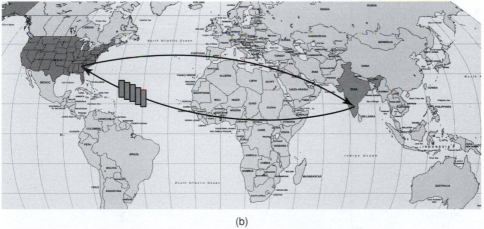

(b)

Figure 13.13 Difference between stop-and-wait and pipelined transmissions.[4]

---

4. World map courtesy of http://www.lib.utexas.edu/maps/world_maps/world_pol02.jpg.

"delivery confirmation" with the postal service. For such applications, we cannot assume that the network is reliable to the extent that we could dispense with ACKs altogether.

13.6.3 Reliable Pipelined Protocol

An intermediate approach between the two extremes of *stop-and-wait* and *pipelining with no-ACKs* is to pipeline the sending of the packets and the reception of the ACKs. The source sends *a set of packets* (called a *window*) before expecting an acknowledgment. The destination acknowledges each packet **individually** as before, but the good news is that the sender does not have to wait for acknowledgements for all the outstanding data packets before starting to send again. Figure 13.14 shows this situation pictorially.

As seen in Figure 13.14, the source (with a window size of 4) sends four packets and waits for ACKs; as soon ACK0 is received, it is able to send Pkt4. In an ideal situation, where there is no loss of packets, the source repeats the cycle. That is, the source sends Pkt4–7 and then waits; upon receiving ACK4, it sends the next four packets Pkt8–11, and so on, until the message transmission is complete.

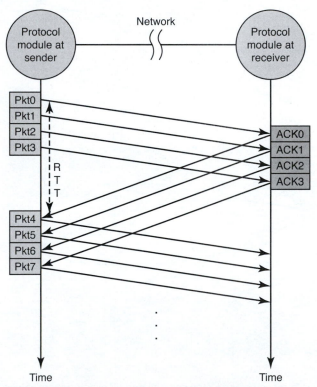

Figure 13.14   Reliable pipelined transmission with ACKs (window size = 4). Sender transmits window of packets before waiting for ACKs.

A packet transmission is complete once the source receives the corresponding ACK for that packet. The size of the window may be a mutually agreed-upon parameter of the protocol between the sender and the receiver, or dynamically adjusted by the sender on basis of the observed *network congestion*.

Network congestion. Let us understand what exactly *network congestion* is and why it happens.

As a simple analogy, consider why the highway starts backing up at certain times of the day—for example, at rush hour. Typically, there are several feeder roads or surface streets that are sending traffic onto the highway. At the other end of the commute, folks are getting off the highway onto surface streets again. Added to this, highways from different directions may merge as they come to the heart of the city. One or more of several reasons lead to the highway backing up. Cumulatively, the surface streets are trying to put more cars on the highway than can be sustained. At the other end of the commute, the cars that want to get off the highway are not able to, due to the limited capacity of the surface streets (number of lanes, speed limit, traffic lights, etc.), which is smaller than that of the highway. When two highways merge into one, the number of lanes of traffic shrinks relative to the density of traffic.

Network congestion happens for almost exactly the same reasons. Consider the following figure:

There are four 1-Gbps (gigabits per second) network flows coming into the pipe that can support up to 10 Gbps. Even if all four network flows are coming in at full throttle, the 10-Gbps fat pipe can sustain their requirements. However, if there are 20 such flows coming into the fat pipe, you can quickly see that the network cannot sustain that rate, and the individual network flows are going to start backing up. This is the reason for, and the manifestation of, network congestion. The result of network congestion is a buildup of the *packet queues* in the routers. Further, the packets no longer have a straight pass through the routers, because they sit in the queues of the routers *en route* to the destination. This results in unpredictable *queuing delays*, closely similar to what we may experience on the highways during peak traffic. Further, if the hardware queues in the routers fill up, the routers will simply drop the packets due to a lack of buffer space, leading to *packet losses*.

You may be wondering why one would design the network in a manner that could result in such congestion. The answer is rather simple. As we have already seen, the Internet is a network of networks. Returning to our example of sending a message from Atlanta to Bangalore (Figure 13.13), we note that the message crosses many network links that are part of different networks, from source to destination. You may have a gigabit connectivity at the sending end, and the core of the network may be able to sustain several such gigabit links, but the ultimate destination in Bangalore may have only a slow dial-up connection to the Internet. This is analogous to the slow surface streets and the fast highways. Unless all the links have the same bandwidth, end-to-end, we cannot avoid congestion in the network.

Each of us may deal in our own unique way with traffic congestion that we may encounter on the highway. Take an exit, get a cup of coffee, stretch our legs for a little while, and so on, before we resume our travel. A transport protocol may do something similar to combat network congestion. For example, it may self-regulate the amount of data it hands to the network layer, depending on the observed congestion in the network. The ubiquitous Internet transport protocol, TCP, does precisely that, and in this sense, works for the common good—a socialistic protocol! The basic idea is that if everybody is equally well behaved, then every network flow will get a fair share of the available network bandwidth, commensurate with the available bandwidth and current traffic conditions. In other words, a well-behaved transport protocol throttles its own contribution to the network load to ensure that it is using only its own fair share among all the competing network flows.

Naturally, there is a downside to this "socialistic" approach. A protocol that incorporates congestion control cannot guarantee how soon the data will get to the intended recipient. For example, if other transport protocols do not follow such self-regulation, then a well-behaved protocol, being the nice guy, will end up the loser. You have seen smart-aleck drivers on the highway, who, noticing a lane closing up ahead, forge ahead on the lane that is ending, all the way to the closing point, and jump into the working lane at the last minute. In other words, there is no *upper bound for delay* that may be experienced when using such a well-behaved transport protocol. Another way of saying the same thing is that there is not even a *minimum guaranteed transmission* rate when using such a protocol. You may have experienced widely varying wait times when trying to access information on the web, since TCP, which is the underlying transport protocol for web-based applications, is a well-behaved protocol that incorporates congestion control. For this reason, network applications (such as video and audio) that need to provide real-time guarantees may choose to use UDP and provide their own reliability on top of it.

Sliding window. The window size serves as the mechanism for self-regulation in a transport protocol that incorporates congestion control. The window size restricts the sender's rate and in turn prevents the buildup of queues in the routers, thus mitigating network congestion.

As we know, the source breaks up the message into a set of packets, each with its own unique sequence number. Thus, for a given window size, we can define an *active window* of sequence numbers as the one that corresponds to the set of packets (with those sequence numbers) that the source can send without waiting for ACKs. This is shown pictorially in Figure 13.15.[5] Looking at this figure, we might wonder what determines the *width* of each packet. The width represents the time it takes at

---

5. This figure is adapted, with permission, from a similar figure that appears in the book by Kurose and Ross, *Computer Networking: A Top Down Approach Featuring the Internet*, Addison-Wesley [Kurose, 2006].

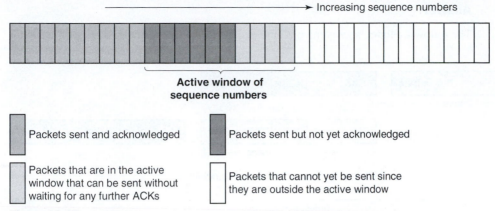

Figure 13.15   Active window (window size = 10) of a sliding window protocol.

the sender to push a packet out of the computer onto the network. As a first order of approximation, we can say that it is simply the ratio of packet size to the bandwidth of the network interface. For example, if you have a gigabit/sec full-duplex network interface, and if the packet size is 1000 bytes, the width of each packet is 8 microseconds. The width is important, as it tells us how many packets we can fit within an RTT. In other words, the width of the packet gives us an upper bound for the maximum window size that is reasonable to use for a given RTT. For example, if the RTT is 2 milliseconds, the maximum window size can be 250 packets (each packet is 1000 bytes), assuming that the ACK packets have negligible width. The actual window size may be chosen to be smaller than this upper bound, for several reasons. These include network congestion (which we discussed earlier in this subsection), buffer space for packets at the sender and receiver, and the size of the field used to denote the packet sequence number in the header. We revisit message transmission time in much more detail in Section 13.12.

In Figure 13.15, as soon as an ACK for the first red packet in the active window is received, the active window moves one step to the right (the first white packet becomes a blue packet). Since the active window slides over the space of sequence numbers (from left to right) as time progresses, we refer to this as a *sliding window protocol*. Whereas this discussion presents sequence numbers as monotonically increasing, as a practical matter, the space of sequence numbers is circular and wraps down to 0 in any real implementation.

Example 13.4

A message has 10 packets, and the RTT is 2 msec. Assuming that the time to send/receive the packet and the ACK are negligible compared with the propagation time on the medium, and given no packet loss, how much time is required to complete the transmission with the sliding window protocol with a window size of 5?

Answer:

The following figure shows the timeline to complete the transmission:

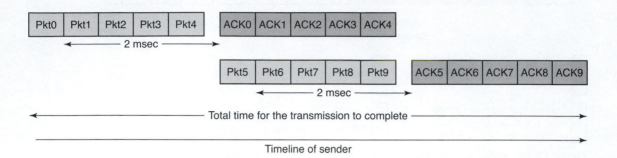

In this example, **RTT** = 2 msec. The source sends a window of 5 packets and then waits for the ACK. The first ACK is received 2 msec after the first packet is sent. Therefore, in one cycle of 2 msec (RTT), the source has successfully completed transmission of 5 packets (since we are ignoring all other times except the propagation time on the medium). Two such cycles are needed to complete the transmission.

The total time for the message transmission = 2 * RTT = 2 * 2 msec = **4 msec**.

We can see that the chosen window size specifies the **maximum** number of packets that can be outstanding at any point in time. For instance, if, instead of 10 (as in Example 13.4), we need to send 12 packets, then 3 cycles of message transmission will be needed. In the third cycle, the last two packets will be sent out to complete the message transmission. (See a variation on Example 13.4 in the exercises.)

An optimization used quite often in transport protocols to reduce the number of ACK packets is to aggregate the acknowledgments and send a *cumulative ACK*. The idea is simple and intuitive. The sender sends a window of packets before waiting for an ACK from the receiver. Let us say that the receiver receives n packets with consecutive sequence numbers. Instead of sending an ACK for each of the n packets, a single ACK for the nth packet is sent. The semantics of the protocol allows this optimization, since the reception of an ACK for the nth packet implies the successful reception of the $n - 1$ packets preceding the nth packet. TCP uses such cumulative ACKs to reduce the overhead of network transmission.

As we mentioned earlier, packets (data or ACK) may be lost. In this case, both the source and destination have to be ready to retransmit the lost packets and ACKs, respectively. The source and destination use a *timeout* mechanism to discover packet losses. The basic idea is for each side to set a timer, upon sending a packet. For example, if the source does not receive an ACK for the packet within the timeout period, it will retransmit the packet. Naturally, the source has to *buffer* the packets (red ones in Figure 13.15) for which acknowledgements have not yet been received.

There are a number of details to be addressed in designing a sliding window protocol. We already mentioned buffering and timeout-triggered retransmissions. Additional details of the protocol include the following:

- choosing appropriate values for the timeouts;
- choosing the right window size;
- dealing with packets that arrive out of order;
- deciding when to acknowledge packets, including sending a cumulative acknowledgement for a set of packets, and moving the active window. (See Exercise 23 at the end of the chapter.)

Such details are outside the scope of our discussion and are left to more advanced courses in computer networking.[6]

Example 13.5

Assume that the network loses 1 in 5 packets, on average. For a message that consists of 125 packets, determine the total number of packets sent by the sender, to successfully complete the message transmission.

Answer:

We would expect to lose 20% (1/5) of the 125 packets, i.e., 25 packets. When we re-send those packets, we will expect to lose 5 of those, etc.

Packets Sent	Lose	Successful
125	25	100
25	5	20
5	1	4
1	0	1
156		125

The total number of packets sent to successfully complete the transmission = **156**.

13.6.4 Dealing with Transmission Errors

First, the destination has to be able to tell by inspecting the packet that there has been an error in the transmission. To enable the destination to identify "good" from "bad"

---

6. For an elaborate discussion of these topics, see Kurose and Ross, *Computer Networking: A Top Down Approach Featuring the Internet*, Addison-Wesley [Kurose, 2006].

packets, the source computes a *checksum,* a value based on the actual contents of the packet, and appends it to the end of the packet. The computation of the checksum can range from very simple to very sophisticated. For example, the checksum in Internet is often computed simply as the sum of the data bytes (viewed as 16-bit integers). The destination does the same computation and compares the result with the checksum in the received packet, to catch erroneous packets. It is also conceivable to use *error correcting codes (ECC)* not only to detect errors in the packet, but also to repair the packet errors. Such discussions are, once again, deferred to more advanced courses in computer networking. However, if a packet is corrupted beyond repair, it is as good as lost in the network. It is the responsibility of the transport layer to recognize and take corrective action when this happens. *Forward error correction* (FEC) gives an ability to repair packets, but it is not a guarantee. Therefore, transport protocols necessarily have to resort to timeouts and retransmissions to overcome transmission errors.

It is interesting to note that, in discussing the transport protocol in this subsection, the size of a packet is the *only* network-specific information used. In other words, the transport protocol specification *abstracts out* the details of the network itself. Thus, the transport layer of the protocol stack provides all the functions explained in this subsection that lie *above* the network level.

13.6.5 Transport Protocols on the Internet

Transport protocols in use on the Internet may be grouped into two broad categories: *connection-oriented* and *connection-less*. TCP (transmission control protocol) is an example of the former, and UDP (user datagram protocol) of the latter.

TCP. TCP involves first setting up a connection between the two endpoints of communication. Once such a connection is set up, the actual data flow between the two endpoints is a *stream* of bytes; that is, TCP does not deal with messages, but streams. For example, let us say that you request a web page from CNN, using your web browser. The web browser application creates a TCP connection with the web server at CNN (or its proxy). Once the connection is made, the client sends a series of requests first, and the server responds by sending a series of objects, in return, that form the web page. The requests and responses between the client and the server appear as a stream of bytes at the TCP transport level. Once the entire page has been sent, the two sides may decide to tear down the connection.

TCP connection is a *full duplex* connection; that is, both sides can simultaneously send and receive data once the connection is set up. Even though one or the other endpoint may initiate the connection setup, the connection is symmetric once established. TCP provides the following major functionalities to facilitate information flow between the two endpoints:

- **Connection setup:** During this phase, the two sides negotiate the initial sequence number for transmission, using a three-way handshake:
    - Client sends the server a connection request message (which has a special field to indicate that it is a connection request), with information about the initial sequence number it plans to use for its data packets.

- The server sends an acknowledgement message to the connection request (once again, with the special field to indicate that it is part of the connection establishment three-way handshake), with information about the initial sequence number the server plans to use for its data packets.

- The client allocates resources (packet buffers for windowing, timers for retransmission, etc.) and sends an acknowledgement (which is the final leg of the three-way handshake). Upon receiving this acknowledgement, the server allocates resources for this connection (packet buffers for windowing, timers for retransmission, etc.).

  At this point, the client and server sides of the newly established TCP connection are ready to exchange data.

- **Reliable data transport:** During this phase, the two endpoints can send and receive data. The protocol guarantees that the data handed to it from the upper layers will be faithfully delivered, in order, to the receiving end, without any loss or corruption of the data.

- **Congestion control:** During the data transport phase, the sender also self-regulates its flow by observing the network congestion and dynamically adjusting its window size to avoid the buildup of queues in the routers (and thus reduces the network congestion, as detailed in Section 13.6.3). For this reason, TCP flows could experience unbounded delays in the presence of network congestion. This spells problems for real-time traffic that needs deterministic guarantees. Despite this inherent problem, due both to its ubiquity and reliable nature, TCP is used for many real-time traffic flows.

- **Connection teardown:** During this phase, the two endpoints agree to tear down the connection, as follows:

  - Client sends a connection teardown request (with a special field to distinguish it from normal data) to the server. The server sends an ACK.

  - The server sends its own teardown connection request (with a special field to distinguish it from normal data) to the client. The client sends an ACK. The client deallocates client-side resources associated with this connection. Upon receiving the ACK, the server deallocates the server-side resources associated with this connection. The connection is officially closed.

Although this discussion assumes that the client initiated the teardown, either the client or the server may initiate the connection teardown. When connection teardown is in progress, no new data will be accepted for transport on this connection. However, all data already accepted for transport previously on this connection will be reliably delivered before the connection is closed.

UDP. UDP sits atop IP and provides an unreliable datagram service for applications. As we just saw, TCP is stream oriented and entails an elaborate handshake to open a connection between the two endpoints before actual communication of information can begin. Similarly, once the communication is complete, there is an elaborate handshake to close the connection. Moreover, TCP has a number of advanced features

Table 13.1 A Comparison of TCP and UDP

Transport Protocol	Features	Pros	Cons
TCP	Connection-oriented; self-regulating; data flow as stream; supports windowing and ACKs	Reliable; messages arrive in order; well-behaved due to self-policing and reducing network congestion	Complexity in connection setup and tear-down; at a disadvantage when mixed with unregulated flows; no guarantees on delay or transmission rate
UDP	Connection-less; unregulated; message as datagram; no ACKs or windowing	Simplicity; no frills; especially suited for environments with low chance of packet loss and applications tolerant to packet loss	Unreliable; message may arrive out of order; may contribute to network congestion; no guarantees on delay or transmission rate

(such as acknowledgements, windowing, and congestion control) to ensure reliable transport over wide area networks, adhering to principles of fairness in the presence of sharing the available bandwidth with other users. Such advanced features translate to overhead for communication. Applications that can function quite adequately with weaker guarantees (*a la* sending a postcard) use UDP, since it is faster, owing to its simplicity. Further, for applications such as Voice over IP (VoIP), latency of getting the packets to the destination is more important than losing a few packets (since there is no time to recover lost or corrupted packets due to real-time constraints). So, the use of UDP has been growing, and the current estimate is that 20% of all Internet traffic is UDP.

There are several cons of UDP, of course: Messages may arrive out of order; messages may be lost; and there is no self-control, so UDP flows may be the source of increased congestion in the network. Similar to TCP, UDP does not provide any guarantees (such as upper bound on delays, or lower bound on transmission rate). Table 13.1 summarizes the pros and cons of TCP versus UDP for networked applications.

The previous discussion makes it sound as though networked applications that require some real-time guarantees can use neither UDP nor TCP. Actually, this is not entirely true. The application developers of real-time applications take the features (or lack thereof) of these protocols into consideration so that the user experience is not negatively impacted. For example, applications that serve audio or video will buffer several minutes of playtime before starting the viewer or the music. Further, they may dynamically increase the buffer capacity to account for network congestion and/or accommodate any application-specific quality-of-service guarantees. Table 13.2 shows a snapshot of networked applications and the transport protocol each uses.

Table 13.2 Networked Applications and Their Transport Protocols

Application	Key Requirement	Transport Protocol
Web browser	Reliable messaging; in-order arrival of messages	TCP
Instant messaging	Reliable messaging; in-order arrival of messages	TCP
Voice over IP	Low latency	Usually UDP
Electronic mail	Reliable messaging	TCP
Electronic file transfer	Reliable messaging; in-order delivery	TCP
Video over Internet	Low latency	Usually UDP; may be TCP
File download on P2P networks	Reliable messaging; in-order arrival of messages	TCP
Network file service on LAN	Reliable messaging; in-order arrival of messages	TCP; or reliable messaging on top of UDP
Remote terminal access	Reliable messaging; in-order arrival of messages	TCP

13.6.6 Transport Layer Summary

In general, operating systems support several protocol families to cater to the differing communication needs of applications. In the early 1980s, the ISO standards body proposed a new transport protocol suite called *ISO-Transport Protocol (TP0 through TP4)* as a potential standard for Internet-based communication. However, TP0-TP4 never really took off, owing to the ubiquity of TCP. Today, although there are concerns expressed in the networking community as to the appropriateness of TCP for transport on the Internet, it is difficult to loosen the stranglehold that TCP enjoys as the protocol of choice for many Internet applications.

Still, one never knows what the morrow will bring. Projects such as GENI (which stands for Global Environment for Network Innovation) and global networking research infrastructures such as PlanetLab[7] may act as agents of change and bring new and better network protocols for different classes of applications on the Internet.

We have given only a brief overview of the fascinating field of transport protocols. You will learn a lot more about these protocols in a more advanced course on networking.

---

7. PlanetLab is an experimental network test bed, with contributed network nodes from across the globe, established to facilitate controlled experiments to be conducted over a wide area network. See http://www.planet-lab.org/.

13.7 Network Layer

At first glance, the role of the network layer seems simple and straightforward—namely, send a packet handed to it at the source, from the transport layer to the destination; and hand off (up the protocol stack) an incoming packet to the transport layer, at the destination. This functionality could be bundled in with the transport layer, but this may not be a good idea. First of all, consider how many different network connections you have on your laptop or your home computer. You may have a wired and a wireless connection, at the very least. In general, different destination hosts may be reachable on different network connections. Second, look at Figure 13.6. The source and destination may not be directly connected to one another, but rather, the packet may have to go through several intermediate hops to get to the destination. At these intermediate hops of the network, there is no need for the transport layer functionalities, since the intermediate nodes simply *forward* the packet toward its final destination. Third, since we have no control over the evolution of the network, the actual path taken by packets from source to destination, referred to as the *route*, is not fixed. All of these reasons point to the conclusion that the decision as to how best to get a packet from a source to a destination host should be left to a different layer of the protocol stack. We refer to the layer that implements this functionality as the *network layer*. Such a separation of responsibility allows the transport layer to be independent of any addition/deletion of network connections to a host. The *destination address* and the *packet size* parameterize the interface between the transport and network layers. The network layer, given a destination address, is responsible for routing a packet. For this purpose, it maintains a table (called a *routing table*) that contains a route, or a path, from this source to any desired destination host.[8] On receiving a packet on the wire, the network layer either forwards the incoming packet on toward its ultimate destination, or passes it up to the transport layer if this node is the destination for the packet.

Let us understand the functionalities needed in the network layer:

- **Routing Algorithms:** The network layer should determine a route for packets to take, from source to destination. Thus, algorithms for determining routes, called *routing algorithms*, are the principal functionalities in the network layer. In this section, we will introduce the reader to some well-known routing algorithms widely used in the Internet.

- **Service Model:** The network layer should forward an incoming packet on an incoming link to the appropriate outgoing link on the basis of the available routing information. This is also often referred to as the *switching* function of the networking layer. This functionality is very much tied to the *service model* provided by the network layer to the upper layers of the protocol stack. In this section, we will discuss well-known switching strategies and service models that are commonly employed in networks in general, and the Internet in particular.

---

8. In Section 13.7.4, we will see that there is another table called the *forwarding table* in the network layer that contains the next hop that a packet must take along its route to the destination address.

The device that performs the functionalities of the network layer is called a *router*. For the purposes of the routing algorithms to be discussed in this section, a router is no different from an end host. The only difference is that a router knows that it is not a terminating point for a packet. In this sense, the protocol stack at a router consists only of the physical, link, and network layers.

13.7.1 Routing Algorithms

The network is a collection of hosts and routers, each with a distinct identity. In the Internet world, the identity is a unique IP address. If the network were fully connected, a packet from any source could be routed to any destination in one hop, assuming that the *cost* of sending a packet between any two nodes is the same. However, in reality, (a) the network is not fully connected, and (b) the cost of sending a packet between any two nodes may not be the same. Let us understand what exactly *cost* means here. Ultimately, the goal is to move a packet with minimal latency from point A to point B. *Cost* can be thought of as some summary quantitative metric that is a composite of the latency (which depends on the bandwidth of the connection) for moving a packet between any two points, and the network traffic between the two points. An analogy is commuting by car. The cost (in terms of travel time) for commuting a given distance depends on both the speed limit *en route* and the amount of traffic. The cost will be higher during rush hour. Sometimes, it may be more cost-effective to take a seemingly longer route and still reach the destination in less time.

Dijkstra's link state routing algorithm. Figure 13.16 shows a network as a graph in which the vertices are hosts and the edges represent physical links available at a given

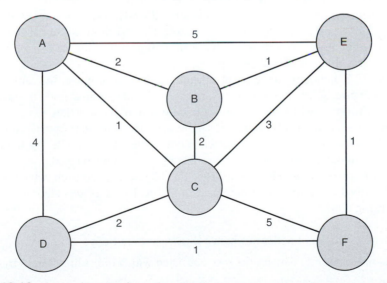

Figure 13.16 A sample network.

The vertices are the hosts, and the edges are the links, with the associated costs (delay), connecting the hosts.

host. We define a node's *link state* as the cost associated with each physical link at any given node. For example, in Figure 13.16, the link state of node A is {B:2, C:1, D:4, E:5}. That is, it costs 2 units to move a packet from A to B, 1 unit to move from A to C, 4 units to move from A to D, and 5 units to move from A to E. Similarly, the link state of B is {A:2, C:2, E:1}, and so on.

The link state (LS) routing algorithm (due to Dijkstra) is a *local* algorithm that uses *global* information. That is, all nodes in the network have *complete* information about the state of the network (i.e., connectivity and costs associated with the links). Given this information, each node can determine the optimal route to send a packet to any destination in the network by running this algorithm locally. Each node gets this information from its peers, since every node periodically broadcasts its link state to all the other nodes in the network.

The algorithm enables a node to find out, iteratively, the least-cost distance to every other node in the network. In each iteration of the algorithm, the node discovers a least-cost route to one more node in the network. Thus, if there are n nodes in the network, the algorithm needs $n - 1$ iterations to discover the least-cost routes to all the nodes.

The reasoning behind this algorithm is quite simple. Initially, you know the cost from A to its immediate neighbors (B, C, D, and E). Out of these, A–C is the least-cost route (1 unit). The direct link A–D costs 4 units. However, if we go through the least-cost link A–C, then the cost from A to D is only 3 units (A–C, then C–D).

The algorithm starts with the known costs of reaching nodes that are directly connected to A. In each iteration of the algorithm, we add a new least-cost route from A to some other node in the network. For example, in the first iteration, using A's link state, we determine one least-cost route, namely, A–C. In the second iteration, we update the cost of reaching other nodes in the network either directly from A or through the newly discovered least-cost route from the first iteration. The algorithm continues in this fashion until all the least-cost routes are discovered. Since the example has 6 nodes, the algorithm goes through 5 iteration steps.

Table 13.3 summarizes the result of running the algorithm on the sample graph shown in Figure 13.16. In each row of the table, the highlighted node in the second column is the one to which a least-cost route is known in that iteration. For example, in iteration 1, A–C is the least-cost route. The routes that have been updated due to the newly identified least-cost route are shown in bold letters. For example, the routes to D, E, and F are updated in iteration 1. The route to B remains unchanged.

Shown next is the pseudo-code for Dijkstra's LS routing algorithm, which we informally described using the graph presented in Figure 13.16. In this algorithm, we use the following notation:

- R denotes the set of nodes to which a least-cost route from A is known.
- link-state(X: value) denotes the cost associated with a direct link from A to X.
- cost(A → X) denotes the cost of the route from A → X.
- route(A → X) denotes the route from A to X, possibly through intermediate hops discovered during the running of the algorithm.

Table 13.3 Dijkstra's Algorithm in Action on the Graph Shown in Figure 13.16. In Every Iteration We Make Progress Toward the Destination by Selecting the Best "Next Hop" on the Basis of the Cost

Iteration Count	New Node to Which Least-Cost Route is Known	B Cost/Route	C Cost/Route	D Cost/Route	E Cost/Route	F Cost/Route
Init	A	2/AB	1/AC	4/AD	5/AE	∝
1	AC	2AB	1/AC √	3/ACD	4/ACE	6/ACF
2	ACB	2/AB √	√	3/ACD	3/ABE	6/ACF
3	ACBD	√	√	3/ACD √	3/ABE	5/ADF
4	ACBDE	√	√	√	3ABE √	4/ABEF
5	ACBDEF	√	√	√	√	4/ABEF √

```
Init:
R = {A} // set of nodes for which route from A known
cost(A → X) = link-state(X: value) for all X adjacent to A
cost(A → X) = ∝ for all X not adjacent to A
// let n be the number of nodes in the network
for (i = 1 to n - 1) {
        choose node X not in R whose cost(A → X) is a minimum;
        add X to R;
        set route(A → X) as the least-cost route from A to X;
        update routes for nodes adjacent to X:
                for each Y not in R and adjacent to X {
                        cost(A → Y) = MIN(original cost(A → Y),
                                          cost(A → X) + cost(X → Y));
                        set route(A → Y); // only if new route
                                          // through X is lower cost
                }
}
```

The link-state algorithm is also referred to as Dijkstra's *shortest-path* algorithm. Apart from the need for global information at each node, one problem with this algorithm is that there is a presupposition of a *synchronous* execution of this algorithm in *all* the nodes of the network so that each node will compute the same least-cost paths. In practice, this requirement is hard to impose, and the routers and hosts run this algorithm at different times, which could lead to some inconsistencies in the routing decisions. There are algorithmic extensions that ensure stability in the network despite such temporary inconsistencies. Discussions of such extensions are beyond the scope of this textbook.

Distance vector algorithm. Another widely used routing algorithm in the Internet is the distance vector (DV) algorithm. By design, this algorithm is *asynchronous* and works with *partial knowledge* of the link-state of the network. Due to the evolutionary nature of the Internet, these two properties make the distance vector algorithm a very viable one for the Internet.

The intuition behind the algorithm is straightforward. Regardless of the ultimate destination, any node has to decide to send a packet to one of its immediate neighbors to which it has a physical link. The choice of a neighbor node to send the packet to is quite simple. The neighbor that will result in the least-cost route to the desired destination is the one to choose. For example, referring to Figure 13.16, if E wants to send a packet to D, it will choose F as the next hop among all the neighbors (A, B, C, and F). Why? Because if we eyeball Figure 13.16, we can immediately see that F has the lowest-cost route to reach D. Note that what E needs to make this determination is **not** the actual route to reach D; it needs to know only the cost of reaching D from each of its immediate neighbors.

Each node maintains a routing table, called a *distance vector* table. This table has the lowest-cost route of sending a packet to every destination in the network, through each of the immediate neighbors physically connected to this node. The name *distance vector* comes from the fact that every node has a cost vector of values for reaching a given destination through its immediate neighbors. Table 13.4 shows the DV table for node E for the sample network shown in Figure 13.16. Each row shows the least-cost route to a particular destination node through each of the immediate neighbors of E. The DV table will contain *only* the cost, but for the sake of exposition, we have shown the actual route, as well, in parentheses. It is important to understand that the actual route information is not needed for choosing the next hop for a given destination. The least-cost route to a destination is shown in gray.

We will just give an informal description of the DV algorithm that is used by each node to construct this table. Each node sends its least-cost route to a given destination to its immediate neighbors. Each node uses this information to update its DV table. A node recomputes its DV table entries if one of two conditions hold:

Table 13.4 DV Table for Node E. Each Row Shows the Cost of Reaching A Given Destination from E Through Each of Its Immediate Neighbors

Destination	Cost Through Immediate Neighbors			
	A	B	C	F
A	5(EA)	3(BA)	4(ECA)	5(EFDCA)
B	7(EAB)	1(EB)	5(ECB)	6(EFDCB)
C	6(EAC)	3(EBC)	3(EC)	4(EFDC)
D	8(EACD)	4(EBEFD)	5(ECD)	2(EFD)
F	9(EABEF)	2(EBEF)	7(ECBEF)	1(EF)

1. The node observes a change in the link state for any of the immediate neighbors (for example, due to congestion, let us say that the link state from E to B becomes 5 from 1).

2. The node receives an update on the least-cost route from an immediate neighbor.

Upon such recomputation, if any of the table entries changes, then the node will communicate that change to its immediate neighbors. The data structures and the algorithm for DV are simple and straightforward. We will leave it as an exercise for the reader to formalize the algorithm with pseudo-code.

We can immediately see the asynchronous nature of this algorithm, compared with Dijkstra's link-state algorithm, as well as the ability of the algorithm to work with partial knowledge. The state of the network is changing continually (e.g., traffic patterns of current network flows, new network flows, addition/deletion of nodes and routers, etc.). We might question the point of computing routes on the basis of the *current state,* given this continuous evolution of the network state. Fortunately, these algorithms have good converge properties that ensure that the route calculation is much quicker than the rate of change of the network state.

Over time, there have been numerous proposals for efficient routing on the Internet, but LS and DV algorithms hold sway as the exclusive algorithms for routing on the Internet.

Hierarchical routing. Perhaps the reader is wondering how the Internet can possibly operate with either the LS or the DV algorithm for routing, given the scale of the Internet (millions of nodes) and the geographical reach. Both of these algorithms treat all the nodes on the Internet as "peers." In other words, the network is one monolithic entity wherein all nodes are equal. Such a flat structure will not scale to millions of nodes. In any organization (political, business, religion, charity, etc.), hierarchy is used as a way of reining in the chaos that could result when the size of the organization grows beyond a threshold. The Internet uses the same principle. Perhaps an equally compelling reason to bring some structure to the Internet, in addition to the scale of the Internet, is the need for administrative control. Especially in this day and age, with the increase in SPAM, an organization may want to control what network traffic is allowed to come in and go out of a corporate network. Both the twin issues of scale and administrative control are dealt with nicely by organizing the routers on the Internet into regions called *autonomous systems (ASs)*. Routers within an AS may run one of the LS or DV protocols for routing among the hosts that are within an AS. Naturally, one or more routers within an AS has to serve the need for communicating with destinations outside the AS. Such routers are called *gateway routers*. The gateway routers of different ASs communicate with one another by using a different protocol called *border gateway protocol,* or *BGP* for short. Nodes within an AS do not care about, nor are they affected in any way by, the evolution/attrition/expansion of nodes within other ASs.

Thus, as shown in Figure 13.17, the network layer in a gateway node supports at least two protocols: one for inter-AS communication and one for intra-As communication.

With reference to Figure 13.18, consider the host connected to router C.1 needing to communicate with the host connected to router C.2. In this case, the communication

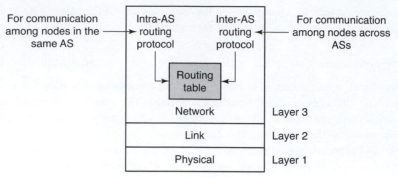

Figure 13.17   Details of the network layer in a gateway node, which supports at least two protocols: one for routing within an AS, and the second for routing across ASs.

is accomplished by whatever intra-AS protocol (LS, DV, or some other variant) is in use in the autonomous system C. On the other hand, consider that the host connected to router A.4 needs to send a packet to the host connected to router B.3. The routing table in A.4 knows that, to send packets outside autonomous system A, they have to be sent to A.G. The routing table in A.G recognizes that, to reach any destination in the autonomous system B, the packets have to be sent to B's gateway node B.G. A.G uses BGP to communicate with B.G, whence the packet is routed using the intra-AS protocol in effect within autonomous system B to node B.3. The routers A.G, B.G, C.G1, and C.G2 will each have a protocol stack, as shown in Figure 13.17, that allows these routers to talk to nodes within their respective autonomous systems, as well as with the gateway nodes in other autonomous systems using BGP.

Note that the network layer in A.4 is completely oblivious of the internal organization of the autonomous system B. For that matter, even A's gateway node A.G is unaware of the specific intra-AS protocol that may be in effect within the autonomous system B.

Details of the BGP protocol itself are beyond the scope of this book.[9]

13.7.2 Internet Addressing

So far, we have used the term *node* to signify either a host or a router. However, a host and a router are fundamentally quite different. As we mentioned earlier, a host is an end device at the edge of the network and typically has a single connection to the network through its network interface card (NIC). On the other hand, a router (see Figure 13.18) allows several hosts to be connected to it. It serves as an intermediary to route an incoming message on one connection to an appropriate output connection toward the

---

9. The interested reader is referred to *BGP4: Interdomain Routing in the Internet*, by J. Stewart, Addison-Wesley [Stewart, 1998].

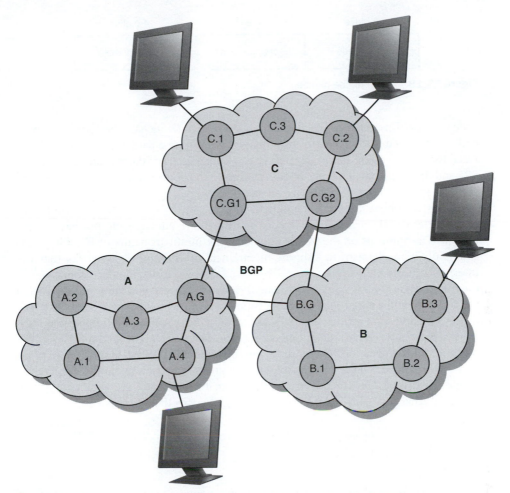

Figure 13.18 Three different ASs coexisting with intra- and inter-AS protocols.

intended destination. Typically, routers have a number of NICs, one for each of the connections that it supports. Further, a host, being at the edge of the network, is both the producer and consumer of messages. Therefore, the protocol stack on the host contains all five layers that we discussed in Section 13.4.1. On the other hand, the router contains only the bottom three layers of the protocol stack, due to its intended functionality as a network level packet router.

Let us dig a little deeper into addressing on the Internet to understand how hosts get network addresses, as well as the number of network addresses that each router handles. You have all heard of IP addresses. As we will see shortly, IP addressing is a fairly logical way of thinking about addressing any networked device that can be reached on the Internet. Consider for a minute phone numbers associated with land lines in the United States. Typically, all the land lines in a given city have the same area

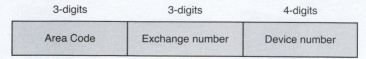

Figure 13.19   A U.S. phone number.

code (the top three digits of the phone number—e.g., Atlanta has area codes 404, 678, and 770 assigned to it). The next three digits may indicate a particular exchange designated for a geographical area or an entity (e.g., Georgia Tech has the exchanges numbered 894 and 385, designated for all campus numbers). The bottom four digits are associated with the specific connection given to an end device.

Thus, the phone number is a multipart address (see Figure 13.19). So are addresses on the Internet. However, as we will see shortly, the IP addresses do not have a geographical meaning, as do the phone numbers. The multipart nature of IP addresses is essentially a mechanism to support hierarchical addressing of networks that the Internet comprises. IP addresses (in IPv4[10]) are 32 bits. Every interface connected to the Internet has to have a globally unique IP address. Thus, if you have a laptop with a wireless card and a wired Internet connection, each of them will have a separate IP address. Similarly, a router that provides connectivity between several independent network segments will have a unique IP address for each of its networked interfaces. The 32-bit IP address is a four-part address, usually expressed in the *dotted decimal* notation—for example, *p.q.r.s*, where each of p, q, r, and s is an 8-bit quantity. Consider the IP address **128.61.23.216**. Each part is the decimal equivalent of the 8-bit pattern that represents that part. The 32-bit binary bit pattern for this IP address is

$$(10000000\ 00111101\ 00010111\ 11011000)_2$$
$$(\ \ \ 128 \ \ \ \ \ \ \ \ 61 \ \ \ \ \ \ \ 23 \ \ \ \ \ \ \ \ 216\ \ \ )_{10}$$

This structure of the 32-bit IP address is a key feature that is used in Internet routing. Some number of the most significant bits of the IP-address constitutes what is termed as the *IP network*. For example, the top 24 bits of the address may be used to name a specific *IP network*, and the bottom 8 bits to uniquely identify the specific device connected to the network. It is customary to denote an IP network with the notation *x.y.z.0/n*, where *n* is the number of bits reserved for the network part of the IP address. In this case, the IP network is 128.61.23.0/24, since the top 24 bits of the IP address constitute the network part. Figure 13.20 shows a number of hosts on a LAN that are connected by a router to the Internet. How many IP networks are there in this figure?

---

10. This discussion pertains to IPv4. IPv6 uses 64-bit addressing and has been proposed to overcome the 32-bit addressing limitation of IPv4. But due to the widespread adoption of IPv4, it is going to be some time before IPv6 can take its place, if ever.

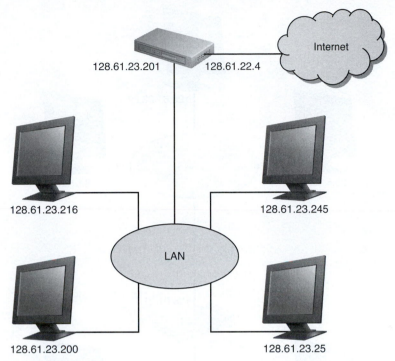

128.61.23.201   128.61.22.4

Internet

128.61.23.216   128.61.23.245

LAN

128.61.23.200   128.61.23.25

Figure 13.20   IP networks.

The answer is **two**. The hosts on the LAN and the interface in the router that also connects to the LAN are all part of the same IP network whose address is 128.61.23.0/24. On the other side, the router is connected through another interface that has an address 128.61.22.4 to the Internet, and is on a different IP network, namely, 128.61.22.0/24.

Example 13.6

Consider Figure 13.21. How many IP networks are in this figure? Assume that the top 24 bits of the 32-bit address name an IP network.

Answer:

There are **three** IP networks in this figure: one for the lower half of the figure connecting the four hosts on the lower LAN with the bottom router (network address: 128.61.23.0/24), the second connecting the two routers together (network address: 128.61.21.0/24), and the third connecting the top three hosts on the upper LAN with the top router (network address: 128.61.22.0/24).

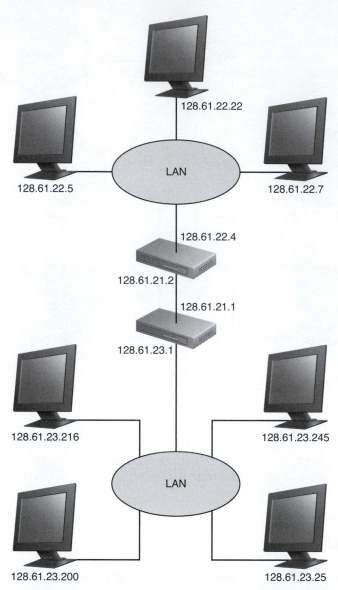

Figure 13.21 Multiple IP network segments.

The Internet is composed of millions of such IP network segments. It is important to understand that it is not necessary that the network part of the address always be 24 bits. Let us say that you are starting a company and need Internet connectivity to hook up 1000 computers to the Internet. You will request and get from an Internet Service Provider (ISP) a range of IP addresses for your organization that will have the top 22 bits fixed. The bottom 10 bits allow you to connect up to 1024 (2^{10}) machines to the Internet. Such a network will have the dotted decimal form *x.y.z.0/22*, indicating that the network part of the address is 22 bits. All the hosts in the organization will have the same top 22 bits for an IP address, and differ only in the bottom 10 bits. The network administrator may further subdivide the 10-bit bottom part of the address to create subnets, similar to the preceding example.

13.7.3 Network Service Model

As should be evident by now, in a large network a packet flows through several intermediate hops from the source before reaching its ultimate destination. For example, in Figure 13.21, consider a packet from the host on the bottom left (with interface address: 128.61.23.200) to the host at the top (with interface addresss: 128.61.22.22). This packet uses three network hops (128.61.23.0/24, 128.61.21.0/24, and 128.61.22.0/24) before reaching its destination.

Circuit switching. How should the network facilitate packet delivery among end hosts? This is the question answered by the network service model. Even before we discuss the network service model, we should understand some terminologies that are fundamental to networking. Let us start with telephone networks. We have come a long way from the days of Alexander Graham Bell (who is credited with the invention of the telephone). No longer is there a single physical wire between the two endpoints of a call. Instead, there is a whole bunch of switches between the two endpoints when a call is in progress. Although the technology has changed dramatically from the early days of telephony, the principle is still the same: *Logically, a dedicated circuit is established between the two endpoints for the duration of the telephone call.* This is what is referred to as *circuit switching*, and to this day it is the dominant technique used in telephony. Imagine that Vasanthi is going to Mailpatti, TamilNadu, India, from Atlanta, Georgia, USA, to visit her grandmother. Being the paranoid person that she is, she makes reservations on every leg of the long journey, right from the airport shuttle bus in Atlanta to the last bullock-cart ride to her grandmother's house. If she does not show up for any of the legs of the long journey, then the seat goes unused on that leg of the trip. This is exactly the situation with circuit switching.

There are a number of switches between the two end points of the telephone call. There are physical links connecting the switches. Figure 13.22 shows two distinct circuits (dashed lines) coexisting over the same set of physical links (solid lines) and switches. Network resources (in terms of bandwidth on these physical links) are reserved, once the call is established, for the duration of the call. Thus, circuit switching gives guaranteed quality of service, once the call is established, at the risk of underutilizing the network resources (for, e.g., *silent time* when no one is talking during a telephone call). The physical link that carries your telephone conversation between the switches may support several simultaneous *channels* or *circuits*. Techniques such as *frequency division multiplexing (FDM)* and *time division multiplexing (TDM)* allow sharing of the physical links for multiple concurrent connections. Given the total bandwidth available on a given link, these techniques allow the creation of dedicated channels for supporting individual conversations. Naturally, if the maximum limit is reached, no new conversations can be entertained until some of the existing ones complete. This is why you sometimes may hear the recording that says, "We're sorry. All circuits are busy.

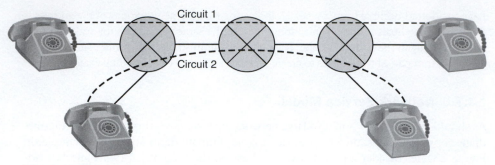

Figure 13.22   Circuit switching.

Two distinct circuits (dashed lines) exist over the same set of physical links (solid line) and the switches.

Please try your call later." Detailed discussion of these techniques is beyond the scope of this textbook, but suffice it to say that these techniques are analogous to having multiple lanes on a highway for transportation.

Packet switching.   An alternative to circuit switching is *packet switching*. Imagine that Vasanthi gets adventurous on her second trip to her grandmother's village. Instead of reserving a seat on every leg of her journey, she just shows up at each intermediate transfer point. The ticketing agent determines the best choice for her next leg of the journey on the basis of the current circumstance. It is possible that she will have to wait if there is no vacancy on any of the choices for her next leg. The basic idea of packet switching is exactly the same as this situation. The idea is not to reserve bandwidth on any of the physical links. When a packet arrives at a switch, the switch examines the destination for the packet and sends it along on the appropriate outgoing link toward its destination. Figure 13.23 shows a conceptual picture of a packet switch. (Router, introduced at the beginning of Section 13.7, is an example of a packet switch). It has input buffers and output buffers. Shortly, we will see the purpose served by these buffers.

Packet-switched networks are referred to as *store and forward* networks. The switch cannot start sending the packet on an outgoing link until the entire packet has arrived at the switch. This is referred to as the *store and forward delay* in packet-switched networks.

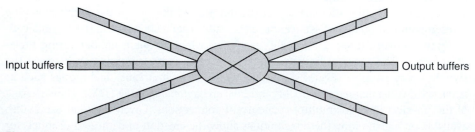

Input buffers   Output buffers

Figure 13.23   Conceptual picture of a packet switch.

Buffers are associated with incoming and outgoing links to and from the switch, to smooth out the burstiness of network traffic and contention for the physical links.

Recall that a switch may have a number of physical links. Associated with each incoming link is an input buffer; the same is true of outgoing links. The input buffers are useful for receiving the bits of a packet as they arrive. Once the packet has arrived in its entirety, it is ready to be sent on an outgoing link. The packet switch examines the destination address and, according to the routing information contained in the routing table, places the packet on the appropriate outgoing link. However, the outgoing link may be busy sending a previous packet. In this case, the switch will simply place the packet on the output buffer associated with that link. Thus, there may be some delay before the packet is actually sent on the outgoing link. This is referred to as the *queuing delay* in packet-switched networks. As you can imagine, this delay is variable, depending on network congestion. Further, since the amount of buffer space available on incoming and outgoing links is fixed, it is conceivable that the buffers are full (either on the input side or the output side) when a new packet arrives. In this case, the switch may have to simply drop a packet (either one of the already-queued ones, or the incoming packet, depending on the network service model). This is the reason we mentioned *packet loss* in such networks, right at the outset (see Section 13.3). Figure 13.24 shows the flow of

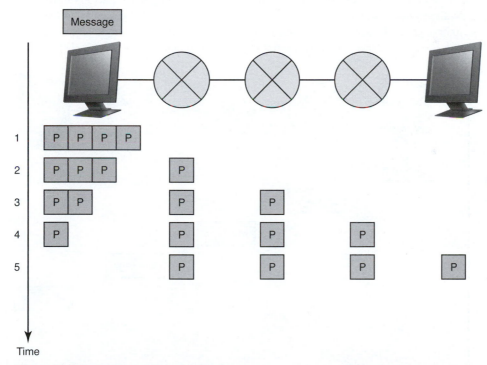

Figure 13.24 A packet-switched network.

The source has four packets to send at the first time step. In the fourth time step, each intermediate switch is working on a different packet of the message to transmit to the next hop. At the fifth time step, the first packet of the message has reached the destination. Thereafter, the subsequent packets of the message will arrive in successive time steps assuming there is no packet loss.

packets of a given message in a packet-switched network. The figure should be reminiscent, for the reader, of the pipelined instruction execution discussed in Chapter 5. Once the packets of the message have started filling up the pipeline, each switch is concurrently working on transmitting different packets.

Message switching. There is an assumption with packet-switched networks that higher layers of the protocol stack (such as transport; see Section 13.6) deal with the scatter/gather of a message into packets, and the out-of-order arrival of packets. It is conceivable that this functionality could be pushed into the network itself. Such a network is called a *message switching* network. In this case, a switch stores and forwards at the granularity of an *entire message,* as opposed to that of individual packets. This is illustrated in Figure 13.25. As should be evident, a packet-switched network leads to better latency for individual messages (by pipelining the packets of a given message; compare Figures 13.23 and 13.24). Further, if there are bit errors during transmission (which can occur due to a variety of electrical and electromechanical reasons in the physical links carrying the data), the impact is confined to individual packets instead of affecting the whole message. As the reader would have inferred already, packet switching will incur a higher cumulative header overhead than message switching, since packets have to be individually addressed, routed, and checked for integrity. It should be noted that message-switched networks also take advantage of pipelined communication; it is just that the pipelining is at the level of messages, not packets within a single message.

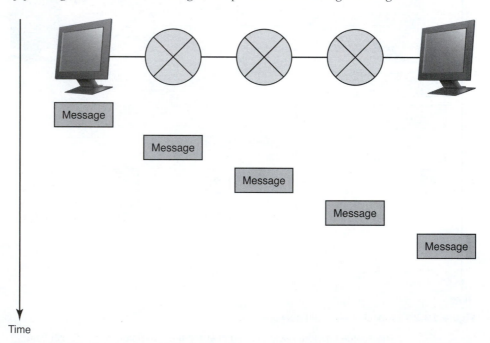

Time

Figure 13.25 A message-switched network.

A message has to arrive in its entirety to each switch before the switch will start transmitting that message to the next hop.

Service model with packet-switched networks. Packet switching offers several advantages over the competition, especially for computer networks:

- Since there is no advance reservation as with circuit switching (using either FDM or TDM), the available bandwidth on a physical link can be fully utilized by a packet-switched network. This is why even telephone networks are starting to adopt packet switching for expensive overseas links.

- The virtue of circuit switching is guaranteed transmission time between the two end points, due to the reservation, which is important especially for voice traffic. However, this is less important for data traffic, which dominates the Internet today. With advances in network technology, even new applications (such as Voice over IP(VoIP), which provides phone service via the Internet) that may need guaranteed quality of service work fine over a packet-switched network.

- Packet-switched networks are simpler to design and operate than circuit-switched networks.

- As we observed earlier, message switching may not use the network as efficiently as packet switching, due to the coarseness of messages, compared with packets. Further, dealing with bit errors during transmissions at the packet level leads to better overall efficiency of the network.

For all the reasons cited thus far, the Internet uses packet switching in the network layer, and IP is the ubiquitous network-layer protocol in the Internet.

With packet-switched networks,[11] there are two network service models: *datagram* and *virtual circuit*. The datagram service model is akin to the postal service. Every packet is individually stamped with the destination address, and the routers *en route* look at the address to decide on a plausible route for the packet to reach the destination. The routers use the routing tables to make this decision, and the routing algorithms that we discussed earlier are used to set up these routing tables, as well as to constantly update them. The Internet, by and large, supports the datagram service model.

A virtual circuit is akin to making a telephone call. We understand circuit switching, in which real physical resources (link bandwidth) are allocated in a dedicated fashion to each independent conversation. A virtual circuit is similar, except that physical resources are not reserved. The idea is to establish a route (called a *virtual circuit*), from source to destination, during the *call setup* phase. The source gets a *virtual circuit number*, which it can use for the duration of the call to send packets along the virtual circuit. The switches *en route* maintain a table (let us call it a VC table) that contains information pertaining to each virtual circuit currently managed by the switch, namely, *incoming link, outgoing link*. Thus, the routing decision to be made by the switch is very simple: Examine the VC number in the incoming packet, consult the VC table, and place the packet in the output buffer of the corresponding outgoing link. Finally, once the message transmission is complete, the network layer at the source executes a *call teardown* that deletes the corresponding entry in each of the

---

11. In discussing of the network service model, we will not distinguish between message and packet switching, since message switching may be considered a special case of packet switching, where the packet is the entire message.

switches *en route* to the destination. This discussion of a virtual circuit is intentionally simplified so as not to confuse the reader. In reality, during the connection establishment phase, each switch is free to locally choose a VC number for the new connection (in order to simplify network management). So, the VC table becomes a little bit more elaborate: VC number of incoming packet (chosen by the previous switch in the route), associated incoming link, VC number of outgoing packet (chosen by this switch), associated outgoing link. Examples of network-layer protocols that support virtual circuits include ATM and X.25. The Internet IP protocol supports only the datagram service model.

13.7.4 Network Routing versus Forwarding

It is important to distinguish between *routing* and *forwarding*. A simple analogy would help here. Consider driving to work every day. Routing is akin to the decision of which sequence of streets and highways to take from home to work, while forwarding is akin to the actual act of driving in that chosen route. We do the former only occasionally, but the latter every day.[12]

Routing and forwarding are both network-layer functionalities. These are in addition to the service model provided by this layer. However, we don't want the reader to get the impression that the network layer has to compute a route every time it sees a packet from the transport layer. As we mentioned right at the beginning of Section 13.7, when the transport layer gives it a packet, the network layer determines the next hop the packet must take in its journey toward the ultimate destination. This is the *forwarding* function of the network layer. To aid in this function, the network layer has a *forwarding table* that computes the next-hop IP address, given a destination IP address. The forwarding table resides in the network layer of the Internet protocol stack.

The foregoing discussion begs the question, "Where is the routing table and how are the routes computed?" In Chapter 8, we discussed daemon processes in the operating systems that carry out certain needed functionalities in the background. For example, a paging daemon runs the page-replacement algorithms to ensure that there is a pool of free page frames available for the virtual memory system upon encountering a page fault. The basic intent is to make sure that such bookkeeping activities of the operating system are not in the critical path of program execution.

Computing network routes is yet another background activity of the operating system. In the UNIX operating system you may see a daemon process named *routed* (route daemon). This daemon process runs periodically in the background, computes the routes by algorithms similar to the ones discussed in this section, and creates *routing tables*. In other words, route calculation is not in the critical path of data transport through the network. The routing tables are disseminated to other nodes in the Internet to update the peer routing tables as network properties change. The routing daemon uses the newly discovered routes to update the forwarding table in the networking layer of the protocol stack.

13.7.5 Network Layer Summary

Table 13.5 summarizes all the key terminologies we have discussed thus far with respect to the network layer functionalities.

---

12. Thanks to my colleague Constantine Dovrolis for this simple, yet illuminating, analogy.

Table 13.5 A Summary of Key Networking Terminologies

Network Terminology	Definition/Use
Circuit switching	A network layer technology used in telephony. Reserves the network resources (link bandwidth in all the links from source to destination) for the duration of the call; no queuing or store-and-forward delays.
TDM	Time division multiplexing, a technique for supporting multiple channels on a physical link used in telephony.
FDM	Frequency division multiplexing, also a technique for supporting multiple channels on a physical link used in telephony.
Packet switching	A network-layer technology used in wide area Internet. It supports best-effort delivery of packets from source to destination without reserving any network resources en route.
Message switching	Similar to packet switching, but at the granularity of the whole message (at the transport level) instead of packets.
Switch/Router	A device that supports the network-layer functionality. It may simply be a computer with a number of network interfaces and adequate memory to serve as input and output buffers.
Input buffers	Buffers associated with each input link to a switch for assembling incoming packets.
Output buffers	Buffers associated with each outgoing link from a switch in case the link is busy.
Routing table	Table that gives the next hop to be used by this switch for an incoming packet, based on the destination address. The initial contents of the table, as well as periodic updates, are a result of routing algorithms in use by the network layer.
Delays	The delays experienced by packets in a packet-switched network.
Store and forward	Delay due to the waiting time for the packet to be fully formed in the input buffer before the switch can act on it.
Queuing	Delay that accounts for the waiting time experienced by a packet on either the input or the output buffer before it is finally sent out on an outgoing link.
Packet loss	Results when the switch has to drop a packet due to either the input or the output buffer being full, and is indicative of traffic congestion on specific routes of the network.
Service Model	The contract between the network layer and the upper layers of the protocol stack. Both the datagram and virtual circuit models used in packet-switched networks provide best-effort delivery of packets.
Virtual Circuit (VC)	This model sets up a virtual circuit between the source and destination so that individual packets may simply use this number instead of the destination address. This also helps to simplify the routing decision a switch has to make on an incoming packet.
Datagram	This model does not need any call setup or tear down. Each packet is independent of the others, and the switch provides a best-effort service model to deliver it to the ultimate destination, using information in its routing table.

To conclude the discussion on the network layer, let us comment on its relationship to the transport layer. It is interesting to note that the intricacies involved with the network layer are completely hidden from the transport layer. This is the power of abstractions. The transport layer itself may be connection-less (such as UDP) or connection oriented (such as TCP), independent of the network service model. However, in general, if the network layer supports virtual circuits, the transport layer will also be connection oriented.

13.8 Link Layer and Local Area Networks

Now that we have covered the two layers of the protocol stack that has implications for the operating system, let us turn our attention to the link layer, which has implications for the hardware. While the top-down approach that we have taken to present the protocol stack makes perfect sense, it is actually innovation at the link layer dating back to the early days of networking that has made the Internet a household name.

Essentially, the link layer is responsible for acquiring the physical medium for transmission and sending the packet over the physical medium to the destination host. Just as a point of distinction, the link layer deals with *frames* as opposed to packets. Depending on the details of the link-layer technology, a network-layer packet (such as that generated by the IP protocol) may require several frames at the link-layer level to transmit to the destination.

Depending on the access mechanism used to gain control of the physical medium, link-layer protocols may be grouped into two broad categories[13]: *random access* and *taking turns*. Ethernet is an example of the former, while token ring is an example of the latter. Today, Ethernet is the most popular link-layer technology that forms the basis for connecting the end devices (hosts) to the local area network first, and from there to the wide area Internet.

The part of the link-layer protocol that deals with gaining access to the physical medium is usually called *media access and control* (*MAC* for short) layer.

13.8.1 Ethernet

Historically speaking, Ethernet is a cable that electrically connects computers together, as shown in Figure 13.26. We use the term *node* to mean a computer or a host connected to a network.

Let us understand the Ethernet protocol. Ethernet cable is akin to a bus.[14] However, this bus is not confined to a box, as we have seen in earlier chapters, but perhaps runs through an entire building. In Chapter 10, we mentioned *bus arbitration*, a scheme for deciding who gets the bus among the competing components connected to it. In a bus that connects the components within a box (processors, memory, I/O devices), *arbitration logic* decides who has control of the bus when multiple units require simultaneous access to the

---

13. We borrow these terms from the textbook by Kurose and Ross, *Computer Networking: A Top Down Approach Featuring the Internet*, Addison-Wesley [Kurose, 2006].

14. As we will see in Section 13.9, modern Ethernet, using switches, is point-to-point and switched. This view of Ethernet as a bus is useful to understand the nuances of the Ethernet protocol.

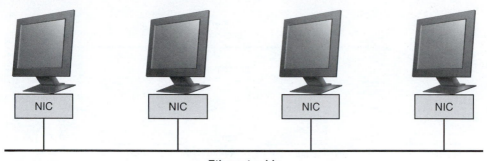

Ethernet cable

Figure 13.26   Computers networked via Ethernet, which is akin to a bus that connects the components inside a computer system.

bus. Arbitration logic is the actual hardware that implements the bus arbitration scheme. Since there are a bounded and fixed number of units within a box, it is feasible to design such arbitration logic. Further, the signals travel a short distance (an order of a few feet at most) within a box. On the other hand, Ethernet connects an *arbitrary* number of units together in an office setting over *several hundreds of meters*. Thus, the designers of Ethernet had to think of some other way of arbitrating among units competing to simultaneously use the medium, in order to deal with the twin problems of large distances and arbitrary number of units.

13.8.2 CSMA/CD

A random access communication protocol called *carrier sense multiple access/collision detect (CSMA/CD)* forms the basis for arbitration of a broadcast medium such as the Ethernet. We will keep the discussion of the protocol simple and superficial, not getting into too much detail on the communication theory behind the data transmission. The designers of Ethernet adopted this protocol to overcome the twin problems of distance and arbitrary number of devices being connected to the Ethernet cable. The basic intuition behind CSMA/CD comes from the way we would carry on a polite conversation among colleagues sitting around a conference table. We would look around to make sure that no one was talking; then we would start to talk; if two or more people tried to say something at the same time, we would shut up and try again when no one else was talking.

CSMA/CD protocol is not much different from this human conversation analogy. Figure 13.27 shows the state transitions of a computer sending a frame, using CSMA/CD.

Let us dig a bit deeper into the protocol name and basic idea behind the CSMA/CD protocol.

1. A *station* (i.e., a computer) wanting to transmit *senses* through the *medium* (i.e., the cable) whether there is an ongoing frame transmission. If yes, the station waits until the medium is *idle* and starts its transmission. If the medium is idle, it can start its frame transmission immediately. Absence of any electrical activity on the medium is the indication of idleness.

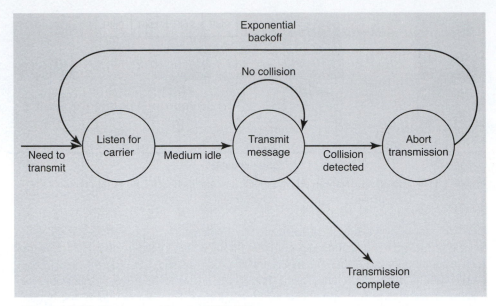

Figure 13.27   State transitions in CSMA/CD.

2. Multiple stations simultaneously sense the cable for idleness. The term *multiple access* in the protocol comes from this fact. Thus, simultaneously, multiple units may come to the same conclusion that the medium is idle, and start their respective frame transmissions. This is a problem. We will see shortly how the protocol deals with this problem.

3. Each station, after starting a frame transmission, listens for a collision. Each station knows the electrical activity it is causing on the medium. If what it observes (via listening) is different from this activity, it knows that some other station has also assumed idleness of the medium. We refer to this as *collision detection* in the protocol. The transmitting station immediately aborts the transmission, and sends out a *noise burst*. (Think of this as static noise you sometimes hear on your radio, or, continuing our conversation analogy, saying "I'm sorry" when multiple people start to talk at the same time.) The noise burst warns all other stations that a collision has occurred. The station then waits for a *random* amount of time before repeating the cycle of *sense*, *transmit*, and *observe for collision*, until it successfully completes its transmission. The algorithm chooses the random number for determining the amount of time a station waits before attempting to retransmit from a sequence that grows exponentially with the number of collisions experienced during a transmission. Hence, this phase of the algorithm is commonly referred to as *exponential backoff*.

We define *collision domain* as the set of computers that can hear the transmissions of one another.[15]

---

15. With the view of Ethernet as a bus, every host connected to the Ethernet is part of the collision domain. However, we will see later on in Section 13.9 that, with modern networking gear, collision domain is limited to the set of hosts connected to the same hub (or a collection of interconnected hubs).

Let us understand how exactly the frame is transmitted and how idleness of the medium is detected. The protocol uses *base band signaling*; that is, the frame is transmitted *digitally* on the medium (i.e., the cable), directly as 0's and 1's.

Just as a point of distinction, *broadband* refers to simultaneous *analog* transmission of multiple messages on the same medium. Different services use different frequencies to simultaneously send their message content. For example, a cable service that you may have in your home is an example of broadband. The same piece of wire *simultaneously* brings in your television signal, perhaps your phone service, and perhaps your Internet connection.

13.8.3 IEEE 802.3

Ethernet uses a particular version of the CSMA/CD protocol standardized by IEEE, namely, IEEE 802.3. In this version of the CSMA/CD protocol, digital frame transmission uses *Manchester code* (see Figure 13.28), a particular type of bit encoding. This code represents logic 0 as a *low followed by a high transition*, and logic 1 as a *high followed by a low transition*. In the IEEE 802.3 standard, low signal is −0.85 volts, high signal is +0.85 volts, and idle is 0 volts. Each bit transmission occupies a fixed amount of time, and the Manchester coding technique ensures that there is a voltage transition in the middle of each bit transmission, thus enabling synchronization of the sender and receiver stations. Therefore, there is always electrical activity when there is a frame transmission on the wire. If there is **no voltage transition** in the duration of a bit transmission, a station assumes that the medium is *idle*. Since Ethernet uses *base band* signaling technique, there can be only one frame at a time on the medium.

It should be mentioned that, whereas early Ethernet used CSMA/CD, most Ethernet LANs in use today are *switched Ethernets* (see Section 13.9) wherein there is *no* collision. It is also interesting to note that 10-gigabit Ethernet does not even support CSMA/CD, since it assumes that the hosts connect via switched links to the network.

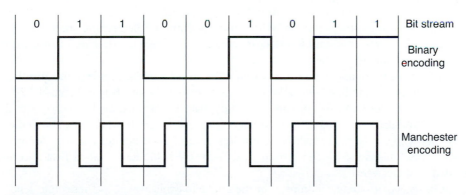

Figure 13.28   Manchester Encoding.

A low followed by a high is a 0, while a high followed by a low is a 1. In other words, there is always voltage fluctuation on the wire when there is data transmission.

However, Ethernet, as a link-layer protocol, continues to use the same wire format (i.e., frame headers), for compatibility.

Example 13.7

What is the bit stream represented by the following Manchester encoding of the stream?

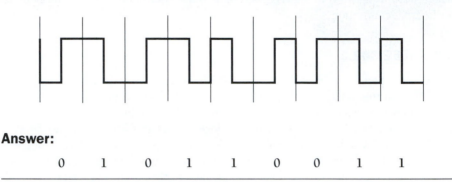

Answer:

0   1   0   1   1   0   0   1   1

13.8.4 Wireless LAN and IEEE 802.11

Wireless networks bring a number of new challenges, compared with wired networks. Just as a point of distinction, we should mention a variation of CSMA protocol that finds use in wireless LANs, namely, *CSMA/CA*. The CA stands for *collision avoidance*. This variant of CSMA is used in situations where the stations cannot determine whether there was a collision on the medium. There are two reasons that detecting collisions may be problematic. The first reason is simply a matter of implementation efficiency. Detecting collisions assumes that a station can *simultaneously* send its own transmission and receive to verify if its transmissions is being interfered with by transmissions from other stations. With wired medium, implementing such a detection capability in the network interface is economically feasible, whereas it is not with wireless medium.

The second and more interesting reason is the *hidden terminal* problem. Imagine that three buddies are standing along a long corridor (Joe, Cindy, and Bala in Figure 13.29). Cindy can hear Joe and Bala; Joe can hear Cindy; Bala can hear Cindy; however, Joe and Bala cannot hear each other. Thus, Joe may try to talk to Cindy while Bala simultaneously talks to Cindy. There will be a collision at Cindy, but neither Bala nor Joe will realize this. This is the hidden terminal problem: Joe is hidden as far as Bala is concerned, and vice versa.

One way of avoiding collisions is for the source to explicitly get "permission to send" by sending a short *request to send* (RTS) control packet on the medium to the desired destination. The destination (assuming that this RTS control packet successfully reaches the destination without any interference) responds with a *clear to send* (CTS) control packet. Upon receiving CTS, the source then sends the frame to the destination. Of course, the RTS

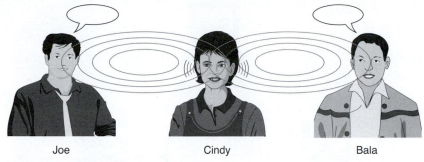

Joe   Cindy   Bala

Figure 13.29 Hidden terminal problem.

Joe and Bala cannot hear each other, but Cindy will hear jumbled words when both of them talk at the same time.

packets from different nodes may collide. Fortunately, these are short packets; therefore, the damage is not huge, and a node that wishes to transmit will be able to get the permission to transmit quickly. All the nodes in the LAN hear the RTS and/or the CTS control packets. Hence, they themselves will not try to send an RTS packet until the data transmission is complete, thus ensuring that there will be no collisions.

The RTS-CTS handshake helps overcome the hidden terminal problem as well as avoid collisions.

The IEEE 802.11 RTS-CTS standard is a wireless LAN specification for the implementation of the CSMA/CA protocol using RTS/CTS.

13.8.5 Token Ring

As we mentioned at the beginning of Section 13.8, an alternative to the random-access protocol such as the Ethernet is for each station to take turns transmitting a frame. One simple idea for taking turns is *polling*. A master node polls each station in some predetermined order to see whether it needs to transmit. Upon getting the "go ahead" from the master, the slave station will transmit its message.

Rather than offering a centralized approach to taking turns, token ring offers a decentralized approach. The basic idea is to connect the nodes of the network in a ring formation, as shown in Figure 13.30.

A *token*, a special bit pattern, keeps circulating on the wire. A node that wishes to send a frame waits for the token, grabs it, puts its frame on the wire, and then puts the token back on the wire. Each node examines the header of the frame. If the node determines that it is the destination for this frame, the node takes the frame. Somebody has to be responsible for removing the frame and regenerating the token. Usually, it is the sender of the frame that should remove the frame and put back the token on the wire. In principle, the token ring also works like a broadcast medium, since the frame travels to all the nodes on the ring. However, if a token ring network spans a geographically large area, it would make sense for the destination node to remove the frame and put back the token on the wire.

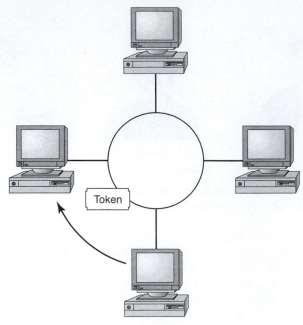

Figure 13.30 Token ring network.

The token passes continuously from host to host. Transmission occurs only when a host has the token.

Figure 13.31 shows the sequence of steps involved in frame transmission and reception in a token ring. By design, there are no collisions in the token ring. But this scheme has its own pitfalls. One disadvantage is the fact that a node has to wait for the token to send a frame. In a LAN with a large number of nodes, this could lead to considerable latency for frame transmission. The other disadvantage is the fact that, if a node dies, the LAN is broken. Similarly, if for some reason the token on the ring is lost or corrupted, the LAN cannot function anymore. Of course, it is possible to work around all of these problems, but the latency for frame transmission is a serious limitation with this technology. Token ring has its advantages as well. Ethernet saturates under high traffic loads. The utilization never reaches 100%, due to excessive collisions under such high traffic. Token ring works well under heavy load conditions. Table 13.6 gives a comparison of the two LAN protocols.

13.8.6 Other Link-Layer Protocols

We conclude this section with a bit of a perspective on LAN technologies. Both Ethernet and token ring were viable link layer technologies in the late 1980s and early 1990s. However, for a variety of reasons—not all technical, as usual—Ethernet has emerged as the clear winner of LAN technologies. While we have studied Ethernet and Token ring as examples of *random access* and *taking-turns* protocols, it is worth mentioning that there are several other link-layer protocols. Some of them showed tremendous promise when

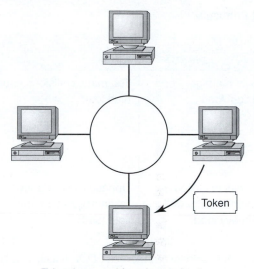

Token is passed from host to host.....

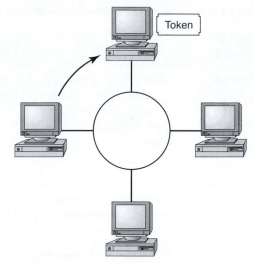

..... until it arrives at a host that has a message to send.

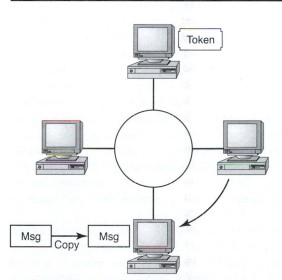

The host holding the token sends a message to the next host on the ring. Each host continues to pass the message to the next host. If a host is the intended recipient of the message it makes a copy but continues the process of sending to the next host. Message will continue to circulate until it returns to sender who will verify that the message is the same as the one sent, remove it, and resume token passing.

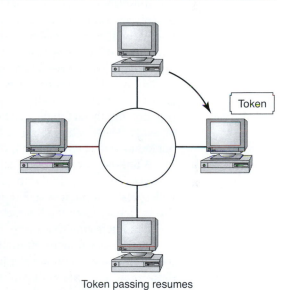

Token passing resumes

Figure 13.31 Sequence of steps required to send a frame on the token ring.

Table 13.6 A Comparison of Ethernet and Token Ring Protocols

Link-Layer Protocol	Features	Pros	Cons
Ethernet	Member of random access protocol family; opportunistic broadcast using CSMA/CD; exponential back-off on collision	Simple to manage; works well in light load	Too many collisions under high load
Token ring	Member of taking-turns protocol family; token needed to transmit	Fair access to all competing stations; works well under heavy load	Unnecessary latency for token acquisition under light load

first introduced, due to their improved performance over Ethernet. *FDDI* (which stands for *fiber distributed data interface*) and *ATM* (which stands for *asynchronous mode transfer*) are two such examples. FDDI was originally conceived for fiber-optic physical medium, and was considered especially suitable as a high-bandwidth backbone network for connecting several islands of Ethernet-based LANs together in a large organization such a university campus or a big corporation. It is also a variant of the taking-turns protocol, similar to the token ring. ATM was appealing due to its ability to provide guaranteed quality of service through bandwidth reservation on the links and admission control, to avoid network congestion. It is a connection-oriented link-layer protocol providing many of the network-layer functionalities as well; thus, ATM facilitates the implementation of a transport layer protocol directly on top of it. ATM has some presence in metropolitan areas and wide area networks (WAN) where it is used by telecommunication service providers. However, it has not found as much traction in LAN due to its relative complexity compared with Ethernet.

A link-layer technology that has widespread deployment today is *point to point protocol* (*PPP* for short). PPP is the link-layer protocol used by dial-up connections, and its widespread adoption is due to the large number of user communities dependent on dial-up for access to the Internet.

It is interesting that every time there has been a threat of obsolescence, Ethernet has found a way to reinvent itself and prevail. In fact, Ethernet has emerged as the network technology of choice not just for LANs. The advent of gigabit Ethernet stole the thunder away, for the most part, from FDDI for interconnecting islands of LANs in large organizations. The advent and maturation of 10-gigabit Ethernet has made the use of 10-gigabit Ethernet common in metropolitan area networks and has driven ATM almost into extinction.

13.9 Networking Hardware

Here we will not get into the physical-layer details such as the electrical, radio, or optical properties of the conduits used for data transport. The interested reader can get such information from other sources (for example [Kurose, 2006; Tanenbaum, 2002]).

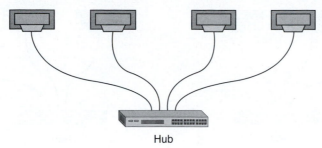

Figure 13.32 Simple application of a four-port hub to interconnect four computers. Electrically, a hub is nothing but a bus.

Instead, we will review the networking gear in common use these days, from homes to offices, in an Ethernet-based LAN.

Repeater

Electrical signals decay in signal strength with distance. Heat dissipation, due to the resistance and capacitance of the physical conductors carrying the signal, leads to the attenuation of the electrical signal. A repeater is a generic name for an electrical device that boosts the energy level of bits on an incoming connection and sends it out on an outgoing connection. Since LANs spread over fairly large geographical distances (e.g., a building or an entire campus), there is a need to boost the signal strength at regular intervals. Repeaters are commonly used in both LANs and wide area networks (WANs) to overcome signal attenuation problems.

Hub

In Section 13.8.1, we mentioned that Ethernet is logically a bus (see Figure 13.26). A hub is essentially Ethernet in a box: As can be seen in Figure 13.32, the Ethernet cable of Figure 13.26 is replaced by a hub. A hub relays the bits received from one host to others (computers and other hubs, forming a logical bus). Hubs allow the fairly easy construction of a more complex LAN, as shown in Figure 13.33. All the hosts reachable via the logical bus, formed by the interconnected hubs shown in Figure 13.33, are part of the same collision domain. Recall that the term *collision domain* refers to the set of computers that hear the transmissions of one another (see Section 13.8.1). Therefore, computers connected to a hub have to detect collisions and follow the exponential back-off phase of the Ethernet protocol in order to resolve collisions so that they can complete their message transmissions. A hub is a *multi-port* repeater, and the two terms are often used interchangeably.

Bridges and Switches

The late 1990s saw yet another landmark in the evolution of local area networking gear, *switched Ethernet*. Bridges and switches separate collision domains from one

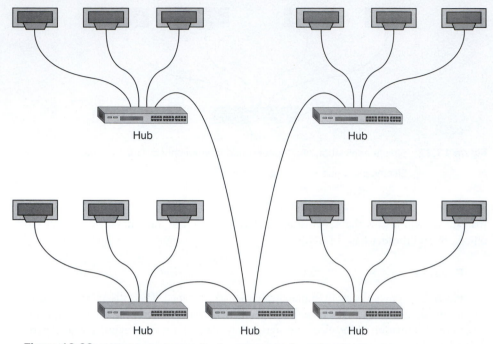

Figure 13.33   Using hubs to construct a more complex network.

All computers shown are part of the same collision domain.

another. For example, Figure 13.34 shows a bridge separating two collision domains from each other. Hosts 1 and 2 form one collision domain, and hosts 3 and
4 form the other. The data packets of host 1 do not cross the bridge unless the destination is one of hosts 3 or 4. This isolation of the traffic allows hosts 1 and 2 to
communicate in parallel with hosts 3 and 4.

What happens when host 1 wants to send a message to host 3 simultaneous
with host 4 wanting to send a message to host 2? The bridge recognizes the conflict

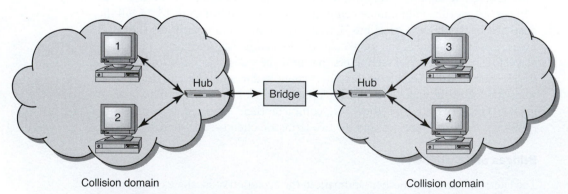

Figure 13.34   Hosts 1 and 2 are on a separate collision domain from hosts 3 and 4.

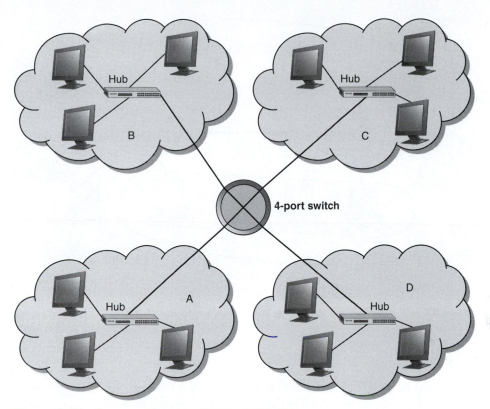

Figure 13.35   Conceptual diagram of a four-port switch.

A host on a collision domain connected to A could communicate with a host on a collision domain connected to C, simultaneous with communication between hosts on collision domains connected to B and D.

and serializes the traffic flow between the two sides (for example, 1 to 3 in one cycle, followed by 4 to 2 in the next network cycle). For this reason, a bridge contains sufficient buffering to hold the packets when such conflicts arise. The hosts never experience a collision unless they happen to be in the same collision domain. The end points of the bridge, referred to as *ports,* pass packets to the other ports on an as-needed basis.

Although the terms *bridge* and *switch* appear interchangeably in the literature, some authors define a bridge as connecting a limited number of collision domains (typically, two), as in Figure 13.34. Functionally, a switch is a generalization of the bridge, supporting any number of collision domains. Figure 13.35 shows a switch supporting four collision domains. (Each of A, B, C, and D represent an independent collision domain.)

In Figure 13.33, if we replace all the hubs with switches, we get a *switched Ethernet* that has no collisions.

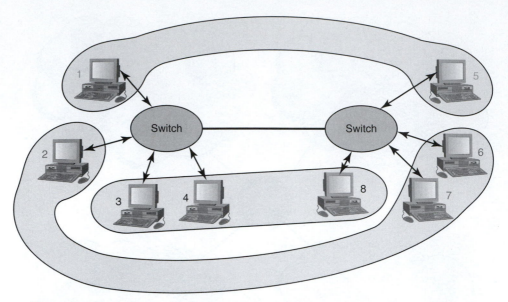

Figure 13.36 Virtual LAN (VLAN): Three VLANs are formed with {1, 5}, {2, 6, 7}, and {3, 4, 8}.

VLAN

Virtual LANs are a natural next step for switched Ethernet, with switches as in Figure 13.36. Nodes 1 and 5 in Figure 13.36 may request to be on the same VLAN; while nodes 2, 6, and 7 may request to be on the same VLAN. If node 2 sends a broadcast packet, then nodes 6 and 7 will receive it, and no other nodes will. Thus, with a hierarchy of switches, nodes that are on different geographical locations (and hence on distinct switches), still form one broadcast domain.

NIC

Network interface card (NIC) allows a computer to connect to the network and allows a host to connect to a hub, a bridge, or a switch. NIC uses half-duplex mode of communication (i.e., at a given time, it either sends or receives packets, but not both) when connected to a hub. A smart NIC recognizes that it is connected to a bridge (when it is) and uses either full- or half-duplex mode of communication. Every NIC has a *media access control (MAC)* address used by the bridge for routing

Figure 13.37 A packet destined to a node on the LAN.
The header contains only the MAC address of the destination.

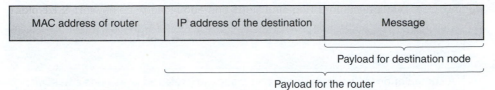

Figure 13.38   A packet destined for a node on the Internet.

The IP address of the destination is part of the payload being sent to the router node.

packets to the desired destination. Bridges automatically learn the MAC addresses of the NICs connected to them.

Bridges and switches understand only MAC addresses. The data traffic flows among the nodes of a LAN entirely on the basis of MAC addresses. A packet looks as shown in Figure 13.37. *Payload* refers to the actual message intended for the destination node. The packet header contains the MAC address of the destination node.

To transmit a packet outside the LAN—that is, to the Internet—a node simply uses the *Internet Protocol (IP)*. As we saw in Section 13.7.2, a packet destined to a node on the Internet contains an IP address, a 32-bit quantity that uniquely identifies the destination node.

Router

In Section 13.7.1, we introduced the concept of a router, which is just another host on a LAN, except that it understands IP addresses. Any node on a LAN that wishes to send a message to a node on the Internet forms a packet, as shown in Figure 13.38, and sends it to the router, using the router's MAC address. The *payload* for the router contains a header for the actual message. Embedded in that header is the IP address of the destination node on the Internet. As we saw in Section 13.7.1, the router has *routing tables* that help it to route the actual message to the node identified by the IP address.

Table 13.7 summarizes the terminologies and gadgetry that are in common use today in deploying computer networks. We have tried to identify each hardware device to the corresponding level of the OSI model (or equivalently, the Internet stack).

13.10 Relationship Between the Layers of the Protocol Stack

It is interesting to note that each of the transport, network, and link layers deal with data integrity at different levels. For example, TCP—the ubiquitous transport protocol and its cousin, IP—the *de facto* standard for network protocol in the Internet, both include error checking in their specifications for the integrity of the packet. At first glance, this may seem redundant. However, in reality, although we say "TCP/IP" in the same breath, thanks to the popularity of the Internet, TCP does not have to run on top of IP. It can use some other network protocol such as ATM. Further, the intermediate routers

Table 13.7 Networking Gear Summary

Name of Component	Definition/Function
Host	A computer on the network; this is interchangeably referred to as *node* and *station* in computer networking parlance.
NIC	Network interface card; interfaces a computer to the LAN; corresponds to layer 2 (data link) of the OSI model.
Port	End-point on a repeater/hub/switch for connecting a computer; corresponds to layer 1 (physical) of the OSI model.
Collision domain	Term used to signify the set of computers that can interfere with one another destructively during message transmission.
Repeater	Boosts the signal strength on an incoming port and faithfully reproduces the bit stream on an outgoing port; used in LANs and WANs; corresponds to layer 1 (physical) of the OSI model.
Hub	Connects computers together to form a single collision domain, serving as a multiport repeater; corresponds to layer 1 (physical) of the OSI model.
Bridge	Connects independent collision domains, isolating them from one another; typically has 2–4 ports; uses MAC addresses to direct the message on an incoming port to an outgoing port; corresponds to layer 2 (data link) of the OSI model.
Switch	Similar functionality to a bridge, but supports several ports (typically, 4–32); provides expanded capabilities for dynamically configuring and grouping computers connected to the switch fabric into VLANs; corresponds to layer 2 (data link) of the OSI model.
Router	Essentially a switch, but has expanded capabilities to route a message from the LAN to the Internet; corresponds to layer 3 (network) of the OSI model.
VLAN	Virtual LAN; capabilities in modern switches allow grouping computers that are physically distributed and connected to different switches, to form a LAN; VLANs make higher-level network services such as broadcast and multicast in Internet subnets feasible, independent of the physical location of the computers; corresponds to layer 2 (data link) of the OSI model.

(which deal with only the network layer) are not required to check the integrity of the packet. Similarly, TCP is not the only transport that may run on top of IP. Therefore, IP specification has to worry about the integrity of the packet and cannot assume that the transport layer will always do the checking.

Similar arguments apply for the network layer not relegating the checking of data integrity to the link layer. Different link layers provide different levels of data integrity.

Since in principle the network layer may run on top of different link-layer protocols, the network layer has to do its own end-to-end assurance of data integrity. Let us return to our original example from Section 13.2 (see Figure 13.3). When Charlie's mom responds to his e-mail from her home computer in Yuba City, the IP packets from her machine use PPP to talk to the service provider, a protocol called *frame relay* to go between service providers, FDDI on the campus backbone, and finally Ethernet to get to Charlie's computer.

13.11 Data Structures for Packet Transmission

Having dived into the different layers of the protocol stack in the previous sections, we will catch our breath for a minute, and slowly surface to the top of the protocol stack. Let us investigate the minimal data structures needed to implement packet transmission.

The transport layer fragments an application-level message or a message stream into packets before handing it to the network layer. Further, the network layer individually routes each packet to the destination. Therefore, the destination address is part of each packet. Further, each packet contains a sequence number to enable the scatter/gather functionality of the transport layer. We refer to such *metadata* that is part of each packet, distinct from the actual data, as *packet header*. In addition to destination address and sequence number, the header may contain such information as source address and *checksum* (a mechanism for the destination host to verify the integrity of this packet).

The transport layer takes a message from the application layer, breaks it up into packets commensurate with the network characteristics, and sticks a header in each packet. Figure 13.39 and Figure 13.40 show the data structures for a simple packet header and a packet, respectively, in C-like syntax. The field named **num_packets** allows the transport layer at the destination to know when it has received all the packets to form a complete message and pass it up to the application layer. For the purpose of forming the entire message at the destination, one can see the need for communicating

```
struct header_t {
  int destination_address;   /* destination address */
  int source_address;        /* source address */
  int num_packets;           /* total number of packets in
                                the message */

  int sequence_number;       /* sequence number of this
                                packet */

  int packet_size;           /* size of data contained in
                                the packet */

  int checksum;              /* for integrity check of this
                                packet */
};
```

Figure 13.39 A sample transport-level protocol packet header.

```
struct packet_t {
  struct header_t header;    /* packet header */
  char *data;                /* pointer to the memory buffer
                                containing the data of size
                                packet_size */

};
```

Figure 13.40 A sample transport-level packet data structure.

the `num_packets` information from the sender to the receiver; however, why should this field be present in each packet header? Once we remind ourselves of the vagaries of the network, the reason for the repetition of this information in each packet will become readily apparent. Recall that packets may arrive out of order. The receiving transport layer needs to know, on the arrival of the first packet of a new message, how much buffer space to allocate for assembling the message in its entirety.

Example 13.8

A packet header consists of the following fields:

> destination_address
>
> source_address
>
> num_packets
>
> sequence_number
>
> packet_size
>
> checksum

Assume that each of these fields occupies 4 bytes. Given that the packet size is 1500 bytes, compute the payload in each packet.

Answer:

Size of packet header = size of (destination_address + source_address + num_packets
                        + sequence_number + packet_size + checksum)

$$= 6 * 4 \text{ bytes}$$

$$= 24 \text{ bytes.}$$

Total packet size = packet header size + payload in each packet.

Payload in each packet = Total packet size − packet header size

$$= 1500 - 24$$

$$= \textbf{1476 bytes.}$$

13.11.1 TCP/IP Header

It should be emphasized that the actual structure of the header at each level (transport, network, and link) depends on the specifics of the protocol at that level. For example, as we mentioned earlier, TCP is a byte-stream oriented protocol. It chunks the stream into units of transmission called *segments* (what we have been referring to as packets thus far in the discussion of the transport protocol). The *sequence number* is really a representation of the position of the first byte in this segment, with respect to the total byte stream that is being transported on this connection. Since it is connection oriented, the header includes fields for naming the endpoints of the connection on which this data segment is being sent. The two endpoints of the connection are called the *source port* and *destination port*, respectively. The data flow in a connection is bidirectional. Thus, the header can piggyback an acknowledgement for data received on this connection in addition to sending new data. The *acknowledgement number* in the header signifies the next sequence number that is expected on this connection. Further, since TCP has built-in congestion control, the header includes a *window size* field. The interpretation of this field is interesting and important. Each end can monitor the amount of network congestion experienced on this connection on the basis of the observed latencies for messages and the number of retransmissions due to lost packets. According to such metrics, the sender of a segment advertizes the amount of data it is willing to accept from the other end as the window size field of the header. The sender also chooses the length of each segment it is transmitting on the basis of such metrics. There are also other special fields associated with the segment:

- **SYN:** This signals the start of a new byte stream allowing the two endpoints to synchronize their starting sequence number for the transmission.

- **FIN:** This signals the end of transmission of this byte stream.

- **ACK:** This signals that the header includes a piggybacked ACK, and therefore, the acknowledgement number field of the header is meaningful.

- **URG:** This field indicates that there is "urgent" data in this segment. For example, if you click *Ctrl-C* to terminate a network program, the application-level protocol will translate that to an urgent message at the TCP level.

The IP addresses of the source and destination are themselves obtained implicitly from the network layer. This part of the header that contains these IP addresses is referred to as a *pseudo header* and is passed back and forth between the TCP and IP layers of the Internet protocol stack during segment transmission and reception.

The IP packet format is quite straightforward. Recall that IP may fragment a transport-layer *message* (*segment*, in the case of TCP) into multiple IP packets and reassemble the packets into the original message at the destination. Therefore, in addition to the source and destination IP addresses, the IP header also contains the length of this IP packet and the fragment offset (i.e., the position of this packet in the transport layer message).

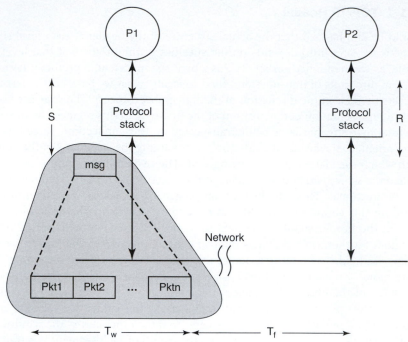

Figure 13.41   Breakdown of message transmission time into four components: delay at the sender (S), transmission delay (T_w), time of flight (T_f), and delay at the receiver (R).

13.12 Message Transmission Time

Now that we understand how messages are transported across the network, let us examine more carefully the time taken for message transmission. In Section 13.6, to keep the discussion of the transport protocols simple, we ignored all other timing overheads except for the propagation time on the medium itself. Let us understand how the network connectivity of your computer affects the end-to-end transmission time. To this end, it is instructive to consider the elements of time involved in message transmission between two end points. This is illustrated in Figure 13.41.

   We will present a simplified understanding of the message transmission time. The total message transmission time is a composite of the following terms:

1. **Processing delay at the Sender (S):** This is the cumulative time spent at the sender in the various layers of the protocol stack and includes

   - transport-level functions such as scattering a message into packets, appending a header to each packet, and affixing a checksum to each packet;

   - network-level functions such as looking up a route for the packet;

   - link-layer functions such as media access and control, as well as framing the data for sending on the physical medium; and

   - physical-layer functions specific to the medium used for transmission.

This factor depends on the details of the software architecture of the protocol stack as well as the efficiency of actual implementation.

2. **Transmission delay (T_w):** This is the time needed to put the bits on the wire at the sending end. This is where the connectivity of your computer to the physical medium comes into play. For example, if you have a gigabit link connecting your computer to the network, then for a given message, T_w will be much smaller than if you had a dial-up connection to the network.

Example 13.9

Given a message size of 21 MB, (a) compute the transmission delay, using a dial-up connection of 56 Kbits/s; and (b) compute the transmission delay, using a gigabit network connectivity.

Answer:

a. Transmission delay = message size/network bandwidth
$$= (21 * 2^{20} * 8 \text{ bits})/(56 * 2^{10}) \text{ bits/sec}$$
$$= 3 * 2^{10} \text{ secs}$$
$$= 3072 \text{ secs.}$$

b. Transmission delay = message size/network bandwidth
$$= (21 * 2^{20} * 8 \text{ bits})/(10^9) \text{ bits/sec}$$
$$= 0.176 \text{ secs.}$$

3. **Time of flight (T_f):** This term simplifies a number of things going on in the network from the time a message is placed on the wire at the sending end to the time it is finally in the network interface at the receiving end. In other words, we are lumping together the delays experienced by a message en route from source to destination. The delay experienced by a message has the following two distinct components:

- **Propagation delay:** This is the time for the bits to travel on the wire from point A to point B. This is dependent on a number of factors. The first factor that comes into play involves the distance between the two points and the speed of light. For example, the further apart the two end points are, the longer is the distance traversed by the bits on the wire, and hence the longer the time taken. This is the reason that we get our web access to CNN faster when we are in Atlanta than when we are in Bangalore, India. In addition to the distance, other factors come into play in determining T_f. T_w already accounts for your physical connectivity to the network. In reality, independent of the specific connection you may have on your computer to the network, the message from your computer may have to traverse several physical links (of different bandwidth) before it reaches the destination. Therefore, in reality, we should account for the propagation delay for each individual physical link en route and add them all up to get the propagation delay. For simplicity, we are aggregating all of these delays together and calling their sum the end-to-end propagation delay.

- **Queuing delay:** Further, as we already mentioned, the wide area network is really a network of networks (see Figure 13.3). There are queuing delays incurred by the message in switches along the way. Besides, several intermediate network protocols come into play as your message traverses the network from source to destination. The details of such protocols add to the latency between source and destination. Finally, the destination receives the packet from the wire into a buffer in the network interface.

We lump all such delays together, for the sake of simplicity, into the term *time of flight*.

4. **Processing delay at the receiver (R):** This is the mirror image of the processing delay incurred by the sender and has all the elements of that delay due to the physical, link, network, and transport layers.

$$\text{Total time for message transmission} = S + T_w + T_f + R \qquad (1)$$

Equation (1) is also referred to as the *end-to-end latency* for a message. From this equation, we can readily see that the bandwidth of the interface that your computer has to the network does not tell the whole story of the latency for network communication experienced by an application running on the computer. Given the message-transmission time, we can compute the *throughput*, defined as the actual transmission rate experienced by an application.

$$\text{Throughput} = \text{message size/end-to-end latency} \qquad (2)$$

As we already know, a message takes several hops from source to destination. Therefore, between any two network hops, a message experiences each of the following delays: processing delay at the sender, transmission delay, propagation delay on the medium connecting the two hops, queuing delay, and processing delay at the receiver. Just to give the reader a feel for the end-to-end delay experienced in message transmission, we have simplified the exposition of message transmission time in this section by lumping all the delays between source and destination (other than the processing delay and transmission delay at the source, and the processing delay at the destination) into *time of flight*.

Example 13.10

Consider the following:

    Processing Delay at the Sender = 1 ms

    Message size = 1000 bits

    Wire bandwidth = 1,000,000 bits/sec

Time of flight = 7 ms

Processing delay at the receiver = 1 ms

Compute the throughput.

Answer:

Total time for message transmission = $S + T_w + T_f + R$, where

S (the processing delay at the sender) = 1 ms;

T_w (Transmission delay) = Message size/wire bandwidth

= 1000/1,000,000 secs

= 1 ms

T_f (time of flight) = 7 ms

R (Processing delay at the receiver) = 1 ms.

Therefore, time for transmitting a message of 1000 bits = 1 + 1 + 7 + 1 ms

= 10 ms.

Throughput = message size/time for transmission

= 1000/(10 ms)

= **100,000 bits/sec**.

The following example illustrates the number of packets needed for message transmission in the presence of packet losses:

Example 13.11

Consider the following:

Message size	=	1900 Kbits
Header size per packet	=	1000 bits
Packet size	=	20 Kbits

Assuming a 10% packet errors on data packets (no errors on ACK packets, and no lost packets), how many total data packets are transmitted by the source to accomplish the preceding message delivery? Every data packet is individually acknowledged.

Answer:

packet size = header size + payload

20000 = 1000 + payload

Payload in a packet = 19000 bits.

Number of packets needed to send the message = 1900000/19000 = 100.

With 10% packet loss, the total number of data packets = 100 + 10 + 1 = **111**.

Total Packets Sent	Lose	Successful
100	10	90
10	1	9
1	0	1
$\overline{111}$		$\overline{100}$

Calculating the cost of message transmission becomes tricky when we have a sliding window protocol.

The following example illustrates the cost of message transmission in the presence of windowing:

Example 13.12

Consider the following:

Message size	=	1900 Kbits
Header size per packet	=	1000 bits
Packet size	=	20 Kbits
Bandwidth on the wire	=	400,000 bits/sec
Time of flight	=	2 secs
Window size	=	10
Processing Delay at the Sender	=	0
Processing Delay at the Receiver	=	0
Size of ACK message	=	negligible (take it as 0).

Assuming an error-free network and in-order delivery of packets, what is the total time to accomplish the preceding message delivery?

Answer:

packet size = header size + payload

Therefore, payload in each packet = packet size − header size

$$= 20000 - 1000$$

$$= 19000 \text{ bits}$$

Number of packets needed to send the message = 1900000/19000 = 100.

Transmission delay for each packet = packet size/wire bandwidth

$$= 20000/400000 \text{ secs}$$

$$= 0.05 \text{ secs}$$

Source side latency per packet = $S + T_w$

$$= \text{Processing Delay at the Sender}$$
$$+ \text{Transmission delay}$$
$$= 0 + 0.05 \text{ secs}$$
$$= 0.05 \text{ secs.}$$

With a window size of 10, the source places 10 packets on the wire and waits for an ACK. The timing diagram at the source looks as follows:

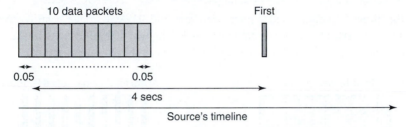

The destination receives the first data packet 2 secs after it is sent.

$$\text{End to end latency for a data packet} = S + T_w + T_f + R$$
$$= (0 + 0.05 + 2 + 0) \text{ secs}$$
$$= 2.05 \text{ secs.}$$

Upon receiving the data packet, the destination immediately prepares an ACK packet. Destination-side overhead for generating an ACK packet

$$= (S + T_w) \text{ at destination}$$
$$= 0 + 0 \text{ (since the ACK packet is negligible in size)}$$
$$= 0.$$

$$\text{End to end latency for an ACK packet} = (S + T_w + T_f + R)$$
$$= (0 + 0 + 2 + 0) \text{ secs}$$
$$= 2 \text{ secs.}$$

Thus, the first ACK packet is received 4 secs after the first data packet is placed on the wire, as shown in the accompanying figure. More generally, an ACK for a data packet is received 4 secs after the data packet is placed on the wire (assuming no loss of packets).

In a lossless network, the 10 ACKs corresponding to the 10 data packets will follow one another with a 0.05 sec spacing, as shown in the next figure:

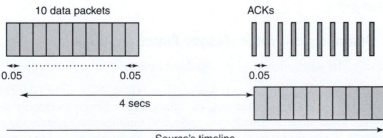

As soon as the first ACK is received, the source can send the next data packet. (Recall that this is a sliding window of 10.) The next 10 data packets follow one another, as shown in the preceding figure.

Thus, in a duty cycle of 4.05 secs, 10 data packets have been sent and 1 ACK has been received at the source. This cycle repeats to send a fresh batch of 10 packets every 4.05 secs.

To send 100 packets, we need 10 such duty cycles.

Therefore, the time to send all 100 data packets = 4.05 * 10 = 40.5 secs.

After this time, 100 data packets have been sent and 91 ACKs have been received, as shown in the next figure. The remaining 9 ACKs (lightly shaded packets in the figure) will arrive subsequently, with a spacing of 0.05 secs, as shown in the figure.

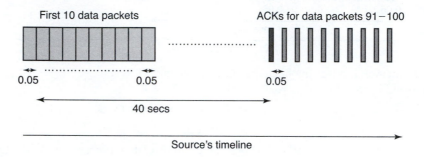

Time to receive the remaining 9 ACKs = 9 * 0.05 secs

$$= 0.45 \text{ secs}.$$

Total time to accomplish the message delivery

$$= \text{time for the 100 data packets} + \text{time to receive the remaining ACKs}$$

$$= 40.5 + 0.45 \text{ secs}$$

$$= \textbf{40.95 secs}.$$

In the preceding example, the processing delays at the sender and receiver are zero. If either of them had been nonzero, it would have increased the overall end-to-end latency for each packet (See Equation 1). The pipelining of the packets follows in a way similar to the foregoing example. (See Exercises at the end of the chapter for variations on the example).

13.13 Summary of Protocol-Layer Functionalities

To summarize, the functionalities of the five-layer Internet protocol stack are as follows:

- The application layer includes protocols such as HTTP, SMTP, and FTP for supporting specific classes of applications, including web browser, electronic mail, file downloads and uploads, instant messenger, and multimedia conferencing and collaboration. Operating system specific network communication libraries such as sockets and RPC (which stands for *remote procedure call*; see Section 13.16) also fall into this layer.

- The transport layer provides delivery of application-specific messages between two communication end points. We saw that the functionalities at this level depend on the quality-of-service requirements of the applications. TCP provides reliable in-order delivery of data streams between the end points, including congestion control, whereas UDP provides message datagram service with no guarantees, message ordering, or reliability.

- The network layer delivers the data, which were handed to it by the transport layer, to the destination. Functionalities at this layer include fragmentation/reassembly commensurate with the link-layer protocol, routing, forwarding, and providing a service model for the transport layer. As we saw earlier, the routing algorithms, which determine possible routes to a destination and functionalities for maintenance of routing and forwarding tables, run as daemon processes at the application level.

- The data link layer provides the interface for the network layer to the physical medium. The functionalities include MAC protocols, framing a packet commensurate with the wire format of the physical layer, error detection (e.g., detecting packet collision on the Ethernet, or token loss in a token ring network), and error recovery (such as a back-off algorithm and retransmission of packet upon collision on Ethernet, or token regeneration on a token ring).

- The physical layer concerns the mechanical and electrical details of the physical medium used for transmission and includes the type of medium (copper, fiber, radio, etc.), the signaling properties of the medium, and the specific handshake for the data link layer to implement the MAC protocol.

13.14 Networking Software and the Operating System

As we mentioned in Section 13.1, there are three strong touch points between the operating system and the networking software.

13.14.1 Socket Library

This is the interface provided by the operating system to the network protocol stack. TCP/IP is the backbone for all the Internet-related services that we have come to rely on in our everyday lives including web browsing, blogging, instant messaging, and so on. Therefore, it is instructive to understand a little bit more about the interfaces presented by TCP/IP for programming distributed applications.

The fact of the matter is that if you are writing a distributed program, you will not be directly dealing with the intricacies of TCP/IP. We will explain why in the following paragraphs.

If you look at the Internet protocol stack (Figure 13.5), you will recognize that your program lives above the protocol stack shown in this figure. An operating system provides well-defined interfaces for programming distributed applications. For example, the UNIX operating system provides the *socket* as an abstraction for processes to communicate with one other (see Figure 13.42).

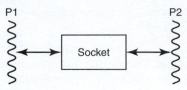

Figure 13.42 Inter-process communication using socket.

Figure 13.42 suggests that the socket abstraction is agnostic as to where the two processes P1 and P2 live. For example, they may both be processes executing on the same processor, or different processors of a shared memory multiprocessor (e.g., an SMP, discussed in Chapter 12), or on two different boxes connected by a network. In other words, the socket abstraction is independent of how the bits move from process P1 to P2.

Protocols such as TCP/IP are vehicles for implementing the socket abstraction. Let us see why it may be advantageous to support *multiple* protocols underneath the socket abstraction. From the point of view of processes P1 and P2, it is immaterial. However, from an efficiency standpoint, it is better to use different protocols, depending on the location of the endpoints of the communication. For example, consider that the two processes are on the same processor or on different processors of an SMP. In this case, the communication never goes on any external wire from the box. Many of the lower-level issues (such as loss of packets, out-of-order arrival of packets, and transmission errors) disappear. Even if P1 and P2 are on different machines of a local area network (say, a home network), where the chances of packet losses are negligible to nil, there is very little need to worry about such low-level issues. On the other hand, the situation demands a more sophisticated protocol that addresses these low-level issues if P1 is a process running on your computer in your dorm room and P2 is a process running on your friend's workstation on campus.

The desired *type* of communication is another consideration in establishing a communication channel, as shown in Figure 13.42. A useful analogy is our postal service. You affix a stamp and send a postcard, with no guarantee that it will reach its destination. On the other hand, if you need to know that your addressee actually received your letter, you pay slightly more to get an acknowledgement back upon delivery of the letter. Analogous to the postcard example, P1 and P2 may simply need to exchange fixed-size (typically, small) messages, called *datagrams*, sporadically and with no guarantees of reliability. On the other hand, Figure 13.42 may represent downloading a movie from a friend. In this case, it is convenient to think of the communication as a *stream* and require that it be reliable and optimized for transporting a continuous stream of bits from source to destination. The desired type of communication channel is orthogonal to the choice of protocol. Application property drives the former choice, whereas the physical location of the endpoints of communication and the quality of the physical interconnect between the endpoints drive the latter choice.

In UNIX, at the point of creating a socket, one can specify the desired properties of the socket, including the type of communication (datagram, stream oriented, etc.), and the specific protocol family to use (UNIX internal, Internet, etc.).

The operating-system-level effort in implementing the socket API is somewhat akin to that involved with implementing the threads library, which we discussed in Chapter 12. Such details are outside the scope of this textbook. The interested reader is referred to other textbooks that deal with these issues.[16]

Other operating systems in extensive use, such as Microsoft Windows (several versions including XP, Vista, and Version 7) and Mac OS X, also support the socket library API.

13.14.2 Implementation of the Protocol Stack in the Operating System

In this day and age, regardless of the specifics of the APIs provided by the operating system for network programming, an operating system necessarily has to provide an implementation of the different layers of the protocol stack to be network ready. While the transport and network layers of the protocol stack are typically implemented in software and form part of the operating system, the link layer (i.e., layer 2) of the protocol stack is usually in hardware. For example, most of you have an Ethernet card in your laptop that provides the functionality of the layer 2 of the protocol stack. With mobile devices, wireless interfaces have become commonplace. These interfaces implement their own link-layer protocols that are variants of the random-access protocol exemplified by Ethernet. In fact, the IEEE standards for the family of wireless LAN protocols are all derivatives of the IEEE 802 family to which Ethernet belongs. We had a glimpse of the wireless LAN protocol when we discussed CSMA/CA in Section 13.8.4. We will defer detailed discussions on wireless LAN protocols to more advanced courses.[17]

As we have seen already, TCP/IP is the dominant transport layer/network layer protocol combination on the Internet today. Correspondingly, standard operating systems (different flavors of UNIX, Mac OS, and Microsoft Windows) invariably include efficient implementation of the TCP/IP protocol stack. Further, most new research endeavors concerning operating system specialization and fine-tuning will invariably use the protocol stack as the compelling example for justifying new operating system mechanisms.

The protocol stack is a complex piece of software, and typically represents several tens of thousands of lines of code and several person-years of software development by expert programmers. The interested reader is referred to textbooks that are devoted entirely to this topic.[18]

13.14.3 Network Device Driver

The discussion of the operating support for networking would be incomplete without a brief look into the network device driver. The network interface card (NIC) allows a

---

16. *The Design and Implementation of the FreeBSD Operating System*, by Marshall Kirk McKusick, George V. Neville-Neil [McKusick, 2004].

17. The textbook by Kurose and Ross, *Computer Networking: A Top Down Approach Featuring the Internet*, Addison-Wesley, has a good basic coverage of wireless LAN technologies [Kurose, 2006].

18. *TCP/IP Illustrated, Volume 2: The Implementation* (Addison-Wesley Professional Computing Series), by Gary R. Wright, W. Richard Stevens [Wright, 1995].

host to be connected to a network. A host may have multiple network interfaces, depending on the number of networks it is connected to. Correspondingly, the operating system has a device driver for each NIC available in the host. As we mentioned earlier (see Section 13.9), a NIC usually incorporates some of the link-layer functionalities of the protocol stack in hardware. The device driver for a specific NIC complements this hardware functionality to enable the NIC to complete the link-layer chores. In Chapter 10, we discussed DMA controllers for high-speed I/O. A NIC incorporates a DMA engine to directly move data in/out of host memory from/to the network. However, there is one fundamental difference between network I/O and disk I/O. The data movement in both directions (i.e., to/from the disk) is initiated by the operating system in response to some user-level or system-level need (e.g., opening a file or servicing a page fault). Now, consider the network. Sending a packet on the network is certainly initiated by a user-level or system-level need. On the other hand, the operating system has no control over the arrival of network packets. Therefore, the operating system has to be ready at any time for this eventuality. This is where the device driver for a NIC comes in. It implements a set of functionality that allows interfacing the NIC to the operating system.

For example, in the case of a NIC that connects the host to an Ethernet NIC, the corresponding device driver incorporates the following functionalities:

- allocating/deallocating *network buffers* in the host memory for sending and receiving packets;
- upon being handed a packet to send on the wire, setting up the transmit network buffers, and initiating DMA action by the NIC;
- registering network interrupt handlers with the operating system;
- setting up network receive buffers for the NIC to DMA incoming network packets into the host memory; and
- fielding hardware interrupts from the NIC, if necessary, and making upcalls (see Chapter 11 for a discussion of upcalls) to the upper layers of the protocol stack (e.g., communicating a packet arrival event up the food chain).

Figure 13.43 captures the actions both in hardware and software for dealing with a network packet arrival. Since the NIC is made aware of network buffers allocated for packet reception by the device driver, it can immediately use DMA to transfer the incoming packet into the host memory, using these preallocated buffers. The NIC notifies the device driver about the packet arrival, using the hardware interrupt mechanism of the processor (Chapters 4 and 10). Using the upcall mechanism that we discussed in Chapter 11, the device driver alerts the upper layers of the protocol stack about the incoming packet. For more detail, the interested reader is referred to literature on developing network device drivers.[19]

---

19. Network Device Driver Programming Guide, http://developer.apple.com/documentation/DeviceDrivers/Conceptual/NetworkDriver/NetDoc.pdf.

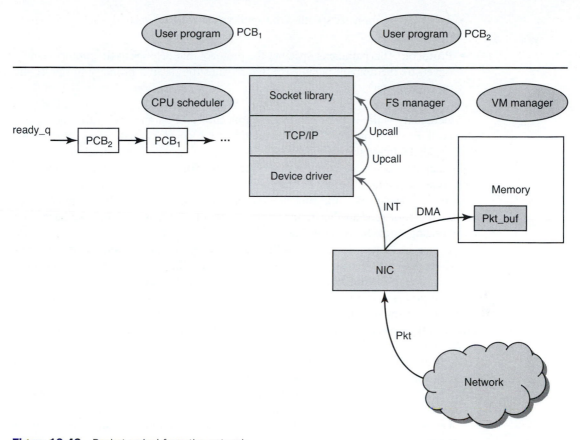

Figure 13.43   Packet arrival from the network.

We are already familiar with the other OS functionalities, such as CPU scheduler, virtual memory manager, and file system manager, from the previous chapters. The figure shows the layers of the protocol stack in the OS for supporting network programming and the actions taken by the hardware (NIC) and the software upon a network packet arrival.

13.15 Network Programming Using UNIX Sockets

To make the network programming discussion concrete, let us take a closer look at how UNIX sockets work, from an application program standpoint.

The socket creation call on UNIX takes on three parameters **domain, type, protocol**.

* **Domain:** This parameter helps pick the protocol family to use for the communication. For example, the choice would be IP if the communicating processes were on the Internet; the choice would be UNIX internal if the processes were on the same machine or a LAN.

- **Type:** This parameter specifies the application property desired, such as datagram or stream.

- **Protocol:** This parameter specifies the protocol that belongs to the protocol family (given by the domain parameter) that satisfies the desired property (given by the type parameter).

Generality is the intent for providing this choice of parameters in the socket creation call. For example, there could be multiple protocols for a particular protocol family (say, UNIX internal) that may satisfy the desired type of communication. In reality, there may be exactly one protocol that belongs to a particular protocol family for a desired type of communication. For example, if the protocol family is IP and the type is stream, then TCP may be the only choice available as the transport. Still, explicitly separating the choices is an illustration of the power of abstraction, which we have been emphasizing throughout in this book.

Figure 13.42 paints a picture as though the two endpoints P1 and P2 are symmetric. However, this is not quite the case—at least, not in the way the communication channel is established. Let us delve a bit deeper into that aspect in this section.

Interprocess communication using sockets follows a *client/server* paradigm. The communication using sockets may be set up as a connection-oriented one or a connection-less one. The **type** parameter mentioned previously allows this distinction to be made at the creation time of a socket.

Let us consider connection-oriented communication using Unix sockets. One can liken the establishment of the connection between a client and a server to making a phone call. The caller needs to know the number to call; the recipient of the call can accept calls from anyone who cares to call him or her. The client is the caller. The server is the callee.

Let us carry this analogy further. The server does the following in preparation for interprocess communication:

1. Create a socket for communication, as in Figure 13.44. Notice that this has resulted in creating an endpoint of communication for the server. This is analogous to having a telephone, but with no connection set up yet to the outside world. To make the phone useful, one first has to get a phone number (which involves getting a line connection from a service provider as well) and associate the number with the phone. That is the next step.

2. The equivalent of the phone number in our analogy is a *name* (also referred to as *address*), a unique identifier to associate with a socket. The system call to associate a name with a socket is **bind**. If the intent is to communicate via the Internet using

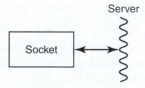

Figure 13.44   Server side socket call.

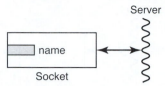

Figure 13.45   Server socket after bind call.

IP protocol, then the name has two parts `<host address, port number>`. The host address is the IP address of the host on which the server is running; the port number is a 16-bit unsigned number. The operating system checks whether the port number specified by the server is already in use at the time of the bind call. (See Figure 13.45.)

Once bound, the name can be given to others who want to communicate with this server. If it is a telephone number, you may publish it in a directory so that others can look it up. The analogous thing to do in the case of client/server communication is to create a *name server,* a well-known machine that potential clients contact to get the name of the server.

3. Of course, to receive a phone call, you have to plug the instrument into the wall socket (where the line connection from the service provider comes in) so that the phone can listen to incoming calls. First, you have to tell the phone company that you want to allow incoming calls, and whether you would like "call waiting"—that is, how many simultaneous calls you are willing to entertain on your phone line. The equivalent thing to do on the server side is for the server to execute the **listen** system call. It tells the operating system how many calls can be queued up on this socket.

4. There is another step on the server side to complete the reception of an incoming connection request. This is the **accept** system call. This is the equivalent of the phone receiver being on the hook awaiting an incoming call once the phone company has turned on your phone service. See Figure 13.46.

Now let us see what the client has to do to establish communication with the server.

1. Create a client side socket, as shown in Figure 13.47. This is equivalent to getting a phone for the caller.

2. To make a phone call, the caller has to dial a number. The **connect** system call accomplishes the equivalent thing on the client side. It connects the client side socket to the **name** published by the server, as shown in Figure 13.48.

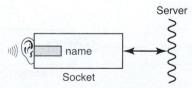

Figure 13.46   Server socket after listen and accept calls.

Client

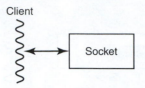

Figure 13.47 Client side socket call.

The client and server are not quite ready to communicate yet. The connect system call is analogous to dialing the phone number. Unless the call recipient picks up the phone, the call is not complete. The **accept** system call on the server side accomplishes the analogous thing in this client–server set up. In a telephone call, one has to pick up the receiver to establish the connection. In the socket world, recall that the server has already indicated its willingness to accept incoming calls on this connection. Therefore, the operating system completes the establishment of the connection between the client and the server, as shown in Figure 13.49. Note that if you have call waiting on your phone, you will be able to know about incoming calls while you are talking to someone. The operating system provides the same facility with sockets. It creates a *new data socket* for the newly established connection. The operating system will implicitly queue up connection requests that may be coming in from other clients on the original named socket on which a listen call has been placed.

At this point, both the client and the server are ready to exchange messages in a symmetric manner. Thus, although there is asymmetry in the way the connection is established (just as in the case of a phone call), the actual communication is truly symmetric.

You may be wondering why both the client and the server have to execute **socket** system calls. From earlier chapters, we know that each process executes in its own address space. The data structures created because of a system call live in the address space of a particular process. Thus, we need a representation of the socket abstraction in each of the address spaces of the communicating processes (see Figure 13.50). All the other system calls (bind, listen, accept, and connect) enable the two sockets to be connected together via the operating system and the network protocol stack to realize the abstract picture shown in Figure 13.42.

Whereas the preceding discussion focused on a stream-type socket that requires connection establishment, the communication is much more simplified if the socket type is a datagram. In this case, the server has to execute neither a listen nor an accept call, at all. The datagram received from a client is simply stored in the datagram socket created by the server. Similarly, if the client creates a datagram socket, it can simply

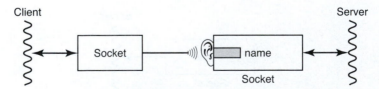

Figure 13.48 Client–server relationship after client executes connect system call.

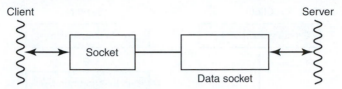

Figure 13.49   Client–server relationship after connection establishment.

send and receive data on this socket by providing the address of the server-side socket (i.e., host address and port number).

To summarize, UNIX provides the following basic system calls for processes to communicate with one another, regardless of where they execute:

- **Socket**: Create an endpoint of communication.
- **Bind**: Bind a socket to a name or an address.
- **Listen**: Listen for incoming connection requests on the socket.
- **Accept**: Accept an incoming connection request on a socket.
- **Connect**: Send a connection request to a name (or address) associated with a remote socket; establish the connection by creating a data socket for this connection if the server has already posted an accept system call.
- **Recv**: Receive incoming data on a socket from a remote peer.
- **Send**: Send data to a remote peer via a socket.

Figure 13.51 shows the protocol between the client and the server for establishing a stream-oriented socket for communication. The listen system call lets the operating system know how many connections are expected to be simultaneously supported on the stream socket. Each time a new connection is established (client connect call matches with server accept call), a new data socket is created by the operating system. The life of this new data socket is determined by the lifetime of the connection. As soon as the client closes the connection, the newly created data socket is closed as well.

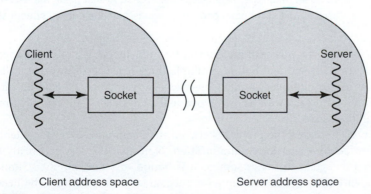

Figure 13.50   Sockets in client–server address spaces.

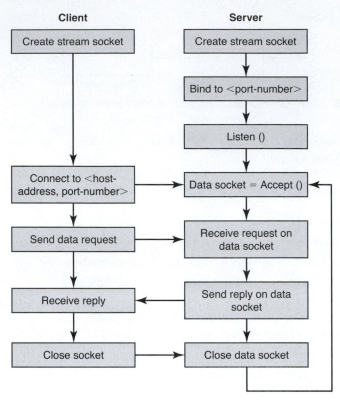

Figure 13.51 Data communication on a stream socket.

The server creates a socket, binds a port number to it, and makes the blocking accept system call, indicating its willingness to accept connection requests. The client creates a socket and connects to the server via the <host address, port-name> tuple. The operating system creates a new data socket for the newly established connection on which the client and server can exchange data streams. The data socket is specific to this connection and will be closed when the client closes the socket. At that point, the server can go back to waiting for new connection requests on the original stream socket.

The listen call is a powerful mechanism for implementing a multithreaded server. Once a socket is created and bound, multiple threads can post **accept** calls on the socket. This allows multiple, simultaneous client–server connections to be entertained on the same socket (each with its own individual data socket), subject only to the limit specified in the listen call.

Figure 13.52 shows the protocol between the client and server for establishing a datagram-oriented socket for communication. Note that the server is ready to send/receive on a datagram socket as soon as it is bound to a port number. Similarly, the client can start sending and receiving on a datagram socket without the need for an explicit connect call.

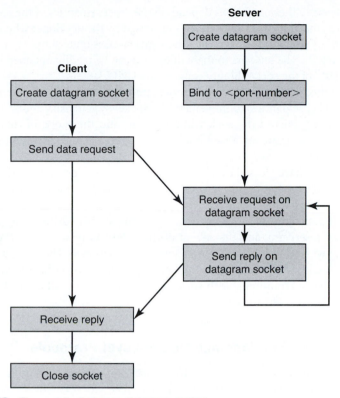

Figure 13.52   Communication on a datagram socket.

Once the server creates a datagram socket and binds a port number to it, data transmission and reception can start on this socket. There is no need for a connect call from the client for the data exchange to occur between the client and the server.

See Appendix for an example of a client–server program using UNIX sockets.

There are a number of issues that demand the attention of a programmer using UNIX sockets to implement a distributed program. Let us itemize some of these issues:

- Can two processes communicate if the associated socket properties (domain and/or type) do not match?
- How does the server choose a port number?
- What does the name translate to for UNIX domain sockets?
- What happens if the name that the client wants to connect to does not exist?
- What happens if the physical link between the client and server breaks for some reason?
- Can multiple clients successfully execute a connect call to the same name?

The answers to these questions depend on the exact semantics of the socket library calls, as well as the implementation choices exercised by the developer who implements the socket library. The purpose of raising these questions is quite simply to pique the interest of the reader. The answers to these questions can be readily obtained by perusing the man pages[20] of the socket library calls on any UNIX system.

The operating system uses the appropriate transport protocol (commensurate with the desired socket semantics) to implement the socket system calls. A discussion of the implementation details of the socket library is beyond the scope of this book. The reader is referred to more advanced books on networking and operating systems for such a discussion.

Of course, we have glossed over many messy details in order to keep the discussion simple. The UNIX operating system provides a number of utilities to assist in network programming with sockets.

With the popularity of UNIX operating systems for network servers (such as file servers and web servers), and the advent of the World Wide Web (WWW), network programming with sockets has taken on enormous importance. The interested reader is encouraged to take advanced courses in operating systems to get hands-on experience with distributed programming with sockets, as well as to learn how to build socket abstraction in the operating system.

13.16 Network Services and Higher-Level Protocols

As a concrete example, let us understand a network application such as *ftp (file transfer protocol)*. There are a *client* and a *server* part to such services. The host machine at the client end opens a network connection with the remote host, using the transport protocol (TCP/IP, for example) to talk to the ftp server on the remote host. Upon completion of the file transfer, the client and server agree to close the network connection. Other network applications such as a *web browser* and *mail*, for the wide area network (WAN), work similarly.

It is interesting to understand how some LAN services work quite differently from WAN services. For example, all of us routinely use file servers in our everyday computing. When we open a file (for example, using **fopen** on UNIX), we may actually be going across the network to a remote file server to access the file. However, such LAN services do not use the traditional network stack. Instead, they use a facility called *remote procedure call* (RPC) in the UNIX operating system. Figure 13.53 shows the idea behind RPC. Process P1 makes what appears to be a normal procedure call to *foo*. This procedure foo executes remotely in process P2 on another machine across the network. The fact that the procedure executes remotely is invisible to the users of RPC.

Network file system (NFS) exists on top of the RPC mechanism. Figure 13.54 shows at a high level the handshake involved in a network facility such as NFS. The **fopen** call of the user becomes an RPC call to the NFS server, which performs the file open system command on the named file residing at the server.

---

20. See man pages online at http://www.freebsd.org/cgi/man.cgi.

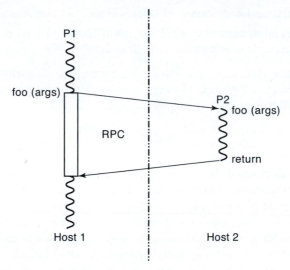

Figure 13.53   RPC in UNIX.

The brief discussion presented in this subsection on network services and higher-level protocols raises several interesting questions:

1. How do we design RPC systems?
2. What are the semantics of a remote procedure call in comparison with local procedure calls?

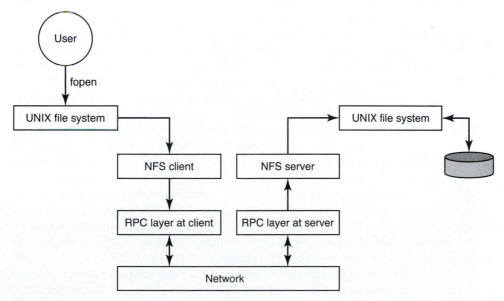

Figure 13.54   UNIX network file system (NFS).

3. How does RPC deal with sources of failures in network transmissions?

4. We have seen implementation of file systems in Chapter 11. What are the semantic differences in implementing a network file system?

This subsection gives a glimpse into the fascinating area of distributed systems. We hope that the reader will pursue advanced courses to get a deeper understanding on these and other distributed systems topics.

Summary

In this chapter, we covered the basics of computer networking. We reviewed the requirements for supporting networked communication in Section 13.3, and introduced the five-layer Internet protocol stack in Section 13.4.1. At the heart of the Internet protocol stack is the transport layer, which we covered in detail in Section 13.6. It is responsible for providing an abstraction to the applications that is independent of the details of the network. Its primary functionality is ensuring in-order delivery of messages, supporting arbitrary-sized messages, and shielding the applications from loss of data during message transmission. There is a tension between fairness, reliability, and eagerness to utilize the communication channel fully, all of which combine to present a number of possible protocols at the transport layer.

We started the transport protocol discussion with the simple stop-and-wait protocol (Section 13.6.1), and ended with the transport protocols used in the Internet today (Section 13.6.5). We covered network-layer functionalities in detail in Section 13.7. This layer is responsible for providing a logical addressing scheme for the nodes in the network (Section 13.7.2), routing algorithms for the passage of packets of a message from source to destination (Section 13.7.1), and offering a service model for packet delivery (Section 13.7.3). The routing algorithms discussed in Section 13.7.1 include Dijkstra's shortest path, distance vector, and hierarchical routing. In Section 13.7.3, we covered circuit switching, packet switching, and message switching as three possible options for using the network resources (such as intermediate nodes and routers between source and destination). Packet switching is the paradigm widely used in the Internet, and we discussed two possible service models on top of packet switching, namely, virtual circuit and datagram. In Section 13.8, we discussed link-layer technologies, paying special attention to Ethernet (Section 13.8.1), which has become the de facto standard for local area networks. This section also covered other link-layer technologies such as token ring (Section 13.8.5), FDDI, and ATM (Section 13.8.6). The networking hardware that connects the host to the physical layer was discussed in Section 13.9. Protocol layering is a modular approach to building system software, and we discussed the relationship between the different layers of the Internet protocol stack in Section 13.10. We discussed the data structures for packet transmission and the components of the message transmission time on the network, in the subsequent two sections (Sections 13.11 and 13.12). We summarized the functionalities of the five-layer Internet protocol stack, in Section 13.13.

Section 13.14 went into the issues involved in incorporating the network protocol stack into the operating system, including a discussion of the socket library that sits at the top of, and the device driver that sits below, the TCP/IP protocol in most production operating systems. We presented an intuitive feel for network programming with UNIX sockets, in Section 13.15, and a glimpse of higher-level network services (such as network file system), in Section 13.16.

This chapter concludes with a historical perspective of computer networking.

Historical Perspective

We start with a journey through the evolution of networking, from the early days of computing.

From Telephony to Computer Networking

Let us first review the evolution of telephony, because computer networking owes a lot to the advances in telephony. Prior to the 1960s, the telephone infrastructure was entirely analog. That is, when you picked up a phone and called someone, the wires that connected the two devices carried actual voice signal. In principle, with a couple of electrical connections and a pair of headphones, one could climb on a telephone pole and eavesdrop on private conversations. In the 1960s, telephony switched from analog to digital. In this system, the infrastructure converts the analog voice signal to digital, and sends the bits over the wire. The network still uses circuit switching (see Section 13.7.3), but the audio signal is sent as 1's and 0's. At the receiving end, the infrastructure converts the digital data back to the original analog voice signal, and delivers them to the end user via the telephone (Figure 13.55).

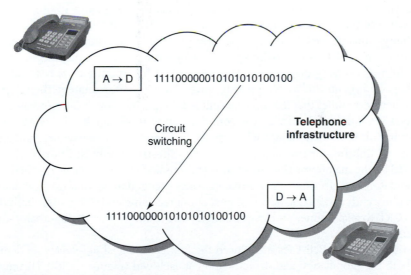

Figure 13.55 Circuit-switched digital telephony.

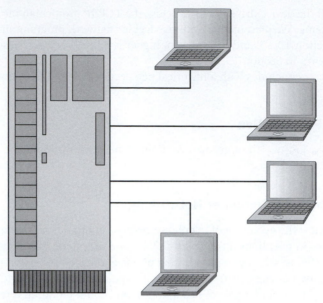

Figure 13.56 Terminals connected to a mainframe.

The 1960s marked the era of *mainframes* in the computing evolution. These machines operated in a batch-oriented multiprogramming environment and used *punched cards* as the input/output medium. *Cathode-ray-terminal-based (CRT-based)* display devices and keyboards made their way, displacing *punched cards* as the input/output medium for users to interact with the computer. This started the era of *interactive* computing and *time-shared* operating systems on the mainframes (Figure 13.56).

With the parallel advances in telephony, the advent of CRTs opened up a new possibility—that is, the CRT need not be near the mainframe computer, but it could be located at a remote location such as the home of a user. After all, the telephone infrastructure was carrying digital data. Therefore, the infrastructure does not really care whether the bits on the wire represent voice or data. Unfortunately, the telephone infrastructure assumes that the input/output is analog (since it is meant for voice transmission), even though internally the communication is all digital. Therefore, there is a missing link from the remote CRT to get to the telephone infrastructure, and a similar missing link from the analog output of the infrastructure back to the digital data expected by the mainframe (Figure 13.57). This missing link is the *modem*—modulator/demodulator—an electronic device that converts digital data to analog (modulator) at the sending end, and analog data to digital at the receiving end. Of course, both directions (CRT to mainframe, and mainframe to CRT) require this digital-analog-digital conversion.

In 1962, AT&T Bell Labs introduced the first commercial *full-duplex* modem that does both the modulation and demodulation at each end (Figure 13.58). This marked the birth of what we know today as *telecommunication*. In 1977, a Georgia Tech graduate named Dennis Hayes invented the *PC modem* that standardized the communication

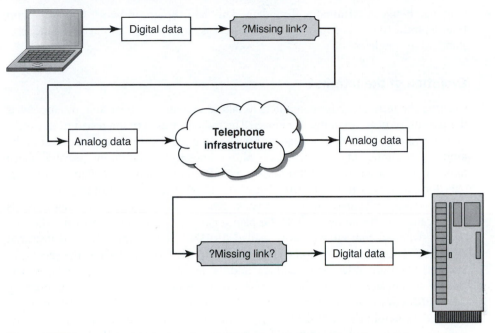

Figure 13.57   Even though the telephone infrastructure operates internally on digital data, the input/output to the infrastructure is analog (voice).

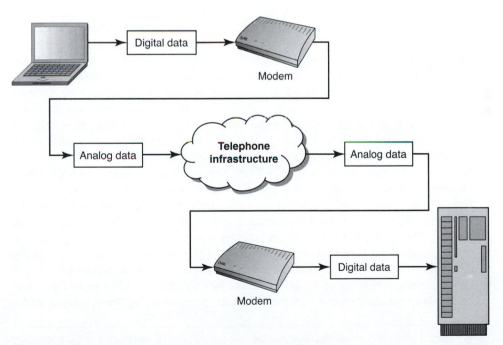

Figure 13.58   Modems connecting terminals to the mainframe.

language between terminal and modem. This laid the groundwork for online and Internet industries to emerge and grow, and to this day has come to stay as the industry standard for modems.

Evolution of the Internet

Creating the technology for computers to talk to one another over long distances was the passion of many a computer pioneer. The military was very interested in this technology coming to fruition, for strategic reasons. In parallel with the development of the modem for connecting terminals over phone lines to the mainframe, several sharp minds both in academia and in industry were thinking about connecting computers over long distances from the early 1960s. In 1968, a federal funding agency, *ARPA* (which stands for *Advanced Research Projects Agency*), with the help of such sharp minds from academia and industry, drafted a plan for the first computer network. The first packet-switched computer network, called ARPANET (short for Advanced Research Projects Agency Network), connected four computers, one at UCLA, the second at Stanford, the third at UC-Santa Barbara, and the fourth at the University of Utah. The "router" in the network, called *interface message processor (IMP)*, was built by a company called BBN (short for Bolt, Beranak, and Newman, Inc.). The IMP system architecture required a careful balance of the hardware and software, that would allow it to be used as a store-and-forward packet switch among these computers. The IMPs used modems and leased telephone lines to connect to one another. ARPANET was first tested in 1969, and the networking luminary Leonard Kleinrock is credited with successfully sending the first network message from UCLA to Stanford.

Of course, after this initial test, ARPANET soon burgeoned into the modern-day Internet. One of the key developments that spurred this growth was the development of reliable communication protocols, namely, TCP/IP, by two networking pioneers, Vinton Cerf and Robert Kahn. Fittingly, in 2004, they were honored with the highest award in computer science, the *Turing Award*, in recognition of their contribution to the development of network communication protocols. It is interesting to note that the basic networking ideas that we covered in this chapter, including transport protocols and store-and-forward packet-switched routing, were fully operational in the Internet by the mid- to late 1970s. Thanks to the Berkeley software distribution effort from the University of California, Berkeley, the TCP/IP protocol stack made it into the UNIX operating system in the early 1980s. Owing to the subsequent popularity of UNIX, initially in the desktop market and subsequently in the server markets, pretty soon the Internet protocol stack became a standard feature in all flavors of UNIX. Even IBM, in the early 1980s, decided to include the Internet protocol stack in its VM operating system, through a partnership with the University of Wisconsin-Madison.[21] Thus, nearly all the major vendors had adopted the Internet protocol stack as the standard offering in their computers. However, it is only in the late 1990s that the Internet really took off as a household name. There are a couple of reasons for that time lag. First, computers did

---

21. The first author of this textbook implemented the mail transfer protocol, SMTP, as part of this IBM project, while he was a graduate student at UW-Madison.

not reach the masses until the invention of the PC and the establishment of its commercial success. Second, there was not a killer application for the Internet until the birth of the World Wide Web. Today, of course, even our grandmother would tell us that a computer is practically useless unless it is connected to the Internet. The explosive growth of the Internet gave birth to companies such as CISCO that focused on making specialized hardware boxes to serve as routers.

Of course, one could write an entire book on the evolution of the Internet, but the purpose here is to give a glimpse of the road we have traversed until now. We have simply to look at the evolution of networking to appreciate the connectedness of the three topics we have been stressing in this textbook—architecture, operating systems, and networking.

PC and the Arrival of LAN

In 1972, a document company called Xerox Corporation designed the world's first *personal computer,* called *Alto,* named after the location of its Palo Alto Research Center (PARC).

In the mid-1970s, Metcalf and Boggs, working in Xerox PARC, invented *Ethernet,* a network for computers within a building to talk to one another. This marked the birth of the *local area network (LAN).* Ironically, Xerox never marketed the PC or Ethernet technology. Other companies, first Apple and later IBM, picked up the PC idea, and the rest is history. In 1979, Metcalf founded 3Com to develop the LAN market and successfully convinced the computer industry to adopt Ethernet as a LAN standard.

Evolution of LAN

Thicknet. A *coaxial cable* serves as the physical medium in Ethernet (Figure 13.59); the innermost thick copper wire carries the signal, and the outer conductor that runs concentric to the first one (separated by the white insulation) serves as the ground. The very first iteration of Ethernet used a thick coaxial cable (called *thicknet* for that reason), and *vampire taps* (Figure 13.60) on the cable, to establish a connection for each computer. The coaxial cable runs through an entire office complex, connecting all the computers together. The cable that connects an office computer to Ethernet is the *attachment unit interface (AUI)* cable, whose length can be at most 50 meters. It is customary to use the notation *xBASEy* to denote the type of Ethernet connection. For example, 10BASE5 refers to an Ethernet supporting *10* Mbit/sec data transfer rate, using *BASE* band signaling, and running a maximum distance of 500 meters between any two computers. Thicknet with vampire taps were in use from 1979 to 1985.

Thinnet. As the name suggests, this kind of Ethernet uses thinner coaxial cable for the Ethernet medium, with BNC[22] connectors for connecting the computer to the coaxial

---

22. BNC connector is the kind used quite commonly for video connections. The letters in the acronym stand for the style of locking (Bayonet mount locking) and the names of the inventors (Neil and Concelman).

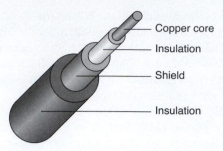

Figure 13.59   Coaxial cable.

cable. Due to the relative thinness of the wire (implying greater resistance and, hence, greater signal degradation with length), 200 meters is the maximum length of a thinnet cable connecting two computers. The logical bus is a daisy chain of these cables from unit to unit, as shown in Figure 13.61. Thinnet (a 10 Mbit/sec data transfer rate thinnet would be denoted 10BASE2) was in vogue from 1985 to 1993.

Fast Ethernet.   The daisy-chained units were a source of connector problems in maintaining the LAN. For example, the LAN is broken even if one BNC connector gets unplugged. Advances in circuit design and VLSI came to the rescue. In the early 1990s, to

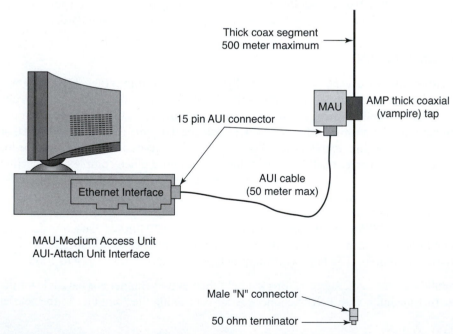

Figure 13.60   Computer connected to Ethernet coaxial cable via vampire tap.

The maximum distance between any two nodes connected by the coaxial cable can be 500 meters.

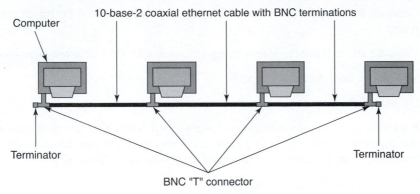

Figure 13.61 Daisy-chain arrangement of Thinnet 10BASE2 Ethernet.

replace the physical wire connecting the units, electrical engineers designed a *hub*, which is a multiplexer/transceiver. The hub is an electronic component that is logically equivalent to a bus. A hub has several *ports*, each of which is a connection point to a computer. Riding on the advances in telephony and the use of modular jacks (called RJ45 connectors), Ethernet switched to using a *twisted pair of wires*, similar to telephone wires, and RJ45 connectors at the two ends, to connect the computers to the hub (Figure 13.32). This changed the landscape of LAN quite dramatically. Deploying an Ethernet LAN is simply a matter of hooking up computers to hubs and connecting the hubs together (Figure 13.33). Logically, all the computers exist on a bus via the hubs. The length of the cable is irrelevant, since the computers connect to a hub over a short distance (a few tens of meters). 100BASE-T (T, for *twisted pair*), often referred to as *fast Ethernet*, denotes a 100 Mbit/sec data-transfer-rate Ethernet using a twisted pair for connecting the computers to the hub.

1GBase-T and 10GBase-T. Since about 2009, gigabit Ethernet has been the standard for LAN interconnects. NICs that provide such high-bandwidth network connectivity for the hosts use a twisted pair of wires to connect the host to a switch. The length of the wire can be at most 100 meters.

Exercises

1. Describe the function of a modem. Include in your answer communication in both directions.

2. Compare and contrast Ethernet and token ring networks.

3. Describe the basic function of a token ring network.

4. What does the abbreviation CSMA/CD stand for and what does it mean?

5. Distinguish between wireless and wired Ethernet protocols.

6. What is collision avoidance and how is it achieved in CSMA/CA protocol?

7. Compare and contrast each of the following: NIC, hub, repeater, bridge, switch, router.

8. Compare and contrast the Internet protocol stack with the OSI seven-layer model.

9. Why do we need network protocols?

10. Distinguish between circuit switching and virtual circuit.

11. A knowledgeable computer engineer designs a switch (such as the one discussed in this chapter) that was made using bridges. In order to save money, he uses repeaters instead of bridges. Would you buy one of these switches? Why or why not?

12. What is the purpose of a sliding window?

13. How do protocols such as TCP/IP deal with problems such as out-of-order delivery, lost packets, duplicate packets, etc.?

14. Discuss why network congestion occurs and how it is handled in TCP.

15. What is meant by an IP network? Assume that you want to start a company and need to connect 2000 computers to the Internet. How would you go about requesting IP addresses from an ISP? What would be the dotted decimal notation of the resulting network for your company?

16. How is a checksum used and why is it necessary?

17. A message has 13 packets, and the time to send a packet from source to destination is 2 msec. Assuming that the time to send/receive the packet and the ACK are negligible compared with the propagation time on the medium, and given no packet loss, how much time is required to complete the transmission, with the sliding window protocol with a window size of 5?

18. Consider the following:

Message size	= 1900 Kbits
Header size per packet	= 1000 bits
Packet size	= 20 Kbits
Bandwidth on the wire	= 400,000 bits/sec
Time of flight	= 2 secs
Window size	= 8
Processing delay at the sender	= 0
Processing delay at the receiver	= 0
Size of ACK message	= negligible (take it as 0)

Assuming an error-free network and an in-order delivery of packets, what is the total time to accomplish the foregoing message delivery?

[Hint: Note that the window size specifies the maximum number of outstanding packets at any point in time. After all the data packets have been sent out, the source has to wait for the remaining ACKs to come back from the destination in order for the transmission to complete.]

19. Consider the following about the transport and network layers:

Data packet size	= 20,000 bits
Size of ACK message	= negligible (take it as 0)
(Each data packet individually acknowledged)	
Transport window size	= 20
Processing delay at the sender	= 0.025 secs per packet (only for data)
Processing delay at the receiver	= 0.025 secs per packet (only for data)
Packet loss	= 0%
Packet errors	= 0%
Bandwidth on the wire	= 400,000 bits/sec
Time of flight	= 4 secs

What is the total time (including the reception of the ACK packets) to complete the transmission of 400 packets with the foregoing transport?

[Hint: Note that, from the point of view of determining the duty cycle at the source, all the components of the end-to-end latencies for a packet (shown in Equation (1) of Section 13.12) can be lumped together.]

20. The following are the sizes of the fields of a packet header:

Destination address	8 bytes
Source address	8 bytes
Number of packets in message	4 bytes
Sequence number	4 bytes
Actual packet size	4 bytes
Checksum	4 bytes

Assuming that the maximum packet size is 1100 bytes, what is the maximum payload in each packet?

21. Consider the following:

Sender overhead	= 1 ms
Message size	= 200,000 bits
Wire bandwidth	= 100,000,000 bits/sec
Time of flight	= 2 ms
Receiver overhead	= 1 ms

Compute the observed bandwidth. Recall that the message transmission time consists of sender overhead, time on the wire, time of flight, and receiver overhead. Ignore ACKs.

22. Consider the following:

Message size	= 100,000 bytes
Header size per packet	= 100 bytes
Packet size	= 1100 bytes

    How many packets are needed to transmit the message, assuming a 10% packet loss? Ignore fractional packet loss. Ignore ACKs.

23. Consider a reliable pipelined transport protocol that uses cumulative ACKs. The window size is 10. The receiver sends an ACK, according to the following rule:

    - Send an ACK if 10 consecutive packets are received in order, thus allowing the sender to advance its sliding window.

    - If a packet is received with a sequence number different from the expected next sequence number, send an ACK corresponding to the highest sequence number received thus far.

        a. 100 packets are sent by the sender. 1 in 10 data packets are lost in transit. Assume that no ACK packets are lost. How many ACK packets are actually sent to successfully complete the transmission?

        b. How many ACK packets would have been sent without cumulative ACKs? In this case assume that the protocol ACKs every packet individually; and if a data packet is received out of order, it resends the last ACK packet.

Bibliographic Notes and Further Reading

Tim Berners-Lee invented the World Wide Web in 1989 [Berners-Lee, 1989]. However, the dots that connect up to this invention go far back. A thought piece entitled "As We May Think," by a visionary named Vannevar Bush, in 1945 predicted a future in which devices (called memex) would hold a complex web of interconnected information, augmenting the human brain [Bush, 1945]. In the 1960s, simultaneously and independently, three different research groups (MIT, Rand Institute, and the National Physical Laboratory in England) invented packet switching [Baran, 1964; Kleinrock, 1961; Kleinrock, 1964], which is the core data-communication technology that drives the Internet. In 1969, BBN technologies built the first version of packet switches, called interface message processors (IMPs), that allowed computers to talk to one another. By the end of 1969, there were a whopping four nodes on the ARPAnet[23] connected by the IMPs! In addition to the ARPAnet, a few other packet-switched networks started to come up in the early 1970s, such as the ALOHAnet [Abramson, 1970], and Telenet, a commercial version of the ARPAnet spun off by BBN. In the meantime, Robert Metcalfe,

---

23. ARPA stands for Advanced Research Projects Agency, and ARPAnet can be considered the granddaddy of today's Internet.

in 1973, laid out the principle of the Ethernet, in his PhD thesis,[24] which resulted in the proliferation of LANs in later years. The time was ripe for interconnecting all these independent islands of networks together. Vincent Cerf and Robert Kahn [Cerf, 1974] did this in their pioneering work, wherein they proposed the architecture for this interconnection, and the Internet, as we know it today, was born. The architecture-specified TCP is the dominant transport protocol that powers the Internet to this day.[25] All of these developments, plus the advances in computing and networking hardware and software, are the enablers for Tim Berners-Lee to invent the WWW.

Implementation details of the TCP/IP protocol stack in the Berkeley UNIX can be found in [McKusick, 1996]. The books by [Stevens, 1994; Wright, 1995] are great resources to learn about the details of the TCP/IP protocol and implementation. There are several excellent textbooks on computer networking [Kurose, 2006; Tanenbaum, 2002] that would serve as references for a student aspiring to know more than what has been previewed in this chapter. Students interested in knowing more about network programming will find these textbooks to be great resources [Comer, 2000; Stevens, 2003; Bryant, 2003].

---

24. Metcalfe and Boggs published the paper that described the Ethernet protocol in 1976 [Metcalfe, 1976].

25. For a three-decade history of the Internet, spanning 1962–1992, visit http://www.computerhistory.org/internet_history/.

Epilogue: A Look
Back at the Journey

This book has been a journey "inside the box." It is worthwhile to look back at each of the topics we covered and see the interrelationship between system software and hardware.

14.1 Processor Design

We saw that high-level language constructs played a key role in the design of the instruction set and related architectural features of the processor. Table 14.1 summarizes the HLL constructs and features that give rise to the architectural decisions in a processor.

We saw that once the architecture is fully specified, there are several implementation choices such as a simple design and a pipelined design. It is fair to say that we have only scratched the surface of the exciting area of microarchitecture. We hope that we have piqued the readers' interest sufficiently for them to dig deeper into this fascinating area.

14.2 Process

The process concept served as a convenient abstraction for remembering all the relevant details of a running program. We know that the processor can run only one program at a time. The operating system gives the illusion of each process having its own processor to run on. To facilitate the operating system in giving this illusion, the architecture provides mechanisms, namely, *trap* and *interrupt*, for taking control back from the currently running program. It is via these mechanisms that the operating system gets control of the processor to make a scheduling decision as to which user program to run next. We saw several algorithms that an operating system may employ to make such a scheduling decision. We also reviewed the data structures needed by the operating system to implement these algorithms. The trap mechanism allows a user-level program to avail itself of

Table 14.1 HLL and Architectural Features

HLL Construct/Feature	Architectural Features
Expressions	Arithmetic/logic instructions, addressing modes
Data types	Different operand granularity, multiple precision arithmetic, and logic instructions
Conditional statements, loops	Conditional and unconditional branch instructions
Procedure call/return	Stack, link register
System calls, error conditions	Traps, exceptions
Efficient execution of HLL programs (expressions, parameter passing, etc.)	General-purpose registers

system-provided utilities (such as file systems and print capability) to enhance the functionality of the program, via system calls.

The processor scheduling component of a production operating system such as Linux or Windows XP is a lot more complicated than the simplistic view provided in this textbook would suggest. The purpose of the book is to provide enough of an exposure to the reader that the mystery is taken out of how to build the scheduling subsystem of an operating system.

14.3 Virtual Memory System and Memory Management

The memory system plays a crucial role in determining the performance of a computer system. Therefore, significant attention is paid in this textbook to understanding the interplay between the memory management component of the operating system and the architectural assists for memory management. We reviewed a number of architectural techniques, such as the fence register, bounds registers, base and limit registers, and paging, from the point of view of supporting such functionalities of the memory manager as memory allocation, protection and isolation, sharing, and efficient memory utilization. We also saw the need for a privileged mode (kernel mode) of execution to be supported in the architecture in order for the operating system to set up the memory area before scheduling a program to run on the processor. We addressed several operating systems issues (such as page-replacement policies and working-set maintenance) that are crucial for achieving good performance in the running of application programs.

The main lesson we learned from both managing the processor (via scheduling algorithms) and the memory (via memory-management policies) is the need for the operating system to be as quick as possible in its decision-making. The operating system should provide the resources needed by a program, quickly, and get out of the way!

The interesting aspect of this exploration was the revelation that very little additional hardware support is needed to realize even the most sophisticated memory-management schemes (such as paging), very efficient page replacement, and working-set maintenance algorithms. This serves once again to emphasize the importance of understanding the partnership between system software and hardware.

14.4 Memory Hierarchy

Related to the memory systems is the topic of memory hierarchy. Program locality (which naturally leads to the concept of the working set of a program) is the key characteristic that enables programs with a large memory footprint to achieve good performance on modern computer systems. The architectural feature that exploits this property is memory hierarchy. The concept of caches pervades all aspects of system design (from web caches to processor caches). We saw how to design data caches in hardware to exploit the locality properties found in programs for instructions and data. We also saw how to design address caches (TLB) to take advantage of locality at the level of pages accessed by a program during execution.

14.5 Parallel System

Parallelism is fundamental to human thinking and, therefore, to the way we develop algorithms and programs. Trying to exploit this parallelism has been the quest both for the systems software and computer architects since the early days of computing. With increasing levels of integration, boxes are now housing multiple processors. In fact, the current buzz in single-chip processors is *multicore,* namely, having multiple processors on a single piece of silicon.

Given these trends, it is imperative for computer scientists to understand the system software support needed for parallel programming and the corresponding hardware assists. We explored a number of topics, from the operating system's point of view, such as supporting multiple threads of control within a single address space, synchronization among these threads, and data sharing. Correspondingly, we investigated architectural enhancements ranging from an atomic read-modify-write primitive in a sequential processor to cache coherence in a symmetric multiprocessor.

This topic is a fertile one, and as can be imagined, it is worthy of further exploration. We hope we have kindled enough interest in the reader to goad him or her to explore further.

14.6 Input/Output Systems

A computer system is useless unless it can interact with the outside world. From the hardware standpoint, we saw how we can interface devices (simple as well as sophisticated) to the computer system through techniques such as programmed I/O and DMA. The hardware mechanism of interrupt was a key to grabbing the attention of the processor. We also saw how the technique of memory-mapped I/O makes integrating I/O subsystems seamless, requiring no special enhancement to the ISA of the processor. Mirroring a device controller that interfaces a device to the processor, software modules in the OS called device drivers and interrupt handlers allow manipulation of the devices connected to the system for input/output.

Two particular I/O subsystems deserve additional attention, namely, the disk and the network. The former is the vehicle for persistent storage of information inside a box, and the latter is the vehicle to talk to the outside world.

14.7 Persistent Storage

The file system is an important component of the operating system, and it is no exaggeration to say that it most likely represents the largest number of lines of code for a single subsystem in any production operating system. Due to its inherent simplicity, a file is a convenient way to represent any device for the purposes of input/output from a program. In particular, files stored on media such as a disk allow persistence of information beyond the life of the program. Here, we studied the design choices for file systems, including naming and attributes related to a file. Focusing on the disk as the medium, we explored space-allocation strategies, disk-scheduling strategies, and organization of files on the disk (including data structures in the operating system).

14.8 Network

Today, with the advent of the Internet and the World Wide Web, connection of the computer system to the outside world is taken for granted. Therefore, we devoted quite some time to understanding issues in networking, from the point of view of both the system software and the hardware. On the hardware side, we looked at the network gear that defines our cyber environment today, such as NIC, hub, switch, and routers. From the system software point of view, we understood the need for a protocol stack that comprises the transport, network, and data link layers. We learned the bells and whistles therein, such as checksums, windowing, and sequence numbers. For example, to combat data loss due to packets being mangled on the wire, error correction codes are used. To decouple the application payload from hardware limitations such as fixed packet size, and to accommodate the out-of-order delivery of packets, scatter/gather of packets is incorporated into the protocol stack. Packet loss en route from source to destination is overcome by end-to-end acknowledgement in the protocol.

Networks and network protocols are fascinating areas of further study. Therefore, we hope the network coverage in this book has whetted the appetite of the reader to learn more.

Concluding Remarks

Overall, the field of system architecture, the meeting point between hardware and software, is an intriguing and fascinating area. This area is unlikely to dry up for a long time, since the application of computing in everyday life is growing by leaps and bounds. To keep pace with this growth in demand, the system architect has to continuously innovate and produce new computing machines that run faster, cost less, consume less power, and offer more services. We hope that this textbook serves as a launching pad for future system architects.

Appendix: Network Programming with UNIX Sockets

A.1 The Problem

Write a simple client–server program for two processes (Client and Server) to communicate by using UNIX sockets. Client executes on a machine whose Internet name is `beehive.cc.gatech.edu`; Server executes on a machine whose Internet name is `mit.edu`; the port number to use with the socket at the Server is 2999. The sockets use TCP/IP as the underlying protocol for communication. Once connected, the Client sends a string, "Hello World! Client is Alive!" Upon receiving this message, the Server replies with a string, "Got it! Server is Alive!" The Client and Server print what they successfully sent, as well as what they successfully received, respectively, on **stdout**, close the connection, and terminate.

A.2 Source Files Provided

In the subsequent sections, the client code, server code, and Makefile are given. Make sure to use the right binary output for your target machine. For simplicity, use the same target machines for both the client and the server. For example, a binary file built on x86_64 architecture will not run on the i686 unless you use -m32 option for compatibility. (Try "uname -m" to check out architecture.) The Makefile provided in the appendix uses "-m32" as the default.

If you are not sure about any system calls in the example, use the UNIX man-pages for detailed explanation. Are you not sure about the "man" command itself? Type "man man." For example, if you want know about the socket system call, type "man socket" on any UNIX machine.

A.3 Makefile

```
#######################################################
##
## Makefile: CS2200 Client/Server Example
##                  Using UNIX Sockets
## Author:    Junsuk Shin
##
#######################################################
```

```
CFLAGS   = -Wall -pedantic -m32
LFASGS   = -m32
CC       = gcc
RM       = /bin/rm -rf


SERVER = server
CLIENT = client


SERVER_SRC  = server.c
CLIENT_SRC  = client.c
SRCS     = $(SERVER_SRC) $(CLIENT_SRC)


SERVER_OBJ  = $(patsubst %.c,%.o,$(SERVER_SRC))
CLIENT_OBJ  = $(patsubst %.c,%.o,$(CLIENT_SRC))
OBJS     = $(SERVER_OBJ) $(CLIENT_OBJ)


# pattern rule for object files
%.o: %.c
        $(CC) -c $(CFLAGS) $< -o $@


#-------------------------------------------------------
all: $(SERVER) $(CLIENT)

$(SERVER): $(SERVER_OBJ)
        $(CC) $(LFASGS) -o $@ $<


$(CLIENT): $(CLIENT_OBJ)
        $(CC) $(LFASGS) -o $@ $<


clean:
        $(RM) $(OBJS) $(SERVER) $(CLIENT) core*


.PHONY: depend
depend:
        makedepend -Y -- $(CFLAGS) -- $(SRCS) 2>/dev/null


# DO NOT DELETE

server.o: example.h
client.o: example.h
```

A.4 Common Header File

```
#ifndef EXAMPLE_H
#define EXAMPLE_H
```

```
#define SERVER_PORT 2999
#define SERVER_MSG  "Got it!  Server is Alive!"
#define CLIENT_MSG  "Hello World!  Client is Alive!"

#define MAXPENDING  5
#define BUFF_SIZE   128

#endif
```

A.5 Client Source Code

```
#include "example.h"
#include <unistd.h>
#include <stdlib.h>
#include <stdio.h>
#include <string.h>
#include <sys/socket.h>
#include <netdb.h>

const char usage[] = "Usage: client [-h] [-p <server port>]
[-s <server address>]\n";

char *server_addr = NULL;
int server_port = SERVER_PORT;

void print_usage(void) {
    printf("%s",usage);
    exit(EXIT_FAILURE);
}

void read_options(int argc, char *argv[]) {
    int c;

    /* read command line options */
    while ( (c=getopt(argc,argv,"hp:s:")) != -1 ) {
        switch(c) {
        case 'p':
            server_port = atoi(optarg);
            if ( server_port <= 0 ) {
                print_usage();
            }
            break;
        case 's':
            server_addr = optarg;
            break;
```

```c
            case 'h':
            default:
                print_usage();
            }
        }
        if ( server_addr == NULL ) {
            print_usage();
        }
    }
}

int connect_to(char *host, int port) {
    int sock;
    struct addrinfo hint;
    struct addrinfo *addr;
    char port_str[8];

    /*
     * making connection from a client side is simpler than
     * a server side
     * It follows 2 steps:
     *        1) make socket (socket)
     *        2) make connection (connect)
     */
    memset(&hint, 0, sizeof(hint));
    hint.ai_family = PF_INET;
    hint.ai_socktype = SOCK_STREAM;
    snprintf(port_str,8,"%d",port);

    /* First, need to find out network address with a given
     * host name.  host can be any form such as
     * host name — tokyo.cc.gatech.edu or
     * dotted decimal notation — 192.168.1.1.
     * When a descriptive name is needed, gethostbyname()
     * or gethostbyname_r() can be used.  The behavior of
     * gethostbyname() when it is passed a numeric address
     * string as a parameter is unspecified.
     * For the dotted decimal notation,
     * inet_addr() can be used.
     * Since the return value from the above two
     * system calls (gethostbyname and inet_addr) are
     * different, the return value
     * should be handled differently.
     * In this example, getaddrinfo() is used, and it
     * simply handles both cases.
     */
```

```c
        /* The getaddrinfo() function shall translate the name
         * of a service location (for example, a host name)
         * and/or a service name and shall return
         * a set of socket addresses and associated information
         * to  be  used  in creating a socket with which to
         * address the specified service.
         */
        getaddrinfo(host, port_str, &hint, &addr);

        /* Second, make socket
         * (use addrinfo set by getaddrinfo() )
         * It can be simply
         * socket(PF_INET, SOCK_STREAM, IPPROTO_TCP) for a
         * tcp/ip connection.
         */
        if((sock = socket(addr → ai_family,
                          addr → ai_socktype,
                          addr → ai_protocol)) == -1) {
            perror("socket");
            return -1;
        }

        /* Third, connect to a socket
         * Since, getaddrinfo() sets the relevant fields of
         * addr variable, we can simply use them for this call.
         * For example, if gethostbyname() is used to resolve
         * the network address, you might code the connect
         * call differently.
         */
        if(connect(sock,
                   addr → ai_addr,
                   addr → ai_addrlen) == -1 ) {
            perror("connect");
            return -1;
        }

        free(addr);

        return sock;
}

int main(int argc, char *argv[]) {
    int     socket;
    int     sent_size, recv_size;
    char    buffer[BUFF_SIZE];
```

```
read_options(argc,argv);

socket = connect_to(server_addr, server_port);
if ( socket <= 0 ) {
    return EXIT_FAILURE;
}

/* send a message on a socket */
/* Usually, recv/send doesn't fail, but always need to
 * check (good programming habit!).
 */
sent_size = send(socket,
            CLIENT_MSG,
            strlen(CLIENT_MSG)+1,0);

if ( sent_size == -1 ) {
    perror("send");
    exit(EXIT_FAILURE);
}
printf("Message sent to %s\n\t%s\n",
                            server_addr,CLIENT_MSG);

/* Receive a message from a connected socket */

/*
 * buffer for the message needs to be provided.
 * It returns the length of the message written to
 * the buffer unless there is an error.
 * By default, it's blocking call.  If interested,
 * check out fcntl(), O_NONBLOCK, and EAGAIN return
 * value.
 */
recv_size = recv(socket,buffer,BUFF_SIZE,0);
if ( recv_size == -1 ) {
    perror("recv");
    exit(EXIT_FAILURE);
}
printf("Message received from %s\n\t%s\n",
                                server_addr,buffer);

/* Close sockets */

/*
 * Not really necessary, since the program terminates,
 * but it's a good habit.
```

```
                      * Same for file descriptors and
                      * sockets.  Also, there's a limit for such
                      * descriptors that a user can open.  Simply,
                      * you cannot
                      * open file/make socket beyond the limit.
                      */
                     close(socket);
                     return EXIT_SUCCESS;
                 }
```

A.6 Server Source Code

```
#include <unistd.h>
#include <stdlib.h>
#include <stdio.h>
#include <string.h>
#include <sys/types.h>
#include <sys/socket.h>
#include <arpa/inet.h>
#include "example.h"

union sock {
    struct sockaddr s;
    struct sockaddr_in i;
};

const char usage[] =
                "Usage: server [-h] [-p <port number>]\n";
int port = SERVER_PORT;
char client_ip[16];

void print_usage(void) {
    printf("%s",usage);
    exit(EXIT_FAILURE);
}

void get_options(int argc, char *argv[]) {
    int c;

    /* read command line options      */
    /* "hp:" means -h and -p <string> */
    while ( (c=getopt(argc,argv,"hp:")) != -1 ) {
        switch(c) {
        case 'p':
```

```
            port = atoi(optarg);
            if ( port <= 0 ) {
                print_usage();
            }
            break;
        case 'h':
        default:
            print_usage();
        }
    }
}

int create_server_socket(int port) {
    struct sockaddr_in serv_addr;
    int serv_sock;
    int opt = 1;

    /* Creation of server socket usually follows these 3
     * steps:
     *      1) make socket / create endpoint of
     *         communication,
     *      2) bind a name (address) to a socket, and
     *      3) listen for incoming socket connections.
     */
    memset(&serv_addr, 0, sizeof(serv_addr));
    serv_addr.sin_family = PF_INET;
    serv_addr.sin_addr.s_addr = htonl(INADDR_ANY);
    serv_addr.sin_port = htons(port);

    /* make TCP socket */
    /* PF_INET : IP protocol family
     *           For more options, check out
     *                        /usr/include/bits/socket.h
     *           (e.g.,  PF_UNIX for unix domain socket)
     * SOCK_STREAM : sequenced, reliable connection
     *           (e.g.,  SOCK_DGRAM for connectionless,
     *                        unreliable connection)
     * IPPROTO_TCP : Transmission Control Protocol/TCP
     *           (e.g.,  IPPROTO_UDP, IPPROTO_RSVP, etc.)
     *                check out /usr/include/netinet/in.h
     *                        /usr/include/linux/in.h
     */
    if ((serv_sock=socket(PF_INET,
                    SOCK_STREAM,
                    IPPROTO_TCP)) == -1 ) {
```

```
            perror("socket");
            return -1;
    }

    /* Set port as reusable */

    /*
     * Port may not be usable if it's not closed properly
     * (e.g.,  segfault, kill process) Specifies that the
     * rules used in validating addresses supplied to
     * bind() should allow reuse of local addresses.
     */
    if (setsockopt(serv_sock,
                    SOL_SOCKET,
                    SO_REUSEADDR,
                    &opt,
                    sizeof(opt)) == -1 )
    {
        perror("setsockopt");
        return -1;
    }

    /* Bind a name (server_addr) to a socket (serv_sock).
     * When a socket is created with socket(), it exists in
     * a name space (address family), but has no name
     * assigned.
     *
     * It normally is necessary to assign a
     * local address by
     * using bind before a SOCK_STREAM socket may receive
     * connections (accept()).
     */
    if (bind(serv_sock,
            (struct sockaddr *)&serv_addr,
            sizeof(serv_addr)) == -1 ) {
        perror("bind");
        return -1;
    }

    /*
     * Listen for socket connections and limit the queue of
     * incoming.
     */
    if (listen(serv_sock,MAXPENDING) == -1 ) {
        perror("listen");
```

```
            return -1;
        }

    return serv_sock;
}

void read_client_ip(int sock) {
    union sock client;
    int client_len;

    client_len = sizeof(struct sockaddr);
    /* get the name of the peer socket */
    getpeername(sock,
                &(client.s),
                (socklen_t *)&client_len);

    /* inet_ntoa() convert the Internet host address to a
     * string in the Internet standard dot notation.
     */
    strncpy(client_ip,inet_ntoa(client.i.sin_addr),16);
}

int main(int argc, char *argv[]) {
    int             server_sock, client_sock;
    int             recv_size,sent_size;
    struct sockaddr_in  c_addr;
    unsigned int    c_len = sizeof(c_addr);
    char            buffer[BUFF_SIZE];

    get_options(argc,argv);

    server_sock = create_server_socket(port);

    /* Waiting on a client connection */

    /*
     * The  accept  function  is  used  with  connection-
     * based  socket  types:
     * (SOCK_STREAM, SOCK_SEQPACKET and SOCK_RDM).
     * It  extracts  the  first connection  request on the
     * queue of pending connections, creates a new
     * connected socket with mostly the same properties as
     *  s, and allocates a new file descriptor for the
     * socket, which is returned.
     */
```

```
            if ( (client_sock=accept(server_sock,
                                (struct sockaddr *)&c_addr,
                                &c_len)) == -1 ) {
          perror("accept");
          return EXIT_FAILURE;
      }

      read_client_ip(client_sock);

      /* Receive a message from a connected socket */

      /*
       * Buffer for the message needs to be provided.
       * It returns the length of the message written to
       * the buffer unless there is an error.
       * By default, it's blocking call.  If interested,
       * check out fcntl(), O_NONBLOCK, and EAGAIN return
       * value.
       */
      recv_size = recv(client_sock,buffer,BUFF_SIZE,0);
      if ( recv_size == -1 ) {
          perror("recv");
          exit(EXIT_FAILURE);
      }
      printf("Message received from %s\n\t%s\n",
                                      client_ip,buffer);

      /* Send a message on a socket */
      /* Usually, recv/send doesn't fail, but always need
       * to check (good programming habit!).
       */
      sent_size = send(client_sock,
                      SERVER_MSG,
                      strlen(SERVER_MSG)+1, 0);
      if ( sent_size == -1 ) {
          perror("send");
          exit(EXIT_FAILURE);
      }
      printf("Message sent to %s\n\t%s\n",
                                      client_ip,SERVER_MSG);

      /* Close sockets */

      /*
       * Not really necessary, since the program terminates,
```

```
 * but it's good habit.  Same for file descriptors and
 * sockets.  Also, there's a limit for such
 * descriptors that a user can open.  Simply,
 * you cannot
 * open file/make socket beyond the limit.
 */
close(client_sock);
close(server_sock);

return EXIT_SUCCESS;
}
```

A.7 Instantiating the Client–Server Programs

The example program uses the following default for the server port:

- Server port: 2999
  This option is changeable via the command line.

To run the program, you have to start the client and server programs:

- Server
  Run server (if necessary, with different options)
  for, e.g.,

```
./server (run with default options)
./server -p 3333 (to set up 3333 as server port number).
```

- Client
  Run client (if necessary, with different options)
  for, e.g.,

```
./client -s < host ip | host name >
./client -p 3333 -s helsinki.cc.gatech.edu.
```

Bibliography

[Abramson, 1970] N. Abramson, The ALOHA system—Another alternative for computer communications, *Proc. 1970 Fall Joint Comp. Conf.*, AFIPS Press, Vol. 37, pp. 281–85.

[Adve, 1996] Sarita V. Adve and Kourosh Gharachorloo, Shared memory consistency models: A tutorial, *Computer*, December 1996, pp. 66–76.

[Agarwal, 1995] Anant Agarwal, Ricardo Bianchini, David Chaiken, David Kranz, John Kubiatowicz, Beng-hong Lim, Kenneth Mackenzie, and Donald Yeung, The MIT Alewife Machine: Architecture and performance, in *Proceedings of the 22nd Annual International Symposium on Computer Architecture*, Santa Margherita Ligure, Italy, June 22–24, 1995.

[Allen, 1987] Randy Allen and Ken Kennedy, Automatic translation of FORTRAN programs to vector form, *ACM Transactions on Programming Languages and Systems* (TOPLAS), Vol. 9, No. 4, October 1987, pp. 491–542.

[Almasi, 1993] George S. Almasi and Allan Gottlieb, *Highly Parallel Computing*, Benjamin/Cummings Series in Computer Science and Engineering, San Francisco.

[Archibald, 1986] J. Archibald and J. Baer, Cache coherence protocols: Evaluation using a multi-processor simulation model. *ACM Trans. Comput. Syst.*, Vol. 4, No. 4, September 1986.

[ARM, 1990] *RISC: Acorn RISC Machine Family Data Manual*, CORPORATE VLSI Technology, Inc., San Jose, CA, Prentice Hall, Upper Saddle River, NJ.

[Backus, 1954] J. W. Backus, *Preliminary Report: Specifications for the IBM Mathematical FORmula TRANslating System, FORTRAN*, Programming Research Group, Applied Science Division, International Business Machines Corporation, New York, November 10, 1954. Available at http://archive.computerhistory.org/resources/text/Fortran/102679231.05.01.acc.pdf.

[Backus, 1957] J. W. Backus, R. J. Beeber, S. Best, R. Goldberg, L. M. Haibt, H. L. Herrick, R. A. Nelson, D. Sayre, P. B. Sheridan, H. J. Stern, I. Ziller, R. A. Hughes, and R. Nutt, The FOR-TRAN automatic coding system, in *Proceedings, Western Joint Computer Conference*, Los Angeles, February 1957, pp. 188–198.

[Baran, 1964] P. Baran, On distributed communications networks, *IEEE Transactions on Communications Systems*, Vol. 12, No. 1, March 1964, pp. 1–9.

[Barham, 2003] P. Barham, B. Dragovic, K. Fraser, S. Hand, T. Harris, A. Ho, R. Neugebauer, I. Pratt, and A. Warfield, Xen and the art of virtualization, in *Proceedings of the Nineteenth ACM Symposium on Operating Systems Principles*, Bolton Landing, NY, October 19–22, 2003, SOSP, ACM, New York, pp. 164–177.

[BBN Butterfly, 1986] BBN, *Butterfly Parallel Processor Overview*, Technical Report 6148, BBN Laboratories Incorporated, Boston, March 1986.

[Belady, 1966] Laszlo A. Belady, A study of replacement algorithms for virtual-storage computer, *IBM Systems Journal*, Vol. 5, No. 2, 1966, pp. 78–101.

[Belady, 1969] Laszlo A. Belady, Robert A. Nelson, and Gerald S. Shedler, An anomaly in space-time characteristics of certain programs running in a paging machine, *CACM*, Vol. 12, No. 6, June 1969, pp. 349–353.

[Bell, 1970] C. G. Bell, R. Cady, H. McFarland, B. Delagi, J. O'Laughlin, R. Noonan, and W. Wulf, A new architecture for mini-computers—The DEC PDP-11, *Proceedings of the Sprint Joint Computer Conference*, AFIPS Press, Atlantic City, NJ, May 5–7, 1970, pp. 657–675.

[Bell Webpage, 2010] *Gordon Bell's CyberMuseum for Digital Equipment Corp (DEC): Documents, Photo Albums, Talks, and Videotapes about Computing History*, 2010. Available at http://research.microsoft.com/en-us/um/people/gbell/Digital/DECMuseum.htm.

[Berners-Lee, 1989] Tim Berners-Lee, *Information Management: A Proposal*, CERN, Geneva, Switzerland, March 1989. Available at http://www.w3.org/History/1989/proposal.html.

[Blackberry OS, 2010] http://www.blackberryos.com/.

[Bobrow, 1972] D. G. Bobrow, J. D. Burchfiel, D. L. Murphy, and R. S. Tomlinson, TENEX: A page time sharing system for the PDP-10, CACM, Vol. 15, No. 3, 1972.

[Bovet, 2005] Daniel P. Bovet and Marci Cesati, *Understanding the Linux Kernel*, 3rd edition, O'Reilly, Cambridge, MA.

[Bryant, 2003] R. E. Bryant and David O'Hallaron, *Computer Systems: A Programmer's Perspective*, Prentice Hall, Upper Saddle River, NJ.

[Burkhardt, 1992] H. Burkhardt, S. Frank, B. Knobe, and J. Rothnie, *Overview of the KSR 1 Computer System*, Tech. Rep. KSR-TR-9202001, Kendall Square Res., Boston, February 1992.

[Burks, 1981] Arthur W. Burks and Alice R. Burks, The ENIAC: The first general-purpose electronic computer, *IEEE Annals of the History of Computing*, Vol. 3, No. 4, 1981, pp. 310–389, commentary on pp. 389–399.

[Bush, 1945] Vannevar Bush, As we may think, *The Atlantic*, July 1945. Available at http://www.theatlantic.com/doc/194507/bush.

[Carr, 1981] R. W. Carr and J. L. Hennessy, WSCLOCK—A simple and effective algorithm for virtual memory management. *SIGOPS Oper. Syst. Rev.* Vol. 15, No. 5, December 1981, pp. 87–95.

[Cerf, 1974] Vinton G. Cerf and Robert E. Kahn, A protocol for packet network intercommunication, *IEEE Transactions on Communications*, Vol. Com-22, No. 5, May 1974, pp. 637–648.

[Chapman, 2007] B. Chapman, G. Jost, and R. Pas, *Using Openmp: Portable Shared Memory Parallel Programming (Scientific and Engineering Computation)*. MIT Press, Cambridge, MA.

[Cocke, 2000] John Cocke and V. Markstein, The evolution of RISC technology at IBM, *IBM Journal of R&D*, Vol. 44, Nos. 1–2, p. 48–55, January 2000.

[Comer, 2000] Douglas E. Comer and David L. Stevens, *Internetworking with TCP/IP, Vol. III: Client-Server Programming and Applications*, Linux/Posix Sockets Version, Prentice Hall, Upper Saddle River, NJ.

[Cooper, 1988] E. C. Cooper and R. P. Draves, *C Threads*, CMU-CS-88–154, School of Computer Science, Carnegie Mellon University, Pittsburgh, June 1988.

[Culler, 1999] David Culler, J.P. Singh, and Anoop Gupta, *Parallel Computer Architecture: A Hardware/Software Approach*, Morgan Kaufmann, San Francisco, CA.

[Dean, 2004] J. Dean and S. Ghemawat, MapReduce: Simplified data processing on large clusters, in *Proceedings of the 6th Conference on Symposium on Operating Systems Design & Implementation—Volume 6,* San Francisco,

December 6–8, 2004. Available at http://www.usenix.org/events/osdi04/tech/full_papers/dean/dean_html/.

[Denning, 1968] Peter J. Denning, The working set model for program behavior, *Communications of the ACM*, Vol. 11, No. 5, May 1968, pp. 323–333.

[Eckert, 1946] J. Presper Eckert and John Mauchly, *Outline of Plans for Development of Electronic Computers*. Document submitted to the U.S. Army. Available at http://www.computerhistory.org/collections/accession/102660910.

[Edler, 1985] Jan Edler, Allan Gottlieb, Clyde P. Kruskal, Kevin P. McAuliffe, Larry Rudolph, Marc Snir, Patricia J. Teller, and James Wilson, Issues related to MIMD shared-memory computers: The NYU ultracomputer approach, *Proceedings of the 12th Annual International Symposium on Computer Architecture*, June 17–19, 1985, Boston, pp.126–135.

[Flynn, 1966] M. J. Flynn, Very high-speed computing systems, *Proceedings of the IEEE*, Vol. 54, No. 12, December 1966, pp. 1901–1909.

[Foster, 2003] Ian Foster and Carl Kesselman, Eds., *The Grid 2: Blueprint for a New Computing Infrastructure*, The Elsevier Series in Grid Computing, 2nd edition, Morgan Kaufmann, San Francisco.

[Fox, 1990] G. Fox, S. Hiranandani, K. Kennedy, C. Koelbel, U. Kremer, C. Tseng, and M. Wu, *Fortran D Language Specification*, Tech. Rep. TR90–141, Dept. of Computer Science, Rice University, Houston, TX, December 1990.

[Gajski, 1983] Daniel Gajski, David J. Kuck, Duncan H. Lawrie, and Ahmed H. Sameh, Cedar: A large scale multiprocessor, in *Proceedings of the International Conference on Parallel Processing*, 1983, pp. 524–529, Columbus, OH.

[Hamacher, 2001] Carl Hamacher, Zvonko Vranesic, and Safwat Zaky, *Computer Organization*, Computer Science Series, McGraw-Hill, Columbus, OH.

[Hennessy, 1981] J. L. Hennessy, N. Jouppi, F. Baskett, and J. Gill. MIPS: A VLSI processor architecture, in *Proceedings, CMU Conference on VLSI Systems and Computations*, pp. 337–346, Computer Science Press, October 1981.

[Hennessy, 2006] John L. Hennessy and David A. Patterson, *Computer Architecture: A Quantitative Approach*, 4th edition, Morgan Kaufmann, San Francisco.

[Hord, 1982] R. Michael Hord, The Illiac IV: The First Supercomputer, Computer Science Press, Rockville, MD.

[IBM system/360, 1964] *IBM System/360 Principles of Operation*, IBM Press, Armonk, NY.

[IBM System/370, 1978] Architecture of the IBM system/370, *Communications of the ACM,* Vol. 21, No. 1, special issue on computer architecture, January 1978, pp. 73–96.

[Intel CnC, 2009] Intel Corporation, Concurrent Collections. Available at http://software.intel.com/en-us/articles/intel-concurrent-collections-for-cc/.

[Intel Instruction set, 2008] Intel Corporation, The *Intel® 64 and IA-32 Architectures Software Developer's Manual: Instruction Set Reference A–M*, Order Number 253666; *Instruction Set Reference N–Z*, Order Number 253667, November 2008. Also available online at http://www.intel.com/products/processor/manuals/.

[Intel System programming guide 3A, 2008] Intel Corporation, The *Intel® 64 and IA-32 Architectures Software Developer's Manual: Volume 3A: System Programming Guide, Part 1,* Order Number 253668, November 2008. Also available online at http://www.intel.com/products/processor/manuals/.

[iPhone OS X, 2010] http://www.apple.com/iphone/.

[Johnson, 1995] K. L. Johnson, M. F. Kaashoek, and D. A. Wallach, CRL: High-performance all-software distributed shared memory, in *Proceedings of the Fifteenth ACM Symposium on Operating Systems Principles*, Copper Mountain, Colorado, December 3–6, 1995, ACM, New York, pp. 213–226.

[Jones, 1996] Richard Jones and Rafael D. Lins, *Garbage Collection: Algorithms for Automatic Dynamic Memory Management*, Wiley, Hoboken, NJ.

[Jul, 1988] Eric Jul, Henry Levy, Norman Hutchinson, and Andrew Black, Fine-grained mobility in the Emerald system, *ACM Transactions on Computer Systems* (TOCS), Vol. 6, No. 1, February 1988, pp. 109–133.

[Katz, 2004] Randy H. Katz and Gaetano Borriello, *Contemporary Logic Design,* 2nd edition, Prentice Hall, Upper Saddle River, NJ.

[Keleher, 1994] Peter J. Keleher, Alan L. Cox, Sandhya Dwarkadas, and Willy Zwaenepoel, TreadMarks: Distributed Shared Memory on Standard Workstations and Operating Systems. *USENIX*, Winter 1994, pp. 115–132.

[Kernighan, 1978] Brian W. Kernighan and Dennis M. Ritchie, *The C Programming Language*, 1st edition, Prentice-Hall, Englewood Cliffs, NJ, February 1978.

[Kleinrock, 1961] Leonard Kleinrock, *Information Flow in Large Communication Nets, RLE Quarterly Progress Report*, Massachusetts Institute of Technology, Cambridge, MA, July 1961. Available at http://www.cs.ucla.edu/~lk/REPORT/RLEreport-1961.html.

[Kleinrock, 1964] Leonard Kleinrock, *Communication Nets: Stochastic Message Flow and Design*, McGraw-Hill, NY.

[Kontothanassis, 2005] L. Kontothanassis, R. Stets, G. Hunt, U. Rencuzogullari, G. Altekar, S. Dwarkadas, and M. L. Scott, Shared memory computing on clusters with symmetric multiprocessors and system area networks, *ACM Transactions on Computer Systems*, Vol. 23, No. 3, August 2005. Available at http://www.cs.rochester.edu/research/cashmere/.

[Krieger, 2006] Orran Krieger, Marc Auslander, Bryan Rosenburg, Robert W. Wisniewski, Jimi Xenidis, Dilma Da Silva, Michal Ostrowski, Jonathan Appavoo, Maria Butrico, Mark Mergen, Amos Waterland, and Volkmar Uhlig, *K42: Building a Complete Operating System*, EuroSys 2006, Leuven, Belgium, April 2006. Available at http://domino.research.ibm.com/comm/research_projects.nsf/pages/k42.index.html.

[Kuck, 1976] David J. Kuck, Parallel processing of ordinary programs. *Advances in Computers*, Vol. 15, Academic Press, New York, pp. 119–179. Available online at http://books.google.com.

[Kung, 1978] H. T. Kung and C. E. Leiserson, Systolic arrays (for VLSI), in *Proc. SIAM Sparse Matrix Symp.*, Knoxville, TN, 1978, pp. 256–282.

[Kung, 1979] H. T. Kung, The structure of parallel algorithms, Carnegie Mellon University Technical Report: CMU-CS-79–143, *Advances in Computers*, Vol. 19, Academic Press, New York. Available online at http://books.google.com.

[Kurose, 2006] James F. Kurose and Keith W. Ross, *Computer Networking: A Top Down Approach Featuring the Internet*, Addison-Wesley, Boston.

[Lamport, 1979] Leslie Lamport, How to make a multiprocessor computer that correctly executes multiprocess programs, *IEEE Transactions on Computers*, Vol. C-28, No. 9, September 1979.

[Lenoski, 1992] Daniel Lenoski, James Laudon, Kourosh Gharachorloo, Wolf-Dietrich Weber, Anoop Gupta, John Hennessy, Mark Horowitz, and Monica S. Lam, The Stanford Dash Multiprocessor, *Computer*, Vol. 25, No. 3, March 1992, pp. 63–79.

[Li, 1988] K. Li, IVY: A shared virtual memory system for parallel computing, in *Proceedings of the 1988 ICPP*, Vol. II, University Park, PA, pp. 94–101.

[Lilja, 1993] David J. Lilja, Cache coherence in large-scale shared-memory multiprocessors: Issues and comparisons, *ACM Computing Surveys*, Vol. 25, No. 3, September 1993, pp. 303–338.

[Love, 2003] Robert Love, *Linux Kernel Development*, SAMS publishing, (A subsidiary of Prentice Hall, Upper Saddle River, NJ).

[Mac OS X, 2010] http://www.apple.com/macosx/.

[Mahon, 1986] M. Mahon, R. Lee, T. Miller, J. Huck, and W. Bryg, Hewlett-Packard precision architecture: The processor, *Hewlett-Packard Journal*, Vol. 37, No. 8, August 1986, pp. 4–21.

[Mano, 2007] M. Morris Mano and Charles Kime, *Logic and Computer Design Fundamentals*, 4th edition, Prentice Hall, Upper Saddle River, NJ.

[McKusick, 1984] M. K. McKusick, W. N. Joy, S. J. Leffler, and R. S. Fabry, A fast file system for UNIX, *ACM Trans. Comput. Syst.*, Vol. 2, No. 3, August 1984, pp. 181–197.

[McKusick, 1996] Marshall Kirk McKusick, Keith Bostic, Michael J. Karels, and John S. Quarterman, *The Design and Implementation of the 4.4 BSD Operating System*, Addison-Wesley, Boston.

[McKusick, 2004] Marshall Kirk McKusick and George V. Neville-Neil, *The Design and Implementation of the Free BSD Operating System*, Addison-Wesley, Boston.

[Mellor-Crummey, 1991] J. M. Mellor-Crummey and M. L. Scott, Algorithms for scalable synchronization on shared-memory multiprocessors. *ACM Trans. Comput. Syst.* Vol. 9, No. 1, February 1991, pp. 21–65.

[Metcalfe, 1976] Robert M. Metcalfe and David R. Boggs, Ethernet: Distributed packet switching for local computer networks, *Communications of the ACM*, Vol. 19, No. 7, July 1976, pp. 395–404.

[Mitchell, 1994] James G. Mitchell, Jonathan J. Gibbons, Graham Hamilton, Peter B. Kessler, Yousef A. Khalidi, Panos Kougiouris, Peter W. Madany, Michael N. Nelson, Michael L. Powell, and Sanjay R. Radia, An overview of the Spring system, *IEEE COMPCOM '94*. Available at http://research.sun.com/features/tenyears/volcd/papers/mitchell.htm.

[Moore, 1965] Gordon E. Moore, Cramming more components onto integrated circuits, *Electronics Magazine*, Vol. 38, No. 8, April 19, 1965. Available at ftp://download.intel.com/museum/Moores_Law/Articles-Press_Releases/Gordon_Moore_1965_Article.pdf.

[MPI, 2009] Message Passing Interface Forum, http://www.mpi-forum.org/.

[Nichols, 1996] Bradford Nichols, Dick Buttlar, and Jacqueline Proulx Farrell, *Pthreads Programming: A POSIX Standard for Better Multiprocessing*, O'Reilly, Cambridge, MA.

[Oliphint, 1987] C. Oliphint, Operating system for the B 5000. *IEEE Ann. Hist. Comput.* Vol. 9, No. 1, January 1987, pp. 23–28.

[OpenMP, 2010] http://openmp.org/wp/.

[Organick, 1972] Elliott I. Organick, *The Multics System: An Examination of Its Structure*, MIT Press, Cambridge, MA.

[Padua, 1980] David A. Padua, David J. Kuck, and Duncan H. Lawrie, High-speed multiprocessors and compilation techniques. *IEEE Trans. Computers* Vol. 29, No. 9, pp. 763–776.

[Patt, 2004] Y. N. Patt and S. J. Patel, Introduction to Computing Systems: from bits & gates to C & beyond, 2nd Edition, McGraw-Hill, New York.

[Patterson, 1980] David A. Patterson and David R. Ditzel, The case for the reduced instruction set computer, *ACM SIGARCH Computer Architecture News*, Vol. 8, No. 6, October 1980, pp. 25–33.

[Patterson, 1981] David A. Patterson and Carlo H. Sequin, RISC I: A reduced instruction set VLSI computer, *Proceedings of the 8th Annual Symposium on Computer Architecture*, Minneapolis, pp. 443–457.

[Patterson, 1998] David A. Patterson and John L. Hennessy, *Computer Organization and Design: The Hardware/Software Interface*, 2nd edition, Morgan Kaufmann, San Francisco.

[Patterson, 2008] David A. Patterson and John L. Hennessy, *Computer Organization and Design: The Hardware/Software Interface*, 4th edition, Morgan Kaufmann, San Francisco.

[PDP-8, 1973] Digital Equipment Corp. *PDP-8/e, PDP-8/m & PDP-8/f Small Computer Handbook*, PDP-8 Handbook Series, Digital Equipment Corp., Maynard, MA.

[Pfister, 1985] G. Pfister, W. Brantley, D. George, S. Harvey, W. Kleinfelder, K. McAuliffe, E. Melton, V. Norton, and J. Weiss. The IBM Research Parallel Processor Prototype (RP3): Introduction and architecture, in *Proceedings of the International Conference on Parallel Processing*, University Park, PA, August 1985, pp. 764–771.

[Prabhakaran, 2005] Vijayan Prabhakaran, Andrea C. Arpaci-Dusseau, and Remzi H. Arpaci-Dusseau, Analysis and evolution of journaling file systems, *Proceedings of the USENIX Annual Technical Conference*, April 10–15, 2005, Anaheim, CA.

[Radin, 1982] G. Radin, The 801 minicomputer, *Proc. Architectural Support for Programming Languages and Operating Systems*, March 1982, pp. 39–47.

[Reid, 2001] T. R. Reid, *The Chip: How Two Americans Invented the Microchip and Launched a Revolution*, Random House, New York.

[Ritchie, 1974] D. M. Ritchie and K. Thompson, The UNIX time-sharing system, *CACM*, Vol. 17, No. 7, July 1974, pp. 365–375.

[Rubini, 2001] Alessandro Rubini and Jonathan Corbet, *Linux Device Drivers*, O'Reilly, Cambridge, MA.

[Russinovich, 2005] Mark E. Russinovich and David A. Solomon, *Microsoft Windows Internals*, 4th edition, Microsoft Press, Redmond, Washington.

[Saltzer, 2009] Jerome H. Saltzer and M. Frans Kaashoek, *Principles of Computer System Design: An Introduction*, Morgan Kaufmann, San Francisco.

[Scales, 1996] Daniel J. Scales, Kourosh Gharachorloo, and Chandramohan A. Thekkath, Shasta: A low overhead, software-only approach for supporting fine-grain shared memory, *Proceedings of the Seventh International Conference on Architectural Support for Programming Languages and Operating Systems (ASPLOS VII)*, Cambridge, MA, October 1996, pp. 174–185.

[Schroeder, 1971] M. D. Schroeder, Performance of the GE-645 associative memory while Multics is in operation, in *Proceedings of the SIGOPS Workshop on System Performance Evaluation*, ACM, New York, pp. 227–245.

[Silberschatz, 2008] Abraham Silberschatz, Peter B. Galvin, and Greg Gagne, *Operating System Concepts*, 8th edition, Wiley, Hoboken, NJ.

[Sites, 1992] Richard L. Sites, Alpha AXP architecture, special issue, 1992 Alpha AXP architecture and systems, *Digital Technical Journal*, Vol. 4, No. 4.

[Smith, 1982] A. J. Smith, A. J. Cache memories, *ACM Comput. Surv.*, Vol. 14, No. 3, September 1982, pp. 473–530.

[Smith, 1985] A. J. Smith, Disk cache—Miss ratio analysis and design considerations, *ACM Trans. Computer Systems*, Vol. 3, No. 3, August 1985, pp. 161–203.

[Snir, 1998] Marc Snir and William Gropp, *MPI: The Complete Reference*, MIT Press, Cambridge, MA.

[SPARC Architecture, 2010] SPARC International Inc., 2010, http://www.sparc.com/ specificationsDocuments.html.

[Stallings, 2010] William Stallings, *Computer Organization and Architecture: Designing for Performance*, 8th edition, Prentice Hall, Upper Saddle River, NJ.

[Stevens, 1994] W. Richard Stevens, *TCP/IP Illustrated, Volume 1: The Protocols*, Addison-Wesley, Boston.

[Stevens, 2003] W. Richard Stevens, Bill Fenner, and Andrew M. Rudoff, *Unix Network Programming, Volume 1: The Sockets Networking API*, 3rd edition, Addison-Wesley, Boston.

[Stewart, 1998] John W. Stewart III, *BGP4: Inter-domain Routing in the Internet*, Addison-Wesley, Boston.

[Strecker, 1978] W. D. Strecker, VAX-11/780: A virtual address extension to the DEC PDP-11 family, *Proceedings of the National Computer Conference*, AFIPS Press, Montvale, NJ, 1978, pp. 967–980.

[Sunderam, 1990] V. S. Sunderam, PVM: A framework for parallel distributed computing, *Concurrency: Practice and Experience*, Vol. 2, No. 4, December 1990. pp. 315–339.

[Swan, 1977] R. J. Swan, S. H. Fuller, and D. P. Siewiorek, Cm*: A modular, multi-microprocessor, in *Proceedings of the June 13–16, 1977, National Computer Conference, Dallas, TX*; AFIPS 1977, ACM, New York, pp. 637–644.

[Symbian OS, 2010] http://www.symbian.org/.

[Tanenbaum, 1987] Andrew S. Tanenbaum and Albert S. Woodhull, *Operating Systems Design and Implementation*, 2d edition, Prentice Hall, Upper Saddle River, NJ.

[Tanenbaum, 2002] Andrew S. Tanenbaum, *Computer Networks*, 4th edition, Prentice Hall, Upper Saddle River, NJ.

[Tanenbaum, 2005] Andrew S. Tanenbaum, *Structured Computer Organization*, 5th edition, Prentice Hall, Upper Saddle River, NJ.

[Tanenbaum, 2006] Andrew S. Tanenbaum, Albert S. Woodhull, *Operating Systems Design and Implementation*, 3d edition, Prentice Hall, Upper Saddle River, NJ.

[Tanenbaum, 2007] Andrew S. Tannenbaum, *Modern Operating Systems*, Prentice Hall, Upper Saddle River, NJ.

[Thornton, 1964] James E. Thornton, Parallel operation in the control data 6600, *Proc. AFIPS Fall Joint Computer Conferences, Part II*, October 27–29, 1964, pp. 33–40.

[Tomasulo, 1967] R. M. Tomasulo, An efficient algorithm for exploiting multiple arithmetic units, *IBM Journal of Research and Development*, Vol. 11, No. 1, p. 25.

[Toomey, 1988] L. J. Toomey, E. C. Plachy, R. G. Scarborough, R. J. Sahulka, J. F. Shaw, and A. W. Shannon, IBM Parallel FORTRAN, *IBM Systems Journal*, Vol. 27, No. 4, 1988, pp. 416–435.

[Torvalds, 1991] Linus Torvalds's posting to the comp.os.minix. Available at http://www.linux.org/people/linus_post.html.

[Ward, 1989] Stephen A. Ward and Robert H. Halstead, *Computation Structures*, MIT Press, Cambridge, MA.

[Wilkes, 1951] M. V. Wilkes, D. J. Wheeler, and S. Gill, *The Preparation of Programs for an Electronic Digital Computer*, Addison-Wesley, Boston.

[Wilkes, 1971] M. V. Wilkes, Slave memories and dynamic storage allocation, *IEEE Trans. Computers*, Vol. C-20, No. 6, June 1971, pp. 674–675.

[Windows CE, 2010] http://www.microsoft.com/ windowsembedded/en-us/default.mspx.

[Windows Version 7, 2010] http://www.microsoft. com/windows/windows-7/.

[Wright, 1995] Gary R. Wright and W. Richard Stevens, *TCP/IP Illustrated, Volume 2: The Implementation*, Addison-Wesley, Boston.

[Wulf, 1972] W. A. Wulf and C. G. Bell, C.mmp: A multi-mini-processor, in *Proceedings of the December 5–7, 1972, Fall Joint Computer Conference, Part II, Anaheim, CA, AFIPS 1972, Fall, part II*, ACM, New York, pp. 765–777.

[Wulf, 1974] W. Wulf, E. Cohen, W. Corwin, A. Jones, R. Levin, C. Pierson, and F. Pollack, HYDRA: The kernel of a multiprocessor operating system, *Communications of the ACM*, Vol. 17, No. 6, June 1974, pp. 337–345.

[Yeh, 1992] Tse-Yu Yeh and Yale N. Patt, Alternative implementations of two-level adaptive branch prediction, *Proceedings of the 19th Annual International Symposium on Computer Architecture*, Gold Coast, Australia, May 1992, pp. 124–134.

Index

Credits

Figure 11.1b	Octus\Fotolia, LLC—Royalty Free
Figure 12.2	Andres Rodriguez\Fotolia, LLC—Royalty Free
Figure 12.7a	© Marzanna Syncerz\Fotolia, LLC—Royalty Free
Figure 12.7b	Courtesy International Play
Figure 12.18	© SimpleStock\Alamy
Figure 12.24	© Jan Remisiewicz\Alamy
Figure 13.1a	Stephen Finn\Fotolia, LLC—Royalty Free
Figure 13.1b	Kirsty Pargeter\Fotolia, LLC—Royalty Free
Figure 13.1c	goce risteski\Fotolia, LLC—Royalty Free
Figure 13.1d	skvoor\Fotolia, LLC—Royalty Free
Figure 13.1e	Incarnatus\Fotolia, LLC—Royalty Free
Figure 13.2	dmitry30\Fotolia, LLC—Royalty Free
Figure 13.3a	Kirsty Pargeter\Alamy Images Royalty Free
Figure 13.3b	pixsell\Alamy Images Royalty Free
Figure 13.6	Paul Fleet\Alamy Images Royalty Free
Figure 13.20	Sean MacLeay\Fotolia, LLC—Royalty Free
UN-12-88	Actionplus\Alamy Images